KT-592-915

THE PRINCIPLES AND PRACTICE OF MANAGEMENT

Edited by

E. F. L. BRECH

B.A., B.Sc.(Econ.), F.B.I.M.
James Bowie Medallist

Associate Authors

R. M. ALDRICH

M.I.P.M., A.M.B.I.M.
Group Personnel Executive, S. Smith & Sons (England) Ltd.

A. W. FIELD

B.Sc., A.M.I.Mech.E., F.B.I.M.
General Works Manager, Mawdsley's Ltd.

J. MADDOCK

A.S.A.A., A.C.W.A., F.B.I.M.
Director, Peter Spence & Sons, Ltd.

FRANK L. WOODROFFE

F.S.M.A.
Sales Consultant

LONGMANS

LONGMANS, GREEN AND CO LTD
48 GROSVENOR STREET, LONDON WI
RAILWAY CRESCENT, CROYDON, VICTORIA, AUSTRALIA
443 LOCKHART ROAD, HONG KONG
PRIVATE MAIL BAG 1036, IKEJA (LAGOS)
44 JALAN AMPANG, KUALA LUMPUR
ACCRA, AUCKLAND, IBADAN, KINGSTON (JAMAICA)
NAIROBI, SALISBURY (RHODESIA)

LONGMANS SOUTHERN AFRICA (PTY) LTD
THIBAULT HOUSE, THIBAULT SQUARE, CAPE TOWN

LONGMANS, GREEN AND CO INC
119 WEST 40TH STREET, NEW YORK 18

LONGMANS, GREEN AND CO
137 BOND STREET, TORONTO 2

ORIENT LONGMANS PRIVATE LTD
CALCUTTA, BOMBAY, MADRAS
DELHI, HYDERABAD, DACCA

FIRST PUBLISHED   1953
NINTH IMPRESSION   1961

PRINTED AND BOUND IN GREAT BRITAIN BY
HAZELL WATSON AND VINEY LTD
AYLESBURY AND SLOUGH

EDITOR'S PREFACE

IN the many discussions that have accompanied the recent spread of interest in the education and training of managers, the supply of suitable literature as a support to organised studies has been one of the recurrent topics. There are some persons who feel that the number of books on the various aspects of management is already excessive, whereas others contend that in a developing subject existing texts soon become out-of-date or relatively superficial. My co-authors and I have no wish or intention to enter into this controversy, nor, in the preparation of the present volume, to imply any comment on the existing texts. We shall have achieved our purpose if readers feel that a useful addition has been made to British literature on management.

This volume is a textbook, offered as a further contribution to those who, at college courses or by private reading, are pursuing the systematic study of management in principle and practice. It has been prepared on the foundation that management is a growing profession, that it has its own specific body of knowledge, and that it is susceptible of study on lines comparable with those of the sciences and the arts.

As to framework, its conception is in the now common pattern, though the sequence of the parts is a point of significance and has been deliberately chosen. In the contemporary economic activities of the human race, the consumption aspects are at once the most fundamental and the most neglected. The study of Distribution is immediately concerned with those aspects: hence its pride of place among the four divisions of management studied in this volume. Production follows, and then the particular topics that bear on the participation of the men and women employed in both fields. Finally, the activities of Control, which can be briefly summarised as the means of assessing management's performance and achievement. The introductory and concluding chapters are, from one point of view, supplementary; but they are, too, an integral part of the whole study, setting its framework and providing the threads that link the specialist sections together.

No attempt has been made to present these specialist sections in any common form or style. Each is the work of an authority with high-level practical experience in his own field. To preserve the full benefit of this expert knowledge, each contribution has been left in its author's own language and presentation. Inevitably, there is a

v

limited measure of overlap in detail, and here and there a little contradiction in practice. But co-ordination of thought from the outset
of the work has prevented disagreement in principle. Perhaps the
only weakness that springs from this independence of treatment is
the irritation of slight differences in terminology: for instance, the
strictness of wording laid down in the Introduction has not
been followed throughout. No apology is offered for this, or called
for. Management is a relatively new field of organised knowledge,
and for some years to come divergencies in word as well as in practice
will necessarily characterise its development.

In framing the content of our various sections and chapters, we
have aimed at presenting the latest known and proven principles
and practices. This is, we hope, an up-to-date study of management,
and one which, subject to detailed revision as the years pass, will
stand the test of time. Its best value will be obtained, we feel, as an
aid to organised studies, where the lecturer can further expound
points of principle set out or bring forward as illustrations other
practices and methods, as well as circumstances in which different
techniques appear to contradict our views. In other words, we lay no
claim to exhaustive or exclusive treatment of the various aspects of
management covered. By the same token, we feel we have avoided
providing in a textbook a substitute for the lecturer's or the student's
own thinking. To the practising manager, too, we hope the volume
has something to offer—a presentation of knowledge and a stimulus
to thought and analysis of his own practice.

Because of the background of its authors, this study of management has necessarily been written in industrial terms, with its bias
mainly to the manufacturing industries and the distributive activities
directly associated with them. A good deal of the matter, however—
in the realm of principle as well as of practice—is of relevance to
such purely commercial fields as wholesale and retail trade or the
management of financial institutions, to the nationalised industries,
and even to many aspects of the local and central government
machinery.

I should like, on a personal note, to pay tribute to the patience
and persistence of my co-authors who, despite the heavy responsibilities which they have to bear as busy senior executives, have
laboured so readily over many months in the preparation of the text
and responded so kindly to my pressure for progress.

E. F. L. BRECH

SEPTEMBER 1952 *Editor*

CONTENTS

ACKNOWLEDGMENTS

ACKNOWLEDGMENTS for permission to include copyright material are due to the following:

Anglo-American Council on Productivity for an extract from the First Report of the Council; The British Institute of Management for a Pre-Production Chart; British Standards Institution for an extract from the Report for 1932; The Council of Industrial Design for material from the Fifth Annual Report; The Illuminating Engineering Society for a section of the Schedule of Recommended Values of Illumination, from the *I.E.S. Code for the Lighting of Building Interiors*; The Incorporated Sales Managers' Association and the United Commercial Travellers' Association for *Standards of Practice*; Industrial Welfare Society for an extract from a pamphlet on Welfare and Personnel Services, and from a document of a Study Group on *The Cost of Personnel Department*; The Institute of Personnel Management for material from the following broadsheets: —*Functions of Personnel Department* by G. R. Moxon, *Personnel Management in Relation to Factory Organization* by L. Urwick, and *A Report on the Administrative and Executive Problems of the Transition from War to Peace—Personnel*; Metropolitan Pensions Association Ltd. for an extract from a pension scheme; The Librarian, Management Library, for quotations from *Letters to Foremen* nos. 17 and 18; Sir Isaac Pitman & Sons Ltd. for three quotations from *The Making of Scientific Management* Volume 1, edited by L. Urwick & E.F.L. Brech; The Controller of Her Majesty's Stationery Office for an extract from the Urwick Committee Report on *Education for Management*.

INTRODUCTION

MANAGEMENT IN PRINCIPLE

By E. F. L. BRECH

CONTENTS

MANAGEMENT IN PRINCIPLE

1. THE NATURE OF MANAGEMENT

WITH some critical insight into the affairs of the times, an American philosopher has christened our epoch that of "the Managerial Revolution".[1] In contrast to the time when rapid progress in scientific and mechanical invention was the mainspring of economic development—the age of the industrial revolution—the affairs of the modern world depend largely for their advancement on the skill of the men and women who can "organise" and "manage" the activities of their fellows. Science still has its part to play, as no citizen of an atomic age could deny. Scientific prowess is, however, no longer able unaided to achieve its potential contribution to man's better livelihood—if indeed it ever could. With the increasing size and complexity of economic units, due to the advancement of technical knowledge, the rôle of the "organiser", "manager", or "administrator" grows correspondingly important.

Perhaps the strangest feature of our times is not the fundamental or widespread importance of management, but the astonishingly limited range of sound knowledge about it. It is a skill or an employment practised by many thousands of persons in every industrial community, but it has as yet no accepted or authoritative principles. It has evolved numerous techniques for more effective daily performance, yet these are "tools" for carrying out a skill of which the real character is still imperfectly known. That there should be many controversies about the relative importance of various aspects of management is but a natural consequence of such a situation. Among the many persons who are professionally engaged in management, most have qualified earlier in their industrial or commercial careers in specialised technical or professional fields—as engineers, chemists, accountants, company secretaries, and the like. They have risen to higher executive positions through years spent in the specialised practice of their profession or technology. Hence they tend, naturally enough, to have a bias or inclination to see management from a certain standpoint, and often lack the capacity to see it as a whole.

Ready illustrations of this tendency come to the mind of anyone with first-hand knowledge of the affairs of industry or commerce

[1] James Burnham: *The Managerial Revolution* (U.S.A. publication. 1941; Putnam, London, 1942; Penguin Special, 1945).

3

To the engineer, for instance, management is primarily a matter of the design of product and the design of tools, associated with the layout of production flows and the field that has come to be labelled "production engineering"; from these it is but a small step to questions of rate-fixing, piece-rates, bonus systems and other techniques that link up the technical operations with the daily activities of the operatives. To the accountant, management looms largely as a matter of figures: he is interested in the statistical data that record progress, usually couched in money terms; the accountant's interest is accordingly centred on procedures which enable him to identify expenditure with its outcome, and which show themselves in summary form in Profit and Loss Statements and Annual Balance Sheets. Recently, new lines of thought are tending to be less concerned with the recording of past financial history and the comparison of this year's progress with last year's, than with routines for the "control" of current expenditure against appropriate predetermined standards. If one turns to yet another branch of technical industry, to the chemist, management appears as a matter primarily of formulæ and mixtures, the flow of semi-solids or liquids through a series of plant in which given chemical changes arc carried out, and in which the most important requirements are the control of temperatures, the control of pressures, the control of ingredients and of the consequent emerging mixtures; the chemical manager's processes are running right if all the dials and readings are in accordance with the best standards, and if the samples of mixtures at various stages of process come up to the formula set.

To pick out the technical bias of managers in a technical field is not to imply criticism of such executives themselves. They have been trained and developed in a given atmosphere: their whole background has been concentrated on certain aspects of their technology, and in the absence of any guide as to what management is or means, one cannot rightly blame them if their rise into the higher executive levels finds them unable to depart from the customary technological or professional standards to which they have for so long been subject.

Recently a lot of attention has been given to the "human factor". Interest in this direction arose out of the war-time need to secure a higher level of labour utilisation, emanating primarily from the shortage of man-power. Experience gained in some munitions industries in the years 1916–18, and in a number of peace-time factories in the inter-war years, taught industrial managers that the productivity of people at work is enhanced by improvements in the physical and social environment of their work and by the promotion of a sense of participation in its achievement—such participation being not only effective performance of the allotted job, but a sense that their contribution is of importance to production and to the well-being of the organisation. It springs from recognition by the managers that their rank-and-file members may have real contributions to make from their own knowledge and experience to the advancement of the organisation.[1] Developments in this more human aspect of management since the early 1940s have, however, unfortunately tended to give rise to yet another specialist bias, this time in the direction of the human being. It has led many persons, erroneously, to the view that the specialist personnel aspect of management should dominate all others. Already there has emerged a new professional field of "personnel management", to parallel the more factual approach of the engineer and the accountant, and those who have been professionally trained in this field will see their own domain with the same specialist outlook as their technical colleagues.

The detached observer can see the true position, that each of these specialist aspects is but a part of management, that all have a contribution to make to the total process. The true character of management must be seen as a process or skill compounded of several essential elements, many of which are steeped in the traditional technologies, and each of which has its own contribution to make to the effective working of that process as a whole.

2. THE BACKGROUND OF MANAGEMENT

Through the misfortunes of war, bad harvests and man-made dislocations of trade, men and women the world over have become acutely aware of the nature and complexity of the contemporary economic system. The basis of that system today, no less than in the simpler days of inter-tribal barter, is the acquisition of goods by the exchange of other goods. The difference in the modern system lies in the fact that usually money serves as the medium of exchange, because the commodities offered on one side are in the intangible form of mental or manual work. A man sells his services for a wage or a salary or a dividend, and with the money received he buys his goods in the shop or market.

The progress of civilisation has turned the simple mechanism of exchange into the complex structure of the twentieth-century worldwide industrial and commercial system, with its innumerable manufacturing units of all sizes and kinds, and its legions of trading and transport houses. This complex pattern of economic activities forms

[1] For further consideration of this trend of thought, see, for instance:
(1) "Management Lessons of the War—Industrial Relations," by E. F. L. Brech, *British Management Review*, Vol. V, No. 3.
(2) *A Study of the Administrative and Executive Problems in the Transition from War to Peace*, Institute of Industrial Administration, London, 1945.

the background of management. Despite its complexity in action, it rests on a simple principle: *all economic activity is directed to a parallel twofold aim of supplying the goods and services that consumers need, and providing the means by which they can purchase those goods and services.* In this principle lies, too, the basic aim of management.

Management finds its rôle in this system because there are different contributory factors to be combined in the effective conduct of economic and social activities. There are the land and buildings, and the materials, whether used in raw state direct from natural sources or as the outcome of synthetic processes; the plant and equipment, machine tools, or, in the case of distribution, ships, rolling-stock and motor vehicles. Such factors of production and distribution are not of themselves productive—they need the skill and effort of man. Throughout the entire range of economic affairs, the dominant feature is the work of the men and women employed—the human effort in part directed to the manipulative and operative tasks, and in part to the mental processes of designing, calculating, drafting, planning, corresponding, selling, deciding, managing. It is the pervasiveness of this human element that gives management its special character as a social process. However these human forces are employed, they need to be unified, co-ordinated, welded into a team effort and directed towards a given purpose. In this lies the rôle of management.

Some emphasis needs to be placed on the duality of aim in the basic principle of economics—the exchange of goods and the maintenance of employment. The rise of a "capitalist system" in the eighteenth and nineteenth centuries, and the emergence of large-scale unemployment in the twentieth, have both tended to add weight to what might be called the "producer" aspect: the current popular interest in "full employment" is ample evidence of this. Yet the same people are, broadly speaking, both the producers and the consumers. The citizens of any community are "producers" when regarded as employers, managers, shareholders, or employees and workers; but they are "consumers" (of themselves and through their families) when they give their attention to spending their earnings.

Neglect of the "consumer" aspect lies at the root of much of the topsy-turvy popular economies of our times, a topic which is outside the scope of the present volume. Management cannot afford to neglect the consumer interests in the daily conduct of its job, because their failure may well result in the breakdown of the whole system.

The setting within which management operates does not call for specific description in the present context. In any country at any time, circumstances determine what the pattern of the economic system is like. At one end of the scale is a highly centralised Government-controlled pattern, such as the Soviet Union. At the other end lies the "free enterprise" pattern of the United States. Our position lies well between. We have our national concerns like the Coal Board and British Railways, and other public corporations set up under earlier auspices, like the Port of London Authority, or the British Broadcasting Corporation. The vast majority of our economic activities are, however, conducted by commercial undertakings: single owners, partnerships, companies. They are of great variety in structure and size, ranging from the one-man shop or market-stall to the mammoth manufacturing and trading concerns whose employees run into the five-figure categories.

The Co-operative Societies represent a different principle in ownership, but from the standpoint of the practice of management, their character is closely comparable to that of any commercial company.

In all these varied types of enterprise, the process of management arises in much the same way. There is, first, the need for lines of direction, the determination of an objective or a purpose, the laying down of broad policy for the achievement of that objective, and the translation of the policy into plans and programmes of action. There are, secondly, the means by which the action is to be carried into effect—the principles and methods for guiding and regulating the personnel of the organisation in the performance of their tasks and for maintaining adequate co-ordination; coupled with these, the techniques of supervision to ensure that performance is in keeping with policy and plan. There are, thirdly, the methods of assessing achievement and results, as well as costs of operation, to ensure that the appropriate tasks are being carried out with adequate effectiveness and economy. Whatever its setting as to type of industry, trade or service, or as to type and size of unit, the responsibility of management is to attain the fulfilment of a given purpose as a contribution to the wealth and social living of the community. The peculiar features of the type of organisation will affect in some details the structure and working of management, but not its basic responsibility or function. Mr. John Mantle, with his tiny workshop for the making-up of women's dresses, has no Board of Directors or elaborate books of account; he has no hierarchy of organisation, no techniques of production control; his personnel management is in his own daily contact with his few workers. But his contribution to real wealth and the character of his function as a chief executive are directly parallel to those of his namesake, Sir Joseph Mantle, the Managing Director of the million-pound Mantle Dressmaking Company, Ltd., employing over 2,000 persons, with elaborate schemes of organisation, planning and control, to ensure the steady maintenance of a large scheme of output, directed to its subsidiary retail shops.

In their respective ways, the two Mantles have the same purpose to fulfil and the same factors to develop; they are responsible for attaining an objective, for providing a policy, an organisation (simple or complex), plans and programmes for production and distribution, planning of rooms, equipment, material supplies, and storage or transport facilities, teams of operatives and staff appropriate to the work to be done, motivation (leadership) of such teams, co-ordination of effort and outcome, financial provisions, means of assessing results. Both, in other words, are managers.

3. WHAT IS MANAGEMENT?

Putting it into broad general terms, "management" is concerned with seeing that the job gets done: its tasks all centre on planning and guiding the operations that are going on in the enterprise. That it is not usually recognised as simply and clearly as this is due to the fact that in most industrial and commercial activities it is over-shadowed by other factors—either the technicalities of operation or the complications of the records, routines, etc., that are adopted for financial control purposes. These things may well be unavoidable accompaniments of modern business, but it is important to realise that they are in fact only the *tools* for the manager's job: they are not the job itself, nor do they really help to explain what that job is.

The true nature of management can be more easily seen in a simple example; for instance, the building of half a dozen houses on a small site:

(1) Obviously, the first requirement is to know what houses are to be built, how they are to be laid out on the site, the type of materials to be used, the dimensions and so on; this may be regarded as the general policy of this building operation, and it is provided by the architect's plans. In addition, there is the question of how to go about the work on the site—where to start, which way to proceed, whether to build one house through and then start the next, or whether to complete each stage on all six at once, how long to take and how many men to use. This may be regarded as formulating the general programme of operations, and is fixed by the master-builder, in agreement with the architect.

(2) On this operation, the establishment of the "authority" in charge of the job calls for no special arrangement: the master-builder takes control; or a General Foreman is put in charge. As the job is comparatively small, will the "manager" remain on the job full-time? If not, arrangements are made to appoint one of the tradesmen as

working Foreman. His responsibilities need to be defined—his relations with the architect's visiting representative, the limits to his powers of independent decision, and so on. Above all, his position as Foreman needs to be made clear to all the tradesmen on the job; he may himself be a bricklayer or a carpenter, but what matters from the management standpoint is his position and responsibility as supervisor.

(3) The allocation of major jobs to the men is largely determined by their own trade skills. But many general jobs will arise for which men will need to be detailed by the Foreman: perhaps unloading lorries, or helping in certain other operations when their own is partially completed or temporarily held up. Quite certainly, from time to time, a "human planning" or allocation of tasks will have to be carried out by the Foreman. The engagement of additional or general labour is another item that comes into consideration here.

(4) A good deal of preparatory work will be done before any operations start on the site—purchase of materials, hire of equipment and so on. As soon as building starts, the detailed planning becomes very important: how the equipment is to be used; the erection of scaffolding; the sequence of jobs; the layout of the materials on the site; where to unload supplies in relation to where they will be used; alterations to programme or planned methods because of weather difficulties or non-arrival of certain supplies and equipment. However much of the planning is done in advance, modifications are bound to occur, and so some continuous replanning activity will be called for. In a building operation, of course, much of the sequence of jobs is predetermined by the type and plan of house, but even here adjustments are bound to arise from circumstance.

(5) To start the job off does not call for any issue of "commands" in the military sense, but it is the Manager's or Foreman's task to issue instructions as the work gets under way, and to keep up the working pace on the job. This is essentially a human task. It is in part concerned with attendance and time-keeping, with meal-breaks and tea-making; but it is in much larger measure a matter of keeping harmony and team-spirit and encouraging all the men to get on with the job with a sense of responsibility and enthusiasm. In other words, it is the task of keeping up morale.

(6) The actual building operations proceed according to the technical dictates of the various trades, and in accordance with programme and plans. They are the activities around which "management" is weaving its pattern of planning, organisation and control.

(7) As the job proceeds, the Manager and/or Foreman (as well as the architect's man and the master-builder) will be keeping an eye on progress. He will be watching to see that all the work is done according to plan and specification, that the correct materials are used, that quality of workmanship is as laid down, that correct dimensions are followed, proper finishing touches given where necessary, no

faults or errors left uncorrected, and so on. He is exercising a detailed supervision of work, and a "control" of progress in accordance with the pre-set plan or programme. The time-factor has also to be taken into account, and the master-builder has a further concern with the progress of actual costs as compared with the planned estimates.

(8) Co-ordination of work is very largely secured by the existence of the plans, but there is still a daily task for the Foreman to undertake. Perhaps at one stage the bricklayers are getting too far ahead of the others. Perhaps the carpenters are dropping too far behind, and will shortly hold up the next operation. In a smaller way, the need for co-ordination will arise whenever a lorry arrives with supplies and has to be unloaded: the Foreman must decide which men to call off, where to put the materials, and so on.

(9) Finally, the Manager and Foreman (as well as the workers) will be all the time acquiring experience of how management and supervision are successfully applied on a building site. In a highly organised manufacturing firm, cards, charts and other records would be used to keep note of progress as measured against programme, and this information would be used subsequently as the basis of management decisions in setting future programmes. In an informal way, every manager and supervisor is acquiring and "recording" in his own mind experience of the best ways of planning and doing this and that. On the building site, the Foreman's keenness in observing and "recording" (remembering) the good and bad incidents in planning and in actual progress will make a big contribution to his effectiveness as a supervisor. So this "recording" process may be regarded as the last essential feature of the whole management activity.

Looking back at these nine items, it will be noticed that only one of them (item 6) is the physical job of building the houses. The other eight are concerned with preparations, with review of progress, with supervision and leadership of the working team, and with co-ordination of men and jobs. In other words, these other eight are the "management and supervising" activities associated with that operation of house-building.

Is it possible to reduce these eight "managerial" tasks to any broad general classifications?

Items 1, 2, 3 and 4 have a strong element of planning. They are concerned with predetermining the lines of operations, the methods, the allocation of tasks, and so on. Item 3, in addition, contributes particularly to co-ordination. Item 5 is primarily a process of inspiration, or "leadership", but also has a strong element of co-ordination in it, by integrating the activities of the working group through the issue of commands. Items 7 and 9 are concerned with checking the performance, i.e. with "control" of the operations to ensure that progress is satisfactory and that the methods applied may be recommended for future use. Item 8 is entirely co-ordination. It would thus seem from this simple analysis that there are four broad classifications in this example of "management":

(1) Planning, i.e. determining the broad lines for carrying out the operations (the policy, the general programme, the overall plans, the organisation), and preparing the appropriate methods for effective action (equipment, tools, material supplies, working instructions, techniques, working teams, etc.).
(2) Control, i.e. checking current performance against predetermined standards contained in the plans, with a view to ensuring adequate progress and satisfactory performance; also "recording" the experience gained from the working of these plans as a guide to possible future operations.
(3) Co-ordination, i.e. balancing and keeping the team together, by ensuring a suitable allocation of working activities to the various members, and seeing that these are performed with due harmony among the members themselves.
(4) Motivation (or ensuring morale), i.e. getting the members of the teams to pull their weight effectively, to give their loyalty to the group, to carry out properly the activities allocated, and generally to play an effective part in the purpose or task that the organisation has undertaken; with this general "inspiration" goes a process of supervision to ensure that the working teams are keeping to the plans and attaining an adequate level of effectiveness and economy of work. (This is the process popularly labelled "leadership".)

An important point to appreciate is that the building of the houses could not be *effectively* carried out without these "management" activities. The building itself could proceed, but there would be waste of skilled men's time and effort through many trials and errors, waste of material through absence of planning, and numerous delays and difficulties through faulty allocation of jobs and lack of co-ordination. In other words, these "management" factors enabled the building operation to be carried through smoothly, economically and effectively. This, in short, is the purpose and function of management.

Since it is chiefly the activities of people that are co-ordinated and regulated by management, it is correctly called a social process. It requires a special skill, in the same way as many other crafts or callings require their own special skills; for instance, that of the watchmaker or the doctor. The chief difference between the skill of management and the skills that are exercised in many other crafts or callings is its human or social character: it is a responsibility exercised over other people, concerned with getting their co-operation and their unified response in the performance of a given task. Admittedly, the skill of management necessitates attention to technical factors, whether relating to the products, materials or equipment, or to the particular kinds of accounting and recording methods that may be in use, but it is the human aspect that calls for the greater degree of attention—the thinking ahead and planning, so that the activities of the people employed can run smoothly, and the understanding of human behaviour, so that morale can be kept at a high level to ensure continuous effective co-operation.

The main social task thus lies in the two elements referred to above as "co-ordination" and "motivation", the other two elements providing the means of regulating, i.e. "planning" the ways and means, and "controlling" the progress against the plans. The whole process of management, whatever the setting in which it occurs, may therefore be conveniently thought of as composed of two major aspects, namely:

(a) One concerned with the routines and procedures for planning and control of activities;

(b) One concerned with the morale or will to work and the co-operation of the people employed.

These two aspects have been given, in contemporary literature, the name of "functions"—respectively the "control function" and the "personnel function".

A problem in terminology needs to be faced at this point. It has long been popular to talk of "four functions of management" labelled: "Production, Distribution, Personnel, Control" (the last-named also called "Financial Accounting"). This division can be found in many textbooks, and numerous enterprises have had a structure of organisation designed on the same basis, often with a specialist executive in charge of each "function". This traditional view, however, is based on an erroneous conception. The process of management is made up of the four elements quoted above, of which two are primarily human in content, and two are primarily procedural. Within any manufacturing enterprise, the activities of production will need to be planned, regulated and co-ordinated, and the morale of the persons employed will need support by good human management. In other words, *within the framework of the production activities*, all *four* elements of the process of management will be found in action. Similarly, in the case of an enterprise concerned with distribution (e.g. a wholesale warehouse), the same four elements will be found: Planning, Co-ordination, Motivation, Control. Since these four elements fall naturally into the two aspects, described as the "function of control" and the "function of personnel", it may be said that both the "functions" can be identified *within* "production" and *within* "distribution".

This gives a solution to the problem: *the four commonly so-called "functions" (Production, Distribution, Personnel, Control) are of different character. The latter two necessarily occur within the former two.* They cannot therefore be classified as the same thing. The correct description is to call Production and Distribution "fields of activity". Personnel and Control are the only two "functions of management", which must, by their very nature, occur *within all* the fields of activity. The term "function" should be strictly reserved for this designation. If a single word is needed as the description of the parts of an organisation which has its executive activities divided into the four traditional groups (Production, Distribution, Control, Personnel), the best choice would appear to be "divisions", i.e. "the four executive divisions of the organisation". It must, however, be recognised that the latter two are different from the former; the nature of the difference and its significance in the working of management will be discussed later in this chapter with reference to the concept of "functional relations in organisation".

For analytical purposes, the simple illustration used above serves to reveal the nature of the social process of management and the elements that constitute it, but throws little light on the way in which the activities of management occur in practice and how they are grouped. The fourfold scheme that forms the framework of the present study—dividing into Distribution, Production, Personnel, Control—uses the common pattern. It would, however, be a mistake to regard this as typical of most industries. The variety met in organisations is considerable, and it might indeed be very difficult to indicate anything that could rightly be regarded as "a typical organisation structure", even within one industry. It is even difficult to classify, in any "typical" form, the activities in which management is seen in everyday operations. A useful presentation of the whole field is to be found in the Ministry of Education Report on "Education for Management": this separates out the nine aspects of the whole management field which have already been the subject of specialisation and in each of which a professional institution is to be found :[1]

"(a) *Financial Management,* including economic forecasting, accounting, costing, statistical control, budgetary control, insurance and actuarial work.

[1] Extracted from the *Report of the Committee on Education for Management,* H.M.S.O., London 1947.

(b) *Production Management*, including work analysis, scheduling, routing, planning, quality control and time and methods study.

(c) *Development Management*, including research into materials, machines and processing, pure and applied, the whole field of application of the physical sciences to industrial processes, laboratories, experimental plants, etc., and the relation between design, consumer demand and production.

(d) *Distribution Management*, including marketing, merchandising, consumer research, advertising, sales management and export.

(e) *Purchasing Management*, including tendering, buying, contract work, storekeeping and stock control.

(f) *Transport Management*, including transportation by road, rail, water and air, packing and warehousing.

(g) *Maintenance Management*, including upkeep of buildings, plant, equipment and estate work.

(h) *Personnel Management*, including selection, employment, placement, training, transfer, promotion, retirement, industrial relations, medical and welfare services and safety.

(i) *Office Management*, including all arrangements for communication and record, planning and control of offices."

The Report indicates that in addition there is the overall field of "General Management", by implication the top planning and co-ordinating activity of the chief executive, responsible for giving the lead to and setting the tone for the subsidiary parts of the organisation.

In this breakdown, "Personnel Management" occurs as a specific item, while the function of Control is represented in part by separate headings, such as "Financial Management" and "Office Management", and in part by detailed items mentioned within other subjects; for instance, Production or Purchasing. These nine (ten, including General Management) can be taken to represent the broad pattern of management activity—each of them might in the larger organisations be represented by a senior manager or official. Following the line of thought of an earlier paragraph, it can be seen that *within* these various headings, the same four elements of management will be in action. In other words, the "functions of Personnel and Control" will recur *within* "Financial Management", *within* "Production", "Development" and so on, throughout the list.

In the smaller firms the position is clearer, particularly in cases where a single owner or manager looks after all the activities of production and distribution, and thus has the whole of the "line" responsibility in his own hands. For discharging these responsibilities, he has to carry out "Personnel" and "Control" activities, which together make up his process of management: these are the means by which he ensures the effective planning and regulation of his manufacturing and selling, and there is no question of any separate "management" activities in regard to either production or distribution. How the two functions are translated into seemingly separate divisions in the larger organisations can be seen, for instance, at the point at which, because of the increasing load on his own shoulders, the owner-manager takes on an assistant to look after certain aspects of either his personnel work or his statistical records and accounts (i.e. control). The process of management is unchanged; only its division among persons has altered.

4. TERMINOLOGY

The absence of agreed or authoritative views as to the definition of management and its fundamental principles has meant that there is as yet no accepted terminology. Through the wider professional interest in the subject over recent years, there is, however, gradually evolving a common pattern of wording, particularly in regard to the day-to-day activities of management, for instance, within such fields as Production Planning or Production Control, Cost Control, Budgetary Control, Personnel Procedures and so on. But with the generic terms "Organisation", "Management" and "Administration" representing the whole process, confusion and controversy persist.

"Management" is gaining ground over the other two, undoubtedly because throughout industry and commerce the title "manager" is widely accepted (with "executive" as a common alternative). The chief complication arises from the influence of the Government Departments, to whose work the title "Public Administration" has long been applied. In some of the larger commercial organisations the term "administration" has been imported to refer to the activities of the higher levels of management; generally speaking, no analytical reason lies behind this, but it can often be traced to the whim of a particular individual, or possibly to a mistaken notion of prestige. This usage is sometimes extended by applying the descriptive term "administrative" to the offices or staffs that are engaged in the control activities; for instance, one sometimes finds the name "Administrative Block" given to the office sections of the buildings of the large combines. References here and there in official reports, and in the title of the Institute of Industrial Administration, have lent support to this use of "administration" in the industrial or commercial world. But even a brief conversation with the managers (or the self-styled administrators) themselves leads quickly to the conclusion that in their everyday thinking and talking, the label "management" is the one they apply to their activities or responsibilities. There is a strong case for following this rather more natural trend of common opinion, and so for adopting "management" as the general title for the process as a whole. The creation within recent years of a British Institute of Management lends point to this argument.

Has, then, the word "administration" any part to play? In any sense that is synonymous with management the answer is "no" Equally, in any sense that suggests a superior process restricted to the upper executive structure, the answer had also best be "no". Popular usage does suggest that the main significance of "administration", wherever it is used, centres on the procedures which form the tools of management, i.e. the techniques or routines of planning and control. To this extent the term "administration" can be a useful label to apply to these aspects of the total process.[1]

In regard to the term "organisation" there does not today appear to be any difficulty: throughout the industrial and commercial world, and in far wider fields, including Government service, the label "organisation" is habitually used to refer to the structure of responsibilities and relationships allocated to the various executive and supervisory posts, i.e. "the Structure of Organisation". A few writers have on occasions used "organisation" in a dynamic sense, thinking of it in much the same way as the process of management has here been described; but this is now so unusual an approach that it can be regarded as eccentric, and set aside as unfortunate.

A further label is needed to designate the particular aspects of management that fall within the domain of the Board of Directors, i.e. the determination of objectives and policy and the exercise of overall control of the affairs of the enterprise. So far no single name has been agreed or is widely used for this purpose, although one school of thought used to call it "administration". As the persons on whom the responsibility rests are habitually known as Directors, it might be useful again to follow the trend of popular nomenclature and to deduce the label "Direction".

A summary of the terms which are recommended as the most appropriate for general usage can therefore be set down as follows:

(1) *Management.*—A social process entailing responsibility for the effective planning and regulation of the operations of an enterprise, in fulfilment of a given purpose or task, such responsibility involving:

(*a*) The installation and maintenance of proper procedures to ensure adherence to plans; and

(*b*) The guidance, integration and supervision of the personnel composing the enterprise, and carrying out its operations.

[1] The question of terminology forms a major topic in a series of papers on "The Principles of Management and their Application", in the *British Management Review*, Vol. VII, No. 3.

(2) *Direction.*—That part of management which is concerned with the determination of objectives and policy and the checking of overall progress towards their fulfilment.

(3) *Organisation.*—That part of management which is concerned with the definition of the structure of:

(a) The responsibilities by means of which the activities of the enterprise are distributed among the (executive and supervisory) personnel employed in its service; and

(b) The formal interrelations established among the personnel by virtue of such responsibilities.

(4) *Administration.*—That part of management which is concerned with the installation and carrying out of the procedures by which the programme is laid down and the progress of activities is regulated and checked against plans.

5. THE FOUNDATION OF MANAGEMENT—POLICY

It is often overlooked that the activities, for the planning, guidance and co-ordination of which management is responsible, are directed to a given purpose or objective. In an earlier paragraph, the character of objectives found in the economic system was briefly examined: industrial and commercial enterprises in the last analysis exist in order to provide something indirectly or directly for the benefit of the citizen-consumer. Each enterprise individually has, as it were, a specific share in this general purpose, according to what has been determined for it by its founders, or their successors in the present-day body of governors or directors. Without such objective, it is difficult to see how management could be carried into effect, because it would have no goal or aim. A primary need in the practice of management is, therefore, to determine the objective and to define it in terms that all members of the enterprise can understand and appreciate. In practice this is seldom done.

Closely allied to the purpose of the enterprise are the principles on which it is to be conducted—what is commonly called "the policy". This, too, calls for clear formulation as a basis for effective management. Responsibility for determining both the objective and the policy (they are usually interrelated) rests first with those who have initiated the enterprise or who have made its existence possible by providing the necessary finance. In the smaller firms, this may be a single owner or a few partners, or perhaps also one or two outside persons who have put in some of the capital. In the case of a Company, the legal formula constituting the Board of Directors sets up a body to which this responsibility is specifically entrusted: a clear line of demarcation can then be drawn between the Directors in their corporate capacity as a Board, responsible for "direction" in the sense just defined, and the individuals acting separately in any other capacity within the organisation. Much the same is true of the National Corporations: in these a "Board" or other governing body is established, having vested in it a similar responsibility for "direction". In the rather dissimilar organisation of the Co-operative Societies, a General Management Committee, locally established, usually undertakes the responsibility in respect of local trading affairs, but often in the larger agglomerations of co-operative trade that have developed in more recent years, a Board of the customary Company type, exercising responsibility for direction at the head office level, is found.

The suggestion that the providers of capital in the typical business units are answerable for objective and policy is not intended to be a reactionary defence of capitalism, but an underlining of the factual position—although recognising that in contemporary Britain, the Boards of Directors have long since ceased to be spokesmen of the shareholders. The chief point is to fasten on to the representatives of the owners or founders the responsibility for direction, whatever their outlook in discharging it.

Policy can be briefly defined as the objective, the mode of thought and the body of principles underlying the activities of an organisation. In an industrial or commercial enterprise, it may be regarded as determining the share that enterprise takes in the purposes of the economic system: the enterprise has been established—let it be repeated—in order to contribute something towards meeting the needs of consumers. For example, the objective and policy of the National Coal Board, and of all its constituent units right down to the pit, are centred on winning and distributing coal for the community. Similarly, in war or peace, a Royal Ordnance Factory exists as part of a central Ministry to supply the country's armed forces with the necessary weapons of war and war-like stores. These two national instances are, however, no different as to objective and policy from, for instance, an organisation such as the Austin Motor Company, or the smallest factory devoted to making, say, fractional horse-power motors on a small scale. Whatever the product on which the factory is engaged, its primary objective is to make adequate quantities of that product available for consumers at high levels of quality, and at the best possible levels of price. The consumers may be either at home or abroad. In the case of concerns that are devoted to the manufacture of machine tools, baking plant or other forms of capital equipment, including basic industries like iron smelting or the making of steel billets, the objective is one or more stages removed from immediate service to the consumers: their task is to provide the equipment by means of which the modern industrial society obtains the wherewithal for its livelihood.

In the field of distribution, illustrations are just as readily found, ranging from the large Co-operative Store or the well-known Departmental Store on the one side, through various categories and sizes of retail establishment, down to the local one-man shop or the stall in the market-square. In each case the objective is to provide the means by which the goods which the consumer wants are put at his ready disposal. Or again, railway and road transport, the activities of the banks, the advances for house purchases from the Building Societies, the travel and theatre ticket agencies, hotels and many other institutions, are there for the purpose of giving to citizens a variety of direct service that they need for the better enjoyment of living.

The objectives of an organisation are seldom explicitly defined in writing, but in many instances they are obvious. The capital structure of our industrial and commercial community has, admittedly, tended to focus a good deal of attention on the earning of profits, and accordingly popular opinion has long tended to see money, i.e. the payment of dividends to shareholders, as the primary objective. This is an inevitable consequence of the fact that the main criteria of effectiveness in a capitalist community are couched in terms of profit and loss figures. Directors and managers mostly overlook the morale value of stating clearly the objectives of their enterprise in relation to social or consumer needs. The war years taught valuable lessons as to the influence on worker and staff attitudes of a clear realisation of "working for the war effort" and of an appreciation of the way in which the equipment, product or service upon which they were engaged made its contribution to known national needs. That the lesson has not been entirely lost has been evidenced by more recent endeavours to secure workers' interest in the export drive, by letting employees know the extent to which their work is devoted to the service of overseas consumers, and thereby to earning the foreign exchange with which essential imports for home needs may be purchased.

Objective is clearly the first element in policy.

In pursuit of the objective, policy is made up of two further elements:

(1) The first may be described as the ethical foundation of the enterprise. This in turn has two aspects: the one can be summarised as its standards of fair trading, i.e. the basic principles on which the enterprise proposes to conduct its relations with persons or firms outside of itself; for instance, its customers, its dealers, and the general public; the other is fair standards of employment, i.e. the principles which the organisation proposes to observe in regard to dealings with its own employees.

(2) The second main element may be described as the organisational or operational foundation, concerned with the structure and conduct of the operations of the enterprise: this will also have two aspects, the one relating to external operations, i.e. channels and methods of trading; the other concerned with internal working, questions of equipment, methods of production, basic practices in personnel or control techniques, and so on.

It will be noted that in both elements of policy there is an "outside" and an "inside" aspect, dealing respectively with—(a) the relations of the organisation to the world outside, and (b) the people and methods making up the organisation itself. Thus a fully developed policy provides management with a basis for discharging effectively the economic and social responsibilities which devolve from its participation in the life of the community:

(a) To contribute to the economic needs of the community by the manufacture and supply of the products which it is set up to produce, or by carrying out the particular lines of trade or service that it is designed to provide;

(b) To contribute to the economic and social well-being of the community by improvements in the quality and volume of the products made available, and by reductions in the price at which they are available; in other fields, by improving the service that is being offered and lowering the cost without impairment of quality. It is by reductions in cost of existing products and services that a community makes advances in its standards of life, because, by having to spend less money on known or admitted needs, consumers have a margin to spend on the satisfaction of further wants, investment for savings purposes, or the pursuit of educational or recreational amenities;

(c) To improve the standards of employment by raising the level of working conditions and enhancing personal and social satisfactions at work;

(d) To respect, or contribute to the advancement of, the local amenities of the particular community in which the enterprise is physically set.

Formulation of its outlook and attitude in these social directions may be said to constitute the general policy of an organisation: such principles as it lays down will apply throughout its activities. In addition, a breakdown of policy will usually be required, especially in those aspects that are concerned with channels and methods of trading and production. In fact once an organisation grows to even moderate size, its activities will need to some extent to be sectionalised, either by division into manufacture, selling, transport, etc., or by geographical divisions with subsidiary premises in other localities, or by the development of functional divisions in management. General policy will then need reformulating so as to set out the guiding lines for these different sectional aspects, to ensure adequate co-ordination of the various parts. Such sectional principles cannot be regarded as separate policies, but only as specialised or sectional expressions of the major general policy from which they all stem and to which they all relate.

The clear formulation of policy, in general and in sections, and its announcement within and without the organisation in a written declaration, can be of the highest importance in promoting the effectiveness of management. Policy is obviously the basis of the structure of organisation needed for carrying on the affairs of the enterprise. Unless policy is clearly defined, it is not possible to frame an organisation, because it is not possible adequately to determine the appropriate executive responsibilities and relationships; nor can the appointed executives carry out these responsibilities with effectiveness and co-ordination. Perhaps more obviously, the clear formulation of policy underlies planning, whether in relation to the capital and equipment required, the premises, the channels of trade, the levels of employment, the purchase of materials, or many other more detailed aspects of the programme for getting the enterprise into operation and keeping its activities moving. It is also important to appreciate that policy has a considerable contribution to make to co-ordination, especially in the larger organisations, and to the maintenance of morale. Where policy is clearly defined, in its general and sectional aspects, the organisation is already a long way advanced towards ensuring that its executives will keep in step in the day-to-day discharge of their responsibilities.

The relevance of policy to morale is not often realised. Information as to objectives and policy is a known means of promoting and securing co-operation. In an organisation where managers keep all these things to themselves, and argue that workers or staff should get on with the job and "do as they are told", morale is often low: ignorance breeds indifference and suspicion, moods which manifestly hinder co-operation and will to work. Clear policy is an aid to information. It removes the sense of aimlessness, and promotes the sense of participation, besides inspiring in employees confidence in the soundness of management. They know what the organisation is trying to do; they know how plans are formulated for the attainment of the known ends; they are aware of the standards of trading and employment that have been laid down. They have in this knowledge a lead towards co-operation and the response of good effort in the performance of their own part of the total job. To the individual managers and supervisors, too, clear definition of policy affords a firm basis for the daily practice of their responsibilities and the continuous promotion of sound employee relations.

Policy is also the basis on which the results of management can be assessed. The establishment of criteria of effectiveness and their use in assessing the achievements of the organisation is the other half of the responsibility of the Board of Directors, the higher level of management. It falls to them to ensure that the objectives of the enterprise are being attained and that the policies that have been laid down are being followed. They have then to ensure that all operations and activities are being carried out at an adequate level of effectiveness and economy: it is in this connection that the various types of control data and higher financial accounts come into play. At the lower levels of control, the function of such data is to ensure that plans are being followed and reasons for departures known, but in addition, the daily, weekly or monthly data are contributing to the overall periodic picture which will enable "top management", and the Board of Directors, to ensure that adequate standards of effectiveness and economy are being achieved and maintained throughout.

Policy must be clearly related to facts; in an industrial or commercial organisation this may mean that policy is based on forecasting, to ascertain market or production requirements and other fundamental factors of economic operation. Accordingly, although the responsibility for the formulation of policy rests squarely with the Board of Directors, the members of the executive organisation may make important and useful contributions. In the first place, their specialist knowledge can be the basis on which accurate and factual forecasts of markets and sales potentials are made. Their daily dealings with the problems of management afford them a more realistic appreciation of the circumstances in which trading has to be carried on—material supplies, machine capacity, man-power, and the many other factors that can so easily play havoc with even the best-sounding policy. They also have a closer view of the structure of management and so of the weaknesses and deficiencies that can be a bar to carrying policy into effect. Apart from such positive contribution from the managers to the formulation of policy, there is also a morale aspect here: if managers are to be expected to carry heavy responsibilities for the affairs of the organisation, they should be consulted on the fundamentals of that organisation. Policy is the chief of such fundamentals. They cannot be expected to show a high level of co-operation, or to secure it from subordinates, if their own superiors adopt the "theirs not to reason why, theirs but to do or die" attitude.

To convey policy from the Board of Directors to the members of the executive structure is the task of the Managing Director. His responsibility can be summed up as the first stage in management, i.e. interpreting policy into terms of operating instructions, and reporting back to the Board on the working of management. To him falls in the first instance the responsibility for ensuring that objectives and policy are known to all members of the organisation, and to set the tone that will govern the level of morale through all subordinate ranks. In the smaller units, particularly in the case of the single owners, this first stage is inextricably intermingled with policy formulation: as his own boss, the single owner lays down the policy and interprets it all in the same breath. The same is largely true of the partnerships and the smaller companies, or of any companies in which the Directors also hold full-time executive appointments. The few men concerned at the top are at one time a Board of Directors sitting round a table in formal array, but for the greater part of the time they are individual managers, with the Managing Director as their chief. To draw the distinction between their two capacities is not always easy in thought and frequently very difficult in action. But in principle the distinction is there.

If there is to be effective interpretation of policy into instructions for executive action, there must be a single source of reference. This, in fact, is the purpose of the office of Managing Director: the individual holding it is at once a Director sharing in the corporate responsibility for determining objectives and policy, and the chief executive in command of the lines of management responsibility leading down to operations. He, in fact, is the first channel through which the process of management will flow.

In larger organisations, the position of the Managing Director is usually clearer. The Board as such may contain a number of persons who carry executive responsibilities within the organisation, and in addition other persons whose services to the Company are restricted to the part-time duties required by attendance at Board Meetings. The Managing Director is specifically appointed and recognised as the executive head of the organisation, responsible to the Board for ensuring that policy is correctly interpreted and that there will ensue effective fulfilment of the policy so as to achieve the objectives. This is not for one moment to suggest that human frailties will not give rise to complications; for instance, any of the Directors also holding executive responsibilities for specific parts of the organisation may usurp the Managing Director's function and issue his own instructions which purport to be the sole interpretation of policy. Such bad practice, however, does not vitiate the principle: only the Managing Director carries responsibility to the Board for the interpretation of policy; he alone holds the dual rôle of Director-cum-executive.

The other Directors must be seen as exercising *two distinct functions* or living two different rôles: they share the corporate responsibility of Directors, as members of the Board, when sitting at Board Meetings; they return to their rather different position as executive subordinates to the Managing Director when they leave the Board Room to take up their responsibilities for specific parts of the organisation. The common habit of talking about "a Director in charge of" manufacturing or sales involves a contradiction in terms.

The formulation of policy is usually a non-current activity, in the sense that the Board of Directors initially lays down general lines and later from time to time introduces adjustments when circumstances specifically dictate. But the interpretation of policy has to be a continuous process, carried out by discussions between the Managing Director and his subordinate executives or by the issue of new instructions to them. Some interpretation of policy also occurs in the form of decisions on specific matters brought forward for consideration. It is an element in the skill of a Managing Director or General Manager that he can make these decisions *ad hoc* in relation to the particular points while keeping truly to the main pattern of policy laid down. Thus, the task of interpreting policy is one readily recurring among the daily activities of the chief executive.

Some interpretation of policy has also to take place at lower levels, especially in the larger organisations. The broad lines of "sectional" policy may have been laid down by the Board in formulating their general policy, or by the Managing Director in his major instructions. There will necessarily have to be some review and reinterpretation in the specialist terms appropriate to the various divisions of the enterprise: this is a natural item in the functional responsibilities of executives in charge of such divisions. In many instances this reinterpretation of policy at the lower levels merges into planning, and serves as the link between policy and programme of action. This is seen especially in the field of manufacturing: at the level of the Production or Factory Manager, policy is reformulated in all the technical terms required for laying down the production plan or manufacturing programme. Similarly, in an enterprise which has adopted the techniques of budgetary control, policy is translated in financial terms into the form of approved expense budgets and related standards of performance.

These aspects of policy show how it is woven into the fabric of management and bring out clearly another important feature— that policy must be flexible, capable of adaptation or reinterpretation in the light of changing circumstances.

6. THE STRUCTURE OF MANAGEMENT—ORGANISATION

As policy is the basis of management in action, so organisation is its framework. It was defined earlier as the structure of the responsibilities allocated to the executive and supervisory personnel and of the (formal) relationships that arise in the discharge of those responsibilities. It was pointed out that it is now customary to use the term "organisation" only in this static sense, and clearly it is thus an aspect of planning—defining the executive and supervisory responsibilities required in order to attain a certain objective and policy is, in principle, little different from the task of deciding what equipment is to be used, how it is to be laid out in the factory, or what materials are to be employed in manufacture.

The foundation of an organisation structure is the descriptive definition of the responsibilities that are to be undertaken. An organisation structure is *not* a chart. The chart is an illustration of the grouping of the responsibilities and of the relations that arise among the groups. Simply to draw lines from a chief executive to his subordinate executive colleagues, including diagonal lines to indicate functional or specialist relationships, may be a useful representation of the facts in any given organisation, but it is only a pictorial presentation of relationships. Of itself it does not codify the responsibilities of the various executive or supervisory posts concerned. This can be done only by clear definitions of the scope and breakdown of such responsibilities, with indication of the official to whom the executive in question is to be held responsible, who in turn is responsible to him, and the particular relations he needs to maintain with other executives not in his own direct sequence. The "relationships" are part of the planned pattern of the working of management. It is conducted from one section to another, not only through the senior to which both of these sections are attached, but by means of lateral or functional relations directly subsisting between the sections, enabling them to co-operate in the pursuit of the common task and in the fulfilment of the common policy. This is readily seen at work, for instance, within a manufacturing unit where there is a Planning Manager and a Factory Manager, both responsible to a senior Production executive. The one has responsibilities, for instance, for laying down the manufacturing plans, the other has responsibility for ensuring that the plans are carried out. Lateral relations exist between these two executives to ensure continuous co-ordination and co-operation in the mutually shared task of translating policy into an agreed output programme and seeing that the programme is fulfilled.

Similar illustrations can be drawn readily enough from the relations between, say, the Factory Manager and the Sales Manager within one organisation, or in the specialist relations between a Personnel Officer, responsible for recruitment, training, welfare and similar procedures, and a Factory Manager who carries full responsibility for the planning and attainment of production programmes. Schedules of executive responsibilities lay down in broad general terms the field that these individual managers or supervisors are called on to cover: illustrations of such schedules are set out in Appendix II.

That the subject of organisation has for some time been of considerable interest is probably due to the many deficiencies or weaknesses that are characteristic of the structure of management in industry and commerce, leading invariably to inefficiency and high costs of operating. It is astonishing how frequently the same deficiencies or weaknesses recur, and how often they are due to the absence of proper definitions of responsibility. There is, of course, the further difficulty caused by lack of agreed principles of organisation structure. That it should be possible to elaborate such principles from analysis of observed strengths and weaknesses is certainly suggested by the very extent to which the same difficulties are found repeated in enterprises of widely different character and size.[1]

From the practical standpoint, the absence of authoritative principles does give rise to a difficult problem in the case of the chief executive who wants to set up a sound structure by defining the responsibilities and relationships of himself and his subordinates. He may, perhaps, have some help from contemporary literature, but he has still to rely largely on his own judgment. If starting with a new organisation, he is in a position to proceed analytically: to start with the formulation of management aims and policy; then to group for his own purposes the particular tasks that have to be undertaken; then deciding in broad outline the planning and control techniques; thus eventually arriving at groupings of responsibilities and duties and relations that will lead to a systematic structure. There may be a textbook that will afford him some principles against which to test his own creation.

When, however, trying to remodel an existing organisation, the problem is more complicated, because some regard must be paid to the present framework. In this case, the formulation of executive responsibilities can best be carried out with the active co-operation of the managers and supervisors themselves. Each can be asked to write down in broad outline the various tasks and activities for which

[1] For further comment on this point, see the author's article in the *British Management Review*, Vol. VII, No. 1.

he regards himself responsible, and the lines along which he proceeds to fulfil them. He can be asked to group these tasks under certain major headings, which have perhaps been broadly formulated in advance. Someone nominated as "Organisation Secretary" would collect these detailed documents, and after scrutiny take up with the individuals concerned amplification or clarification of obscure points. Note should particularly be taken of items of duplication or omission that the Organisation Secretary can recognise from his own more central standpoint. He would then proceed to analyse the completed documents, in order to obtain a comprehensive picture of how the total responsibilities of management are distributed, to ascertain how they contribute to the fulfilment of policy, and to mark out the instances of overlapping, duplication, deficiency or omission. The chief executive is then in a position to examine with his subordinates the "map" of the organisation territory as at present laid out, and to agree with them the ways in which certain fields or parts would be better regrouped, to ensure a higher degree of co-ordination, a better cover of management responsibility, a closer fulfilment of policy, a better distribution of load, or remedies to correct such deficiencies and gaps as have been revealed. The review would be rounded off by writing up the schedules along the lines indicated in Appendix II.

The task thus set out may appear to be formidable and to lend support to the view that organisation is an aspect of management pertinent only to the larger units. Nothing, in fact, could be farther from the truth: even the smallest organisation can gain from knowing exactly how its management works. As soon as two or three managers and supervisors are brought into existence by growth from the very small stage, the need for demarcation of responsibilities becomes not only valuable, but essential to good management; and such demarcation is nothing else than the determination and definition of responsibilities and relationships, i.e. setting up an organisation structure.

It might be useful at this point to enter a warning against any search for "a typical organisation". There is, admittedly, a broad common pattern of organisation to be found in the average British company. A Board of Directors represents the owners (shareholders) and carries a corporate responsibility for the objectives, the policy and the overall progress of the enterprise. Responsible to the Board is the Chief Executive, the Managing Director or General Manager, called on to translate policy into instructions for executive action, to initiate the whole process of management, and to answer to the Board for its effective operation throughout the enterprise. This responsibility is discharged by the processes of delegation, and is reported back to the Board through the medium of accounts, reports and statistics. Below the Managing Director come the hierarchy of senior, intermediate and junior managers, smaller or greater in number according to the size of the enterprise, and appropriately divided along varying lines according to the tasks to be undertaken, the prevailing needs and other factors. Some managers carry direct responsibility for the immediate operations of the enterprise; others hold appointments of specialist (functional) character. In either case the executives are sharing part of the total responsibility for the planning and regulation of the activities of the enterprise according to the particular division or function allotted to them. To enable these executives or managers to carry out their responsibilities effectively, they are assisted at the working level by "supervisors", whose responsibilities are less, if at all, concerned with planning, but mainly centre on the oversight of operations to ensure that plans are followed or departures from plan promptly reported to the responsible executive.

This rather characteristic general pattern is, however, only in a superficial sense "typical". The outward similarity of responsibilities at each major executive level cloaks the very varied distribution or arrangement of them that will be found within even a small number of seemingly comparable organisations. It may broadly be said that there is no general pattern for the distribution of executive responsibilities: there would appear to be certain basic principles of organisation structure commonly applicable, but with considerable differences in actual application. Paramount among these is the principle of the unity of management. Whatever the character, size or aims of an enterprise, the organisation structure represents from top to bottom the framework of a single process. Starting in "direction" and moving right down to the immediate supervision of the routine activities of making, distributing or recording, the whole scheme of executive responsibilities is an integrated pattern, designed to carry out effectively the planning and regulation of these activities and to ensure that a given purpose is fulfilled at the optimum level of operating efficiency and cost.[1]

The fallacy of referring to a "typical organisation" is often paralleled in the error that there are "types" of organisation, the three most commonly referred to being labelled: (i) the line or military type; (ii) the line and staff; (iii) the functional. In the first, all responsibility is direct from subordinate to senior, and conversely; there are no specialist executives who bring to bear a subsidiary responsibility

---

[1] For an interesting analytical study of the breakdown and grouping of executive and supervisory responsibilities, see Alvin Brown, *Organisation of Industry*, chaps. 10–12 (Prentice-Hall, New York, 1947).

cutting crosswise into the up-and-down pattern. The second is described as a mixture of direct and functional responsibilities, and is illustrated from widespread experience of everyday practice: the factory which has an executive in charge of production or manufacturing paralleled by a specialist (functional) personnel executive providing direct to the factory the numerous customary services. The third type is sometimes illustrated in the textbooks in chart form as a pattern of diagonal lines without up-and-down lines below the top level. It is a conception not easily illustrated from industrial practice and difficult to understand in theory—if indeed it has any validity at all.

From the descriptions of the practice of management that make up the later parts of this volume, it will be seen that, except in the very small enterprises, some form of specialist activity is nearly always present, even if only carried out by a secretary on behalf of an owner-manager. This means that the pure (so-called) "line" type is seldom found, while the functional pattern, in simple or complex form, tends to be the commonplace one. The notion of "types" of organisation is thus one that serves little useful purpose, and from analytical consideration may be definitely written off as a somewhat pointless conception that has been allowed to go unchallenged.

There are, however, *"types of relationship" within an organisation*, and an understanding of these is essential to proper appreciation of the working of management. Four kinds of relationships can be distinguished, and they can be conveniently summarised as: direct, lateral, functional, staff (personal).

(1) *Direct Executive Relations.*—The relationship existing between a senior and his subordinates, and conversely. The senior may be a Managing Director or other manager, and his subordinates the junior managers, supervisors and other grades down to the operative levels. The relations involved here are those of instruction on the senior's part and compliance by the subordinates. (This is not, of course, to suggest any authoritarian approach, as obviously the element of motivation requires a proper human flavour to the instructions and appropriate consultation with subordinates.) In principle, the relationship is that of "direct authority", in the customary sense in which a senior may give valid orders to subordinates within his jurisdiction: these relations are customarily described as "direct" or "line", and are readily illustrated from the position of a factory manager, chief accountant, supervisor, and many other managerial or supervisory positions in industrial organisation, *vis-à-vis* their immediate subordinates.[1]

[1] Because of confusions with the military terminology in the phrase "line and staff", there is a very good case for recommending use of the term "direct" instead of "line" to designate relationships of this category.

(2) *Lateral Relations.*—The working relations between executives or supervisors at the same level of responsibility. In the exercise of management two executives may both be responsible to a common senior for different sections of the activities of the enterprise, both of them holding "direct" responsibilities. The smooth working of management calls for collaboration between them on points of mutual interest, without reference back to the common senior: the executive relationship thus set up between the two managers is described as "lateral".

(3) *Functional Relations.*—Those which arise in the case of a specialist executive contributing a service to the managers and supervisors who compose the rest of the organisation. His executive position and the service that he gives arise primarily from specialised knowledge, i.e. within a certain field he has a body of knowledge and experience which is germane to the working and effectiveness of management in the organisation as a whole. Usually, it is only in the larger enterprises that such specialist services can be separated out into a distinct executive post, though the services will arise in organisations of any size. The specialist (or "functional") executive has a responsibility for ensuring that the particular field of activities allocated to his jurisdiction are carried into effect throughout the organisation at a high level of effectiveness, a responsibility which has three aspects: the first is to assist in the formulation of the relevant sectional policy; the second is to advise his "line" colleagues and subordinate members of the organisation on the working of management in that particular regard; the third is to be answerable to his immediate senior, usually the Managing Director, for the effective conduct of the particular specialised activities concerned, i.e. he is responsible for assisting the other managers and supervisors in carrying out those activities and for ensuring that their "line" instructions conform to the relevant sectional policy. If a "functional" executive has subordinates or staff of his own, his relations with these persons are obviously of the "direct" type already described; similarly, his own relations with his immediate superior have the same character. But relations with other executives, supervisors and members of the organisation are of an indirect category, and are customarily labelled "functional". Referring back to the argument of an earlier paragraph (see page 12), it will be appreciated that in the general working of industrial and commercial organisations, the functional relationship arises chiefly in regard to the personnel and control aspects of management. Illustrations can be drawn from the Personnel Manager responsible for ensuring that personnel policy is carried out by appropriate procedures and by an adequate standard of human relations at all levels of management and supervision; or from a Clerical Methods Manager, responsible for sanctioning routines and procedures, the design of forms, the purchase and the use of office equipment, etc., throughout the organisation.

(4) *Staff Relation.*—A distinct relationship arising from the appointment of a (personal) assistant to an executive. The arrangement is not often found in industry, and occurs mainly in the top levels of the organisation, e.g. a Personal Assistant to the Managing Director. His terms of reference may be of general or specific character, but the nature of responsibility is clearly defined as assisting the executive to whom he is allocated. The Personal Assistant is, strictly speaking, not an executive at all, and certainly of his own right carries no authority; he is best regarded as an extension of the personality of the executive he serves, either for general or for specific purposes according to the terms of reference. In such a capacity he clearly discharges his chief's responsibilities and equally clearly dispenses his authority; of himself he has no subordinates (except perhaps a secretary) and issues no instructions. Whatever he does within that organisation, he does on behalf of and with the authority of his chief. In consequence, it is only with his chief that he has any formal relations, and for these the title "staff relation" is used. No label can be applied to his relations with other parts of the organisation because *of himself he has none*; his activities and his daily contacts with the executives are part of the working of management within the organisation, but the character of his responsibility is such that he can have *no formal relations*, direct or functional, with other members of the organisation, apart from his chief.

Of these four types of relationships within an organisation the first and second are most frequently met. The "direct" contact of senior and subordinate arises in even the smallest working unit of a man and a boy, or a plumber and his mate, or the village shopkeeper and her girl. The "lateral" relationship can only emerge when there is more than one member in any one grade, for instance, two partners, both operating as principals, or two supervisors responsible to a Works Manager, each in charge of a separate department or section of the factory. The alternate Day Shift and Night Shift Managers of a department are related laterally—and many other illustrations can readily be quoted. "Functional" relationships develop as the unit begins to grow to larger size, though no numerical test can be laid down. Sometimes, the need for specialist service emerges early in growth, as is most commonly seen in regard to accounting and secretarial activities: even when still of quite small size, a manufacturing enterprise may need to engage specialist accountancy assistance, perhaps on a part-time basis in the person of a professional Secretary. The human problems of management are another field that often give rise to the need for expert assistance early in the growth of an enterprise, and the functional position of Personnel Officer is frequently brought into existence among the first few executive appointments below the Managing Director.

It is these groups of executive relationships that give a meaning to an organisation structure: they form the "lines" as portrayed in the chart. Direct relations are the verticals; lateral relations are the horizontals. Functional relations are customarily shown in dotted or broken form for distinction, and portrayed as diagonals from the executive concerned directly to all other major points of relevant contact. In strict principle, however, they should be shown parallel to the horizontal and vertical lines. The distinction is illustrated in Fig. 1 opposite: the dual portrayal there brings out the important point that, while in everyday practice a functional executive will deal with subordinates of other executives on matters within his jurisdiction, in principle he is doing so with the concurrence of the immediate superior of such subordinates. In practice, this means that the functional executive should keep that superior fully informed of instructions or decisions given to his subordinates.

In regard to his colleagues on the same executive level as himself, a specialist executive's functional relations are identical with lateral relations. But his responsibility is different. The particular features of a functional responsibility are:

(a) It originates in expert knowledge of a given field, and exists in order to provide specialist service to the "direct" executives and supervisors;

The chart illustrates five functional relationships; in the organisation depicted there will, of course, be very many more.

The broken lines (– – – –) show functional contacts between the Personnel Assistant and—

(1) The three Foremen of Component Manufacturing Sections (perhaps in regard to progress of apprentices or absence of some operatives);
(2) The Supervisor of the Accounts Department (perhaps in regard to recruitment of a new junior or a problem regarding one of the staff).

The dash-dot lines (–·–·–·) show functional contacts between the Clerical Methods Manager and—

(3) The three Foremen of the Assembly Departments (perhaps in regard to Work Tickets or Stores Notes);
(4) The Supervisor of the Personnel Department Office (say, in regard to Record Cards);
(5) The Supervisor of the Sales Office (perhaps in regard to customer records or addressing of letters).

The broken and dash-dot lines show the functional relationships:

(i) Parallel to the horizontal and vertical relations, they represent the formal pattern of contact, i.e. the path along which *in principle* the contact flows;
(ii) Diagonally they represent the customary direct contact between the parties concerned, though involving the Functional Executive in a responsibility to keep the senior managers informed of the decisions or "instructions" given to their subordinates.

N.B.—The varying levels portrayed in this chart are for convenience of printing and not to be read as indicating status.

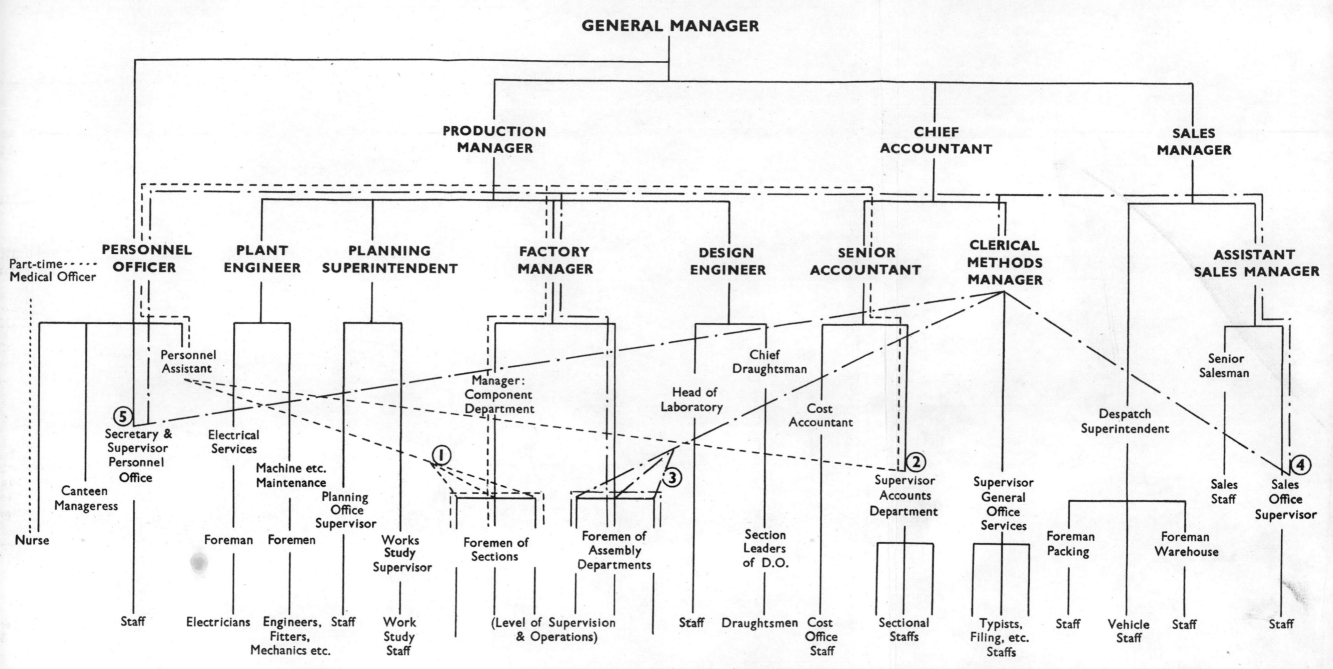

Fig. 1   CHART ILLUSTRATING FUNCTIONAL RELATIONSHIPS IN AN ORGANISATION

(b) The functional executive is always to be consulted before any decision is taken pertinent to his jurisdiction;

(c) He must ensure the attainment of the relevant sectional policy throughout those parts of the organisation where his jurisdiction extends; and

(d) His decisions, rulings or instructions with the given field, and within the agreed policy, must be followed by other executives, and cannot be gainsaid, overruled, or set aside except by his immediate senior executive.

His responsibilities are mainly discharged by *other* executives and supervisors, and his "instructions" therefore pass through the lateral and direct channels of the organisation.

One special problem calls for mention here. The personnel aspects of management, when separated out as the sphere of responsibility of a specialist executive, are now readily recognised as "functional" in character, and the Personnel Officer's relations with his colleagues in the hierarchy are similarly—and correctly—described. This accords with the analytical presentation of the personnel element in the process of management set out in an earlier section. The comparable position of the "control" element is, however, not so readily recognised. The character of "control" as a "functional element of management" in an exact sense was diagnosed alongside the personnel element. Yet in the working of management, it is more usual —though incorrect—to regard the control executives as "line" managers. The reason probably lies in the rather large subordinate staffs that such executives (Chief Accountant, Comptroller, Company Secretary) customarily have under their jurisdiction. What are often described as the "administrative and clerical offices" of a large organisation can sometimes employ hundreds of accountants, clerks and secretaries, and so the responsibility of the Chief Accountant or Comptroller appears to have very much of the same "direct" character as that of the manager in charge of manufacturing operations; he seems to have much the same task as the Factory Manager, watching over the activities of a large number of people, and thus the analogy of position as a "line" executive is easy to draw. Within the Chief Accountant's own domain that argument is sound: that is to say, he has a direct executive responsibility for and over the activities of his subordinate staffs. But *in relation to the process of management as a whole his responsibility is of a functional kind.* This can be seen quite readily by examining the purpose of the activities within his jurisdiction: accounts, records, correspondence, and the like. Their purpose is an obvious one, to assist the effective performance of the major activities of the enterprise—whether these be manufacturing, selling, transport, catering, loans to house purchasers, or any other economic field—by forecasts and plans or budgets for directing operations in the factory or sales departments, and by currently keeping the executives informed of the progress of their activities, in physical and financial terms, as compared with plans or budgets. He records financial transactions, and periodically renders an account of them to reveal the financial outcome (profit and loss, etc.); he keeps a record of work done and time worked; he calculates wages and salaries, prepares statistics of stocks, sales, orders, costs, etc., and provides facilities for correspondence, filing, telephone, and so on. By function, therefore, the Chief Accountant is providing a service of information and communication for the managers; apart from this contribution to the effective planning and control of the major operations, he has no *raison d'être*. This clearly establishes the *functional* character of his responsibility.

Reference was made earlier to the common view that organisation is one of the refinements of management, that the definition of responsibilities is all very well for the bigger and more ambitious enterprises, or those which like doing things with a sense of display. With the practical man, it is argued, there is no call for an organisation structure; he knows what his colleagues are doing, and they all get along quite well together by their mutual knowledge of each other and of the business as a whole. Experience has, unfortunately, proved this rather common view to be utterly erroneous, even in the case of quite small units. Again and again, difficulties in the operations or management of a factory or store can be traced to weaknesses in organisation—either faults in the allocation of responsibilities and the determination of their relations or, more usually, to the absence of any real pattern of known responsibilities. Inevitably in such circumstances there occur overlapping, duplication of effort, and misunderstandings, and many important things are omitted because no one seems to be responsible for them.

Such casualness in regard to organisation springs from failure to appreciate its position as the framework of management: without a framework management cannot be effective. Organisation is closely related to policy, to planning, to control, to co-ordination and even to motivation. In the first place, the responsibilities that make up an organisation structure cannot be determined until policy is known, at least in outline. For the policy indicates what is going to be done, and in broad terms how: this alone makes it possible to draw up the proper framework for the necessary operations to achieve that policy. Conversely, of course, the existence of a stable and clear structure makes the dissemination and interpretation of policy easier, and enables its fulfilment to be more readily checked. The known distribution of responsibilities provides a foundation for more detailed planning of operations, methods, lines of working, equipment, routines and the like. Obviously it contributes enormously to co-ordination: the mere knowledge of who is doing what, and how the various responsibilities are interrelated, is in large measure a guarantee of co-ordination in the working of management. There is also a relevance to morale: much of the frustration that characterises so many of the executives and supervisors in Britain's industrial system springs from irritations due to lack of knowledge of their own and their colleagues' jurisdiction, from unfortunate experiences of wasted duplicated effort, or from a sense of despair due to lack of clarity as to limitations imposed on the exercise of responsibilities. The clear definition of responsibilities and relations contributes to better understanding of objectives and of policy, to a keener sense of orderliness and purpose, and so to a higher level of morale; this in turn is reflected in a greater measure of self-responsibility, of co-operation, of will-to-work, of effectiveness in daily action, and so of productivity. This is not to argue that organisation structure alone can achieve efficiency; that could not be so, because it is only one aspect of the process of management. But it is in a special sense a fundamental aspect, because it is the framework without which the process cannot be carried out.

A major problem that comes up in any consideration of organisation structure is the question of "personalities". There has long been a controversy of "personalities versus organisation", a conflict of view as to whether an organisation should be formulated according to deductive principles and in the abstract without any reference to personalities, or whether the grouping of responsibilities should be built around the available personalities. The controversy is easily resolved, by the answer that neither argument is entirely true. In smaller units it is often inevitable that the distribution of responsibilities should conform to certain personality requirements, while in the larger unit, experience suggests that it is safer for the structure to be built up independently of persons. In neither case can it be safely said either that principle should be disregarded or that the personal element should be entirely neglected. The wise line of procedure would seem to involve treating organisation as a technical issue and adopting the following steps:

(1) Work from the known objective and policy of the enterprise.
(2) Define the responsibilities needed to secure fulfilment of the policy, and determine their appropriate groupings and relationships.
(3) Determine from these definitions specifications of the qualities qualifications and experience required to discharge the respon- sibilities effectively, i.e. prepare specifications for the various executive and supervisory appointments.

(4) Select the persons to be appointed to the responsibilities in accordance with the specification; or, if it is decided to appoint someone not exactly conforming, set down the known objective reasons for the departure from the specification.

(5) Set the structure (responsibilities and relationships) to work according to the definitions, but if it is decided that certain departures should be countenanced, the known objective reasons for such departure should be set down; in every instance of departure it should be clear that basic principles are not being contravened.

(6) The test as to the soundness or otherwise of such departure will lie in whether or not harmonious and balanced working of management is attained throughout the organisation, so that management is in fact ensuring true efficiency of operations and a high level of morale in the working teams.

One special aspect of the personal factor in organisation structure is that of the span of responsibility or supervision of an executive over subordinate executives or supervisors. The point arises with most significance where the activities of the subordinate sections are inter-related in their current working. A widely accepted notion is that the number of such subordinates should be "limited to five or six", as though there were virtue in either figure. This notion originated from a Rumanian Management Consultant working in Paris in the early 1930's; he calculated the combinations of reciprocal interrelationships that must arise in the course of contacts between a superior and increasing numbers of subordinates. With five subordinates, the total relationships ("direct and cross" as he called them) is 100. With six, the total increases to 222, and with seven to 490. This last figure he regarded as beyond the range of expected competence of the average individual executive. There is undoubtedly substance in the argument, and a clear conclusion can be derived that a definite limit is to be imposed on the span of responsibility (or "span of control" as it is popularly, but rather loosely, called). Personal make-up and the specific character of the responsibilities covered and circumstances concerned must, however, be taken into account. Some men, in certain circumstances, might easily be overburdened with only four subordinates, whereas here and there an individual may well be able to carry eight or nine persons reporting to him. This again is a matter on which considerable thought is to be exercised before a decision is taken, and a sound management appraisal will always counsel choosing the lower number of subordinates, at the executive or supervisory levels, rather than the higher one, if there should be any uncertainty in the decision.

7. PRINCIPLES OF MANAGEMENT

At many points in this Introduction, reference has been made to the absence of accepted authoritative principles of management. This has undoubtedly been one of the factors contributing to the persistence of weaknesses in industrial and commercial practice, chiefly because it has hampered the systematic study of the subject on a professional or scientific basis. It may at first sight seem strange, since management has been carried on so widely and for so long, that no common fundamentals should have been agreed. Four factors have contributed to this:

(a) Managers have been too exclusively concerned with the practice of their profession; it is frequently deeply set in technical surroundings, and much of their attention is attracted to the technical factors rather than to the managerial; accordingly, they tend to be more concerned with practical issues than with the principles that underlie such practice.

(b) There is a long-standing tradition that management is a special aptitude, which is to be found inborn in some individuals and missing from others. Industrial developments in more recent times have proved this view to be fallacious, but its persistence has hindered recognition of the underlying fundamental principles, common to management wherever it occurs and whoever is responsible for it.

(c) In most industrial countries, and particularly in Great Britain, economic progress was made mainly on technical foundations; that is to say, the improvement of machines and equipment, the development of better methods of transport, the improvement of materials, and so on; it is only in comparatively recent times that management has been identified as contributing specifically to industrial and commercial progress.

(d) The few writers or thinkers who have been attracted to the fundamental aspects of management, with a view to elucidating basic principles, have shown a marked tendency to approach their analytical task on a purely individual basis; they have not normally taken as their own starting-point the body of knowledge already existing as the result of contributions from earlier writers. In consequence, their writings have tended to conflict, or to lead to confusions, instead of building up a cumulative "science" of management. A particular instance of this isolation is seen in the terminology tangle centring on the three words "management", "administration" and "organisation".

The possibility of defining principles of management has been the subject of a good deal of writing and discussion in the past decade, in both Britain and the United States. In part this has come from increasing awareness of the extent to which observed weaknesses in management have common characteristics. It has also been fostered by the professional Management Consultants, whose whole activity is the diagnosis and remedy of management deficiencies. A number of the more expert professional Consultants have contributed to knowledge of the "laws" of management, and their efforts have been assisted by such professional bodies as the Institute of Industrial Administration, the Office Management Association, the Institution of Works Managers, and the corresponding societies in the United States.[1]

Among the various suggestions put forward, there have been some that cannot rightly be called "principles" at all: they are rather methods for the better practice of management. A principle means a fundamental truth as the basis of reasoning, a primary element, a general law. It is commonly understood in this sense in the world of science or any other field of systematic knowledge: it must carry the same meaning in regard to management—the fundamental "principles" must mean the basic laws on which the practice of management is to be built up. They must necessarily be couched in general terms, because they have to be applicable within organisations of varying size and character. Moreover, they must be so formulated as *not* to include suggestions for *specific methods* by which they are to be implemented. The term "method" points always to a way in which principles are carried into effect: thus, any given *principle* of management could be carried into effect in different organisations by different methods. The value of principles of management in this fundamental sense lies in the foundation that they provide for its effective conduct, by marking out the essential features that must characterise the practice of management, irrespective of where it is occurring.

Principles of management could be deduced by *a priori* reasoning from the nature of the process of management itself, but a greater degree of acceptance is likely to be accorded to a body of principles drawn from practice, say, from a comparative study of observed strengths and weaknesses. This would necessitate a volume of first-hand research that has not so far been contemplated in this field. A full set of principles must relate to the total process of management in action, and so to the essential elements which constitute it, i.e. the elements of planning and control, co-ordination and motivation. It has been noted above that one of the special aspects of planning is the determination of the executive responsibilities and relations that comprise the framework of management in action, i.e. the organisa-

---

[1] Brief notes on the contributions from earlier writers on the subject are set out in Appendix I. A study of contemporary thought is to be found in the papers referred to earlier in the *British Management Review*, Vol. VII, No. 3.

tion structure; because of its particular importance in the working of management, separate "principles of organisation" should be identified.

The following set of principles covering all these elements is put forward as an addition to existing knowledge: they have been deduced from analytical study of the practical working of management and checked by observation of strengths and deficiencies. They have also taken into account contributions from earlier writers on the subject.[1]

Definition

Management is a social process entailing responsibility for the effective (or efficient) planning and regulation of the operations of an enterprise in fulfilment of a given purpose or task, such responsibility involving (a) the installation and maintenance of proper procedures to ensure adherence to plans, and (b) the guidance, integration and supervision of the personnel composing the enterprise and carrying out its operations.

The process consists of the four essential elements summarised on page 11.

A. Principles of Management (General)

1. In economic affairs, the purpose or task of the enterprise, and so of management's responsibility, is the provision of goods and services in accordance with the requirements of the consumer.

   N.B.—(i) This does not imply that the consumer requirements are to be the *sole* determinant of economic activity, without reference to other factors, such as the technical needs of production or design.

   (ii) In many enterprises the product handled is such as to contribute only indirectly to consumer needs: the ultimate purpose is still as stated, though one or more stages removed.

2. The interpretation of the purpose of an enterprise or organisation lies in the formulation of its policy. Sound policy, in relation both to overall purpose and to the activities of the various divisions or sections of the organisation, is an essential factor in effective management.

3. The formulation of policy is the responsibility of the highest level of management; for instance, in a Limited Company, the responsibility of the Board of Directors acting on behalf of the owners (shareholders).

4. The formulation of policy, and the exercise of all aspects of management directed to achieving its fulfilment, must be based on adequate consideration of the relevant facts without and within the organisation.

[1] A first approach to "principles of management" presented in a similar form is to be found in a paper published by the author in *British Management Review*, Vol. VII, No. 1.

5. The aim of management is, in achieving the purpose or task to which it is directed, to attain and maintain an optimum level of effectiveness of operation in all the activities of the enterprise. Among the essential ways of attaining such effectiveness is the promotion of contentment and morale of the persons composing the organisation.

6. Management thus acquires a secondary social aim in the promotion of contentment and morale.

7. Because of its nature as a social (human) process, management responsibility must be carried into effect as a continuous and living activity on the part of the appointed executive(s), and cannot be replaced by techniques or systems designed for operation by subordinate personnel in the prolonged or recurrent absence of the executive(s).

8. Irrespective of the size of the organisation, or of the divisions into which its activities may in practice be divided, the process of management within that organisation is a unity, and its several parts or aspects must be recognised as related items in the one integral process.

9. The only reliable basis of approach to effective management in action is a systematic method based on: diagnosis of situation—ascertainment of facts—assessment and interpretation—decision—check results.

10. The criterion of management is to be sought in—(a) achievement of purpose; (b) the effectiveness of operations, measured usually in terms of productivity per man-hour employed or cost per unit of product produced or work performed; (c) the contentment of the members of the organisation.

B. *Planning and Control*

1. Ascertainment and assessment of all relevant facts, without and within the enterprise, are essential factors in sound planning and control.

   N.B.—(i) These two elements are *essentially* interrelated, control being the obverse of planning.

   (ii) Both are largely carried into effect by means of techniques or procedures, and form the "administrative" aspect of management. They provide "tools" of management, and so are always *means*, never *ends* in themselves.

   (iii) Apart from the techniques by which these elements are carried into effect, they are also to be reflected in the attitude of managers in discharging their responsibilities.

2. Two essential preliminary stages in the determination of plans are:

   (a) The formulation of policy, in general as well as in appropriate sectional terms;

   (b) The laying down of the responsibilities or tasks allocated to the various members of the group or enterprise, and of the (formal) interrelations consequently arising among them.

   N.B.—It is this definition of responsibilities which constitutes *"the organisation structure"*.

3. Sound planning and control require the determination and setting down of appropriate standards of performance in respect of the various activities or operations of the enterprise: these are to be determined by systematic analysis and assessment of the relevant facts.

4. The effectiveness and economy of activities or operations are controlled by a continuous comparison of actual achievements or results against these predetermined standards.

5. The selection of the personnel, equipment, materials, methods, processes, etc., to be used in carrying out the operations, should be based on a continuous review of all relevant factors, and determined on an analytical basis.

6. Effectiveness and economy of operations can be assisted by—specialisation, simplification and standardisation.

7. In striving for economy of operations, as the counterpart of effectiveness, it is important to keep a balance between long-term and short-term results or consequences.

8. In the application of techniques of planning and control, full regard must be paid to the human needs of members of the organisation: the techniques alone cannot secure effectiveness of operations, and neglect of human requirements inevitably militates against their successful application.

C. *Organisation Structure*

1. Organisation is an aspect of planning, concerned with the definition of:
    (a) The responsibilities of the (executive and supervisory) personnel employed in the enterprise; and
    (b) The formal interrelations established by virtue of such responsibilities.
    N.B.—An "organisation chart" is an illustration of these responsibilities and relationships appropriately defined.

2. The structure of organisation of an enterprise is the framework for carrying out the responsibilities of management, for the delegation of such responsibilities, for the co-ordination of activities or operations, and for the motivation of members; the design of the structure must be directed to promoting the effective working, at all levels, of the four elements of management.

3. The responsibilities or activities of all (executive and supervisory) members of an enterprise, or of all its main and subsidiary divisions or sections, should be clearly defined, preferably in writing: the definition should also specify the (formal) relations of each particular member or section to any others with which there is to be active contact.

4. When the size of the enterprise necessitates subdivision of (executive and supervisory) responsibilities, the most useful division is into specific primary groups, determined by specialisation of function or operation.

5. When the increasing size or activity of an enterprise (or any other factors) threaten to impair the effectiveness of management through the overloading of (executive and supervisory) members, appropriate provision is to be made for the delegation of responsibilities to lower levels in the direct line or to the specialist members; appropriate provision has then also to be made to ensure continuous effective co-ordination.

6. The definition of responsibilities and relationships forming an organisation structure should provide:

   (a) A single chief executive responsible to the policy-forming body for the effective conduct of all the operations of the enterprise;

   (b) Adequate decentralisation of decision through the delegation of responsibility;

   (c) Clear lines of responsibility linking the chief executive with the various points of decision or operation;

   (d) The span of responsibility or supervision of a superior limited to a reasonable number of (executive or supervisory) subordinates, if their activities are interrelated. (See page 36.)

   (e) The integration of functional (specialist) sections in such a way as not to impair the clear lines of responsibility and command.

7. If responsibilities are properly defined, the delegation of responsibility, and its acceptance, automatically implies delegation of the corresponding authority to take decisions and to secure the carrying out of the appropriate activities. If limitations are intended to apply to any executive's responsibilities, they should be specifically mentioned in the definitions.

   N.B.—When responsibilities are delegated, a superior is still to be held accountable for all the relevant activities of subordinates within his jurisdiction, whether he has issued specific instructions for such activities or not.

8. An organisation structure cannot be regarded as immutable. It must be flexible enough to admit of adjustment when required by changes in basic circumstances.

D. Co-ordination and Motivation

1. The aims of management, in the achievement of a given purpose or task through effective and economical activities or operations of persons associated in an enterprise or organisation, can be attained only if there is willing co-operation from and co-ordinated activity among those persons.

   N.B.—Willing co-operation may be alternatively described as "will to work" or "high morale".

2. However sound the framework provided by the policy, plans and organisation structure of the enterprise, effective management implies a responsibility for deliberate and continuous co-ordination, and specific mechanisms to this end may be required.

3. The effectiveness of operations and the maintenance of co-operation among members of an organisation is in part determined by the

personal and social contentment derived by them from their participation in the tasks of the enterprise.

N.B.—(i) A person employed in any organisation necessarily goes into that employment as a "total person", continuously subject to influences derived from temperament, background, domestic circumstances and many other factors external to the working situation.

(ii) It is now becoming increasingly recognised that inherent in management as a social process is a *direct* responsibility for the promotion of personal and social satisfactions of the persons under its jurisdiction; the attainment of such satisfactions in a "group situation" is one of the reasons for persons taking up employment.

4. Co-ordination of operations requires balance of activities as well as unification; it can be most effectively attained by direct continuous contact among the persons concerned, starting at an early stage of their activities, and proceeding with due regard to the relevant facts.

5. The issue of instructions (command) and the supervision of operations are among the channels through which the element of motivation is carried into effect.

6. Communications (instructions, etc.) should flow along the lines of responsibility and relationship set out in the organisation structure.

7. High morale (will to work) among members of an organisation is promoted by:

   (a) Keeping them informed of matters concerning the activities of the organisation;

   (b) Consulting them in regard to its regulation and further development;

   (c) Fostering in them a sense of self-responsibility for the performance of their tasks;

   (d) Affording them opportunities for self-development, compatible with the purpose and interests of the organisation.

   (e) Encouraging them to contribute to its effectiveness and development apart from the performance of their allotted tasks;

   (f) Fostering their responsible participation in its management.

8. High morale is in part determined by the confidence and respect felt by subordinates for their superiors; outstanding among the factors promoting such confidence and respect is an unquestioned basis of fairness and objectivity in dealings with subordinates.

9. Members of an organisation cannot be expected to develop a spirit of willing co-operation in its purposes and tasks, unless they are able to anticipate reasonable security of tenure of their membership of that organisation.

10. Discipline means acceptance of the necessary rules or regulations of the enterprise, and is the natural concomitant of high morale: the need for special provisions for "the maintenance of discipline" is an indication that morale is not adequate.

11. Discipline, as a reflection of high morale, is best attained by fostering the sense of responsibility of subordinates—by enlisting their co-operation in the formulation of the code of regulations and by providing for independent review in cases of alleged grievance or dispute as to the application of that code.

12. However democratic its principles and structure, the level of morale of an organisation (its "tone") is largely a reflection of the human attitude and outlook of its chief executive.

8. THE PRACTICE OF MANAGEMENT

In the analytical review in the foregoing sections, management has been revealed as a process involving four essential elements—planning, control, co-ordination, motivation. The process has a single aim in attaining the stable, smooth, integrated and effective carrying out of operations directed to the fulfilment of a given purpose. Underlying this process there are certain principles, which, if adhered to, will ensure the sound working of management. As a whole, the process of management is not readily seen, its inner character being frequently hidden by the techniques used to carry it out. How management appears to the onlooker is illustrated in the remaining portions of this study.

Modern developments in the practice of management have given rise to a variety of techniques or procedures. These form the "tools" of the executive; they apply chiefly in respect of the elements of planning and control, but there are some applicable to the human responsibilities—techniques of selection and placement, training, wage analysis, merit rating, lost-time control, suggestion schemes, and so on. These many and varied procedures, however, must not suggest that management is but a matter of routine application of systems. There is a basic human responsibility, a personal task of consideration and decision. The keynote of management is its *responsibility* for the planning and guidance of other people's activities. Within each element of the process the personal attitude of the individual executive is an important part in attaining effectiveness of operation. Herein lies part of the true skill of management—the "art" that parallels the "science" comprising the basic principles and systematic knowledge of methods. There is a good analogy in the craftsman—he needs basic knowledge of the principles underlying his craft, of materials and tools, of methods and lines of work, and so on. His training and skill make possible the proper application of his craft that results in high-grade work. Well-designed and efficient tools make his task easier and his work better, his quality and finish of a higher order; they certainly do not replace his skill, nor can they. So too with management, the "tools" cannot be a substitute for the executive's personal task of responsible consideration and decision. It is when the "tools" take the place of the manager that the process breaks down, to give place to the rule-of-thumb "management" that has become so widespread in modern industry.

True management is a continuous, living process in which an individual must take specific responsibility. It begins with an examination and assessment of the relevant facts; with these properly appreciated the broad plans can be formulated and then the more detailed programmes laid down, including provision for the necessary equipment, materials, and so on. The definition and allocation of tasks to the members of the organisation is a further stage in the planning, and while the work and activities are proceeding, a further human responsibility for co-ordination and motivation arises. The management process completes its round in the supervision of activities and the checking of progress to ensure performance at an adequate standard of effectiveness, in accordance with plans. Underlying the whole process is the policy of the enterprise, the statement of the objective and the principles that form the basis of management.

In the general pattern of industrial or commercial organisation, management is found in three broad levels: the Board of Directors, the Managing Director (chief executive), and the hierarchy of managers and supervisors.

(1) The responsibilities of the Board of Directors may be summed up as the formulation of policy and the overall control of the organisation. The major tasks arising are: the determination and statement of policy on general lines as well as the chief features of the sectional aspects; the provision of adequate financial means; schemes of control by which the activities and progress of the enterprise are to be assessed; the appointment of the executive authority designated to manage the concern (the Managing Director); provision for the legal responsibilities towards the community (in respect of the legal requirements of Company Law, the custody of property and so on). From among its number the Board elects a Chairman to preside over its deliberations. This Chairman is *not as such an executive official of the Company*, but the president of the Directors, who holds office only at their formal deliberations and those of the shareholders. Frequently, the same individual is both Chairman and Managing Director, but this should not mislead as to the true character of the Chairman's position.

(2) The Managing Director holds a dual office—as a member of the Board he shares the corporate responsibility of the other Directors. But his special position of chief executive he holds alone. It falls to him in this capacity to be the link between the Board and the rest of the organisation: to present the objective and to interpret policy; to encourage participation in the formulation of policy;

to issue the appropriate instructions that will set the organisation to work; and to maintain effective co-ordination and a high level of will-to-work. His responsibilities for morale are especially important, because it is from him that the "tone" of the organisation is set—his attitude and outlook are likely to be reflected by the executives at lower levels, even down to the ranks of supervisors and operatives. Naturally enough, there will be certain differences in the detailed make-up of the responsibilities allocated to individual Managing Directors, but the character of such responsibilities will be broadly the same throughout: the pattern is illustrated in the one schedule set out in Appendix II.[1]

(3) Various executives and supervisors responsible to the Managing Director make up the rest of the organisation. This is where all the differences in the size and character of the enterprise will come out. A small trading unit may have only a Managing Director and half a dozen junior assistants: the chief executive is really an owner-manager, whose business is clothed in Company form as a matter of legal convenience. A small manufacturing company may have a Chief Engineer serving as a technical executive to assist the Managing Director on matters concerned with design, plant, tools and quality, while an Accountant looks after the financial and selling aspects, and such clerical routines as are carried out; the Managing Director may himself look after the factory and all general aspects of production, with the assistance of a Senior Foreman. In the medium-sized and larger enterprises, whether in manufacturing or commerce, the total process of management is customarily split up among a hierarchy of executives and supervisors, who together form "the organisation". Their scope and character are necessarily varied: this is where the definitions of responsibilities come into play. According to the needs and circumstances of the enterprise, and in accordance with its objectives and policy, the total process of management under the Managing Director is divided into appropriate sections, groups or functional units, each with its responsibilities and relations determined as part of the whole. Each executive or supervisory post, in other words, is specifically set up to play a given rôle in the total pattern of management. Some of the tasks may be temporary ones—for instance, work of a special technical development kind undertaken in order to bring out a new product; or looking after a subsidiary factory evacuated for security purposes; or the building up and running of an Export Sales Department, for subsequent merging into the general sales activities. In such cases, a temporary executive appointment may well be made, with specific responsibilities which will be terminated or modified or merged in due course, as required. Briefly, then, the organisation of any medium-sized or larger concern, whatever

---

[1] A comparative summary of the responsibilities of the Board of Directors and of the Managing Director is contained in the author's paper on "The Responsibilities of Higher Management", *British Management Review*, Vol. VI. No. 1.

its field of economic activities, will consist of a complex of responsibilities and relations, determined by reference to the approved objective and policy and providing a framework within which the whole process of management (including supervision at the operating level) can be effectively carried out.

What these managers (and supervisors) do, how they spend their working hours, is the subject-matter of the following parts of this study. The core of their task lies in the definition of management itself—to take responsibility for the planning and guidance of the sections of activities entrusted to them and for the motivation of the persons entrusted to their jurisdiction. The human element in this task is very much the same in most executive and supervisory posts, whatever their field of activity. Some differences of degree can be found, as between, say, a manager and foreman: the latter has a more circumscribed human job in the guidance and supervision of men and women at the working level, and in promoting a high sense of morale among them. The manager's personnel responsibility, on the other hand, may be more remote, directed more to the supervisors themselves, getting a good team spirit among them, encouraging them and helping them in their own direct motivation task, thus setting the human "tone" of the department or section as a whole. Among themselves, managers may again find differences of emphasis due to particular circumstances: in highly technical manufacturing operations, largely process-controlled, the human responsibility may be less prominent than the technical. Similarly, the character of the staff and work under the jurisdiction of, say, a Chief Accountant or a Retail Store Manager, may give rise to quite a different pattern of human relations and problems from that of the large-scale light engineering factory.

So far as the other half of management is concerned, the techniques and procedures, differences are more usual than similarities. These techniques, as the methods or "tools" for carrying the process into effect, necessarily reflect the policy and organisation of the enterprise and are largely interwoven with the planning and control activities. They must therefore be specific to an individual enterprise.

For instance, the routines for production control may need to be quite differently worked out even in two factories with much the same product and layout, and working from the same fundamental principle of measured standard times. In this fact lies the weakness of the "systems" that are sometimes offered to executives by firms specialising in the sale of a given type of equipment or advisory service. Superficially, the "system" is widely applicable in a set way; but in reality its application in that set way may cause serious weaknesses in the working of management in some organisations. The advances made in the study of management in recent years have, however, led to the widespread use of common forms of techniques or control schemes. These may often differ in detail from factory to factory, or office to office, but they are based on the same principles and may broadly follow similar lines of application. In other words, these techniques do conform to a coherent pattern, as is evidenced by the many textbooks that are available to describe, for instance, the principles and practice of production control, budgetary control, office methods, market research, or merit rating. Illustrations of most of these activities appear in the following parts of this volume.

It is important to note that these techniques, or "tools" of management can be classified in accordance with the four elements of the process of management itself, although they are mainly concentrated in the elements of planning and control. This emphasises their character as the means by which management is applied. The classification may be illustrated by taking each element in turn and setting down in relation to it some of the techniques that are found in current use in many organisations. The classification is made more revealing if the illustrations are drawn from different divisions of an organisation, as shown in the following summary:

A. *Planning*

(i) The primary management responsibility arising under this element is the determination of policy, i.e. the laying down of the aims of the organisation and the general principles on the basis of which it will operate. This is required not only in a general sense, but also in relation to each of the major divisions. Without a known policy in respect of all its activities, an enterprise cannot function effectively, if at all. A well-defined policy relating to all aspects of an organisation can be of considerable value in promoting co-ordination and smooth working.

(ii) A second general responsibility under the element of planning is that of organisation structure.

(iii) *Production.*—Some of the management activities concerned with planning in the field of production are:

Link with distribution to ascertain forecast of sales requirements and so to establish a true (potential) programme of output.

Preparation of programme and breakdown into sections.

Technical layout of operations.

Analysis of operations for allocation of jobs and machines.

Materials specification.

Budget of material supplies; pre-purchasing; pre-allocation (linking up with "control" element).

Method and time study to determine operation times and rates.

Machine loading and production planning.

Inspection routines.

(iv) *Distribution.*—Some planning activities are:
Market research ("assessment of potentials").
Layout of sales territories and budgets.
Preparation of sales campaign, including advertising.
Budget of stocks to be carried.
Transport programme.

(v) *Financial Management.*—The planning activities in this field are closely related to the "control" element and are best considered there. Special features are: the provision of capital, the maintenance of working capital; availability of cash (for wages and other short-term disbursements).

(vi) *Personnel.*
Planning of labour supply; requisitions
Selection and placement.
Training and job instruction.
Working hours, holidays, substitute man-power, etc.
Cloakroom accommodation, canteen facilities and other amenities.

B. *Control*

Planning lays down the programme to be followed and the standards to be attained. Control watches to see that the programme and the standards are adhered to, or brings to light the reasons why not. In some recent methods of management (especially "Budgetary Control" and "Higher Control"), the two elements are actually combined in one procedure.

(i) The Board of Directors has a general oversight of all the activities of the organisation and looks to the General Manager to bring forward the "control" information that will enable progress to be checked against the policy and programme laid down. In this sense, top management frequently uses the field of financial activities for providing the means of "control".

(ii) *Production.*—The usual management activities relating to observing the productive performance or the progress of output are:
Progress control (often called "production control").
Utilisation of man-power and machine-hours.
Material or stores control (to foresee and prevent shortages of material).
Balance of components, work in progress, etc.
Quality control (perhaps by statistical methods).

(iii) *Distribution.*—Stock control (quantities of goods in stock).
Sales progress control, broken down into territories, products, salesmen's quotas, or any other desirable subdivision.
Delivery control (to check for transport delays).

(iv) *Financial Management.*—Here the planning and control activities are interlinked. The whole accountancy system of a business is a scheme of control, or recording and checking the expenditure, but certain aspects of it are more readily recognised as "tools" of management; for instance:

Labour cost control (perhaps on the basis of work study standards).
Materials cost control.
Sales expense control.
Overhead expense control.
Standard costing systems.
Budgetary control (by which a complete plan of financial needs in relation to every aspect of production, distribution and personnel is prepared in advance and used for planning purposes and for subsequent continuous checking).
Higher Control (a specialised system of pre-planned expense control, on simpler lines than the "budget").

(v) *Personnel.*—All forms of record and report, employee-rating, merit-rating, and so on.

C. Co-ordination

This element in management does not call for or use any special techniques, but is achieved by the active skill of the manager or supervisor himself. As already indicated, any form of planning scheme is a help to co-ordination. Committees can also be used for this purpose. But co-ordination is achieved in the main by the conscious "management efforts" of the individual manager.

D. Motivation (Leadership)

This again is an element in which special techniques are not available, but in which the human skill of the manager and supervisor is called into play. The task is to fuse the varied individual human capacities and powers of the many people employed into a smoothly working team with high morale and so high productivity. It is a task closely linked up with the element of co-ordination. It is an element in their responsibility of which managers and supervisors have hitherto too frequently been ignorant and negligent. There is a great deal to be said as to how this task can be carried out, but in brief the major points may be summarised as follows:

Securing interest, by keeping people informed of proposed developments and of progress.
Maintaining loyalty, by fairness in allocation of work, rates of pay, discipline, etc.
Maintaining personal keenness by fostering a sense of participation.
Promoting group harmony, by joint consultation.
Preventing frustration, by providing a sympathetic outlet for grievances and grumbles.
Preserving impartiality, by ensuring co-operative discipline and fairness in judgment.
Encouragement of responsibility in the affairs of the organisation.

The chart in Fig. 2 shows how these techniques may be grouped and distributed among executives in an organisation set up on the basis of the four major divisions.

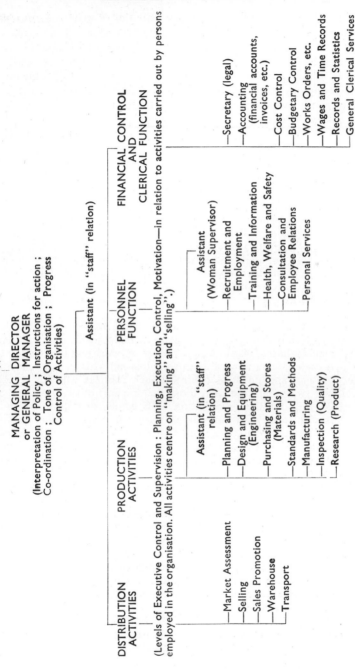

Fig. 2.—Chart of Organisation illustrating the Activities of Management.

This presentation of the everyday activities of management recalls what was said some pages back about the two aspects of the manager's job: his routines, and his personal contribution of consideration and decision in applying these routines. He has not just to apply his "tools" blindly, but to study the facts and use his "tools" as the means of carrying out his decision in the light of how he interprets the facts. Alongside this task he has the continuous human responsibility implied in the elements of co-ordination and motivation.

Taking a broad view, it may be said that, whatever their specific differences as laid down in the definitions of responsibility, management appointments all partake of a threefold character—a technical aspect, an administrative one, and a human one:

(a) *The Technical.*—Applying the particular knowledge of processes, products, materials, equipment, procedures, etc., pertinent to the operations or field allocated to the manager. For example, in the case of a Factory Manager, this will cover consideration of, and decisions on, quality standards, the suitability of a certain tool, the design of product, investigation into complaints of faults, and so on. In the case of the Chief Accountant, it will cover questions of classification of expense, liability for income tax, interpretation of financial law, and so on.

(b) *The Administrative.*—Concerned with the routines or procedures by which planning and control are carried into effect, in relation to manufacturing, distributing, or other activities that the organisation is dealing with, as well as to such internal matters as employment routines and financial controls. Such routines will fall generally into two groups, namely, those that are part of the overall scheme designed for the organisation as a whole, and those which are specific to the division, unit or section of the individual manager. The tasks of the manager in this connection are often delegated to clerical or secretarial staffs engaged on the compilation of records, the writing of reports, or the preparation of other documentary matter.

(c) *The Human.*—The motivation of the working teams, all those daily activities which the responsible manager must undertake in order to ensure that the morale of his team is high. Part of this activity may be delegated to a specialist personnel officer or assistant; for instance, matters concerned with the engagement or training of staff, or the routine handling of welfare activities. For *every* manager, however, there is a human element in his own responsibility which he cannot delegate and which is in effect the impact of his own leadership or motivation on the people working under his jurisdiction.

The technical group of activities is not, strictly speaking, part of management at all. There will be found many managers who have very little of a technical character within their responsibility: for example, a manager in charge of a packing department for which no special knowledge of products or processes is required; or the superintendent of a group of straightforward clerical and typing activities. But with many of the executive appointments in industry and commerce, the manager would be at a loss if he had no technical competence in regard to the particular products or processes with which he was dealing, whether in production or distribution. Similarly, in the field of accounting, the executive in an industrial organisation has a high "technical factor" in the tasks entrusted to him. Yet it remains true that these aspects of his responsibility are parallel to and associated with his real management activities, rather than forming part of them.

With the other two groups, the administrative and the human, the position is different—they contain the elements of the process of management itself and in varying degree they will occur in the responsibilities of all executive and supervisory appointments. "In varying degree" has to be stated, because necessarily the make-up of any particular executive appointment depends on the responsibilities allocated, determined in relation to the aims, policy, plans and methods of the enterprise. In this, of course, lies the difficulty of any textbook on the practice of management: it can suggest and describe an approach to organisation and methods of planning and control that have been tried and found satisfactory in perhaps a number of enterprises, but it can rarely prescribe them safely for universal use irrespective of circumstances. This is true even in regard to the human element in management, where it *could* be argued that, as men and women are much the same the world over, the principles and practices of "personnel management" could be set down in fairly standard terms. Experience has proved this argument, however logical it appears, to be untrue—the particular circumstances of different organisations, activities and persons give rise to differences in the human situation and so need to be met by differences in management approach and techniques. Perhaps the only factor that remains persistently the same in the practice of sound management is the attitude and outlook of the manager: the executive who discharges his responsibilities with a personal approach that is characterised by the four essential elements (plus a scientific method) is always on sure ground. He needs to have a "planning and control" outlook, to watch always for "co-ordination", and to maintain a human attitude that will secure unbroken morale ("motivation") among his subordinates. Essential to this approach is the method of the scientist: get the facts together first, examine and marshal them, assess them objectively, and only then, after due consideration, take a decision.

The present study illustrates this line of thought. In the following Parts the various chapters examine the principles of management applied in practice, through the description and illustration of certain proved methods. It is not practicable to give at every turn the particular circumstances that characterised the evolution or development of the method put forward, and as far as possible the techniques described are those which have been found capable of widespread and varied application. Yet it would be a mistake to imagine that the techniques described can be applied without further analysis to any and every business. Their purpose rather is to explain and illustrate how the process of management is carried into effect—and the student should respond, if he wants to carry them into practice, by analysing his own particular situation to see how far these techniques would be relevant, and how far the circumstances are sufficiently different to require some alteration in the treatment of the problem or the design of the techniques. The easy accessibility of "systems" in recent years has been an obstacle to better management, mainly because it has led managers away from making a critical appraisal of their own situation and of the methods of management best suited to it.

*   *   *   *   *

Parts I and II of the present study are devoted to the description of management at work within the fields of distribution and production, the main branches of the economic system. In regard to distribution (Part I), emphasis is deliberately placed on those aspects that concern the manufacturer; less attention, and in only a more incidental way, is given to wholesale and retail trade and to transport. These latter form separate fields of activity for which specific management techniques have been developed: the process and elements of management there are similar, but it would take the present study too far out of balance between the Parts to have treated at length the specialist trading aspects.

Parts III and IV are an examination of the "functions of management" in the sense referred to earlier, as they are carried out within the fields of production and distribution. The matter contained in them does not overlap with that of the preceding parts, but should be studied alongside of them. There is a danger in this method of presentation, in so far as it repeats the practice of industry, in the separation of the parts of the management process. The appointment of a specialist Personnel Officer or Controller may often lead "line" executives to feel relieved of responsibility for human relations in their domain or for the effective control of operating costs. Such a mistaken notion can just as easily arise if these functions are separately studied. The gain from specialist treatment, bringing more authoritative knowledge to bear, must not be offset by any suggestion that "Personnel" and "Control" are outside management or outside the responsibility of the managers in Production and Distribution.

*   *   *   *   *

Perhaps the best way of closing this Introduction is to refer once more to the position of the smaller firms. They are still characteristic of British industry and commerce. Their owners or managers are often apt to be frightened or misled by textbooks on management. Modern methods have evolved mainly from the larger organisations and are too often couched in terms which suggest greater applicability to such organisations. Even the separate consideration of "Distribution", "Production", "Personnel" and "Control" rings untrue with the smaller unit, whose owner or manager may move throughout the day from one field to another, unconscious of any differentiation. On reflection, he could recognise that at one moment he is dealing with a manufacturing problem (Production), shortly afterwards meeting a customer (Distribution), then settling questions of excess expenditure on certain operations (Control), and later dealing with a difficult employee (Personnel). The separation of activities which larger scale enterprise has made possible has no meaning for him—but this is not to argue that he does not meet the same problems nor need much of the same knowledge and skill in the different fields. He may not need the same techniques, certainly will not in their more elaborate forms; yet he may well need the better approach and the greater effectiveness that underlie those techniques. In other words, from the seeming complexity of methods used in the larger units, the small man may often learn a new skill and be able to adapt the method more simply to meet the narrower scope of his own problems.

In this very process, however, of examining a situation, considering all the relevant factors, and deciding on an appropriate course of action, he is displaying his skill in management and proving the value of a study of its principles and practice.

AN OUTLINE HISTORY OF MANAGEMENT THOUGHT

EDITOR'S NOTE

THE following is a brief review of the contributions to the evolution of modern knowledge of the principles and practice of management. For readers who may be interested, a more detailed review is to be found in:

The Making of Scientific Management

Vol. I—*Thirteen Pioneers.*
Vol. II—*Management in British Industry.*
Vol. III—*The Hawthorne Investigations.*

By L. URWICK and E. F. L. BRECH (Management Publications Trust, London 1945–1948).

* * * * *

While in the course of Britain's industrial revolution during the nineteenth century, a certain amount of attention was given to the development of management techniques, it was only in the later decades of the century that this subject became one of any width of interest. The technical periodicals and journals began from about the 1870s onwards here and there to carry articles on certain aspects of production management, and the analysis of costs, and gradually in the following ten or twenty years there emerged a category of recurrent topics which would today be classified as "management". An odd book or two had been published bearing on this subject prior to 1870, but it can rightly be said that the first volume to aspire to a title as an outstanding nineteenth-century contribution to the British literature of management was GARCKE and FELLS *Factory Accounting*, published in 1887. Here for the first time was the combination of the accountant and the engineer, representing the co-ordination of the two major aspects in management development at that period.

In 1894, F. G. BURTON began his occasional series of articles in *Engineering*, on the subject of engineers' estimates and cost accounts, two or three years later republishing some of them in the form of a small book. Just before the end of the century (1899), he brought out a full-length book of some merit: this was *The Commercial Management of Engineering Works*. Its character was more that of an accounting and office handbook than a textbook of management in the present-day sense, though it has two or three very interesting chapters on the managers' responsibilities. (Burton was Secretary and General Manager of the Milford Haven Shipbuilding and Engineering Company.) But between his two publications, however, Burton lost a good deal of his pride of place, when in 1896 J. SLATER-LEWIS published his historic study entitled *The Commercial*

Organisation of Factories. This was a new work by a General Manager, a highly qualified engineer, who had not previously written for the technical press. Here was a textbook of organisation and management in the best sense of the term, with many features that were astonishingly modern, decades ahead of their time—even an organisation chart, an illustration of the flow of documents, and interesting comments on the human aspects of management.

The next noteworthy contributor did not appear until 1908; this was a writer using the pseudonym "A General Manager" for a long series of articles on "Commercial Engineering". His identity was revealed as A. J. LIVERSEDGE in 1912, when the series appeared in book form. Its content was even more a commercial handbook than Burton's, largely consisting of market information.

Apart from the articles in the periodicals, presumably written for the growing middle-class readership employed in industry, even greater interest was beginning to be taken in management among the professional ranks of the technical societies, such as the Institution of Mechanical Engineers and one or two of the local Engineering Associations, notably in Manchester. In the annals of such bodies one or two names figure prominently, particularly after the turn of the century, as the main exponents of the "new" approach to management, and the first references to F. W. TAYLOR's pioneer work (published in U.S.A. in 1895) began to appear.

No further textbook of any note, however, came on the market until 1914, when the first edition of *Factory Administration and Accounts* was brought out by ELBOURNE, assisted by two colleagues (HOME-MORTON and MAUGHLING), once again representing the combination of accountant and engineer. This book is a review of the best features of contemporary management practice, though with a significant degree of pioneer thinking in its presentation. It is perhaps a tribute to the foresight of its authors that the book has lasted down to our own day and remained one of the classics of production management under the revised title *Factory Administration and Cost Accounts*. ELBOURNE's other great work, *The Fundamentals of Industrial Administration*, first appeared in 1934, specifically prepared as an interpretation of the principles and practice of management for the benefit of students pursuing courses for professional qualifications in that field.

Nineteen-fourteen was the year of another classic in early British management literature, *Engineers' Costs and Economical Workshop Production*, by DEMPSTER-SMITH and PICKWORTH. Whereas it probably attracted more contemporary attention, as being of stronger practical appeal, it did not have the seeds of prosperity within it, and disappeared with the passing of the years. It may be of interest to point out how frequently in the thirty years between 1885 and 1915 the subject-matter of articles and textbooks centre on estimates and costs—a theme reflected in the practice of management in the considerable contemporary interest in premium bonus and similar incentive systems in the hands of HALSEY, WEIR, ROWAN and others, following in the wake of Taylor.

While this general interest in management was emerging in Great Britain in the fifty years after 1870, the American scene was witnessing lively debate centring on the progress of *Scientific Management* under the direction of F. W. TAYLOR and his associates. This little team of American pioneers—of whom the best known were TAYLOR, GANTT and GILBRETH—were more concerned with elaborating the techniques for the application of systematic management than with writing up their findings in literature; they did, however, each produce two or three volumes, all of which have lived down to our own times.[1] Taylor and his associates were, broadly, concerned in the first place with diverting attention away from the struggles over the division of the proceeds of industry, to the need for a concerted effort to increase those proceeds for mutual benefit by better planning and a better will-to-work, supported by incentive methods and other forms of bonus technique. But much of their effort went into the elaboration and advancement of techniques for the planning and control of production, including such methods as time study, motion study, the division and definition of responsibilities, planning charts, job tickets, and many other of the features that are currently recognised as essential to production control systems. They have perhaps come down through the years more by their contributions in these directions than by their more important fundamental contribution to the philosophy or principles of management applied in human terms. In their own country they gained, through accidental circumstances a publicity that inevitably entailed increasing public interest in the more easily understood and the more pleasantly acceptable aspects of their work. In this country, the publicity engendered serious suspicion in the minds of the leaders of organised labour, and generated an emotional opposition that has persisted even to our own day.

It would not be unfair to describe the first ten to fifteen years of the twentieth century in Great Britain as a barren period in management literature, even though the technical press and the journals of the societies frequently published articles and papers, many of them devoted to the exposition of Taylor's teachings and methods. "Barren" is a fair description, because of the superficial character of so much of this writing, and because of its failure to secure any serious acceptance among the industrial owners and managers. The outbreak of war in 1914 found British industry ignorant of contemporary advances in management thought and practice, save for such rare exceptions as Hans Renold, Ltd., or the Cadbury organisation.[2]

Overlapping on the one side with Taylor, and on the other with the First World War, was HENRI FAYOL, General Manager of a large French mining and metallurgical concern. Almost at the close of a long executive career, Fayol took the opportunity of a paper to a Congress of a Metallurgical Society in 1908 to review, as he saw them, the processes that went to make up his everyday practice as a chief executive; but it was some eight years later before this paper appeared in published form in the *Bulletin* of the Society, under the title, "Administration Industrielle et Générale", and

---

[1] F. W. Taylor's main writings are available in collected form under the title, *The Principles of Scientific Management* (Harper, New York).
[2] See *The Making of Scientific Management*, Vol. II, chaps. xi and xii.

another ten years before it appeared in English. The text was reproduced exactly as given in 1908, even to the extent of the note which foreshadowed additional sections to follow, intended to elaborate the author's basic conception of management as a process built up of the five elements: Planning, Organisation, Command, Co-ordination and Control. It is a matter of considerable regret that Fayol, despite his interest, did not see fit to complete the work or to add any further publication to his legacy in this field. It was only after his death in 1925 (then aged well over eighty) that his one and only paper on this subject secured wider recognition by its publication in book form, first in French and later translated into English.[1] The importance of Fayol's contribution lay in two features: the first was his systematic analysis of the process of management; the second, his firm advocacy of the principle that management *can, and should, be taught*. Both were revolutionary lines of thought in 1908, and still little accepted even in 1925. The seemingly unedited and unfinished state of Fayol's matter makes the real value of his analysis difficult to appreciate at first reading. Confusion is the reader's main reaction to the juxtaposition of overlapping "principles of administration" and "administrative duties". Yet in his simple deduction of the five elements of the process of management he reached a conception that has stood the test of time, and has even been closely reproduced from an entirely different and independent analysis (cf. Introduction to this volume).

Throughout this first quarter of the century, MARY FOLLETT was gaining her experience of social and industrial problems, though she had not yet turned her attention at first hand to the principles and practice of management. It was not until 1924 that she gave her first paper to a Conference of the Bureau of Personnel Administration in the United States, and over the next four or five years she contributed the remarkable series of papers on the fundamentals of management, illustrated from practical events, that form such an outstanding addition to the literature of the subject. (*Dynamic Administration*: collected papers reproduced from the Bureau's Conferences.) Mary Follett, broadly, was less interested in the practice of management than in the extent to which the everyday incidents and problems reflected the presence or absence of sound principle. She was chiefly concerned to teach principles in simple language, amply illustrated from everyday events—not the mechanics of management, but its special human character, its nature as a social process, deeply embedded in the emotions of man and in the interrelations to which the everyday working of industry necessarily gives rise—at manager levels, at worker levels, and, of course, between the two. Bearing in mind she was speaking of America in the early 1920s, her thinking can be described as little less than revolutionary, and certainly a generation ahead of its time. There is no evidence that Mary Follett ever had any contact with the persons who sponsored or conducted the Hawthorne Investigations, but the findings of those investigations, when they appeared in their full form in the 1930s, were a striking testimony to the soundness of her teaching. Again

---

[1] A new British edition, under the title *Industrial and General Management*, appeared in 1948 (Pitman).

and again an incident described or a conclusion drawn from the Hawthorne studies can be recognised as reflecting a principle or a fundamental tenet that Mary Follett had advanced from her own observations of the industrial situation.

In Great Britain the 1920s were marked by two or three publications which have lived down to our own times as still having a value in the study of their subject: o. SHELDON's *Philosophy of Management* (1924); *Factory Organisation*, by NORTHCOTT, URWICK and WARDROPPER (1927); URWICK's *Organising a Sales Office* (1928); POWELL's *Payment by Results* (1924). Perhaps, however, the really outstanding work of the decade was one that has become lost to posterity because its contemporary sales did not justify keeping it in print. This was the DICTIONARY OF INDUSTRIAL ADMINISTRATION, published by Pitman in 1927 as a collection of writings on the principles and practice of management by all the known authorities of the day, under the editorship of JOHN LEE. It is a misfortune that this volume should have been born out of time, almost twenty years ahead of the day when its full value would have been appreciated.

During these years, the interest in costing was beginning to spread into its management aspects, and a few small publications were to be found, a notable one being EMSLEY and LOXHAM: *Factory Costs* (1924), now extant as *Factory Costing and Organisation*.

The corresponding period in the United States was considerably more fruitful, probably because a larger industrial population provided the publishers with the certainty of an adequate market. Again, many of the books published then have come down to the present day, as, for instance, LAMBURGH's *Industrial Administration* (1923), the two classics in the personnel field: TEAD & METCALF's *Personnel Administration* (1920) and *Personnel Management*, by SCOTT, CLOTHIER and OTHERS (1923). E. SCHELL's *The Technique of Executive Control* also dates from 1924. The climax of these series of comprehensive studies was reached in America in 1931 in the appearance of THE HANDBOOK OF BUSINESSS ADMINISTRATION followed by its more specific companion THE (COST AND) PRODUCTION HANDBOOK (1934.)

By this time, the subject of management had become, both in Britain and in America, one of considerable contemporary interest, supported not only by professional institutes, but as well by systematic studies at University level. The way was open for the great flow of textbooks and treatises that make it so difficult for the historian to pick and choose. Inevitably many of the studies were of a "bread-and-butter" kind, concerned with the description and illustration of techniques for production management, for production control, for cost control, for sales management and stores control, for personnel practices, and the many other aspects of the day-to-day activities that go to make up the pattern of executive control in any medium or large-sized organisation. Inevitably also, many of such studies were short-lived, of passing interest only, because as practice developed, new techniques would be evolved and new textbooks called for. One can perhaps avoid the difficulty of selecting among this literature by refraining from specific mention, except to pay tribute to such pioneer British classics as T. H. BURNHAM's *Engineering Economics*, ELBOURNE'S *Fundamentals of Industrial Administration*, and T. G. ROSE's *Higher Control*—all dating from the 1930s.

Throughout these years there had been relatively little contribution to what might be termed the "theory" of management, i.e. the systematic study of the principles upon which the everyday practice of the executive process rested. Outstanding in this field was L. URWICK's first major contribution to the literature of management, which appeared as a section of the "Dictionary" referred to above, under the title of "Principles of Direction and Control", a systematic scheme of the fundamentals of management, obviously the product of far-reaching and painstaking analytical thought, which even today has a valuable relevance to the study of the subject. (These "Principles" are available to present-day readers in a reproduction in ELBOURNE's *Fundamentals*.) An equally useful American study was WEBSTER ROBINSON's *Fundamentals of Business Administration*, first published in 1928. In 1931 came *Onward Industry* by MOONEY and REILLEY, an American classic in the study of organisation principles. This, not confining itself to industry, roamed over the whole field of organised human endeavour, in an attempt to find a common pattern of principles that would serve to prescribe a sound foundation for effective action. Subsequent editions appeared in 1939 and 1947 under the title *The Principles of Organisation* (with MOONEY now as sole author). Historically, this book in its earlier edition may be regarded as the first systematic study of organisation on scientific lines. Though concerned with the static aspects of the structure of organisation and the formal lines of relationship, it had inevitably to deal with many aspects of an organisation at work, and so many "dynamic" considerations came into the study: this gave rise to a short-lived fashion in the terminology of management—the use of "organisation" as the name for the total process as well as for the structure of responsibilities.

In 1933 came URWICK's second book, *Management of To-morrow*, a combination of principle and practice, following largely on the lines of Mary Follett in the endeavour to discuss effective management in action in simple terms of everyday life in the factory and the office, but at the same time attempting to lay down the fundamental principles upon which such effective management must rest. It followed Mooney and Reilley in the use of the term "organisation" as the generic name, and brought out specifically for the first time the dual concept of the "dynamic" and "static" aspects. In spite of its limited issue, this book made a very important contribution to British literature and to the advancement of management thought: it was the equivalent in this country of its equally well-known contemporary in America, *Organisation Engineering*, by H. S. DENNISON (1931).

By the mid-1930s the possibility of a science of management was being canvassed, though by now the terminology tangle was already well to the fore. Many writers were using, not only the existing two terms "management" and "organisation", but beginning also to bring in the third member of the trilogy, "administration". This can be illustrated, for instance, by the joint Anglo-American publication (1937) of *Papers on the Science of Administration*, written and edited by GULICK and URWICK.

Apart from the two or three monumental works on the Hawthorne investigations, the last outstanding contribution to the literature of management before the outbreak of war in 1939 was CHESTER BARNARD'S *Functions of the Executive*, a penetrating analysis of the process of co-operation that is inherent in every aspect of management. Here the findings of the Hawthorne investigations were being used as an analytical instrument for examining the process of management, for the special purpose of throwing into relief its human or social character. Management, Barnard concluded, has an objective or economic aim which finds its achievement in the manufacture and sale of products, the provision of transport services, the establishment of banking facilities, the supply and distribution of electricity, and many other such technical fields. But management is essentially a co-operative human process; the pursuit of the economic aims necessitates the working together of many people offering different skills and different levels of ability, but all needing to be co-ordinated in the pursuit of the common task, and given through that association the permanence of a stable equilibrium. This, Barnard argues, can be done only if there is genuine co-operation and effective co-ordination. In turn, such co-operation and stability can be attained only when there is real contentment in the men and women who make up the organisation. Management, therefore, is a dual process: in part it has techniques and technical operations; but it also has an inherent social content without which effectiveness or efficiency cannot be attained.

*   *   *   *   *

The publications of the past ten years have been too numerous to permit of more than passing mention. Much of the new literature has been concerned with techniques for the practice of management in its various divisions. It is perhaps in the fields of PERSONNEL RELATIONS and INDUSTRIAL PSYCHOLOGY that most additions have been made, a very large proportion of them from American sources. Naturally enough, the American contributions in all fields far outweigh the British, a fact which is partly explained by the existence in the U.S.A. of the many College and University Courses in Management, with considerable numbers of lecturing and research staffs devoted to the study and teaching of the subject.

New British literature in these past few years has on the whole been of higher quality. A few references may serve to illustrate the trends.[1] Books covering the human factor in management may be usefully represented by G. S. WALPOLE'S *Management and Men* (1944), W. C. PUCKEY'S *What is this Management?* (1944), and BROWN and RAPHAEL'S *Managers, Men and Morale* (1948). Or among those with a more specialised approach: C. H.

---

[1] Mention of the following books is not intended to imply superiority over others not referred to; a full selection of titles in various fields may be found in the Reading Lists published by the professional management Institutes and the Management Library. An outline bibliography of recommended titles for further study is also appended in each Part of the present volume.

NORTHCOTT's *Personnel Management* (1945) and MAY SMITH's *Introduction to Industrial Psychology* (1943). Techniques for production management have also figured in a variety of publications, illustrated by two such different works as WILLSMORE's *Modern Production Control* (1946) and VERNON's *Manual of Industrial Management and Maintenance* (1946). Similar studies have appeared in other fields, including those of Budgetary Control and the special applications devised by T. G. ROSE under the title *Higher Control*. During the later years of the war (1944–45), the BRITISH STANDARDS INSTITUTION brought out an interesting series of booklets on management methods called *Office Aids to the Factory*, and a similar contribution to the wider spreading of knowledge of management practice was made in 1947–48 by the MANAGEMENT LIBRARY in a series of *Letters to Foremen*.

In the more fundamental field of management principles, additions to British literature have been sparse, the only outstanding publication being L. URWICK's *Elements of Administration* (1943). A pioneer study was E. F. L. BRECH's *Management: Its Nature and Significance* (1946–48), an attempt to analyse the process of management into its basic elements and so reach the basis for a "theory of management". An American author ALVIN BROWN published two works, similarly endeavouring to expound the essential factors in the structure of organisation, virtually in logical line of succession from MOONEY and REILLEY. These two books are *Organisation—A Formulation of Principle* (1945) and *The Organisation of Industry* (1947). A parallel study from a background of American public service administration (though more concerned with the executive processes of delegation and decision than with organisation structure) is SIMON's *Administrative Behaviour* (1947). Another important American addition to literature in the more practical field is COPELAND and TOWL's *The Board of Directors and Business Management* (1947), almost the only study of its kind, systematically analysing the functions of the Directors.

Two representatives of British thought will serve usefully to conclude this brief outline of management literature. The first is GILLESPIE's *Free Expression in Industry* (1948), an interesting and original plea for recognition of the morale factor in human relations by the inclusion in the structure of management of freely elected "morale leaders" parallel to the "technical" executives and supervisors. The other comes from Britain's oldest teaching establishment in the field of management: the Manchester College of Technology founded its Department of Industrial Administration in 1918, but its first systematic publications began in 1946 as *The Manchester Monographs on Higher Management*.

This outline would not be complete without mention of the *British Management Review*, a quarterly journal devoted to the serious study of management in principle and practice on a level comparable to that of academic journals in other fields. First appearing in the later 1930s, its publication was much interrupted by war-time difficulties, but it has continued its regular appearance since 1946 and begun to win wide recognition as Britain's "journal of the study of management" as distinct from a magazine or technical periodical.

The study of principle is gaining ground, a recognition of the point that without sound principle effective practice is impossible. Time was when any mention of a "theory" of management brought smiles of scepticism or smirks of contempt to the faces of the practical men. But the practising manager is today gradually coming to realise that, just as in the fields of engineering or chemistry or other scientific subjects the correctness of practice rests upon the stability of principle, so too in the human process of management it must be possible to have a fundamental body of doctrine of principle, i.e. of theory.

*   *   *   *   *

It is fitting to close this brief historical review by reference to the co-ordination activities of the British Institute of Management, which may well mean that the decade of the 1950s will be characterised by full catalogues of management literature, drawn up in the main to meet the everyday needs of the man on the job.

SCHEDULES OF EXECUTIVE RESPONSIBILITIES

THE following schedules are submitted as illustrations, especially from the point of view of approach and layout. They are extracts drawn from various companies, in which full definitions of executive responsibilities had been laid down, though they have been remodelled to conform to the common pattern of presentation. They may be used as guides for drawing up similar schedules, appropriate to the organisation concerned, but they should *not* be regarded as models to be reproduced or as suggestions for the content of responsibilities of corresponding executives in other organisations. The content and pattern of responsibilities and relationships necessarily vary with the policy and circumstances of the enterprise, and the particular conditions pertaining in each case must be taken into consideration in formulating the schedules.

It is also relevant to point out that titles vary considerably: those used in the following illustrations are the ones adopted in the organisations concerned, and are *not* necessarily recommended as standards.

The illustrations set out are:

Title	*Code Reference* (*imaginary*)
Managing Director	LG/1
General Production Manager	LG/2
Factory Manager	LG/3
Work Study Supervisor	LG/4
Company Secretary	LG/5
Chief Accountant	LG/6
Clerical Methods Manager	LG/7
Personnel Officer	LG/8
Marketing Manager	LG/9
Sales Manager	LG/10

N.B.—i. Except in the cases of 6–7 and 9–10, these ten illustrations are NOT INTERRELATED.

   ii. In the imaginary code references quoted on each illustration, sheet numbers have been omitted.

The method adopted here is to set down the main responsibilities in general terms, without attempting to specify duties or activities in detail. Some Directors prefer to follow the latter practice. Whatever its merits, it has two disadvantages: the one is the danger of fastening attention on specific details and so of stifling initiative; the other is the possibility of instability because changes in duties or daily activities may be frequent and so lead to frequent amendment of the schedules. Definitions of responsibilities in the sense here illustrated provide quite an adequate basis for determining the scope of each executive and for pointing to the interrelations. At the same time, they leave scope for initiative and a progressive outlook in interpretation. On the other hand, they require greater vigilance in the Chief Executive to ensure continuous co-ordination and balance.

Sheet Ref.: LG/1
Date of Issue: May 1948.

Title: MANAGING DIRECTOR
Responsible to: Board of Directors.

Responsible for

1. Carrying into effect the policy laid down by the Board of Directors as set out in the statement entitled "The Objectives and Policy of XYZ Manufacturing Company Ltd.", dated 12th September, 1947, and subsequent amendments as agreed by the Board and set out in the minutes of meetings.

2. Communication and interpretation of policy for the information and instruction of subordinate executives and, through them, of other members of the organisation.

3. Keeping the operations of the Company under constant review and presenting to the Board of Directors periodically accounts and statistics showing the progress and current position of the Company's affairs.

4. Submitting to the Board the definitions and structure of responsibilities of the executive and supervisory positions in the organisation, and appointing suitable persons to fill such positions. Also keeping the definitions and structure-up-to date in line with requirements.

5. Approving manufacturing, distributing and development plans submitted by the senior executives concerned, and ensuring that these fall within the agreed policy of the Company.

6. Giving decisions and interpretations of policy in cases where a proposed course of action by an executive entails, for good reason, a departure from agreed policy.

7. Ensuring adequate arrangements to safeguard the continuity of supplies to customers in times of emergency.

8. Giving adequate attention to a continuous study, in association with the executives concerned, of the effectiveness of operation of all parts of the organisation. (In practice this responsibility will be carried out to a large extent by the customary periodical review of operating performance against budget standards.)

9. Determining and/or approving arrangements to ensure that adequate contact is maintained on the Company's behalf with Government Departments, and Technical, Trade and Research Associations, including those devoted to the advancement of management.

10. Ensuring adequate co-ordination of activities throughout the organisation.

11. Ensuring adequate facilities for the training and developm executive and supervisory staffs and the encouragement of managem research.

Special Duties

1. To consider suggestions from subordinate executives in regard to the promotion of the Company's policy and organisation and to submit them objectively to the Board of Directors.

2. To review, from the standpoint of the Company as a whole, reports received from specialist executives in relation to their own field.

3. To ensure that all members of the executive and supervisory staff understand the nature and importance of budgetary control principles and are familiar with the application of such principles to the activities carried out within their own jurisdiction.

4. To give adequate attention to promoting and maintaining a high level of morale among the executive and supervisory staffs, and throughout the organisation.

Limitations

1. Not authorised to incur capital expenditure in excess of £5,000 in any one financial year without the specific consent of the Board of Directors.

2. Not to dispose of the Company's properties or assets, other than stocks in trade or waste materials, without the consent of the Board of Directors.

Immediate Subordinates
Factory Manager.
Sales Manager.
Chief Accountant.
Personnel Officer.
Research Engineer.
Personal Assistant.

Functional Contacts—Nil.

Committees—*Ex officio* member of all Committees set up in connection with the management of the Company's affairs. Empowered to appoint a subordinate to represent him on any such Committees, except those concerned with Finance and Technical Development.

Sheet Ref.: LG/2
Date of Issue: July 1947.

Title: GENERAL PRODUCTION MANAGER
Responsible to: Managing Director.

Responsible for

1. The formulation of production plans and programmes within the agreed policy, suitably designed to carry such policy into effect.

2. Co-ordination and control of all production activities throughout the organisation.

3. Co-ordination of production plans and progress with sales programme.

4. Adequate supervision of production activities to ensure that progress is in conformity with plans: day-to-day responsibility for production activities rests with the local Factory Managers.

5. The maintenance of the Company's plant, machinery and tools in effective working condition, including the purchase of such additional items as are necessitated by the agreed production plans, and within budget limits.

6. Maintenance of the Company's premises and buildings, including adequate provision for renewals, redecorations, etc., as required to maintain the premises in good order.

7. Ensuring that local Factory Managers maintain factory services, power supplies, internal transport, etc., appropriate to requirements in accordance with production plans.

8. Co-ordination of the purchase and delivery of raw materials, tools etc., with progress of production.

9. Co-ordination of work in progress and finished stock levels at the local factories with sales programmes and with the current delivery position.

10. The establishment of suitable procedures for the effective control and prevention of waste of materials, tools, etc., in the local factory stores.

11. Ensuring provision for adequate research and technical development services in relation to the Company's products, materials and equipment, and also provision for adequate test of raw materials received, to ensure conformity with standards.

12. Ensuring that Assistant Managers and Supervisors within the production divisions carry out the Company's personnel policy as advised by the Personnel Officer.

13. Continuous review of the Company's manufacturing operations in all aspects, to ensure the maintenance of a high level of effectiveness.

14. Keeping continuous effective control over expenditure on account of manufacturing and development activities in accordance with approved budgets.

15. Ensuring that statutory and other legal records in respect of the Company's manufacturing activities are properly maintained and that internal records approved by the Managing Director are maintained.

16. Submitting to the Managing Director as required statistical and other reports in regard to manufacturing and development activities and expenses, and such other data as may be called for.

17. Attending, as representative of the Company, Trade Union or Joint Industrial Council negotiations dealing with matters of policy affecting the Company's manufacturing activities or employment (as distinct from matters of routine procedure or local disputes).

18. Representing the Company at Trade Association or Technical Association meetings concerned with manufacturing or development matters.

Special Duties

1. Preparing for submission to the Managing Director at the appropriate time a budget indicating proposed manufacturing and development plans, designed to fit in with the Company's policy and Purchasing Budget in respect of plant, equipment, tools, materials, etc.

2. Determination of standards of manufacturing and development activity as a basis for continuous control over relative expenditure (see item 14 above).

3. Collaboration with the Personnel Officer in determining wage rates and supplementary payments to concur with agreements reached within the Joint Industrial Council.

4. Collaboration with the Personnel Officer in regard to adequate provision for the training of supervisory staffs and skilled operatives.

Limitations

1. *Re* item 5 above: the General Production Manager is not authorised to incur expenditure on plant, etc., outside the agreed budgeted items without the specific consent of the Managing Director.

2. Direct responsibility for manufacturing operations is in the hands of the Factory Manager at each Works, unless for special reasons in times of emergency the General Production Manager decides otherwise.

Immediate Subordinates

Factory Managers at North, South and East Works.
Planning Manager, at Head Office.
Chief Engineer, at Head Office.
Purchasing Agent, at Head Office.

Functional Contacts

Sales Manager, at Head Office.
Chief Accountant, at Head Office.
Cost Accountants at North, South and East Works.
Group Personnel Officer, at Head Office.
Assistant Personnel Officers at North, South and East Works.

Committees

1. *Ex officio* member of Group Works Council.
2. Company's representative on Joint Industrial Council.

Sheet Ref. LG/3
Date of Issue: April 1946.

Title: FACTORY MANAGER
Responsible to: Managing Director.

Responsible for

1. Advising and assisting the Managing Director in determining the programme of production.

2. Planning and supervising all manufacturing activities for carrying out the programme of production when agreed.

3. Maintaining suitable procedures for the effective planning and control of production.

4. Maintaining quality standards of the Company's products as laid down.

5. Determining and maintaining scales of wage rates and piece-work prices in accordance with Agreements and local levels.

6. Maintaining in all sections of the factory and subsidiary services adequate labour supply to ensure achievement of the programme of production.

7. Determining conditions and regulations of employment affecting all members of the factory personnel. For these and other matters concerned with personnel, the Factory Manager has a Personnel Officer as his immediate subordinate in an advisory capacity.

8. Promoting a high level of morale among members of the factory personnel in order to ensure a good standard of productivity.

9. The maintenance of discipline.

10. Conducting all contacts and negotiations with Trade Unions on the Company's behalf.

11. Maintaining all equipment, plant and tools in good working condition.

12. The purchasing and storing of all raw materials for production purposes.

13. Adhering to cost standards laid down.

14. Keeping contact with Development and Design Engineer in respect of quality standards, improvements, modifications from production standpoint, etc.

Special Duties—None specified.

Limitations

Not entitled to purchase plant or materials in quantities in excess of £100 per month without the sanction of the Chief Accountant.

Immediate Subordinates

Personnel Officer.
Buyer and Stores Keeper.
Chief Inspector.
Manufacturing Department Supervisors.
Maintenance Engineer.
Production Control Supervisor.

Functional Contacts

1. Chief Accountant, for all financial matters.

2. Cost Accountant, in relation to Cost Standards.

3. Sales Manager, with particular reference to delivery, special orders and complaints.

4. Development and Design Engineer, in relation to design and quality standards.

Committees—Member of Technical Development Committee and Chairman of Works Committee.

Sheet Ref.: LG/4
Date of Issue: June 1948.

Title: WORK STUDY SUPERVISOR
Responsible to: Works Manager.

Responsible for

1. Carrying out Work Studies of manufacturing operations as instructed by the Works Manager and in collaboration with the responsible foreman concerned.

2. Establishing accurate time standards as a result of such studies, and notifying these to the interested parties in accordance with the agreed procedures.

3. Determining appropriate time allowances in respect of operations carried out under conditions which depart from those laid down as standard.

4. In collaboration with the Personnel Department, classifying operations into appropriate rate grades.

5. Determining and recommending to the Works Manager standard methods and equipment for all manufacturing operations.

6. Determining and recommending to the Works Manager the correct sequence of operations and the appropriate personnel grades to be used.

7. Assisting the Works Manager in determining standards for material utilisation, reject percentages, etc.

8. Collaborating with the Office Manager in the determination and establishment of appropriate procedures to ensure the communication to all interested parties of time standards, job specifications, route cards, study sheets, work tickets, piece-work tickets, etc.

9. Co-ordination of work study activities with Production Control Office, Design Department and Drawing Office, Personnel Department, and Raw Material and Tools Stores.

Special Duties—Nil.

Limitations

1. The Work Study Supervisor has no authority to issue or alter work standards without the approval of the Works Manager.

2. No authority to alter methods of operation without the approval of the Works Manager.

3. No authority to fix or quote rates of payment or piece-work prices.

4. Not to give any instructions or orders to operatives.

Immediate Subordinates—Work Study Staff.

Functional Contacts

Assistant Works Manager (Production Control Office).
Drawing Office Supervisor.
Toolroom Foreman.
Foremen of Manufacturing Departments.
Foreman of Inspection Department.
Personnel Officer.
Office Manager.

Committees—Co-opted member of Joint Production Committee.

Sheet Ref.: LG/5
Date of Issue: March 1947.

Title: COMPANY SECRETARY
Responsible to: Board of Directors.

N.B..—(a) The Secretary is also the Chief Accountant, and in this respect is responsible to the Managing Director according to the schedule set out on Sheet Ref. BC 2/1 (not shown here).

(b) In respect of the routine work of the Secretarial Department and the control of staff engaged in those activities, the Secretary has a functional responsibility to the Managing Director.

Responsible for

1. Fulfilment of the Company's legal responsibilities under the Companies Acts.

2. Preparation of agenda, minutes and other documents for regular and special meetings of the Board of Directors.

3. Attendance at Board Meetings.

4. Preparation of documents for Annual General or Extraordinary Meetings of shareholders and attendance thereat.

5. Dealing with the issue of shares and maintaining the statutory share registers and conducting appropriate activities connected with share transfers.

6. Ensuring that the Company's properties and interests are adequately insured and dealing with all insurance matters arising. (In matters connected with industrial insurance, or other aspects of National Insurance, this responsibility will be discharged in collaboration with the Personnel Officer.)

7. Custody and administration of the Company's property investments, patents and trade-marks.

8. Signing and sealing of agreements, leases and other official documents on the Company's behalf.

9. Advising the Managing Director in respect of legal matters pertinent to the Company's affairs, and conducting on behalf of the Board and/or Managing Director legal negotiations in connection therewith.

Special Duties—Nil.

Limitations—None specified.

Immediate Subordinates—Nil.

Functional Contacts—With Personnel Officer in respect of Item 6.

Committees—Nil.

Sheet Ref.: LG/6
Date of Issue: July 1948.

Title: CHIEF ACCOUNTANT
Responsible to

1. Managing Director in respect of all activities set out below.

2. The Chief Accountant also assists the Secretary by the supervision of the activities of the Staffs engaged on secretarial routines (share matters, etc.) and in this respect is responsible to the Secretary.[1]

Responsible for

1. The planning and control of all expenditure connected with the fulfilment of the Company's policy as interpreted by the Managing Director. Also for carrying out the financial policy laid down by the Board.

2. Preparing and issuing budgets designed to express the Company's policy and to ensure the necessary control of operations.

3. Keeping adequate accounts and records covering all aspects of the Company's business transactions and preparing Annual Accounts for presentation to the Board and shareholders.

4. Keeping appropriate records and accounts designed to show the current position in respect of outside commitments and charges, and also designed to keep the Managing Director adequately informed in regard to the control of costs.

5. Preparing and issuing as agreed periodic statements to show the current operating and financial position in relation to the budget.

6. Drawing the Managing Director's attention to departure from policy, plans or budgets, or any other special features revealed by the periodic reports.

7. Passing all accounts for payment.

8. Receiving, banking and accounting for all moneys received, including foreign currency, bills of exchange and petty cash.

9. In collaboration with the Sales Manager, ensuring adequate provision for collecting money due to the Company in respect of sales of products.

10. Maintaining and issuing to executives concerned information pertinent to the control of costs in respect of labour, material and overhead items.

11. Preparing reports or statistics required by the Managing Director or for other executives as approved by the Managing Director.

12. Keeping statutory records regarding salaries and wages, and other internal records approved by the Managing Director.

[1] In this Company, the Secretary is a part-time professional appointment.

13. Planning control and co-ordination of clerical methods throughout the organisation (in this responsibility the Chief Accountant is assisted by a specialist executive, the Clerical Methods Manager: see details set out in Schedule LG/7).

Special Duties

1. Collaborating with the Secretary in respect of secretarial routines (see note in opening item).
2. Collaborating with the Secretary in respect of statutory and other official records (see item 12 above).
3. Collaborating with the Personnel Officer in regard to salaries, engagement, employment and working conditions, and similar matters in respect of accounting and clerical staffs.
4. Advising the Managing Director on matters of taxation or other statutory financial matters on the Secretary's behalf.
5. Maintaining contacts on the Company's behalf with Government Departments or other organisations in respect of matters pertinent to the Company's finances, when so required by the Secretary.
6. Attendance at Board Meetings for routine matters of financial character, or when called for.

Limitations—None specified.

Immediate Subordinates

Assistant Accountant.
Cost Accountant.
Clerical Methods Manager.

Functional Contacts

1. All executives on financial matters.
2. All executives on matters concerned with cost control procedures or clerical methods, through the appropriate Assistant.
3. Personnel Officer on matters concerned with accounting and clerical staffs.

Committees—Available for attendance at Works Council when required.

Sheet Ref.: LG/7
Date of Issue: July 1948.

Title: CLERICAL METHODS MANAGER
Responsible to: Chief Accountant.

Responsible for

1. The planning of all clerical activities throughout the organisation, including methods of work, equipment, supplies and personnel required.
2. Sanctioning and/or refusing appointment of permanent or temporary clerical staff not in accordance with agreed budgets.

3. Authorising purchase of office machinery and equipment.

4. Provision and maintenance of records of office machinery and equipment.

5. Examination and approval of all proposals for forms, stationery, printing and other office supplies, to ensure that they conform to general policy and plans, and are such as to attain the desirable standards of simplification and economy.

6. Determination and sanctioning of office layout and use of accommodation available.

7. Determining office procedures and clerical methods and compiling a manual setting out details thereof.

8. Collaborating with the Personnel Officer in respect of records of accounting and clerical staff.

9. Installing and maintaining records of output, expense, etc., as necessary for the effective control of clerical operations and clerical costs.

10. Planning and supervision of central office services, namely, telephone and messenger services, inward and outgoing postal services, copy-typing pool.

11. In association with the Personnel Officer, ensuring the provision of office hygiene and the welfare of staffs.

Special Duties

1. The Clerical Methods Manager is entitled to undertake investigations or to call for a report on matters which he may consider to be departures from current policy or practice.

2. Before taking any decisions on findings of such investigations, he must report back to the Chief Accountant.

Limitations

1. While responsibility for the planning and requisitioning of additional members of clerical staff rests with the Clerical Methods Manager, the recruitment of such staff shall be handled by the Personnel Department and selected candidates submitted for approval to the Clerical Methods Manager.

2. Clerical methods, routines, forms, etc., relating to production planning and control shall be determined in collaboration with the Factory Manager.

3. Accounting routines can be determined only with the direct sanction of the Chief Accountant.

4. Clerical methods, routines and forms relating to Sales Office procedures shall be referred to the Sales Manager for approval.

Immediate Subordinates—Nil.

Functional Contacts—All executives and supervisors on matters pertinent to clerical methods, routines and documents.

Committees—Nil.

Sheet Ref.: LG/8
Date of Issue: September 1947.

Title: PERSONNEL OFFICER
Responsible to: Managing Director.

Responsible for

1. Advising and assisting the Managing Director in preparing the Company's personnel policy for formulation by the Board.

2. Ensuring that the Company's personnel policy is made known to all executives and supervisory staffs and to all employees of the Company.

3. Ensuring that the Company's personnel policy is effectively carried out throughout the organisation.

4. Developing and maintaining procedures for recruitment of personnel in accordance with the budgets and programmes laid down and in collaboration respectively with:

(*a*) Factory Personnel—the Works Manager and Manufacturing Department Supervisors.

(*b*) Office Personnel—the Chief Accountant.

(*c*) Sales Personnel—the Distribution Manager.

5. Developing and maintaining training facilities in accordance with the Company's policy and output programmes. These should include arrangements for juveniles' attendance at outside educational establishments.

6. Determining, for the approval of the Managing Director, the terms and conditions of employment for all personnel up to, but excluding, the senior executive level.

N.B.—"Senior executive level" means those members of the executive staff directly responsible to the Managing Director.

7. Defining, in collaboration with the Factory Manager and/or Chief Accountant, regulations and rules for the conduct of Factory and Office personnel while on the Company's premises.

N.B.—In accordance with the Company's policy, such regulations shall be worked out in consultation with representatives of the staffs concerned.

8. Carrying out on the Company's behalf all contacts with officials of the Ministry of Labour and National Service, including the Factories Inspectors.

9. Maintaining on the Company's behalf correct relations with and handling all negotiations with Trade Unions, Employers' Associations, Educational Establishments, and other bodies concerning matters affecting employment in the Company's service.

N.B.—In the case of formal negotiations with Trade Unions, this responsibility is to be discharged in collaboration with the Factory Manager.

10. Providing appropriate secretarial services for the Company's Works Council and subsidiary committees.

11. Advising on and ensuring, in conjunction with the Factory Manager and Supervisors, the maintenance of adequate standards of working conditions, safety precautions, first-aid and factory welfare services.

12. Maintaining suitable records and statistics of employment. This responsibility will be carried out on the basis of collaboration with the Accounts and Office Methods Departments to ensure co-ordination with procedures in respect of wages, etc.

13. Interviewing and assisting employees in regard to personal difficulties and problems affecting ability and contentment in work.

14. The provision of canteen services within the financial limits laid down by the Company, and executive control of Canteen Manageress and staff.

15. Providing adequate medical and health advisory services within the financial limits laid down by the Board. The Personnel Officer is the primary executive contact for the Medical Officer (part-time) and the executive responsible for Nursing and First-aid staffs.

16. Providing within the Personnel Department adequate current information regarding local and industrial wage rates and other matters pertinent to the fulfilment of the Company's policy, including statutory orders, regulations, etc., with a view to ensuring that such ir lormation is available to the Managing Director or other executives as and when required.

17. Ensuring the correct fulfilment of the Company's obligations with regard to employment, including the maintenance of Official Registers and Returns.

Special Duties

1. Advising the Managing Director on the formulation and development of personnel policy, in order to keep it up-to-date and in respect of special conditions arising, e.g. in times of emergency.

2. Assisting the Managing Director in the development of training schemes for executive and supervisory staffs and carrying such facilities into effect on the Managing Director's behalf.

3. Acting as an arbiter in cases of dismissal, to ensure that no employee is dismissed from the Company's services except on grounds that conform with the agreed personnel policy.

4. Negotiations: except in the event of a local dispute, or in the formal discussion of policy matters, the Personnel Officer will be the Company's representative in all Trade Union negotiations and contacts. In the case of formal negotiations, the Factory Manager will serve with the Personnel Officer.

5. The Personnel Officer will attend all Trade Association meeting on the Company's behalf when questions of employment or personnel are under discussion.

6. He is expected to maintain in the Company's interests adequate contacts with organisations and activities devoted to the development of personnel management.

Limitations

1. The Personnel Officer carries no absolute right to engage staff, whether for Factory or Office employment. In filling requisitions submitted by

executives or supervisors, he will submit suitable candidate(s) for their acceptance.

2. He has no authority to determine rates of pay, salaries or wages without reference to—

(a) The senior executive concerned; or

(b) The Managing Director.

3. He has no authority to transfer or dismiss members of the Company's personnel without the approval of the senior executive concerned.

Immediate Subordinates

Personal Assistant (female staff).

Canteen Manageress.

Nursing Staff.

The Medical Officer (retained on a part-time basis for professional services).

Functional Contacts

1. All executives and supervisors regarding matters pertaining to employment and personnel.

2. Chief Accountant in respect of Personnel Department routines, records, etc.

Committees

1. *Ex officio* member of Works Council, normally serving as Honorary Secretary to the Council.

2. *Ex officio* member of any Sub-committees set up by the Council including Canteen Committee.

3. Co-opted member of the Sports and Social Club Committee.

Sheet Ref.: LG/9
Date of Issue: January 1948.

Title: MARKETING MANAGER

N.B.—See Note at end of document LG/10.

Responsible to: Managing Director.

Responsible for

1. Within the limits of interpretation of policy specified by the Managing Director, planning and carrying into effect appropriate activities for—

(a) The assessment of markets and potential customer demand;

(b) The sale of the Company's products;

(c) The storing of finished products and dispatch to customers.

2. Preparation of sales budget showing anticipated sales and expenses in attaining them.

3. Keeping market conditions under continuous review in order to obtain the necessary information for the preparation of sales budgets and to assess the trend of actual and potential consumer demand.

4. Keeping price levels of the Company's products under continuous review in order to ensure that they are competitive and profitable.

5. Fixing prices for special qualities or orders on the basis of known costs and overhead margins.

6. Within the limits of the agreed policy, determining special conditions of sale in particular cases, e.g. appropriate discounts.

7. Keeping a continuous watch on the acceptability of qualities of the Company's products, and recommending lines for research or investigation in respect of improvements in quality, new design, or the correction of deficiencies.

8. Investigating serious or recurrent complaints from customers in respect of qualities, delivery or service, and passing forward to the Production Manager the findings of such enquiries.

9. Ensuring adequate control of distribution activities, so that costs are kept within the agreed budget levels.

10. In collaboration with the Personnel Officer, appointing appropriate staff for sales, clerical and warehouse purposes, and determining appropriate levels of remuneration and conditions of employment.

11. Undertaking appropriate activities for the developing of and promotion of sales of the Company's products.

12. Keeping contact with the Trade Association in respect of all matters concerned with prices and conditions of sale.

Special Duties

1. To submit to the Managing Director at six-monthly intervals a report of general economic conditions bearing on current and future sales of the Company's products.

2. To have available in the Marketing Department current information regarding qualities and prices of products sold by competitors.

3. To encourage from members of the Sales Staff contributions in respect of design or improvement of the Company's products.

4. To organise and advise in each financial year a Conference of the Sales Staff.

Limitations

1. No special market investigations involving a cost of more than £500 in any one financial year may be undertaken without the Managing Director's sanction.

2. No discounts outside the standard range may be granted without the Managing Director's sanction.

Immediate Subordinates

Sales Manager.
Advertising Manager.
Assistant Sales Manager.

Functional Contacts

1. Factory Manager.
2. Chief Accountant, in respect of financial matters and clerical methods.
3. Personnel Officer, in all matters regarding staff.

Committees

1. Member of Managing Director's Development Committee.
2. Chairman of Sales Conference.

Sheet Ref.: LG/10
Date of Issue: January 1948.

Title: SALES MANAGER
N.B.—See Note at end of this document.
Responsible to: Marketing Manager.

Responsible for

1. Planning and control of selling activities and associated warehouse and transport activities, in order to carry into effect the agreed sales budget.

2. Co-operation with Marketing Manager in determining sales budgets.

3. Ensuring adequate control of the selling expense in accordance with agreed budget.

4. Maintaining adequate records of the Company's sales activities suitably analysed to show trends in conformity with budget and to reveal sources of excess costs.

5. Determining boundaries for sales territories within the United Kingdom.

6. The issue of instructions and information regarding conditions of sale to home salesmen and overseas agents.

7. Handling all contacts with overseas agents in respect of export sales.

8. The training of sales staff and supervision of all selling activities.

9. Maintaining adequate control of stocks in the main warehouse and in local warehouses in Northern and Western territories.

10. Considering and deciding on requests from salesmen or customers for special consideration in relation to qualities, prices, discounts or delivery.

11. Maintaining close contact with salesmen, and through them with customers, and making visits to customers at suitable intervals.

12. Taking up as a matter of urgency and dealing with complaints received from customers and passing report to Marketing Manager.

13. General supervision of Sales Office staffs and activities.

14. Ensuring the maintenance of adequate transport services within the budgeted costs.

Special Duties—None specified.

Limitations—None specified.

Immediate Subordinates

Warehouse Supervisor.
Transport Supervisor.
Salesmen.

Functional Contacts

1. Production Manager, in regard to customer complaints.
2. Chief Accountant, in respect of financial matters and clerical methods.
3. Personnel Officer, in regard to staff matters.

Committees—Attendance at Sales Conference.

NOTE.—The titles used in these last two schedules (LG/9 and LG/10) are unusual: the title "Sales Manager" is more frequently used for the senior post, carrying the wider responsibilities. The division of items between the two posts portrayed here may also be found a little unusual, being determined by specific circumstances in the organisation concerned.

BIBLIOGRAPHY

WITHIN the past few years, a considerable number of books on the general subject of management have been published in Great Britain and the United States. The selected bibliography set out below claims to be no more than a pointer to some of the more useful texts, relevant to the content of the foregoing Introduction.

1. *The British Management Review.*
   Various issues.
   (Publishers: The British Institute of Management.)
2. *The Manchester Monographs on Higher Management.*
   Various issues.
   (Publishers: The College of Technology, Manchester.)
3. L. Urwick: *The Elements of Administration.*
   (Pitman, London, 1944.)
4. A. S. Wilson: Paper on "The Mechanics of Management."
   (Published by the Australian Institute of Management, Melbourne Division, 1948.)
5. Alvin Brown: *Organisation—a Formulation of Principle.*
   (Hibbert, New York, 1945.)
6. Alvin Brown: *The Organisation of Industry.*
   (Prentice-Hall, New York, 1947.)
7. C. I. Barnard: *The Functions of the Executive.*
   (Harvard, Cambridge, Mass., 1939.)
8. James D. Mooney: *Principles of Organisation.*
   (Harper, New York, 1947.)
9. H. A. Simon: *Administrative Behaviour.*
   (Macmillan, New York, 1947.)
10. J. A. Scott: *The Measurement of Industrial Efficiency.*
    (Pitman, London, 1949.)
11. Various Papers in the *Proceedings of the International Congress on Scientific Management, Stockholm,* 1947.
    (Published in Great Britain by The British Institute of Management.)
12. M. T. Copeland and A. R. Towl: *The Board of Directors and Business Management.*
    (Harvard University, Boston, 1947.)
13. Editor, G. E. Milward: *Large-scale Organisation.*
    (Macdonald & Evans, London, 1949.)

DISTRIBUTION

By FRANK L. WOODROFFE

CHAPTER I

SALES ACTIVITIES AND SALES MANAGEMENT

Sales Potential—the Basis of Industry. The Sales-Production-Finance Triangle. Sales Management. The Cost of Distribution. Terminology.

SALES POTENTIAL—THE BASIS OF INDUSTRY

ASSUMING that the laws of supply and demand operate normally, it is prudent to base the whole structure of an industry upon the amount which it can sell. From the mines, the quarries and the fields and all sources of raw material, from the factories and workshops, the dairies and vineyards, from every place of production, from the laboratories and studios and desks and wherever industrial services are created, throughout the whole range of production, goods and services have to be sold and have to find their market at an economic price. Selling may therefore be considered as the basis of industrial economy and the factor on which all other activities depend. This applies equally to a one-man shoemaker or to a vast concern. It governs every factor, the amount of capital or plant which is installed, planning the operations, the raw materials required and so on.

The first stage in Management, therefore, is sales forecasting. There are many methods of approach to the problem of sales forecasting and many factors which must be considered before the actual work of planning a commercial programme is commenced. Fortunately, it is seldom necessary to start the whole operation from ground level, as each business has some experience to draw upon, and must have built up their undertaking over a period of years, so that sales planning is more a matter of development, expansion and rearrangement upon existing trading, and can be carried out with greater confidence and sounder judgment. Whether starting a completely new industry, however, or progressing with one already established, the planning of a sales programme is equally necessary, and varies only in the margin of error, which is a normal hazard of commerce and which is reduced as far as possible by sound judgment and detailed examination of every problem.

THE SALES-PRODUCTION-FINANCE TRIANGLE

It is not practical to consider only the total volume or value of goods sold, that is only one aspect of the matter—frequently an unimportant or even misleading consideration. The vital factor in commerce is the amount of profit which will accrue from the total sales, and this again is dependent upon the gross profit taken on the goods and the expenses of distribution. In reverse, the price factor has an important bearing on sales and the expenses have a bearing on the efficiency of both production and selling methods. This suggests, therefore, that finance and financial control, production and sales are entirely interdependent, and no sales programme can be either conceived or executed without the closest co-ordination between all three at the highest level. The lack of this co-ordination has been a major fault in many of the larger industries in the past, and it is only in recent years that the executives have developed the technique of pooling their knowledge in committee or conference work to achieve complete harmony in planning. The same error does not usually apply to the smaller concern because of the greater intimacy of those in executive posts, but such firms are often lacking in efficiency in other ways, their size limiting the selling organisation available to them.

Whatever the organisation, large or small, the administration of sales must come under one heading, and this is generally under the title of Sales Manager. There may be some variations in responsibility, e.g. where the work is divided in the larger companies and the Sales Manager and the Advertising Manager are separately responsible to the Managing Director, but this is for convenience in operation rather than because there is any difference in the purpose of their work. At the other extreme, the Sales Manager may be also responsible for other work, such as production in a smaller firm.[1]

In practical application it therefore becomes necessary for the Sales Manager not only to take the initiative in sales planning, but to decide the fundamental issues, finance, production and sales in concert with the others. The sales plan is submitted by the Sales Manager with estimated profits gross and net, against which are considered production problems and financial resources. The amendments are re-analysed by the Sales Manager, and from these discussions a plan is produced which is workable by all sections of the Company.

Sales plans must always be flexible, because of the many factors outside the control of any one Company, even outside the control of a State monopoly. It is therefore desirable to organise the Sales-Finance-Production co-operation on a continuous basis. A practical method to achieve this is by a Management Committee of the three sections, presided over by the Managing Director.

[1] See Part IV, Chapter II of this volume, "Outline of Control in Operation".

SALES MANAGEMENT

Management in the various fields of distributive activity, i.e. Sales Management, is only a specialised application of the process of management as a whole. It requires the same systematic basis of approach, and the necessary body of specialised knowledge. For this reason it has been thought advisable to devote rather a high proportion of this section to a description of the various functions in the processes of selling. Sales organisation is not a science, and the first thing is a clear understanding of the normal procedure. Management is not so much a solution of technical problems as skill and resourcefulness in adapting a sales team to ever-changing circumstances and constantly probing for new and more effective ways of finding and supplying the market.

One important difference, however, from management in other fields lies in the imaginative conception of the selling "idea" as a necessary part of the operation before the more normal function of management in organising a team of sales personnel to put the "idea" into operation. So often a homely thought will make its appeal to millions. In the serious business of management, this may seem a fantasy; nevertheless, the idea that "night starvation" injures the health, the idea of calling children's teeth "ivory castles" are examples of appeals which have built up substantial sales. Perhaps these are unusual methods of sales promotion, but even steel tubes and small electric tools have developed their markets in this way. Examples of creating new uses and new markets by inspiration are legion. In the spheres of design and packaging the importance of art has to be recognised as a considerable influence on the development of sales.

If this aspect of Sales Management is taken to have a bearing on the development of sales, it is to introduce another element into the study of the subject, not one that can itself be acquired by learning perhaps, but one which should be ever kept in mind, as part of the equipment of any sales organisation.

It has long been the criticism of foreign buyers that British goods have merit in themselves, but are designed and sold without imagination.

Another aspect of Sales Management which should be considered is the wider variety of costs incurred and the greater potential of waste than is normal in other fields. The matter-of-fact procedure in controlling expenditure on production and other sides of a business enterprise allows for greater measure of control than on selling activities, because they are dealing with more definable facts, whereas there can be a great deal of speculation in the selling side of a business, particularly advertising. As far as ever possible, sales policy must be kept within the bounds of assessment of expenditure and results, but prudence can, on occasion, be carried too far, and bold enterprise often plays its part in the field of Sales Management, even if it does not conform to the strict tenets of scientific management.

THE COST OF DISTRIBUTION

The expenditure on the various needs of distribution is not only a vast amount in total, but a substantial percentage of the ultimate cost to the consumer. It is only necessary to consider the great number of people employed in the distributive industries, in the shops and warehouses, in commercial travelling and advertising, in road and rail transport to visualise the expenditure which must be added to the cost of goods before they are finally sold to the consumer. It is no uncommon thing for the cost of an article to the public to be twice the factory cost of the finished product.

Considerable study of this position has beenmade in every sphere of economics and business management to devise methods of cheapening this cost.

The trend in recent years has been twofold:

(a) There have been reductions in the cost by increasing the scale of operations. This is noticeable in the cases where competition and advertising have reduced a multiplicity of lines to a few well-known brands. Such a position not only makes for economy in handling the goods, but enables the wholesaler and retailer to trade on a reduced margin of profit because of the steady public demand. It is also noticeable in the development of large multiple retail groups, where cost per unit to operate may be substantially lower than the smaller groups and single shops. In both these cases, the tendency has been to pass the saving on to the public in reduced prices.

(b) There have been factors which have tended to increase the cost of distribution. The low wage standards of certain retail trades has been raised and standardised. The trend of carriage rates has been upward and the cost of packaging has risen both by increased costs of materials and the public preference for the improved types of packings. Increased rates, gas, coal and electricity together with social services and, above all, rates and taxes, have placed a heavy burden on the costs of distribution.

It would seem, therefore, that the overall tendency is to save by better organisation, but to utilise the saving, at least in part, by better presentation of the goods and better conditions in the distributive trades. A forecast of the future of this trend would be to suggest that the process of efficient management will continue to operate over and above all other factors and in time reduce the proportionate cost of distribution.

To examine the distribution system critically is to reveal certain faults and considerable waste, but the present position must be recognised as representing a stage in evolution which will ultimately develop towards greater rationalisation and the improvement of the national economy.

TERMINOLOGY

In the absence of a term generally understood to embrace all the various functions of marketing—Sales Management, Advertising and Selling by Manufacturer, Wholesaler and Retailer, together with the physical warehousing and distribution of goods—this section bears the title "Distribution" in the sense in which it was known in the earlier part of the century. It will be realised that this is not an expression used in a wide sense in present-day practice, where it is normally taken to mean the limited functions of satisfying an existing demand such as those performed by the wholesaler and retailer. Nevertheless, it is the only one which is general enough for the purpose of expressing all those processes which go to make up the vast business of bringing goods from producer to consumer, and it will be used here in an even wider sense to embrace Sales Management and Marketing, which are concerned, in modern practice, not only with satisfying a demand, but in creating and stimulating markets to the highest possible degree.

It may also be necessary to give a more accurate definition to the meaning and functions of "Sales Management", "Marketing", "Merchandising" and "Advertising" than these words may convey. As the interpretation varies considerably in different quarters, it would be expedient to agree the meanings as they are applied here, even if such meanings are not universally used.

"Sales Management" is applied to the overall organisation of the whole field of selling, the Sales Manager being the director of all these activities. "Marketing" is confined to the planning side of these activities excluding the field of active selling. "Merchandising" is used where the predominant factor is a technical knowledge of commodities and markets, with day-to-day variations in prices or qualities mainly in the "commodity" and fashion markets. It implies skill in assessing market values and trends, rather than working to a planned production and sales programme.

The general field of "Advertising" and "Sales Promotion" is usually understood to come within the sphere of Sales Management. It may or may not be delegated to those responsible for marketing according to its importance in the firm concerned, whether there is a self-contained Advertising Department or not. It is therefore referred to separately under "Advertising". At the same time, some advertising plans must necessarily be included in the work of marketing, but only as an overall consideration, the practical application being carried out by the Advertising Department or Advertising Agents.

CHAPTER II

SALES PLANNING

Design, Packaging and Trade-marks. Assessing Consumer Demand—Market Research. Price Maintenance Policy.

A DISTINCTION needs to be drawn at the outset between "sales policy" and "sales planning". Those factors which affect the business as a whole, where decisions can only be concluded in team with the executives responsible for the Production, Finance, etc., form the *policy* of the Company. To carry out this policy on the distribution side is the purpose of *planning*. The responsibility for planning may be shared by others, but it is primarily the responsibility of the Sales Manager.

The factors which have to be considered in Sales Planning fall broadly under the following headings:

(1) The preparation of goods for the market, including Design, Packaging and Trade-marks.

(2) Assessing the probable market (Market Research).

(3) Deciding the channels of distribution through which the goods will flow.

(4) The provision of a suitable sales force and sales office to meet the task.

(5) The plan and appropriation of funds for advertising the product.

(6) The provision of the necessary warehousing and transport for the physical distribution of the goods.

Within this chapter the subjects of (1) Design, Packaging and Trade-marks, and (2) Market Research will be considered, together with some notes on price maintenance.

The consideration of both planning and execution of policy under the other headings is made in subsequent chapters.

DESIGN, PACKAGING AND TRADE-MARKS

In planning a distribution policy, whether for home or abroad, due consideration must be given to the presentation of the goods for sale. It is contended that this truth extends very widely and may even be universal. One sees today a steel girder delivered to the builder branded with the name of the great steel manufacturer who made it and brilliant advertisements for the most prosaic raw chemicals or steel tubes. Even where the goods do not lend themselves to a brand or trade-mark, this may be done by packaging or labelling. In many such cases the branding and presentation may have no bearing on the immediate sales which are based on price and quality, yet the attractive presentation does enhance the standing of the firm who take enough pride in their products to see that they bear their name or trade-mark.

In the majority of cases, however, particularly where goods are sold to the general public, these matters are of the utmost importance.

Industrial Design

It has taken more than a generation to develop the idea that design of consumer goods plays an important—often spectacular—part in their sale and in the pleasure of using them. The remarkable success of well-designed articles has long been noted. Yet the union between the designer, living in a world of art, and the manufacturer, whose outlook is that of sheer utility, has been long delayed. No real breadth of outlook has yet taken its proper place in this matter, and it is still a commonplace in industry to see a conflict between designer and Production Manager instead of the co-operation so urgently needed.

In order to resolve these difficulties and to accelerate the process of raising the standard of Design in British manufactured goods, the Council of Industrial Design was set up in 1944 by the President of the Board of Trade. It is financed by the Government, and the objective is to improve the design in the planning of goods, including structure, texture, form and decoration.

The Council offers manufacturers, designers and others a general advisory service for the promotion of improved industrial design. The main activities include:

> The purpose of the Council is to promote by all practicable means the improvement of design in the products of British industry, and its main functions are:
>
> (a) to encourage and assist the establishment and conduct of Design Centres by industries, and to advise the Board of Trade on the grant of financial assistance to these Centres;
>
> (b) to provide a national display of well-designed goods by holding, or participating in, exhibitions and to conduct publicity for good design in other appropriate forms;
>
> (c) to co-operate with the Education Authorities and other bodies in matters affecting the training of designers;
>
> (d) to advise, at the request of Government Departments and other public bodies, on the design of articles to be purchased by them, and to approve the selection of articles to be shown in United Kingdom

Pavilions in international exhibitions and in official displays in other exhibitions; and

(e) to be a centre of information and advice, both for industry and for Government Departments, on all matters of industrial art and design.[1]

Manufacturers who are willing to devote the necessary time and thought to this objective need have no difficulty in achieving a high standard of design in their products. The skilled personnel is available, and may be sought through the Council of Industrial Design or by direct contact with the designers themselves. Given the opportunity, they can ensure that British products are produced with a quality, style and "finish" equal to anything in the world.

Manufacturers who are in frequent need of new designs, such as manufacturers of printed fabrics, will staff a department for the purpose, selecting those designers most suitable to the task. Others may rely solely on the services of free-lance designers. Many of these work independently, but, to ensure the flexibility and variety needed to bring the right artistic conception to each job, such designers frequently work in groups, each designer being a specialist in one aspect of the work. Such groups are rapidly acquiring some knowledge of production, so that their designs are becoming more and more practical, but whether the balance between beauty and utility is preserved at the optimum height depends to a great extent on the amount of co-operation between the designers and those responsible for production. The Sales Manager should devote thought to this problem, for it is often he, by virtue of his interest in the matter, who can best promote the harmony of art and efficiency.

Packaging

This may be no less important in attracting the buying public than design of the goods themselves; indeed, it is only by attractive packing that many goods of standardised quality, e.g. some foodstuffs and cleansers, that public acceptance can be fostered. By creating an attractive pack, the Industrial Designer can often enhance sales. In the past, package design has usually been left in the hands of the printer. It is good counsel to suggest that the best available talent is selected and the results checked and amended, checked and amended again, until packaging is finally proved to measure up to the highest standard judged by public acceptance. It will not be sufficient for the manufacturer to see a design and consider it is good. He is usually a man and a man who lives a different life from those who buy his goods. If it is the woman with her shop-

[1] Quoted from the Council's Annual Report, 1950/51.

ping basket who is the ultimate buyer, it is the woman with the shopping basket who must finally decide the design for goods or package, and as many such women as possible should be given a hand in choosing every important proprietary pack before it is put on the market. Advertising Agents and Market Research organisations well know the methods by which those things are tested.

The selling value of package design does not end with attractive appearance. Frequently its utility is of equal importance. However well-designed a food carton may be, for instance, it will defeat its object if it is difficult to open and spills its contents. It must give adequate protection to the goods, it must pack and store well and the contents must be readily accessible.

In the more elaborate packs, the container may be designed as a permanent storage to be refilled, such as a tea canister; and in extreme cases the container is of greater value than the goods, as in the case of a charming vase filled with bath crystals.

Trade-marks

The use and importance of trade-marks is universally accepted. The development of a brand or trade-mark is largely in the field of advertising, but the trade-mark itself should be given considerable thought in sales planning, both as a name itself and in the design in which it is drawn or lettered. The trade-mark register is so full that it is difficult to conjure up a good name for a new product, yet no efforts should be spared to find one suitable for the goods, one easily spoken and remembered. In lettering, too, a distinctive design with its constant repetition on the package and in advertising builds up the public's memory of something which they will choose when buying.

ASSESSING CONSUMER DEMAND—MARKET RESEARCH

The sales policy of a manufacturer can be resolved into two parts, making goods for sale and making sales, but the two are so closely interrelated that they become a common problem. The articles which are manufactured must not only have intrinsic merit at a saleable price, but they must be an exact fit to a particular market and so prove acceptable to a sufficiently wide public to maintain a steady flow of production. The Sales Management must find that market by the most direct and economical way and must ensure that the goods are of the design, quality and price or adapted until they will meet wide acceptance.

The process of assessing the suitability of the goods and their prices to the market and that of learning what further markets are available comes under the heading of market research. It is gradually replacing the older method of trial and error, a method which has proved very costly in the past and which few manufacturers can afford in modern times of stringent economy and active competition.

The term "market research" is all too often taken to mean an academic study remote from practical considerations. This is entirely erroneous; in fact, the very essence of market research is its practical and factual application. It must be so, because its purpose is to inform the manufacturers of facts about their products and markets which they do not already know, perhaps after a lifetime in their business.

A very simple example could be given of a manufacturer who had been quite successful during his lifetime producing a health beverage. He was persuaded one day to rent a demonstration stand in a large store—a type of sales promotion not previously used. He was interested, and stood for several hours at the stand talking to women who were sampling the product. He was taken for an assistant, and was told frequently and emphatically how they disliked the flavour of his beverage; they took it as a medicine but with distaste. A little chocolate flavour was suggested. It was tried on the spot with most satisfactory results. The outcome was that the beverage was packed thereafter in two ways, with and without the flavouring. The old type still maintained some of its previous sales, but the new pack sold in far greater quantities.

Product research resolves itself into asking the right people the right questions about your products and extracting the truth from the answers. Occasionally this truth can be obtained by asking a few people, but the manufacturer of consumer goods usually requires a far more representative enquiry.

In rare cases of the largest marketing companies, a complete department is staffed for market research. This, however, is not the general practice, as the larger operations of research are only carried out at intervals, and there are a number of well-equipped organisations expert in this work, with large, trained staff available for the purpose. It is as well, therefore, to divide this work into two parts. First, the systematic assessment in the Sales Department of all the knowledge collected by the sales force and others of relevant information as to reception of the goods by trade and public, of criticism and suggestion, of competition and market trends, of every constructive suggestion for development and so on. The advertising and methods of competitors may be studied with advantage. Every opportunity should be taken of personally contacting the actual users of the products.

A trade survey, covering those who distribute the goods, is often a good preliminary but by no means conclusive. It is more helpful in assessing the merits of distribution methods than as a guide to public taste. It deals with those who have preconceived ideas and therefore is often misleading.

An important feature of Market Research is its value in checking plans and ideas. Having projected a major plan, whether it be launching a new line on the market or a major alteration in the present articles in quality, composition, design or pack, whether a new use for the product is to be advertised or a change in appeal—in brief, whenever an important step is suggested—it is most hazardous to proceed without learning everything possible about the probable effect of such a step upon those who buy such goods.

Where the users are few or all of the same outlook, the matter is simply to ask them the right questions. The real importance of market research is in the case of goods sold to a wide public of varying tastes and conditions. It is here that there is so much at stake in any major plans, and the research acts as an insurance against a false step as well as a guide to the best methods of development.

The methods of conducting the many types of surveys are the subject of a more detailed study in the appropriate textbooks. The Sales Manager, however, must first plan his survey by deciding exactly and precisely what facts are required and list them in a questionnaire. The preparation of this questionnaire is difficult, because there is so much information which will be useful, yet the scope must be limited to such questions as can be answered in a brief interview and these must be of a kind which are readily understood and to which simple, direct answers can be given. In framing the questions, too, nothing must be asked which will suggest the answers, as no information is of use which is not fact or honest opinion. The questions, therefore, must be reduced to the vital information on which manufacturing and selling policy is based.

In the public survey, the test is carried out through a representative sample of consumers throughout the country or such part of it where the goods are to be sold. The questionnaire is devised, and a team of research workers contact such consumers on a prearranged plan of selection, asking of each identical questions and noting the replies. These are collected and subjected to the closest analysis and tabulation for the final report.

A simple example will illustrate typical methods.

A Company with a substantial sale of a breakfast cereal called "Sunshine" in an old-fashioned packet wishes to bring this design up-to-date, because it is suffering in display value in the shops against that of its competitors. At the same time the Company do not wish to lose the goodwill of the present users of the product, many of whom have taken it from childhood and to whom the packet is so familiar. It is therefore decided to "clean up" the design, retaining the essential features, but introducing brighter colours, painting it in broader lines and strengthening the lettering. Sketches are commissioned, and when the advice of designers and advertising agents have finalised the new packet, it is decided to conduct a research.

A "window" display is arranged, showing the old packet, the new packet and a representative selection of competitive packs shown in as normal a manner possible. Care must be taken to see that every packet has an equal chance in the display, and if there is a bias it should be against those being tested. These displays are then arranged in a number of centres throughout the districts where the goods are to be sold, cities, market towns, etc., and housewives of various classes are asked, at random, to come in, given a free packet, or other present for their trouble. They are then asked such questions as:

1. Which packet do you notice first?
   (*after a pause*)
2. Which packet do you consider most attractive?
3. What breakfast cereals do you regularly buy?
To those who use your product:
4. Would you recognise this as the old "Sunshine"?
   (*after a pause*)
5. Do you like it better?

A summary of the results produced the following:

	Seen first Per cent.	Most attractive Per cent.
"Sunshine" old . . .	8	6
"Sunshine" new . . .	18	19
A competitor . . .	23	22
B competitor . . .	9	10
C competitor . . .	4	4
D competitor . . .	10	9
Indefinite	28	30
	100	100

This was very satisfactory, considering that "A" competitor was a famous brand in a well-recognised packet of good strong design.

The question, "What breakfast cereals do you regularly buy?" produced a percentage of 22 in favour of "Sunshine"—a very substantial proportion, although slightly higher than the known all-over percentage of sales.

It was shown that these regular users accounted for almost all those who chose "Sunshine" in the above table. Further, they produced the following table of preferences:

	Recognise new packet Per cent.	Prefer it Per cent.
Yes	56	42
No	23	38
Uncertain	21	20
	100	100

This latter table came as a surprise, for it showed that there was a strong tendency among present users to cling on to the old, well-recognised design. Yet the answers to questions 1 and 2 showed that the new design had so much more display value that an alteration was necessary to attract the eye of more buyers. The new design had obviously gone so far away from the old one as to be a revolutionary step.

A compromise plan was decided. The alteration was not made forthwith, but a series of four designs, each with a stage of alteration towards the final design, was put in hand and the changeover made in these stages over a period of three years.

Public Surveys.—On a wider issue a complete poll of opinion can be taken throughout the country to determine the public views on any subject, from political tendencies to preferences in perfume. It is specialist work by a few organisations devoted to the purpose. Their teams of investigators are highly skilled, and they contact a representative section of the public throughout the country with the questions.

Mechanical statistical departments provide analyses of the answers in every necessary variation. A high degree of accuracy can be achieved on public opinion in any reasonable subject. The selection of classes can be carried out according to need, such as income groups, age-groups, etc., all of which can be tapped at will.

PRICE MAINTENANCE POLICY

British manufacturers and traders have been increasingly leaning towards a policy of price maintenance for their products in recent years as a step towards the more orderly distribution of goods and the provision of a fair margin of profit at all stages of production and distribution. Their case has been that such goods, although sold at fixed prices, are in free competition with other goods, and that therefore no restrictive practices are in operation. They maintain that cutting prices by the retailer is only a temporary expedient to gain trade at the expense of his fellow traders, and having achieved this the price-cutter turns to other goods, and so there is no permanent benefit to the public. On the other hand, there is much benefit to both public and distribution to have a fair margin of profit ensured and a known standard of value universally accepted. Paring margins by price cutting inevitably cuts the standards of quality and service which are generally rated as highly by the buying public as the purchase of the goods themselves.

To this end, therefore, there have been groups of manufacturers, notably of toilet and medicinal preparations and proprietary foods, which have combined together through their trade associations to maintain fixed prices throughout the trades concerned, and by combined action have withdrawn supplies over a wide range from traders cutting the price of only one member's product.

Some conflict has arisen over this, and it was suggested that such methods constituted a restrictive ring which was not in the public interest.

The President of the Board of Trade, therefore, set up a Committee on Resale Price Maintenance, and the Report,[1] published in 1949, will serve as a reference in the consideration of a policy of price maintenance. The conclusions and recommendations reached (one member making reservations) were that the present growth of branding and standardisation would probably continue, and that the manufacturer of a branded article remains responsible for the quality of the goods sold under his own brand; he cannot therefore be indifferent to the terms on which his goods are sold to the public. Well-known branded articles are particularly liable to be used as loss-leaders by distributors, and the Committee were satisfied that their use in this way has not brought any permanent advantage to manufacturers, distributors, or the shopping public as a whole. Resale price maintenance offers a convenient means of protecting brands against misuse by distributors in this or other ways, and it is recommended that nothing should deprive the individual manufacturers, wholesalers, importers, etc., of power to prescribe and enforce resale prices for goods bearing his brand.

On the other hand, the distinction is drawn between the fixation and maintenance of resale prices by an individual manufacturer and the collective administration of resale price maintenance schemes. Manufacturers are not, in the opinion of the Committee, entitled to use resale price maintenance to obstruct the development of particular methods of trading, to impede the distribution by another manufacturer of competitive goods, or to deprive the public of the benefits of improvements in distribution. Collective price maintenance schemes appear to have led to the comprehensive regulation of competition in the distributive trades and are undesirable.

[1] "Report of the Committee on Resale Price Maintenance." H.M. Stationery Office, 2s. 6d.

CHAPTER III

THE CHANNELS OF DISTRIBUTION

Distribution through Retail Stores. Selling Direct to the
Public. Selling to Industrial Users. Export.

THE main structure of the system of distribution may be said to be clearly defined and not unduly complicated from the point of view of the manufacturer, however intricate the administration may be within the distributive trade itself. Well-established methods of wholesale and retail trading carry the great bulk of goods to the public in every part of the country, and most manufacturers and producers are content to have their goods distributed in this way. Such distribution is not in their hands, but on the whole the manufacturers and the distributive trades work well together, and the latter are willingly subject to influence by such things as advertising and the persuasion of representatives in promoting the development of sales.

It is advisable for the manufacturer's Sales Manager and Sales Staff to have a very thorough understanding of how these distributors operate both for the purpose of planning the sales policy and its execution. Special methods of distribution, often complex and difficult, have their place to a smaller extent. These, in the main, relate to the raw materials of industry or to the partly manufactured requirements of the factory.

In deciding the channels of distribution required by a manufacturer or producer, it should be remembered that the nature of the goods themselves will determine the methods to be employed. They are made for and appeal to a certain market, either actual or potential. That market is either known or must be sought out. There may be one customer or ten thousand. A maker of flags must know that the market for authentic Royal Standards is limited, but that sixpenny National flags can be sold to thousands of toy shops, bazaar stores and novelty dealers.

The main channels of distribution are as follows:

(1) Through retail stores.

This is approached through a combination of channels in varying degree; (*a*) wholesalers; (*b*) direct to multiple stores; (*c*) direct to retail stores.

(2) Direct to the public.

This is a method of distribution usually reserved for highly specialised goods, and may entail a high number of traveller-calls, door-to-door.

A well-developed aspect of this is selling by Mail Order, which may be direct on a widespread scale to the public or used as a method of approach to traders offering the goods for resale. It is sometimes used as an adjunct to other methods to reach potential buyers less expensively than by personal calls and for its advertising value.

(3) Direct to industrial users.

Goods and materials used for the process of manufacture. Goods and services for industrial concerns. Special materials and packs for factory and office use. This type of product is usually sold direct to industrial concerns, and includes raw materials, accessories, tools and machinery, cleaning materials, office machinery and equipment, etc.

(4) Export.

This is approached in the main through (a) Export Corporations, (b) overseas representatives and (c) overseas agents.

DISTRIBUTION THROUGH RETAIL STORES

The Retail Store is the final link in the chain of distribution for the great bulk of consumer goods. Retail distribution is one of the major industries of the country and part of the national life. It is so complex and varied, performs so many functions, that it is difficult to grasp all the implications of the system by outlining its economic functions. For example, retail stores contribute to the social life of the country as a meeting-place for millions of women daily. They have considerable influence on the habits of the people. By their influence, homes are better equipped, clothes are more attractive, cosmetics are more suitably applied—and they circulate advice on countless subjects, from food to medicines, from the garden to the nursery.

Furthermore, the success of retail trading does not necessarily depend on strict economics in a great many cases. The element of service is often a factor of considerable importance, and the variation between the cash-and-carry store and the service store can be over a wide range. It is all a matter of what the individual can afford. The public likes "service" and demands it, provided the cost is not apparent. The primary function of the Retail Store is to provide a selection of goods easily accessible to the public as conveniently near their home as possible. The display of goods is a feature in that the public can see and select at will, and the public is provided with a fund of suggestion to remind them of their needs.

In the main, retail stores are in small units, each devoted to a particular group of products, and even the large stores retain this principle in dividing the store into departments, each with its group of products even more specialised than the average small retail shop.

It is not suggested that this system, which has grown up to meet the needs of the public, is the most economical method of getting goods to the individual members of the public. We have seen under various dictatorships the allocation of supplies according to a pre-arranged plan of standardisation and ration, and this can be done at much lower cost. But as freedom is very essential to the British way of life, the public has built up its retail system according to its own preference as it exists today.

Much of the retail system is, however, carried out in a well-organised and most economic manner. The distribution of food and all other staple household goods in regular demand is done at a very low percentage of cost; in fact, this became so low as to jeopardise the provision of a fair wage to those employed in the trade, a fault which has now, to some extent, been remedied.

The major fault in the system is the countless numbers of small shops with insufficient turnover and consequent need for high margins of profit. This is again caused by the scattered populations who have the habit of buying at their small, local shop when they could buy more economically at busy shopping centres. If the manufacturers provide a fixed margin of profit sufficient to cover the inefficient shopkeeper, they are setting a standard of profit unnecessarily high for the modern, well-run multiple shop. This process is, fortunately, giving way under the more critical outlook of the buying public and the extension of the more efficient trader to wider areas. One may deplore the elimination of the "small man" in the retail trade, but he is not eliminated of necessity, only when he ceases to trade efficiently and well.

(a) Selling to the Retail Stores through Wholesalers

The wholesalers perform a function not generally appreciated by the public and not always valued by commercial interests. The repeated slogans about "cutting out middlemen" and "direct from producer to consumer" are misleading, and do not necessarily reduce the costs of distribution.

The wholesaler normally carries out his work of redistribution in small quantities at a cost below that which would occur if any but the largest manufacturers were to do it direct. His travelling costs are lower because of the great number of lines he carries, his credits are better organised because he is in more intimate touch with his customers and his warehouse is laid out to assemble and deliver in his area.

Wholesalers, collectively and individually, will increase or decrease in importance according to their efficiency and operating costs. If they realise their responsibility to the trade and organise to meet its requirements, they can make their usefulness greater, and so attract a larger volume of goods for distribution as has been done in America. On the other hand, many wholesalers are tending to lose their place and force manufacturers to set up their own direct distribution. They are mostly too small to be economic units, they are housed in buildings unsuited to handling merchandise in the most efficient manner, and they lack equipment and good transport.

A wholesale warehouse must be planned and mechanised for its work. Goods must be unloaded and loaded with a minimum of labour by the provision of well-designed bays, with conveyors and other equipment of the appropriate type. There must be a well-run fleet of the right type of transport vehicles and their operation scheduled for maximum running time with full loads and a minimum of standing.

The buyers must be skilled men who keep their pulse on the selling side and alert for opportunities to develop the volume of sales. It is a mistake to devote too much time to seeking large percentages of profit. In view of the considerable overheads, large and rapid turn-over is the keynote to growth of net profits.

To the manufacturers the facts are quite easily ascertainable, and the economy or otherwise of finding a distribution through whole-salers is resolved by experience or can be calculated with some degree of certainty, according to the nature of the goods sold, the quantity of output, the extent of public demand and the margin of gross profit. Apart from the multiple and departmental stores, there are many thousands of retail stores in each of the main trades. They range from the larger stores with a brisk turnover to the remote "general" stores in the smallest village. On a given line or range of goods, it is known, or can easily be discovered, what would be the margin of profit which the wholesaler would require to distribute such goods. Experience will tell that travellers can be employed to sell at a given percentage to various classes of traders and in a given volume. As soon as this becomes a greater percentage than the wholesaler's margin, plus the cost of selling to him, it no longer pays to go direct to the class of retailers he serves, but such trade should go through the wholesaler.

It is important, however, to take some other considerations into account in deciding the extent to which a distribution through whole-salers is employed. It cannot be expected that they will put any sales effort behind the distribution of any one manufacturer's products. They will seldom distribute show-cards, leaflets, or other advertising material to the retailer as the manufacturer's travellers would do. They will not give service or informed advice about your products

If, therefore, the manufacturer requires these things done, he must make the necessary arrangements and take the costs into account in arriving at the true cost of distribution through the wholesalers. To achieve the contacts required with the smaller retailers, the usual method is to employ a team of travellers who call on those retailers who are served by the wholesalers. They will be special pleaders for the merits of their goods, but will not take orders, or if they do, they will pass them on to the appropriate wholesaler for execution. They will deliver or arrange show-cards or display material where necessary and generally do whatever is needed to promote sales and distribution. They do not, as a rule, call often, as the physical distribution of their goods is already arranged.

Another method to achieve the same ends is employed by some wholesalers themselves. Subject to a special arrangement of terms, they will themselves give special selling efforts to a limited number of lines. Their travellers are "briefed" for this, usually by the manufacturer's Area Manager, and show-cards are distributed. In short, the wholesalers' organisation performs the same function as the special sales staff of the manufacturers.

(b) *Selling to Multiple and Departmental Stores*

This section of the retail trade will account for a large percentage of most manufacturer's sales to the public. It falls roughly into four groups: the multiple private traders, the multiple bazaar store, the Co-operative store and the departmental store. The latter is classed as a multiple store, even if it should be a single unit, because it has a number of separate departments or "shops", which approximate to a group of multiple stores in one area.

The multiple private traders approximate to a number of individual shops, each with the advantage of tapping the trade of its locality and the personal day-to-day contact of manager and staff with their customers, combined with the benefits of central organisation for buying, standardisation of economy in administration and widespread goodwill. This is an important and growing method of retail distribution, and is noteworthy for skill in bringing the right selection of goods to the smaller shopping centres at very low percentage cost.

The range of goods distributed in this way is fairly comprehensive but the main achievements have been in merchandise of everyday consumption, notably food, household goods and medicines. Certain types of smaller articles of clothing, particularly shoes, newspapers and books are also represented.

Co-operative trading plays a prominent part in the distribution of goods to the public, particularly food. The Co-operative movement consists of the Retail Societies scattered throughout the country and the Co-operative Wholesale Society with its counterpart in Scotland. The Retail Societies are many autonomous groups, ranging from a single shop in a small, remote village, to large organisations with hundreds of shops and their bakeries, dairies, delivery vans and central offices. The Co-operative Wholesale Society and Scottish Co-operative Wholesale Society are the producers and wholesalers for all the groups of Retail Societies—vast concerns with factories of many kinds, large warehouses and many other activities.

The mutual benefit system, where the customers own, govern and share the profits, applies to the Retail Societies and in turn through them to the Wholesale Societies. Their primary function, therefore, is retail trading, but this has extended so far beyond such field that this fact, together with their political activities, makes a marked division between them and normal retail businesses.

The Bazaar Store companies are few in number, but between them account for a great volume of business, particularly in the less-expensive and small merchandise. They differ from the usual methods of selling in their self-service system of selling openly from their counters and racks and the fact that they offer only the quick-selling goods of each range at low prices. Originally one-price or maximum prices, this policy has perforce been suspended, but it must be a low price limit to maintain the basic principle of such stores.

Departmental stores differ from other types of retail stores in the concentration under one roof of a great variety of merchandise for display and selection. Unlike the smaller stores, they are not dependent on local trade, but must draw their customers from a wide area, and this they are well able to do by the attractions they can offer. Advertising and display constitute a major part of their operations, and the opportunities of making a grand spectacle for the delight of the shopping public bring many people to their stores.

In the main, the basis of their trade is in women's clothing, particularly fashion goods, where a large selection of styles and sizes can only be provided at such a store far greater than the capacity of the small shop. The larger items of household furnishing are also an important feature of the store business, where again a wide selection is only possible in such premises.

Although clothes and furnishing play an important part, Departmental stores cover the whole gamut of shopping, and many such stores make it possible to buy everything you need under one roof, from food to fashions, from pins to pianos.

The Department Store has certain administrative advantages over the smaller unit. The organisation is more flexible, in that it can exploit whatever section of the business shows greatest opportunity at the moment and move departments to greater and less prominence at will, concentrate advertising and window display on the most saleable goods. Stock control and buying are more easily managed than for scattered small units. Their advertising is more effective because it draws buyers who purchase other things beside the specific goods advertised, particularly the development of a food section and restaurant for this purpose.

No plan for selling on any substantial scale to the public, through retail stores, can be complete without the co-operation of the multiple, departmental and Co-operative stores. The selling methods must be right, the goods strictly competitive in price and quality, and a service of prompt delivery assured before they are approached. In most cases it will be necessary to be sure of a public demand for the goods before such stores will buy them.

Buying is almost, without exception, carried out centrally. It becomes necessary, therefore, to make plans which will satisfy the highly skilled and sceptical buyers employed by these firms, and do so in the face of the keenest competition on price, presentation and quality. Any weakness in these essentials will prejudice future relations with these traders and so should be eliminated beforehand. At the same time, the outlook should be flexible enough to meet every situation to retain their goodwill. The buyer's judgment is important, but there is a court of appeal—the public demand. By creating public support for the products, buyers everywhere will usually distribute such goods if there is a fair margin of profit, but the multiple stores can play an important part in moulding buying tastes, so it is preferable for them to take a line willingly rather than be forced by advertising alone.

The physical distribution of goods through all these stores presents the least problem of any type of distribution. Most deliveries are effected in bulk to central warehouses or depots. Where detailed distribution is required to the individual stores, instructions are clearly defined on printed lists and simply require multiple dispatch.

A variation of the multiple store system sometimes employed is for the manufacturer to open his own chain of retail stores for the distribution of his goods. The same end is achieved through "tied" stores. Tied stores (or public-houses in the case of a brewer) may be financed and partly controlled by the manufacturer primarily to distribute his goods to the exclusion of competitors, but may be privately managed. This system overcomes the difficulties of obtaining distribution through independent retailers, but gives added problems in other ways, such as retail organisation and selling. Apart from this, all other problems of marketing, advertising, etc., are similar.

(c) Selling Direct to Retail Stores

The small retailer is in a separate class, but within that class provides infinite variety. There are many thousand small shops very successful either because they give outstanding service, sell exclusive goods, or have some distinct character which places them in a position outside the competition of the larger groups. There are many more thousands who earn their proprietors no more than a modest income, but have a very definite place in distribution by reason of their personal service and often their geographical location near their customers' homes. They are at some disadvantage in their buying, but in the main this only reduces their profits and is not passed on to the consumer, as they are usually competitive in price with the multiple and other store groups. Beyond this there are still many more of the smallest shops which are not strictly economic units, and which exist either because they are run under so little expense, such as being run by the wife of a man earning in other ways, or because the customary margin of profit in certain cases is higher than it should be in a well-ordered trade.

In the case of a normal, widespread distribution, selling to this group should be considered in conjunction with distribution through wholesalers (q.v.), because only manufacturers with the largest sales organisations can hope to call on all retail stores direct. These larger firms, for example the great soap companies, achieve direct distribution to, perhaps, a hundred thousand or more shops through a staff of some hundreds of travellers, but only because they have so many lines in daily demand and so great a total turnover that even the smallest shop can order sufficient to justify a direct traveller call.

Of the smaller manufacturers, the only ones which normally deal direct with individual retail stores are those with specialised sales, where distribution is required through a picked type of store, either because of their special type, e.g. a fitting service for clothes, or because of a technical service, e.g. wireless sets.

In these cases service, prestige and location all play their part. Retailers are selected; they are usually appointed Agents, and a written agreement is concluded. On the manufacturer's part, he usually agrees that he will not sell through others in the locality. He will train the retailer's staff in sales methods to suit the products and give technical information on servicing. The retailer will undertake to give attention to the goods, afford displays and limit his competition with other lines.

In "exclusive" lines, a less formal agreement is undertaken, but sales are rigidly kept to such stores as can maintain the prestige of the goods, such as fashion goods, which must be sold only through such retailers as can uphold the exclusive style of the designers. Prices and margins of profit in these cases are in keeping with the limitation of quantity.

SELLING DIRECT TO THE PUBLIC

This is an important and generally the only means of selling the variety of public services—passenger transport, entertainment, catering, etc. (see introductory chapter). It seldom includes a direct selling organisation as such, but all those in touch with and serving the public in the course of their duties have the opportunities of salesmanship, in which they should be trained so far as it may affect them. An example of this would be the hall porter of an hotel or any other member of the staff, who can do much to ensure the return of their visitors.

The promotion of business in public services is largely conducted by advertising and other forms of publicity. The technique of the Public Relations Officer frequently promotes the public goodwill to institutions of this kind.

In the case of the manufacturers of consumer goods, this is a type of distribution which has hitherto received only a limited measure of support; and of those who use it, a high proportion change over to a retail distribution when they are sufficiently well-established to command the support of the retail trade. It involves a very large and expensive force of salesmen to reach the public wherever they may be found, in their houses, at exhibitions, sports meetings, etc. The organisation to control such salesmen, both office and supervisory, needs considerable work and constant watchfulness to make it work smoothly.

The class of manufacturers using this method mainly consists of makers of household appliances. The necessity to concentrate intensive salesmanship on the particular line, free from the competitive distraction of rival lines, is the usual reason for this choice of method. It is normal to higher-priced goods, e.g. vacuum cleaners and refrigerators, although it is sometimes applied to general household requisites. In these expensive goods, the necessity to sell on hire-purchase terms is an added reason for this personal and individual selling. Servicing may also enter into the reasons for considering such a method, as it may be more convenient to sell direct to the user when direct servicing is a necessary part of the contract.

Against the undoubted expense of direct distribution, the saving in both selling to the retailer and the retail profit is a not inconsiderable item. The decision as to which is the cheaper and most effective will probably depend on whether the goods will flow naturally and easily through retail channels or require the more forcible attack direct to the public by direct selling.

Selling by Mail Order

By direct-mail selling it is understood that the complete transaction is conducted without personal contact, but entirely by mail. In other methods of selling the approach by post may play its part as a "sieve" to economise in sales staff, but the final contact is personal. To justify the term "Direct-mail Selling", however, the personal call is entirely absent.

As a complete method of selling this is rarely practised by manufacturers as an outlet for their range of products. It does, however, assume some proportions as a trading method for distributors as an alternative to retail methods.

In countries where there are large rural populations, isolated from shopping districts, there is a very substantial mail-order business, particularly the United States of America, where the great mail-order houses issue detailed catalogues in large numbers. In Britain the mail-order houses dealing in general merchandise are few, and it is probably safe to say that the bulk of this business is done as an extra outlet for their goods by the larger departmental stores. Overseas buying also accounts for a not inconsiderable proportion of this trade.

Any comparison of the selling costs against the cost of selling in a store must be largely speculation, but it is usually assumed that the cost of selling by direct mail is at least as high as the store costs and in many cases considerably higher. Printing catalogues, mailing, correspondence, advertising, special packing, etc., amount to a substantial percentage in the turnover, particularly as so many of the catalogues and circulars do not produce results and postage costs are at the present high level.

If a manufacturer embarks upon direct-mail selling, it is usually for one of three reasons: (*a*) that the users of his products are in remote places, as, for instance, farmers, or are widely scattered overseas buyers and therefore are difficult and expensive to reach through usual trade channels; or (*b*) where the nature of the goods requires elaborate listing and studying in the home, such as garden seeds, or (*c*) that he is either content or counselled to sell to a limited number of customers of a strictly limited classification where the expense of a sales staff is not justified. Even in this case, direct-mail selling is seldom the best way unless customers are widely scattered. At best, advertisement and mailing matter can rarely have the force of personal salesmanship, and if potential customers can be approached personally, it must be more effective. The resistance to sitting down and writing an order is a very real one compared with saying "yes" to a salesman.

Within those limits, however, there are some manufacturers who would be wise to decide upon the direct-mail method of selling their goods. They should therefore lay their plans to use all the devices at their disposal to reach the righ class of public in as convincing a way as possible.

The use of outside experts is very important in this kind of campaign. The first line of attack is by advertisement to produce enquiries, which are then followed up by post, and the Advertising Agent should produce results in this way.

The specialised Direct-mail Advertising Agents with their selected mailing lists and skill in producing the most effective mailing "shots" should be called in, as their advice is of great value. At the same time the internal systems and mailing lists should be built up and buyers and prospective buyers should be mailed with regularity. The key in most cases to direct-mail selling is persistence. Reminder after reminder is usually necessary to produce results.

SELLING TO INDUSTRIAL USERS

Apart from the main structure of distribution of consumer goods, i.e. goods which are passed through channels of distribution to their ultimate consumers, there must be a secondary group where the goods or services are only a part of the complete chain, and where the sale is to a factory or other place where further process is necessary before being distributed to the final user.

The range of such goods covers such raw materials of every kind which are the basic needs of the factory: iron and steel and other metals, wood and cotton and wool, and all the many materials of manufacture. Such materials are sold on the exchanges, are sold direct from mines or forests, are handled by brokers and are dealt with by importers.

The second group of sales to industrial users is that of manufactured articles which are not complete in themselves but form part of the finished products. Examples of this are component parts of motor-cars and plastic mouldings for wireless sets, etc.

Professional services are in a similar category, as these are for the use of industry as part of the process of manufacture and distribution.

In addition, there are many finished products required by industry for which a specialised type of selling is required: the machinery and plant, the transport vehicles, the office and canteen equipment and the buildings in which these things are housed.

There are many minor products which are necessary to the running of factory and office, all of which require a sales organisation to distribute. The list of such products is wide and varied, ranging from books and stationery to cleaning preparations and paint, from food supplies for the canteen to disinfectants. In this category, the bulk of the products are those already sold to the general public, but special packs and probably a special sales staff develop the sales to industrial users.

If, therefore, the main headings are considered in more detail, they would fall broadly into the following classes:

(a) Raw material.
(b) Manufactured articles for incorporation in other products.
(c) Professional services.
(d) Plant, machinery and transport.
(e) Sundry adjuncts.

(a) Raw Material

Buying and selling of the main groups of the basic raw materials of industry have reached the point of standardisation where the process is relatively simple. The majority of metals are dealt with through their appropriate exchanges, where a known quality can be purchased at a settled price. A similar position occurs in such materials as cotton, wool and grain. There are variations to meet particular needs, as, for example, the cotton exchange or its equivalent where a spinner may contract for the delivery of a specified grade on given dates to meet his future production programme.

Whether sold through organisations set up for the purpose, however, or direct from production or importing to the factory, quality and price are main factors in effecting sales of raw material. The market is open and readily accessible, the buyers are anxious to receive any product better or cheaper than they are at present using and are usually few in number, so that sales organisation on a large scale is rarely necessary. At the same time the market is one of the most difficult to capture, but the problem is more one of production than selling, because the user of such material is buying on cold facts of quality and price, and these depend on production efficiency. On the research side the producer of raw materials has almost unlimited scope for the scientific development of his products, and on the cost side the works management can never cease to plan economy in production.

On the purely selling side, however, there is much to be done. The first essential is to develop sales personnel of the highest possible technical efficiency. The second is to classify fully and in great detail all the necessary information about potential buyers, what material they now use and in what quantities, how they could be approached and with what products, who are the key people in such firms and their background. It is then necessary to maintain contact with them frequently and skilfully to become on terms of the closest relationship to them individually and to their problems in order to work out with them the processing of the materials. Every kind of service must be given generously, and a team spirit built up between the two companies where the mutual interest is known and recognised on both sides.

The most productive development in this field of recent years has been the establishment of research teams by producers of raw material which are entirely at the disposal of their customers. The steel industry, the chemical industry, the great oil-producing companies and the makers of light alloys, among others, have set up research laboratories of considerable size and efficiency for this purpose. The advice of such a team is invaluable to a progressive manufacturer, and in turn develops the market for the raw material to the benefit of both concerns.

(*b*) *Manufactured Articles for incorporating in other Manufactured Goods*

A similar set of circumstances occurs in this field, as such articles, even if manufactured, may be considered as the raw material of the finished product. Manufacturers of electrical equipment or wireless sets may buy their plastic mouldings from a specialist manufacturer, most motor-car and aeroplane manufacturers contract for a considerable number of component parts from outside sources, almost every manufacturer orders the necessary containers, bottles or cans from other firms ; in fact, some of these industries, plastics, containers, glass bottles and cans or metal boxes, are very large organisations in themselves, entirely devoted to serving other manufacturers. They maintain their position by the scale on which they produce, often combined with a high degree of standardisation which is far greater and higher in efficiency than their customers could produce themselves. The degree of concentration, not only in production but in selling, places them in the forefront, and this is noticeable in the service they can render in research and advice as to the best methods to use.

Other manufacturers of component parts owe their position to their patents or their high technical skill in production, thus creating an industry within an industry closely linked to their customers.

(*c*) *Professional Services and Operations*

This group is wide and varied, and the details of the selling methods can only be worked out according to the individual problems. To many, the conduct of the service is, in itself, the selling medium required, such as in Public Utility Companies and Banking. Others, such as Insurance and Insurance Brokers, Consultants in Management and other aspects of business, Advertising Consultants and Agents, Commercial Art Studios and Industrial Designers, all require highly specialised and skilful selling methods peculiar to their particular approach. Service, rather than goods, is the feature of publishers and of some specialised printers of advertising material and fine art.

The primary consideration of selling all such services is a sound appreciation of the object and purpose of the task to be performed, not from the point of view of those who create and carry out the service, but from that of a possible user. It is not sufficient for the salesman to believe wholeheartedly in the project, he must step into the shoes of the prospective customer to find out what will convince him of his need. In all selling of specialised services, it is important to know and understand the facts about the potential customer and his business. Very skilled and highly paid men are essential. The provision of a social atmosphere and entertainment sometimes plays its part in overcoming the barriers which occur largely through prejudice, and to promote friendly co-operation so often necessary in achieving the objective.

(d) Machinery and Plant and Transport

This group requires specialised knowledge of the products to be sold and a wide general knowledge of the manufacturing processes or purposes for which they are to be used. It is essential that sales personnel should have sufficient background of technical training and experience together with a keen interest in the customers' requirements. "Service" is of vital importance. A first-class organisation, allied to the sales department, should maintain the most alert watch over the installation and working of every item of plant and machinery to build up a reputation for "service"—sometimes as important as the products themselves.

(e) Sundry Adjuncts

The range of the smaller articles used by industry must be very wide and conforms roughly to the needs of a household in that a factory, like a house, must be cleaned and painted, and the workers usually need food and clothing. As a rule, therefore, the manufacturers of similar goods for household consumption can develop a trade with industrial users as an addition to their domestic business. Some firms, say, overall manufacturers, may specialise in this type of business but that is exceptional.

This is, in the main, a straightforward selling problem, although it

P.P.M.—5

is usually necessary to devote specialist salesmen and bulk packs to the operation. It requires regular and thorough calling on the buyers. Some technical knowledge may be required ; e.g. in selling detergents, the nature of the foreign matter to be removed and the particular product required to do this need some instruction, but in general the buyers know what they want, and the firm which supplies the right article at the right price with efficient service can win a share of the business without undue elaboration of sales methods.

EXPORT

Export sales constitute a wide study, and export sales management is a profession in itself. As with advertising, the reference to the subject which can be given here must of necessity be inadequate except as a guide for the general principles of management. Furthermore, world economic conditions undergo frequent change, and any detailed study of the subject must always be flexible to current influences.

The first consideration is to examine the problem briefly from the point of view of a manufacturer for the home market who wishes to enter the export market or expand export sales. For this purpose export is treated as a general market throughout the world, although such is not strictly possible. Each country or group of countries should be considered as a market in itself and generalities may be misleading. If, however, the problem is studied as a whole, it gives a basis for general procedure, always provided that the fact is well understood that as the sales develop a more detailed study of each market will be necessary to obtain any substantial results.

The consideration of an export programme may be examined under three main headings :

1. Research and planning.
2. Representation.
3. Home organisation.

(1) *Research and Planning*

The first essential is to consider the suitability of the products which are produced for the different markets of the world and if necessary to decide what are the adaptations or alterations in either the products themselves or their packing. This entails a wide and detailed survey of the markets of the world or such markets as are considered suitable. Such research on a wide scale is a big undertaking and may be very costly. Fortunately, it can be taken in stages over a period of time, or one section of the world may be taken first, followed by others as progress is made. Even a Company with a substantial export business is well advised to make such survey from time to time. With a Company embarking on export sales for the first time it is essential.

There are various ways in which the matter can be approached. I₁ Great Britain the Government-sponsored British Export Trade R₁ search Organisation (B.E.T.R.O.), a non-profit making and indepen⸱ dent organisation, is ready-made for the purpose, and can carry ou⸴ the desired research for reasonable fees and carry them to the stag⸴ required.

There are many other ways of getting the information, but in the main they would prove less accurate and usually more costly. Commercial attachés at the various Embassies provide very valuable help, but obviously they are not equipped to deal with more than the general proceeding for the various markets and are not able to give a detailed examination of consumer demand. A personal visit to the countries concerned is an important step to take, perhaps in any case, even though other means of market research are employed. In this way samples can be shown to the distributors and even to the consumers on the spot, and as a result of personal contact with those who really know the market, much information may be obtained which could be gathered in no other way. At the same time, such a journey should be made with due discretion. There are many pitfalls, and it may prove as easy to be led astray as to be put on the right track. Those who are contacted abroad must have been proved to be reputable people of standing in their trade before action is taken on their advice.

The larger importers and distributors in the various countries of the world maintain offices or shipping agents in Great Britain and America. Their addresses can be obtained from the trade directories and it is generally useful to make contact with such firms, where a fund of information about their particular market may be obtained. In London, for example, agents for importers of many lands have their offices, and themselves constitute a complete network of facilities to distribute to a large section of the world. Similarly, British Export Corporations in London, Liverpool and Glasgow will be in a position to transact business throughout the world. These latter, however, are mainly trading companies buying in the best market and exporting. It is not necessarily in their interests to develop any one particular product overseas as a proprietary in a way the manufacturers themselves would do it. While such Corporations remove the manufacturers' necessity of building up an export organisation, the policy is reflected in the price obtained for the products, and seldom can valuable proprietary export markets be built up in this way. If, however, bulk selling on day-to-day markets is the policy of the Company, a quick and often considerable business can be done.

Particular attention should be given to the services of the Board of Trade and the Institute of Export, together with the various periodical publications issued by subscription from various publishing houses. World conditions of imports, import licences, duties, currency arrangements, etc., are listed to form a complete record of the current position for day-to-day reference on these matters.

With these various methods available, the exporter can proceed to find out all relevant facts about the export of his goods to the various countries of the world.

The following headings will suggest the type of information useful in arriving at the plan for further procedure:

(a) Suitability of the goods for the market or adaptations necessary.
(b) Import licences, financial restrictions, quotas, law relating to the sale of the goods, labelling regulations.
(c) Shipping, freights, duties, packing.
(d) Final landing costs, cost of distribution, resultant consumer prices.
(e) Competition in price and quality to be found in each country.
(f) The desirability of assembly or packing abroad to facilitate import or save shipping costs.

A questionnaire on these lines could be prepared and the answers sought through one or more of the sources of information previously listed. The answers could be analysed under two headings: first, the factual answers relating to costs, restrictions, etc., and secondly, the matter of opinion, such as the suitability of the goods for the market. When these answers are completed, it should considerably simplify the problem. Attention will then be focused upon a manageable number of markets for further progress.

Having selected these markets for approach, the manufacturer can proceed by appointing agents or representatives and try to develop sales forthwith, or can embark on consumer research in the country or countries concerned before doing so. A good deal depends on the nature of the product. If the goods are to be established as an advertised proprietary, it is wise to make investigations before spending money on advertising and building up a brand name. If, however, it is a normal trading transaction, the difficulties can be learnt while proceeding and methods adopted while feeling the way into the market.

(2) *Representation*

The fact cannot be too strongly emphasised that selection of the agents to distribute throughout the markets abroad is of paramount importance. Where a firm can set up their own organisation and have direct representation, the selection of personnel is of equal importance. A firm distributing through agents, which is the usual practice, must take all possible steps to ensure that the man or Company appointed to represent them is suitable in all respects.

The agent must, of course, attain to the necessary standard of integrity, and commercial standards in this respect vary considerably throughout the world. His other agencies must fit in precisely with the manufacturer and he must be connected with the right class of trade for distribution of the products. These, and many other factors, should be carefully considered before appointing an agent overseas.

(3) *Home Organisation*

It is essential to have a competent Export Department at home to control efficiently the various functions necessary to ensure the smooth flow of export business. The main functions of this department are:

(*a*) *Export Office* to deal with shipping documents, accounts, export finance and currency.

(*b*) *Export Correspondence Section*, where correspondence is handled by those who know the special requirements and if necessary the languages for the purpose.

(*c*) *Packing and Shipping Department* for the physical handling of goods for export. An alternative is to employ a good shipping agent for the purpose.

(*d*) *Factory Representatives.*—The full development of export markets calls for one or more travelling representatives to visit the agents and principal customers direct from the factory. It may be a Director of the Company, the Export Manager, or representatives selected for the purpose.

(*e*) *Export Advertising Department.*—Where advertising is conducted overseas, it should be dealt with by a special section, either of the Advertising Department or Export Department. Overseas advertising calls for separate treatment from home advertising, and unless it is devised specially for the nationals to whom it appeals, it will almost certainly miss the mark.

CHAPTER IV

SALES ORGANISATION AND MANAGEMENT

Sales Management. The Travelling Staff. Departments of the Sales Organisation. Budgetary Control and Sales Forecasting.

IN accordance with the general pattern of management, it must be the aim of Sales Management to co-ordinate every member of the sales organisation into playing his part in a concerted plan of operations. There is, however, this complexity that a sales staff is usually widespread, and contact between themselves and with the concern itself is less frequent than is the case with other units of organisation. Furthermore, the personnel are almost certain to have highly developed individualism. The qualities of leadership would seem to be required in a high degree in addition to the more normal skill in organisation and management. Nevertheless, system and order are essential in the smooth working of a sales team, but working controls should be as simple and clearly defined as possible.

SALES MANAGEMENT

The overall management of sales is in the hands of the Sales Manager, and it is being accepted generally that the most effective plan is to unify the control of all departments concerned with sales in his hands. The Sales Manager is frequently a Director of the Company (when he usually assumes the title of Sales Director) in order to achieve the unity of Sales Management with other aspects of planning and control and to provide the authority required for his task.

In a Company with a fully developed sales organisation, the Sales Manager, responsible for both planning and execution of the sales campaign, will have the Marketing Manager at his side, who will provide him with the relevant information and ideas and with whom he will develop all sales planning. The active execution of all selling operations is carried out through various managers directly responsible to him.

An example of this would be:

On the other hand, the Sales Manager of a smaller concern will perform the functions of many of these managers himself. The Marketing Manager's work is almost certainly incorporated. Actual calling on the principal buyers is generally done by the Sales Manager himself, and the travellers are under his direct control instead of through Area Managers. His advertising department is in the hands of a junior, and he operates advertising policy direct with the Advertising Agents.

An example of this would be:

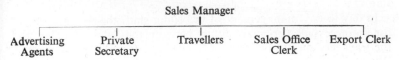

Whatever the manner be in which he carries out his work, it makes little difference to the principle that all selling functions should be a concerted effort under unified control.

The main exception to this system in current practice is for the Advertising Manager to function independently and be responsible to the Managing Director instead of the Sales Manager. There may be a case for this procedure in Companies with a high advertising expenditure, where the Managing Director requires to keep in close contact with advertising activities and where the Advertising Manager is a highly placed official. This arrangement does not seem a logical one, as it would seem that the Managing Director is assuming the work which should belong to the Sales Manager if the right degree of co-ordination between sales and advertising is to be achieved, and can only be justified as an expedient rather than the rational delegation of responsibility.

THE TRAVELLING STAFF

Excepting the extent to which advertising may dominate the sales plans, the primary responsibility for carrying out the Company's sales plans rests with the outside staff. To achieve the maximum development of the sales policy through travellers, two aspects of their place in the Company's organisation should be considered:

(1) That they are fully and clearly instructed on the precise tasks which they are to fulfil and are supported in every way in carrying out their duties; and

(2) That the routine organisation to which they must conform should be made as light as possible, so that it will not interfere with the time and thought needed for actual selling on the ground.

With regard to (1), emphasis is laid on the human side of salesmen and travellers, because selling is a human and personal thing and salesmen are (or should be) men of human understanding and of character. So it must follow that skill in managing salesmen is very largely a matter of personal contact. Travellers are notoriously casual in their treatment of letters, circulars and bulletins from the office. The spoken word is the tool of their trade and the method they understand. The impact between man and man, face to face, is the one thing which really influences them. It is important, therefore, that an adequate system of personal contact should be established and maintained to instruct, to stimulate and to control an outside staff.

In day-to-day management of travelling staff, the free movement for the necessary personal contact between the Sales Manager and the travellers should be planned as a frequent and regular routine. With a small force, the Sales Manager or his deputy should have regular meetings on the grounds, so that he can make calls with his men on important buyers or help solve difficult problems with customers. With a larger force, Area Managers should perform this function, and be always on their ground with regular visits to the Sales Office or the visits to the ground by their chief.

On important occasions, such as the launching of a new campaign, the commencement of the "season" or introducing a new line, the policy and purpose of the activities may be introduced in a more definite and emphatic way by calling a Sales Conference. This would be attended by all sales executives, all Area Managers and Representatives with production and accountancy management attending. The Sales Manager would normally be in the chair, and the Managing Director could profitably open such a conference with an outline of policy.

Every conference should have a purpose and a theme and each item planned and carried through with precision. The management should aim to convince the representatives of the merits of the forthcoming plan of action and show the precise way in which they are to execute it. Speeches should be clear and to the point. Charts, demonstrations, displays, films or other devices should be employed to illustrate the theme. In these ways every representative returns to the road with full and exact information, enthusiasm and the confidence born of contact with the executives at Head Office and the factory.

Regarding routine organisation (2), office system and statistics play their part in control of outside staff, but they should not be rated above their merits. They provide information, but do not of themselves produce action. The representatives, on the other hand, find the office demands for reports and figures irksome, having to write them at the end of a heavy day on the road, and the temptation to finish a little earlier when there is a lot of writing to do cannot be overlooked.

Much can be done by so devising the stationery that quick marking of information reduces writing to a minimum. Similarly, the information which the traveller needs, such as records of customers' purchases and accounts, should be as simple as possible and be in his hands at exactly the right time.

The Selection of Salesmen

Much can turn on the skill of the Sales Manager in choosing his men. There are few guiding principles which can be laid down, because the knowledge which leads to good judgment can only be gained by experience over a number of years in the selection and handling of men. It is not only important to select men who are of good character and who are either good salesmen or potential salesmen, but also men who are adapted to the kind of work you wish them to do. A first-class commercial traveller well able to handle a country round may be quite out of place as a speciality salesman in a big city unless he is exceptionally versatile. A brilliant salesman may, and often does, prove a complete failure when promoted to the management of a group of travellers in an area.

Before considering a man's ability, it is important carefully to judge his character. If a man has those qualities of high integrity, loyalty and will to succeed, it gives great promise and goes far to balance other shortcomings.

It is advisable to set down some standard tests to apply to all candidates for the post of representative which will summarise the qualities required. Such a test must, of course, be adapted to the special requirements of each particular sales force. The questions may be marked with "points" or by marking the general terms of "good", "average" and "poor", or it may be more advantageous to make more detailed notes.

The style in which such a questionnaire can be formulated may be suggested as follows:

	Good	Average	Poor

Character

Is his demeanour honest and straight-
forward?
What do his references indicate?
Does he speak loyally or disparagingly
of others?
Is he ambitious for success?

Appearance and Manner

Is he correctly dressed and tidy?
Is his manner likeable?
Is his speech clear and convincing?
Does he look healthy?

Intelligence and Knowledge

Does he grasp the point quickly and
accurately?
Is he adaptable?
Does he know our trade?
Has he a good connection on the
ground?

The selection of salesmen will also be governed to some extent by the training available after they are engaged. While every effort should be made to introduce and maintain a good system of training, this is not always carried out, and as an alternative it will be necessary to lay considerable emphasis on a man's already proven ability as a sales-man when engaging outside staff. There is also to be considered the Company's standing with the trade it serves. If they are well-established, it is less important to have a man with knowledge of the ground, but otherwise it is as well to choose those well-connected with the trade.

Training of Salesmen

An aspect of Sales Management which rarely gets the attention it deserves is the scientific and systematic training of salesmen. The theory that salesmen are "born and not made" falls short of the truth, and the reliance so often placed on the value of training with a senior man on the ground leaves many gaps in complete training. A thorough system of training both at Head Office and on the road has many advantages apart from the ultimate efficiency of the man's work, the chief of which is that it enables a Company to select promising "inside" men for posts on the road, a plan of very great value in most concerns, for those men have the right kind of knowledge and usually have the interests of the firm at heart. Furthermore, they are generally keen to take advantage of the opportunity, and this in turn promotes keenness among the inside staff for similar promotion. It also gives the opportunity to engage outstanding men who have no practical experience of either the particular business or of travelling.

The system of training must follow a definite course and be in the hands of someone fitted both by temperament and ability for the post. He must not only have skill in selling, but have the art of imparting knowledge, and of bringing out the innate qualities from his "pupils". It may be advisable to have the training course divided into two parts under different instructors, one for the technical side of the business to cover the information a traveller must know about the products and a second part in selling. In this a definite curriculum must be laid down and followed. After a thorough grounding in the information about the products, the policy of the Company, methods of handling accounts, complaints, office systems, as far as they affect the representative, a theoretical course of sales approach, arguments and generally presenting the case for the Company and its products are stated, rehearsed and if necessary learnt verbatim, not to induce a parrot-like repetition, but in order that the necessary argument may come easily as and when required. Objections which will be met with are stated and the replies provided. The student takes the floor, and is criticised until he is competent before he approaches the buyer.

This does not take as long nor is it as difficult as many people imagine, and can well be done as the spare-time occupation of a member of the outside staff in all but the larger organisations. Unless it is routine, however, before a traveller goes on the road, there will be fundamental errors in his methods which become ingrained and difficult to detect and eliminate afterwards.

These methods of training can be carried out in even the smallest firms engaging (say) one or two new travellers a year. The Sales Manager, the Office Manager, the Works Manager and others can devote the necessary time to give the training provided the information has been duly scheduled beforehand.

Area or Branch Management

In most sales organisations, the outside work must be divided into two parts, selling and administration. Selling must come first, and it still must be the main preoccupation of even those engaged on administration. There are, however, certain functions to be performed, particularly with the larger forces, in the control, routeing and discipline of sales staff, where it is wise to delegate some of the administrative work to those on the ground, where an assessment of the situation is far simpler than at Head Office. Area or Branch Managers provide this in whatever degree required. They also serve as senior representatives who can deal with the larger buyers on the necessary level.

The degree of authority afforded an Area Manager, the staff, if any, given to him, whether or not he has a branch office or depot for invoicing and delivery of goods will depend on the nature of the Company's operations and its size.

Territory Division.—Available statistics for the Sales Manager in planning his territories are all too few. It is only with a long study of the problem that one can assess the amount of ground a man can cover to the best advantage and the amount of business he should obtain from it. The geographical problem can be scheduled in terms of distances, number of calls—but even in these there are wide margins of error through local habits of buyers being brisk or lengthy in their interviews—and according to the prevalence or otherwise of multiple stores on the ground.

In assessing the extent of the ground in terms of the amount of business it should produce, many other factors are to be taken into account, the prosperity of the area, the number and size of multiple or big buyers, the local preference or otherwise for the particular commodity being sold, etc. It is therefore only possible to make a reasonable compromise between population figures and the known facts about the area to arrive at the best possible conclusions, which are reviewed from time to time in the light of development.

It may be as well to keep in mind that the territory is the salesman's world, his living. He is anxious to get the maximum ground possible in terms of the production of business and is jealous of encroachment. If alterations are necessary, they should be negotiated rather than forced, or a disgruntled traveller may lose heart. Where a territory is reduced in size due to expansion and putting on additional travellers, it is the practice of reputable houses to guarantee average commission of the past year or two for, say, a year until the commission on the new ground builds up. In this and other ways such changes should be made to maintain the spirit of the outside team and goodwill of the customers.

Sales Quotas.—Total sales quotas have been dealt with elsewhere but it is necessary to allocate the total quota to each area and each traveller. This is done in proportion to the assessment of the territory, and results in a figure for the ground which should appear against sales in all statistics as a plus or minus figure for discussion with the representatives. The success or otherwise of sales against quotas is a useful tool in the hands of a Sales Manager in promoting the efficiency of his outside staff. It can be used critically as occasion demands to censure the laggard, but its more important use is positive in stimulating effort by competition, with praise and reward to those who produce the best percentage increase in quotas.

Remuneration.—The remuneration by salaries, commissions or bonus, together with agreement about travelling expenses, is a matter for negotiation, and should be arranged according to the particular circumstances of the business, the traveller and the nature of the work. Some selling of well-advertised and popular brands is by nature a stable occupation, where commission enters far less into the matter than in the case of goods depending almost entirely on the salesman's skill for their sales. The payment of commission is becoming less and less a practice as the work of salesmen becomes more systematically controlled and as other factors such as advertising become the mainspring of sales.

There are sound reasons why a Company, building up a good name in the trade for which they cater, should be fair and even generous in their treatment of travellers, as they are assessed by this as well as by the quality and price of their goods, and a traveller who has the security of a living wage, an opportunity to earn well by commission or by promotion and his expenses reimbursed is in a position to be proud of the firm and its goods, an outlook which is reflected in his work.

There is as yet no remedy for the occasional exploitation of travellers which still exists in some quarters, fortunately to a less extent than the past. It is still possible to employ travellers on commission terms with exaggerated statements of the possibilities which the traveller is unable to check until he has done valuable spadework in introducing the goods, and a succession of such men are employed without any check on such activities. The joint statement by the Incorporated Sales Managers' Association and the United Kingdom Commercial Travellers Association "Standards of Practice intended to govern the Employment of Representatives" is commended for careful consideration. It is set out in full as an Appendix to this Part.

The Sales Agent.—As an alternative to the employment of a full-time travelling staff, a manufacturer can use the services of one or more Sales Agents to introduce and sell his goods.

Organised selling agencies have developed quite substantially of recent years. They were a feature of the nineteenth century and have again come into vogue with the growing need for better representation current today. A manufacturer with a limited output cannot afford, or for some other reason does not wish, to provide the sales staff necessary to cover the country. It is economic policy to combine his selling with that of other manufacturers whose goods are sold to the same class of trade. A Sales Agent is therefore appointed who has a staff of travellers throughout the country carrying the goods of, say, a dozen manufacturers. Alternatively, a number of agents, each covering an area, are appointed separately. A third plan is to cover certain parts of the country, usually those in the vicinity of the factory, with the Company's own representatives and appoint agents for the outlying areas.

The good agents are a valuable contribution to the scheme of distribution. They usually work on commission only and afford a great economy in working. Their calls are productive in relation to the cost of travelling because of the number of lines they carry, and they are well known to buyers—a great consideration when introducing a new line. Their drawback to a manufacturer is that they are unable to give the highest degree of concentration on his particular line, and this must be weighed against the advantages which an agent can provide in other ways.

DEPARTMENTS OF THE SALES ORGANISATION

The sales organisation, apart from the main structure of the actual selling team, requires subdivision into each of the specialist sections according to extent and nature of the sales operations.

The more important sections or departments coming under this heading are:

(1) The Advertising Department.

(2) Public Relations and Propaganda Department.

(These two may be separate or divisions of the one department according to the nature of the publicity used by the particular Company.)

(3) The Sales Promotion Department.

(4) The Sales Office.

(5) The Sales Service Department.

The functions and operations of each of those sections will be found in the following chapters. In the overall management of their various activities and their place in the general sales plans, some notes may be useful here.

Market Research is considered outside departmental organisation, as it is rare for such work to be undertaken as part of the sales operation, but is generally performed by outside organisations.

Each of these departments requires its appropriate officer in charge of its operations, and his standing will be in relation to the importance which his department plays in the affairs of the Company.

(1) *The Advertising Department.*—The post which varies most in significance is that of the Advertising Manager. It can rank in importance from Director to junior according to the part which advertising plays in the affairs of the Company. It also depends upon the extent to which the Advertising Agent is given a trusted position in handling the Company's advertising. The ethical standards of Advertising Agents are high, so that the better firms can well be trusted to act in their clients' interests, and their proficiency is greater than could be obtainable, as a rule, in the Company's own department for producing effective advertising. Nevertheless, it is most important that, however good the agent and however well he knows the Company's products, there should be a competent officer to represent the Company's interests, their point of view, to stimulate the agents to better work, to criticise intelligently and maintain the relationship between agent and themselves at the pitch of efficiency. There are also many other tasks to be done which may not be suitable for passing to the agents. Handling of print usually is more economical and efficiently done directly with the printers, and this is a matter for the Advertising Department, particularly if it includes advertising-printing, such as show-cards and leaflets. There is the checking of the agents' accounts, of voucher copies of newspapers and magazines and consequent study of the positions and reproduction of the advertisements, the checking of posters, etc. These and many other details of a firm's advertising require the constant supervision of the Company's Advertising Manager.

The Advertising Manager.—It is assumed, therefore, that all publicity is under the direction of the Advertising Manager. By training and experience he is fitted to deal with both the creative and the administrative activities of the department and bring together the various and complex methods of selling goods by publicity into one concerted plan:

(1) Planning with other executives the amount of the advertising appropriation.
(2) Allocating the total appropriation among the various methods of publicity, e.g. Press, Poster, Print, etc.
(3) Liaison with the Advertising Agents in the devising and conduct of the advertising campaigns.
(4) Directions of the Advertising Office and creative sections.
(5) Direction of the Public Relations Department.

(2) *The Public Relations Officer (P.R.O.)* is of growing importance in the larger organisations. The changing conditions under which we are living have produced a completely new set of circumstances with regard to the dissemination of information and a new technique to

meet them. More and more information is demanded by employees, customers and the public generally about all the things which affect them. The employees today are keenly interested in their Company's affairs, and must be met by a skilled treatment of the news in a way which makes for understanding between employers and employees. The relationship with customers and prospective customers can be immeasurably improved by the use of the P.R.O.'s handling of news which comes from the factory, office and sales staff, and in larger organisations there is much news of still wider interest which is suitably issued to the Press for general publication, and so guided that it is presented with imagination and ability to enhance the Company's prestige.

In considering the place of the various officers in a sales organisation, the P.R.O. is in a unique position, and it may be that he should be considered as outside the jurisdiction of the Sales Manager. This will depend on whether his functions mainly concern building up sales or whether they have a wider application. In any event, the P.R.O. must be given a wide independence in his terms of reference. It is necessary that he should have complete and unimpaired access to every section of the business; it will be required to take him fully into the confidence of every executive of the business on all matters which may have bearing on both outside and inside relationships. He, on the other hand, must be given a roving commission to make outside contacts with the Press and others and suitable facilities for the social obligations usual in such contacts.

It will be appreciated that only men of the highest calibre are proficient as P.R.O.s, and unless such a man is justified by the scope of his operations, it is as well to restrict such work to the more usual channels of the Advertising Department.

(3) *The Sales Office* is usually the one in closest liaison with the Sales Manager, and its head is responsible for the inside working of the whole of the Sales Department. (It is more fully studied in the following chapter.) It combines the secretariat to the Sales Executive with statistical control of sales operations. There are two differing views on filling the post of manager for this department: one, that he should be a capable office man, and the other, that the post is a stepping-stone to Sales Management, in which case he should be essentially a salesman in outlook. In either case, one or other side of his work must lose something, because it is necessary for the manager of a sales office to be competent at his office work, but his outlook must be the development of sales and salesmen. If a manager able to combine these qualities can be fitted to the post, it must be the best solution.

(4) *The Sales Promotion Department*, where it is a separate depart-

ment, is for the purpose of developing fully the many ways in which sales to the public can be improved by the provision of publicity and exhortation to feature the manufacturer's goods at the actual point of sale in the shops, thus making a specialised task of work which would be done by traveller and Advertising Department in the smaller firms. The provision and distribution of display material—showcards, window bills, window display sets, etc., is a first consideration. This material, which is provided by the Advertising Department, may be distributed through the travellers or by a separate staff, in which case they would have small vans complete with bill-posting equipment to put up small posters and window bills as they go around. The arrangement of demonstrations in retail shops and a comprehensive plan of window dressing with special displays of the products would come under this department.

In the larger manufacturer's organisation, the Sales Promotion Department often controls a substantial outside staff calling on the stores and working in co-operation with the travellers for the above purposes and to persuade retailers to feature the goods. In many cases this staff also calls on a large number of "indirect" stores, i.e. those who buy through the wholesalers.

The organisation necessary for stands, equipment and staff at public exhibitions would come under this department.

(5) *The Sales Service Department* only exists as a separate department in such firms where after-sales service is an extensive operation, otherwise it is part of the factory organisation to be called upon by the Sales Manager as required. Where, however, it is an important part of the selling plan to give after-sales service, it should come directly within the province of the sales organisation, but with all the technical assistance possible from the factory. The reason for this is that the contacts with the customer on the matter of service are maintained by the representatives, and it therefore facilitates the smooth working of the service to be embodied in the sales organisation.

The personnel must be skilled men on the technical requirements of their job, but it is not difficult to find such men with a selling outlook or to train them in such a way that they promote the Company's interests whenever they are meeting the firm's customers.

BUDGETARY CONTROL AND SALES FORECASTING

The methods of control under a sales budget is considered in detail in Part IV of this volume (see especially page 583). The Sales Manager is concerned with two aspects of this matter: (*a*) the preparation of the forecast for the period ahead, which he carries out in co-ordination with his fellow executives concerned with production and finance, and (b) the practical operation of using budget and performance figures as his daily guide to maintain the selling machine at the right pitch of efficiency.

In the case of (a) preparation of the forecast, it is necessary to take many factors into account, first in the field of ascertainable facts, statistics and records, together with the results of market research and the needs of the production departments, and secondly to call upon experience, imagination and ideas for the less tangible trends which may influence future sales. Some reference to these matters is made in Chapter I and to Market Research in Chapter II.

The extent to which factual knowledge can decide the sales forecast, and therefore its accuracy, depends upon the nature of the goods and the methods by which their sales are developed. Fashion goods require the judgment of trends first and foremost, advertised proprietaries may depend on the effectiveness of the advertising "copy", seasonal goods may depend on the weather. On the other hand, certain basic materials may depend on the ascertainable facts of the programme in a particular industry; (b), exercising control by the use of budget figures is fully discussed in Part IV of this volume, particularly Chapters II and IV.

CHAPTER V

FUNCTIONS OF THE SALES DEPARTMENT

The Sales Office.   Statistics of Sales, Budgets and Forecasts.
Sales Correspondence.   The Order Department.

THE SALES OFFICE

THE importance of the Sales Office lies in the detached and factual assessment of sales performance which is carried out in recording all transactions on the one hand and in issuing instructions impartially on the other according to the decisions of policy laid down by the Sales Manager.

The office is under the control of a manager, who receives his overall instructions from the Sales Manager, and reports regularly to him all the information and statistics compiled in the office.

The Sales Office cannot be built up to a stereotyped plan: it must be moulded to the needs of the business. It has certain main functions which can be outlined, but details of methods must be adapted to individual requirements. For example, a section of many Sales Offices is devoted to a sale room, a sample room or a show-room. This does not properly come into the work of a Sales Office at all, but it is convenient to have it so attached, and it gives the Sales Office staff the opportunity to meet customers and perhaps prepare for promotion to positions as travellers. At the other end of the scale, some Sales Offices carry out functions which properly belong to the General Office, and there are many where the ledgers are posted and balanced.

Accountancy can hardly be in the province of Sales Management, and if a choice must be made, it is better for the Accountant to be in charge of the Sales Office than for accounting to come under the Sales Manager. There is, however, in most organisations, an easily defined line where accounting ends and sales records begin. That line must be clearly understood by both or duplication will occur. While the Sales Office must draw many of its figures from the General Office, the use to which such figures are put is a matter for interpretation only by those with a sales outlook.

The sound plan, therefore, will be for the compilation of all money figures to be carried out by the Accountant in his office and made available to the Sales Office Manager, who will make them up in suitable form for sales control. All other figures, such as sales package units, travellers' mileage, number of calls, etc., should be compiled by the Sales Office. The two are then united to form the complete basis for statistical control of sales.

The main headings under which Sales Office records and statistics are grouped are:

(1) Records of customers and their purchases.
(2) Record of travellers, their sales, commission and costs.
(3) Record of territories, journeys and groupings.
(4) Statistics of sales budgets and performance.

(1) *Records of Customers*

The sales ledgers seldom give more than a fraction of the information necessary to keep in touch with customers in all but the smallest and simplest sales organisations. It is therefore necessary to keep a record of customers and their purchases in the appropriate form. This is generally provided by a visible index card or simple card index according to the frequency with which purchases occur and the number of customers involved.

The form in which the record is kept should be the subject of careful thought when planning such a record, as it is difficult to make alterations without loss of comparative figures at a later stage. The headings with the permanent information should be as full as possible. The buying information—address, name of executives or buyers, discount and terms, special preferences, etc., should be marked, and this is a point at which some information can be available for other departments to be recorded and marked on the order before the invoice is typed, such as delivery instructions. Credit rating may also be marked and credits worked with the Accounts Department through the record.

Figs. 3 and 4 show an example of a customer's record as used in visible index trays. A loose sheet (Fig. 3) folding over the card (Fig. 4) records day-to-day sales, the card itself accumulates the monthly totals off this sheet. There are six lines which are numbered and quantities are in "units"—a unit being a gross in one case and a dozen in others. There are no comparative figures with the previous year's sales, but this could be provided by an extra column if required. The divisions at the foot of the card are for tabbing and a coloured tab is moved along each quarter (1, 2, 3 and 4) for each of the six lines, and shows instantly where the customer has failed to buy for more than that period.

The cards are arranged in trays and grouped under each traveller and divided into six sections covering his six journeys, thereafter alphabetically, so that they broadly follow the sequence of his journeys. Any card can be located geographically first and then alphabetically.

In recording sales, it is a matter of individual preference for each business to devise the information required. It is always a good plan to discuss the problem with the manufacturers of the card indices, who have a variety of standard cards and wide experience of other firms' records to draw on.

The various alternative sales information required should be first scheduled, and when decided upon, a suitable card should be made up to fit the needs. The main decisions will be:

(1) Whether sales should be recorded in total sales, in dozens, grosses, tons, units of packing or money values, or some combination of these.

(2) What number of divisions or classifications are required and will be required in the lifetime of these records.

(3) What kind of accumulative or comparative totals are and will be required over a long period.

(4) Whether it will be required to record invoices and payments on the card. If this is done, it will be a duplication of the ledgers, and it is only justified where collection of moneys is an important part of the work of the salesmen. It is difficult to combine this with a record card, and the more usual practice is to create a separate set of cards for this purpose worked on the shuttle principle (backwards and forwards) between the traveller and the office.

(5) What "tabbing" is required to throw up vital information at a glance. There are various systems of movable tabs which can indicate frequency of orders, routine of calls, classification of customers, etc. Their function is an automatic reminder for action as and where required.

When these various alternatives are decided and scheduled, they should be made up into the necessary card index system and continue unaltered as long as possible.

(2) *Record of Travellers, their Sales and Commissions*

The difference between a traveller as an individual and his territory as a section of the business should be established. The traveller should have a record as to his service, remuneration, contract or agreement, together with a compilation of his earnings month by month or whatever period is established for his commissions. A separate record should give particulars and totals of his sales in the territory, and from these his commissions are totalled. In this way travellers may come and go, be moved or promoted without interference with the continuity of the sales records of a territory. Similarly, the territory can be divided or re-allocated without rewriting the travellers' records.

NAME................ ADDRESS................

DATE	INVOICE No.	1	2	3	4	5	6	DATE	INVOICE No.	1	2	3	4	5	6

Fig. 3.

19	1 MONTHLY TOTAL	1 ACCUM. TOTAL	2 MONTHLY TOTAL	2 ACCUM. TOTAL	3 MONTHLY TOTAL	3 ACCUM. TOTAL	4 MONTHLY TOTAL	4 ACCUM. TOTAL	5 MONTHLY TOTAL	5 ACCUM. TOTAL	6 MONTHLY TOTAL	6 ACCUM. TOTAL
JAN												
FEB												
MAR												
APR												
MAY												
JUNE												
JULY												
AUG												
SEPT												
OCT												
NOV												
DEC												

EXECUTIVES COMPETITION TERMS

ADDRESS

TEL. No.

CONSIGN.

NAME

1 |2|3|4| 2 |2|3|4| 3 |2|3|4| 4 |2|3|4| 5 |2|3|4| 6 |2|3|4|

135

Fig. 4.

A traveller's card will show the name, address, age, territory, terms of contract, particulars of car and any other relevant information as headings. It should not be necessary then to put more than the following totals as monthly or other period summaries:

Traveller: Jones, A. F.   Territory: S.-W. London.
Address: 21, Progress Way, London, S.W.7.
Date of Birth: January 20th, 1910.   Car: Austin 10, FXE428, 1939.
Contract: £480 per annum salary. Car fixed: £3 10s. per week.
Postages, stationery, etc. No lunch allowance.
1¼ per cent. on all sales in territory, excepting House Accounts (listed on Contract).

	Salary			Expenses			Commission			Total			Total Sales			Per cent. as to Sales
	£	s.	d.	£	s.	d.	£	s.	d.	£	s.	d.	£	s.	d.	
Jan.	40	0	0	15	11	6	14	9	5	70	0	11	1156	13	2	6·1
Feb.	40	0	0	15	12	4	14	10	11	70	3	3	1163	12	1	6·0
Mar.	40	0	0	15	14	2	16	2	5	71	16	7	1289	11	3	5·5
Apr.	40	0	0	15	11	3	18	1	0	73	12	3	1444	1	7	5·0
May	40	0	0	16	1	0	21	2	9	77	3	9	1691	3	2	4·6
June	40	0	0	16	2	1	23	1	6	79	3	7	1845	17	8	4·3
July	40	0	0	15	18	2	21	13	3	77	11	5	1733	2	2	4·5
Aug.	40	0	0	15	14	0	20	4	2	75	18	2	1616	16	9	4·7
Sept.	40	0	0	15	12	3	17	18	8	73	10	11	1434	11	2	5·2
Oct.	40	0	0	15	13	0	15	0	4	70	13	4	1201	8	7	5·9
Nov.	40	0	0	15	11	2	16	1	11	71	13	1	1287	8	3	5·6
Dec.	40	0	0	15	14	1	12	19	0	68	13	1	1038	16	2	6·0
TOTAL	£480	0	0	£188	15	0	£211	5	4	£880	0	4	£16,903	2	0	5·2

FIG. 5.

Analysis of expenses should be carried out from expenses sheets and analysis of sales in the record of the territory.

The totals of all travellers under this heading could be brought together and listed for the Sales Manager's regular review. The individual records are important, but are examined one at a time. These overall figures would be examined in the full list to obtain the necessary comparison between the different territories.

(3) *Analysis of the Territory*

The territory card or analysis sheet must have much greater detail. It should show the sales in every subdivision considered necessary, such as (a) each line or group of commodities, (b) to different classes of trader discounts, (c) subdivisions for different parts of the territory. For example, a manufacturer of cleansers might have six lines. Each is sold to grocery and hardware trades at three discounts off the basic price to the retailer: a wholesale discount of 15 per cent., a multiple and co-operative discount of 7½ per cent. and the retail price net. Thus, each of the six lines will be recorded in six divisions—wholesale, grocer, multiple and co-op. grocer, retail grocers, wholesale hardware, multiple hardware and retail hardware. It will then be possible to see whether each classification is handling its share of the distribution, and whether at any time there is a drift to or from the wholesale channel in supplies to the smaller retailers.

STATISTICS OF SALES, BUDGETS AND FORECASTS

Where possible, the market forecast should be divided into the assessment for the territory and this figure shown as the potential or target. A column for plus or minus the target would then give the periodic standing of sales in relation to targets. It is usual to keep this on the territory card or sheet.

In addition to the record of sales, a journey order for the regular travellers' round should be kept, usually territorially. This not only serves to locate the travellers' movements, but is convenient for the Accounts Department in sending statements in advance and to enable a new man quickly to pick up the routine in the event of sickness, holidays, etc.

SALES CORRESPONDENCE

It is desirable that correspondence on all matters affecting customers and travellers should come directly into the Sales Department and not be part of the Company's general correspondence.

There are several reasons for this. In the case of travellers, it will cause confusion if they are receiving instructions and advice (sometimes contradictory) from several departments of the firm; on the other hand, it is embarrassing to the Sales Office not to know what the travellers are told. When such communications are passed through the Sales Office, there can be uniformity of approach and varying sets of instructions can be grouped together. For example, the Factory Manager might wish to congratulate a traveller on moving a difficult pile of stock and the Accountant to reprove the same man for failing to get the accounts settled for the same items. By bringing the two points together the Sales Manager or his deputy can link the two together to produce the desired effect.

Correspondence with customers is equally the task of the Sales Office, whatever the subject may be. There should be a particular outlook of courtesy, friendliness and understanding always present in letters to customers, together with a clarity of expression without which there is misunderstanding and friction. Writing sales letters is an art rarely understood by any whose job is not selling. Most Sales Managers have experienced the difficulty of placating angry customers and travellers over letters written by office personnel who are not skilled in writing the right kind of letters. It is therefore better as far as possible that the relevant information be passed to the

Sales Office for all such correspondence where the matter can be handled in a diplomatic manner.

The Sales Office correspondence section can also perform a useful function in sales promotion. Build-up letters to prospective customers, sales-aid letters, etc., can form a regular part of the routine of the office, and the typists can be fully occupied in this way as additional "salesmen" whenever the regular correspondence slacks off.

In the matter of more formal communications to travellers, advice on the stock position, statements, salary cheques, notices from the Welfare Office and the many such items, the Sales Correspondence Section act as the collecting centre and forward daily to each traveller in one envelope. It is usual to have a set of pigeon-holes tabbed with the travellers' names, and as the varying communications are received, they are placed in the appropriate pigeon-holes and assembled for posting at night.

THE ORDER DEPARTMENT

Incoming orders pass first through the Sales Office, or the Order Department if it is a separate section. The first process is scrutiny to see that all relevant information is written and correct, such as prices, discount and rating. Approval of credit can be made at this point or later according to whether this is the business of the Sales Office or the Accountant's Section. It is usual to pass on orders at once for immediate invoicing, and make up records from a statistical copy of invoices, but this can be done off the actual orders either before or after invoicing where the number of orders is few. Whichever method is employed, it is always necessary to provide a check to see that orders are executed as written, as any alteration, say, in the Dispatch Department will render the records inaccurate.

CHAPTER VI

ADVERTISING

The Purpose of Advertising. Advertising Budgets. Advertising Agents The Advertising Department. The Public Relations Department.

PUBLICITY and propaganda play a very active part in the distribution of goods and services. Vast sums of money are spent annually on this means of promoting sales. Advertising has been the means of building up many great concerns, sometimes the only means, often the principal reason for their progress. On the other hand, great sums of money have been spent only to be lost, and it has been truly said that the quickest way to lose money in trading is by mistaken advertising.

In more adventurous and less scientific days, advertising was a highly speculative pursuit which made and lost fortunes with great rapidity, and was characterised by blatant showmanship and sometimes total disregard for the truth. Throughout the years, a very determined effort has been made by those concerned with advertising to remove the abuses, and today the scientific approach and the strict code of ethics imposed by the newspaper proprietors and professional advertising associations have resulted in advertising becoming a skilfully used and honest tool in the process of distribution, the effect of which can be calculated with a moderate degree of certainty.

The production of all kinds of publicity is, however, mainly the production of ideas, and to this extent it must be a variable factor. There are well-known and perhaps well-worn methods of giving any product publicity which produce fairly certain results, but the development from time to time of a brilliant idea in advertising will have an increased effect out of proportion to the expenditure and with spectacular results. In the main, the speculative element of advertising applies mainly to launching new lines, but with existing proprietaries there is more solid basis on which to judge how sales can best be developed by the use or extension of advertising.

THE PURPOSE OF ADVERTISING

The usual purpose of advertising is to reduce percentage costs of production and distribution. Whatever other reasons may be ascribed to its use—and there are always many other repercussions from extensive publicity—the constant aim of a producer or distributor is to handle sufficient volume of goods so as progressively to reduce on-cost percentages.

The principle is simple, and should always be well to the fore in the mind of every manager, not only the Sales and Advertising Managers but the Production Manager, and others concerned with the administration of the Company's affairs. It is in application of this principle that there are such wide variations of methods and views, and many of the difficulties which arise in this field are caused by managements taking too little interest in the principles and too active an amateur part in the practice of the craft.

ADVERTISING BUDGETS

In theory there is an optimum amount which should be spent on advertising, but there are so many varying and changing factors that there must be wide latitude in judging such a figure. Economic conditions of the buying public change, labour conditions change, production methods change, all having bearing on the amount of the advertising appropriation, so that the only practical course is to plan the allocation by sound judgment on as many available facts as can be ascertained. Advertising budgets are generally taken annually. They are usually a compromise between a percentage figure of sales, an assessment of the results of last year's advertising and a studied forecast of the following year's prospects. Weighed in with those factors may be the production and distribution cost analyses which may show urgent necessity for increased volume.

The scale of advertising in terms of percentage of turnover has wide variation according to the nature of the business, ranging from a fraction of 1 per cent. in the case of a basic raw material to quite a high percentage in the case of exclusive fashion goods sold to the public. The variation is only a matter of degree, and whether large or small and whether the total amount of money is large or small, its employment should take its place in planning distribution.

The Advertising Appropriation

Reference has been made earlier to the place of the advertising appropriation in the general sales budget, and the Advertising Manager's special contribution to this is his expert knowledge and judgment as to the probable effect of various sums of money on the sale of goods or services. The many factors involved are judged together, and among the other items of the budget the amount to be spent in advertising is allocated as a whole, and thereafter its employment is largely the responsibility of the Advertising Manager. It is as well to allow a firm allocation for a reasonable period, and if variations are necessary from time to time, to anticipate them as fully as possible. Advertising requires planning far ahead to obtain the necessary continuity of appeal. Space must be booked and ample time allowed to write and draw good advertisements. Frequent changes of plans tend to undermine the work of any advertising campaign. Whether the amount is large or small, the right selection of media can make a great difference, but the smaller it is, the greater the need to make the right choice. With a large campaign, the advertising will carry weight whatever media are chosen, but even then the proportion of expenditure as between, say, Press and poster must be nicely balanced.

The consideration above all others to be studied is the degree of concentration and repetition achieved by the advertising. If a fund, particularly a small fund, is scattered, it can lose its effect so rapidly as to be almost wasted. Judging by the frequency with which this error is made, it would appear that the important truth that advertising needs concentration is not widely understood.

To achieve concentration, a sufficient weight of advertising must be provided to impress the public, i.e. those of the public who are potential buyers, in a reasonably short space of time. If the appeal is to a wide section of the public, e.g. a general household article for all purses, this cannot be effected on a national scale without the expenditure of a very large sum of money which is outside the scope of many manufacturers of such articles. In such cases a method of achieving concentration is to advertise on a substantial scale in one area only until sales develop sufficiently to extend to wider fields.

Areas are selected (or select themselves) where sales of the product show promise, and public acceptance of the particular brands is encouraging without the support of advertising. Every reasonable medium of local advertising is brought into service, but the basis of the campaign must, of course, be the local newspapers, and perhaps posters backed up with special efforts to encourage the shop to display the goods. The limited funds can then be enough to provide substantial weight in the area, and there is the added advantage that the particular methods of advertising can be tested out on a limited scale and proved right before increasing the commitments.

Equally to achieve concentration with goods of a limited appeal to a certain class of the public, it cannot be economic to advertise widely and reach all types of people who could not possibly be interested in them. For example, to advertise salmon-fishing tackle in the national daily and Sunday papers one or two insertions a year would absorb all the available appropriation, and the circulation would be mostly wasted, as only a small percentage of the readers are likely to buy such goods. For a similar sum of money an adequate size of space could be purchased with frequency in such papers as *The Fishing Gazette*, *The Field* and *Country Life*, thus concentrating on a more limited number of readers of the right type and with substantial emphasis.

Concentration by the selection of media and by the size of space and frequency in those media is a subject of detailed study with the particular product and its distribution in mind. There are so many variations, such a wide choice of media and so many types of appeal that one must approach each problem with an open mind and work out the various combinations according to the circumstances.

First, the size of the necessary space for an advertisement must be studied. It is wasted effort and expense to put a large number of insertions in papers and magazines if the space is too small to carry the necessary message and be noticed by readers. A well-known proprietary name in a small space is seen and has some value, but a little-known name will convey nothing unless supported by an exposition and probably an illustration. Therefore, the size of space must be adequate for those purposes. As a rule, it must not be crowded; only articles which are eagerly sought by potential buyers can be set in small type and still be read. The size of space is then decided as a minimum, always remembering that increase over and above this size greatly adds to the value, and the increase in pulling power is proportionately greater in excess of the increased size. The budget of expenditure is then applied to the size of space and the number of periodicals selected and if necessary ruthlessly pruned. With a limited appropriation, therefore, the necessary size and frequency to effect concentration is given in a limited number of periodicals.

Selection of Periodicals

In the selection of the particular newspapers and magazines, an analysis of each periodical can be obtained, often in some detail. The leading journals publish their audited net circulation. Some general idea of the class to which readers belong can be ascertained—indeed, many are published solely for a particular class of readers, particularly the magazines. All such information is available from the Advertising Agency. They can also advise on the relative cost and value of the various periodicals. It will be noticed that the advertising rates per thousand copies will vary over a very wide range. If the circulation should meet the exact needs in reaching a particular class of customer, the rate may be much higher in proportion to others but well worth the extra cost. If a wide public is to be reached, wide circulation at low cost per thousand copies is desired, and the right judgment of space value can contribute to the economical running of an advertisement campaign.

Poster Advertising

Poster advertising is the "heavy artillery" of advertising, and is rarely brought into action except as a support for "front line" advertising in the Press. With minor exceptions (theatre, cinemas, and appeals of such nature) poster advertising is not generally used to *impart* information, but to remind the public of information they already possess. It has great force which can be applied at the right place—located in the exact areas where it is of greatest value. In this medium again, the importance of concentration must not be overlooked and is easily achieved. Posters widely scattered lose one of their greatest assets, the power of repetition.

Railway, bus and van advertising can also be classed as poster advertising and treated in the same way except that it is often possible to impart more information when using bills and cards in certain places, inside buses, railway compartments, etc. It is important, however, to study the class of traveller using such places. The city tube, for example, may be a wasteful way to reach the suburban housewife.

Special Methods of Advertising

In all smaller campaigns, indeed in many of the larger ones, the importance of many of the minor methods of advertising should be carefully studied. Direct mail advertising is not spectacular, but of first importance to all those with a limited number of potential customers. Point-of-sale advertising, window displays, demonstrations, etc., is always a method to be skilfully developed, but is vital to those whose product has a visual appeal.

Cinema and radio advertising are highly specialised media and not suitable for those with limited resources except in the case of cinema slides. To make and circulate an advertising film or embark on a radio advertising programme is a considerable programme and the emphasis must first and foremost be placed on the quality and originality of the production. Exhibiting films in the cinemas and broadcasting are so costly that production costs may need to be heavy to ensure the highest standard of perfection.

A medium in growing popularity is the film for private showing, a method of considerable potential. Such a film need not be costly to make, but its impact upon those who see it can make a deep-rooted impression. It has many applications, it may be shown to quite a wide public in meetings of Institutes, Associations, etc., or it may be for private showing to invited audiences of specialists, technicians, etc. It is being widely used in travelling cinema vans and portable units.

Public exhibitions are a medium of advertising which play an important part in many operations and can often be combined with considerable immediate business.

There are, therefore, many conflicting claims in these and other methods of allocating an advertising appropriation. It is advisable that serious planning should be undertaken, and when the right methods are chosen they should be pursued with determination. Except for the largest advertisers, many attractive suggestions will have to be negatived, but there is no alternative or the funds will be frittered away.

ADVERTISING AGENTS

The position of the Advertising Agent in the world of business is a deservedly high one. Advertising by Press and poster as well as many other forms of publicity is almost universally placed through agents. By reason of their professional conduct, their ability and their organisation, they are able to provide a service which it would be difficult for the advertiser to develop for himself, apart from the expense of doing so.

The Press and other media of advertising reserve a fixed percentage of their rates which is paid to the agent as his fee. This system has grown up from the earliest days and is one that has been the subject of considerable controversy. In theory, it is liable to prejudice the advice of agents in the placing of advertisements, but in practice they take a wider view. The welfare of the client comes first, and it is generally realised that impartial advice rather than temporary gain is the wise policy, so that the apparent anomaly of the system has, in fact, no adverse reactions in the conduct of the good agencies. The system of payments, too, is well regulated by the Newspaper Proprietors' Association and other bodies. Commissions are only payable to accredited agents who are under specific obligations to maintain certain standards of conduct.

It is frequently a private arrangement between agent and client to depart from this system and for the client to pay a fixed percentage for the agent's service, instead of the various commissions he receives from the Press and others. This commission must not be less than the standard rates under his professional agreement. The method has much to commend it in many ways.

The choice of Advertising Agent can be an important step in the marketing programme, as much can depend on the agent's approach to the problem. Having appointed an agency, it is advisable to allow a fair measure of freedom in their plans and operation. The success or otherwise of these can considerably influence the progress of sales. Furthermore, there are advantages in maintaining continuity, for a change in the Advertising Agent is often a serious step which is only taken with reluctance.

An Advertising Agent should therefore be chosen carefully and deliberately, taking the time and trouble to find out the relevant information about his suitability for the task. Each agency has its definite characteristic: some will have a particular type of presentation, some will display a flair for fashion goods, some will be at their best with technical advertising, some well known for their handling of poster campaigns, others specialist in colour work. The biggest agents may have sections capable of handling all of these and other fields. The question of the size of an agency should be considered. A big campaign usually (but not necessarily) requires the resources of a big agency, but a smaller one may well be handled better by a smaller concern, where the account is in the hands of one of the principals.

A practical plan in the selection of an Advertising Agent is to study current advertising as widely as possible and select the type of approach suitable to the particular product, but not competitive lines. A reference to the *Advertisers' Annual* will show a comprehensive list of agents and their clients from which the type of advertisement chosen can be located to the agents producing it. The agents who are selected, perhaps two or three, will be very ready to put forward the information required about themselves, their resources and often practical suggestions as to the way they would approach the campaign. An advertising Agent will not handle products or services in direct competition unless it is agreed to do so between the respective principals.

When the appointment of an Advertising Agent has been made, a great deal can be done by building up the right relationship without which the best results are difficult to obtain. All relevant information about the Company's background and policy, the products and methods of distribution should be freely and clearly placed at the disposal of the agent, together with the full details of the budget of expenditure. When the appropriation is not fully in the hands of the agent—for example, where orders are placed direct for window displays and show-cards—they should have details of this. The Advertising Manager and Advertising Agent should establish and maintain complete confidence in each other's operations.

In the production of advertisements, it is usual to give the agent wide freedom in methods, subject to approval at each stage of their preparation and final placing. A schedule of advertisement insertions is prepared and approved. Copy and rough sketches are passed and art work commissioned. Blocks are made and type set, and the final advertisements are passed before going to press. All this can be carried out with constructive criticism on both sides aimed at the production of the highest standard of inspiration.

The operation and results of all Market Research should be fully understood by the agents and taken into account in the planning and execution of their work. Many of the leading agencies have their own Market Research sections, and in these cases it will probably be found convenient to carry out investigations through them. In any case, the agency can contribute a great deal both to the conduct and assessment of research from their wide knowledge of marketing problems.

In the more complex marketing organisations, it is frequently the practice to employ more than one Advertising Agent, each for a specific group of goods, and this plan may well be developed further. It has many advantages. One agency is not overloaded with conflicting claims on their resources, but works singlemindedly on the one problem. There is a healthy rivalry for the best results. The agent best equipped for the particular line can be selected in each case.

A division is also sometimes made between home trade and export advertising. There are many considerations to be taken into account when placing overseas advertising through a home agency, particularly their experience in this work and the strength of their overseas connections. It is not always an advantage for the same agent handling the home market to place advertising abroad. He may be liable to issue the advertising he has so painstakingly prepared, without considering whether it is suitable for overseas markets. Export advertising must be given fresh consideration and if necessary be completely redesigned for its purpose.

THE ADVERTISING DEPARTMENT

The Advertising Department embraces the Advertising Office for purposes of control and the various production sections. The latter will be built up according to the needs of the business and can be eliminated altogether if the production is all carried out entirely by the Advertising Agent.

The Advertising Office records both expenditure and commitments, and provides the facilities for the Advertising Manager to keep in close touch with outgoings in relation to his budget. The necessary statistics are built up to this end, and analysed to show dissections of expenditure on each type of advertising in relation to the internal allocation of the total appropriation.

Advertising Production

The creative and production sections, whether carried out in the Advertising Department or by the Advertising Agent, both follow the

same plan. At its fullest scale it can be a large and complex organisation because of the many and varied activities associated with the
production of all the different types of advertising. Reference to
these in detail should be made to a comprehensive textbook on the
subject.

The production of the more general forms of advertising in the
newspapers, magazines, posters and other printed messages is a combination of the work of the copy-writer and artist, coupled with the
skill of the blockmaker and typesetter. The Director is responsible for
initiating the ideas and for co-ordinating the working production.

The general plan of the campaign, its "message" in terms of the
qualities of the goods or service to be advertised, the type of media to
be employed, have been discussed and settled on broad lines by all
executives responsible for distribution. The interpretation of these
plans, the production of the actual advertisements, is taken over by
the Advertising Manager, the Advertising Agent or executive in
charge of advertising production. He or his staff will "visualise" the
message in terms of the printed word and the supporting illustration
with the layout to combine the two.

"Copy" is drafted and a "rough" sketch is prepared, so that the
general plan of the finished advertising can readily be understood.
When this has been agreed, the artist is commissioned to produce a
"finished" drawing and the blockmaker and typesetter instructed as
to the precise requirements of the work.

The first consideration should always be "copy", particularly those
few words of "copy" (the fewer the better) which contain the main
message. The lay mind will be impressed by the illustration, the layout and the appearance of an advertisement. These devices are of
great importance, and without them the advertisement will not be
seen and read. The vital part of the advertisement, however, is and
must be the message—what the advertisement has to say. It may, in
the case of a famous product, be only the name of that product, but
it should have more than that: it should convey a definite idea. The
simplest illustration is to reflect on well-known "slogans" of the
leading advertisers: "Guinness is good for you", "Bovril prevents that
sinking feeling", "Hoover—it beats as it sweeps as it cleans", "Parker
51—the world's most wanted pen". It is these and other words that
call you to buy.

Much can turn on the merit of advertising illustration, because this
draws the eye to the words you wish to say and occasionally suggests
an idea in itself. The selection of the right artist for each type of work
is the key to successful commercial art. Few agents or Advertising
Departments can fully occupy all the artists needed for their varied
work, and the most efficient and economical way is to commission,

direct or through a commercial studio, the one exactly suited to the particular drawing required.

In advertising production it is generally wise to consider production of every phase of advertising on the one plan so as to have the same message and design running through the whole campaign. Thus, the Press and poster campaign will set the standard which is interpreted at the same time in the production of all the secondary forms of advertising to support the campaign such as direct mail, window displays and show-cards, cinema slides, or whatever else is used, and so the message gains the force of repetition.

THE PUBLIC RELATIONS DEPARTMENT

It was suggested earlier that the dividing-line between certain aspects of public relations and advertising is flexible. By this it is meant that certain functions could be allotted to either section, provided that the skilled personnel is available. There are many aspects of this work, particularly in the large companies and undertakings, where specially trained staff is required, staff which has developed an outlook on publicity that is different from that associated with advertising. This is particularly true of Press relations, and in this respect the advantage is twofold. The production of material for issue to the Press must be undertaken with an editorial outlook, free from noticeable advertising as such, and of news value as understood by an editor. It should also be issued to the Press by an officer who is known and trusted by the Press, and "news" which emanates from an Advertising Office is suspect from its inception. The P.R.O., therefore, who has these qualities is able to prove effective where others fail.

This "editorial" mind and training of the P.R.O. is the keynote to all work of the department, and is applied to many forms of publicity. The type of work allocated to this department usually falls into the following headings:

(*a*) Press relations.

(*b*) Special printed productions—the House Organ, booklets, catalogues, etc.

(*c*) Direct consumer contacts and propaganda, goodwill missions.

(*d*) Trade fairs and exhibitions.

(*a*) *Press Relations.*—The application of Press propaganda is largely political, but has its place in the commercial life of the community.

In the sphere of distribution, with which we are concerned here, its application is still more restricted, because the greater part of the propaganda in the distribution of goods and services must of necessity come within the normal methods of advertising. In those organisations, however, particularly the larger groups where there is news

value in their activities, the opportunities of enhancing the prestige
of the Company, its goods and services, through the columns of the
Press should be pursued with vigour. Even the smaller companies
may well have much useful information to impart in this way, particularly through the trade and technical press. In this case it may not
be possible to employ a full-time P.R.O., but there are many capable
free-lance Press Officers who can be commissioned for the work.

As an instance of the work of the P.R.O., the motor-car industry
is producing products which are of absorbing interest to the public
and therefore to the readers of newspapers. The Press realise this, and
are willing to give space to news of the productions and achievements
of motor manufacturers, a right given equally to the small and large
manufacturers. A well-conceived programme to give the Press a
service of information about the features of each car, vehicles placed
at the disposal of motoring correspondents for testing and comment,
news of reception and use of the car overseas, and notable personages
driving one, etc., etc., will prove of benefit to both the news editor and
the Company. Special occasions are created, such as track tests or an
unusual reliability trial, entries are made in races or rallies, and so
every available method is used to bring the product to public notice
as genuine news which the Press will publish.

To take an example of a small firm using this type of sales promotion, even the smallest book publisher can obtain mention for his
books in a wide Press, and by the nature of his calling has the knowledge at hand to devise sound methods of approach to the editors. On
the largest scale we have Film Corporations with a considerable
network of Press publicity services.

The approach to general Press publicity and to trade Press notices
is rather different. In the majority of cases, the use of the trade Press
is more easily obtained and can be very valuable. The material should
be prepared very carefully, because the readers are well-informed
and more influenced by factual information than are the general
public, but this method, if successful, can develop sales widely and
with immediate effect.

(b) *Printed Productions*.—The P.R.O., who is responsible for the
printed propaganda of his Company, has two main considerations,
the material and literary merit of the productions on the one hand
and the design, layout and printing on the other. The first part
properly belongs to the work of the P.R.O., and it is his authorship
and editorial skill which are the basis of this work. On the technical
side of producing and printing, it is important that this should be done
well, and if he or his staff are not versed in these matters, he should
call in experts from the Advertising Department or outside sources
for the undertaking.

The House Organ is one of the P.R.O.'s best vehicles for spreading information to the right quarters. Its virtue as a periodical is that it can become known by regular repetition and operates to a schedule. Its purpose must be decided by each enterprise, whether it is for internal circulation to inform and stimulate the workpeople, to develop good relations within the organisation and enhance the community spirit, or whether it is for outside circulation to promote a wider interest in the Company and its products and to sell the goods and services.

Of the remainder of the printed productions they are many and various—catalogues, technical books and leaflets, propaganda booklets of all kinds, each to suit the particular purpose. They may be cold schedules of scientific data or, in the case of a travel agency, lead your thoughts to gay social life on the French Riviera.

(c) *Direct Contacts.*—As a rule, there is no officer in a Company better fitted to stage important direct contacts on a social level than the P.R.O., and to him is deputed the special organisation required to make such occasions a success. Each Company has its own requirements in these matters, and whether it should be to herald a visit of the Managing Director on a mission to the Southern American Republics or to arrange a cocktail party to the winner of a slogan competition, the P.R.O. has that opportunity to demonstrate his flair for creating the right atmosphere which will ensure the success of the occasion and attract favourable publicity. On these occasions, too, his experienced eye will note much which is of value, in that he meets the users of the products or services on a footing of friendliness and can assimilate candid opinion which will be a valuable guide to policy.

(d) *Trade Fairs and Exhibitions.*—The P.R.O. is normally in charge of the planning and presentation of the Company's exhibits at Trade Fairs and Exhibitions and of the entertainment of visitors.

Liaison with the Press and sponsors of the fair is also his responsibility. The staff of the exhibit, however, is usually drawn from the sales staff or engaged for the purpose.

Designing exhibition stands has become a highly specialised art, and the creation of a notable stand can do much to attract buyers and enhance the prestige of the Company and its goods. The graphic presentation of the goods or services on an exhibition stand is an art which is not easily attained and well worth careful planning.

Visitors to the exhibition, particularly overseas buyers, will always reward the right arrangements for their reception. A buyer on such occasions has the various alternative products before him for his selection and is there to buy. He is therefore amenable to good selling tactics and, other things being equal, orders will come through skilful handling of the situation and a well-presented case, together with the artistic merit of the display.

CHAPTER VII

PHYSICAL DISTRIBUTION

Warehousing.   Stock Control.   Dispatch and Transport.

In the aggregate, a very great quantity of material from raw material to finished products must be handled, stored and moved from place to place in the course of progress of consumer goods through the factory to the ultimate user. The skill and management of this movement can advance the smooth flow of industry and effect substantial economy in the total cost of distribution.

The whole system is complex, but the distribution of any particular product may present few or many difficulties, according to the nature of the products and the method used to carry them to their destination. In the main, the machinery of distribution is outside the scope of those manufacturers who use external transport, as the bulk of the movement of goods is undertaken by nationalised transport, which presents few opportunities for the manufacturer to organise alternatives. Apart from actual transport, however, there are many considerations in methods of routeing, in warehousing and stock-keeping, packing and avoiding transport losses which should be organised for maximum efficiency.

Each branch of the handling and distribution of goods is a matter of detailed study in itself, particularly that concerned with transport. The consideration in this section is that of the overall management of distribution, and a very brief review of the management problem involved should serve to indicate the types of organisation necessary to achieve a smooth flow of goods from factory to customer.

WAREHOUSING

The principles of good warehousing would seem to apply equally to all types of products, the only important distinction being that special precautions must be taken where goods are perishable. Good stock control is important in any case, but a margin of error in control of perishables may result in a loss of goods which would not occur with non-perishable types.

It may serve the purpose of illustration if one system of storage is considered. An example would be a large food manufacturing firm, making proprietary foods which are packed in cans, bottles or other containers with a wide distribution to wholesalers, retailers and direct consumers, and which have a variable turnover according to seasons and with goods of variable keeping quality. Such an organisation has all the essentials of warehousing, stock-keeping, handling and transport, and adaptation to other types of handling can readily be made. Many things essential to this complete system will be found unnecessary for other types of goods, but such adjustments will be apparent.

Four types of storage would be provided, and while they are, to some extent, interchangeable, it is as well to consider them as separate categories as far as possible to avoid confusion and overlapping. In any case, it is necessary to have four entirely separate stock-keeping records for them:

(*a*) Raw material.

(*b*) Containers.

(*c*) Goods in continuous production.

(*d*) Seasonal goods.

The warehousing and stock-keeping of raw material and containers is a matter of factory organisation and should be considered in the factory programme. If possible, a separate storage should be provided. The raw material storage is situated at the receiving end of the factory and the distribution storage at the dispatch end.

The operation of the factory is in two phases. There are lines in continuous production for those goods where the raw material is available at all times. Such production is tuned to the demand, and the finished products flow out of the factory. There must, however, be a certain proportion kept in stock in case of breakdown in the manufacturing or distribution systems. This stock is kept partly at the factory and partly at depots throughout the country.

The second phase of production is seasonal. Fruits and vegetables under contract to the factory are delivered in substantial quantities over short periods and the factory keyed up to process and pack the resulting products. The finished products, however, are not immediately sold, but are stored, often for long periods, and provision must be made according to the particular circumstances of each product.

Provision must therefore be made for two types of storage— "rotational" storage and "bulk" storage. Goods in continual production are dispatched as far as possible immediately, going direct from the production line to the dispatch floor. If there is a surplus over requirements, the balance is sent to the store. These goods are handled in rotation. They are so stacked and marked that the goods which have been longest in store are dispatched first, and new goods coming into the store are on no account placed in front or on top of goods already there. A part of the store nearest to the dispatch is usually allocated to this type of storage, and bulk storage, which remains undisturbed for some time, is placed in the less accessible parts of the store.

Mechanical handling by "spade" trucks and platforms is employed throughout. A carefully calculated procedure in each stage of the movement of goods reduces the amount of man-power to a minimum.

STOCK CONTROL

The exertion of stock control at every stage is a fruitful means of economy (see Part IV of this volume), and in the case under discussion would be of the "perpetual inventory" type, where all arrivals and withdrawals are continuously recorded and the stock position can be assessed at any time.

DISPATCH AND TRANSPORT

The organisation and control of dispatch can be considered in three phases:

(1) The dispatch of goods is tied to a document, which in turn is tied to the invoice for the goods.
(2) The document is clearly marked by the transport office with the route or method of conveyance.
(3) The loading of vehicles for conveyance of goods must be of the optimum quantity and speed consistent with service to customers.

The first requisite is the simple matter of office routine. Dispatch is usually authorised on a dispatch note or notes typed with the invoice, and on completion tied back to invoice and/or warehouse stock.

The second need is for the Transport Department to decide the most economical route for the goods and mark the order accordingly before invoicing. Considerable economy can often be effected by a detailed study of transport methods and rates in order to route goods at the lowest rates consistent with service and to avoid pilfering and breakages.

The third consideration is one for more detailed organisation. Where dispatch is effected in the Company's own vehicles, it is prudent to arrange loads in sufficient quantity to work the vehicles economically and to assemble them beforehand in order to save waiting time for each vehicle. It is necessary to load in journey order, so that the goods are delivered in the reverse order to loading, i.e. goods loaded last are delivered first in order to save time locating the goods in the vehicle on its rounds. Economy in the use of transport can be more readily effected by prompt loading and unloading of full tonnage than by any other means. Nevertheless, attention must be given to vehicle maintenance in order to avoid the losses incurred while the vehicle is idle for repairs, breakdowns and high running costs.

Overriding all considerations of transport economy must be considered the sales aspect of service to customers. It is false economy if the delivery of goods is unduly delayed, thus losing sales, or the goods arrive in anything but the best condition. It should therefore be the pride of the dispatch and transport section of any business, no less than the sales departments, to see that the goods arrive promptly and at their best.

STANDARDS OF PRACTICE INTENDED TO GOVERN THE EMPLOYMENT OF REPRESENTATIVES

Preamble

1. These Standards of Practice have been framed by the Incorporated Sales Managers' Association and the United Commercial Travellers' Association of Great Britain and Ireland (Incorporated), in consultation.

It is proper that they should be prefaced by some indication of the causes which gave rise to their creation, and the attitude in which they have been framed.

During this most disastrous war of all, it has been the concern of the two Associations separately to prepare themselves for the onerous duties they will have to perform in helping British trade to prosper after the war. None knows better than they the magnitude of their task. Than their combined experience of the distributive end of British trade, none greater can be found.

Certain that the integrity of the British trader stands high among the trading nations, in the belief that British traders are proud of this and desire to do all in their power to maintain it, and knowing well that the bulk of British business is conducted along sound and fair lines, the two Associations have sought to codify those standards which exemplify the practice of the majority. By many they will be recognised as minimum standards indeed, because by no means are they the terms which join the most capable men to the best employers.

But always has there been a minority of less responsible traders which has shown itself ready to use all those devices which may be the most profitable, whilst permitting the men employed no right whatever. The effects of this, in times of difficult trading, and upon newcomers to the profession in any times, are bad. It is in the national interest to endeavour to prevent them: and it is fitting it should be done in time for men returning from service with His Majesty's forces to receive the protection these standards are designed to give.

Towards solution of this one of their problems, by separate ways, the two associations reached the same point, and there combined their efforts, of which these Standards of Practice are the result.

Definition of the term "Representative"

2. Throughout the following Standards of Practice the term Representative means—Sales or Technical Representative, or however otherwise qualified, Commercial Traveller, or Travelling Salesman.

Agreement

3. All terms and conditions of employment should be embodied in a properly drawn service agreement, clearly setting out the terms of

engagement and embodying the principles set out in these Standards of Practice.

Restrictive Clauses

4. Clauses in agreements which aim at preventing the fair movement of a representative from one firm to another in the same trade and area are undesirable.

Territories

5. The boundaries of the territory to be worked should be defined as precisely as possible. Delineation on a map of suitable scale may aid considerably the clear definition of the territory. Normal progress frequently demands territory revisions. Provisions for any reduction of territory area should be made, but in such cases it should not cause the representative originally working the whole to suffer a reduction of his remuneration.

Remuneration

6. The basis of pay shall be salary, commission, or some combination of the two: with or without bonus. It is essential that a minimum remuneration be established, but it must be recognised that the wide range of businesses makes it impractical at this stage to stipulate a figure. It is recommended that each employer should establish a minimum that is fair to their representatives and in line with that paid in the trade. The minimum should be such that every representative can adequately support himself and his family.

Trial or probationary periods shall be held to be governed by these conditions, except for men employed additional to the regular selling staff in training schemes which provide definite conditions of advancement.

Expenses

7. It is recommended that payment of all out-of-pocket expenses for travelling, hotel accommodation when away from home, office accommodation, advertising, or any other expenses, be paid as legitimately and reasonably incurred by the representative in his duty of maintaining his employer's and his own prestige.

House Accounts

8. House accounts, existing or potential, contained in the boundaries of a territory should be the subject of a clear agreed statement from the commencement. For the terms of employment to permit any particular account to be withdrawn, without recompense, from the general territory by claim of it having become a house account is not equity.

Samples

9. Representatives should not be required to pay for samples or sales aids used for the purpose of obtaining business except where they consist of finished goods, and then they should be the subject of proper accounting.

Bad Debts

10. A representative should not be held liable for any proportion of bad debts incurred in his territory other than the refund of any overriding commission or bonus which he may have drawn in respect of the business resulting in the bad debt. In no circumstances should the basic salary be liable to such deduction.

Transference

11. Provision against financial loss should be made for a representative being reasonably required by the employer to move his home. Merely to pay the removal expenses is not necessarily adequate. Arbitrary removal from one territory to another is to be discouraged. A representative's and his family's entrenchment socially in a given neighbourhood is something which deserves reasonable consideration.

Engagement and Termination of Employment

12. An essential part of all service agreements should be provision of adequate notice of termination of employment. The period held to be fair is widely variable. It is considered that the initial period of employment should be not less than three months, and the engagement be terminable thereafter by not less than the same period of notice except where otherwise mutually agreed. Long and faithful service to one Company may make desirable a long period of notice—the time it may reasonably require to secure a parallel situation—and similar circumstances should all be taken into account in fixing the period of notice.

Welfare

13. There should be payment of full remuneration for a reasonably defined period in case of sickness.

Representatives should be given holidays for at least the same period as members of the Sales Office staff, with full remuneration.

Superannuation arrangements for representatives, as indeed for all other employees, are much to be desired.

Conclusion

14. The same spirit which fairly claims conditions of equity for the representative makes it incumbent upon him to give his absolute best to his employers. Finite terms to suit each case must after all result in something of a partnership, and the spirit of an agreement will at all times sway its execution to the letter. Only gain to both can accrue from the representative doing his best in all circumstances to maintain the dignity and integrity of his firm and, incidentally, his own calling.

(Issued by joint authority of The Incorporated Sales Managers' Association, 4 Holborn Place, London, W.C.1, and The United Commercial Travellers' Association, 180 Tottenham Court Road, London, W.C.1.)

BIBLIOGRAPHY

THIS list is intended to suggest some of the many books of interest in this field, referring mainly to those of a more general nature rather than the specialist study of any one aspect.

1 Robert Ferber: *Statistical Techniques in Market Research.* (McGraw Hill, New York, 1949.)
2. F. T. Clarke: *Marketing and Market Research.* (Pitman, London, 1948.)
3. Harold Whithead: *Administration of Marketing and Selling.* (Pitman, London, 1950.)
4. H. R. Todsal: *Introduction to Sales Management.* (McGraw Hill, New York, 1940.)
5. J. R. Doubman: *Fundamentals of Sales Management.* (McGraw Hill, New York, 1947.)
6. J. C. Aspley: *Sales Managers' Handbook.* (Dartnell Corp., U.S.A., 1947.)
7. R. Simmat: *Principles and Practice of Marketing.* (Pitman, London, 1933.)
8. C. L. Bolling: *Sales Management.* (Pitman, London, 1946.)
9. R. Simmat: *Scientific Distribution.* (Pitman, London, 1948.)
10. F. B. Lane: *Advertising Administration.* (Butterworth, London, 1931.)
11. R. Simmat: *Principles and Practice of Advertising.* (Pitman, London, 1935.)
12. F. P. Bishop: *Economics of Advertising.* (Robert Hale, Ltd., 1944.)

PART II

PRODUCTION

By A. W. FIELD

CHAPTER I

ACTIVITIES FORMING THE PRODUCTION DIVISION

The Meaning of Production Management. Types of Production. Organisation Structure. Production Administration. Supervision

THE MEANING OF PRODUCTION MANAGEMENT

PRODUCTION can be defined as the organised activity of transforming raw materials into finished products. In this sense raw materials can include anything from rough ore to an electric motor; the finished product of one industry is frequently the raw material of another. Production therefore includes all manufacturing and extractive industries.

Following the definition of management arrived at in the introductory chapters, Production Management then becomes the process of effectively planning and regulating the operations of that part of an enterprise which is responsible for the actual transformation of materials into finished products.

The physical features of production vary from industry to industry and are usually specific to each one, or even to particular companies. They can be seen and can be fairly easily appreciated in a tour of any particular factory. But the intangibles which go to build up effective management are not at all apparent and, as with expert performers in the arts or games, the more skilful the performance, the less apparent the effort; a well-run factory looks so easy to manage. In dealing with the management of production, therefore, less attention has been paid, in this part of the book, to the physical or material features than to the human factors, and to principles which are common to many, if not most, industries and companies. For this reason much of what is said has a wider application than to production in the narrow sense; it will be found to apply in many cases to the provision of services, such as transport.

It will be realised that principles by themselves are not enough, and that only experience and practice in applying them will give the aspiring manager that style, that apparently effortless success which is the hall-mark of skill. Adherence to sound principles is important —the man who adheres to them is less likely to run into difficulties of his own making than the man who works by rule of thumb or instinct or takes refuge in expedients which, at best, are temporary. The road of compromise and expediency leads to muddle, if not chaos, particularly in production. This does not mean that identical problems must be solved in the same way, or that two businesses of exactly the same size, making exactly the same product, would be identical in structure and organisation. People differ and organisations reflect and are a compound of the personalities of which they are composed.

One of the essentials in securing effective management is the separation of "planning" from "doing", both in organisation and in persons' minds. Work should be planned in advance and standardised as far as possible, so that those who supervise others, the managers and foremen, are free to fulfil their proper function of training and directing the doing and ensuring that operators conform to standard practices and methods. And in training and directing operators, supervisors must themselves plan ahead. Chapters II and III therefore deal with "planning" activities (Designing the Product and Production Administration), and Chapters IV and V with "operating" activities (Supervision and Ancillary Services).

Activities Covered

In dealing with production, all those activities are covered which enter directly into the design and manufacture (process or production) of goods or materials. They are the activities which are generally understood to be done in the "works"—where workers clock in and wear overalls. Not every student manager will find his job, or the job he hopes to have, described in detail, but all normal activities carried on in the "works" are dealt with, as far as it is possible to do so in a book of this kind.

The following major activities are covered:

(1) Designing the Product

This is done by the Technical Department which is concerned with specifying what is to be produced, and includes those activities usually associated with the Chief Engineer or Designer in an engineering factory, or the Chief Chemist in a process factory. It includes the design of the Company's products, the preparation of drawings, specifications, formulæ, or other instructions to the Production Departments, experimental and development work, and the preparation of estimates and contracts for new enquiries or for orders from customers.

(2) Production Administration

This is dealt with in its specialised parts:

(a) *Production Engineering*—which is responsible for deciding and

specifying how work is to be done and covers production metho
and the preparation of process specifications, jigs and tool design
and the measurement of work and establishment of standard times
(in shop language, rate-fixing).

(b) *Production Planning*—which decides and issues schedules for
when work is to be done, and covers materials and stock records,
preparation of long- and short-term manufacturing programmes,
shop and machine loading, and progress chasing.

(c) *Production Control*—which is a specific application of the control function, and is concerned with recording results and correcting
for deviations from programmes and variations from standards.

(3) Execution

This is concerned with the organisation and supervision of the
actual doing, i.e. with people more than paper. It is general management on a smaller scale. The activities are considered under the following headings: inspiration and co-ordination and the integration of
supervision and skill, selection and promotion, training, remuneration and incentives, performance, meetings and joint consultation.

(4) Ancillary Services and Departments

This section deals with those departments which are not strictly
production departments, i.e. they do not make any part of the product. They are dealt with under the following headings:

(a) Buying.

(b) Storekeeping.

(c) Inspection.

(d) Works Engineering—covering buildings and services, plant and
tools, and maintenance.

Integration with Distribution Function

Production is integrated with the distribution activity by the
General Manager or other chief executive, through the co-ordination
and reconciliation of the sales forecasts and programmes with production programmes. Production is not self-sufficient, but it can be
looked upon as the middle links in the chain of activities, starting
from the obtaining of an order or receiving an enquiry and ending
with the dispatch to customer or sale over the counter. The production policy, forming part of the general company policy, must
tally with the distribution policy. If the distribution policy is to go for
seasonal markets, production must be flexible enough to respond; if
the policy is to keep production steady, stocks must be built up in
preparation for the seasonal demand. Long-term production pro-

ammes must reflect long-term distribution plans, building up apacity of plant or sections of the works to meet changes in demand or emphasis in advertising. Technically too the policies must agree. Continual small modifications to design or product may prove disturbing to customers because of existing stocks; less frequent but more radical changes may be a better distribution policy. Similarly, production must not place too much emphasis on quality with the consequent higher price if the distribution policy is to go for a low-priced market where quality is not required.

There is often a tendency for sales and production staffs to be antagonistic. Certainly, ideal requirements for each do not always appear to coincide; to please the customer sometimes disrupts production. This antagonism is likely to develop in the very concerns where the production and distribution divisions are well led by vigorous capable executives with a pride in their departments. The antagonism must be curbed and the departmental prides related to a co-ordinated whole. The biggest factor in bringing this about is the general sharing in the formation of policies. When the Board, who are primarily makers of policy, and the top management clearly define the wider purpose of the business, insisting that a primary purpose is to serve its customers well and to make a profit in doing so, and when the chief executives concerned share in formulating the secondary policies required to achieve this purpose, then there is likely to be unity of outlook, and production men will recognise that they have a duty to serve the sales departments and through them the customer.

It is not always possible to explain to operators at the desk, bench or machine exactly why certain instructions or actions are necessary (and indeed these can often look senseless or useless), but it is possible to explain policies and the reason for them. Instruction and actions can then be seen as a part or an expression of these policies whereupon the need for them will be understood; and understanding is the first essential to correct performance.

TYPES OF PRODUCTION

Production is a very wide term indeed, and it is not made much narrower through being qualified by the term "industrial". If it is assumed that all those persons engaged in the professions, central and local government service, and wholesale and retail distribution are not engaged in production, then according to the Government's Economic Survey, published as a White Paper in March 1948, out of a total of 18,887,000 persons employed, 12,244,000, or 65 per cent. are engaged in production.

A classification of all the types of production thus segregated can be divided into five main groups:

(1) Mines and Quarries, employing . . . 831,000
(2) Agriculture and Fisheries, employing . . 1,090,000
(3) Building and Civil Engineering, employing . 1,364,000
(4) Transport, Dock and Public Utilities, employing 1,708,000
(5) Manufacture, employing . . . 7,251,000

Size and Diversity of Industry

Within each of these groups there are, broadly speaking, three types of production, or put in another way, production is carried on on three scales. They are: Job (usually small scale); Batch (usually medium scale); and Flow or Mass (usually large scale).

Job production is concerned with the manufacture of single products to a customer's individual requirements, i.e. "one-off". Each job or order stands alone and is unlikely to be repeated. No two jobs are exactly alike and long runs on a single product are uncommon. Job production is carried on by a large proportion of the small manufacturing companies in Britain, and by many quite large companies. Because they are small and the proprietor so often discharges many or all of the executive functions of large companies, it is usually considered that small companies cannot use or have no need of all the "systems" and modern developments of scientific management, but the truth is that it is just in these small companies that the application of sound production Management principles and the use of simple methods of production administration can effect so large an improvement in effectiveness.

Batch production operates in those companies where a batch or quantity of products or parts is made at a time, but where production on a part or product is not continuous. This occurs when there is a variety of products manufactured to stock and when orders are diverse, but for fairly large quantities and not for "one-offs". But perhaps the most common reason for batch production—and one which creates the complexities and many of the difficult problems of production administration—is the use of standard components in different products and models. This type of production is typical of industry, not only in Britain, but in most industrial countries, including the United States. It calls for general-purpose equipment, and machine tools, flexibility in organisation, and a high standard of skill at the foreman and executive level. Whilst the skill of all operators may not be as high as in factories on jobbing production, and tooling may not be so complex as on mass production, a high degree of skill is required in setting up tools and jobs and in deciding rapidly the most effective way to do a job. It is on this type of production in all industries that control is most difficult to secure and where badly designed and elaborate systems and paperwork can so easily clog the wheels and bog down production.

Flow or *mass production* is limited in general to the large-scale units, although continuous or flow operation is used, frequently and with advantage, for certain products or processes in factories mainly on batch production. In this type, products or parts of identical kind are in continuous production, going through exactly the same sequence of operations, and all processing units (machine, plant, or operation) are always employed doing the same operation. Mass production has resulted in and depends on the development of the single-purpose type of machine. Frequently, only one product, and one or perhaps two or three models or grades only, are produced, and the production rate is high. Mass production reaches its most advanced stage in the large process industries like flour-milling and in factories making such standard articles as domestic refrigerators and vacuum cleaners. Factories operating on a mass-production scale are usually large, and employ thousands rather than hundreds. Many of the problems of management in this type of factory arise from the very size of the units and the consequent lack of contact between the higher management and operators, and the de-skilling of jobs, resulting in lack of interest in them.

The table opposite illustrates this diversity of type and scale, and gives examples of each type of production for each group of industries.

The development of a factory from job production to batch production occurs naturally, and creates as a rule no major problems. It is usually the logical result of a gradual increase in volume of turnover, or of the application of standardisation of parts, as the business grows and its customers' needs become known. But it is the decision to apply mass-production methods that is fraught with danger and has proved so disastrous in many cases. The premature application of mass-production methods in the U.S.A. to the manufacture of domestic refrigerators, and of wireless sets in this country, are examples of the results to be expected. A factory laid out on mass-production lines is a single-purpose machine in itself, and a change in fashion, inventions and radical improvements in design may make it obsolete almost overnight. The loss of profit entailed by a shut down for a changeover can be expensive, as even Ford found out. It is dangerous to set up a factory for mass production for a product still in its early commercial stages, or when it is subject to fashion or public taste, or if the market potentialities are not definitely known. The decision to

Industry	Type of Production		
	Job ▨	*Batch* ▨ ▨ ▨ ▨	*Flow* ▨ ▨ ▨ ▨ ▨ ▨
Mines and Quarries .	Quarries on special work for architecture	Normal mines	Oil wells
Agriculture and Fishing	Normal mixed farm	Special stock and poultry farm Large market gardens	Whaling, herring, kippering and salmon canning
Building and Civil Engineering	Bridges Individual houses	Housing estates Public works maintenance	Modern road surfacing
Manufacture . .	Special-purpose machines Prototype work	All manufactured articles and most engineering and consumption industries	Cars, vacuum cleaners, telephones, electric lamps and motors, sugar refining, flour milling, paper making
Transport . .	Furniture removal Plane chartered	All forms of transport	Public transport and special industries, e.g. milk

do so therefore must be a deliberate one and taken only by the Board of Directors as a matter of high policy.

Size of Factory

In order finally to get in perspective the average or typical size of a manufacturing unit in Great Britain, the following table is reprinted from the Ministry of Labour Gazette for April 1948. It will be seen that 55 per cent. of the total number of factories employ less than 50 persons each, although they account for only 11 per cent. of all those employed. On the other hand, 23·5 per cent. of all factories employ between 100 and 1,000 persons, and account for 48 per cent. of all those employed. Excluding factories employing less than 100 persons (such factories call for a very simple form of organisation), 93 per cent. of the remainder employ between 100 and 1,000 persons, and account for 62 per cent. of those employed. This, then, is the size and type of factory with which we are chiefly concerned.

MANUFACTURING INDUSTRIES IN GREAT BRITAIN

	Establishments		Number of Employees		
	Number	Per cent. of Total	Males (000's)	Females (000's)	Total (000's)
11–24 employees	15,640 ⎫	55·0	179	83	262
25–49 „	12,730 ⎭		290	156	446
50–99 „	9,710	19·0	420	263	683
100–249 „	7,810 ⎫		734	478	1,212
250–499 „	2,920 ⎬	23·5	629	388	1,017
500–999 „	1,330 ⎭		596	312	908
1,000–1,999 „	590 ⎫		580	221	801
2,000–4,999 „	250 ⎬	2·5	592	151	743
5,000 or more „	60 ⎭		342	96	438
Total with 11 or more employees	51,040		4,362	2,148	6,510

ORGANISATION STRUCTURE

The importance to effective management of a sound organisation structure and of the understanding and application of its principles has been emphasised in the Introduction. In the present context it remains only to look briefly at the organisation structure needed for the Production Division. Frequently, this Division covers by far the largest number of persons and departments, and there is always the danger of having too many persons individually responsible to the head, i.e. the Works Manager, Production Manager, or whatever his title may be. This is a common fault: fifteen or even twenty people answerable directly to a Works Manager is no unusual situation and is a frequent cause of mediocrity, sluggishness and downright inefficiency in many of our factories today.

There are good reasons for thinking that the optimum size of a manufacturing unit is between 500 and 1,000 employees. In such a unit advantage can be taken of specialisation of activity and the use of production engineering and planning staff without losing the personal touch which comes from close contact between directors, executives and employees at all levels. This is recognised in the U.S.A. The productivity report on Welding made by the team which visited the United States in 1950, and published by the Anglo-American Council on Productivity, stated (page 55): "It is of interest that one major company had 125 separate works of which all but eleven employed fewer than 500 people. These smaller works were considered an advantage because they afforded a closer contact between employers and labour, which resulted in a better relationship between the two."

For a typical unit of any size between, say, 300 and 750 employees in the factory, the following diagram shows the basic structure for the Production Division, with suitable alternatives for the head of each department. (Titles of course are less important than definitions of duties.)

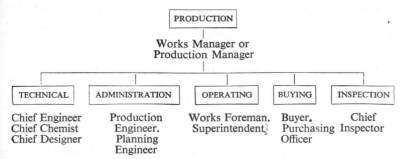

PRODUCTION

Works Manager or
Production Manager

TECHNICAL	ADMINISTRATION	OPERATING	BUYING	INSPECTION

Chief Engineer   Production   Works Foreman.   Buyer.   Chief
Chief Chemist   Engineer.   Superintendent.   Purchasing Inspector
Chief Designer   Planning   Officer
              Engineer

The technical activity is clearly a production activity, and is treated as such in this book. It is therefore shown in the diagram as responsible to the executive in charge of production. In some concerns, however, particularly where it is closely tied up with the distribution division, the technical division is responsible directly to the Managing Director. In these cases Production Engineering and Planning may be separately responsible to the Works Manager. Or there may be two or three main operating divisions; for example, Processing, Packing and Storeroom in food manufacture, Printing and Binding in printing, Cutting, Making and Warehouse in clothing, and Machining and Assembly in engineering, each responsible to the Works Manager, without exceeding unduly the latter's span of control. On the other hand, if the technical activity is small and intimately bound up with works facilities, as is common in small jobbing businesses, it is often more satisfactory for one person to be responsible for the technical and administration activities. In a small factory of under 100 people, one person might be responsible for the technical, planning and inspection activities, the Works Manager himself directly supervising the several foremen or chargehands.

In the medium-sized factory employing 500–1,000 people, a more elaborate structure may be necessary. This may take the form shown in Fig. 6. On this chart departments are shown in panels with activities listed below. In still larger organisations, each of the second-line departments may be further divided. In all cases, however, the general form would remain the same, and the line of responsibility shown should not be departed from except in unusual circumstances. In factories in which a Chemist is the technical executive, e.g. chemical processing and food factories, he is likely to be responsible for formulæ and methods, and not the Production Engineer. He may also be responsible for factory inspection and test.

Charts of this nature are insufficient by themselves; they can only indicate broad responsibilities and give a picture of the organisation as a whole. In order that each person in a supervisory position is quite clear about his detailed responsibilities and duties, definitions of duties should be drawn up and handed to him by the senior executive. In addition, each person should be given a copy of the definitions of duties for other supervisors in the form of a loose-leaf manual, including a copy of the organisation chart. Finally, it must be remembered that such organisation charts and definitions of duties soon get out-of-date; they should not be considered fixed and invariable for all time. As developments take place in Company policy, size or personnel, amendments may become necessary. If they do, they should be put into effect in a clear and definite manner; new or amended definitions of duty and an amended chart should be issued at the time.

Illustrations of definitions of responsibilities have been set out in Appendix II to the Introduction. To assist those who are already engaged in the management of production and who have decided to tidy up their own organisation, a list of duties is set out at the beginning of each section in the present Part.

PRODUCTION ADMINISTRATION

A word or two is required as an introduction to what is after all a relatively recent development of industrial organisation—the delegation to specialists of that function of Production Management concerned with forms and figures and forethought. Not that there has not always been a lot of figures and forethought required in business. But the setting up of a central department charged specifically with the task of doing all the planning and issuing of works orders and of keeping check on progress is relatively new. It is a development associated with the growth of scientific management, which had its birth at the end of last century, and with large and complex organisations.

Frederick Taylor, the "father of scientific management", back in the early days of this century, having set out to determine what precisely was a "fair day's work", discovered two things:

(1) that planning, work flow, material supply and other factors, which are the responsibility of management, affected output in addition to the effort of operators;

(2) that a tremendous amount of time and energy was wasted by skilled men in finding the best way to do a job or in doing it the wrong way,

whereas the one best way could be determined scientifically and laid down in precise instructions for future repetition.

It is clear that although Taylor did not use the term "production administration" as a function of management, he recognised its content, and what is more, recognised its two parts, one connected with work flow or planning, and the other with methods.

Several common words have been pressed into service to describe the various activities of this branch of management, and most probably because it is not an exact science, but has developed in the solving of day-to-day problems, there is as yet no definition of their meaning. Terms such as planning, progress, production control, progress chasing, shop planner, progress clerk and so on have been used with different meanings, or to refer to different activities in different organisations and textbooks. The word "planning" is perhaps the most widely used. In some organisations it refers exclusively to the activities concerned with and the department responsible for determining the way in which a job is to be done, and the preparation of jigs and tools, operation times and so on. In others, particularly where there are few changes of method, and where new methods are not being continually studied, it is applied to the activity of preparing production programmes in relation to time, issuing shop schedules, and generally steering work through the shops. In other organisations the term is used for the whole process of production administration, including methods, programmes, shop orders and progress. There is indeed some justification for using the word "planning" for all the activities covered by Fayol's—"*prévoyance*". All forethought or work put into arranging beforehand how and when a job is to be done can be called planning, but with the need to specialise on the various activities of production administration, it is better in industry to be more specific and to use other terms for divisions of the activity. One of the earliest terms used, at least in England, for that activity of production administration dealing with programmes, particularly on the shop floor, was "progress". It has been widened from its use in describing the work of the assistant to the foreman who looked after the clerical work attached to programmes in the shop (as a progress clerk or progress chaser) to include all the activities associated with preparing production programmes. There are many variations of these terms, and of others in use, evidence that there is no clear idea of what is meant by production administration, nor what are its activities, duties and responsibilities. It may be thought that the technical characteristics of industry vary so widely that a common treatment of production administration, or a common terminology, is unlikely to be of any use

Managers usually claim that their business is "different"—and with justification. No two businesses or organisations are exactly alike, any more than two persons are alike—and businesses are built up of persons. Nevertheless, not only the principles, but also the techniques of administration, and particularly of production administration, apply to all businesses. In this sense, businesses do not differ; production administration can be equally effective in them all, large or small, and whether they produce silk stockings or sewing machines, chemicals or cars. In order, therefore, that it can be discussed in relation to all industries, it is essential to define terms and to build up a commonly accepted use of such terms.

Definition of Terms

There are three distinct, though related and sometimes combined, activities concerned with getting production into stride and keeping check on its progress. They may be briefly described as follows:

(1) *Methods.*—Finding and deciding the one best way to do a job, laying down standards for its performance, and designing the tools and equipment required. This can be best described as *Production Engineering*.

This term is valid whatever the industry; it is not specific to engineering, although the activities covered by Production Engineering have been developed rapidly and intensively in engineering. The study of methods and of the best way actually to do a job in a factory is an engineer's or requires an engineer's training and outlook. The product may be pottery or chocolates, or even farming, but in this age of mechanisation and the application of power, the plant for producing and the best way to use it is an engineering problem. It is therefore a production engineering problem. The fact that there is a professional Institution of Production Engineers gives added force to the term.

(2) *Programmes.*—Arranging for what work shall be produced, and when. It is the activity concerned with the clerical routines, pre-planning production, preparing schedules of work to be done, the issue of work orders and control of stocks of materials and components. Since the word "planning" is usually associated with this kind of activity, and is the most commonly used, the term *Production Planning* best describes it and will be used in this book.

(3) Checking up on performance against standards and programmes. This activity can best be described as *Production Control*, in line with the analysis of management activities (page 49). It must not be confused with its frequent use for the whole process of Production Administration. It is concerned with comparing actual results with standards which have been laid down by either of the two other activities and the statistics are prepared and used by them or by the Accountant. Action is ultimately taken by supervision, i.e. managers or foremen, as a result of any differences that are revealed.

The terminology position may now be summarised:
"Production Administration" consists of:

(1) *Production Engineering.*—Methods, tools, standards of quantity and time, etc.
(2) *Production Planning.*—Programmes, works orders, production schedules, shop loads, material stocks.
(3) *Production Control.*—Recording results and performance, checking against programmes and standards, and pointing out corrective action required.

"Production Management" involves the use of these activities, coupled with the human task of supervising the actual execution of the work to be done, ensuring morale and co-ordinating the team.

There is one further term "Tools" which requires explanation— having a special significance in engineering. The machines used for cutting and forming metal are called "machine tools", and tools handled or put into the machines just "tools". But tools are used in all industries—moulds in potteries, lasts in boot and shoe manufacture, trowels and hods in building, formes in printing and boxmaking, and so on. In this book, therefore, the word "tools" will be used to cover all such uses.

Systems and Dangers

It is necessary to sound a note of warning against believing many of the claims made by "systems", visible card records, movable bar or line charts, duplicating machines, and so on, in particular that they "control" production. They do nothing of the kind. Correctly designed, they make records rapidly available and present a mass of data in a simplified, easily comprehended form that can be grasped with a minimum of time or effort. They are tools of production administration, and as such can be very effective tools indeed; but like all other tools, they have to be used by workmen and cannot work of themselves. A few such tools effectively used are more successful than elaborate systems. There is a tendency to measure the effectivenesss of "production control" systems by their complexity and by the amount of information that can be gathered from them. In this way small firms unwittingly cumber themselves with elaborate records and procedures and refinements of technique suitable only for the large-scale organisation—and even then of doubtful value. For this reason techniques and procedures described in Chapter III will be kept simple and sufficient to illustrate principles only.

It is important to remember that what is wanted in production administration work is a firm grasp of principles and the methods of setting about a problem, and that the actual methods adopted and forms used may have to be fitted to the particular case, modified and certainly simplified if possible, as experience is gained and conditions change.

Persons engaged on the administration of production must be aware of dangers like the following:

(1) Tendency to overrate the relative importance of production administration and to forget that it is only *part* of the total process of management—and never the most important. It appears increasingly important to persons who become wrapped up in it.

(2) Inclination to forget that production administration is a *tool* of management—and like all tools, must not be allowed to become rusty, but must be kept sharp (or up-to-date).

(3) Losing sight of the fact that production engineering, production planning and production control in action all bear on people and inevitably create reactions—good or bad.

(4) Failure to realise that production administration is a service to supervision and not an end in itself. It supplies information to production but must not dictate to supervision.

(5) The recurring temptation to make manufacture fit production control "systems", to compromise sound management principles for the sake of simpler production planning procedures, particularly when these have been in operation for some time. Systems must be flexible, adaptable and as simple as possible.

SUPERVISION

When designs have been prepared, and drawings, specifications, or formulæ issued, when methods of production and programmes have been worked out and the plant and tools provided, someone must still do the work or actually make the job. And when there are more than two or three persons jointly concerned with the doing, i.e. there is an organisation or a team, then someone must be responsible for generally overseeing the job, i.e. for supervision. If the team is larger than ten or a dozen, a full-time supervisor is needed, and we have management in action on a small scale. As the team or organisation gets larger, management becomes a bigger job, detailed supervision has to be delegated, and the title for persons performing the function changes becoming Managing Director or General Manager at the highest level. Whatever the position in the organisation and whatever the title, this job of management involves supervision of people. Supervision is primarily and in the main a human problem—it is concerned with persons not forms. David Lilienthal, the man through whose leadership the great adventure in regional development in the U.S.A., the T.V.A., was so successful, said "making decisions from paper has a dehumanising effect, much of man's inhumanity to man is explained by it". And persons differ, they are not all cast in the same mould. It is a fundamental law of mechanics that every action has an equal and *opposite* reaction. But in the realm of management commands and actions of a supervisor must induce reactions in the *same direction* and not in an opposing one. The personnel activity has developed in industry to advise and assist management in dealing with human problems. But just as on production matters a manager is advised by the technical departments, planning, production engineers, chemists, inspectors and so on, but must remain responsible for ultimate action and what goes on in his department, so on personnel problems he is responsible for their ultimate solution. There has been a tendency to look upon the person responsible for the Personnel Department as a Personnel *Manager* with authority to make decisions relating directly to problems of supervision in a department. This is a mistaken view of the personnel activity and a dangerous surrender of authority for a supervisor. A supervisor must always be responsible for all persons in his division of the organisation, and must therefore study the personnel or supervisory part of his job as keenly as he does the technical part—and the higher up the organisation structure he rises the more need there will be to deal with persons and situations instead of things. We have the technical knowledge today to raise productivity and with it our standard of life beyond all previous rates of increase; what is needed to do so is the ability to get people to work effectively and willingly together and as a co-ordinated enthusiastic team. The advice of the Personnel Officer should be sought whenever it might be helpful, but a supervisor should learn to deal with day-to-day problems himself. As in so many other cases, prevention is better than cure; it is better to prevent personnel problems by good management in day-to-day affairs.

The wider aspects of leadership, morale, welfare and what makes people want or be willing to work are dealt with in Part III. In Chapter IV of this Part we shall consider the problems to be faced by the supervisor on his shop floor. These will cover such topics as: inspiration and co-ordination; selection, training and promotion; remuneration and incentives; performance; meetings and joint consultation.

A special topic calling for mention here is that of status and titles. Between the Managing Director and the chargehand in a manufacturing company there are many grades of supervisor. In a Company employing some 7,000 people, there were nine definite grades, and in a medium-size engineering firm employing 500–600 there were seven. In all grades management is, or should be, actively in action, although the degree of responsibility involved and the proportion of time spent on the two functions of management, control and supervision, vary

Generally speaking, in each division of an organisation the grade varies with the number of individuals for whom a person is ultimately responsible, but this is not true as between different divisions. The rank or status of a supervisor depends on factors other than responsibility for the performance of those under his charge; these are technical knowledge or skill, responsibility for money, information and goodwill as well. For example, a foreman in the works may have the same rank or status as the chief clerk in the general office or a section leader in the drawing office, though he may supervise many times more persons.

The proportion of time spent by supervisors on administrative work and on supervision varies with the grade, the chargehand spending almost all his time on actual supervision of persons and the

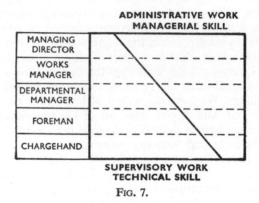

FIG. 7.

Managing Director spending the greater portion of his time on administrative work. This can be illustrated as in Fig. 7.

It is to be noted too that the amount of technique and managing ability required by a supervisor varies in the same way. A chargehand must himself be able to do all jobs for which he is responsible and his management ability need not be of a high order. The reverse is true of the Managing Director.

There is much heartache suffered by those of small mental stature on account of supposed or imagined lack of status or inadequacy of title. Those who worry about their status have none to worry about. Although by many much store is set on the title of foreman or manager, it is not the title, but the duties that are covered by it, which are important. A person's value to a Company and hence to the community, and therefore to some extent his status, is measured by his grade, which carries a certain remuneration and certain privileges. A chief chemist may be on the same grade as a works manager, and the chief inspector may be in the foreman's grade and remunerated accordingly. But a person's status to a large extent, like the respect he receives, is earned by him and extended to him by those around him, of their own free choice—it cannot be handed out by order or pro-clamation. To have earned respect and the status due to him is the hall-mark of a good supervisor.

CHAPTER II

DESIGNING THE PRODUCT—THE TECHNICAL DIVISION

Duties. Design. Estimating and Contracts. Development and Research

DUTIES

BETWEEN the customer and the production departments there must be someone who interprets the customer's requirements and sets them out in a way which enables production to make exactly what the customer wants with the facilities available. The Sales Department may collect the information and make a first interpretation of requirements, but it must still be set out for the production departments in the form of working instructions. In engineering and similar factories these take the form of drawings with associated lists of parts, in others they consist of specifications, formulæ or recipes. Associated with this activity of specifying what is required, i.e. Design, is the problem of anticipating, or trying to do what will be required in the future and improving what is already produced—that is, Development. Development is a broad term covering research, experiment, invention and development to full production scale.

These associated activities of design and development should normally constitute a department of the production division under the authority of a single individual, and can most appropriately be called the Technical Department. It must be recognised that the Technical Department is a vital link in the chain of production; it must not be thought of as a non-productive department. It is just as important therefore to study its effectiveness and plan its output as it is in the case of direct operations in the factory. The importance and extent of the activities of the department vary greatly. Many small firms manufacture articles or do work on parts entirely to customers' designs or specifications. Others, and often quite large firms, take up a patent or design or the manufacture of a standardised product and, resolutely refusing to consider orders for small variations, maintain a large production without any design department. In the case of the firms manufacturing to customers' orders, estimates and quotation must be prepared and submitted, and this is normally a job for the Technical Department; but when a firm manufactures standard products only, even this is not required, the Sales Department varying prices only in the form of discounts off price lists. Firms of the first type depend for success mainly on their production "know how" and efficiency, the latter need also marketing skill.

In between are the many firms in all industries which manufacture a range of products which either have to be modified for individual customers or continually improved to keep up with, if not ahead of, the market.

Since in business there is no standing still—stagnation is the first stage of decline—there must always be some development activity. In the firm manufacturing to customer's orders, such development activity is mainly concerned with production technique and facilities, and is most likely to be a responsibility of the Production Engineers. In all other firms there is, or should be, active and continuous development of the firm's products, and because of the need for a close liaison between design and development, these should be the responsibility of the same person.

The title of the head of the Technical Division varies more perhaps than that for any other activity. His job demands an intimate knowledge and experience of the processes and techniques of the particular industry and until recently his title usually indicated the old craft from which the industry developed (Head Brewer is still used in the brewing industry). Whatever the title, the following is typical of the duties for which he is responsible:

(1) Interpret the Company's policy in relation to design of its own products and interpret customers' requirements in relation to their enquiries and orders.

(2) Translate these designs and requirements into clear and adequate working drawings, specifications, or other instructions in a manner satisfactory to the Works Superintendent and issue to the production departments.

(3) Lay down and specify standards of quality and accuracy to maintain the Company's reputation and minimise production costs and to ensure standardisation and interchangeability as far as possible.

(4) Prepare estimates of the cost of producing a job to customers' requirements and send to customers tenders covering cost and the margin of profit laid down from time to time by the Managing Director. Maintain such records as are necessary to enable this to be done quickly and accurately.

(5) Keep abreast of developments in the design, use and manufacture of the Company's products, and carry out development, research and experimental work to this end.

(6) Keep and store safely and tidily accurate file records of all drawings, specifications and calculations.

(7) Supervise work done and maintain discipline in the department. Ensure that all members of the department are adequately trained

in their duties and particularly that juniors and apprentices receive a good technical and practical training.

(8) Adhere to the Company's personnel policy.

DESIGN

Factors Influencing Design

Customers' Exact Requirements

A satisfied customer is one of the best salesmen a firm can have; he is a perpetual recommendation. It is essential therefore for designers to find out exactly what the customer really requires. When the product is a shelf product sold ultimately to the public, it is mainly a market research job, although even then the designer has to seek information which the marketing staff and even the customer may not realise affects the design. In the large number of firms which supply equipment and intermediate products to other companies, it is usually left to the designer to ensure that he has all the information he requires. The salesman finds the markets and the customer and secures the order with a specification of requirements and conditions of service. But it is repeatedly found in practice that certain conditions and factors are taken for granted by the user and assumed by the designer, and when the product is put into service, it is found to be faulty in some respect. The designer therefore must ensure that he has all the information.

A good way to meet this point is for designers to have by them a detailed and comprehensive questionnaire relating to the kind of products with which they deal. Whenever the designer tackles a new design, he should fill in the answers himself, seeking from either salesman or customer those which he cannot supply, or submit the whole questionnaire in the first place. An alternative is to submit a detailed statement of the design before final acceptance, but a customer is less likely to check this accurately than to give correct answers to specific questions.

A product need not be better than the market for which it is intended. At the same time, however good a design may be, it fails to satisfy the user if maintenance is difficult or troublesome or it is inconvenient in use. For example—motor-cars and factory equipment which are difficult to get at for service and repair, machines which are inconvenient for the operator, containers, bottles and cartons which are difficult to open or use, furniture which is comfortable but heavy to move and difficult to clean, cannot be considered well designed and do not help sales. This means that designers must have a commercial outlook and should see their products in use in all kinds of conditions as often as possible.

Operator

One of the factors too often ignored, more particularly with designers of machines, is the convenience and comfort of the operator or user. With the development of production engineering and work study techniques, there has been much improvement in this respect in recent years, but one still meets plenty of glaring instances of this neglect. Power presses are seldom comfortable to operate, and it is quite common for the working position and operation of wrapping, packing and weighing machines to be unnecessarily tiring or to need a most unnatural stance. For example, tables or delivery chutes of machines cause operators to bend over, yet are so obstructed below that the operator cannot sit with knees bent and feet supported. How many sink units for the modern house have been designed with an eye to appearance, yet the user cannot stand with feet under the sink and must therefore work with the body off balance, with the consequent strain on back muscles. In other cases, operation handles require an unnatural stretch or action, or are hard to work.

Materials

It might be thought that all designers are aware that materials affect design. This is probably true, but it is worth emphasising that improvements and new materials are constantly being developed, and that there is a tendency always for busy designers to work in materials to which they are accustomed and of which they have had long experience and to neglect the newer ones. It means a continual reading of technical and scientific journals, close collaboration with the buyer —and an open mind. It is always worth while making suppliers aware of new requirements; there are always some who are ready to consider new uses and needs—they are the designers of another product.

Works Methods and Equipment

It is the general impression in most works departments that the designers have little idea of how a new product or part will be made— or could be made most economically. This is an indication of the lack of consideration given to the point by designers. Small modifications to designs can often result in considerable economies in production costs. This is a well-known fact to production engineers in engineering, but is often not realised in other industries. It can of course be overdone, and result in stereotyped design when improvement may be an asset. It is usual for engineering draughtsmen to spend some time in the works departments (it is ideal for them to go through every department), but it is by no means universal. There are so many processes in industry today that it is unusual for any one firm to employ a large proportion of them and impossible even then for technicians to have practical experience of them all. Chemists and other "designers" or technicians often have a scant knowledge of engineering or factory methods. Indeed, their profession is so specialised that it is difficult for them to gain such knowledge. It is important, therefore, to emphasise the need for the establishment of a routine or procedure which ensures that, where designers have not an intimate knowledge of production methods and technique in their own works, the works staff or production engineers have an opportunity of scrutinising designs or specifications before their form is finally determined.

It is essential for designers in the first place to understand and take into account the plant available and methods used, and to design with the method of production in mind. A common fault is to leave too much information to be supplied by too many people. There is a temptation always for the design or technical department to leave manufacturing and process details which become general practice in a works—"old Spanish customs"—to foremen, operators, or inspectors. This is dangerous. All goes well as long as there are no staff changes, but when there are changes, often unexpected and due to death, sudden resignation, or need for expansion, the new people on the job take some time before they pick up the "know how", and mistakes occur. It is essential in specifications and on drawings to be specific and complete. For example, in process industries instructions like heat, soak, dry, etc., should be defined as to degree, and in engineering the limits in dimensions should *always* be stated on drawings and not be left to be remembered (or forgotten) in the production departments. All these factors can affect the quality of the product. Specifications and drawings therefore must be clearly, accurately and minutely defined.

Organisation of Department

The purpose of the Design or Technical Department is to prepare and issue instructions to the Works Department to enable them to manufacture. This is done with the aid of some or all of the following documents:

Drawing.—This may be a pencil sketch, carbon copy, tracing or print (blue or white), showing the object, usually in three views (plan, elevation and end view) with dimensions. It should include all information required in manufacture, such as material, limits or dimensions, jigs and tools, etc.

Specification.—A written description of the product (and its parts), process or formula.

Part List.—A list of all parts of a product, with brief particulars of each.

Material Collation List.—A list of all material required, summarised.
Amendment Note.—A written statement of an amendment to either of
the above.
Log of Design.—A classified record of designs or formulæ.
Register.—A record, indexed, of drawings, specifications and formulæ.

Drawings

A drawing should be an accurate pictorial specification of exactly
what the object it represents must be. It must be accurate and complete. It is important, therefore, that drawings should be fully
dimensioned, and that every dimension should be accurately defined.
This means that the variation permitted for each dimension is stated,
and this is done by stating the tolerance permitted. An explanation of
tolerances, fits and limits is given later in Chapter IV, on page 380[1].
It is important to remember that a dimension has no real meaning
unless the permissible variation from it is known. A statement should
therefore be included on all drawings giving the general tolerance on
all dimensions which are not individually limited. The following is
a good example:

TOLERANCES ALLOWED

UNMACHINED SURFACES $\pm$ $\frac{1}{16}$ IN.

MACHINED SURFACES AND CRS OF MACHINED
HOLES $\pm$ 0·015 IN. UNLESS OTHERWISE STATED

The principle of one part one drawing is now generally accepted
for details and there is everything to be said for it. Drawings can be
kept smaller—a great many parts can be satisfactorily reduced to a
scale which enables 13 × 8-in. drawings to be used and, as this is a
standard stationery size (foolscap), it simplifies filing. It also avoids
the troubles and waste of time which occur in the works when several
parts are shown on one drawing and more than one part is in production at the same time (a very frequent occurrence).

Specifications

Because technical people often have a poor command of language,
specifications are sometimes not as clear as they should be. They
should be written, bearing in mind that they are most likely to be used
by persons having less knowledge of the subject than the writer. Short
sentences should be used, the matter set out in headed paragraphs,
and illustrated where it is difficult to explain adequately in words.

[1] See also BSS 308, Part II, Engineering Drawing Office Practice, Dimensioning and Tolerancing (H.M. Stationery Office).

Part Lists

Part lists vary from very brief lists of parts, most of which are illustrated by drawings, to fairly lengthy and adequate descriptions of many of the parts listed. In practice a good deal of trouble is experienced with them because small items are omitted by oversight on the part of the person preparing the list. For this reason they should always be checked by another person. To avoid the lengthy and expensive job of writing them out on tracings and printing, they can be run off on duplicators.

Material Collation List

Since a part list is prepared in a form to suit the works departments, if it is necessary either to purchase or allocate material for each order, then it is a great convenience to both the Stores Records and the Buyer to have a Material Collation List. This is a list of all material included on the part list, material of the same kind and size being totalled and grouped and like materials being grouped together. It should be prepared by the Drawing Office and issued at the same time as the part list.

Amendment and Revisions

It is always difficult to keep specifications, drawings and part lists up-to-date, to ensure that all copies are corrected when alterations are made, and that no old copies are in use. Failure to do so can result in work being done incorrectly, with the consequent increase in costs. It is essential therefore to lay down a reliable procedure for dealing with the problem. Where it is impracticable to withdraw and reissue a corrected document, a standard Revision or Amendment Note should be issued by the originator of the document to be amended, and copies sent to *all* departments that receive the original document. It is unsafe, in practice, to issue copies only to the departments who appear, at the time, to be affected. In normal circumstances certain departments may not need information which only concerns others; but unusual circumstances always arise, and it is then that all the information, including amendments, is required.

In the case of drawings, however careful the reissue of new drawings and the withdrawal of old ones, there are always wrong drawings left in existence. A simple and very safe method of issuing amended drawings is to differentiate between those which affect interchangeability and those which do not. For the former the drawing must be reissued with a new number and the part given a new number (if not the same as the drawing). When interchangeability is not affected, the number need not be changed (a suffix R1, R2, etc., to the original number, changed for each revision, is an added precaution). In both cases, if the original tracing is altered and not redrawn, a note of each amendment, numbered, should be made on the tracing.

Log or Record of Design

When there are many variations of design for various products continually being prepared, a log or record book should be kept, in which is entered every design, and against each, in headed columns, brief particulars of the various major parts of the design. It is surprising how often such a record is found to be of value to both the technical and production engineering staff and often to the sales staff too.

Sections and Specialisation

In line with the development of industry generally, designers and other technical men have become specialised, and in the larger firms the technical departments tend to be sectionalised, each section being headed by a senior man. Depending on whether there are many small designs or projects being dealt with at a time, or one large one, so sections either deal with all similar projects or all the same parts of each large project as it comes along. In either case, persons become highly specialised in their own class of work, and as this means that they become very familiar with and memorise all the details, which are never very easy to record and index, work is dealt with quickly, and the maximum use can be made of standardisation and previous experience. There is, however, an element of danger in such specialisation, not to be overlooked. When specialised knowledge, and a memory of unrecorded detail, are suddenly removed, as must happen from time to time, there can be a serious loss. For this reason it is important for the head of the department to keep in touch with all jobs and all divisions of work in the department, to examine and talk over with his staff all the new work coming into the department, and to insist that all vital information and data are adequately recorded.

A good deal of design work involves intricate and advanced mathematical calculations, and a special section is often set up to deal with them for the whole of the department. Such problems as the stresses in parts of machines, the strength of materials required and the quantities for large projects are dealt with in this section. The advantage of specialist skill has to be set off against the delay to which this arrangement almost inevitably gives rise, but in a large engineering drawing office, where it is impracticable for all draughtsmen to have the requisite knowledge, it is essential.

A much less certain case can be made out for the frequent arrangement of a separate section for checking all designs, or work produced in a technical department, before issue. The aim, of course, is to ensure that all work is absolutely correct when issued to the works—faults found afterwards (or not found) are always expensive. Nevertheless, in practice the tendency is always for the designers to rely on this check. It promotes a better sense of responsibility and a higher standard if each man is responsible for his own work, arranging for such checking as may be necessary with his senior. Where 100 per cent. accuracy is vital, a final check is unavoidable.

In the same way part lists, generally speaking, should be prepared by the man producing the design, since only he can be certain that everything is included. To avoid tracing part lists for standard reference as is usual in engineering concerns, a tedious and expensive job, the modern duplicating machine should be used, the part list being written in pencil directly on to the master sheet. Since the designers must in any case write out a list of parts somewhere, this overcomes the draughtsman's usual objection to the purely clerical or elementary work associated with the preparation of part lists. Where, however, designs or projects incorporate standard designs or subassemblies, and material collation lists are also required, a special clerical section to deal with lists, compiling the material lists and gathering together copies of the standard subassemblies, can be effective and economical. Such a section should be responsible also for the issue of work from the department, ensuring that copies of originals and revisions are circulated correctly and superseded copies withdrawn.

Work Planning

The Design Department or Drawing Office is as much a production department as any in the works; it is in the direct line of manufacturing processes from receipt of an order to its dispatch. That its cost is usually included in overheads does not alter the fact and in some companies handling large projects the design and drawing time is included in the final price as a direct cost. It is just as important therefore to plan and measure work done in the Design Department as in a department of the works. To do this it is unnecessary to have time sheets or to clock on jobs, neither of which is popular or usual for office staff.

Since it is impossible to plan reliably without a measure of the time likely to be taken to do the work, let us first of all consider the problem of measurement. The usual reaction of designers and technical staff to any suggestion that their work should be measured is that it is impossible to say beforehand exactly how long it will take to think out a new design or solve an awkward designing problem. This may be so for completely novel designs never before attempted, but experience shows that in dealing with the normal run of work forming a Company's regular production it is possible with practice to estimate the time normally taken within sufficient accuracy for it to be used for a measure of individual performance and for planning.

In a small office, the head of the department, and in a large one, the section leaders, should, when scanning each new job before allocating it to a designer or section, assess the standard time required for dealing with the job, i.e. the time which an average designer on that class of work in the department would take to deal with it, giving conscientious attention to it. Each job is allocated and the "standard time" for it recorded. As each job is completed and issued to the works, the designer (or group) is credited with the "standard" time on his weekly record. The total of the "standard" hours produced for the week, or other period, is compared with actual hours worked, and the weekly figure and cumulative total are recorded for each man and the department as a whole. Experience at estimating the "standard" time and in studying records of results enables the person doing so to become quite accurate. There is no need to use the times for any method of payment by results. If results and doubts about probable times are discussed fully with the person concerned, it has a beneficial effect on output. When such a scheme is first introduced, it will be found that the total standard hours produced in a period for each man and for the whole department is considerably less than the actual hours worked, but after a time, six months or so, performance improves (and estimates are made more accurately) and the standard hours agree quite closely with actual hours. Even if performance does not improve, the estimated time will at least adjust itself to actual time, so that planning can be accurate, but inevitably such a method of *measuring* and *examining* results has a beneficial effect on output.

Planning of work should then be dealt with in much the same way as it is dealt with for factory departments. Again in practice the most effective way is to show the length of standard time allowed each designer (or group) on a Gantt-type chart on a time base. A more flexible way is to mark the time along the edge of a card representing the job and place in pockets of a load board marked horizontally in weeks and months. In this way, not only can the load on each designer be seen and overloading avoided, but the date for completion of each job and new jobs coming in can be given and the effects on existing promises of dealing with urgent orders out of turn can be assessed. To ask a designer to drop a job to take up a more urgent one is inimical to concentration; to do so repeatedly is to invite small and large errors and too many of them. Planning can go a long way towards avoiding this.

Indexing and Filing

The correct filing and indexing of technical documents, specifications, formulæ and drawings is an important matter, but one often neglected. It is essential that there is no loss of time in finding them when they are required (and time so lost can be considerable), and that they are not damaged during storage or in the filing process; for they are valuable documents. Moreover, it is even more essential that designers, whose time is valuable, can readily refer to data which has a bearing on a present problem when the filing number of the document containing it may not be known.

Dealing first with safety, it has been found that the most satisfactory method of filing all technical documents, except books, is a drawer-type metal filing cabinet. For maximum protection of documents, care in use, and most rapid reference, the suspended-type folder should be used, and in general the foolscap size is most satisfactory. The suspended folder method is also satisfactory for larger drawings if they are folded, although for very large drawings drawers are not suitable and cabinets opening from the top should be used. If drawings are standardised on commercial stationery sizes, e.g. foolscap (and this size is quite satisfactory for the majority of detail drawings), standard equipment can be used.

Protection against the hazard of fire should be given serious consideration; drawings, formulæ, specifications and the like are extremely valuable documents, and in most cases it would be physically impossible to replace or remake them unless another copy existed. It is advisable, therefore, either to store all such documents in genuinely fireproof equipment (much so-called fireproof equipment is only partially so) or to store one copy of the document some distance away from, and certainly in another building from, the master copy— or as a safeguard against a general conflagration to do both. An alternative to an exact copy is micro-film copies. These need special photographic equipment, but there are firms in most large towns who specialise in the service, and such copies have the great advantage of taking up very little space. Perhaps the most satisfactory way, if space is available, is to file the master copy (tracings of drawings) in a strong room and have copies available in the department for reference purposes. This has the added advantage of preserving the master from damage and defacement in normal use.

In order to identify and file drawings and other documents, it is usual to give them an individual number. The simplest method, but one which has no other purpose than mere identification, is to number from one up, i.e. start at number one and number each successive document made or filed with the next unused number in a register. It is possible, however, to devise a system or code which ensures that the documents are filed in some sort of useful order and which facilitates memorising and identification. Such a code involves the separation of the items into groups or categories and their classification which makes a code useful and effective. In technical departments where the data, including specifications, abstracts from technical journals, etc., cover a very wide sphere, then the general classification used in public libraries in Britain can be used, and any public library will give detailed particulars or a demonstration. In general, however, the data or documents to be filed cover a limited field peculiar to the firm's activities or products. It is then necessary to build up a classification and code to suit this limited range. For specifications and formulæ dealing with processes, it will be found most useful either to classify according to name of processes, subdividing for subsidiary processes, or according to products. For drawings there are in general two alternative methods of approach, either to classify according to product or according to type of part. Where it is possible to use standardised parts in different products (and this should be encouraged), classifying should be according to part.

In order that items can be identified individually and in classes, they must be given symbols, and the symbols and the method of allocating them must satisfy the following requirements:

(1) Provide a logical classification.
(2) Result in a simple and flexible index.
(3) Allow of easy insertion of new classes.

Several forms of symbolisation have been suggested, but generally either alphabetical or numerical ones or a combination of both are found most satisfactory. The following example used in the aircraft industry in this country, taken from B.S. 1100 (page 19), illustrates a method suitable for a single product:

The number is VA521317 but each portion is thought of and spoken independently, thus: V.A5.21.317.
The first portion V indicates the firm;
The second portion A5 indicates the aircraft type;
The third portion 21 indicates the subassembly;
The fourth portion 317 is the part number.

The part number may be modified to indicate for example the hand of parts, odd numbers being used for left-hand parts and even numbers reserved for right-hand parts.

Another example, taken from a firm building cranes, used an eight-figure code, all figures.

The number of the part is 61012314.

Figure six is the product category;

The second two figures 10 indicate the model;

The fourth and fifth two figures 12 indicate the tonnage in the code, in this case 5 tons;

The last three figures 314 indicate the part number of the model 61012.

Perhaps the best method of all, providing maximum simplification and standardisation, is a decimal classification. For example, in a case where it is desired to file or store all like parts together, irrespective of the model for which they are used, in order to make reference to all such parts quick and complete, the class of part is coded in the first three figures, and the part number by figures following the decimal point, thus:

126.14 represents the 14th design of Part 26 in Group 1 of the firm's products.

If there are more than 99 parts to a group or product, three figures before the point must be used for parts; and if the number of products or groups exceeds 9, the number before the point would become 5 figures; e.g.: 11001.1, being the first design of part 1 of group or product 11.

Part numbers are allocated in a block to subassemblies. As drawings are filed in numerical order, all designs of the same part are filed together and all associated parts are filed adjacent to each other. From the Drawing Office point of view this is perhaps the most effective way of numbering drawings.

In practice, it is found that a symbol build-up of numbers only is most satisfactory; it can be extremely flexible within wide limits, and leads to less confusion on the telephone than one containing letters, many of which sound similar. Also to most people figures are easier to remember than letters.

Finally, it is good practice and generally accepted nowadays that part numbers and drawing numbers should be identical. This again simplifies identification and aids memorising frequently used parts and saves space and writing on documents. It certainly avoids errors and confusion in the works.

Standardisation

Standardisation to some extent has become commonplace. Indeed, it is taken for granted, in industry and everyday life. Many objects in common use, the telephone, motor-car, cycle, household articles (particularly electrical ones), boots and shoes, and even the ready-made suit, would not be so cheap as they are, were it not for the extensive, and intensive, use of standardisation. Yet a good deal more could be done to gain the advantages of standardisation both between different firms manufacturing the same product and within individual firms. And the benefits of standardisation begin, and its application for the most part must be worked out in the Design Department. More could be done between firms that make or use intermediate products, e.g. water and steam valves, household plumbing and fittings, books, bottles and similar articles, to ensure that overall sizes which make for interchangeability between one brand and another are standardised. And within a firm it is quite usual to find different draughtsmen designing similar parts for different products with only small differences, when an identical part would be quite satisfactory for both cases. Or again, materials are specified which have to be purchased specially when, with a little thought, a standard material or size in stock could be used.

The advantages of standardisation are:

To the producer:

(1) Bigger production batches and more continuous runs resulting in lower tooling and set-up costs.
(2) Possibility of breaking down operations, of increasing mechanisation and of using special-purpose high-production plant.
(3) Reduction in idle plant, tools and space.
(4) Reduction in stocks of materials, components and finished products.
(5) Reduction in overhead staff costs (drawing, design, planning and clerical).
(6) Less service and maintenance of products.
(7) Possibility of concentrating marketing effort and costs on smaller range.
(8) Generally, increased output and productivity and lower costs.

To the user:

(1) Lower prices.
(2) Interchangeability whatever the supplier.
(3) Improved stocks and supplies, service and maintenance.

It is as well, however, to remember that there are disadvantages, or rather, dangers in standardisation. If carried too far or adhered to too rigidly, it can sterilise design and make desirable or worth-while changes slow in adoption until too late (until, for example, a market is lost. Henry Ford nearly ruined his business by hanging on to his Model T just a shade too long). Standardisation is possible for most articles, the design or performance of which satisfies all normal requirements, e.g. bolts, pipes, roller chain, electric plugs and domestic irons. Complete standardisation is unwise for complex machines like lathes and electric motors, or to tie standardisation of dimensions to performance, when ultimate performance is not known. Furthermore, however desirable it may be to standardise and mass-produce certain articles, there is always a need for a special design for a special purpose. But the firm that adopts as its production policy mass production based on standardisation cannot economically deal with specials—in practice they do not mix—and it may well be that in this country with the accumulated skill and "know how" of generations with a high level of craftsmanship reinforced by general education, the special product and not the mass-produced one will continue to be the normal, and indeed the most suitable for British manufacturing industries, for a long time to come.

The objects of standardisation are to facilitate the interchangeability of parts and to reduce costs by limiting variations of material, nomenclature, set-up, or process, as far as possible. It can be effectively used in the following wide variety of applications:

Nomenclature.—The sciences are built up on the application of defined terms. Similar precise definitions should be used in all technical work, and this applies particularly in the industrial Design and Technical Departments, and in the case of drawings, specifications and similar documents.

Dimensions.—Standardisation of dimensions and their definition by limiting the variation has become almost universal. By the use of such standards and tolerances and the rejection of parts whose dimensions do not conform to them, interchangeability of parts has become possible. Whitworth started the good work on screw threads, and today most articles and materials in general use, such as sheet metal, wire, rolled-steel sections, commercial stationery, boots and shoes, electric plugs and sockets are standardised as to certain vital dimensions. The method of specifying the desired accuracy of dimensions is dealt with in Chapter V under "Inspection", page 380[1].

Quality.—Only by the standardisation of quality of raw material can a manufacturer ensure a reliable performance of his product, and without reliability there would neither be the safety nor the absence of trouble and inconvenience which we take so much for granted today. A standard quality is ensured by specifications laying down tests and performance.

Tools.—This is a special case of quality, but is of special significance, because without standardisation of tools, interchangeability of parts and standard times and performance would be impossible, and on this depends all planning in factories. It also ensures accuracy of dimensions in such cases as drills for holes and taps and dies for screw threads.

Performances.—This again can be a special case of quality when applied to finished products. Standards for testing ensure that a product will do what it is designed or specified to do within prescribed limits. Standard times are a measure of performance for human operation (see page 219).

[1] See also B.S.S. 308, Part II, Engineering Drawing Office Practice, Dimensioning and Tolerancing (H.M. Stationery Office).

Processes.—There is always one best way, and in certain industries like the chemical industry, only one correct way, of doing a job. With standard materials and tools and specifications, methods can be standardised and a uniform product ensured.

Standardisation applied to industry in this country has been developed and organised by the British Standards Institution, which explores the need for, and issues British Standard Specifications in, the following four divisions: Engineering, Building, Chemical and Textile. In recent years the Institution has spread its activities to other industries, for example, clothing, and this widening interest can be expected to continue if the need is there. The activities of the Institution are briefly explained as follows:

"The Institution exists to assist British Industry by preparing British Standard Specifications, of which up to the present over 1,700 have been issued, exclusive of some 300 for Aircraft Materials and Component Parts issued in co-operation with the Air Ministry and with the Society of British Aircraft Constructors.

"The British Standards Specifications are based on what is best in present practice (and do not attempt to attain an ideal which might be too costly to adopt) providing a generally suitable standard of performance, quality, or dimension, and an equitable basis for tendering. They help to eliminate redundant qualities and sizes, and enable manufacturers to provide stock during slack periods and purchasers to obtain their requirements more rapidly. The specifications are kept up-to-date; they do not interfere with individual initiation and invention, and they leave the producer as much freedom as possible in his methods of production. Wherever possible, the Specifications deal mainly with performance."

ESTIMATING AND CONTRACTS

Nature of the Activity

Estimating the total cost of a product or a job before manufacture is an activity which is carried on continuously only in those companies who manufacture to customers' special requirements. It is not a continuous activity in companies whose products are completely standard and made for shelf or warehouse stock. This means that it is not usually found in factories manufacturing articles which are eventually bought by the general public, like sewing machines, furniture, food, confectionery and ready-made clothing, but is limited, by and large, to firms making (or repairing) plant and equipment for other manufacturing companies and, of course, civil engineering and public works contracting. Standard products can be costed accurately and the selling price determined for repeat sales, this being varied only according to the quantities ordered or the type of customer and the service he renders to the ultimate consumer. This adjustment of prices is a Sales Department function. But when it is necessary to quote a prospective customer a price for supplying an article, machine, or plant before he is prepared to order (i.e. against an enquiry) some kind of an estimate of the ultimate costs has to be prepared. This can vary from an extraction from previous costs of the cost of each part or item to what may be called "guesstimating"—or intelligent guessing. When preliminary designs are not prepared in detail, the accuracy of the estimate depends on the skill with which the estimator interpolates from records of previous costs. Obviously, the more complete the records and the more effectively they are indexed, the more accurate will be the estimate. It is possible, of course, to estimate each detail, piece by piece, and to build up a complete estimate, but in practice this generally takes too long, and is too expensive, so that something between this and a pure guess is required.

The job of the estimator then is to arrive at as accurate a forecast as possible of the ultimate cost of a product or project before work on it commences or is authorised, and in the shortest time and at a minimum cost.

It is obvious that continually under-estimating will involve the risk of a loss on the year's trading and ultimate financial failure. It is not always realised that over-estimating can be equally serious. It not only loses individual orders, but, by thus limiting or reducing turnover, increases the burden of overheads and particularly of selling and estimating costs (since costs will be absorbed on unfruitful enquiries).

Methods and Practice

As the accurate determination of the correct price to be charged for a standard product is decided from a study of figures prepared by the Cost Department from actually recorded costs, or from a study of the market, we shall deal here only with estimating as it must be carried on in firms which have to quote for special orders.

Customers' Requirements

When dealing with an enquiry, the first and essential job is to find out exactly what the customer wants. This is not always as simple as might be thought. It is very easy for an estimator, experienced in his own firm's usual work and products, to make unwarranted assumptions. Also users of equipment may know what they want in general terms, but not be aware of the need to state certain working conditions or limiting factors. Furthermore, a customer may think he knows what he wants and ask for it, not knowing exactly what is available or what might be more satisfactory for his purpose.

It is very necessary therefore for the estimator to scrutinise the enquiry in detail and with the greatest care, looking for any gaps in the information and doubtful requirements. If in doubt, or if there is any information lacking, he must ask for confirmation before proceeding with the estimate. If there is not time to do this, the assumptions that are made should be noted and explained to the customer with the quotation for confirmation. If the estimator, from his knowledge of the trade or the customer, thinks that the customer really needs something different to fulfil the purpose he has in mind, then it should be suggested, even if it would mean a smaller order or no order at all. There is no sense in selling a customer something which he will later find he does not want, or which is inadequate; good advice given in this way establishes confidence and ensures future enquiries.

Certain standard information may always be required. For example, manufacturers of overhead travelling cranes always require to know, in addition to the weight to be lifted and the span across the track, the speed of lift required, the height, roof clearance, electric supply and atmospheric conditions (if in a foundry or chemical plant or similar situation). In such cases a standard data sheet should be printed, and either filled in by the estimator before beginning his estimate, or sent to the customer immediately on receipt of the enquiry for him to fill in and return. The latter course is advisable if only for confirmation.

Data

The basis of an estimator's work is the cost data. In order to do his job effectively he must have available records of costs, recorded and filed in such a way that they can be simply and rapidly referred to and used. The best method of filing will depend on the kind and extent of the data recorded, but the loose-leaf ring binder is very satisfactory in practice.

It is sometimes suggested that only elementary data is required, such as for example the times to do operations, labour rates, and the cost of materials as bought. These detail facts may be required in rare cases, but to build up estimates in such detail is expensive and usually unnecessary. What is wanted is costs of normal products or parts of them for each size or variation likely to occur, with some indication of extra costs incurred for additional special equipment. Standard costs (see Part IV) is the answer to this problem, particularly when a detailed estimate is required.

If standard costs are not available, past costs of whole products (to take crane manufacturers, again, of whole crane) and of parts and normal materials (such as crabs, blocks, carriages, motors and girders) should be recorded. For the whole product and for major subassemblies the costs should be plotted on graph paper against the variable factor, horse-power, load, weight, or whatever it is. If there are several variable factors, it will be necessary to plot several graphs. It is not necessary to plot the cost of each value of the variable factor: four or five points will indicate the nature of the curve, which can then be drawn in for other values with sufficient accuracy. The values of costs can be plotted as detailed estimates are made, or better still, from previous actual costs. Gradually, a very comprehensive set of figures can be accumulated from which it is comparatively simple to find the cost for any set of factors, interpolating for values of a variable between those plotted.

Fig. 8 is an example (figures not actual) of the kind of graph referred to. In this case it is assumed that there would be a graph for

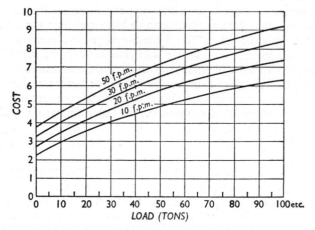

Notes.—Add 10 per cent. for variable speed.
Add £x for each 5 ft. lift above standard (15 ft).

FIG. 8.—Cost Chart for Estimating

each major subassembly and a set of curves for each type of each subassembly. The important thing is to find the variable factors against which the cost varies in a uniform manner; in the case of structural steelwork of a standard design it may be weight, for packing-cases superficial area, for electric motors horse-power, and so on.

In addition to such records of costs, it is necessary to have recorded information concerning limiting factors of the works plant capacity. The works will be able to handle production within a certain range without abnormal arrangements or equipment, but outside these limits, usually above a certain size or weight, it is impossible to produce, or special arrangements have to be made. For example, the kinds of limiting factors often overlooked, with disturbing results in the factory, are the maximum lifting capacity of cranes (and sub-assemblies or parts of special machines may be above this capacity), the size of machine tools, particularly the swing of lathes or the table of boring machines, the size of doorways or exits from erecting shops. It is essential to note all such capacities, and whenever an estimate is being considered for something outside previous experience, all unusual features must be examined for such snags.

Co-operation with Other Departments

It is most essential that, when a new type of job or one outside previous experience is being considered, special features should be referred to other departments interested, if there is the least doubt in the estimator's mind as to whether he has accurate information. The Production or Methods Engineers should be consulted whenever there is any question of tooling or special processes, and the Drawing Office if the design is unusual in any way. If tools and drawings are included as a direct charge in the estimate and it has not been possible to plot costs for reference purposes, these departments should be asked for their estimate. If this is normal procedure, a standard form can be used, relevant information being filled in by the estimator and sent to each department for completion and return. These departments should also be consulted on the delivery period to be quoted if special drawings, tools, or methods are required, unless the Planning Department are entirely responsible for progress through these departments as well as for production programmes.

A close liaison must also be maintained with the Sales Department and technical engineers or representatives. They are likely to be able to interpret a customer's real requirements when these are stated ambiguously in the enquiry, and can decide the best way to approach the customer if it is considered desirable to suggest an alternative or modified product. In many cases correspondence and contacts of this nature with the customer must go through the sales channels.

Delivery Dates

When new orders take their place immediately at the end of the queue or order book, there is usually no difficulty in deciding on what delivery to quote. The period is arrived at by dividing the total orders on hand measured in £ s. d. or some unit of volume by the works capacity per week in the same unit. This may be done for all products or each particular type according to whether each type is limited to the same rate of output or not. This measure can be in terms of value, volume, man-hours, or whatever unit is found to be sufficiently accurate, sales value is obviously the simplest and is often adequate, but it frequently does not accurately represent works capacity (or the proportion of bought-out parts or materials per pound of sales value and varying profit margins make it an inaccurate measure).

When, however, orders are booked for delivery at a definite time and some of the dates are beyond the period when all orders on the books could be completed at normal output rate, obviously some orders can be completed earlier. It is then not so easy to determine exactly when an order can be delivered, i.e. to know for what periods the works capacity is booked. The Planning Department will have this information, of course, and will have to be referred to if departmental detail programmes must be consulted. If, however, it is possible to allocate capacity in terms of a unit (value or some unit of volume), a simple production chart can be constructed. Production periods are marked off horizontally on a time scale. The capacity absorbed by orders already booked in each production period (week or month) is marked off vertically on the scale of unit of capacity. A line is drawn horizontally at the level of the capacity absorbed (with steps for planned increases or decreases). This should be corrected weekly or monthly and will show at a glance in what periods capacity is available and how much.

Whatever method is adopted, it is essential for all delivery promises to be made in line with the Planning Department programmes, or on a basis agreed by them and confirmed periodically.

Final Build-up of Estimate

The method of finally building up the estimate to include all charges, works overhead, administrative selling and profit margin, should be agreed upon with the accountant. Because the estimator cannot be expected to have the broad view of affairs and of sales policy in particular which is necessary in dealing with estimates, the estimator is sometimes only permitted to build up to the total works cost, or perhaps total cost, but not selling price, the final margin being added either by the Sales or General Manager. In many cases, however, the estimator compiles the final selling prices. When the appropriate overhead expenses and profit margin have been added (if not already included in the synthetic cost data) to make the selling price, it is advisable in any case for the final estimate or tender to be confirmed either by the Sales Manager or General Manager. To reduce the work on senior executives which this may involve, small tenders below a stated value can be sent to customers without reference, those above a high value referred to the General Manager and those in between to the Sales Manager. In practice, it is sometimes found necessary to vary the profit margin or the competitive strength of the price as a measure of selective selling. In times of depression and when orders at normal prices for any reason do not fill the works to capacity, it may be sound management to take work at little or no profit to help to carry the standing charges or overheads. On the other hand, because of inadequate plant, unwillingness to lock up a large part of works capacity, or for other commercial reasons, it may be desired to ward off certain orders unless an unusually high margin is considered to override such considerations. Only the General Manager is in a position to decide such matters.

An effective method of adjusting the selling price to attract or repel orders according to their material or labour content is to add different profit margins to each element of total cost, adding a higher percentage to that element which is in short supply. If, for example, an average profit margin on cost of 15 per cent. (13 per cent. on selling price) is required, material is on the average 70 per cent. and labour 30 per cent. of total direct cost, and it is desired to attract orders with a low rather than a high proportion of labour content, the following differential margins could be used:

Material	.	plus 11 per cent.
Labour	.	plus 25 per cent.
Overheads	.	plus 15 per cent.

This would yield 15·2 per cent. on total cost when material and labour are in the normal proportion, since:

11 per cent. of 70 per cent.	. .	7·7 per cent.
25 per cent. of 30 per cent.	. .	7·5 per cent.
		15·2 per cent.

But when the labour content is high, say 50 per cent. of direct cost, then the total margin would be:

11 per cent of 50 per cent.	. .	5·5 per cent.
25 per cent. of 50 per cent.	. .	12·5 per cent.
		18·0 per cent.

which is higher than normal, and would tend to make such orders more uncompetitive. The total margin can be divided so as to attain the selection of orders desired.

Tenders

A tender or quotation is a written offer to do a certain amount of stated work or supply certain goods at a definite price and in accordance with stated conditions. Such a tender or quotation, when accepted by letter, note, or order, constitutes a contract in law. It is clearly set out and conditions clearly defined. Such conditions should be reasonable in character and stated in terms as precise and unambiguous as possible to avoid dispute and legal action. Simple English should be used as far as possible, and the long sentence with too many qualifying phrases avoided. It is not possible to cover here all the information, terms and conditions which at times have to be covered, but the following are the more generally used. Model forms of contract and tender can be obtained from most trade associations and professional institutions.

Specification.—The goods, work, or services to be supplied should be precisely stated by the use of a standard form of specification where possible. Outline drawings may have to be included if certain overall dimensions have to be adhered to. The specification must include limiting figures for performance and duty.

Price.—The net price must be stated and any discounts allowed. Terms of payment must also be stated; for large installations part payment on delivery or during erection may be required.

During times when costs are fluctuating (particularly rising) rapidly, as during and after the last war, the right is claimed to adjust prices to costs ruling at the time of dispatch. It is not a very commercially sound practice in normal times.

Delivery.—It should be made clear whether the delivery date is when it leaves the works or is delivered to customer.

Inspection.—The right or necessity for the customer to inspect may need to be specified.

Guarantee.—Any actual or implied guarantee should be most clearly defined. This question is a prolific source of dispute. The responsibility for equipment included, but bought from other manufacturers, should be made clear. Often the final supplier disclaims responsibility. Service for a limited period is sometimes included in the contract price; if so, the precise nature or limitation of such service should be defined.

Penalties for Non-fulfilment.—If any penalty for non-fulfilment of any part of the contract is accepted, it should be most precisely defined, as dispute can easily arise and legal action follow any non-fulfilment under penalty.

Conditions Specified in Order.—Any conditions which have been stated or referred to by the customer in his enquiry or order must be specifically referred to in the tender; such conditions must be either accepted or repudiated.

DEVELOPMENT AND RESEARCH

A business cannot stand still: it must either develop or perish. There is no permanence or security in self-satisfaction. If a Company for long remains satisfied with its products or productivity, it becomes moribund, and ultimately goes out of business or becomes absorbed by a more successful competitor. To flourish, a Company must continually improve its products or services or develop new ones, and to do this it must not only be receptive to new ideas, it must continually search for and develop new materials, new methods and new products. This process of research and development is a specialised activity, must be recognised as such and not left to the spare-time activity of those who may be interested in it. Whilst some discoveries of value have been accidental, most have been the result of thorough and painstaking experimental work, and certainly the development of most new ideas to successful production has meant continuous and purposive application of time and ingenuity. Rule of thumb and trial and error can find the solution to development problems, but they are expensive and uncertain methods. Results are more reliable and less costly if development is organised scientifically. In those firms who do keep abreast of the times, development of some kind or another is always going on, but it is frequently not recognised as a definite or separate activity, nor is it consciously or continuously directed by anyone. Consequently, it is much less effective than it could be; progress is haphazard and results patchy. Moreover, experimental work that is carried out in the shops by foremen or operators on production does not get the concentrated attention it requires, is not likely to be scientifically carried out, and anyway interferes with the main activity of production.

This all means that development should be conceived of as a whole and should be the responsibility of a single individual in a concern who is (or is responsible to) the chief technical executive. It may be convenient to have experimental sections of the works responsible to the works executives, but the responsibility for development work as a whole, its conception, planning and results, should be the responsibility of the technical department. In fairly large firms, there is likely to be experimental work of one kind or another being carried on in several departments or divisions of the organisation, the design department experimenting with new products, the production engineers or toolroom developing new tools or machines, and production seeking for ways to improve processes. Each of these activities is development work, differing only in the matter of process, but not in the nature of the activity. On the other hand, all development work involves three stages:

First, research, either fundamental, seeking to find the fundamental laws of cause and effect, and seeking knowledge for its own sake with little thought for what the results may be, or applied, finding ways of applying these laws to practical purposes.

Second, experimental and development work, in which the findings of research are developed and proved on a practical scale, on pilot plants or prototypes.

Third, the initiation of full-scale production and as a service to production.

If there is any need to divide up the activities of development work because of its scope or the size of the organisation, it is more correct to do so on the basis of these three stages, research, prototype or experimental, and process assistance, than to do so according to the type of work.

It is vital therefore that this important development activity should be controlled and staffed by men with good scientific training and experience; it is not only knowledge, but also the ability to comprehend the possibilities of new knowledge and to carry out scientific investigations that are essential. Development work properly co-ordinated in all its stages and imaginatively directed can then be of immense value to any Company.

Obviously small companies are likely to find it impossible to conduct fundamental and original research work and must rely on bodies like the Universities, the Department of Scientific and Industrial Research and trade research associations and laboratories for such work. More support to and use of all these bodies could quite well be given by industrial firms, particularly the smaller ones who are unable to undertake research work on their own account. Some firms make arrangements for a University to do their research work for them, and others, particularly in areas where there is a local industry, are encouraging the technical colleges to help. The Department of Scientific and Industrial Research conducts research in its own laboratories, e.g. the National Physical Laboratory, but in addition it encourages and gives financial support to a large number of research associations formed and supported by firms in particular industries. There are over thirty British industries now supporting such research associations, a complete list of which is given in the annual reference book *Industrial Research* (Geo. Harrap & Co.). These associations are primarily concerned with problems related to specific industries, undertake long-term applied research on basic problems, and publish results in language which can be understood by the manufacturers. They can be called upon to give advice and information concerning any problem submitted by an individual member. But all firms should carry out their own, or commission on their own behalf, development work aimed at improving their products or services and their tools and processes. In development work connected with a Company's products, it is essential for the development engineers and chemists to work in close co-operation with the sales or marketing staff; indeed, most of the investigations which they will be called upon to make will arise from market research or investigations. Similarly, close co-operation and active collaboration with both production staff and production engineers are essential.

It is sometimes recommended that development and experimental work should be made to pay for itself in terms of yearly economies or profits. This is a mistake. It usually results, and inevitably must tend to do, in too careful a selection of the work undertaken and a reluctance to take a long view. This is understandable, since only the chief executive or the Directors are in possession of all the relevant facts to be able to take the long view and to assess the probable value of such work. Its actual value can rarely be accurately assessed in advance; it is seldom possible to calculate even the actual return on costs incurred. Nevertheless, such work can of course absorb too high a proportion of available resources, and this should be guarded against by budgeting of expenditure. For details of how to do this see Part IV.

Finally, it should be remembered that employees in the production departments are always interested in development and the experimental department, and anything which can be done to encourage and satisfy this interest in the firm's products and affairs is sound management. The results, therefore, of research, experimental and development work which are applied in the factory or incorporated in the firm's products should be explained to all employees and particularly to those closely involved.

A word of warning is called for against the tendency for the Managing Director of small firms, who is usually the proprietor as well, to be too actively associated with research. It is a common weakness where the proprietor has built up the business around his own technical knowledge or skill. But when the business is big enough to require the usual four or five senior executives, if a Managing Director continues to be actively interested in detail research, it inevitably results in his devoting too much time to the subject to the detriment of "general management". If the Managing Director has peculiar abilities or knowledge which make it advisable for him to direct technical and development work, the solution may be to appoint a staff assistant to relieve him of detail work, but to work under his immediate supervision, or to appoint a General Manager responsible to him for all other activities except technical. The danger must still be avoided of such work absorbing a disproportionate amount of the Managing Director's time.

CHAPTER III

PRODUCTION ADMINISTRATION

Production Methods. Measurement of Work. Tool and Equipment Design. Production Planning. Production Control. Principles

PRODUCTION METHODS

Definition of Activities

IT was shown in Chapter I that one activity of the administrative side of production is concerned with finding and stating the one best way to do all jobs. No longer is this left to the skilled and interested operator, proceeding by trial and error, successive operators making the same trials and the same errors to arrive at the same, or sometimes a different, result. As more machines, tools and equipment, some of them highly specialised, have been designed and become available, and new materials and processes developed, it has become increasingly a skilled technical job to keep abreast of developments and always to know the up-to-date or best way to do a job. It would be quite impossible today for the craftsman at the bench or machine to keep himself so informed and do a job of producing. Skilled men are still required, but increasingly today they become setters, minders, or maintenance men.

The old type of foreman is apt to think that the appointment of a production engineer, process engineer, or chemist, reduces his usefulness, his value to the Company, or his status. It does nothing of the kind, of course. It is true that, before the development of production engineering, and the use of chemists in the works as well as in the analytical laboratory, the Works Manager and his foreman supplied the production "know-how", and decided how a job should be done But it is now recognised that the training and supervising of persons is a much more complex job than it once was, and to relieve a foreman of a large amount of administrative work makes a higher general performance possible and his job more valuable, not less. It is essential to separate planning from doing, administration from execution.

When a new material is developed or a new product designed, the method of production is obviously either known or worked out. But from then onwards all is change. Better methods of production are being discovered continually. Furthermore, in many factories, particularly those engaged in engineering, the detailed method of production for each part to be manufactured, the machines to be used and equipment required, is decided subsequent to design. The task of deciding the best method of production, of saying how a job shall be produced, and of finding new and better ways of doing so, should be the responsibility of a Methods or Production Engineering Department. Similarly, in a Company where the technical knowledge is supplied by chemists, production methods would be the responsibility of the works laboratory.

In deciding the one best way of doing a job, the production engineer or chemist must have regard for the costs of production, and therefore for the time to do the job. He must have some say also in new tools or equipment required. These are the three divisions into which the activities of the production or methods engineer usually fall—that is to say, work study or methods, work measurement or time study and tool design.

These three aspects all call for close collaboration with the designer and works departments. The design of jigs and tools might be thought to be a logical development of the Design or Drawing Office work and in some works it is done in the Drawing Office. But it cannot be effectively developed without detailed study of methods and work being done in the factory, and, as will be shown later, this study forms the basis of standards for time, and hence for payment by results, production planning and costs. This study work calls for a specialised technique and training quite different from Drawing Office work. The outlook required is different too. It is more successful in practice therefore if it is recognised as a separate activity, and combined with the design of tools and equipment. To avoid it becoming too remote from or independent of the Drawing Office, Design Department, or Technical Department, new drawings, designs, or technical developments should always be referred to, and discussed with, the production engineers before final issue.

The development of production engineering as a special skill and the extensive use of specially designed tools and equipment have contributed largely to the very much greater output per man-hour in the U.S.A. than in this country. There is no doubt that it is through such development, adding horse-power to man-power, and taking out the manual effort from jobs, that the way lies to reduce man-hour requirements.

"The records of the United States and the United Kingdom have demonstrated that over a period of many years productivity in industry bears an important relationship to the amount of energy which is available per employee. In the U.S.A. the figure is approximately twice that in the U.K. This fact, in our opinion, accounts in large measure for the greater output per man-hour in many industries in the U.S." [1]

[1] " The First Report of the Anglo-American Council of Productivity."

Because production engineers tend to get machine or gadget minded, they are apt to forget or neglect the human factor. Machines cannot yet operate without human agency, and men should not be made into robots. The foremen may have something to say if the division of labour, for example, is carried too far, or if new methods are forced on them without consultation. Continued and close cooperation between the production engineers and works departments is absolutely essential.

Broadly, then, the function of the Production Engineering or Methods Department is to determine, in collaboration with the Design and Works Departments, the most effective, economical and suitable method of production, to lay down standards for material and time, and to design special tools and equipment required. The following can be taken as typical of the duties of the head of the department:

(1) Scientifically investigate processes and operations in order to:
    (a) Establish the correct way of carrying out processes and of performing operations.
    (b) Eliminate unnecessary and ineffectual operations.
    (c) Reduce operators' fatigue to a minimum and examine all drawings and jobs to this end.
(2) Prepare drawings for all jigs, tools, or gauges that are required.
(3) Carry out time studies to determine the amount of work involved in operations.
(4) Establish standard times which, when used as a wage incentive, will enable an average qualified operator, working well within his or her capacity, to earn at least the standard amount of bonus agreed between the operators and management, including an appropriate allowance for rest and fatigue.
(5) Collect, collate and file data relating to operation times to enable standard times to be rapidly and easily prepared.
(6) Investigate and report when required on all forms of excess cost.
(7) Establish and cultivate mutual confidence between the department's staff and supervisors and operators.
(8) Adhere to the Company's personnel policy and see that subordinates do so.
(9) Train staff in the effective performance of their duties.
(10) Keep abreast of modern developments in manufacturing methods of all kinds, but particularly where related to the manufacture of the Company's products. In particular, recommend to the management the purchase of modern or improved designs of machines which will improve production, or reduce costs.

Work Study

There has been some confusion in industry and in technical literature dealing with the measurement of work and payment by results, because of the indiscriminate use of terms like time study, motion study, micro-motion study, dynamic motion study, rate-fixing, time setting and so on. Indeed, there is a good deal of confusion in the minds of men engaged in the work. And because the more generally used term, time study, has been associated with attempts by untrained persons to do rate-fixing rather more accurately, and has occasionally been misused by shortsighted or impetuous managements, it has come to mean to some, particularly organised labour, something synonymous with speeding up, nigger driving, or inducing persons to work harder than is reasonable. Furthermore the use of the word "time", coupled with the ostentatious use of a stop-watch and insufficient explanation to all those affected, has made the term suspect.

In point of fact, all these terms are particular applications of the general process of work study which has been going on since man first thought of the wheel and cart to save him carrying loads himself. What is relatively new is the emphasis given to the time aspect of work study. Engineers in particular have always been interested in better ways of doing things, and the present industrial civilisation is the result of finding better and quicker ways of doing them. We have, however, mainly concentrated on designing equipment and mechanisms. It is only in recent years that men, chiefly engineers, have studied the ways men do the jobs that men, and not machines, must do. F. W. Taylor, who established and popularised the scientific approach to this matter, began his studies into better methods of doing work in the Midvale Steel Works in the 1880s. Taylor was appointed, at an early age of twenty-four or so, chargehand of the lathe operators in the factory. He soon realised that the men were not giving an output that he knew was reasonable and easily attainable, and at first he had to use the disciplinary methods customary in those days (and for many years since). He discovered, however (and Taylor was a searcher for facts and reasons), that the difficulty and disagreements generally encountered lay in different ideas, rather abstract ideas, which everyone had of what constituted a "fair day's work". No one really did know in fact what did constitute a "fair day's work". He realised that if it were possible to find a way of measuring this abstract value in terms which had a basis in fact and could be understood, then most of the bitterness and mistrust would be eliminated. He determined to find a way, and adopted the scientific approach to the problem. He began a series of carefully controlled and recorded experiments on lathes, and started on his career of work study and scientific management.

"Taylor started with an individual worker at a lathe, started, as the trained research worker starts, to find out all about it, to observe what he was doing and leaving undone, to analyse and to measure every factor in his task which could be made susceptible to measurement. In short, he began to build up a 'science' of cutting metals on a lathe. Gradually he isolated the various elements and set to work to improve the factors which made for high performance, to eliminate causes of delay and interruption, to reduce the craft of the tradesman to precise and detailed written instructions." [1]

In addition to discovering exactly what the work content of a job in the lathe was, he discovered then that there were certain factors which affected total output. The method adopted by different operators for doing the same job varied—there was no one best way—and operators lost a good deal of time experimenting and trying out various ways themselves. In addition, planning of work and flow of material was uncertain, and caused a good deal of waste of time. Both these factors are management's problems; they are, in fact, the major part of management's administrative task.

It is a long time since Taylor made this approach to the study of the work content of a job and of factors affecting it, and today there can be no doubt that the scientific approach and the establishment of the one best way under correct conditions is essential to obtain a measure that is factual and will be accepted by the operators concerned of what constitutes a "fair day's work".

It is possible to say with reasonable accuracy exactly how many parts an automatic machine will produce per hour; the designer or machine setter can state precisely the rate of output of e.g. a cigarette-making machine, an automatic machine producing screws, a printing machine, or an automatic loom on a given weave. But how many articles will be produced in a day or a week in a given factory; how many looms or automatic screw machines can an operator look after, and how many cigarettes can be made by hand per hour, chocolates wrapped, orders packed, or customers served in a Department Stores? You will notice that the question is, how many can, not how many are. The answer to these questions can only be obtained with any degree of accuracy by studying the work being done, at the time it is done, the effort required, and the skill of the operators, and including in the study the conditions under which it is or may be done, and delays that may occur. It is not sufficient to take an average of past performance, to ask the operator or the foreman, or to take a spot check. That may tell us how many are being done, either the maximum, minimum, or anywhere in between, but it will not tell us how many can be done. Only work study can do that.

Furthermore, there are few methods of doing jobs which cannot be

[1] *The Making of Scientific Management*, vol. I, by Urwick and Brech, page 30.

improved upon, however much they have been developed and however well they are being done today. New materials, new techniques, new equipment are being developed continually. Filling powder by scoop or chute was a slow as well as a dusty job until someone studying the dust problem remembered that fluids are filled by vacuum; insulation materials were cut by hand with scissors until someone studying how to increase production remembered how printers cut paper and cardboard to shape. Unexpected, and often substantial, improvements in output can frequently be obtained by objectively studying the way work is done with the aim of finding what is the best and quickest way to do it.

Gilbreth, the pioneer of motion study, who devoted the greater part of his career to the search for "the one best way to do work", was able quite early in his search to eliminate unnecessary movement and effort from bricklaying in the U.S.A., and obtained outputs, *without undue fatigue*, which trade union bricklayers in England consider impossible nearly fifty years later.

"Even in his very early days the results that Gilbreth achieved were remarkable. Thus, for instance, the work of bricklaying was so simplified that the eighteen motions formerly thought necessary to place a brick were reduced to four or five, and, indeed, in one case, to two. Those which remained were made as simple and effective as thorough study could make them. The final result was that Gilbreth's men, who had formerly worked to their limit to lay 1,000 bricks per day, were able, after a short period of instruction, to reach a daily output of 2,700." [1]

The daily approved output in England today is somewhere between 400 and 800!

Work study therefore can be defined as the scientific study of work to find:

Exactly what has to be done;
The one best way to do it with present equipment and conditions;
What impediments or inefficient work can be eliminated;
What equipment, or conditions, or methods would make it easier and quicker;
What effect have present methods and conditions and modifications to them, on the operator;
How long should it take with a normal operator with normal skill and in normal conditions.

(The establishment of what is meant by "normal" is dealt with later.)

---

[1] *The Making of Scientific Management*, vol. I, by Urwick and Brech, page 138.

Work study thus defined includes the other more limited terms mentioned on page 207.

Time study is used synonymously with the more general and descriptive term work study. As carried out quite frequently, however, time study has a more limited aim, namely, that of finding the correct time for a job as at present being performed.

Motion study directs emphasis on to the study of bodily movements, and is most intensively developed in mass production or continuously repetitive production. This study of bodily movements is fundamental to all work study, but the neglect of the other factors involved in doing work, i.e. environment and administration, by those engaged on motion study, has warped their conclusions and judgment on its value and equity by those concerned.

"Motion study has been very much misunderstood. Possibly, some responsibility for this attaches to the Gilbreths' own definition of their quest—'the one best way to do work'. They have been misinterpreted as seeking to tie the worker to a monotonous repetitive round in his daily task, although their only field of interest was to make movement simple and economical. It is too often forgotten that the study calls, not only for an analysis of motions, but also—and to an equally important extent —for an analysis of the environment in which the work is being carried out. In short, motion study calls for a complete analysis of the whole job with all its attendant circumstances. When it is regarded thus in its proper light, the criticism of motion study becomes meaningless."[1]

Time and motion study is a term often used combining these two aspects of work study.

Micro-motion study is the study of very small elements of motions frequently with the aid of a special camera. It was first developed by F. B. Gilbreth, who called these ultra-small elements "Therbligs" (Gilbreth spelt backwards) and defined them as "motions or mental events made by different members of the body, of too short duration to be observed with stop-watch". It is claimed that units of time as short as 0·0005 minute can be easily measured by these means and can be built up synthetically into an overall time. They can, but whether the results on and from the operator justify the trouble and expense involved, and whether ordinary time-study methods would not obtain adequate, if not better results is open to question.

Dynamic motion study is a term used by J. J. Gillespie (who denies that micro-motion study gives all the picture) to describe the study of the whole work situation, including the psychological or human factors—in short, work study. Gillespie states his case against

[1] *The Making of Scientific Management*, vol. I, by Urwick and Brech, page 141.

the narrow conception of motion study, and sets out certain "principles" in his book *Dynamic Motion Study*, published by Paul Elek.

Rate-fixing (time setting) is a term given to the rather approximate or workshop method of assessing a time or piece-rate for a job. As practised by the man who has been promoted from the shop floor without any training in scientific work study it is unsatisfactory. It aims at setting a task or rate for a job as it is being performed with only an approximate allowance for ignorance to cover all factors likely to affect the actual time. A measure which is merely the overall time taken with a watch is unfair. There is no certainty that it can be maintained or reduced over a day and is therefore unreliable. It usually leads to bargaining with operators and permanently hides any real knowledge of how much longer a job is taking than it really should.

What is the Need for Work Study?

Since work study or any kind of time study is still unknown in many factories and some industries, and is looked upon with suspicion by operators, it is pertinent to ask why it is required and why it is not more universally practised. The answer is in two parts. No one will deny the need to increase production per man-hour, now and always; only by so doing can we continually increase our standard of living. In order to do so, all wasteful, ineffective and unnecessary work or effort must be eliminated, and the only way to be sure of doing this is to study the work situation, establish the one best way, and standardise the method for future reference and training. Having established the work to be done and the way to do it, management must measure the amount of work involved. This measure is required for planning, and for control (see "Labour Cost Control", Part IV), and it can be used for payment by results. A measure which is a guess is no use for planning or control, a measure which is inaccurate is unfair to both operator and Company and leads to suspicion and distrust, and a measure which does not exclude ineffective work is uneconomic; and to get an accurate measure requires scientific work study.

This does not mean that economical production is impossible without work study or that work study or any kind of time study is a cure-all for inefficiency. Nothing is more effective than high morale; and small units can be, and frequently are, more efficient, because they are more personal than big concerns, have a higher morale, and because all workers in them, from the manager down, feel a personal interest in their success. On the other hand, work study does not produce goods; it provides information and reveals inefficiency, but operators must still produce and management manage. The most modern tools and methods will not avail under poor management and low morale.

It will be noticed that we said work study *can* be used for payment. by results. Payment by results is impossible without some kind of work study and unsatisfactory without scientific work study, but the absence of piecework or other form of payment by results does not mean that work study is not required. If anything, it is then even more necessary. The mere measurement of production and work done, and publication of the results, has a beneficial effect on daywork shops, and anyway some form of planning and control is essential. It is always essential to improve and standardise methods and reduce ineffective and unnecessary work whatever the method of payment. But having obtained a reliable measurement of work, it might just as well be used for payment by results. Under good management a fair and equitable financial reward for work done is a powerful incentive to maintain a high output.

It is important to consider the operators' point of view and their reaction to work study; after all, they are the persons most affected, and without their co-operation, understanding and support it will not succeed as it should. There has been and still is a good deal of opposition to it, based mainly on the fear of consequent unemployment and the reputation gained by the early efforts of "efficiency experts" who rode roughshod over workers' feelings and over unions, without the elementary courtesy of explaining fully to the persons most affected what it all meant and what was its purpose. The operator stands to gain appreciably from the sympathetic application of work study. In the first place it reveals where unnecessary effort is being used and where operating conditions are unsatisfactory. It is also a measure of protection to operators on piecework or other method of payment by results, because, in obtaining a fair and accurate measure of the work to be done and laying down the method, conditions and standards to be maintained, it:

(1) Ensures equality of reward for the same skill and effort, whatever the job;
(2) Ensures that adequate time is allowed for relaxation and all personal needs;
(3) Establishes a standard price or rate for a job which cannot then be cut;
(4) Avoids delays and the consequent frustration and loss of earnings.

It is sometimes thought that the main or only object of work study or rate-fixing is to increase output or operator performance, but this is not true. Actually, performance and output can be improved by—

(1) Improving conditions, methods, tools, or layout;
(2) Eliminating ineffective work and movements;
(3) Ensuring better balance between operators, groups, or machines;
(4) Better services (labouring, etc.);
(5) Ensuring a steady flow of material and jobs to do (planning).

None of these items calls for more effort from the operator; they do call for a good deal more attention and effort from managements. It is along these lines that any substantial increase in output can be obtained.

Technique of Work Study

The only sound and reliable approach to work study is on a basis of scientific method, but always with the full realisation that it is a scientific study of human beings and not of inanimate machines or chemical actions which is being undertaken.

The scientific method is a logical process of:

Observation—involving diagnosis of situation and getting the facts;
Action—translating theory or recommendations into action;
Control—checking the results.

Applied to work study, this means a study of the work being done on the job, recording all relevant details of materials, method, operation and variations; an analysis of the records and comparisons with other studies to derive a standard method and a standard measurement; and finally trial runs with any changes considered necessary and a check study.

There are two distinct, though interrelated, objects of work study:
To establish the one best way of doing a job;
To establish the standard time for doing it.

Neglect to give due attention to the first object and the unscientific methods so frequently adopted to attain the second are a cause of much disappointment, inaccurate work and disputes with operators over rates. All too often men are appointed solely to fix a time or rate for a job straight from the machine or bench, without any training and little knowledge of the subject and given the title rate-fixers or time-study men. With some knowledge of the processes (this is wrongly considered essential) they go on to the job, make sure that it is being done correctly in their estimation, and proceed to record the time for doing the job half a dozen or so times. An attempt is usually made to find an average operator (though none exists in this context) or a skilled one. A floor-to-floor time being found, an allowance (the same for all jobs and often too little) is made for fatigue and incidental delays, and a time or rate for the job fixed. This is not work or time study; it may be rate-fixing. It usually gives rise to bargaining with operators so that a rate is first fixed which is known to be low, and when the operators claim a rate known to be high, a compromise somewhere near normal is accepted. This procedure misses altogether the real value of work study, which is the improvement of existing methods and the revelation of where and how management can reduce delays and unnecessary effort.

Work study is carried out in two broadly different circumstances:

(1) When information is required for one particular job. This may be to find the standard time for a job already being performed correctly or to try to improve a job under continuous production.

(2) When data is required from which process layouts and standard times can be determined synthetically for new jobs before they commence.

In the first case it is necessary to analyse the operations being done in fair detail and to consider whether methods, materials, tools, equipment and working conditions need to be changed. If it is a job in continuous production, the usual case in mass production and process factories, it obviously warrants a most careful and detailed study and may justify motion study. Motion study is unlikely to be justified if the operation or process is likely to be changed within a known period. The first thing to do is to find out or agree with the foreman and inspector what the operation is intended to do, what standard is required, and whether the operator is working correctly. A detailed list of all operations performed is then made, noting anything doubtful and requiring further investigation or modification. Special attention must be paid to such things as material-handling methods, convenience of tools, arrangement of work-bench, supply of material and its condition, comfort and stance of operator. It is usual to use a standard printed form or study sheet to suit the particular factory and the type of work being done in it. For preliminary analysis of repetitive operations Flow Process Charts are especially useful. By using symbols to designate different elements such as operation, inspection, transport or move, storage or lay by, and delay or ineffective work, rapid analysis is facilitated, the frequency of each type of element, the disproportionate time spent on carrying on ineffective work and so on being shown up diagrammatically.[1]

The study or process chart is then analysed and further investiga-

---

[1] Examples and a more detailed description of analysis work are given by R. L. Morrow in his book *Time Study and Motion Economy*, published by Ronald Press, and also in *Operation Analysis*, by Maynard and Stegmerten (publishers McGraw-Hill).

tions made of points noted at the time the study was made. Finally, a process layout or specification is built up for the best and therefore correct way of doing the job, laying down in as much detail as is necessary for the particular job, methods, tools, inspection, standards and so on. Before this is issued as a standard specification or instruction, it should be tried out and proved, to the satisfaction, not only of the study man, but also of the foreman and inspector.

This process layout or standard specification is a most vital and valuable product of work study, becoming as it does a standard of reference in all cases of query or doubt at a later date. This is especially important when it is suddenly realised that standards of performance or quality of the product have fallen, or piecework earnings slump or become inflated. In such cases, it is found, on checking current practice against the original standard specification or process layout, that something is different. Methods should be either brought back into line, or the specification modified (and if necessary the standard time). The point is that there is a standard of reference which avoids all argument and reliance on memory.

When data is required in order to be able to build up in advance (i.e. synthetically) process layouts and standard times for all jobs, as in general engineering, printing, and other batch type of production, individual jobs are not studied with the sole aim of improving that particular job. Instead, a complete study is made of the department, section, or machine over many jobs in order to establish—

What operations are used from time to time and the best method of doing them;

The standard time for each operation and elements of operations;

Machines, tools, or equipment available or required and their limitations;

Incidental operations and their frequency;

What service work is required and who does it.

The standard time or rate for a job can then be built up synthetically by adding together the times for all elements of operation in the job.

When scientific work study is first undertaken in a department, even one apparently well run, it often involves a re-layout of the department, the provision of more suitable equipment, particularly portable tools, trays, holding devices, etc., the standardisation of tools or reorganisation of planning or services. When jobs do not run continuously, detailed motion study is seldom called for. Instead, investigation is directed towards finding the best of the several ways (which are invariably found) of doing the same operation and getting this established as standard practice. As in the first case an agreed process layout or specification is finally built up to which all work must adhere. As each new job is considered preparatory to production, a process layout and, if necessary, a detailed operation layout is prepared for it.

No.	OPERATION	STATION	TRAVEL	CUTS	FEED	R.P.M.	JIGS AND TOOLS
1	Chuck feed to stop & true	T1					3 jaw chuck & stop
2	Rough & finish face	RP	.64	2	H80 H120	750	H81
3	Rough bore for 1½"gas	T2	.75	1	A80	465	FS cutter
4	Finish ditto	T3	.87	1	H120	"	E91
5	Chamfer for tap	T4	.14	1	"	"	FS cutter
6	Tap 1½"	T5	.87			74	1½"taper gas tap NH STD

OPERATION LAYOUT

LAYOUT No. 1   OPERATION No. 2   PART Body   No. XXXX

DRG. No.	MATERIAL	BATCH QY	DEPT.	M/C OR GROUP	GRADE OF LABOUR	OPERATION
1072/1	GM CSTG		CAPST	1	MF2	Bore, face & tap

GAUGING PROCEDURE

DETAIL	GAUGE	FREQU.
1½"thrd	1½"taper gas M:	1/10

NOTE: Spigot in chuck to suit bore in 1st end to prevent crushing.

AUTHORISED   30-8-45   DATE

PREPARED BY   DATE 30-8-45

TIME ALLOWED
SET-UP 2.00   PER 100 5.85
HOURS   HOURS

Fig. 9.

A typical example of a detailed operation layout for machine work in an engineering factory in a very suitable form for issue to the shops is shown in Fig. 9, and a simple example of a process specification taken from engineering is given on page 217.

PROCESS SPECIFICATION
Welding Shop Operating—Profile Cutters

I. *Process*

This specification covers gas cutting in the Welding Department, procuring sheet metal (assisted by Service Operators), the disposal of all "off cuts" and scrap material, but not the disposal of waste and slag from the base of cutting machines.

II. *Operations*

1. Procure raw material sheet (assisted by service operator) from stock area and position on profile cutting machine stand.
2. Procure template or jig from template maker.
3. Position template in such a way that material is cut in the most economical manner.
4. Trace round template, or template tracing, using the oxygen pressures and feeds specified in table.
5. Where possible, remove all slag during machine cutting period.
6. "Firsts off" must be passed by the inspector before all production runs commence.
7. Change bottles of Propane gas.
8. Dress work on grinder, removing all burrs or slag where possible.
9. Book "on" and "off" job.

III. *Standard Times*

The standard time (or allowed time) covers all operations included in this specification.

When for any reason additional operations appear to be necessary, it must immediately be reported to the foreman. If it is found that they are necessary, either the standard time must be adjusted, or an allowance will be granted by the time-study engineer. Additional time not normally required is to be recorded as excess. No allowance will be made for additional time not reported.

Operators are to book off a job *immediately* it is completed, and on to the next job (or waiting time) at the same time. Waiting time must be booked to the appropriate cause.

First offs, after each set-up or reset, are to be submitted by setter for an inspection for approval before commencing production. Operators are not to book on to production until job has been passed for production.

The natural tendency and up to a point one of the objects of work study is to simplify work and operations. There are dangers in pressing it too far, however, dangers to the operator's outlook, and a risk of going beyond the point of minimum overall cost. Simplification of method or operation reduces the work content of a job, and therefore the operator's interest in that job. The emotional disturbance induced may be very real and entirely negative any reduction in effort achieved. It may be possible to counteract these effects by continually making the operators aware of, and interested in, the significance of the job—and this is management's responsibility. A remedy which can be effective and economical is to switch operators about, or to get them to do several or all the operations, however simplified, on a part or product. Over simplification may also induce cramped or taut muscles; a variation of motions or a deliberate insertion of a fetching or waiting operation may prevent this.

One well-remembered case illustrates the danger of restricting output by over simplification. An article was assembled from several components, some of which formed small subassemblies. There were many different types and sizes of the article. In order to get the benefits of simplification, assembly was arranged along two sides of a conveyor belt, each operator doing one operation. Work study revealed that because the times required for individual operations varied with the size and type of article, there were always some operators who did not have to work as fast as others. The conveyor belt was taken out, each operator supplied with an individual bench and a complete set of tools, and set to do the whole assembly. Output per operator was actually more than doubled—and the operators were undoubtedly more interested and contented.

In work study the outlook and method of dealing with operators and foremen are important. A study man must preserve a completely open mind and start off with no assumptions. Nothing must be taken for granted. He must not only be observant, missing nothing, but also be critical, accepting nothing without query and confirmation. Normally he will accept the assurance and authority of the technical expert, but even then if still in doubt should insist on proof. At the same time he must be quite impartial in all issues and decisions and maintain a strict mental honesty in his own work. All improvements and modifications must be made through the foreman and operator, enlisting their unreserved interest and co-operation; such improvements must not be imposed as an order without the fullest opportunity for understanding and acceptance. To do this the study man must discuss his findings with both operator and foreman and invite their comments and suggestions. Old hands and skilled craftsmen do not, as a rule, believe that an outsider can suggest better ways of doing a job, or even be capable of knowing whether it is done correctly. They must be convinced that the ability to study work scientifically is a craft as skilled as their own—and that "the looker-on sees most of the game"—if he is skilled in observation.

Study men should be trained by qualified persons. This is particularly so if their work is to include, as it most certainly should, measurement of work. So much of the technique has been proved, learnt and formalised into a science that it is wasteful and unnecessary for a person taking up the work to start at the beginning, and learn by trial and error as the original workers in the field had to do. As it is usually necessary to train several persons at the same time and to undertake a general programme of study work in whole departments or works, it is strongly recommended that a first-class firm of management consultants be engaged—the training they give both study men and supervisors is well worth the fees incurred.

MEASUREMENT OF WORK

The Need for a Standard of Measurement of Work

In an engineering sense efficiency can be simply stated as the ratio of useful energy obtained to energy applied. We can all understand that. Put succinctly, that is what is really meant by efficiency of production, but the difficulty is to see the relationship between input and output of production, or to measure performance. Which brings us right to the heart of the problem of efficiency of production: how to measure performance.

There is usually some difficulty about measuring the comparative performance of several departments in a Company or different companies. If two factories are turning out the same product which is measured in tons or feet, then the overall cost per ton or per foot is a measure of performance which can be obtained readily and used for comparison. But how does one compare the costs or efficiency of two factories or departments making dissimilar products? Cost per ton or unit is no good. As between two different firms, only the percentage net profit is any measure, and that is affected by the type of market and selling costs which are not production costs. And between different departments in the same firm there would seem to be, at first sight, no measure of efficiency on a common and therefore comparable basis.

If, however, the amount of "effort" (or cost—material, labour and overhead services) which should have been used to make a given quantity of a product is known and also the amount actually used, then surely the correct amount as a proportion of the actual amount is a measure of performance or efficiency. It is in reality an efficiency formula again, output over input. The real value of output, in effort, hours or £ s. d., is the amount of cost which goes out of the factory or department in a useful form, i.e. it does not include all wastage and excess costs, avoidable, and of no benefit to customer or company. And input is the total of all effort and costs absorbed, including excess costs. What is required therefore to measure efficiency of production is—

(1) A measure of the amount of cost (material, labour and on-cost) which should be used per unit (the standard);

(2) A measure of the excess over standard.

Engineers have defined a unit for work done by machines; it is horse-power, usually written h.p., and is the power expended when working at the rate of 550 foot-pounds per second (i.e. 550 lb. through 1 foot per second). No such precise definition of the amount of work which can be done by man, even an "average" man, is possible. Nevertheless, it is obvious that some measurement of the amount of work in a job, under known circumstances, is essential.

Furthermore, quite apart from the question of total and relative costs, it is obviously necessary for a foreman to be able to judge objectively and fairly the relative performance of his operators and for higher management to be able to compare the performance of departments, in terms of effort and the utilisation of man-hours. It is even necessary for operators themselves to know the comparative results of their efforts; not always the most conscientious or most skilled operator makes the most effective use of his time. What is required again is a method of measuring work done in terms of a common and standard unit, a unit that does not depend on a foreman's opinion or the condition of equipment.

Again, it is essential to have some measure of the work content of a job in order to do any planning of production programmes. Those who have endeavoured to plan production with only the roughest of estimates of what work is involved, fully appreciate the impossibility of doing so satisfactorily.

Finally, the value as an incentive of payment by results, i.e. payment according to the work done or effort put in, is generally accepted. This raises again the problem of what is a fair day's work, and it has been shown earlier that one of the objects of work study is to obtain a standard measurement of the amount of work in a job. The old rate-fixing assessment was unsatisfactory, for it failed to take into account the following factors:

(1) The skill and experience of the operator;
(2) The speed, effort and attention during the observed performance;
(3) The strain on the operator and the specific fatigue involved;
(4) The results of a critical analysis of each element of the operation.

An accurate unit of work must allow for all these factors; the first two are dealt with by a rating factor, the third by a relaxation allowance, and the fourth by work study.

There are therefore four purposes for which some unit of measurement of the work content of a job is essential, they are:

Cost control;
Assessment and comparison of performance;
Production planning;
Payment for results.

In each case the results cannot be more accurate than the unit of measurement used. And as time is a factor common to all four purposes, it is obviously desirable to use a unit based on time, and this is done by expressing the work content of a job in terms of the time required to do it in "standard units".

Where the same article is being produced repeatedly, the work done is frequently calculated as "so many per hour", but this may be reversed to read "time to produce one or 100". If, then, the "time to produce" any article or to do any job of work is measured in terms of a common unit, we have a measurement of work which can be used for production control, planning, costing, payment, measurement of performance, comparisons and so on.

Units of Work

In measuring work in terms of time, it is to be remembered that there are three ways in which time may be spent when doing a job of work:

(1) *Effective.*—Time spent effectively doing the job required.
(2) *Ineffective.*—Time spent in doing things not essential to the task.
(3) *Relaxation.*—Time spent in resting and other forms of relaxation in order to be able to maintain a steady rate of effective work.

Any unit of work must include items (1) and (3), but not item (2). The unit used is defined as the amount of work performed in one minute at a standard rate of working, including time for relaxation. This unit involves a definition of a standard rate of working. A standard rate of working is taken to mean the normal or moderate rate which can be kept up without undue fatigue by an average qualified operator working well within his or her capacity. In industry this is roughly equivalent to normal "daywork" rate. Long investigation and study has revealed that in normal industrial conditions a person can put in such extra effort for continuous periods as will produce one-third more work, i.e. work at a rate one-third faster than at normal day-work rate.

From this definition it will be seen that at a standard rate of working a person can be said to produce 60 units of work in one hour, and this is taken as the basis for rating speed, effort, skill and attention during the time-study investigations, and is referred to as a "60 rating".

Any other base figure for units per hour could be used, and is used in some cases. For example, 100 units per hour can be taken as standard. It so happens that there are 60 minutes in an hour, and this was adopted by the early workers in the field and is now in common use. Much confusion exists as to what is a normal daywork rate of working and it is important to get the issue clear. It is difficult to illustrate it to inexperienced observers, but trained observers get to recognise it quite clearly and keep their standard absolute for all practical purposes. Perhaps the simplest way to illustrate it is to imagine a person walking (a person of normal physique of course and not deformed or crippled in any way). If walking at 3 miles per hour over level ground, as one would when out for a stroll, but not dawdling, is taken to be roughly equivalent to a 60 (or standard) rating, then a brisk speed, 4 miles per hour, at which one would walk when getting to one's destination on time would be equivalent to an 80 rating, and loitering, e.g. taking in the scenes of the country, usually averaging 2 miles per hour, equivalent to a 40 rating.

When practically no effort is involved, e.g. tying knots in thread or wrapping very light articles in paper, a rating of 90 coincides with the blur point, when it becomes practically impossible to distinguish with the eye the separate movements of fingers and hands.

Ratings as low as 20 or as high as 120 may occasionally be seen, but the times to which they apply should be treated with suspicion and if possible ignored. Generally, it is unnecessary to use times with ratings outside the limits of 50 and 100; there is usually something wrong if the rating is low and it should be corrected.

Recognition of the skill factor is perhaps the most difficult. Long experience and close association with trained observers are essential before reliability can be acquired. The learner always tends to underrate the highly skilled and overrate the unskilled operator, as he will at the beginning with speed and effort.

The standard rate of working assumes that a person, by taking the necessary rest or relaxation, is able to keep it up indefinitely over the normal working day. This means that the unit of work must include time for personal needs and relaxation. Experience and study have given us reliable information on the relaxation required under different conditions. It is a good deal more than is generally recognised, and may be as high as 50 per cent., or even 100 per cent. of working time in extreme cases, although when these figures are required it is obviously a case for improving conditions and reducing the effort and hence the fatigue involved.

Criticism is sometimes levelled at the use of relaxation allowances because so little is known about the subject. Certainly there is need for more information on industrial fatigue, but in practice the

relaxation allowances given later have been found to give satisfactory results and in normal circumstances involve no serious errors.
Very abnormal conditions should be improved if possible, and if
not, special studies should be made to obtain data specific to those
conditions.

Finally, in order that the measure of work shall apply to conditions
in the shop where the work is being done, it is almost always necessary to add an allowance to cover incidental delays which do occur
even in the best-run factories. These delays are least in continuous
process work and on automatic machinery, but in general vary from
2½ per cent. to 10 per cent. Only study on the shop floor can determine an appropriate and adequate figure. Morrow, in his *Time Study
and Motion Economy*, discusses in detail methods for finding the
correct allowance required.

Technique of Measurement—Tools

The tools required for making a time study are few, and unless
micro-motion technique is to be employed, are quite simple, they are:

(1) *Pencil and Paper.*—Preferably a standard printed form or study sheet
is used, designed to suit the kind of study and work being observed.
On this sheet a complete record of operations and times is made for
one or several complete cycles of operations.
(2) *Timepiece.*—A stop-watch is most convenient but is not essential.
In some cases an ordinary pocket or wrist-watch is quite sufficient.
In extreme cases, when the use of a stop-watch is for some reason
objected to by the operators, it can be dispensed with and the technique of counting substituted.
(3) *Study Board.*—This is preferably of plywood, or other stiff material,
and arranged with a clip to hold the study sheet, and a pocket or clip
for the watch.
(4) Cine camera, or similar special equipment, for micro-motion study
work.

A specially printed form should be used for recording a time study.
A suitable form is shown in Fig. 11 (see page 230). On the reverse
of the sheet an adequate description and details of the operation and
notes should be recorded. Referring to Fig. 11, ratings are entered in
the column headed R, the time at the end of each element in the
column headed T, and later, the elapsed time calculated by deducting
each time from the subsequent one, entered under E, as shown.
As there is a column for running times, an ordinary watch can be
used; if a fly-back stop-watch is preferred and always used, two
columns only are required. Several types of stop-watch are in use,
with the following variations: one hand, split hands, single knob or

knob and slide for operating; minutes and seconds, minutes in decimals, or hours in decimals, calibration and so on. Either can be used and are equally effective when experience has been gained on the particular type and its operation has become completely automatic (in the same way that instantaneous operation of motor-car controls becomes automatic to a driver). It is claimed that the two-hand type (one hand can be stopped whilst the other continues) gives an observer more time to note the time. An observer, however, must be trained to note the time instantaneously, for it is essential when small elements are being timed, and studies involving such elements are frequently met with. The decimal division type (one revolution for one minute, reading to 0·01 minute) facilitates calculations from observed times.

For micro-motion study work special camera equipment incorporating a timing device is used. It requires expert observers to use and analyse its results, and because of the expense and the rather elaborate arrangements which have to be made, its use is generally limited to laboratory work, detail assembly and similar work in continuous production. An electric counter, called the Wink-counter, which enables slightly shorter elements to be recorded, has been used in the U.S.A.

Techniques of Measurement—Rating

The actual elapsed time for an operation or job of work can be recorded accurately, since a watch is an accurate instrument of measurement. But this observed actual time must be converted to "standard" time, i.e. the time at a "standard rate" of working. As shown above, this is done by "rating" the observed time and "levelling" or converting the time to standard by multiplying by the observed "rating" and dividing by the standard rating (usually 60).

It will be obvious that the accuracy and effectiveness of work measurement depend on the reliability of the technique of rating. Rating is affected by the time-study engineer's

(1) Concept of normal performance.
(2) Ability to rate consistently the same performance at different occasions and by different operators.
(3) Ability to consistently detect and rate proportionate changes in performance (i.e. different ratings).
(4) Discrimination in selecting the "normal" time from several observed times.

To attain and maintain accuracy and consistency on all these counts, not only are training and experience essential but also the continuous, conscientious analysis and criticism of one's consistency of rating. A simple and effective method of doing this has been developed by D. J. Desmond, M.Sc. (for his theory and detailed explanation see *Engineering* for October 20th, 1950).

In Desmond's method, actual observed times are plotted against the "Reciprate" (reciprocal of rating). When the times for several observations of an operation or element are so plotted a mean or average line can be drawn through them so that the scatter about this line is at a minimum. This is called the Study line. A similar line drawn from the origin through the points so that the scatter of the points about the line is a minimum is called the Operation line. The time corresponding to the point where the operation line intersects the normal rating (60) is the normal time for the operation. See Fig. 10 which illustrates the observed times plotted as above for the example of a study given on page 232 and Fig. 11.

In a perfect study all points would lie on the operation line and both operation line and study line would coincide. If the study line does not coincide with the operation line it indicates an inability to appreciate accurately proportionate changes in rating. The "Flatness" (of rating) is the amount by which the rate of slope of study line to slope of operation line is less than unity $\left(\dfrac{OA}{OB}\right)$. If studies so plotted always show a degree of flatness, the study engineer's estimate of normal time is incorrect as indicated by the intersection of the study line and operation line in relation to normal rating. The graph also shows at which ratings the study engineer is most in error. By regularly plotting studies in this way, study men can keep their measure of performance (rating) in line with "standard"; the normal tendency to flatness can be corrected and inconsistency between studies and between engineers minimised.

Techniques of Measurement—Making the Study

When making a work study it is usual to include observations of times taken, since, if the times are not wanted for measurement, they are required for analysis purpose. It is not possible here to describe in detail the exact procedure to be followed in all the various kinds of work met with in industry, but the following is a general outline of the procedure which is satisfactory in all but exceptional cases; it can be varied when particular problems are met with:

(1) Put the operator at ease.

It is obviously necessary to observe the work being done under normal circumstances; the circumstances are not normal unless an operator is working entirely at ease. It is therefore important to explain to the operator as much as is necessary of what is required of him, or of what is being done. For the first study in a department this is especially important, later on it is not so necessary. It is essential to tell the operator that he is being studied and advisable for the study man to stand where he can be seen by the operator, and not behind his back. Nothing is more certain to put the operator on edge

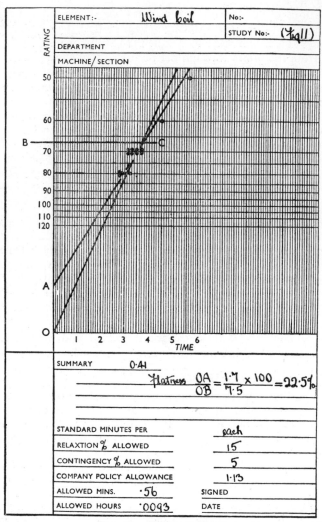

FIG. 10.—Reciprate Graph.

than to know he is being watched from behind. It is also advisable to ask the operator to carry on at his or her normal pace, neither speeding up nor slackening off, and making no especial efforts because an observer is present.

(2) Note all particulars of a job—brief description, conditions, inspection standards and so on. In machine-shop work it may be necessary to make a note of the machine, part number and even a description of the part. The nature and extent of the particulars will depend on the kind of study and the work being performed.

(3) List all operations in the sequence in which they are being performed. It may be necessary to run through the cycle two or three times in order to be quite sure that operations are being performed in the same sequence and none is omitted. It is at this stage, before any times are taken, that it may be found necessary to recommend immediate improvements in method, and this should be done if records taken would otherwise be wasted.

(4) Record the time taken and the rating for each operation as it is performed. An example of the records made is shown in Fig. 11. It is important to make a mental note of the rating for each element of time recorded during the time the element is being performed, and to record the rating before recording the time for the element. It is also important to be able to recognise accurately a break point between elements of operations so that each repetition of an element is strictly comparable. (This is absolutely vital when the records are to be used for synthetically built standard times.) It is this process of recording times and ratings that requires skilled training, and no records should be used until an observer is fully qualified and his records reliable.

In machine operations, elements of time which are entirely automatic or machine controlled are given a normal rating (e.g. 80); it is assumed that a machine maintains a normal "piecework" rate, and time so rated yields a normal piecework bonus for payment by results.

(5) Rating. The rating for each observed time must take account of the four factors—speed, attention, effort and skill. As compared with an element which is so simple as to require negligible skill, effort, or attention, e.g. folding letters or circulars, an operation which is performed in exactly the same time, but requires effort in addition, would be rated higher and so on. It requires concentrated and prolonged experience to enable an observer to take account of all factors and assess a correct rating almost instantaneously as is required for short elements of time.

(6) Record all time spent during the study and how it is spent, indicating any ineffective time. In order to be able to check that no time has been missed, it is advisable to make a note of when a study starts and when it ends. The continuous running method of recording time used in the illustration, instead of the method of noting the elapsed time by stopping the watch for each element, takes care of this point. It is important to record *all* ineffective time from whatever cause and however small—it may be required later during analysis. The observer must be quite clear as to what is ineffective time. Waiting time and inattention of the operator, talking, smoking and so on

are obvious, but wrong ways of doing an operation are not always so obvious, but may be just as ineffective.

(7) Record the times for a number of complete cycles. It is unsatisfactory to rely on one observation of a cycle of operations for a job. The number of complete cycles of an operation which need to be observed depends on the nature of the job and the information required from the study, and only experience of the particular circumstances can be any guide. With a trained study-man, the accuracy of the results of the normalised ratings for an element is not appreciably increased by taking more than nine or ten observations.

(8) Convert each recorded time into a standard time, and calculate and select the standard time for each operation. This is dealt with later under "Analysing and Working up the Study".

Thereafter, the procedure followed will depend on the use to be made of the information obtained. If a standard time is required for the job which is being studied, and it is considered the job is being done correctly, then the standard time is worked up immediately from the study. If it is thought that improvements can be made, the study is analysed to see whether improvements might be possible, and if any potential ones are revealed, arrangements are made with the foreman for them to be tried out, and further ones made until a satisfactory method is evolved. When improvements have been made, a check study should be made before the standard time is finally established for the job. If standard times are required for all operations, or elements of an operation, likely to be used in future jobs, as is frequently the case in batch production and general workshop practice as distinct from process work and mass production, then the times obtained for each operation must be tabulated and later analysed, selected and recorded for future use. The method of using such records for synthetic times is explained on page 239.

Examples of actual studies are given in Figs. 11, 12 and 13, and they will be used for explaining how to work up a study. The description of elements and figures are in type; in actual use they would be written in, of course.

Fig. 11 is of an operation consisting entirely of manipulative elements: 16 cycles were recorded and, as so often happens, the observer, who was not very experienced at the time, missed three elements in cycle 11 and one in cycle 13. No ineffective time occurred during this study and the operator worked fairly consistently.

Fig. 12 is an operation consisting of three elements not performed as a cycle, the first preparing sufficient material for a short run, the second operating the machine at a speed entirely controlled by the operator, and the third emptying the container of completed work periodically.

Fig. 13 is an operation on a machine involving a cycle of opera-tions, some purely manipulative and others (for which no ratings are entered) entirely controlled by the machine. In the first cycle the observer evidently made an error in reading the time at the break point between two operations, and these two readings would not be used. In the second cycle the rating for the last but one element is doubtful and would also not be used. In the fifth cycle the item marked D includes ineffective time due to the operator, and would not be used; similarly, the elements marked E and F in the sixth and seventh cycles would not be used, as they are not normal, and such occurrences would be covered by the contingency allowance. (They are noted, as the extent and frequency of occurrence of such contingencies may need to be assessed.) The observer has noted that the last but one element "check" could be done during a machining element. It will be noted that the total elapsed time checks that all time has been accounted for.

Working up the Study

Briefly stated, this consists of calculating the standard time for each element of an operation, making due allowance for relaxation and contingencies, and either—

(a) Adding together the standard times of each element of the operation to find the total standard time for the operation; or
(b) Recording the results for building up synthetic times of whole operations in the future.

There are, however, three distinct steps:

(1) For each element each observed time is converted to standard minutes and an average figure for all observations calculated or selected.
(2) This average figure is increased by an allowance for relaxation.
(3) The resulting figure is, if necessary, further increased by an allow-ance for contingencies. Usually this contingency allowance is added for the whole operation or job and not for each element.

Conversion to Standard.—To obtain the time at a standard rate of working, an actual observed time is multiplied by its rating and divided by 60, thus: if the actual time for an element is 0·6 minute, and the rating 80, then the time at standard rate is:

$$\frac{0{\cdot}6 \times 80}{60} = 0{\cdot}8 \text{ standard min.}$$

This calculation is made for each recorded time of an element, and the average, minimum selected, or commonest time of the results is

WORK STUDY SHEET (Fig. 11)

Element	R	T	E	R	T	E	R	T	E	R	T	E	R	T	E	R	T	E	R	T	E	R	T	E
Attach wire	80	·09	·09	80	·86	·08	80	4·00	·10	80	·70	·10	80	·60	·10	75	·43	·10	80	·20	·10	80	13·06	·08
Wind coil	80	·40	·31	50	2·42	·56	60	·32	·32	70	6·15	·45	70	·93	·33	80	·75	·32	80	·57	·37	80	·34	·28
Hammer coil	80	·49	·09	80	·46	·04	80	·41	·09	80	·24	·09	80	8·00	·07	80	·81	·06	80	·63	·06	80	·43	·09
Tie coil, 2 places	70	·80	·31	80	·80	·34	80	·70	·29	80	·52	·28	70	·35	·35	80	10·16	·35	70	12·00	·37	70	·77	·34
Half turn and cut	80	·89	·09	80	·89	·11	80	·81	·11	80	·61	·09	70	·45	·10	80	·21	·05	80	·10	·10	80	·87	·10
Hammer coil	80	·98	·09	80	3·00	·11	80	·90	·09	80	·69	·08	80	·54	·09	80	·29	·08	80	·16	·06	80	·95	·08
Tie coil, 2 places	80	1·38	·40	70	·40	·40	70	5·25	·35	70	7·08	·39	75	·95	·41	70	·75	·46	60	·55	·39	60	14·43	·48
Form, unload and reset	70	·78	·40	80	·90	·50	80	·60	·35	70	·50	·42	70	9·33	·38	80	11·10	·35	70	·98	·43	70	·87	·44
Attach wire	80	·96	·09	80	·97	·09	80	·66	·13	80	·50	·10				70	·32	·12	80	·22	·12	80	·98	·10
Wind coil	80	·25	·29	80	17·25	·28	70	·98	·32	70	·85	·35	40	·85		70	·65	·33	70	·57	·35	70	28·35	·37
Hammer coil	80	15·30	·05	80	·30	·05	80	19·05	·07	80	·90	·05	80	·90	·05	80	·70	·05	75	·62	·05	80	·42	·07
Tie coil, 2 places	80	·67	·37	75	·70	·40	80	·45	·40	80	21·30	·40	80	23·20	·30	75	25·05	·35	80	·97	·10	75	·75	·33
Half turn and cut	80	·76	·09	80	·80	·10	80	·58	·13	80	·39	·09	80	·30	·10	80	·20	·15	80	27·07	·10	80	·83	·08
Hammer coil	80	·86	·10	80	·86	·06		·58	·13	80	·46	·17	80	·39	·09	80	·29	·09	80	·14	·07	80	·92	·09
Tie, 2 places	75	·34	·34	70	18·25	·29	70	20·00	·42	80	·79	·33	80	·72	·33	80	·63	·34	60	·50	·36	60	29·50	·58
Form, unload and reset	60	·88	·68	80	·53	·28	70	·40	·40	75	22·14	·35	70	24·20	·48	70	26·10	·47	80	·88	·38	80	·85	·35

WORK STUDY SHEET (Fig. 12)

Element	R	T	E	R	T	E	R	T	E	R	T	E	R	T	E
A. Wipe down, 20 strips	80	—	1·4	80	—	1·3	80	—	1·3						
B. Feed strips, blank 7 and discard waste		(See below)													
C. Empty container	80	·25	·25	80	·25	·25	80	·3	·3						
B:—		(140)			(138)			(142)							
	80	·20	·20	80	·34	·20	80	·73	·22	80	·90	·18	80	·28	·24
	90	·37	·17	90	·57	·23	90	·95	·22	100	7·07	·17	100	9·45	·17
	90	·57	·20	90	·83	·26	90	5·15	·20	90	·25	·18			
	90	·80	·23	100	3·03	·20	100	·33	·18	80	·49	·24			
	85	1·00													

230

WORK STUDY SHEET (Fig. 13)

R	T	E	R	T	E	R	T	E	R	T	E
95	·60	·18	80	·83	·24	90	6·10	·20	90	·32	·21
95	·74	·14	80	4·10	·27	90	·30	·26	80	·58	·26
80	·97	·23	90	·29	·19	100	·47	·17	80	·86	·28
90	2·14	·17	80	·51	·22	80	·72	·25	90	9·04	·18

Element	R	T	E	R	T	E	R	T	E	R	T	E	R	T	E	R	T	E	R	T	E	R	T	E
Load and start machine	80	·13	·13	60	3·49	·17	80	·78	·18	80	·95	·14	90	13·44	·11	80	17·02	·29	80	·23	·13	80	·34	·14
Box up and lock	70	·35	·22	80	3·68	·19	90	·98	·20	90	10·12	·17	80	·63	·19	60	·21	·19	80	·48	·25	80	·54	·20
Face inside	—	·68	·33	—	4·03	·35	—	7·33	·35	—	·45	·33	—	·95	·32	—	·57	·36	—	·61	·33	—	·89	·35
Form vee	90	·91	·23	—	·25	·22	—	·65	—	—	·70	·25	—	14·21	·26	—	·79	·22	—	·84	·23	—	25·10	·21
Box away	90	·98	·07	90	·32	·07	70	·76	·11	80	·80	·10	90	·29	·08	80	·85	·06				70	·21	·11
Index, turret and up	80	1·09	·11	90	·42	·10	40	8·49	·73	80	·99	·19	80	·39	·10	80	·96	·11	80	21·02	1·73	70	·35	·14
Bore and turn, outside dia.	80	1·83	·74	—	5·20	·78	60	·63	·14	80	11·74	·75	80	15·03	·74	80	18·13	·77	—	22·75	·13	80	26·15	·80
Turret back, index and up	70	2·01	·18	80	·36	·16	60	·68	·05	80	·95	·21	80	·19	·16	90	·16	·07	80	·88	·13	—	·32	·17
Centralise reamer	70	2·09	·08	80	·43	·07	—	9·09	·41	80	12·04	·09	80	·44	·25	70	·07	·43	80	·96	·08	80	·40	·08
Ream	—	·51	·42	—	·86	·43	60	·19	·10	70	·47	·43	90	·90	·46	80	19·39	·43	80	23·44	·48	80	·82	·42
Turret back and index	80	·64	·13	80	6·05	·09	70	·26	·09	90	·61	·14	90	16·02	·12	80	·47	·08	80	·54	·10	80	·93	·11
Tool box away	90	·68	·04	70	·30	·25	60	·49	·23	90	·70	·09	90	·18	·16	80	·54	·07	80	·62	·08	80	27·11	·08
Remove burr	80	·90	·22	70	·52	·22	85	·74	·25	60	13·00	·30	80	·40	·22	90	·78	·24	80	·93	·31	80	·34	·23
Check (A)	60	3·23	·33	85	6·60	·08	85	9·81	·07	80	·25	·25	80	·66	·26	90	20·03	·25	90	24·12	·19	90	·54	·20
Stop machine and unload	70	3·32	·09							80	13·33	·08	85	16·73	·07	80	20·10	·07	80	24·20	·08	80	27·61	·07
Check complete																						80	28·02	·41

B   C   D   E   F

Commenced 10.22
Completed 10.50
Elapsed 28 mins. (which checks up)

Notes: **A** This operation should be done during next operation.
      B ? break point correct.
      C Faulty rating.
      D Includes some ineffective time.
      E Work reset in chuck (covered by contingency).
      F Overhead tool reset (covered by contingency).

231

calculated or selected. Under normal circumstances the average, after rejecting doubtful or obviously incorrect times, is satisfactory, but if ratings are not dead accurate, the mean calculated time is better. In practice, calculating work is reduced by taking all recordings of the same rating together, or still further by averaging all times and all ratings. The former method is to be preferred in the early stages of training, and occasionally thereafter in order that the consistency of the observers' rating can be checked. For example, taking the second element, wind coil, in Fig. 11, the calculations would be set out thus:

Rating	Times	Total	At Std.	Std. for element
50	·56	·56	·47	·47
60	·45	·45	·45	·45
70	·32, ·33, ·37, ·32, ·35, ·37, ·35, ·33	2·74	3·20	·40
80	·31, ·32, ·28, ·29, ·28	1·48	1·98	·39
	Total for 15 observations	5·23	6·10	

6·10 ÷ 15 is an average of ·407 standard min.,
or approximately ·41 standard min.

The quicker though more approximate method is:

Total of all times 5·23 mins. for 15 observations
Average 0·348 min.

Ratings 1 at 50 =   50
1 at 60 =   60
8 at 70 = 560
5 at 80 = 400
           1,070 for 15.

An average of 71·3

0·35 min. at 71 rating = $0.35 \times \dfrac{71}{60}$

= ·414 std. min.
or approximately ·41 min.

A study of the first method will show that the most nearly accurate time at standard would be ·40. Had all the ratings been dead accurate, there would be no discrepancy whichever way the average was calculated. It also shows the tendency in the early days of training for time-study men to overrate low effort or skill and to underrate high effort or skill. Working out each element as shown in the first method above brings this to light, and helps the study man to get his rating accurate. It is also possible to select the more nearly correct time.

A still better way of maintaining accuracy and consistency of rating is to use the form shown in Fig. 10 for determining the normal or standard time for operations or elements. It will be seen that the operation line in Fig. 10 cuts the standard rating (60) at a time ·41 min. which the above calculations gave.

Relaxation.—The time so calculated is the time which would be taken for that one element at a standard rate of working. But this rate cannot be kept up all day long without some break and allowance therefore has to be made for relaxation, i.e. to compensate for fatigue and the time required for personal needs. This is done by adding a percentage allowance to all elements. For example, if an allowance of 15 per cent. is appropriate, the time for the above element becomes:

$$0{\cdot}41 \times \frac{15}{100}$$

or $0{\cdot}41 \times 1{\cdot}15 = {\cdot}472$ standard min.

When all elements of an operation are of the same type or involve the same effort, then the same relaxation allowance can be used for each different element, but in many cases certain elements of an operation require a higher relaxation allowance. For example, during an operation in a machine shop it might be necessary to lift a heavy casting of 50 lb. weight or more on to a machine, or in a warehouse to lift heavy parcels after packing on to a trolley or the floor, and the time for lifting would need to be increased by a far bigger relaxation allowance than for the other elements. Relaxation allowance therefore should be added to each element.

A good deal of thought and study has been given to the problem of industrial fatigue and the time required for relaxation to offset its effects and to enable a worker to maintain a steady output without permanent fatigue. In practice allowances between 10 per cent. and 20 per cent. are found to be satisfactory. In assessing relaxation there are five factors to consider:

(1) Whether the operation is sitting or standing.
(2) The weight of the thing moved, i.e. effort required.
(3) Concentration or attention required.
(4) Frequency of the cycle of operations.
(5) General conditions.

A basic allowance of 8 per cent. can be considered satisfactory in normal industrial conditions when the correct type of labour is doing the work sitting down and no physical effort, concentration, mono-tony, or trying conditions are involved. When the work has to be done standing up, then an extra 2 per cent. should be added, making 10 per cent. Obviously the heavier the article moved, whether it is tool or job, then the more the relaxation necessary to overcome fatigue. The following figures have been found satisfactory in practice. Above the weights given, arrangements should be made to do the lifting mechanically, but if this is impossible, as in some cases it is, an extra 1 per cent. relaxation per lb. weight above these figures should be added (and this includes the basic figure of 8 per cent.).

*Table of relaxation to be added to
basic figure of 8 per cent.*

Lb.	Male Per cent.	Female Per cent.
5	1	2
10	3	6
15	7	14
20	12	24
25	17	34
30	22	44
40	32	—
50	42	—

For concentration or especial attention, 2–5 per cent. should be added. Jobs calling for the maximum amount under this heading are those like careful inspection of process work or engraving. Occasionally the whole operation is of very small duration, sometimes of the order of 10 seconds. In these cases an allowance of between 2 and 5 per cent. is made to provide relaxation from monotony.

In spite of the recognition by sound management that trying conditions of temperature, dust and so on are unwise, nevertheless they cannot always be avoided. For example: loading ovens and attending to vats can rarely be done mechanically. An allowance of up to 10 per cent. (sometimes in extreme cases an even higher figure) is added in such cases.

As an indication of how total relaxation allowances are built up, the following examples are given:

Job	Basic	Weight	Con-centration	Fre-quency	Con-ditions	Total
Wrapping by hand (sitting) . .	8	—	—	2	—	10
Bench assembly, operating m/c.s etc. (standing) . .	10	—	2½	—	—	12½
Engraving (sitting) .	8	—	5	—	—	13
Attending to and filling a vat . .	10	2½	—	—	7½	20

Contingency Allowance.—When the total standard time for the whole operation has been calculated, it is usually necessary to add a contingency allowance. This entirely depends upon the conditions in the particular department, but if the figure would appear to be higher than 5 per cent., then there is obviously a large uncontrollable factor, and efforts should be made to improve the condition, since the incidence is likely to vary, and so therefore will the actual results and piecework earnings. In a machine shop, wear and tear of tools, and in a warehouse, queries with orders, are the kind of examples of contingencies which must be allowed for. Since they cannot be entirely prevented, it may be necessary to make prolonged studies in order to obtain a measure of the incidence of delays, and a figure should never be used without some such study.

Machine-controlled Elements.—Machining elements, that is elements or operations which are performed entirely automatically by a machine at a predetermined speed, are rated at "normal" i.e. an 80. This means, of course, that the machine is reckoned to be producing at exactly "piecework" speed. But the operator may only need to work for a portion of the machine cycle, and the standard time for the operator's work within the cycle may be less than the standard time for the cycle. The effective rating of the operation then cannot ever be as high as 80. For example, an operator working a machine producing an article, or completing an operation, in 3 minutes (or 20 per hour), and during this time having to do only 1·5 standard mins. of work, would be restricted to an effective rating of 1·5 × 20 = 30. The dilemma is whether to assess the work done as

$$3 \times \frac{80}{60} = 4 \text{ std. mins. or } 1\cdot5.$$

In some cases it may be possible to arrange for the operator to look after more than one machine, in the above case it could be two, but even then the rating would only be $2 \times 1\cdot5 \times 20 = 60$. Where this is not possible, it is usual to credit the operation with compensating time of either all or some portion of the difference between the effective work and standard mins. at the 80 rating. If the machine time is a small part of the total operation, that is, there is considerably more work outside the machine cycle, then the operator does not have time to take any real relaxation during the machine cycle, and the whole of the difference should be credited as compensating time. But if the machine cycle is a large proportion of the total time, then only a proportion of the time is credited, depending on the amount of relaxation which can be taken during the machine cycle instead of at some other time. In any case, operators on payment by results expect to be able to be paid for the whole time, and at a piecework rate if putting in a piecework effort whenever possible.

It is always advisable to record the amount of compensating time in a Standard Time in case it should later be found possible to utilise some of it; that there is any spare time may be disputed.

Typical Examples

The following is an example of how a Standard Time is calculated from a study using the study shown in Fig. 13.

Operation—Blanking size X main pole plates.

Element A.—Wipe down 20 strips (7 blanks per strip = 140 blanks)

Rating:—80   Time per strip.:—1·4, 1·3, 1·3

$$\text{Average} = \frac{4 \cdot 0}{3} \times \frac{80}{60} = 1 \cdot 78 \text{ S.M.s.}$$

$$\text{Time} = \frac{1 \cdot 78 \text{ S.M.s.} + 12\frac{1}{2} \text{ per cent. relaxation}}{20 \times 7} = \cdot 014 \text{ per blank.}$$

Element B.—Feed strip, blank, and place waste on floor.

Rating	Time per strip	Total time at Std.
80	·20, ·23, ·23, ·26, ·24, ·27, ·22, ·22, ·25, ·24, ·19, ·26, ·28, ·24	4·45
85	·20, ·22, ·20, ·20, ·23	1·49
90	·17, ·20, ·17, ·20, ·20, ·19, ·19, ·22, ·22, ·20, ·20, ·20, ·18, ·18, ·25, ·21, ·18	5·10
95	·18, ·18, ·18	0·86
100	·17, ·18, ·17, ·18, ·17, ·17, ·18, ·17	2·31
	(48 observations)	14·21

$$\text{Time} = \frac{14 \cdot 21}{48} + 12\frac{1}{2} \text{ per cent. relaxation} = \cdot 336 \text{ per strip.}$$

$$\text{or } \frac{\cdot 336}{7} = \cdot 048 \text{ per blank.}$$

(NOTE.—The recorded time 0·14 (Fig. 12) at a 90 rating has been discarded as doubtful.)

Element C.—Empty container (every 20 strips).

Rating:—80   Time per 20 strips:—·25, ·25, ·30

Average $= \dfrac{\cdot 80}{3} \times \dfrac{80}{60} = \cdot 354$ S.M.s for 140 blanks.

Time $= \dfrac{\cdot 354 + 15 \text{ per cent. relaxation}}{140} = \cdot 003$ per blank.

Total for operation $= \cdot 014 + \cdot 048 + \cdot 003 = \cdot 065$ per blank.
Add contingencies at 5 per cent. $= \cdot 0683$ or 6·83 per 100 blanks.

STANDARD TIME $= 6·83$ per 100.

Payment by Results or Piece-rates

Having arrived at a time for measurement of the work content of a job, it is obviously convenient to use the unit, i.e. time, for piecework rates and calculations. In this case the Standard Time becomes the Allowed Time. That is, an operator is allowed this time in which to do the job, at daywork rate of wages. Many methods have been evolved and used in the past for paying the operator a bonus increment on his daywork earnings for saving time, i.e. doing the job in less time than standard. Some encourage high effort by paying at a higher rate when the job is done faster than at piecework rate, whilst others, like the Rowan, by paying for a proportion of the time saved endeavour to minimise the effects of variations due to inaccurate measurement.

Such systems are largely academic today, and it is generally accepted that straight piecework, i.e. payment pro rata with work done, is the only fair and satisfactory basis of payment. It is understood and accepted by operators and Trade Unions.

For straight piecework payment therefore the operator is paid for doing the job in the Standard Time, however long it actually takes. Since operators like to think in terms of bonus earned above their flat rate, they are interested in the time saved, so that the total time they save on all jobs done in a week, expressed as a percentage of the time worked, is a measure of their performance commonly understood, and known, as the Percentage Bonus. For example, if an operator completes jobs for which, in total, 60 hours were allowed, by working at a steady piecework effort (an 80 rating) in $\times \dfrac{80}{60}$ $= 45$ hours in a week, then the time saved is 15 hours, and the bonus is—

$$\frac{15}{45} \times 100 = 33\tfrac{1}{3} \text{ per cent.}$$

The operator is paid for the whole of the 60 hours, but payment is usually shown thus (assuming for example that the hourly rate is 2s. per hour):

$$
\begin{array}{lrrr}
 & \text{£} & s. & d. \\
\text{Actual time, 45 hours} = & 4 & 10 & 0 \\
\text{Bonus time, 15 hours} = & 1 & 10 & 0 \\
\hline
\text{Total earnings} & \text{£6} & 0 & 0 \\
\hline\hline
\end{array}
$$

This is obviously 60 hours at 2s. per hour.

If it is desired to pay per piece (the original derivation of "piecework") instead of for time allowed, then the Standard Time (time allowed) is multiplied by the rate per hour. For the example worked out above, the piece-rate would be:

$$\frac{6 \cdot 83 \text{ mins.}}{60} \times 2s. = 2 \cdot 75, \text{ or } 2\tfrac{3}{4}d. \text{ each.}$$

It is to be noted that the number of pieces to be finished per hour at dayrate is 60 divided by the Standard Time in minutes, and at piecework rate this figure is multiplied by $\frac{80}{60}$. For example, if the Standard Time is 5 minutes then:

$$\text{Standard (or daywork) rate per hour} = \frac{60}{5} = 12 \text{ pieces per hour}$$

$$\text{and piecework rate per hour} = \frac{60}{5} \times \frac{80}{60} = 16 \text{ pieces per hour,}$$

which is one-third faster.

Finally it occasionally happens that for good and sufficient reasons it is desired to pay more than one-third of the daywork (or basic) rate extra for a piecework effort. (The most straightforward way of paying more for a piecework effort is obviously to increase the basic rate, but the many agreements between employers and operators have been reasons for avoiding this.) If this should be so, then the Standard Time is first calculated (and clearly retained in calculations and records) and then increased in the desired ratio to obtain the Allowed Time. If, for example, it is decided to pay 50 per cent. of the basic rate extra for a piecework effort (i.e. one-third more effort than daywork) then the Standard Time would be increased in the ratio $\frac{1 \cdot 50}{1 \cdot 33}$ or $\frac{90}{80}$.

Formulæ.—The above calculations can be reduced to the following formulæ, with certain convenient terms for common use:

(1) *Standard Minutes* (S.M.s) = actual minutes $\times \dfrac{\text{rating}}{60}$.

(2) *Works Units* (W.U.s) = S.M.s + relaxation allowance

$$= \text{S.M.s} \times \left(1 + \dfrac{\text{relax. per cent.}}{100}\right).$$

(3) *Standard Time* (S.T.) = W.U.s + contingency allowance.

(4) If piecework effort is to be paid for by some bonus percentage B other than 33⅓, then—

$$\text{Allowed Time (A.T.)} = \text{S.T.} \times \dfrac{1 \cdot B}{1 \cdot 33}.$$

(5) Time to earn normal piecework (i.e. at 80 rating)

$$= \text{Allowed Time} \times \dfrac{60}{80} = \tfrac{3}{4} \text{ Allowed Time.}$$

(6) Output rate for normal piecework (i.e. at 80 rating)

$$= \dfrac{60 \text{ mins.}}{\text{Allowed Time in mins.}} \times \dfrac{80}{60} \text{ pieces per hour.}$$

$$= \dfrac{80}{\text{Allowed Time in mins.}} \text{ pieces per hour.}$$

Synthetic Standard Times

One valuable advantage of scientific work measurement over ordinary rate-fixing, in factories engaged on batch or jobbing production, i.e. where machines or operators are not continuously engaged on the same job, is that Standard Times can be established for operations or elements which are combined in different ways for different jobs. In such circumstances, when jobs are of short duration, quite a large staff of time-study men are required if every job is to be studied whilst it is running, but if basic data for each likely operation is first established, then a much smaller staff is adequate for preparing Standard Times.

From a large range of studies of all types of work and operations, and for all operators, Standard Times for each element are recorded. From a study of these, with rechecks when necessary, one Standard Time is selected either by average, mean, or other method. Once the process or operations required are decided and laid down, the total Standard Time for a job can be built up by merely selecting and adding together the appropriate times for elements. To reduce clerical work, groups of elements which are frequently found in combination are summarised. Examples of this technique for machine operations are given in Figs. 14 and 15.

BASIC TIMES FOR SYNTHETIC STANDARDS
MANIPULATIVE ELEMENTS—No. 4 HERBERT CAPSTAN LATHE

No.	Element	Selected Standard Time	Study Number							
			1	2	3	4	5	6	7	8
1	Start machine	·020	·019	·016	·015	·023	·010	·019	·016	—
2	Stop machine	·060	·068	·050	·050	·080	·063	·060	·056	—
	Pick up and load:									
3	A. Simple location	·150	·106	·073	·184	·176	·161	·153	·165	·133
4	B. Difficult location	·250	·365	·209	·291	·250	·327	·233	·223	·300
5	Load bar	·300	·380	·250	·123	·365	·300	·150	—	—
6	Feed bar to stop (including turret up)	·300	·364	·253	·460	·360	·154	·300	·232	·310
	True up:									
7	A. Bar work	·150	·140	·160	·175	·153	·195	·148	—	—
8	B. Chuck work	·300	·199	·324	·355	·330	·274	·225	·350	·320
	Unload and put down:									
	A. from chuck:									
9	(i) Light work, easy to remove or finish un-important	·180	·162	·165	·185	·197	·129	·188	·171	·172
10	(ii) Heavy work, difficult to remove or easily damaged	·260	·206	·308	·273	·219	·262	·290	·315	·358
11	B. from collet	·070	·059	·059	·069	·064	·100	·078	·056	·087
	Tighten down:									
12	A. Small effort	·140	·117	·147	·185	·111	·140	·190	·157	·137
13	B. Great effort	·300	·287	·277	·287	·300	·300	·295	·320	·410
14	Turret up	·070	·061	·066	·067	·062	·068	·065	·079	·096
15	Turret away to stop	·065	·058	·066	·062	·056	·064	·064	·056	·048
16	Turret away	·050	·070	·058	·050	·058	·057	·057	·040	·030
17	Index turret (away, index and up)	·095	·077	·108	·107	·094	·097	·088	·096	·089
18	Index front tool post	·095	·096	·096	·070	·084	·145	·083	·078	·080
19	Rear tool post up } Front tool post up }	·090	·073	·075	·086	·093	·084	·072	·081	·086

FIG. 14

GROUPS OF ELEMENTS FOR SYNTHETIC STANDARDS
No. 4 HERBERT CAPSTAN LATHE

Constant Elements	S.M.s	S.M.s	S.M.s	S.M.s	S.M.s	S.M.s	S.M.s	S.M.s
Start machine . . .	·020	·020	·020	·020	·020	·020	·020	·020
Stop machine . . .	·060	·060	·060	·060	·060	·060	·060	·060
Pick up and load:								
A. Simple location .	·150	·150	·150	·150	—	—	—	—
B. Difficult location .	—	—	—	—	·250	·250	·250	·250
Tighten down:								
A. Small effort . .	·140	·140	—	—	·140	·140	—	—
B. Great effort . .	—	—	·300	·300	—	—	·300	·300
Unload and put down:								
A. Light work, each to remove or finish unimportant . .	·180	—	·180	—	·180	—	·180	—
B. Heavy work, difficult to remove or easily damaged . .	—	·260	—	·260	—	·260	—	·260
Totals . . .	·550	·630	·710	·790	·650	·730	·810	·890

FIG. 15.

Which can be summarised thus:

SUMMARY OF MANIPULATIVE ELEMENTS
No. 4 HERBERT CAPSTAN LATHE

Constant Elements Depending on Type of Article	Light work, easy to remove or finish unimportant S.M.s	Heavy work, difficult to remove or easily damaged S.M.s
Easy to locate, small effort to tighten ·	·550	·630
Easy to locate, great effort to tighten .	·710	·790
Difficult to locate, small effort to tighten	·650	·730
Difficult to locate, great effort to tighten	·810	·890

It is frequently found that the time varies with certain factors, such as weight, size, shape and accuracy. Time can be saved in determining the time for each variation, and a valuable check on results made, by finding the factor which controls the variation in time and plotting the standard times from a few studies along the range of variation. If the correct factor has been found, the results will lie approximately along a straight line or regular curve. If they do not, either the factor is wrong, the studies inaccurate, or there are unknown variations occurring during the studies. An example is given in Fig. 16. Such curves also form a valuable means of averaging results and of checking the accuracy of results. A curve (or straight line) drawn through plotted results indicates the mean result, and should be used for reading off standard times for values of the variable factor. Points which lie some way off the line are suspect, and should either be ignored or better still checked up.

This method of synthetic building up of times is not recommended for micro-motion technique as being too elaborate and impracticable. Figures which are quoted in this connection, such as "grasp a piece of wire $\frac{1}{32}$ in. diameter ·00313 min.; $\frac{1}{8}$ in. diameter ·00314 min.", only have significance in continuous operation conditions, and an

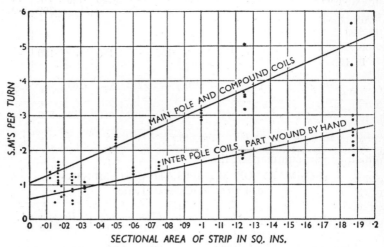

FIG. 16.—Standard time from studies plotted against variable factor.

individual study is then more satisfactory. The difference in time between the $\frac{1}{32}$-in. and $\frac{1}{8}$-in. wires is ·00001 min., only ·3 per cent. of the element, which is of little practical significance.

The use in a factory of standard times measured and established in another factory is not recommended. It is difficult for operators to accept their validity; in case of dispute there is no proof of their accuracy in the new conditions. Synthetic times developed in *the factory in which they are to be used* are likely to be more acceptable, no more expensive to establish, and from the work study necessary yield valuable results in improving methods.

Special Cases

It frequently happens in process work that although the time for the process or reaction which has to take place is entirely controlled by the operator, there is an absolutely correct time. If the time is exceeded for any cause or reduced to increase output, then the resulting product is not up to standard. In such cases it is an easy matter to determine the Standard Time. But if it is desired to apply payment by results, payment obviously cannot be according to output. The solution is to pay full or piecework rate for standard output, and to decrease the rating, and therefore payment, as output falls below or rises higher than the standard figure.

It sometimes happens too that because operators think it is something inimical to their interests, they object to the use of a stop-watch, and their trade union organisation refuses to co-operate. Fortunately, this restrictive practice is dying, but its possibility must still be provided for. Correct time studies can still be made by counting the time interval. It is possible for a time-study engineer to train himself to count at the rate of 60 per minute with a small degree of error, no more than a second per minute either way. When using this method, it is necessary to break up an operation into short elements, because of the difficulty of counting as the count gets into high figures; it is preferable not to exceed 30 seconds. Generally, it is not possible to do long continuous studies, involving many short elements, by this method. It is very important to check the speed of counting regularly, preferably at least twice per day, and important too to check rating on other work, or with other study men. It is important to avoid external impressions, such as loud noises and visual interference. Periodic noises tend to confuse, and if the time interval is round about one second accurate counting becomes impossible. Providing these precautions are taken, quite satisfactory studies can be obtained.

TOOL AND EQUIPMENT DESIGN

It is impossible, in a book of this kind, to discuss in detail the technique and practice of tool design, usually referred to in engineering as Jig and Tool Design. Nevertheless, it is important for the student of production management to be aware of its importance, not only in engineering, but in all industries, and the part it can play. In England we have not been backward at inventing. Indeed, the Industrial Revolution started here, and the use of steam power for driving machinery was developed by Watt. But in this century we have tended to rest on our oars of tradition in the factories. We have lagged behind America in the use of horse-power and of specially designed equipment. As a result of the lead given by the mass-production automobile factories, we are rapidly taking up the slack in our engineering factories, but there is still much to be done and great scope for special equipment in the non-engineering and process factories.

One has only to go through the factories of well-known companies who make consumable goods such as Boots (pharmaceutical products), Cadburys (chocolates), The Metal Box Company (boxes), Lever Bros. (soap), and some of the shoe factories, to appreciate the use that can be made of conveyors, special machinery, gadgets and power.

In such factories cans are conveyed up and down buildings, and even along the ceiling; powder is filled by vacuum, like fluids, to avoid dust; articles are wrapped and packed automatically; and conveyors are used to avoid persons lifting or carrying wherever possible, and most of the equipment is designed by the firms' own engineers. These engineers are equivalent to the jig and tool draughtsmen of the engineering industry, but whatever their title, the important thing is to recognise the need for such specialists, to employ capable men, and to make use of their abilities. The tendency usually is to make insufficient use of them, either because of a reluctance to make the capital expenditure on special plant they recommend, or because of resistance to change to new methods in the factory. Most of the productivity reports of the Specialist Teams from this country which visited the U.S.A. under the auspices of the Anglo-American Council on Productivity in the years 1950-52 give evidence of this.

Tool designers have two spheres of activity. First, the design of new tools, department layout and special machines for new programmes or models. This applies more especially in engineering, and has intensive application in the motor-car and aeroplane manufacturing industries. In this case the tool designers must be brought in at the design stage of the new product or model, the design of which can only be settled in relation to production methods. Tool design and tool making must be integrated with production programmes. This is a good reason why the production engineers should be closely connected with production planning.

Their second sphere is in designing improvements to present methods, and in this they must work closely with work-study engineers. It is in this work that there is most scope in factories producing consumable goods. Work-holding devices, fixtures, special tools and departmental layout can be handled by a firm's own staff, but the design of special machinery usually has to be given to firms who specialise in this class of work.

In engineering factories the battle between special-purpose and general-purpose machines is not settled, and is never likely to be. It would appear that the British manufacturer generally must look for export business where quality and special skill are required, rather than mass production. This means more general-purpose machines, and the user, the tool designer and production engineer can help the machine manufacturers by taking their problems to him.

Tool designers and draughtsmen should develop a critical and inventive outlook, never being satisfied with past practice. There is a danger of their becoming stale, and to guard against this they should be given every facility and encouragement to visit other factories, and to invite designers into their own. Methods often have a common use in quite different industries and processes, and nothing but good can come of such interchange. For example, the sight of cardboard being cut in a printing factory gave an engineer the idea of how to cut insulation and conversely printers have used paint-spraying technique to prevent offset.

PRODUCTION PLANNING

Definition of Terms and Activities

It is necessary to be clear about the meaning and use of certain terms used rather loosely in connection with production planning in industry. Certain words which are in common use in normal speech and writing have a specific use in industry, and others are used with different meanings in different places. The meanings which will be attached to such words in this text, therefore, are set out below.

Production Planning.—The meaning and content of this term have been explained in Chapter I. It is used instead of the term Production Control, as defined in British Standards Booklet B.S. 1100, page 2, "the means by which a manufacturing plan is determined, information issued for its execution, and data collected and recorded, which will enable the plant to be controlled through all its stages".

Planning Department.—The department charged with the responsibility of planning production in the above sense.

Schedules.—Lists or charts setting out work to be produced in a period, or in order of priority or to stated dates. It is commonly used synonymously with programmes.

Capacity.—The amount of production which can be done in a period with the labour and facilities available in assumed conditions.

Loading.—The process of setting the amount of work to be done against the capacity available, for operator, machine, department, or factory.

Stock Records.—The maintenance, usually by a system of records, of adequate stocks of materials and components to enable production to continue according to plans.

It would be as well before we go farther to examine the aims and objects of production planning. There are two aims of an economical production policy, one to ensure that goods are produced to a delivery date or at a required rate, the other to keep down costs; and for both of these effective production planning is essential. Delivery promises can be broken if assessments of capacity are wrong, and congestion, bottlenecks, idle time and other excess production costs can arise if all supplies (including information) are not forthcoming when they are required. Guesswork is not good enough and memory is an unreliable servant. In all but the smallest organisations a person cannot carry all the details of delivery dates, supplies and capacities in his head without making mistakes or neglecting something. Waiting for work, instructions, or tools, is one of the biggest contributory causes of high costs—or at least of costs being higher than they should be, i.e. excess costs. Well-thought-out schemes of production planning substitute facts for guesswork and reduce waiting time considerably. In general, therefore, orders must be delivered to time, and for economical production there must be a minimum of interruption to flow due to lack of work or information, and in order to maintain steady employment a balanced load of work must be maintained between departments. The object of production planning therefore can be stated to—

(1) Relate orders and delivery promises or plans to capacities available or conversely to provide the capacity and production to meet agreed or accepted demand.
(2) Ensure that material and components are available when and where required.
(3) Produce a steady flow of work through all departments.
(4) Preserve a balance of work between the various departments.
(5) Provide adequate manufacturing instructions to enable management and foremen to concentrate on supervision and production technique, and relieve them of detailed clerical work.
(6) Provide management with information to correct for possible delays and difficulties before they arise or become serious.

It is sometimes objected that production planning increases clerical staff and involves a large increase in paper work. This is not usually true; it is more usual for there to be already a large amount of paper work, often on scrap pads and memo books, spread throughout the factory. Simple and effective systems of planning merely replace this scrappy paper work with well-designed forms, which ensure that the information required is recorded in a form most convenient to those who have to use it.

A frequent objection, particularly from the old and experienced manager, to planning or departmental loading is that his business is different, and there are so many day-to-day alterations to suit customer or supplier that it just is not worth drawing up plans or programmes. Experience proves that good production planning inevitably reduces the frequency of change, and that in any case the existence of some plan reveals quickly the precise effect on production and promises already made which any new alteration will have. Too often factories flounder from one week to the next, attempting to meet the demands of pressing customers, nearly all of whom get their goods later than promised merely because too much has been promised.

It will be obvious that the tools of the production planner are formed of figures and facts. For the tools to be effective the figures and facts must be accurate and available when required. It is understood that figures used by designers and accountants must be accurate, but not always recognised that they must be equally so for the planner. Too often the times for operators, or figures of output, are approximate within wide limits, and then there is surprise because plans do not appear to be realistic.

The type of person employed on the work is also of vital importance. He must not only have a very good memory, but also must be logical and have an analytical type of mind—but not a single-track mind. That is, he must be able to take a wide view of his field of operations and take in and memorise many details and keep several major jobs or problems alive in his mind together. At the same time he must be resourceful (and not merely in finding excuses) but not easily flustered. Quite a specification! It certainly cannot be fulfilled successfully by a shop clerk who may happen to have a good memory of the firm's products but is without training or experience.

Executives in small factories of say less than 100 persons (and we have seen that there are more factories in Britain smaller than this than there are larger) need not be apprehensive that planning involves expensive "systems" and large clerical staffs. Planning is a mental process, the result of an attitude of mind, a determination to do things in an orderly way, and to do them in the light of facts and not of guesses. Simple records and schedules of weekly priorities with an accurate measure of capacity and demand can be as effective as the most elaborate systems.

The characteristics of effective planning are:

(1) That it has a clearly defined objective in view.
(2) It is simple and flexible.
(3) Provides for and uses accurate records and data.
(4) Establishes standards for measurement of results and progress.

Duties

The following can be taken as an example of the duties of the head of a Production Planning Department:

(1) Carry out the Company's manufacturing policy in relation to production programmes.

(2) Determine capacity of all manufacturing departments and prepare long- and short-term loads.

(3) Translate orders received from the Sales Departments (via Design or Drawing Office) into orders on the Works Departments.

(4) Prepare schedules of production for all departments and issue them in such a form, and at such a time, as to enable the departments concerned to produce the work required at the right time.

(5) Maintain progress records to show actual against planned production, and take necessary action to correct deviations as far as possible.

(6) Advise the Sales Department when it becomes known that delivery promises cannot be maintained.

(7) Answer enquiries from customers as to the progress of their orders, remembering that good delivery and the honouring of delivery promises is an important part of the Company's reputation and manufacturing policy.

(8) Maintain accurate records of all material and component stocks and movements in and out of stores in such a way as to anticipate future requirements and always to have material available for production to customers' requirements.

(9) Requisition from the buyer materials and supplies required, giving the necessary information, including the time when goods are required. Prepare schedule of requirements for suppliers and integrate with the Company's production programmes, progressing as required.

(10) Train staff in the effective performance of their duties.

(11) Adhere to the Company's personnel policy and ensure that subordinates do so.

(12) Keep abreast with developments in modern production planning and technique.

A word is required on the inclusion of Stock Records under the Chief Planner's authority. Both in text-books and in practice it is frequently put under the authority of either the storekeeper or buyer on the misguided assumption that because the storekeeper is responsible for actual stocks and the buyer for obtaining them, one or the other ought therefore to be responsible for records. The records are a tool and used mainly by the planners. The same records can be used once a year for stock valuation purposes, but their main purpose is to ensure that a proper production flow and balance between departments is facilitated by accurate stocks—and production flow and balance between departments is a Planning Department responsibility. It is fundamentally wrong for clerical work which can be done just as easily in an office, away from noise and under specialist supervision, to be done in a works department—and the stores is a works department. The buyer's job, on the other hand, is to buy and is concerned primarily with external agencies—he should not be responsible for level of stocks or accuracy of records.

Organisation of Department

The work of a Production Planning Department generally falls into three sections, dealing with three stages of the sequence of operations. They are:

(1) Compiling and recording facts.
(2) Developing plans.
(3) Putting plans into operation and controlling results.

In the first stage and section, information is gathered together recorded and filed in a way which is suitable for use by planners, and so that reference to it is easy and rapid. The information is of three kinds, relating to:

(a) Customers' orders and requirements;
(b) Stocks of materials and components;
(c) Plant available, capacities, operations and times.

Unless the organisation is of such a size that each kind of information is dealt with in a separate section, it is advisable for all of it to be handled by one section under the supervision of a person skilled in the work. Its organisation is mainly a problem of filing and entering-up figures or records from vouchers, i.e. transferring information and striking balances. It can usually be staffed with juniors, female, or relatively unskilled labour, but must be carefully supervised and checked by very reliable people. The absolute accuracy and therefore double checking required in banks is not essential, but inaccuracies can be troublesome and costly.

The second stage and section comprises the vital part of planning. It is here that the effectiveness or indifference of results is ensured, and where the ability to scheme, think ahead and take all factors into account is so essential. It is a job mainly done on paper, juggling as it were with figures and charts. Sales budgets must be broken down into or integrated with long-term production plans, factory and departmental plans formulated, and weekly or daily or even hour-by-hour loads prepared. In small factories a few simple charts or schedules suffice, but in very large organisations a vast amount of detailed information, in the form of masses of figures, flows into the section, and must be rapidly and regularly collated and reissued for action. Extreme tidiness is essential, and if those concerned are not to be bogged down by a continuous stream of insistent enquiries demand-

PRODUCTION ADMINISTRATION SHOWING STAGES AND TOOLS USED

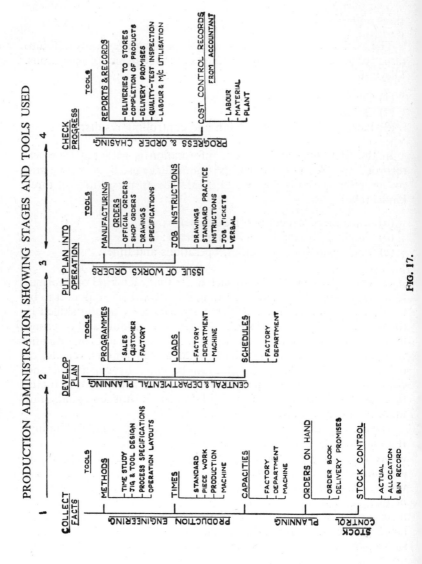

FIG. 17.

ing attention, much of the work must so be organised as to be dealt with in a routine manner by juniors.

The third stage consists of translating the plans into shop instructions and can be mainly of a clerical nature. In practice, however, it is at this stage that a certain amount of decentralisation is advisable, and the hour-by-hour machine or operation loading and the actual issue of jobs to operators is done either in or adjacent to the foreman's office, or in a shop office. Progress work, that is, checking performance against plans and reporting results (with recommendations for corrective action and requests for urgent actions) to foremen or other supervisors, which is really an aspect of control, is frequently carried out from the same office and even by the same persons.

These stages and the tools used are shown diagrammatically in the chart opposite (Fig. 17).

The complexity of an organisation structure for production planning depends on the type of industry or manufacture rather than its scale. In mass-production and continuous-process manufacture, production planning consists of balancing the flow of materials (or components) from outside or component manufacturing departments, with consumption by the factory or assembly departments. Particularly is this so in the automobile or similar industries, where a good deal of preliminary work on materials is subcontracted, no large stocks of materials are kept (or could be for the immense consumption rate) and a small interruption to production affects a large part of the factory and is very expensive. In those factories engaged on batch production of partly standardised products (by far the greater number in Great Britain), there is the added complexity of setting-up (time and cost), varying batch sizes, and the synchronisation of finishing dates for parts and subassemblies when batches vary so much. It is predominantly a question of continual adjustment in order to maintain balanced loads on departments and to correct for unforeseen delays. When the product is designed to customers' requirements, the total process time is increased by the time required for design or preparation for each order, and consequently the period over which planning must extend is greater, making the problem more complex. Production planning is most complex when the product is mainly to customers' requirements, but is designed to incorporate many standard parts kept in stock. When the number of orders exceeds something like 50 per week, the amount of information to be handled becomes large and the department correspondingly so.

Installing Production Planning

The question is often asked by those who become aware that they must do something about the need for an effective planning scheme, how long will it take to put in? As usual it all depends on the scheme, the job it has to do, and the limiting factors of the shortage of skilled staff, the continuity of sales programmes, market stability, and the delivery periods of stationery and special equipment. But unless all or most of these conditions are unusually favourable, it is found in practice that it takes between one and two years to put in a complete scheme and to make it work effectively and permanently. The factor which most affects the time is the availability of skilled staff. But in whichever way it is tackled it takes time to get it running smoothly, and for everyone in the works, unaccustomed to "systems", to understand and support it. One cannot graft on something new and expect immediate fruit. It is preferable first to prepare all process data and times, as these are seldom available in the form required. To plan on approximate data gives only approximate results—hit and miss—and the misses can be annoying, disturbing and discouraging to the works —but sometimes immediate results can be obtained with approximate figures and the Sales Department may be grateful for them.

Universality of Technique

The writer has had active experience of production planning in many industries, and has always found that the same principles, techniques and procedures are effective in each. Production planning is a universal science, and the tools developed, systems, indices, forms, procedures, office machinery, and so on, are not peculiar to one industry. What follows in this section, therefore, can be taken to be of general application. The only illustrations which the writer has available that are up-to-date and have not been quoted elsewhere relate to engineering, but because they can be adapted and modified to suit particular circumstances and requirements, they should serve their purpose as illustrations of method and principle. Students, particularly those primarily interested in engineering, are recommended to obtain and read the more detailed exposition of the principles and practice of production planning given in the small booklets published originally by the British Standards Institution B.S. 1100 (but now obtainable from the British Institute of Management):

Part 1—*Principles of Production Control,*
Part 2—*Production Control—the Small Factory,*
Part 3—*Application of Production Control,*

Compiling and Recording the Facts

The science of production planning consists broadly of relating what is wanted to what is available, on a time basis. Obviously, this can only be done if all the facts are known—facts relating to what has to be produced and when, and facts relating to capacities and materials available. This in turn involves still more detailed facts of materials, stocks, plant, methods, labour, times, production, scrap, delays and amendments. To plan an operation like the erection of a bridge calls for the collection of all facts relating to that one operation only, but in a factory, production of one kind or another continues indefinitely, so that we have the added requirement that *all* the facts should be *always* available in a suitable form. One of the skills of production planning therefore is to be able to compile, record and index all the information required, so that it can be kept up-to-date and be readily and effectively used.

In the logical sequence of events, the orders from customers or sales requirements provide the first set of facts, but since we must consider a unit which is operating on a continuous basis, it will be more helpful if we consider first the permanent records which form the background as it were to all the planning operations. The first of these is Stock Records.

Stock Records

In a very few of the large mass-production units, materials flow straight into production within a day or two of receipt, but nothing like this is possible in the majority of factories. In most factories some materials or components must be kept in stock against a probable or a known future requirement, and it is therefore essential to know what stocks are available and when they need replenishing and when orders must be placed for further supplies. There are two rather different methods in use, one depending on a knowledge of the *actual* stock at any time, and the other on the amount of *free* stock, that is, the amount available and *not allocated* to or absorbed by future production. Which method to use depends on circumstances and the kind and extent of control required. The free stock method ensures that all future commitments are covered by orders, whereas the actual stock method only ensures that there is sufficient material in stock or on order to cover *normal* requirements with normal delivery periods from suppliers. It is difficult to be sure what will be normal, so that the actual stock method is dangerous and results in frequent trouble due to stocks becoming exhausted, when consumption is liable to fluctuate irregularly. For example, a stock equivalent to two months' normal demand of a material may be exhausted in two weeks if an unusual order absorbs an abnormal amount of this material; and it may not be possible to replace it in two weeks. The free stock method is almost essential in times of continually rising demand, but when production periods in the factory exceed the time for delivery of materials, excessive stocks may be created. Neither method prevents stocks running out if suppliers take longer than expected or promised to deliver the goods. Perhaps the simplest method of controlling actual stocks and one quite suitable where demand and delivery periods are steady, and actual quantity in stock is only required to be known for annual stocktaking purposes (and is then counted), is to box or parcel the minimum stock quantity as described on page 353. When in similar circumstances a clerical record of actual stock is also required, the Bin Card record of stock movement and balance is satisfactory. Normally, however, conditions are not so stable and the job must be done clerically. The information which then has to be utilised or recorded is:

Amount required (for allocating).
Amount ordered (for allocating).
Amount used (for actual).
Amount received (for actual).
Balance—free or actual.
Date and Job or Order No. (for reference).
Specification of material or part (for re-ordering).
Minimum stock (safety margin).
Re-order quantity (normal batch).
Unit value (for stock-taking purposes).

Because rapid reference is essential, it is usual to do all recording on visible edge cards, and much ingenuity has been used in their design and the equipment for housing them. There are numerous types from which to choose to suit varying uses and commodities, and three only are illustrated:

(1) For allocating future requirements from a free stock.
(2) For replacing stocks when actual stocks are reduced to a minimum figure and for recording orders placed.
(3) For allocating from a free stock and at the same time revealing actual stock.

Illustrations of suitable forms are given in Figs. 18, 19 and 20, with a few typical entries shown.

Allocating from Free Stock (Fig. 18)

This is the simplest form of record. The same columns and entries can be used for Actual stocks, "issues" replacing "allocation" and "receipts" replacing "ordered", the "balance" being actual stock and not free. To open such a record the total present known requirements is deducted from the total stock available (ordered, in progress, and in stock) and entered as an opening "free stock". An opening figure of 15 is shown in the illustration (from which subsequent entries can be followed). A new order is placed, or batch put into production,

Date/Job No.	Alloc.	Ordered	Free	Date/Job No.	Alloc.	Ordered	Free	Date/Job No.	Alloc.	Ordered	Free
			15								
14·2·48	4	–	11								
3·5·48	12	–	–1								
AB	–	40	39								
5·5·48	5	–	34								
6·5·48	1-Scrap (No 3)	–	33								

BATCH ____ 40 ____

DESCRIPTION ____ BUSH ____

PATT No. ____

FRAME ____

PART No. ____ /111 ____

FIG. 18.

either when "free stock" is reduced to nil or to a minimum reserve. The latter is only required if a very urgent order, using this part or material, is likely to absorb any existent stock and is likely to be required immediately or before other orders booked.

Replacing Actual Stocks (*Fig.* 19)

In this case further supplies are ordered or put into production when the actual quantity in stock falls to a predetermined minimum

RECEIPTS					ISSUES			
DATE	ORDER No.	QUANT.	REC?	OUTSTAND.	DATE	ORDER No.	QUANT.	STOCK
								14
					4·5·48	BP	4	10
10·5·48	AA	40		40				
16·5·48	AA		20	20				30
					20·5·48	BQ	3	27
24·5·48	AA		20					47

ORDER PT. 10   BATCH .40

DESCRIPTION   PART No. /111

FIG. 19.

(order point). This minimum quantity must be sufficient to supply normal issues from stock over the period normally taken to obtain replacement. The left-hand half of the record deals with the orders for replacement, the right-hand half with issues and actual stock balances.

Replacing Free Stock and Recording Actual (Fig. 20)

This record is a combination of allocation and actual stock records. It could be made comprehensive by adding a column for balance-on-order as in the second illustration. For all normal purposes it gives all the information required for maintenance of stocks; in the few

DATE	ORDER N°	ORDERED	FREE	ALLOC	REC?	STOCK	ISSUED	DATE	ORDER N°	ORDERED	FREE	ALLOC	REC?	STOCK	ISSUED
			4			14									
4-5-48	BP					10	4.								
6-5-48	124		-1	5											
10-5-48	AA	40	39												
16-5-48	AA				20	30									
20-5-48	BQ					27	3.								
22-5-48	125		32	7											
24-5-48	AA				20	47									

DESCRIPTION　　　　　BATCH 40　　　　　PART N° /111

FIG. 20.

instances when the balance on order is required, it can be found by totalling receipts and setting off against the quantity ordered. It needs greater care and skill from clerks than the first two illustrations, but when accurately maintained and checked periodically, the record of actual stock can be accepted for stock-taking purposes to avoid the annual physical check and the problems this involves. It will be noticed that the free stock and actual stock entries and records are independent of each other, and that actual stock at any time may be more or less than the free stock.

It may sometimes happen that there are a few items of stock which, because of their importance to production, require to be specially watched. The basic materials in certain process industries, like grains in flour milling, flour, sugar, etc., in food and confectionery, and linseed oil, solvents, etc., in paint, are important in this way, and the head of the Planning Department or Works Manager himself may wish to have a visible record or wall chart of stocks of these items. A simple chart can be constructed as illustrated in Fig. 21. It is corrected daily or weekly by the Stock Records clerks. There are similar moving

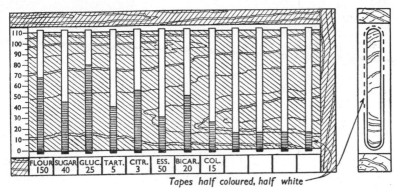

Tapes half coloured, half white

FIG. 21.—Movable Bar Chart.

bar charts available from office equipment manufacturers which show three facts on each bar.

Records of Times and Capacities for Processes and Operations

The second type of basic data which must be compiled and made available is that which has to do with processes and operations carried on in the factory.

It is essential to have readily available the operations, plant required and production times for all products, parts and assemblies. This can be done in the form of a standard practice manual, or process book, or stock catalogue, but some kind of card filing is more convenient. In engineering and general manufacture, where there are many parts, many of which are standard, the information is best set out on Process Layouts or Master Route Cards. An example of such a process layout is given in the appendix to this chapter, Fig. 31, Operation Master (page 293).

In whatever way it is set out, the following information should be on one record:

Description and reference number of product or part.

Material and amount required for one unit.

Normal production quantity, i.e. production batch.

Operations or processes involved in manufacture.

Plant or machine and tools required for each operation.

Production time for each process or operation.

The production time is best expressed as the time allowed or standard time. To avoid a conversion to actual time for planning purposes, all charts and measures of capacity should be in terms of standard time. Thus, for a week of 45 actual hours, the available standard hours in a factory, where the normal bonus is 33⅓ per cent., would be 45 × 1·33 = 60 hours.

The Production Engineers will supply all of the above information (set out on Process Layouts, when these are used), deciding the normal production batch in collaboration with the Production Planning Department.

It is also necessary to have an accurate record of the plant and labour force available and their capacity. This may sound obvious to those in factories where a few continuous processes are in operation, but in the many factories on batch production with general-purpose plant and machines, it is often neglected, plant being taken out of commission because of breakdown and new plant or equipment installed without the Production Planning Department being informed. The Production Planning Department, therefore, should have a copy of the plant register, or at least a list of all plant, should be advised of all changes, and should keep the record up-to-date, it being the duty of either the foremen or Maintenance Department to inform them of changes. Similarly, either the foremen or Personnel Officer should inform them of changes in the labour force which will affect capacity.

Orders on Hand

Finally, the Production Planning Department must know what has to be produced, and therefore must know of all orders on hand and delivery promises made. This again can be a simple or elaborate job, depending on the type and number of orders. When customers are supplied from shelf stock, the Sales Department keep stock records of finished products and requisition (or order) on the Production Departments as free stock is absorbed. In other cases Production Planning are advised of the customer's actual order and requirements. In either case orders are recorded as received in the Production Planning Department, and marked off as completed. In most cases it will be found that the best way of doing this is on visible edge card records. The card must be designed to suit the kind of order and the information frequently required in connection with it, e.g. portion completed. Either one card can be used for one order (if there are always several items per order), or one line of the card for each order. The cards should be filed in some logical sequence, and it is of considerable help for reference purposes in the works and sales offices if it is arranged with the Sales Department for order numbers to be allocated to orders in the works in some code which designates the type of product. Orders are then filed in production groups and number sequence, providing a logical reference for planning purposes.

It is important to log each order *immediately* it is received, to allocate a works order number immediately (if the sales order number is not used) and to cross off or enter the date immediately it is completed. Failure to do either of these things results in false computations of balance of work on hand and neglect to produce or over production of orders.

Developing Plans

Long-term Plans or Budgets

Production plans must, of course, be based on sales demand. When there is no positive sales programme, plans can only be based on trends. Normally there are sales programmes both long term and short term, and broad or long-term production plans are developed from general conferences between all executives and the Managing Director when future sales programmes are discussed. In the case of the larger mass-production factories manufacturing consumption goods for the general public, such as cars and radios, proprietary foods, toilet preparations, etc., a definite sales programme is agreed upon, and this must be broken down by the Production Planning Department into a pre-production programme for the new product or sales push. When such a programme involves drawings, special tools, or plant, and detail manufacture or assembly, it should be set out in chart form on a time basis, so that the interrelated completion dates for each stage or part can be seen. Such a chart is shown in Fig. 22 taken from BSS. 1100, Part 3. Difficulties, due for example to lack of capacity to meet the programme, lack of equipment and need for special tooling, etc., are discussed by all concerned at the pre-production stage, and general agreement on all stages obtained before the programme is confirmed.

Usually no radical departure from previous demands is planned or expected. A more or less continuous flow of orders for the Company's products or services is received, varying in volume from time to time. But it is still necessary for the Production Planning Department to take a fairly long forward view and to develop long-term programmes. In the first place, it is essential to know what is the total load on the factory represented by all orders on the books in order to know what delivery period can be promised to customers for manufacture to customer's order, or what finished stocks to carry when manufacturing to stock. It is also necessary to know whether this load will keep the departments or processes equally loaded. In this we encounter the problem which vexes all those interested in measuring overall output, planners, statisticians and economists—what measure of output to use in firms or industries manufacturing many different lines or products. A ton of cement is much the same wherever it is

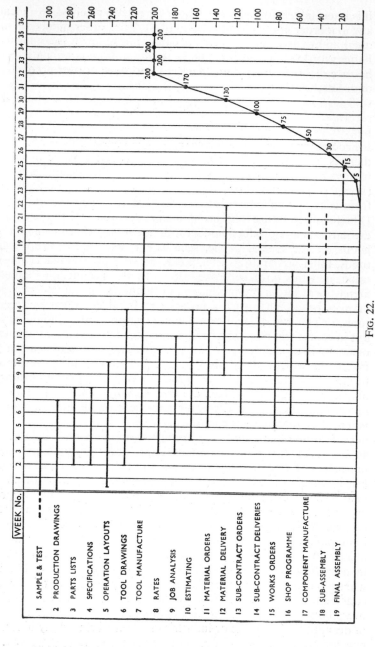

FIG. 22.

manufactured, but two yards of cloth may be very different in quality and in the amount of machine-hours and man-hours required for production, and two electric motors even of the same horse-power can be very different in design. The only accurate measure is machine-hours or man-hours, but the breakdown of every order into detailed man-hours for long-term planning is impracticable. It is frequently sufficient to use man- or machine-hours for the process or department common to all products or otherwise controlling (total) output. If a simple measure of volume is not possible, it will usually be found that value in £ s. d. is adequate, if the spread of kinds of product remains fairly steady and corrections are made for appreciable variations. The total load divided by the factory capacity per week (actual or budgeted) gives the time in weeks it would take to manufacture everything on order, and therefore the delivery period.

If there is only one or a few very similar products, and orders are executed in strict rotation, then little more information on future load is required. More often, however, there are many dissimilar products, each absorbing different amounts of each department's capacity, or orders are taken for delivery at a specified time, and not merely in rotation, and sometimes both conditions apply.

In either case, either orders must be taken for delivery according to capacity available, or capacity must be adjusted to suit orders received and delivery required, and in practice forward plans are made to reconcile these two alternatives. The problem revolves itself into a matter of setting off orders received against capacity, actual or budgeted. Taking first the case when orders are to be executed in rotation and not at a specified time, the period it would take to manufacture the total load (value, units, etc.) of orders on hand should be assessed periodically, weekly, or monthly. If the period varies, it must be decided either to adjust quoted delivery periods accordingly, adjust capacity, or (if the period is falling too rapidly) ask for more sales effort. When output measured in value, or volume, does not reflect capacity proportionately, and the only accurate measure is hours (man-hours or machine-hours), then it is necessary to divide the products made into categories of like kinds (if they do not fall naturally into definite categories) and, for each category, to select the most representative unit, taking into account demand and hours capacity absorbed. Orders are then recorded and assessed for capacity in terms of these representative units. Capacity can be checked departmentally in this way without a great amount of statistical work (see Fig. 23). Since for a given overall volume of production definite financial and production facilities are required, it is necessary to budget total volume and to allocate this to the various categories. An example of the build-up of such a production budget using typical

ASSESSMENT OF DEPARTMENTAL LOAD

Departments and Standard Hours of Load

Product	Load in Units	Welding 1	Welding 3	Welding 5	Machine 11	Machine 12	Machine 13	Assembly
A	258	—	—	—	0·062 / 31·4	0·6 / 304·2	0·42 / 212·9	1·25 / 633·75
B	9	0·133 / 7·5	—	0·1 / 5·7	0·16 / 9·1	0·6 / 34·2	2·135 / 121·6	2·25 / 128·2
C	200	—	—	—	0·125 / 50·6	1·55 / 627·7	0·25 / 101·2	1·25 / 506·2
D	12	—	—	0·1 / 28·8	0·16 / 46·0	0·7 / 201·6	2·38 / 685·4	2·75 / 792·0
E	147	0·142 / 48·5	—	0·18 / 61·5	0·625 / 213·7	1·85 / 632·7	0·2 / 68·4	1·5 / 513·0
F	57	0·65 / 137·8	—	0·93 / 197·1	0·3 / 424·0	2·0 / 398·5	1·88 / 165·3	3·25 / 689·0
G	132	0·27 / 68·5	—	0·495 / 125·7	0·65 / 165·1	0·92 / 233·6	0·422 / 107·1	1·63 / 414·0
H	70	1·76 / 286·8	3·0 / 489·0	0·75 / 122·2	0·85 / 138·5	1·46 / 237·9	1·06 / 172·7	3·5 / 570·5
I	435	0·256 / 91·9	—	0·38 / 136·4	0·78 / 280·0	1·0 / 259·0	0·6 / 215·4	1·75 / 628·2
J	69	0·135 / 110·8	—	—	1·85 / 651·2	2·36 / 830·7	0·95 / 334·4	4·0 / 1408·0
K	77	0·496 / 121·0	—	1·17 / 285·4	1·01 / 246·4	1·1 / 268·4	1·3 / 317·2	2·0 / 488·0
L	112	0·57 / 205·7	—	1·02 / 368·2	2·5 / 902·5	2·55 / 920·5	1·46 / 527·0	4·25 / 1534·2
M	68	0·17 / 5·1	—	0·4 / 12·0	0·9 / 27·0	1·3 / 39·0	1·27 / 38·1	2·14 / 64·2
Total required	—	3422·378	7624·2	2933·37	etc. 6697·579	etc. 8570·79	6140·193	20378·22
Capacity	—	111	234	144	200	220	250	410
Weeks	—	31	32	20	33	39	25	50

average units for each category of product manufactured is given in Fig. 24.

Having established such production budgets, or assessed the capacity required to meet the demand reflected in all orders on hand, the effect on plant and labour requirements and material supply (long-term contracts and minimum reserve stocks) must be assessed, and the information passed on to the appropriate department. Plant and labour requirements are not usually neglected, but the adjustment (particularly for a marked increase in output) of minimum stocks is also essential; it is frequently forgotten.

Factory Loads

In the case of orders which are quoted for delivery at a specified date or when it is necessary to build up a broad programme of the load on the works (or departments) represented by orders to be produced, it is necessary to log orders as they are accepted or put into the programme in the week (or period) concerned. This can be done either graphically or by merely listing orders on a sheet for each period. Perhaps the simplest is to record the value, in £ *s. d.* or other unit, of each order on a card in a visible edge system, one card for each week. If necessary, separate series of cards can be used for each department or process. A sliding coloured tab is slipped inside the visible edge of the card holder and is adjusted horizontally as each addition is made. The result at any time shows the load in each week, and, across all cards, the way the load varies. Alternatively, a wall chart can be used, being adjusted periodically. This can be done by small nails driven into a board in lines vertically to represent the scale of units, and horizontally in weeks. (The nails in effect being at the points of intersection of lines on a graph.) Coloured elastic is stretched round or through the nails to form a graph, separate colours representing budgeted and scheduled capacity. A similar result can be obtained by using squared paper blocking-in or crossing through squares as units of volume are absorbed or booked. Such charts show clearly where capacity is unabsorbed and available for new orders.

When the number of orders per week is small, it is possible to plan orders into a load board. An effective way of doing so is to originate a card or ticket for each order, and to draw a line along the top edge to a scale, equivalent to the number of hours or capacity absorbed by the order. These cards can then be slipped into horizontal pockets of a load board (see Fig. 25), behind each other and overlapping, with the load lines end to end, the board being marked with the same scale and divided into weeks. One pocket should be used for each unit of capacity (products, department, or group). In this way the

SALES AND PRODUCTION BUDGET

BASED ON 30 PER CENT. INCREASE ON SALES FOR FINANCIAL YEAR 1948

	1948 Sales			Average Unit		Prelim. Budget Uniform Increase for all Categories		Final Budget Adjusted for Present Trends	
	Total Sales Value	No. of Units	Average Value	Unit taken as Std.	Est. Value of Av. Unit	1948 Sales + 30%	Est. Prodn. in Units	Est. Total Sales	No. of Units at Av. Unit Value
	£		£		£	£		£	
Group 1: A	51,786	45	1,150	5-ton	1,200	67,400	56	67,400	56
B	56,178	35	1,585	5-ton	1,600	73,000	46	73,000	46
C	15,201	89	171	2-ton	150	19,760	131	19,760	131
Total	123,115	—	—	—	—	160,160	—	160,160	—
Group 2: A	6,065	101	60	½-ton	77	7,880	102	11,470	149
B	17,458	132	132	2-ton	115	22,700	105	14,470	125
C	10,028	44	228	5-ton	175	13,040	75	18,542	106
Total	33,551	—	—	—	—	43,620	—	47,982	—
Group 3	23,287	—	—	—	—	30,250	—	30,250	—

Group 4: A	28,519	160	170	5-ton	150	37,020	247	34,500	223
Group 4: B	6,964	75	91	3-ton	90	8,870	98	11,390	126
Total	35,483	—	—	—	—	45,890	—	45,890	—
Group 5: A	17,285	906	19	2-ton	17	22,450	1,320	19,038	1,120
Group 5: B	6,105	211	29	2-ton	25	7,950	328	7,000	280
Group 5: C	3,580	h288	12·4	2-ton	10	4,650	465	4,650	465
Group 5: D	3,780	88	42	1-ton	—	4,910	118	4,910	118
Total	30,980	—	—	—	—	40,190	—	36,826	—
Group 6	9,242	—	—	—	—	12,000	—	12,000	—
Group 7	7,371	—	—	—	—	9,580	—	9,580	—
Group 8	23,150	—	—	—	—	30,030	—	30,030	—
TOTAL	£286,179	—	—	—	—	£371,720	—	£371,720	—

Fig. 24.

265

load can be built up as far ahead as wished, it is readily visible, the completion date of existing or new orders can be seen, and it can be used for progress checking. The pockets can be made of metal or

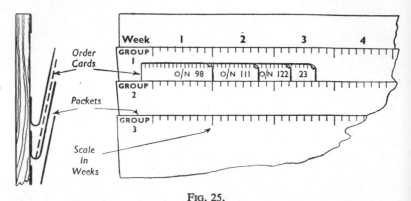

FIG. 25.

wood or even print paper stuck on to a board, the ends wrapped round the edges of the board, the scale being printed on the face of each pocket.

Departmental Loads—Long-term

Unless all orders received absorb the same proportion of capacity for each department and thus preserve a balanced load between departments, it is necessary to check regularly forward loads on departments in order to preserve balance. To do this the procedure outlined above should be followed in a more detailed manner on a departmental basis. When output of the product is easily measured in terms of volume, this is not difficult, but when hours is the only measure because the individual jobs vary so much, the method of grouping into categories should be followed. All orders in hand should be analysed to find the number of units in each category. For each category the number is then multiplied by the hours required in each department and the figures for each department totalled and divided by capacity to find the load in weeks. Periodically (weekly or monthly) net differences in units for each category between orders received and dispatched should be extended similarly and added (or subtracted) from previous loads. These periodic loads should be plotted to reveal any trend. An illustration of the assessment of capacity absorbed, calculated in this way, is given in Fig. 23. In such a case the loading in departments is obviously not balanced, and either orders must be increased to correct the underloading, or capacity in the overloaded departments must be expanded.

Departmental and Machine Loads—Short-term

Actual orders at some time have to be issued to the works for production.

In process and mass-production industries, where processes are in continuous operation on the same product (cement, steel, margarine, etc.), this amounts to little more than instructions for starting and stopping. When different grades of the same product are made, as in papermaking, or glass container manufacturing, an order of priority for each grade or kind must be determined. If each order takes its turn and there is no delivery period problem, no more need be done, but if it is required to know when orders will be completed, then the production scheduled must be measured and related to capacity. In most manufacturing industries a variety of different products, articles, or components is manufactured in each department, and few departments, machines, or operators make the same article continuously and permanently. It is then essential only to issue instructions for production at the rate at which it can be completed. This means actually measuring the amount of work it is proposed to schedule for immediate production over a period. An approximate measure is no longer of any use, and if capacity and output cannot be measured accurately in some unit of volume, man-hours or machine-hours must be used. Thus we get what is commonly called *departmental or machine* loading. When instructions for production are issued in the form of a list of jobs or orders to be done in a period or in order of priority, such lists are usually termed *production schedules.*

It is at this stage that the planning problem becomes complicated and the technique needs most skill. The methods and techniques in use are many and varied, and indeed must be so to suit the widely different types and scales of production. In a book of this kind it is impossible to refer to them all. As, however, the principles underlying them all are the same and can be applied to all industries, a few illustrations will serve for an understanding of how the problem is tackled. Planning for batch production for a variety of machines or processes is about the most difficult, and will therefore be referred to in any specific illustrations.

At the loading stage of planning there are always opposing forces to be kept in equilibrium, the desire to meet customers with urgent demands and the undesirability of disturbing existing programmes; the need to keep inventories low, and the preference of the works for large batches, and so on. All such factors have to be remembered and allowed for when building up programmes or loads prior to issuing production schedules.

This detailed loading can either be done directly to machine or operator, or in two stages, first to department or groups, and then to individuals. If all machines are exactly the same and there is absolutely no difference in operator skill or aptitude, then loading immediately to machines or individuals is permissible. But where there are operator differences or idiosyncrasies it is far better not to lose the personal touch and to arrange for the production supervisor to have some or the last say in allocation of job. This can be arranged by first loading to department or group in the Production Planning Department, and then either the foreman or planning clerk in the department loading to individual or machine. The importance of this personal touch at the final stage of planning at the point of impact on the man or woman cannot be over-emphasised, and is too little appreciated. With Shakespeare,

> "We fortify in paper and in figures,
> Using the names of men instead of men,
> Like one that draws the model of a house
> Beyond his powers to build it".

dehumanising administration just where it most requires the personal touch. This accounts not a little for the indifference and even hostility to "systems" and to operators "leaving it to the planner" when a word or suggestion at the right time could do so much to help the job along.

The simplest form of scheduling—it is hardly loading—is by priority, keeping supervision informed at least several jobs ahead, and as far ahead as possible of the order of priority of each job. In its simplest form this is a written list. If a graphical or visual method is preferred, job tickets can be hung on hooks, one hook for each machine or operator, the next job always being uppermost.

A more comprehensive planning board consists of a series of four pockets for each machine and operator. The top two pockets each hold one job card, the lower two several. Into the top pocket is placed the job in production, in the second the next to be commenced, in the third jobs ready for production in order of priority, and in the fourth jobs waiting for material, tools, or completion of a previous operation.

Loading to capacity can be done by list, graphically or in a load board. If a list is used there should be three columns in which are entered respectively—job reference (name or number), capacity absorbed (hours, quantity, etc.), and the cumulative capacity.

Perhaps the most widely used graphical method is the Gantt chart. It suffers from the one defect that it is not easily modified, rubbing out and re-drawing lines being a time-absorbing occupation. When loads can be built up simply and are unlikely to be altered, the Gantt chart can be extremely useful and can be used to indicate progress.

There are many variations, and illustrations are given in most books dealing with charts or production planning (e.g. see *Management's Handbook*, Ronald Press Co., New York); Fig. 26 is an illustration of a simple version showing the loading for two machines. The lines are drawn horizontally on paper specially printed, or on graph paper.

There are several methods of building a load board from materials likely to be available in any factory. They are usually made to take cards or strips of cardboard which are used to indicate the load. Perhaps the simplest is a board built-up of pockets as illustrated on page 266. To avoid preparing special cards, one of the cards used in

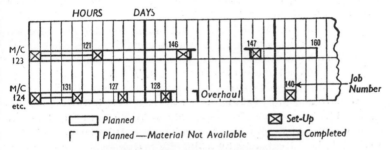

FIG. 26.—Gantt Chart for Planning.

connection with the issue of jobs, for example the job or time card, should be used, marking along the top edge a line representing the time required to do the job. It facilitates drawing the line to have a scale printed along the top as shown in the illustration of a Move Note in the Appendix to this chapter (Fig. 36). If the boards are large, the pockets can be made of metal, but for small ones they can be made of strips of strong paper when the scale can be printed on each strip, which is folded backwards and gummed to a backing board. A portable board can be made in this manner for chargehands and foremen of small sections by using a piece of stiff cardboard as the backing board. There are of course several types of planning boards sold under proprietary names by office equipment suppliers.

Planning Problems

So much for the tools of loading; the technique can only be learnt by practice, but there are several precepts which are generally applicable. The first essential is to use an accurate measure. It cannot be too strongly emphasised that the accuracy of planning varies directly with the accuracy of the information and measurement of capacity and performance. However much skill is used in loading, if the figures used are not accurate, departments will sometimes be over-loaded and at others short of work, resulting in overtime and idle capacity alternating violently, to the extreme annoyance of foremen and operators, and engendering a hostility to the planning engineers when co-operation is required. Furthermore, promises given to customers or the Sales Department are not kept, resulting in urgent action to retrieve the position, adding further disturbance in the shops and incurring excess costs due to "breaking down" jobs which are running to put in the urgent ones. In extreme cases the jobs super-seded themselves become urgent, and eventually there are more urgent than normal jobs and planning becomes a continuous purge and a discredited instrument.

It is also important to allow for plant breakdown and maintenance and for absence of operators. For normal conditions this can best be done by loading to the normal standard hours produced per week as revealed in weekly Labour Control reports. This allows then for the average performance of operators. But over and above this the Plan-ning Department must take steps to see that it is informed of any unusual breakdowns or absence likely seriously to affect plans, so that any necessary readjustments can be made. It is always advisable to schedule below capacity by a definite margin, which can then be filled up in the current period by urgent or rush orders.

In factories on batch production it will be found that a week is the optimum period for planning and shop loading purposes. Longer periods are apt to need too frequent revision, and a day is not long enough for collecting like batches together and for balancing up between machines or groups. Weekly schedules should be issued to departments long enough ahead for them to be given adequate con-sideration and preparation. The schedules themselves should be pre-pared far enough ahead by the planning engineers to enable their effect to be seen on work-in-progress and over- or under-loading of certain machines in sections.

In factories on batch production of components for assembly into machines or units, the aim is to arrange for all components to be com-pleted as nearly as possible together and in time for assembly to be completed by due date. For continuous assembly of one product or assembly of a special order, it is ideal to arrange for delivery of com-ponents to the job or to a work station or lay-by in the assembly shop at the rate required, or just in time, for assembly. In other cases com-ponents are delivered to a component stores, and if manufacture of components is not synchronised reasonably well with assembly, the stores will have to be larger than it need be. In assessing the pro-duction time for components (that is, the total time it takes to get them from the raw material stores to finished part stores), it is not sufficient to add up the time taken in each process or operation. In continuous-flow production, where conveyor assembly is in use, this may be nearly so, but in intermittent or batch production, where batch sizes differ, all parts do not need the same operations, and operator times vary, there must always be a float of work behind each machine or operator, and this fluctuates. In addition, some kind of inspection or checking and some transport are required after each operation, so that a job seldom moves to the next operation immediately the previous one is finished. This in-between operation time is frequently longer than the direct operation time. In any case, it must be allowed for and can only be found from experience. It will be found to vary with the component and normal time for a batch on any machine or section. The more effective the planning and subsequent control, the less is the work in progress between operations, the smaller the total production time, and the better the production flow.

Example of Procedure

In order to illustrate the method of applying these planning techniques and to show how they hang together in practice, an actual example is described briefly below. The factory concerned manufactures products to delivery dates. The products all require an assembly stage and a variety of components, some of which are standard and others designed and manufactured for a particular order.

Copies of all works orders, which are identified by a number coded to indicate type of product, are sent to all departments concerned. The orders give the customer's name, a certain amount of technical data needed by the various departments, and state the delivery date promised. This date is in line with the general delivery period agreed with the Production Planning Department, and with the appearance of the sales load board (Factory Loads, page 263) kept up-to-date for the Sales Department by the Production Planning Department. The Production Engineers' and Production Planning copies go via the Drawing Office, who enter the date by which drawings will be ready after reference to their own planning board. The Planning Card used by the Production Planning Department is produced at the same time as the copies of the order and is attached to Production Planning copy.

As orders are received daily by the Production Planning Department they are recorded by the Records Section in the visible edge card record, one per line on cards filed in numerical order which automatically divides them into groups. Vertical columns of the card are used for indicating progress of main stages of the order. At the same time the number of units in each group on the order are added to the weekly list of orders received and dispatched, to be added to the cumulative total of units on order (dispatches are deducted).

The copies then go to the Forward Load section, where each order is scrutinised for special features which will affect planning and any notes of these are entered on the planning card. The measure of the capacity of the factory absorbed by the order is entered on the card and the card is filed into the appropriate week nearest the week indicated by the delivery date, according to existing load and budgeted capacity for each group of products. Each week is numbered, and the week number into which the card is filed is entered on the Order Record for cross-reference purposes. The week number is entered on the Production Engineers' copy of order to tell them (after allowing for normal production time) by when process information and tools will be required. The copy of the order is then filed.

The load (factory capacity and assembly capacity) is transferred periodically from the planning card file to a visible edge card index book, one card for each week, a coloured tab indicating the load. This reveals the distribution of load as far as orders are booked, and is used as a reference for scheduling, building of planning card load, and keeping sales load board up-to-date.

As soon as the Production Engineers receive their copy of the order they examine it and any drawings attached, decide on the method of production of the whole and each part, and prepare process layouts, including standard times for each operation (calculated from synthetic data). All tools required are listed and any new ones noted for designing. The draft process layout is typed as a master, and is then available for use by Production Planning whenever they decide to initiate production. When tools have been designed, a tool manufacturing requisition is raised, giving the date the tools are required, and a process layout is prepared for these so that Production Planning will have documents for planning and control.

Each week, and at a date some 10 or 12 weeks ahead (time for the manufacture of components, assembly and test, and for planning routine) of the week to which it will apply, a provisional assembly schedule is prepared from orders in the Planning Card file. Slight adjustments may be made at this stage to allow for changes in capacity or urgency of orders, or other special circumstances. This provisional schedule is passed to the Stores Record Section.

The Stores Record Section takes the part list for each order listed and allocates all materials and components on free-stock records, throwing up requisitions for new manufacturing orders or buying orders on which is stated the week number by when delivery must be made. Special parts are not allocated, but a requisition to manufacture is raised for them. The requisitions to manufacture are sent to the Document Printing Section, who run off all works documents. These, in sets, are returned to the Component Planning Section of the Production Planning Department, where they are filed under the week number first entered on the requisition for manufacture. This file, in week numbers, forms the provisional schedules for component manufacturing departments.

Final schedules for the assembly departments are prepared and issued one full week before the week to which they apply, and copies are given to Stores and Test. At this stage certain orders included on provisional schedules may have to be deleted because of non-delivery of special material, or delay in component manufacture. At some time it may be necessary to bring forward other orders to meet urgent demands for customers (after checking material and component position) or to balance the assembly capacity.

Final schedules for component manufacturing are built up by Component Planners at least two to four weeks earlier than the completion week to which they apply, using standard times on the production documents as a measure of load. This involves a good deal of juggling and skill to ensure that each section in each department is fully loaded, but not overloaded. Loading to machines and operations is done in the departments.

When building up loads, consideration has to be given to the following factors:

Urgent orders;

Special parts or tools;

Availability of raw materials (suppliers may have to be chased);

Need for sub-contracting to cope with overloads;

Effect of change in demand on capacity of certain plant;

Excessive illness of operators, or breakdown of plant.

That maximum flexibility is provided for at each stage.

A department schedule is only made final just before it must be issued, and even then is just short of capacity for the department to allow for additions during the current week. This flexibility is of the utmost importance, especially in those factories on batch production and working to customers' orders. A production planning system which cannot respond quickly to urgent orders, changes in demand and difficulties with suppliers is not doing its job properly.

Putting Plans into Operation

Having decided when work shall be produced, authority must be given for it to commence and instructions given to get material on the move and actually to do the work. Methods for doing this vary from a copy of the customer's order to a detailed specification with part list and drawings and detailed manufacturing instructions, with all supporting documents for each part. Procedures are simplest at the opposite extremes of industrial organisation, i.e. in the small business with a working proprietor who can give verbal instructions and personal supervision, and in the continuous-flow mass-production factories where all work moves automatically through an established standard sequence of operations so that planning instructions are almost limited to starting the right amount of material at the first process. In between are the intermittent flow or batch production units, and it is in these that paper work becomes more complicated, and where consequently there is most need to find ways of reducing the work involved. Where personal supervision is adequate, there is no need to impose unnecessary or complicated systems. This is possible in small process units and in those factories where it has been possible to arrange for conveyors (either power or gravity) to control operators and the flow of work. In most cases, however, the managers, supervisors and operators must be provided with written instructions, and in their turn must render written records. It may appear a truism to say that paper work and systems must be simple in order to get all the information to all the departments requiring it promptly, accurately and regularly. But there are many executives who readily recognise this, yet only consider one form at a time and neglect to work out a co-ordinated system or procedure. Odd scraps of paper and memo books may be good enough for occasional use, but they are not effective vehicles for regular information and records. Specially printed forms should be designed for the purpose. The preparation and movement of forms should be considered as a co-ordinated whole just as production is. Foremen, storekeepers, checkers and all and sundry should not be allowed to start their own records and design their own forms without reference to a master plan and design, and it is advisable for one person to be made responsible for designing and authorising all new forms. The Chief Production Planning executive should be competent to do so. Wherever possible, forms should be made to serve more than one purpose or record, and steps should be taken to ensure that they are promptly dealt with so that the last person to use a form is not unduly delayed. This means that design and layout of forms must be well thought out, providing for all the essential information and displaying it in a way that enables those who have to use particular information to recognise it quickly. For most purposes it will be found that forms are most effective when designed with headed panels for each item of information, the same information, such as Job No., appearing on all forms in the same place, heavy lines drawing attention to significant information. The appendix of this chapter contains good examples of well-designed forms. When forms are to be used on a typewriter, spacing of information or panels should suit typewritten spacing—on normal machines 10 per inch horizontally and 6 per inch vertically.

A manufacturing order is the executive authority to the works or department for production to commence. In the simplest cases this may be a copy of the customer's order on the firm, but in companies manufacturing proprietary lines to warehouse stock the works may never see a customer's order or know a customer's name. In most manufacturing units the order as received from the customer has to be translated into shop language with a good deal more information than is given by the customer. This is usually done by the Order Department or Contracts Department. Even when a customer's order is accompanied by a complete specification, there is usually much more technical information required in the way of formulæ, instructions or drawings, which have to be prepared. This is given on the documents described in Chapter 2, page 182. In most cases, of course from shoes to ships and toys to telephones, this involves instructions for the manufacture of individual components, and for their assembly. The manufacturing order for the whole product and the kind of information it gives varies widely according to the product and industry, and it would be of limited interest to describe a specific case, but in batch production at least, one component is very like another so far as arranging for its production is concerned. Material for it must be drawn from stores, it is subjected to one or more operations, delivered into a component or finished-part stores, and is subsequently reissued with others for assembly. It will be sufficient therefore if we understand the principles and procedure for putting previously prepared plans into operation as they apply to a component, knowing that they will apply to subassemblies and final assemblies by treating these as a unit.

Fig. 27 shows in the simplest form the order routine and documents used for production of a component. Information is required to authorise and record:

(1) The movement of material from stores to a production point;
(2) The identity of material as it is processed;
(3) The preparation of machine and/or tools in readiness for work to be done;
(4) Actual commencement of work, where and when;
(5) The time allowed and actually taken to do the work;
(6) Date when completed, and quantity good and scrapped.

In addition to the Production Engineers' and Production Planning Departments, this information is needed by some or all of the following departments:

(1) The manufacturing department concerned—foreman or shop planner or progress clerk and time clerk;
(2) The Inspector in the department;
(3) Stores Department—material and finished;
(4) Wages Department;
(5) Accounts Department or Cost Office.

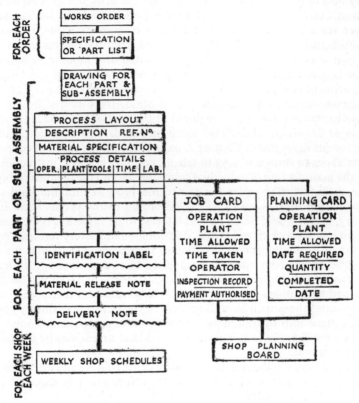

FIG. 27.—Documents for Production Planning.

The following documents are required, at least:

(1) Process Layout (Master Route Card or Ope ration Instruction describing the method of production.—For each component;
(2) Identity Label.—For each part;
(3) Material Release Note (Requisition) for obtaining material.—For each part;
(4) Job Card (Time Card)—describing and authorising operation.—One for each operation;

(5) Planning Card (Move Note or Delivery Note)—for planning and progress information (the Job Card can sometimes be used).—One for each operation.

(6) Cost Card—for calculating cost (standard or actual).—One for each part.

In many systems in operation more documents than this are in use, particularly for each operation, and whilst this may be justified in certain cases, usually the same results can be obtained with a smaller number. Certainly supervision must be better and the work and documents must be dealt with more quickly after operations are completed, but this is a strong argument in favour of the smaller number of documents. In fact, it cannot be too strongly emphasised that paper work and the appearance of paper work must be kept to a minimum in an organisation—and on the shop floor especially. It is disliked by operators and foremen alike. As far as possible all writing and paper work of any kind should be done in offices by trained operators and not on the shop floor by operators at the machine or bench.

This is one of the two compelling reasons for the development and widespread use of pre-printed documents. The other is that they reduce to an absolute minimum the risk of errors due to transcription and recording of information. By pre-printed documents is meant production planning documents which are prepared, and bear, in printed or some variety of duplicated form, all information pertaining to a job or operation which is known before it is issued (e.g. job number, drawing number, tools required, etc.). There are two principal forms, one using a special carbon impression on chromo-surface (or ordinary) paper as a master, and the other using a stencil. Both have their advantages and adherents. In some cases they can make a substantial reduction in the amount of clerical work and labour required in the works.

Since generalities are not very helpful when studying planning in action, or devising procedures for the use of the documents involved, a specimen set of instructions and of all documents used is given as an Appendix to this chapter (pages 292 et seq). It covers the use of pre-printed documents, but these are not essential, and only the instructions dealing with the operation of pre-printing would be affected if hand-written documents were used; more information, of course, would have to be written in the shops. The instructions describe in detail how each document is used for authorising work to commence, recording work done and when, and the time taken and hence payment to be made. It is emphasised again that though this particular set of documents was obviously prepared for an engineering factory, the same documents of substantially the same design can be used in any factory making piece parts.

Documents for each part (or operation) should be sent to the department concerned with the weekly (or daily) schedule on which they are listed. A bundle of documents can, of course, constitute a schedule, but there is a risk of loss or misplacement which makes this inadvisable. Schedules should be sent to departments in time for the latter to make their own plans with ancillary departments, e.g. material and tool stores, so that everything is ready when the operator requires it.

Availability of Tools, etc.

The availability of tools, or their equivalent, formers, templates, etc., is frequently a problem in factories on job or batch production, particularly when these have to be manufactured specially for each order. When the tools have already been made previously, the problem is one of getting information to the tool stores in time for them to have the tools ready for when they are required by the operators. In this case it is advisable for the tool stores to be supplied with a daily or weekly schedule, or work sheet, as far in advance as it is necessary for them to prepare tools. If possible this should be limited to one day, and the schedule can then be given to the tool stores by the planning clerk in the shop concerned. The tool stores are then able to prepare the kit of tools, including drawings or other instructions, for each job, ready to be handed to the operator immediately it is asked for. When new tools have to be made for a job a suitable routine procedure must be worked out to ensure that tools are available when they are required. This procedure must be strictly adhered to in practice; there is often a tendency to allow such procedures, which involve ancillary departments like the toolroom to go by default.

Although the procedure has been covered in the instructions given in the appendix to this chapter, it is a problem peculiar to itself, and the following additional notes might be helpful.

The Drawing Office or whatever the technical department is termed, must discuss tooling and special manufacturing methods with the Production Engineers during the design stage to enable special measures or tools, which will take an unusually long time to produce, to be dealt with. A copy of the works order or part list, with any drawings and other technical information, is sent to the Planning Engineers, who enter on it the date when tools must be ready and send it on to the Production Engineers. The latter prepare process and operation layouts, and decide what tools are required, sending a list of the tools, or the documents for each tool, whichever is more convenient, to the Planning Engineers. The Production Engineers should then record all drawings which have to be prepared and the date by which they have to be completed, in order to enable tools to be prepared for when they are required. The Planning Engineers plan and schedule and progress the production of tools in the same way as they do production, including them on the normal production schedules when they are made or dealt with at all in production departments, to ensure that they receive the same attention as other work (they are one-offs, and production departments are very inclined to neglect one-offs and special work). If tool production is left entirely to the Toolroom and not controlled by the Planning Department, there are bound to be instances when tools are not ready when they are required, particularly when plans are revised, or jobs brought forward, as they must be at times.

Unless jobs are planned to individual machines by the Production Planning Department centrally, departmental schedules must be broken down into machine or operator loads in the department—foreman's office of shop planning office. The same technique is used as already explained for departmental planning (page 267), but more use is likely to be made of load boards. The one chosen will depend on the nature of the work and the complexity of operations. A board which helps to accumulate and reveal the load on a machine or operator, and when jobs are due to start and finish, is more useful. The Move Note (Fig. 36 in the Appendix to this chapter) has been designed so that it can be used in this way.[1]

PRODUCTION CONTROL

In this chapter on Production Administration we have so far discussed preparing and establishing standards for operations and time plans for carrying them out. Supervision, that is managers and foremen, then take over the execution of the plans. But no matter how accurate the standards, or how perfect the plans, since human nature is fallible and not all the factors affecting production are under the control of management, there are in practice mistakes and failures to achieve plans and reach standards of performance.

To enable corrective action to be taken to limit and reduce the effect of these mistakes and failures and to prevent their recurrence, there must be some means of measuring deviations from plans and shortcomings in performance. This is an activity of *Control* discussed in detail in Part IV, of which Production Control is a specific case. There are four aspects of Production Control in which Production Management is interested:

---

[1] For an alternative and rather fuller treatment of the subject of Production Planning, the reader can refer to *Modern Production Control*, by A. W. Willsmore (Pitman).

(1) The control of variations from plans or programmes, commonly known in industry today as PROGRESS.

(2) The control of manufacturing costs by measurement and limitation of the excess costs of production referred to as COST CONTROL. In this part we are concerned with MATERIAL COST CONTROL and LABOUR COST CONTROL.

(3) The control of quality of the product. This has become a specialised activity, since it is a highly technical matter demanding a knowledge of the specific processes and skills in the particular industry. Control is maintained by inspectors and testers, and the activity is dealt with as an ancillary service in Chapter V. It is significant that the modern application of inspection to quantity and process production has become known as QUALITY CONTROL.

(4) The control of MACHINE UTILISATION by drawing attention to the effective use of machines in terms of machine hours.

Progress

It will be recognised at once that controlling variations from production plans, or progressing, can only be done from a detailed knowledge of plans and results, and in any but the smallest organisations this means records of results. Since in practice it is usually found advisable, and is in fact recommended, to appoint special men as progress men or chasers, there is a danger that duplicate records are set up. The Planning Engineers must have records of results to keep their plans up-to-date and to adjust for them in future plans. If Planning and Progress are not integrated nor production planning documents and procedures designed to cater for both activities, each will have its own system of recording results. It is not unknown for the Planning Engineers to spend a good proportion of their time frantically adjusting their plans, *after* the progress men have made theirs! Planning schemes introduced by inexperienced persons have been held to scorn and failed on this account. It is particularly likely to happen when progress men have been operating before planning is installed or are appointed by or are responsible to foremen of departments.

In the first place, therefore, it is essential for progress to be a responsibility of the Production Planning Department, and for the progress men to be under the authority of the head of this department. Secondly, all planning and production documents and procedures should be designed to incorporate records which the progress men will require. This has been done in the documents included in the Appendix to this chapter. Thirdly, it is important to choose and train the right type of person. Because a progress man is likely to be frequently changing programmes or asking for urgent action, he must enlist the ready co-operation of supervisors. It is essential for him to have a cheerful and friendly disposition, and yet be determined. If he is too assertive and overbearing, he will get little co-operation from supervisors; if he is too easy going, he will not get the results required. A retentive memory for detail is also essential and an extensive knowledge of the firm's products is advisable.

Progress can be organised in two ways:

(1) Each progress man responsible for a section or department.

(2) Each progress man responsible for one product or group of components.

In the larger units both methods may be seen in operation.

If it is laid down and clearly understood that a production schedule is an assignment which it is a foreman's duty to complete, then the former method is likely to be most satisfactory. Even then it may be found advisable to have one man responsible for the progress of customers' or urgent orders, throughout the factory, in addition to departmental progress men. What must be guarded against is a progress man building up so much authority that he wrecks planned schedules in his enthusiasm for short-term results.

The progress man's main "standards of reference" are the production schedules, weekly or daily, and lists of orders promised. It is one of the advantages of departmental production schedules that they are a department's assignment for completion by a given date. If work is crossed off as completed, work not completed, and, therefore, behind programme, can be immediately seen by the progress man. It is even better of course to know what jobs have been started late or are running behind programme. This means a record of when jobs started in addition to a record of when jobs are completed. It is not usually justified if most jobs do not last for longer than one day. In either case in factories or departments on batch production the best way of keeping an eye on whether jobs have started or finished *to time*, is by using a planning or load board, provided with a scale of time. Normally, however, sufficient control is obtained by checking jobs finished against the weekly or daily schedule, and it requires far less paper and clerical work.

Another aspect of progress work which is important is respect for delivery promises to customers. There is an unfortunate tendency in industry, more prevalent in a seller's market, to assume that a slight lateness on delivery promised is not very serious, and that to quote a better delivery than it is possible to maintain in order to get orders is good business. Both are bad business, bad for planning in the customer's factory and damaging to a firm's reputation, however good that might otherwise be. Broken promises should be looked upon like any other broken promises—it is just "not done". The incidence of broken promises is sufficiently important for a special report to be made weekly to the Works Manager. This should at least show the number of deliveries made overdue and its percentage of all deliveries. The incidence should be so small that the Works Manager should be able to see and deal either daily or weekly with a list of all orders promised and not delivered to time. Each order should be recorded at the time the promise is made, on a weekly (or daily) promise sheet. At the end of each week (or day) orders delivered should be crossed off, leaving broken promises. Prevention being better than cure, a duplicate of the promise sheet should be given to a progress man some time before the due date—time enough to check progress and take urging action if necessary.

It is important for tools to be completed on time, since tools not ready when required will throw production programmes out of gear. Therefore, tool orders must also be progressed, and the method recommended above for dealing with delivery promises by recording and throwing up deliveries due is effective, since it directs attention to jobs likely to be held up, in time for corrective action to be taken.

Shortage lists for raw material and components should be prepared regularly by the progress men for urgent action either by the buyer or component-producing departments. These can be collected from the stores or thrown up automatically by return of requisitions or material release notes. It is useful for stores, particularly component stores, to post up on a blackboard or wall chart all items out of stock. There are always some items or aspects of production which senior executives need to keep an eye on personally. Charts, wall boards, or special forms are useful for this purpose if—and only if—their number and the number of items on them are few, and the items which need attention "hit the eye". In process factories stocks of scarce materials may need especial attention, in others output of important products or the load on departments may need watching from time to time. Charts are most convenient for the purpose, lines being drawn vertically to a quantity scale for each item listed horizontally. In practice the weakness is that whilst a line can always be extended, it must be rubbed out to be shortened. A simple home-made board which provides adjustable lines is shown in Fig. 21 (page 257). If it is desired to keep an eye on the progress of a few important orders in a factory with a limited number of processes, as in printing, a chart can be used (as in Fig. 28); a circle or diagonal line can indicate that the process is required, and a tick or an opposite diagonal line that the process is completed. If a board is used, cardboard discs can be hung on hooks and removed as the process is completed. Dates written on the discs add a time element to the control.

Suppliers of office equipment can provide very ingenious adjustable visible charts or boards for progress work. Keen and impressionable planning and progress men sometimes see in them a cure-all for progress problems. It is assumed that they work. They do not: they are tools, and as such must be operated by people who must be trained to be skilful and reliable in their use. It is unwise to use visible boards when the number of items is large, hundreds or more, as just

ORDER	COMPS.	ENGRS.	PLATEN	WHARFE	MIEHLE	C. & C.	BIND.		
212 B. JONES	O		O				O		
215 SMITH & WELLS		O		O	O				
216 BRA. ENG.	O	O			O	O	O		

FIG. 28.—Order Progress Board.

as good results can be obtained by cards or paper and at less cost in labour or space. But, for a small number of items, they can be most effective.

Cost Control

Meeting the term Cost Control in this section dealing with production may cause the reader to pause and think—but this is an Accountant's job. True the Accountant is responsible for calculating and accounting for all costs, but only the person immediately responsible for actual expenditure can control the cost—and that means the man on the shop floor, the operator and the foreman. And for a supervisor to be in control of the costs for which he is responsible he must know what costs should be, and what they actually are, so that he can take action to reduce or entirely avoid differences, i.e. excess costs. A supervisor has neither the time nor the facilities to record and calculate his own costs, so that he must be provided with the information; that is, he must be provided with another administrative service, just as he is by the Planning and Progress Engineers on programmes and deviations from them for controlling production flow. For controlling costs the Accountant supplies the information in the form of Cost Control Reports showing:

(1) *For Material.*—The cost of material used in excess of standard with an analysis of the causes of such excess.

(2) *For Labour.*—The cost of labour used in excess of standard analysed in the same way as for material, the effective performance of each operator and department, and the total cost per unit of production.

The supply of these reports and their interpretation is a production administrative activity and, as such, is dealt with here.

It may be necessary first to distinguish clearly between the terms Cost Control and Costing, lest they should be confused or assumed to be synonymous.

(a) *Costing*, as normally practised, is the computation of the total actual cost of a product or process *after* manufacture.

(b) *Cost Control*, in the modern sense, is the control of all items of expenditure by regular and frequent comparison of actual expenditure with predetermined standards or budgets, so that undesirable trends away from standard can be detected and corrected at an early stage.

The former is historical, and whilst comparisons can be made between total cost and selling price of a product to reveal the profit (or loss), little can be done about any excess cost except to deduct it from any total profit for the period, since the cause of the excess is not known. Even if the cause can be found for any particular product or component, its incidence cannot easily be detected, so that little can be done about it. On the other hand, well-designed Cost Control techniques reveal the actual cause of *all excess costs* in some detail, their magnitude, and their trend, i.e. increasing or decreasing. They are revealed too, immediately after the event, so that foremen and all concerned are aware of cause and effect and can take immediate steps to improve unsatisfactory results. In this chapter we shall deal only with Direct Material and Direct Labour Costs. Overhead expenses, which are controlled by comparisons with budgets, is dealt with in Part IV. Suffice to say here that supervisors must be presented with reports of actual expenditure, preferably compared with budget, regularly and immediately after the period to which they refer. Supervisors must be held accountable for all the expenses over which they have authority and control (e.g. loose tools, but not heating).

It has been explained earlier how the Production Engineers determine the correct material for use on a process or on a job, and the standard time for doing it. In practice, more material is used and more time spent over a period (e.g. a week) than the standard necessary for the total production for the period. The excess, of either labour or material, on any job usually has nothing to do with the job itself, but is due to such causes as careless operating and waiting for tools. What is wanted, therefore, to control these excesses is a record of them, not by job but by *cause*. And since the absolute cost of such excesses for a department is likely to increase in total production, to get a true measure of performance it is necessary to know the relative cost and therefore to express the incidence of total excess costs as a percentage of total costs.

Finally, it will be appreciated that Cost Control figures must be presented to the persons who are responsible for the expenditure; that is, to the foreman or supervisor of the department. And to enable effective action to be taken, the reports must be rendered immediately after the end of the period to which they refer, e.g. by Tuesday of the following week. To be fully effective they must be broken down to sections of a department where this is appropriate. In order to avoid duplicating work and extra operations in the accounts or wages office, the preparation of these reports should be integrated with the preparation of the payroll and operating accounts.

Material Cost Control

Excess material cost is revealed either as scrap or as an excess withdrawal from stock compared with standard for the amount of finished product manufactured. The most effective way of controlling scrapped material is to prevent the disposal of such scrap by anyone except an authorised person, and then only to a stated receiving depot, e.g. stores, against a document, such as a scrap note stating the cause and signed by an inspector or foreman. The scrap notes can then be valued and summarised either daily or weekly in the form of a report showing the cost under each cause heading compared with previous average and budget. Since it is usually impossible to prevent all waste or scrap, it is not enough to record actual scrap and its value; it must be compared with some standard (previous average or best or a budget) so that differences on the wrong side are immediately apparent. A suitable form for this purpose is illustrated in Fig. 29. Other headings by cause can be used according to the type of product or process. For example, in a Foundry they would be:

Total Melt, Cupola, Risers, Moulding, Fettling, Total.

It is usual for the Accounts Department to provide an overall control as a check on whether all material is accounted for as good product or scrap. (In the absence of such a check, there is a tendency for scrap to be understated or "lost".) Such control is effected by comparison of standard amounts (as laid down in process layouts) with amounts actually used. It will relate to each material used and apply to each department or process. The difference should be accounted for by the scrap recorded; where it does not, steps should be taken to explain the discrepancy; it may reveal unsuspected waste.

When material is issued in bulk from stores or drawn on as required by operators in the department, and scrap, waste, or over-usage is not identified as such, as e.g. in industries using materials in sheets (press work) or reels (wire) or planks (casemaking), etc., it is impossible to issue only the correct amount for a job, and so to control usage in that way. A control can still be provided, however, by the Accounts Department rendering periodical reports showing the standard amount which should have been used for the products completed

EXCESS MATERIAL COST

WEEK	TOTAL MATERIAL OR LABOUR		DUE TO OPERATOR		DUE TO MACHINE		FAULTY MATERIAL		OTHER CAUSES		TOTAL		REMARKS
	AMOUNT £ s d	%	AMOUNT £ s d	%	AMOUNT £ s d	%	AMOUNT £ s d	%	AMOUNT £ s d	%	AMOUNT £ s d	%	
BUDGET		100											
1													
2													
3													
4													
5													
6													
7													
8													
9													
10													
11													
12													
13													
TOTAL													

Fig. 29.

compared with actual bulk issues for the period. In any one period there will be slight differences due to variations in the amount of material in progress in the department, but over a period the difference should remain substantially constant (for a constant proportion of scrap) and a gradual improvement or deterioriation will be revealed.

Labour Cost Control

Excess labour cost can arise from the following causes:

(1) Waiting time paid to operators for periods when they are not able to work on jobs;
(2) Low effectiveness where a guaranteed minimum rate is paid;
(3) Premium payments, e.g. overtime, learning, etc.;
(4) Wrong grade of labour;
(5) Unused capacity, i.e. low output for same indirect operators.

Only excesses under the first heading are brought to the foreman's notice immediately and in detail, and only then when he personally signs or scrutinises each record of waiting time. Immersed as he is in the day-to-day problems of shop management, he cannot watch the incidence of each cause of excess cost, far less the total cost or its trend. It is necessary therefore to provide him with a weekly statement—his weekly operating statement as it were. Very detailed ones are often recommended, and daily reports are even used, but these involve the Wages Department (or some other Department) in a considerable amount of extra work and the foreman in an interpretation which is too detailed for him to give to it the necessary thought and attention. Of the several methods of presenting the essential information which the foreman must have, the form shown in Fig. 30 is a good example. It is not suggested that this form covers all cases or includes all causes of excess costs or indices of performance that may be required, but it will serve as a basis for preparing a suitable form for any specific need, and it is one which with slight modifications only has been used in industry and proved most effective, giving the foreman the picture he requires of his labour costs and the necessary control.

The form covers a thirteen-week period, and is entered up weekly by the wages clerks, sent to the Works Manager, and thence to the foreman for information and action, and report back to the Works Manager if requested. It is returned to the Wages Office in time for the next week's entries to be made. The average figures for the previous quarter (or budget figures if preferred) are entered as the opening line, so that continuity is preserved, and, as each week's results are added, trends are revealed.

The top portion of the front of the form brings home to a foreman the total costs for which he is responsible and their make-up. It is an analysis of the payroll for the department rapidly summarised by the wages clerks from the different classes of time or job cards. The total excess costs are shown and expressed as a percentage of the relevant figure. The unmeasured labour cost, i.e. the amount paid on day-work, is shown, as this can be considered uncontrollable, and should be kept to a minimum. The difference between standard and actual wages is the total excess labour cost and is analysed by cause on the back of the form.

The standard for indirect wages is arrived at by agreeing on the number and therefore weekly cost of supervisors and labourers for a given number of operators. This number of operators can be expected to produce a normal number of standard hours per week. The total cost of supervision divided by the normal total standard hours gives a cost per standard hour for supervision, which, multiplied by the total standard hours recorded for the work, gives the standard cost for supervision for that week.

The bottom portion of the front of the form is used for remarks by wages clerks, Works Manager, or foreman, and for indices of per-formance. The total hours earned divided by total hours on standard (on piecework) is the *index of piecework performance*. A figure of 1·31 is equivalent to 31 per cent. bonus, of course. If work measurement is done correctly, as recommended earlier, this figure is a true measure of performance, and can be used for comparisons between depart-ments. Dividing the earned hours by total clock hours (including daywork hours in both figures) gives the *overall effective performance* of the department.

The *cost per unit* is the total wages costs of the department divided by the total hours earned or tons produced or other unit of produc-tion, and shows the trend of the true effectiveness of the department. The cost per unit goes up if—

(1) Piecework performance goes down;

(2) Excess costs go up;

(3) The total output goes down with the same supervision and other indirect wages cost.

Excess costs are analysed on the back of the form under two head-ings, those for which the foreman of the department can be held responsible, and those for which other members of the management team are responsible. The Works Manager may have to deal with the latter, but the foreman is expected to act on the former. The analysis of waiting time is picked up from the reason given on the time card record and the headings are self-explanatory; others can be used to suit circumstances. The item "To equal P.W. Guarantee" is the amount which has to be paid to pieceworkers over and above their piecework earnings when these are below the minimum guaranteed.

Such operators were working below a satisfactory standard and well below normal. The cost of using a wrong grade of labour is picked up by the wages clerk from the job card when the grade of operator who does a job is different from that laid down by the Production Engineers and appearing in the standard data on the job card. It is ineffective use of labour by supervision. Excess cost due to faults in other departments is transferred out and vice versa.

In practice, when excess costs due to one or more causes are high or begin to rise, it is wise for the foreman to arrange to investigate personally over a limited period each incident recorded for these causes immediately it is reported. He is then able to find quickly the exact cause and to take effective remedial action. The report points to where such close attention is required, and it throws up the bad spots. To those unaccustomed to such reports, it is surprising how effective they are in drawing the attention of senior executives to increasing costs and deterioriating performance.

It is noted that in the example, provision is made for assessing a foreman's bonus, on the basis of his success in controlling excess costs in his department. The particular method used will depend on circumstances, but the report does reveal a measure which can be used in this way.

Machine Utilisation

At one time machine utilisation was considered to be more important than labour utilisation, idle machines more expensive than idle men. Although it is now realised that it may be wise to have a little spare capacity and machines available for operators thrown idle by breakdown on others, nevertheless it is still necessary to keep an eye on machine utilisation to ensure that there is no unnecessary idle productive capacity or capital. This is particularly true of automatic machines and plant, and plant in belt assembly or continuous production plant, where many delays on one machine may ultimately affect the whole plant.

Where, as in most cases, machines are attended or operated by individuals, the overall machine utilisation of a department can be calculated from operators' job cards by the wages office and included in the labour cost controls. Provision has been made for this on the form referred to above (Fig. 30). When this report, or other information, reveals that utilisation is unsatisfactory, it may be necessary to have a more detailed analysis for each machine. This is best done, as with excess labour cost, by recording the actual loss at source, that is, the delay or machine down-time, at the time it occurs with a note of cause. The simplest method is to provide a daily log sheet for each machine, preferably fixed on a board or holder, on which the operator or attendant can enter the time machines stop or start, and the cause. The principal causes of machine delays are mechanical breakdowns, setting-up troubles and unsatisfactory material. The first can be reduced by an effective scheme of preventive maintenance (see page 370), the second by a great deal more attention to the training of setters and to design of tooling (particularly important in specialists and short-run production so common in Britain), and the last either by better inspection of incoming material, or by more attention to regularity of product from previous processes or operations.

PRINCIPLES

As in everyday life, so also in the particular activity of management, experience proves that as a basis for all conduct it is wise to adhere as closely as possible to sound fundamental principles. The more one departs from principles, the more necessity there is for hasty decisions and expedient action to meet awkward situations which ought not to have arisen. One cannot always be certain of where some decisions are likely to lead, but if they are made in accordance with proved principles, then they are certain to lead in the right direction and to satisfactory results in the long run. It is useful, therefore, to have a body of principles, if only of limited application, in this relatively new science of management.

From experience and the study of the operation of the administrative activities discussed in this chapter, the following principles emerge. They are *specific* applications of the *general* principles of planning and control given in the Introduction on page 40.

(1) Planning is a function of management to be distinguished from doing. In the structure of an organisation the two should be separated and those persons responsible for doing (executives and foremen) should be supported by administrative staff whose duty is to supply information on how and when work is to be done, standards of measurement, and reports on results compared with standards.

(2) There are three divisions of the administrative activities:
Production Engineering (concerned with methods and standards);
Production Planning (concerned with programmes or time plans);
Production Control (comparing results with standards and plans).
Each should be separately recognised, and its specialised techniques developed.

(3) To reduce human effort to a minimum and to increase output per man-hour, work must be studied scientifically.

(4) Work can be measured in a common unit and the work content of a job assessed. Standard Times expressed in a unit based on the rating of speed, effort, attention and skill, with a due allowance for relaxation, provide an accurate measure.

(5) Standards to be used as a basis for planning and control for the material and labour content of production can be established.

(6) The only satisfactory basis for payment by results is an accurate measure of the work content of a job.

(7) Production planning is impossible without reliable information; and accuracy of results (given constant performance by supervision and operators) varies directly with accuracy of information.

(8) The more the information which has to be transmitted, the less effective the results of planning are likely to be.

(9) As far as possible paper work must be done in offices by trained operators and not on the shop floor by operators at machine or bench.

(10) To be effective, planning must—
be simple, flexible and balanced; be based on accurate measurement, and provide means for measuring performance against plans;

(11) For production control to be effective, results must be compared with standards (of performance, cost or programme) in reports which reveal the extent and cause of any discrepancy. Such reports must be rendered promptly, and corrective action must be taken immediately.

PRODUCTION PLANNING DOCUMENTS

A. GENERAL DESCRIPTION

I. PURPOSE

THIS instruction describes a method of preparing and using Production Planning Documents which makes use of modern techniques and duplicating machines for preparing pre-printed documents for use in Planning, Production and Cost Accounting. The main purpose of pre-printed forms is to ensure that as much information as possible is entered on works production documents before they are issued to the works, and that such information, after careful check of original entries, is automatically transferred to all copies from a Master document. The method adopted has three important advantages; it prevents transcription errors, prepares all documents rapidly and economically, and reduces the amount of clerical work in the shops to a minimum.

II. DESCRIPTION OF FORMS

A Master Document is prepared for each component and each machine to be manufactured.

This Master is in two parts:

A. A permanent Master (Fig. 31), on which is entered all permanent information relevant to production of the component or machine, including a summary of each operation in list form (i.e. process layout or master route card), and in the case of the technical design documents, design data required in the works.

B. A Variable Heading, on which is entered information relating to the particular order or batch to be manufactured.

The two portions married together form a complete Master Document for the particular batch.

C. Production Documents—From the Component Master the following documents are prepared immediately an order is created:

1. *Material Release Note* (Figs. 32, 33)

Specifying type and quantity of material required for 100 units and for the batch. Only the total amount of material specified is "released" in the first instance, and more can only be obtained by presenting an Excess Material Requisition. After materials are issued it is returned to Planning, who adjust stock and progress records. It is then sent to Accounts, who debit and credit appropriate inventory accounts.

ORDER HEADING MASTER													

CUSTOMER Stock | **QUANT.** 40 | **DESCRIPTION** Shaft· | **PART NO.** 140.2 | **JOB OR MACH. NO.** 342.E

DATE ISS. 10/8 | **MATERIAL RELEASE** 40 Billets | **SPECIAL INSTRUCTIONS** | **DATE DUE** Wk.35

LAYOUT ISS. 1 | **MATERIAL SPEC. & QUAN. PER** M.152.9 2½"D 21.7/16"L | **PATT. No.** | **DESCRIPTION** Shaft 70R A1 | **PART No.** 140.2

ROUTE	DEPT.	1	2	3	4	5	6	7	8	9	10	11	12
		9	9	9	9	9	3A						
	M/C OR GROUP	527	42	61	527	54							

OPERATION MASTER

TYPE ON DOTTED LINE ONLY

OP. NO.	DEPT.	MACH. OR GROUP	OPERATION	JIGS, TOOLS AND GAUGES	LABOUR GRADE / O'HEAD REF.	TIME ALLOWED SET-UP	HOURS PER
1	9	527	Centre face turn		M7 C	.25	.5
2	9	42	Grind		M7 D	.2	.48
3	9	61	Keyseat		M5 C	.2	.18
4	9	527	Screw		M6 C	.2	.16
5	9	54	Drill Peg Hole		M1 C	.05	.01
			(These times are purely imaginary)				

FIG. 31.

2. *Identity Label* (Fig. 34)

Used for identifying a batch and specifying each operation and the department where performed, i.e. the route. This label accompanies the work throughout all operations, and on it is recorded details of scrap and good work produced.

MATERIAL RELEASE NOTE — FABRICATIONS

CUSTOMER			QUANT.	DESCRIPTION	PART No.	JOB OR MACH. No.
			10	Bracket CE/OB/FV	120.25	350.B

DATE ISS.	MAT'L RELEASE	SPECIAL INSTRUCTIONS				DATE DUE
22/8	10 sets					Wk. 50

REQUIRED BY	Layout Iss	FROM STORES		DRG. No.	DESCRIPTION		PART No.
	1	$\frac{3}{11}$	Sht 1 of 1	120.25	Bracket CE/OB/FV		120.25

STORES CONTROL	QUAN. PER PART	MATERIAL CODE No.	MATERIAL DESCRIPTION	Wt/Part	Total	QUAN. THIS BATCH	VALUE
	1	M190-4	18"x18" Temp 1	46 lbs			
	1	M190-3	14"x14" Temp 2	21			
	1	M190-1	6½"x18" Temp 3	8.9			
	2	M190-3	8"x13½" Temp 5	25.5			
	2	M190-1	6½"x8½" Temp 4	8	109.4		
	1	M181-76	1"x2¾"x4¾"	3.2			
	4	M181-11	3½"x3/16"x1⅛"	1			
	12	M181-8	1¾"x3/16"x⅝"	2.2			
	2	M181-8	1¾"x3/16"x¾"	.4			
	4	M181-6	7/16"x5/16"x1"	1.34	8.14		

CUT	ISSUED	STORES SIG.			TOTAL COST	

FIG. 32.

MATERIAL RELEASE NOTE

CUSTOMER		QUAN	DESCRIPTION	PART No.	JOB OR MACH No.
		40	Shaft	140.2	342.B

REQUIRED BY	Date Iss.	MATERIAL RELEASE	SPECIAL INSTRUCTIONS		DATE DUE
	10/8	40 Billets			Wk. 35

PROGRESS	Layout Iss.	MAT. SPEC. & QUAN. PER	PATT. No.	DESCRIPTION	PART No.
	1	Steel M 152.9 2⅛" dia 21.7/16" long		Shaft 70R A1	140.2

STORES CONTROL	STORES SIGN.	DATE ISSUED	WEIGHT cwts. qrs. lbs. ozs.	RATE	VALUE

FIG. 33.

3. *Job Card* (Fig. 35)

One for each operation as specified on the Master, giving the Time Allowed for the operation, and the Jigs, Tools and Gauges required.

On this is recorded the operator's name and check number and the number to be paid for. It is later used for wages computation.

IDENTITY LABEL

CUSTOMER		QUAN.	DESCRIPTION	PART No.	JOB OR MACH. No.
		40	Shaft	140.2	342.E

DATE ISS.	MATL. RELEASE	SPECIAL INSTRUCTIONS		DATE DUE
10/8	40 Billets			Wk. 35

LAYOUT IS.	MATL. SPEC. & AMOUNT	PATT. No.	DESCRIPTION	PART No.
1	M.152.9 2⅛"D 21.7/16" L		Shaft 7OR A1	140.2

¹ 9	² 9	³ 9	⁴ 9	⁵ 9	⁶ 3A	⁷	⁸	⁹	¹⁰	¹¹	¹²
527	42	61	527	54							

FIG. 34.

CHECK No.	OPERATOR'S NAME		**JOB CARD**			WEEK ENDING
Standard times marked thus * are provisional for special or small batches and are subject to re-study and revision for quantity production.	CUSTOMER	QUAN.	DESCRIPTION	PART No.	JOB OR MACH. No.	
	Stock	40	Shaft	140.2	342.B	
	DATE ISS.	MATL. RELEASE	SPECIAL INSTRUCTIONS		DATE DUE	
	10/8	40 Billets			Wk. 35	
	OP. No.	DEPT.	M/C or GRP. No.	OPERATION	JIGS, TOOLS & GAUGES	LABOUR GRADE	SET UP.	HRS. PER
	5	9	54	Drill peg hole		C	.05	.01
	TOTAL TO PAY FOR	PREVIOUSLY PAID FOR	PAY FOR THIS WEEK	PREVIOUS ACTUAL HOURS	Std. Hours at Base Rate		Standard Hours Earned on run
					Actual Hours at Nat. Bonus.		
					TOTAL		Total Hours Earned

FIG. 35.

4. *Move Note* (Fig. 36)

One for each operation specified on the Master. On this is recorded the quantity passed forward, scrapped and to be rectified. It is returned to Planning Office when the operation is completed, where it is used for progress records.

5. *Delivery Note* (Fig. 37)

For the final operation only. On this is recorded the quantity finally delivered to Stores. The information is checked by Stores and entered on progress and stock records by Planning Office. It is then sent to Accounts, who debit and credit appropriate accounts.

6. *Progress Envelope* (Fig. 38)

In which all works' documents are kept until issued and after use, and on which is recorded the progress of the job (quantity and date) through the works.

FIG. 36.—*Note :* Layout of Move Note and Delivery Note should be identical—alternative forms are shown in Figs. 36 and 37.

7. *Cost Card* (Fig. 39)

A facsimile of the complete Master, with additional columns for Cost Account purposes.

8. *Tool Requisition* (Fig. 40)

Advice of tools required and receipt for tools taken from Tool Stores.

From the Technical Specification Master the following documents are prepared:

9. *Official Order Record*

This is a complete copy of the Master, and includes all information, technical and commercial, relating to the order, i.e. Customer, Machines and Spares ordered, Prices, Delivery Instruction and Design Data.

DELIVERY NOTE	CUSTOMER			QUANT.	DESCRIPTION		PART No.		JOB OR MACH No.	
	Stock			40	Shaft		140.2		342.B	
SCHEDULE	Date Iss.	MATERIAL RELEASE	SPECIAL INSTRUCTIONS						DATE DUE	
	10/8	40 Billets							WK 35	
PROGRESS	OP. No.	DEPT.	M/c or Group No.	OPERATION		JIGS, TOOLS, GAUGES	LABOUR GRADE		TIME ALLOWED	
									SET UP	Hrs. Per 100/Ea.
	5	9	54	Drill peg hole			C		·05	·01
STORES CONTROL	OPERATOR'S NAME		Quantity Passed and Sent Forward	RECTIFICATIONS					INSPECTOR	
				No.	CAUSE					
	CHECK No.			SCRAP					No. TO PAY FOR	DATE
				No.	CAUSE					

FIG. 37.

PROGRESS ENVELOPE		CUSTOMER		QUAN.	DESCRIPTION		PART No.		JOB OR MACH. No.		
		Stock		40	Shaft		140.2		342.B		
		DATE ISS.	MATL. RELEASE	SPECIAL INSTRUCTIONS					DATE DUE		
		10/8	40 Billets						Wk.35		
		LAYOUT is.	MAT. SPEC. & QUANTITY PER		PATT. No.		DESCRIPTION		PART No.		
		1	Steel M 152.9 2¼" diam 21.7/16"long				Shaft 70B Al		140.2		
SCHEDULE	DEPT.	1 9	2 9	3 9	4 .9	5 9	6 3A	7	8	9	10	11	12
ORDER PART LIST	M/C or GROUP	527	42	61	.527.	54					
	START										
	FINISH										
	OPRS. No.										
	No. GOOD										
	No. SCRAP										

FIG. 38.—*Note*. Envelope open at top and right-hand end for rapid use.

									MATERIAL		

COST CARD

CUSTOMER		QUANT.	DESCRIPTION			PART NO.		JOB OR MACH. NO.	· %		
Stock		40	Shaft			140.2		342.B	LABOUR		

DATE ISS.	MATERIAL RELEASE	SPECIAL INSTRUCTIONS						DATE DUE	A		
10/8	40 Billets							Wk.35	B		

LAYOUT ISS.	MATERIAL, SPEC. & QUAN. PER		PATT. NO.	DESCRIPTION				PART NO.	C		
1	M 152.9 $2\frac{1}{8}$"D 21.7/16"L			Shaft 70R Al.				140.2	D		

ROUTE

DEPT.	9	9	9	9	9	3A			10	11	12	E		
M/C OR GROUP	527	42	61	527	54							TOTAL COST		

OP. NO.	DEPT.	MACH. OR GROUP	OPERATION	JIGS, TOOLS AND GAUGES	LABOUR GRADE O'HEAD REF.	TIME ALLOWED SET-UP	Hours Per	STD. RATE	LABOUR COST		
1	9	527	Centre face turn		M7 C	.25	.5				
2	9	42	Grind		M7 C	.2	.48				
3	9	61	Key seat		M5 C	.2	.18				
4	9	527	Screw		M6 C	.2	.16				
5	9	54	Drill Peg Hole		M1 C	.05	.01				
			(These times are purely imaginary)								
									TOTAL		

FIG. 39.

10. Technical Specification

A complete copy, as in 9, but omitting price details.

11. Invoice Order

A copy of the commercial portion of the Master, including delivery details and prices of all items.

12. Dispatch Instructions

A copy of the commercial portion of the Master, omitting prices, but including data required for nameplates, etc.

13. Instruction Card

One for each assembly operation and for certain components. This card will give the operator all the technical data required at this operation.

14. *Planning Card*

One for each order. This will have only a brief description of the order as given at the head of the Master, but will have planning data added, and be used for building the Forward Master Load on the Works.

Part No.		Opn. No.	Clock No.	
Date Issued		Date Reqd.		
REMARKS :—				Total Tools Received
TOOL REQUISITION	Received Tools & Drwgs. to this Reference			
	Date		Signed	

FIG. 40.

B. PROCEDURE FOR USE OF DOCUMENTS FOR COMPONENT ORDERS

In the following procedure it is assumed that each person hands on a document to the person dealing with the next subsequent operation. The procedure is illustrated in the Flow Chart, Fig. 41.

I. ORIGINATE ORDERS

A. STANDARD COMPONENTS

By *Standard* components is meant those parts which are made against job numbers through a stock control routine.

1. *Stock Record Clerk*

(*a*) Originate order when order point on stock of a component is broken by writing out a Requisition for Manufacture.

(*b*) Calculate quantity of material to be released (i.e. length of bar or number of castings, etc.), and enter on Requisition for Manufacture.

(*c*) Enter on Requisition for Manufacture the actual stock of castings or fabrications.

2. *Shop Schedules Clerk*

Receive Requisition for Manufacture from Stock Record Clerk, and scrutinise and amend batch quantity if circumstances call for this.

3. *Typist*

Type Component Order Heading Master from information on Requisition for Manufacture.

4. *Duplicating Machine Operator*

(*a*) Take Operation Master for Component from file.

(*b*) Marry Order Heading Master and Operation Master, and run off documents on duplicating machine, thus:

> 1 Material Release Note. (For Fabrications two notes are usually required—one for Bar Stores and one for Plate Stores.)
> 1 Job Card for each operation.
> 1 Move Note for each operation.
> 1 Delivery Note (in lieu of Move Note for last operation).
> 1 Identity Label.
> 1 Progress Envelope.
> 1 Cost Card.

The Cost Card is only necessary for the initial issue of a Master Operation Layout, and for Standard items is to be run off without Component Order Heading Master.

(*c*) Refile Master, and scrap Order Heading Master and Requisition for Manufacture.

5. *Shop Schedules Clerk*

(*a*) Receive Progress Envelopes containing all documents. Draw load line on all planning tickets and replace tickets in envelopes.

(*b*) File in the appropriate section of the "Standard" Waiting File under machine size sequence.

(*c*) Send Cost Card for new components to Cost Office.

B. SPECIAL COMPONENTS

By *Special* Components is meant those parts which are made only to special order numbers, and not to minimum and maximum stock requirements.

1. *Forward Load Planner*

(*a*) Scrutinise Order Parts List of machines on Assembly schedule for availability of material.

(*b*) For machines where material is not available, write out appropriate urge notes and pass to Buying Department.

(*c*) Where all material is available, raise Requisition for Manufacture for each special part on the Order Parts List.

(*d*) Obtain Operation Master copy and calculate quantity of material to be released, and enter on Requisition for Manufacture.

(*e*) Send Requisition for Manufacture to typist.

2. *Typist*

Type Component Order Master Heading from information on Requisition for Manufacture.

3. *Duplicating Machine Operator*

(*a*) Take Operation Master from file (or obtain from Production Engineers).

(b) Marry Order Heading Master and Operation Heading Master and run off documents as for Standard components.

(c) File Master, and scrap Order Heading Master and Requisition for Manufacture.

4. Shop Schedules Clerk

(a) Receive Progress Envelopes containing all documents. Draw load line on all planning tickets and replace tickets in envelopes.

(b) File in the appropriate section of the "Special" Waiting File under machine size sequence.

(c) Send Cost Card for components to Cost Office.

II. BUILD COMPONENT MANUFACTURING LOAD

1. Shop Schedules Clerk

(a) Each week, when departmental Assembly Schedules are built, scrutinise all jobs in both Standard and Special Component Waiting Files, and build up load on each department in priority order (i.e. according to date due on Heading). Write out draft schedules of loads.

(b) Should special circumstances warrant reduction of size of batch, arrange for duplicate documents for the second half of the batch.

2. Typist

Type departmental schedules from drafts.

3. Forward Load Planner

Record on Order Parts List week number of schedule for any special parts that have been scheduled.

III. ISSUE SCHEDULES

1. Shop Schedules Clerk

(a) Issue schedules to Shop Planners of department concerned one week ahead of the scheduled week.

(b) With the schedule, issue Move Notes and Job Cards to the department in which operations are performed, and send Material Release Notes and Identity Labels to the department in which the first operation is performed.

IV. MANUFACTURE

1. Shop Planner

(a) Build up load on planning board with Move Notes for each section.

(b) Send all Material Release Notes to Stores concerned, as requisition for raw material, and to enable Stores to prepare all the material in advance of requirements, stating day on which material will be required.

(c) On day previous to when job is to commence, send Identity Label to Stores marked with the machine number or operator to which the material is to be delivered, and the time by when it will be required.

(*d*) On day previous to when an operation is to commence, make out Tool Requisition and send to Tool Stores.

2. *Tool Stores*

(*a*) On receipt of Tool Requisition put up kits of tools for job operation specified, and place Requisition with tools.

3. *Foreman or Chargehand*

As instruction for commencement of job, hand Move Note to operator.

4. *Operator*

(*a*) Take Move Note for new job and Identity Label for job finished to Time Clerk. Having been clocked on, retain Move Note for new job, and refix Identity Label to finished job.

(*b*) Present Move Note to Tool Stores for drawing, jigs, tools and gauges. (Retain Move Note.) Enter clock number on Tool Requisition and sign.

5. *Time Clerk*

(*a*) Clock the time on Job Cards of new job and job finished.

(*b*) Enter operator's name and department, with the week number, on the new Job Card, and place in current job tray.

6. *Inspector*

(*a*) After operator has completed job, make a final inspection, and make out Scrap Note for any scrap. If there is any faulty work which can be rectified, arrange for rectification, if possible, by the operator responsible.

(*b*) Enter on Move Note the quantity passed forward, the number to pay for, and, if any, the number scrapped. Date and sign Move Note.

(*c*) If batch must be passed forward before rectification, enter quantity to be rectified, and complete Move Note, and make out new Move Note and Job Card for this operation, and Identity Label, by hand. The foreman to arrange for completion of batch and any further documents, if required. If operator is to be paid for any scrap or rectifications not sent forward (fault lying elsewhere), enter quantity to be paid for in panel of Move Note.

(*d*) Enter on Identity Label number of parts passed forward.

(*e*) Hand Move Note to Time Clerk.

(*f*) Sign Move Note each time a check inspection is made.

(*g*) For a final operation, on receipt of Delivery Note from Time Clerk, arrange for immediate transfer of batch to destination.

(*h*) If part deliveries are made from a batch, make out a part Delivery Note for any partial delivery with the part Delivery Note number.

7. *Time Clerk*

(*a*) When job is "clocked off", transfer Job Cards to "completed" tray.

(*b*) When Move Note is received from Inspector, transfer quantity to be paid for from Move Note to Job Card.

(c) Extend actual hours for job and enter on front of Job Card in panel immediately at right of "Actual hours at Nat. Bonus".

(d) At end of week write out new Job Cards when operator has to be paid for work done on a job not completed in that week.

(e) Enter on front of new Job Card the quantity previously paid for and actual hours for this quantity in panel "Previous Actual Hours".

(f) When completing a carried forward Job Card, deduct the quantity previously paid for, as shown on Move Note, to leave quantity to pay for on this card.

(g) Send Job Cards to Cost Office, and hand Move Notes to Shop Planner.

(h) For a Delivery Note of a final operation, mark off schedule and hand Delivery Note immediately to Inspection.

8. Storekeeper

(a) On receipt of Material Release Notes, prepare material, castings, or components, ready for issue.

(b) Enter on Material Release Note for raw materials the quantity (or weight) of material for batch to be issued.

(c) On receipt of Identity Label claiming the material, enter date issued, and sign Material Release Note. Send material to machine or operator indicated on Identity Label at, or before, time specified.

(d) Send all completed Material Release Notes to Planning Office once daily.

(e) On receipt of Finished Components from a manufacturing department, check description and quantity of goods with Identity Label and Delivery Note. Sign back of Delivery Note, with the date, and send to Planning Office. See that Identity Label is firmly fixed to special batches, and where necessary to standard batches.

9. Progress Record Clerk (Planning Office).

(a) On receipt of Move Notes, record completion of operation on Progress Envelope. File Move Notes in envelope.

(b) On receipt of Delivery Note for all components, mark off Office copy of Shop Schedule, and hand Delivery Note for Standard components to Stock Record Clerk.

(c) For Specials, in addition to marking off Final Operation on Progress Envelope, enter on Order Parts List that manufacture of component is complete. Send Delivery Note to Cost Office.

(d) File Progress Envelope in Orders Completed File.

(e) For weldings delivered to Casting Stores, mark Progress Envelope for Machine Shop batch "Weldings ready".

10. Stock Record Clerk

(a) On receipt of Material Release and Delivery Notes for Standard components, record receipts and issues on Stock Record Cards.

(b) Sign Material Release and Delivery Notes and send to Cost Office once daily

C. PROCEDURE FOR USE OF DOCUMENTS FOR ASSEMBLY ORDERS

I. ORIGINATE ORDERS

1. Forward Load Planner

(a) At the time Requisitions for Manufacture are raised for special components (see item B. 1(c) on page 300), write out in pencil with carbon the Variable Heading for Assembly Master. See that any special instructions of general interest are included in the Variable Heading.

(b) At this stage, when there is more than one machine on an order, decide on the number of machines to be put through as a batch, and make out the Variable Heading for each batch quantity.

(c) Send Variable Heading to Duplicating Machine Operator.

2. Duplicating Machine Operator

(a) Take Operation Master for Assembly from file (or obtain from Production Engineers).

(b) Marry Order Heading and Operation Masters and run off documents as follows:

1 Move Note for each operation for each batch or machine.
1 Job Card for each operation (except Test) for each batch or machine.
1 Delivery Note in lieu of Move Note for Finishing and for Machine Painting Operation.
1 Identity Label for each machine.
1 Progress Envelope for each batch.
1 Cost Card for each order.

(c) Refile Master and Order Heading Master until advised that order is complete.

3. Shop Schedules Clerk

(a) Receive Progress Envelope containing all documents. Draw load line on all planning tickets and replace tickets in envelopes.

(b) File in Waiting File under machine number sequence.

(c) Send Cost Card to Cost Office.

II. BUILD ASSEMBLY LOAD

1. Shop Schedules Clerk

(a) Each week build up assembly load from load in Waiting File. Adjust, if necessary, to preserve as near as possible a uniform load through all Assembly sections.

(b) Write out draft schedules of load.

2. Typist

(a) Type departmental schedules from drafts.

(b) Record scheduled week number on Order Book Card Index.

III. ISSUE SCHEDULES

1. *Shop Schedules Clerk*

(a) Issue schedules to Shop Planners of Department concerned one week ahead of the scheduled week.

(b) With the schedule, issue Move Notes and Job Cards to the department in which operations are performed, and send Material Release to Assembly Notes and Identity Labels to the department in which the first operation is performed.

(c) With the schedule, issue Job Instruction Cards.

IV. MANUFACTURE

1. *Shop Planner*

(a) Build up load on planning board with Move Notes for each section.

(b) Send Material Release to Assembly Notes to Stores concerned two days previous to when machine is to be built, to enable Stores to prepare material in advance.

(c) In Assembly Shop, components for building will be put out on stillage platforms and parked by Stores inside Assembly Shop, identified by a handwritten tie-on label. Assembly Shop Labourer will collect and move platforms to Fitter.

2. *Foreman or Chargehand*

As instruction for commencement of job, hand Move Note to operator.

3. *Operator*

Take Move Note for new job and Identity Label for job finished to Time Clerk. Having been clocked on, retain Move Note for new job, and refix Identity Label to finished job.

4. *Time Clerk*

(a) Clock the time on Job Cards of new job and job finished.

(b) Enter operator's name and department, with the week number, on the new Job Card and place in current job tray.

5. *Inspector*

(a) After operator has completed job, make a final inspection. If there is any faulty work which can be rectified, arrange for rectification, if possible, by the operator responsible.

(b) For Subassemblies, enter on Move Note the quantity passed forward, the number to pay for, and, if any, the number scrapped. Date and sign Move Note.

(c) For dealing with rectification in Detail Assembly, see paragraph B. IV. 6, page 302.

(d) Hand Move Note to Time Clerk.

6. *Time Clerk*

(a) When job is "clocked off", transfer Job Card to "completed" tray (*b*) When Move Note is received from Inspector, transfer quantity to be paid for from Move Note to Job Card.

(*c*) Extend actual hours for job, and enter on front of Job Card in panel immediately at right of "Actual Hours at Nat. Bonus".

(*d*) At end of week make out new Job Card for uncompleted jobs, and mark "Brought forward". On Job Card to be closed mark "Continued".

(*e*) Send completed Job Cards to Cost Office, and hand Move Notes to Shop Planner.

(*f*) For Delivery Note of a final operation mark off schedule and hand Delivery Note immediately to Inspection.

7. *Storekeeper*

(*a*) On receipt of Material Release to Assembly Notes, prepare material ready for issue.

(*b*) Mark off Part Lists for items issued. Send Part Lists to Cost Office when all materials on the order have been issued.

(*c*) Sign Material Release to Assembly Notes and send to Planning Office daily.

(*d*) Assembly Stores. Gather together all parts required, put up on stillage platform, write machine number on manilla label, tie on batch, and park in Assembly Shop.

For Subassemblies follow same procedure, using trays and Identity Labels supplied.

8. *Progress Record Clerk* (*Planning Office*)

(*a*) On receipt of Move Notes, file in Progress Envelope, and mark off progress on envelope.

(*b*) On receipt of Delivery Note, mark off Order Book Card Index.

(*c*) When Delivery Note on last machine is received, transfer Progress Envelope to Orders Completed File.

9. *Stock Records Clerk*

(*a*) On receipt of Material Release to Assembly Notes, adjust records.

(*b*) Sign Material Release to Assembly Notes and send to Cost Office once daily.

D. PROCEDURE FOR USE OF ANCILLARY DOCUMENTS

I. GENERAL

A. The following ancillary documents are to be used in conjunction with the pre-printed documents, and are to be filled in by hand when required:

1. Excess Time Card.
2. Excess Material Requisition.
3. Stores Credit.
4. Waiting Time Card.
5. Scrap Note.

With the exception of the Stores Credit, these documents all record excess costs, i.e. money spent on either material or labour in excess of what need have been spent. It is vitally important, therefore, not only that they are accurately made out, but are authorised by a Foreman, so that the head of the department is aware of the excess costs in his department.

B. If either of the Material Documents, i.e. Stores Credit or Excess Material Requisition, or Scrap Note, are spoilt, they must not be thrown away, but must be marked across the face "cancelled", and sent forward with the other completed documents.

II. EXCESS TIME CARD (Fig. 42)

A. This is to be used whenever extra Standard Time is allowed on a job because of some unusual cause, i.e. when, because of some temporary

		EXCESS TIME CARD						
	DEPT. NO.	CUSTOMER	QUAN.	DESCRIPTION		PART No.	JOB OR MACH. No.	
OPERATORS NAME		REASON FOR EXCESS					ACCOUNT No.	
	DATE	OP. NO.	DEPT.	MACH. OR GROUP	OPERATION	JIGS, TOOLS & GAUGES	LABOUR GRADE	EXCESS TIME
								PER
OPERATORS NO.	ACCOUNT NO.	QUAN. TO PAY FOR		EXCESS HOURS ALLOWED	RATE	COST	£. s. d.	
		AUTHORISED BY						

FIG. 42.

condition in the shop, more time will be required to do a job and the extra time can be assessed. It is not to be used when Standard Times are permanently adjusted.

B. It is only to be made out and authorised by a Work Study Engineer.

C. It is important to give the account number on which the excess cost is to be charged, and to state the exact reason for the excess, particularly showing the responsibility.

D. Excess Time Cards are to be attached to the Job Card to which they relate, and sent to the Wages Department.

III. EXCESS MATERIAL REQUISITION (Fig. 43)

A. This is to be used when an extra issue of material is required, because it will be impossible to finish the job with the amount of material available, due to scrap, loss, or shortage on original requisition.

B. Normally it will only be used when the amount of scrap is unknown, or material has been cut to waste.

C. Under "Reason for Demand" the exact details and the reason excess material is required must be shown.

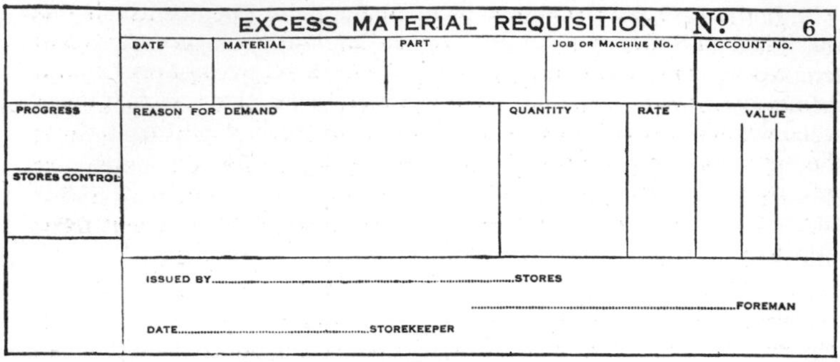

FIG. 43.

D. Excess material will only be issued against the signature of a Foreman or some higher authority.

E. The Material Requisition is to be forwarded to the Planning Office with Material Release Notes.

Note.—See Scrap Note for replacement of scrap.

IV. STORES CREDIT (Fig. 44)

A. This is to be used when, for any reason, job cancelled or material found to be surplus to requirements, material or components have to be returned to Stores.

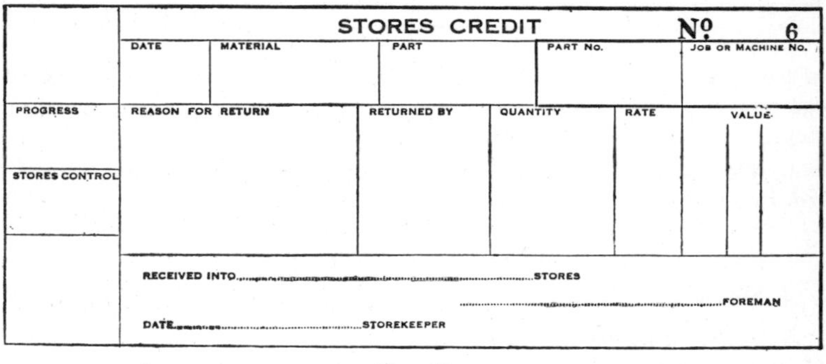

FIG. 44.

B. It must be signed by the Foreman of the Department returning the material or components.

C. Stores Credit Notes are to be forwarded to the Planning Department with Material Release Notes.

V. WAITING TIME CARD (Fig. 45)

A. This is to be used whenever an operator has to be paid for waiting time, i.e. the operator is prevented from, or delayed in, doing work.

B. It is to be made out in total by the Foreman or Chargehand, including the "time on" and "time off". Because an operator can, and might be tempted to, claim more waiting time than has actually occurred in order to artificially increase bonus earnings, it is most important that the exact time when waiting time commenced and finished shall be known and checked by the Supervisor responsible. It also gives the Supervisor the opportunity to investigate the cause, and to take steps to prevent its recurrence. It will be advisable for one card to be used for each incident. One card must never be used for waiting time on different account numbers.

C. The exact cause for the lost time must be stated, indicating the responsibility. When the responsibility is considered to belong to another department, the card should preferably be countersigned by the Foreman

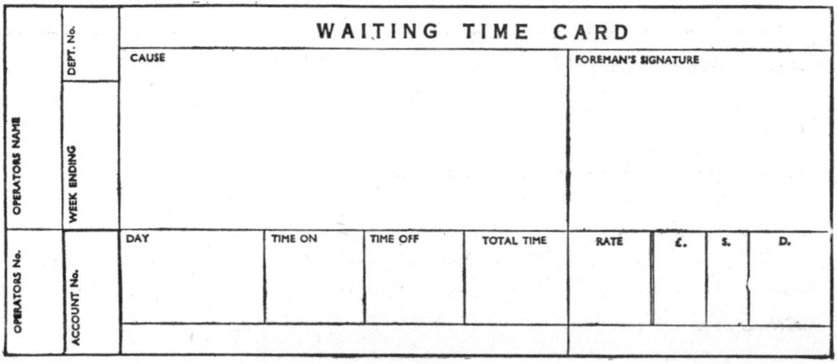
WAITING TIME CARD

OPERATORS NAME | DEPT. No. | WEEK ENDING | CAUSE | FOREMAN'S SIGNATURE

OPERATORS No. | ACCOUNT No. | DAY | TIME ON | TIME OFF | TOTAL TIME | RATE | £. | s. | D.

FIG. 45.

of the other department on the day the card is completed, in order that he can be made immediately aware of the lost time and excess cost, and take steps to prevent its recurrence.

D. Waiting Time Cards are to be handed in to the Time Clerk, who will confirm that all time in the day is accounted for.

VI. SCRAP NOTE (Fig. 46)

A. This is to be used to record components completely rejected as scrap.

B. It is to be made out by the Inspector rejecting the work, and the cause of the scrap must be clearly stated, and the account number indicating the responsibility entered, consulting the Foreman concerned if there is any doubt.

C. A Scrap Note is to be used for each job and operation, i.e. the scrap from several operations or different jobs *must not* be included on one Scrap Note.

D. Should it be necessary to replace the component scrapped, and therefore obtain further material, as may occasionally happen on the first operation of a special part, the material required may be drawn from the Stores by completing the bottom of the Scrap Note, and using the Note as a requisition instead of using an Excess Material Requisition. It is the Inspector's responsibility to find out whether it will be necessary to replace the material at this stage.

When replacement of scrap must be put through separately and cannot go with the original batch, the Scrap Note must not be used as a material requisition, but a new set of documents must be issued from the Planning

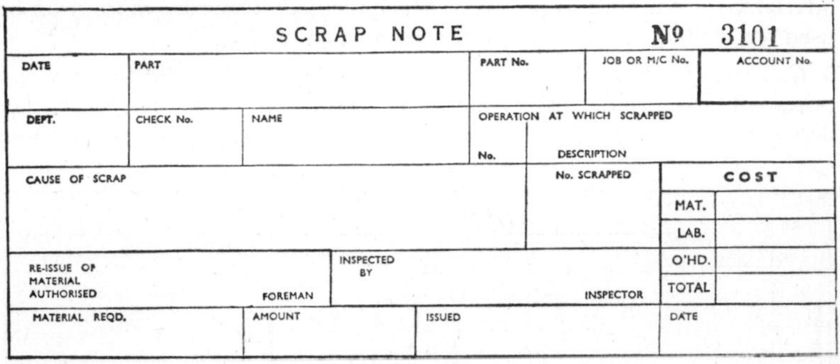

SCRAP NOTE				Nº 3101	
DATE	PART		PART No.	JOB OR M/C No.	ACCOUNT No.
DEPT.	CHECK No.	NAME	OPERATION AT WHICH SCRAPPED		
			No.	DESCRIPTION	
CAUSE OF SCRAP			No. SCRAPPED	COST	
				MAT.	
				LAB.	
RE-ISSUE OF MATERIAL AUTHORISED		INSPECTED BY		O'HD.	
	FOREMAN		INSPECTOR	TOTAL	
MATERIAL REQD.	AMOUNT	ISSUED		DATE	

FIG. 46.

Office. The Planning Office will decide whether to issue a replace order on receipt of a Scrap Note for which replace material has not been drawn. It will help the Planning Office, in the case of urgent jobs, if the Inspector refers the Scrap Note immediately to the Progress Engineer or Planning Office direct.

E. After summarising by Inspection Department, Scrap Notes are to be forwarded to the Planning Office, who will forward on to Cost Office.

CHAPTER IV

SUPERVISION

Supervision—a Human Problem. Selection, Training and Promotion. Remuneration and Financial Incentives. Performance

SUPERVISION—A HUMAN PROBLEM

PRODUCTION MANAGEMENT is concerned with getting things made or done. The technical function of this management is primarily concerned with material things, designs, processes and machines, the administrative function is concerned with facts and figures. The actual doing, execution of plans and supervision of the persons involved, is a human problem. It is concerned with people, who have emotions as well as capabilities, rights as well as duties, free will as well as good will, and reactions that cannot be predicted with the accuracy of machine movements. It is a problem at least as old as civilisation; what makes it still so little understood apparently and so difficult to solve today is that conditions have changed, and changed rapidly in the comparatively short industrial era. So much work now must be done collectively under supervision and at so intensive a pace. Recently, too, with the changing political atmosphere has come "industrial democracy". The feeling of equality on the part of operators with management—a by-product of industrial democracy —reduces the automatic obedience to orders, complicating tremendously the relationships between supervisor and supervised. Unfortunately, the attitude of willing, informed, intelligent obedience is not inherent nor automatic—it must be engendered and developed, and this is only possible in an atmosphere of mutual trust and belief in a worth-while common purpose and of enthusiasm for attaining the purpose. In such an atmosphere people enjoy what they are doing, and work willingly and effectively and with continuous high effort. The supervisor's job mainly consists of creating this atmosphere by word and action, decision and example, orders and organisation; it is a job of leadership. Although the new type of leadership must permeate management from top to bottom (no section, department, works or organisation can be better than the man at the top), it is at the foreman level that serious lack of it causes most unrest and most reduces individual effectiveness. The foreman, alone of the management hierarchy, is in constant daily touch with operators, and is most frequently giving orders and making decisions. Today he is often the weakest link in the chain of command. The reasons and the difficulties are not far to seek. During the first half of the twentieth century the duties and responsibilities of supervisors of all grades have been steadily reduced or changed. Certainly their power "over" people has been reduced even if their effective power is more. Specialists are now employed to do most of the work which, in the earlier days of the industrial era, occupied a foreman's time. Processes and methods are laid down by technicians and production engineers, the order of production is decided by planning clerks, piece rates are worked out by ratefixers, costs and performances calculated by accountants, and even engaging and discharging and trade union negotiations are largely performed by (though not the ultimate responsibility of) the Personnel Officer. Frequently, the foreman is not on or represented on works councils, joint-production and similar committees, and is obstructed by shop stewards. Furthermore, the effects of taxation have reduced the differential between him and his skilled subordinates' earnings, reducing the incentives to acceptance of the job for all its status. Finally, foremen and other supervisors are often promoted from the ranks because of proficiency as operators and not for abilities as leaders of men and receive no training for the job of supervision or management. Yet from the foreman grade, higher grades of management are, in the main, ultimately recruited. All this has a depressing effect on the standard of management as a whole.

The solution of course is to select supervisors mainly for their abilities, even if latent, as leaders, and not only for their skill, and then to train them for the job of supervision. This job consists, in addition to knowing something of the technical work being done by subordinates and associated specialists, of putting the right man in the right place, seeing that he is suitably rewarded for his efforts, giving him all the information he needs or should have, making decisions on the innumerable occasions which are not covered by standard practice, instructions and procedures, and continuously to inspire all his team to work willingly and well.

Inspiration

No one will doubt these days that inspiration is one of the greatest incentives to action. History has given many outstanding examples, the efforts of the British people after Dunkirk being not the least among them. Such tremendous events as were occurring at the time of Dunkirk and such conditions do not (fortunately) occur in everyday life. But inspiring leadership in everyday work can have astonishing results in raising men's efforts much above the ordinary level. To do so, supervisors must show by their enthusiasm and example that they have faith in the purpose of the job in hand and of the Company's products or business and are loyal to the Company's policies, their own seniors and to all their subordinates. It is not enough to do so on important occasions, it must be shown *always* in every small decision and action, in giving orders and receiving unpleasant ones, in reprimands and in commendation, in attempting the impossible and carrying out the routine jobs, in dealing with disputes and correcting or reporting grievances, in setting tasks and ensuring reward. Free men can be led : they cannot be pushed. It is easier to pull a chain than to push it in the direction desired—and it is the same with a group of people. To inspire his team and maintain a high morale, the supervisor must set himself a high standard and live up to it. One occasionally hears a supervisor lament that he does not get the respect due to his position. Respect, like authority, cannot be handed out or ordered, it must be earned. Men on the shop floor have an accurate assessment of their supervisor's character ; they know him at least as well as he knows himself, and usually better. He has presumably been chosen for his superiority, and they therefore tend to set their own standard of behaviour by his. People learn most easily by imitation and habit. If a supervisor is loyal and is trusted, is enthusiastic and co-operative, so will his subordinates be ; if he is not, he cannot make his subordinates so.

In a very small group of unskilled operators the chargehand usually has no difficulty in getting over the purpose of high production ; even the need for quality is readily appreciated. How the group fits in to the general scheme and contributes to the finished product or total output of the factory is not so easily appreciated, but must be put over. Nor should this be left entirely to the chargehand, nor even the foreman. All supervisors up the chain of command should take the time and trouble to do so and to be interested in their subordinates and their work. The most significant fact which came out of the long detailed and now famous experiments carried out at the Hawthorne factory of the Westinghouse Company in America, known as the Hawthorne experiments[1], was that the powerful incentive behind the continuously increasing production of a group of girls was not the many physical amenities or the financial reward, but the fact that, in the words of the girls themselves, "they mattered". Directors, Managers, Professors, were interested in them and their results, visited them and their department, and they felt that they were important—they mattered. Of such is the elusive spirit of loyalty and morale made ; we must all, and the purpose for which we work, matter.

---

[1] *The Making of Scientific Management*: Vol. III, *The Hawthorne Investigations* (Urwick & Brech) (Management Publications Trust).

Inspiration, then, is the essence of leadership. Loyalty is a principal ingredient—loyalty to subordinates, to management and to the purpose of the enterprise. Others are keenness, which is infectious; absolute honesty in all things, but especially in discussions; interest in and liking for people, resulting in personal sympathy and understanding; readiness to face awkward situations and to accept responsibility, but unwillingness to ask others to do anything one would not or could not do oneself; an ability to make prompt and resolute decisions, however unpleasant; and finally a sense of humour. These ingredients cannot be distilled from mere meditation or reading, nor are they entirely inherited. They must be learnt and practised daily, and become an integral part of a supervisor's character.

Communication

The communication of information, ideas and decisions is a basic necessity for management. It is a "tool" of supervision which is in constant use and must always be in good condition. It is perhaps true that what makes leaders inspiring and outstanding, in addition to that vital spark of enthusiasm and an unshakeable faith, is the ability to convey ideas and information clearly, vividly and convincingly to others. Generally, in industry, supervisors at all levels are not very fluent or even able to pass on information accurately and clearly. As a result of prolonged concentration and specialisation on technical skill, often encouraged at school and college, they have neglected the art of speaking and writing good English. It is the cause of much misunderstanding of what has been said and the reason why much information that should be passed on is not.

How can employees understand and appreciate the purpose of their work if it is not explained to them? If facts are withheld or suppressed there is suspicion, where information is lacking there is rumour—which has a high rate of circulation. This is true, not only of matters of policy, higher management, decisions and wage rates, it is also true of the hundred and one decisions taken every day down the line of supervision. Information must circulate like fresh air and permeate the whole organisation. Secrecy separates people, common knowledge of a common purpose unites them. It is therefore essential for a supervisor to become proficient at communicating essential and accurate information and decisions; and the more effective in doing so he becomes, the more power *with* people he will have—the more he will inspire.

The essential ingredients of information is, of course, facts. Many disputes and misunderstandings arise because *all* the *facts* of a case are not known to *all* the people concerned. Busy supervisors intent on their own job and immediate problems have difficulty in finding the time necessary to obtain all the facts bearing on their own work or that of their department, and to see that all essential facts are passed on. But it is essential, and they should make particular and constant efforts to do so. Especially in dealing with matters affecting individuals, it is essential to be objective and not personally influenced in assessment and communication of the facts of a case. Absolute honesty and scrupulous fairness are vital in such matters.

This does not mean that the manner of passing on information is unimportant. In supervision we are dealing with persons who have feelings and emotions, and just because facts can be so cold and impersonal it is essential to present them with a certain amount of warmth and preferably in person. The spoken word is more effective (though less permanent) than the written, talks more effective than notices on the board, a word of encouragement often a stronger incentive than financial reward. A flash of humour is worth a good deal of legal argument and a ready sense of humour is an attractive and popular trait.

There is a reluctance, on the part of managers and foremen, particularly of practical and technical persons, to hold forth in front of a crowd, however small. But it is one of the essential techniques of management that must be learned. It is good for a leader sometimes to stand in front of all his team and to talk to them collectively, inviting questions and giving straight answers. It is dynamic and effective in maintaining morale. It can of course be overdone—and abused.

However desirable it may be to convey information verbally and in person, it is sometimes necessary to do so in writing. Occasionally, notices have to be displayed, standard practice instructions laid down, the results of meetings minuted, and letters and reports written or dictated. In such cases it is not only necessary for a manager to say what he means, he must say it in a way that will be understood—and not misunderstood—by those for whose benefit it was written. Written communications like these, to achieve their purpose must be set out simply and clearly, must not be verbose nor involved, must be accurate and not ambiguous, and must read well, i.e. have a certain amount of style and be free from official jargon. In a word, they must be good English. It is essential therefore for managers of all grades to learn (or relearn), to study and practise, the art of writing well—not literature, but technical English. Like any other craft, it can only be learnt by practice and critical study of one's own and other's efforts. It is an important part of their craft, and due time and thought should be given to it.

Two recently published books giving a great deal of useful advice and information which will help those wishing to improve their power of self-expression by the written word are *The Presentation of Technical Information*, by R. O. Kapp (Constable), and *Plain Words*, by Sir Ernest Gowers (published by H.M. Stationery Office).

Decision

Decision is an important element of leadership, and the nice balance between the impetuous, too hasty decision and a hesitating one or procrastination has to be cultivated. One is certainly not born with it. There are some people who find great difficulty in making up their minds and sticking to a decision. Highly skilled, technical persons and those trained in research often do not make successful managers or supervisors for this reason; they have been so used to looking all round a question in every detail that they are unable to make a decision rapidly. It is in times of war when the power of rapid and correct decision is so vital that so many fine leaders are developed. But although it is essential to be able to make a decision, it must not be thought that it is possible to do so without a knowledge of the facts and a good deal of thought. During a war, those in command are living at a high pitch of intensity, and at such times the brain is tuned to a like intensity and is able to comprehend rapidly and assess a wide range of factors. One does not usually live at quite the same intensity in times of peace, yet something like the pitch must be reached for a short period when decisions are being taken, and the practice of intense concentration for the purpose must be cultivated. Behind this sudden concentration of thought there must be, however, a continual observation and reception of facts, an awareness of what is going on, of likely reactions of people concerned (a General studies his opponents' character and behaviour minutely), a feeling for the atmosphere of a situation. A manager therefore must not always be forcing his ideas, he must be a good listener as well as a good talker, and above all must be able to get others to contribute their ideas and facts, and as far as possible, to share, or feel they share, in the decision.

Sharing of decisions adheres to what Mary Follet called the "law of the situation".[1] When all the facts of a situation are found (the law discovered), all concerned, supervisors and operators, obey the law; there is not the same feeling as when obeying orders. Authority can still be exercised, but it is the authority of the facts of a situation.

Co-operation, Co-ordination and Integration

These are elements of the technique of organising action. Co-operation is really a state of mind that can exist only on a basis of

[1] *Dynamic Administration*, page 58 (Metcalf & Urwick) (Management Publications Trust, 1945).

knowledge and appreciation of a common purpose that is understood by all. Likewise, co-ordination needs all concerned to have all the information necessary at the time common effort is required. Integration requires a pooling or gathering together of all the facts and ideas for the purpose of arriving at a best solution of a problem, one which is likely to be better than any one person's solution. In each case a sharing of information is required. In practice it means that there must be frequent meetings between those concerned; not necessarily large or formal meetings, but at least some opportunity to exchange views, ideas and facts. Under wise leaders this co-operation, co-ordination and integration ensures harmony, progress and effectiveness of the whole team. This is not a plea for formal meetings or committees; far from it. The atmosphere of committee rooms is apt to be deadening and sterile. But it does mean that the practice of getting together by these whose activities interlock is a good one and should take place at all levels. On the shop floor such meetings need not be regular, but should be quickly arranged as necessity arises and be limited in time. When members of a team are frequently, if quite informally, together as a team, they see themselves as such and co-operation becomes more of a habit than a formal process.

Co-ordination of plans and activities can be ensured by regular meetings, daily, weekly or as required, of those concerned, under the supervisor ultimately responsible, and each supervisor in turn should hold meetings, smaller and less formal perhaps, of his subordinates. At such meetings, in order to integrate ideas, to arrive at the best solution, it is essential not to allow a discussion to crystallise into an either-or situation. To do so invites the taking of sides, conflict instead of integration. If such a situation tends to develop, efforts must be made to keep the discussion open until a good deal of thought has been concentrated on the issue. Finally, when an agreed solution is arrived at, it should not be made a "decision" of a committee, but the person responsible for action and results should take responsibility for decision and issue of instructions. A committee is too impersonal a body to be responsible for decisions. (This does not apply when objective judgment and not action is required, as in selection of candidates or assessment of blame or merit.) A person cannot be responsible to more than one person and hence to a committee of which he is not a member. In the same way a person cannot be loyal to two masters. This latter is a compelling reason for finding the solution to a problem of modern industry, the dual loyalty to employer and trade union, which puts an impossible stress on those subjected to it. It should and must be possible to integrate the separate points of view and purposes. This particular problem is a challenge to modern management.

SELECTION, TRAINING AND PROMOTION

Because selection and training schemes are matters in which the Personnel Officer advises and undertakes a good deal of the work, this does not mean that they are no longer the line executive's responsibility. Ultimately, the head of a department is responsible for the people he has working for him, he must retain the final right of decision about people added to his staff, retained or promoted. He has the duty, of course, of requesting, if necessary, and at least of listening to and considering, the advice of the Personnel Officer, but he himself must make the final decision.

The skill of choosing subordinates is one which the young or newly promoted supervisor must learn if he is to be successful. Many re-organisations would not have been necessary, and many unhappy organisations would not be so, had the executive at the head been skilled in the choice of men. Square pegs in round holes are obviously wrong, and no doubt do not usually remain in the hole for long, but the perfect fit, just the right person who not only fits but also makes his sphere of activity vital and stimulating, is the ultimate aim. There is, however, another aspect of choosing. Few persons remain what they are at an early age. All are susceptible to training—particularly good and stimulating training. So it is equally important and makes for more stability and loyalty than introducing persons into an organisation from outside at a high level, to choose good material at an early age and then to train. Each promotion then is also a selection, so that Selection, Training and Promotion, vital elements in supervision, form as it were a triangle (Fig. 47).

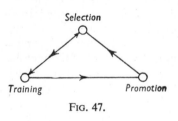

Selection

Training   Promotion

FIG. 47.

Skill in selection of staff demands of executives that they shall be good listeners and better observers. Dominant men usually get "yes-men" round them. To learn a man's abilities and potentialities one must draw him out and encourage expression of views and abilities; this can only be done by giving him his head as far as possible. Although much-improved techniques have been developed to aid selection by interview and test, they are not sufficient by themselves, and personal evaluation, particularly of character and personality, has still to be relied on. Such evaluation should be continually practised if it is to be reliable. For it to be practised only in the case of important appointments and for the inevitable mistakes to be made is expensive and wasteful, but it can be practised without actual appointments being involved by studying the behaviour of people one meets and checking one's judgment later. It will be found, except in rare cases, that a conscious effort of evaluation has to be made, else the decision will be affected too much by emotional reactions and personal likes and dislikes.

There should not be the same difficulty when making promotions. There is no better way of knowing a person's abilities, potentialities and faults than by living or working with him. At the same time it is not always certain how he will react to responsibility and the power of authority. Opportunity should be taken or made of trying out likely men in the absence of or in the place of existing executives and supervisors. All concerned benefit by the trial, leaders and those led, and for every supervisory position in a structure there should be a person trained, or selected privately by the superior, to be promoted immediately in case of necessity. There is much to be said for training in the position. Most important of all is that it ensures continuity of policy, tradition, and the knowledge of the innumerable details which are never recorded in standard practice instructions, but are part of the "know-how" of the department.

In many ways there is no more important job which a supervisor has to do than train—train his subordinates and see to it that all training in his department or organisation is effectively carried out. In the complex organisations of modern industry, in which every person needs some skill, but a relatively small proportion are "fully skilled", it is not satisfactory to the trainee or to the company to leave training to other operators. A systematic plan is called for. While a Training Centre may be employed in some cases, the supervisor still has an important part to play. An essential part of the training of a new employee is bound up with the psychological atmosphere of the department which he joins, learning to belong to and co-operate with the team.

This subject is more fully dealt with in Part III, Chapter III.

REMUNERATION AND FINANCIAL INCENTIVES

Remuneration, salary or wages, is one of the provisions which go to make up a contract of service, written, verbal, or implied, and as such is a matter of legal importance. Although it is one of the duties of a Personnel Officer, where one is employed, to ensure that all legal conditions are complied with, a supervisor must make himself acquainted with such conditions lest by implication or otherwise he breaks the law or creates misunderstandings. Where there is no Personnel Officer, it is especially important for the chief executive to make sure that all foremen and other supervisors, and particularly newly appointed ones, understand the wage structure and conditions attached to it.

It is generally known that the payment of wages under contract of service is still governed by the Truck Acts (1831, 1887, 1896) and the Shop Clubs Act (1902), and that under these Acts payment of wages other than in the coin of the realm (money) is illegal. So is the condition of compulsory membership of works societies and of deductions, with certain exceptions, for bad work, or supply of material. In most industries minimum wages and additions for overtime and special working conditions are enforceable by law and, in some, piece rates also.

In most large industries, rates of wages are settled by mutual negotiation and agreement between representatives of employers and employees, in others they are laid down by decisions of Wages Councils set up by the Minister of Labour where, in his opinion, there is inadequate machinery for regulating wages. The management of a new company must make certain whether its employment conditions are affected by existing Wages Councils or other agreements. In industries covered by Wages Councils, schedules of rates and conditions must be posted up in the premises.

"The labourer is worthy of his hire." The economic worth is the value in cash which the community places on a person's services. Ultimately, whether we like to think so or not, this means the scarcity value of services either individually or collectively. The higher collective value, of course, gave rise to trade unions and the use of strikes or organised absence. But there are other rewards for work (see Dorothy Sayers' booklet *Why Work?*). Recent authoritative surveys and individual investigations have revealed that financial reward is not the first, and is sometimes placed as low as the fifth, reason for remaining in a job. This may come as a shock to older foremen and those in mass-production industries, and gives point to what has already been said under Inspiration. Nevertheless, a satisfactory level of earnings and method of wage payment is a basic necessity of a job, an essential requirement which must be satisfied before other factors begin to operate to engender the "will to work".

Kinds of Payment

Remuneration to employees takes two main forms:

Daywork or Time Rate.—Payment at a flat rate per hour, week or year, independent of the amount of work done or output achieved.

Payment by Results.—Payment which varies in some way according to work done or other measure of effort or results. Piecework is a form which is different from all other payment by results methods, in that payment varies *directly* with the amount produced at all levels of production.

Since most persons are inherently conscientious, it is probably thought by everyone, at some time or other, that a flat-rate weekly wage is an adequate incentive. But in cold, hard fact there are few of us who do not work harder for the stimulus of more reward for more effort. Hence it is that more and more employees in industry, hourly paid and staff, are being paid some proportion of their total earnings (even if annually) according to results. Provided that management is sound and is trusted and respected by operators, payment by results is effective as an incentive to higher output. Payment by results is not, however, a universal panacea. It goes only some way to meet one of the essential requirements of a job, the possibility of higher earnings for greater effort. It is a financial incentive, and as such is only one of many incentives. Financial incentives cannot be considered as an isolated factor affecting morale, or as producing predicted or invariable results depending only on the incentive, its type or power. But as part of the larger factor of financial reward or remuneration, they are a vital part of the personnel policy, which in turn is one aspect of the management policy, which in turn is an aspect of company policy.

Before going on to consider each form in detail, it might be as well if we get the advantages and disadvantages of the two main forms into perspective. Broadly speaking, time rate involves the minimum of administrative and clerical work, but provides no financial incentive. Neither does it provide a measure of what labour cost should be, but only what it has been. It hides excess costs of low producers. Piecework provides the most direct financial incentive, and also, if properly applied, the most powerful incentive, but for maximum effectiveness it does involve adequate study and measurement of work done and clerical labour in calculating results. No one will deny that under certain circumstances there are adequate incentives to work well even with time-work payment. At the same time such circumstances are comparatively rare, and in industry it is generally found that output of all manual operators and most clerical workers is higher on some form of payments by results. The disadvantages, or rather difficulties, of payment by results are, in addition to the extra clerical labour:

(1) By putting the emphasis on output, quality tends to suffer. (This can be neutralised by including quality in the "results" and by adequate supervision.)

(2) It can lead to disputes with operators over rates. (This is a function of the quality of supervision.)

(3) It requires careful and thorough preparation and measurement. (This is in reality an advantage, since it puts the emphasis where it is most required, i.e. on work study.)

(4) Methods other than direct piecework tend to confuse and be mis-understood and mistrusted by operators. This is particularly true of premium bonus methods (which share savings in cost between management and operator), and of so-called profit-sharing systems.

These disadvantages, or difficulties, should be read as signals for caution, not as reasons for not proceeding with some form of payment by results. There is no cheap or easy way to better results—all ways call for better management. Even where time rates or staff conditions are preferred to payment by results, it is necessary to measure results against standards either by department or by job, or both, for effective management control.

Prior to the introduction of any incentive scheme, it is essential to establish a sound wage-rate structure for all jobs and all grades of labour. It is advisable to do so whatever method of payment is used. This involves an analysis of all jobs, grading them, and fixing rates for all grades.

Job Grading

There is a strong case for the objective assessment of all jobs and operations carried on in industry in the country on a standard basis in order to establish once and for all the relative value of all jobs. For example, has mineworking a greater intrinsic value than skilled engineering say in the toolroom, and is the man at the coal face of more value than the shot firer, and the toolroom operator than the blast-furnace operator, bearing in mind responsibility, skill, risk, effort and so on? It should remove the cause of much argument and many disagreements and strikes if all jobs could be rated on a point system which would place them in correct relative position. Or would it? After all, the final arbiter of a person's value to the community must be what the community is prepared or forced, by scarcity, to pay for his services. An actor, or painter, or chief brewer, may earn far more than any such assessment would indicate. Nevertheless, in any one company, and certainly in one factory, it is possible to assess, in relation to all other employees in that concern, the scarcity value (due to long experience or local factors) of any job. Inequalities of reward are far more obvious in a small community like a factory and create as much dissatisfaction, no less damaging to morale because it is hidden, as in industry as a whole. For this reason an analysis and assessment of all jobs should be undertaken whenever possible or opportune. This job grading, as it is called, should most certainly be done before any form of payment by results is introduced or changed in a factory. In some industries certain occupations or grades are laid down by custom, agreement, or regulation, but even in these there are usually many jobs not defined or not covered by them, such as, for example, service labourers, semi-skilled operators, storekeepers, trolleymen and many others.

Job grading analysis is a method of giving a value to all jobs in an organisation according to certain characteristics of the jobs or required of the persons doing them. It is now generally recognised that there are four main groups of job characteristics:

1. Skill,
2. Effort,
3. Responsibility,
4. Working conditions;

and each group can be divided into sub-characteristics, effort for example consisting of mental and physical effort. All these major characteristics are present to some degree in all jobs, the degree varying from job to job. If the relative value of each group and each sub-characteristic is agreed upon at the start in terms of points or percentage, then each job can be assessed or rated for each characteristic and the total value of the job found. Such an evaluation will be as nearly objective as is possible, and, in any one company at least, jobs will be valued and rated strictly according to their relative importance to that company, and not as a result of bargaining or pressure. When the points value of jobs have been fixed, they can be given an hourly wage rate in relation to the minimum in the industry or company. In tackling such an analysis, there are four problems to settle:

(1) To determine the headings or characteristics for which each job shall be rated.
(2) To fix the maximum number of points to be given to each characteristic.
(3) To adopt a procedure which will ensure consistent rating.
(4) To set up a panel or team to do the actual analysis and rating.

Characteristics

The above four main headings can be further subdivided thus:

Skill	Responsibility	Effort	Conditions
Basic knowledge	Equipment	Physical effort	Surroundings
Experience	Material and product	—	—
Complexity	Safety of others	Mental effort	Hazard
Judgment	Supervision given	—	—

At this point one has to decide whether to go for still further subdivision, as obviously each of the above subdivisions can be qualified in many respects. However, to do so makes for considerable complexity, and consequently more time and effort to do the job, whereas the above divisions are adequate for most purposes and work well in practice. In a particular factory or organisation it may be found that one or two of the divisions only need be further divided.

Maximum Point Rating

With the particular organisation in mind and the kind of work carried on, a point rating is given to each main characteristic and allocated to each subdivision. Checks are then made with a number of well-defined jobs and the results reviewed critically. It may be found that some correction is called for. For example, they might be assessed first as Skill 40, Responsibility 30, Effort 20, Conditions 20. It may then be judged that Skill should have 45 points, allocated as to Basic Knowledge 15, Experience 10, Complexity 8, Judgment 12, and that in the particular factory Conditions are extremely good and safe, so that a rating of 12 points is adequate for this characteristic. Checks and rechecks are made until reasonable satisfaction is obtained. If there are certain jobs which have a rate established by agreements in the trade, these should be used as key checks (although it does not always follow that their established wage rate is correct).

Rating

When rating a job, it is absolutely essential that it is done objectively, and that all the persons on the rating panel use the same kind of scale for good, medium and poor. Where records are available, such as time for training or number of accidents due to specific causes, these should be used. Otherwise good, medium, poor and none can be thought of in terms of percentage and then applied to the maximum points. It is important that each member of the panel should make his assessment first and jot it down before comparing assessments to arrive at an agreed figure.

Panel

The panel should not be too large, but should consist of at least the Personnel Officer, Foreman of department concerned, possibly a representative of operators, and Works Manager or other senior executive. Being directly affected by the results, it is obviously more difficult for the operators' representative to be objective than for members of the management, and there is usually a tendency for them to rate higher. Nevertheless, if agreement between all members of the panel is always insisted on before fixing a rating, results are satisfactory, and it is elemental that those affected shall have a say in the assessments.

Wage Rates

In order to fix appropriate wage rates to each grade, it is usual to take as a basis the wages paid in the industry or company for the lowest and highest grades and to fix other wage rates pro rata. In certain circumstances it may be necessary to work within certain wage rates already established by agreement or by Wages Councils and rates may have to be paid for certain jobs whatever the job grading value is assessed at. If maximum and minimum rates are already established, then the job grading results will enable a satisfactory scale of rates to be established for grades in between and beyond the limits. When existing rates must be incorporated these should be plotted against points rating for the appropriate job. A mean line then establishes rates for all ratings (a permissible difference plus or minus can be allowed for).

Since it is so important a matter to all concerned and so little understood yet, readers who decide to tackle the job are recommended to read first or at least refer to Lytle's *Job Evaluation Methods*,[1] particularly Chapter IV, and *Job Evaluation and Merit-Rating in Theory and Practice*, by J. J. Gracie.[2]

Daywork or Time Rate

This is simple enough to be generally understood. Payment is at a uniform rate for every hour worked up to a maximum number of hours in a day and a week, above which premiums are paid according to the industry and local agreements or arrangements. Premium payments are also usual for Sunday, holiday and night work. Until recently, staff employees were paid for a week whatever and whenever the hours worked, but with the diminishing difference between staff and works privileges, there is a tendency for staff to be paid for regular (as distinct from occasional) overtime.

Apart from premium payments for overtime, earnings of the operator on time rate are constant per hour or day. On the other hand, the labour cost to the employer increases for outputs below standard and decreases for outputs above standard. This means that the employer bears losses and retains savings with variations from standard output as shown in Fig. 48.

This should be compared with piecework (see pages 326–8).

Where output can be maintained at or near to standard, more or less independently of the operator's control, then daywork is satis-

---

[1] *Job Evaluation Methods*, by Lytle (Ronald Press, New York).
[2] *Job Evaluation and Merit-Rating in Theory and Practice*, by J. J. Gracie. Series of Monographs published by Manchester College of Technology.

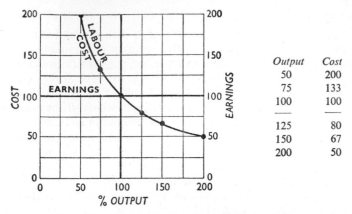

Output	Cost
50	200
75	133
100	100
125	80
150	67
200	50

FIG. 48.—Graph for Time-work Earnings and Cost.

factory. This occurs on production assembly lines and where output is governed by the speed of machine or conveyor. In these cases, financial incentives, if required, should be tied to quality, overall output, or some other such factor.

Payment by Results

The various kinds of payment by results fall under three headings:

(1) *Piecework*—being payment at a constant rate of pay per unit of work produced correctly for all units whatever the number.

(2) *Premium Bonus Systems*—being methods of varying the rate of pay per unit or of sharing savings between Company and operator above or below a standard task.

(3) *Profit Sharing*—methods of distributing a portion of overall profits earned by the Company over a period (usually a year) to employees.

Piecework

Although piecework is perhaps the oldest form of payment by results (it was used in cotton spinning in Lancashire as early as 1876), it is still the most widely used, at least in England. No doubt because of its overriding advantages of simplicity and fairness, it is rapidly replacing the other forms of payment by results. The most frequently raised objection to it, the fear of rate cutting, is not inherent in the method of payment, but arises from faulty measurement of work or rate fixing, which can occur however payment is made for work done.

Piecework can be paid on either a price per piece basis or on a time per piece basis. The result is the same in either case. For example, take the case of an operator whose hourly rate is 1s. 8d. or 20d., doing a job for which the "standard" output is 10 per hour:

Piece price is 20 ÷ 10 = 2d.
Piece time or time allowed is 1 ÷ 10 = 0·1 hour.

If actual output were 13 pieces per hour:

	On price basis	On time basis
(1) Earnings per hour would be	13 × 2 = 26d.	13 × 0·1 × 20 = 26d.
(2) Bonus earned would be	26 − 20 = 6d.	(1·3 − 1·0) × 20 = 6d.
		i.e. time saved at hourly rate.

There are distinct advantages in working on the time per piece basis and it is strongly recommended. The objection to the time basis frequently raised by operators, that they cannot calculate earnings or judge the output they must make for normal earnings, is not justified in practice. When operators have worked on the time basis for a week or so, they have no difficulty in calculating earnings or rate of output. In either case each rate can be given to operators as an output per hour for standard as well as price or time per piece as the case may be. Output is calculated thus for example, assuming above figures and a desired earning of 26d. per hour.

In a price basis
Desired earnings divided by piece price
26 ÷ 2 = 13 per hour.

On a time basis
Desired earnings divided
by earnings for time allowed
26 ÷ (20 × 0·1) = 13 per hour.

The advantages of working on a time basis are:

(1) Emphasis is given to the time aspect of a job and the need to save time.
(2) Since work on a job must first be measured in time required to do it before fixing any rate, it avoids a calculation to translate time into price.
(3) Planning uses time, and therefore must have a time for a job. Piece prices have to be translated back to time.
(4) The time is constant whatever the hourly rate of the operator doing the job; a piece price must be recalculated for each hourly rate. This is a most important point on the shop floor and when changes in rate occur. (In a factory where there are thousands of piece prices, it is obviously a job of some magnitude to alter all prices when an all-round change in rates occurs; piece times do not have to be changed.)

The effect on earnings and on labour costs is shown in the diagram at Fig. 49.

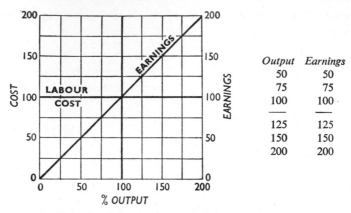

Output	Earnings
50	50
75	75
100	100
——	——
125	125
150	150
200	200

FIG. 49.—Graph for Piecework Earnings and Cost.

It will be seen that it has two most desirable features. Earnings of the operator increase pro rata with effort, a 50 per cent. increase in effort bringing a 50 per cent. increase in pay, and the *labour cost* to the Company is *constant*. (Total cost is reduced of course, due to greater absorption of overheads.)

In practice the principle of a guaranteed minimum earning modifies the result somewhat. Whilst earnings still increase above the minimum pro rata with effort, below the output equivalent to the minimum guaranteed earnings, pay is constant, but labour cost increases as in the time-rate diagram. In many industries this minimum is fixed at some level higher than day rate or standard, but why this should be so is difficult to see. A daywork rate should be paid for a daywork effort, and some other method found of paying an incentive to operators like labourers, for whom it is difficult to measure their output. The simplest and quite effective way is to pay such operators the same or some proportion of the percentage bonus earned by the department or group they serve or belong to. (They must not be paid *out of* the earnings of the piecework operators.)

It is usual for operators and management to think of piecework results in terms of "bonus", i.e. the earnings above standard. Its significance to the operator is obvious; to the management it is a most valuable measure of performance if work measurement has been done accurately. Referring to the calculation above, it was seen that earnings for an hour when production was 13 was $13 \times 0.1 \times$ hourly rate, or 1·3 hours × hourly rate. This can be expressed as time wages (1 hour at hourly rate) plus wages saved (0·3 hours saved at hourly rate). That is to say, the operator is paid his hourly rate wages plus *all* wages saved, because he has done a job in less time than standard. This is the vital point and the reason why straight piece-work is the only satisfactory method of payment by results for direct operators and the only one really acceptable to them because it does pay to operators all the savings made due to their efforts, is simple in operation and easily understood. It provides a positive and strong incentive at all levels (above any guaranteed minimum) and no other method is so satisfactory in practice. If it would seem that one of the other premium bonus schemes is required, there is strong reason to think that conditions are wrong somewhere and should be corrected rather than by-passed by inherently weak methods of payment.

At the time of writing there is a complication in some industries in Britain, particularly the large engineering industry, due to piece rates being calculated on a Base Rate which is less than the full day rate. For example, the *base rate* for a skilled fitter is 66s. per week (1s. 6d. per hour), but to this is added a "National Bonus" of 33s. (9d. per hour), making 99s. in all. Piecework earnings are calculated on the hourly

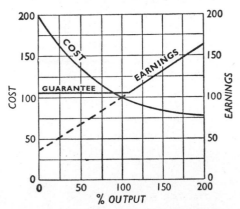

FIG. 50.—Graph for Piecework Earnings and Cost (Eng. Industry).

base rate of 1s. 6d. only, the 9d. "National Bonus" being added for each hour worked. The effect on earnings and costs is shown in the diagram at Fig. 50.

Output	Earnings per Week		Cost
	Piecework	Total	
50	33·0	66·0	1·32
75	49·5	82·5	1·10
100	66·0	99·0	0·99
125	82·5	115·5	0·92
150	99·0	132·2	0·88
200	132·0	165·0	0·82

It will be seen that the earning curve is still a straight line, but it starts at a minimum figure (in practice the minimum guarantee is 8s. above the total day rate, i.e. 107s.) and the cost is not constant, but decreases with increasing effort.

Premium Bonus Systems

These were first introduced around the turn of the century, in the U.S.A. by Halsey, Taylor & Gantt, and in Britain by Rowan, the underlying thought being that employer and employee shared savings or profits resulting from outputs higher than standard. To operators on time rate this appeared "fair shares". As the mathematics of the idea were studied and understood, the proportion of the savings paid to the employee and the level taken as a basis for savings were varied to provide stronger or different incentives. In some schemes the proportion of savings going to employer and employee changed at different levels of output; in one, the Barth system, the proportion varied (geometrically) as output varied. In the original Bedaux system, which for calculation of savings was straight piecework, 25 per cent. of savings due to increased output was paid to supervisors in a department. It was this particular arrangement which proved so noxious to British workers, and so discredited the very sound methods of work measurement used by the Company from which the system took its name. The idea has since been completely dropped from all modern applications of premium bonus system.

The Rowan system, much used in Britain—before accurate methods of work measurement were well known—paid to operators, over and above a minimum day rate, the proportion of their base-rate wages represented by the ratio, time saved to time allowed. The effect of this was to cause earnings to rise rapidly immediately above standard output, but less rapidly the higher output became. Under this system it is impossible for an operator ever to exceed twice his base-rate earnings. It thus avoids high earnings due to loose rates, but has a low incentive to high effort.

In general, all premium bonus systems suffer from the marked disadvantage that they are difficult to understand by the operator and as such are suspect. The result is that whatever intrinsic incentive they may have is more than neutralised by the effect on general morale.

Readers who are interested in such systems are recommended to Lytle's *Wage Incentive Methods* (Machinery Publishing Co.) for a detailed and penetrating analysis of most if not all of them, and of other incentive schemes.

Installation of Payment by Results Schemes

A word of warning will not be out of place to all those who contemplate introducing some form of payment by results. Trouble with, or actual failure of, attempts to introduce financial incentives into wage payment may probably be traced to lack of preparation and of sufficient detailed explanation to the employees concerned, foremen as well as operators. The writer has found that the ability of operators in industry to grasp completely and understand the calculations and implications of the simplest and most direct schemes is unbelievably low. One is apt to forget that what looks simple to the initiated is a bit mysterious to people who left school long ago and are conditioned to their existing method of payment. And what appears mysterious is suspect. Furthermore, both foremen and representatives of the operators will understand quite clearly themselves, yet be quite unable to convey the facts to operators or to convince them of the fairness of a scheme.

For this reason it is essential to take trouble to ensure that all the main body of operators do understand what is involved and exactly how their efforts will be rewarded. It will require a great deal of patience. The first essential, of course, is an introductory meeting, either with all operators or their elected representatives, and an agreement on principles. This should be followed by smaller meetings of departments, sections, and groups with explanations and illustrations in full. Finally, but most important, foremen and other supervisors must be completely "sold" on the scheme. It is to court certain trouble to put in any scheme against the wishes of or with the least doubts of the supervisors concerned. They must be 100 per cent. behind the scheme and show real enthusiasm for it. It helps considerably to give supervisors and a shop steward or other representative some training in the methods of work measurement used and methods of calculation and interpretation of results.

Profit Sharing

The popularity of profit-sharing schemes ebbs and flows according to the general level of prosperity. They are popular with employees when there is profit to share, but become suspect and lose their savour when profits decline, and remuneration accordingly. Such schemes are more in the nature of sentimental attempts to meet the complaint of those who maintain that workers (as distinct from owners) do not get a fair share of increasing profits or prosperity, than deliberate financial incentives. Nevertheless, they are usually looked upon as forms of payment according to results, incentives to think of company prosperity and to work accordingly. As incentives to individual effort they fail in their purpose, and the mortality of such schemes is evidence that there is something unsound about them. There is no doubt that in certain circumstances particular forms of profit sharing can be effective, but success in a specific case is no guarantee, nor can it be expected to be, in other cases or in general. Such schemes are more likely to be effective or permanent in very small organisations where owner and employees work closely together, and business problems, as distinct from workshop problems, are apparent and can be understood and appreciated. They are likely to fail in general and in large concerns for two reasons:

(1) They are based on false premises—in particular that profits can be shared but not risks.

(2) As incentives they are too remote and lack power—reward is too remote from effort.

An arrangement which gives to persons a share in the profits of investment, other than as a simple loan, without any sharing of risks is unbalanced and bound to be unstable. Profit-sharing schemes do not usually incorporate any sharing in losses; that is, there is no deduction from current or future earnings if the Company makes a loss or less than a normal profit. Employees' earnings are "guaranteed", but earnings of capital are not. Furthermore, in steady years most employees come to look upon their share of profits, whether paid monthly or yearly, as normal, and to adjust their standard of living accordingly. Frequently, the expected share out is actually mortgaged in advance. When the first lean year arrives, as it so frequently does, there is much disappointment, disillusion and bitterness. The slump in morale then appears to far outweigh the advantages, and in fact this is likely to be true.

As an incentive to individual effort, schemes of profit sharing, which depend on yearly results and on the actions of high executive who by single errors (like faulty buying of a major material, faulty decisions on sale policy, or bad design) can wipe out any efforts of the body of employees, have little direct effect. They are too remote from individual effort except to the few top executives, who can see the effects of their own individual actions. Operators on the bench cannot see the cumulative effect of their own individual efforts, indeed they are swamped or may be negatived by the efforts or lack of effort elsewhere.

One type of profit-sharing scheme which has attracted a certain amount of attention recently, goes some way to meet this last weakness, but it does not appear to have been tried in companies where the make-up of total cost as between labour and material may vary appreciably from year to year. In process and mass-production shelf goods industries it may have some success. It is the scheme operated in America by the Nunn Bush Co. A wages fund, out of which all works operators are paid, is credited with a fixed percentage of gross sales, so that employees as a whole benefit by all of any increase in the productivity of their labour. They are guaranteed 52 weekly wage payments, and are paid on account until the final results of the year are known.

If it is thought that Company loyalty and co-operation should be engendered or bolstered by financial methods, then some form of co-partnership or purchase of shares in the Company may be successful, although there are not many schemes in operation. Certainly, for executives, senior and long-service employees, a stake in their company's assets should foster a feeling of joint ownership and responsibility.

PERFORMANCE

High, Normal, Low.—These are the terms frequently used to describe performance. But usually they are an expression of a person's own opinion based on his own abilities. In respect of the performance of a whole department, it is likely to be even more a matter of personal judgment. Whilst such judgments are good enough for personal belongings like cars or radios where performance is largely a matter of opinion, they are not adequate in industry where the ultimate measure is the customer's decision conditioned by competition. The basis for comparison, the standard, must then be not what has been, but what is possible. All those in supervisory positions, manager and foremen, must be in a position to assess performance on the basis of measured results compared with an accepted standard. This is the basis of management and cost controls referred to in Chapter III, page 283.

In order to use his own time effectively, a manager must so organise his department and his own job that others take care of the routine work of the department, and must delegate to subordinates everything within their competence and covered by standard procedure or instructions. He can then give his specialised attention to the difficult and exceptional or new problems. This is the principle of management by exception. To do this every supervisor must have information which not only reveals exceptional performance, bad as well as good, but in such a way that his attention is directed to the high and low spots. There are some supervisors who prefer to deal with knotty problems as they crop up instead of making conscious efforts to trace and eliminate cause, and others who love to have reports and graphs but do nothing about them. Managers must be continually alive to the need for good and better performance, of labour, machines and their product, to seek continually the cause for results which are below standard and take energetic steps to remove the cause.

Labour

The main source of information on the performance of labour is the weekly results of individual bonus percentages (or other record of results where piecework is not in operation), and the weekly Labour Cost Control report (see page 287) is used for this purpose. Weekly bonus results should be scrutinised regularly. Particularly good performances should be complimented: an ounce of appreciation is worth a ton of reprimand. Poor performances should be approached in a spirit of enquiry, and efforts made to find out whether there is anything which can be done to help the operator either by training or relieving (by advice or sympathy) the worries arising from personal situations outside the factory. The help of the Personnel Officer may be sought on occasion.

The Labour Cost Control report should be watched for signs of a falling off in performance, of rising cost per unit, and of rising percentage of excess costs. If the figures are normal or falling, no action is called for, but significant rises should be further investigated. In particular a continual rise in excess costs for one particular cause should be followed up, and may call for examination of each instance recorded for a week or two. This often reveals a trouble unsuspected or unnoticed.

In particular, chargehands of small sections should be trained to appreciate the significance of such records and to make their own investigations into means of improving performance or reducing excess costs. A bonus based on reductions in excess costs is an incentive satisfactory to supervisor and company alike.

Machines

Machine utilisation for the department as a whole is revealed in the Labour Cost Control report, and this normally is an adequate index. If the results are unsatisfactory, or performance begins to fall, it may be necessary, until the cause is found, to arrange temporarily for a detailed record of down-time (idle machine time) on each or certain machines. Such detailed records should not be continued beyond their usefulness if they involve any clerical labour away from the machine or which affects an operator's output. At all times, records which are not used bring themselves and their originators into disrepute.

It is sometimes recommended that detailed records of maintenance and repair costs for each machine should be made. If such costs are heavy, it is necessary, but it is clerical work which can be avoided except when the comparative maintenance costs of similar machines are, or are likely to be, in question. If the difference is appreciable, a foreman knows without records; if there is doubt, detailed records must be kept for a period.

Material or Product

The performance of finished machines or parts, or the quality of products, are other aspects of performance. It is often thought that this is the inspector's responsibility. It is not. Quality of product is the supervisor's (manager's or foreman's) responsibility; the inspector is really the representative of the customer (or Assembly Department or Sales Department), and is employed as a guardian of quality. The production supervisor must, in the end, produce a good-quality article, and it is for him therefore to get and use reports on the performance, or quality, of his product. As with labour, he must look for incidence of cause and follow up in an endeavour to cure the cause. Nor is it right to assume that there must always be some waste or scrap, or that a normal figure needs no further efforts to reduce it. It is surprising to how low a figure scrap and faulty work can be reduced if the effort is made.

For process and continuous production work there is no better index of performance and guide to cause than the statistical method of quality control (referred to in Chapter V, page 379).

CHAPTER V

ANCILLARY SERVICES OR DEPARTMENTS

Buying. Storekeeping. Works Engineering. Inspection

BUYING

BUYING, or purchasing as it is alternatively called, is very much a specialist activity calling for the commercial rather than the technical training and outlook. Skill in the specialist activity can be taught, but it is one of the instances where long experience in the industry, or even in the same company, is very valuable. For many years now managements have been concerned with the productivity or effectiveness of the direct-labour content of cost, and have usually failed to appreciate that the Buyer is frequently responsible for by far the largest single item in total cost; the average figure for industry as a whole is something like 30–50 per cent. of the total sales value. It is obviously important, therefore, that this activity of buying should be just as effectively performed as any other operation in the organisation. The word "effectively" is purposely used, because the measure of a Buyer's value is not always the reduced prices at which he can obtain goods from time to time, but the success with which he can obtain satisfactory materials, find alternative better materials at an economic price, and at the same time obtain adequate service from his suppliers.

A Buyer has to build up dependable sources of supply; it is wasteful and unnecessary to send enquiries to *all* suppliers for every order. There must be mutual trust and fair dealing between buyer and supplier. This means that strictly ethical standards and methods are adopted by the Buyer encouraging competition without taking unfair advantage of position or circumstances. The reception of customers' representatives should always be prompt, courteous and businesslike. It would be a good education and experience for a Buyer to become a salesman or representative for a time. It is fatally easy not to be interested in a new line, or a product competitive to one already giving satisfaction, and to miss very many opportunities of buying better or more economical materials through not being energetic enough to find out what is available. To tell a salesman that his price is high when it is low, to refer to imaginary competition, or otherwise to misrepresent directly or by implication in order to coax a lower price or an extra discount from a salesman induces instability into relations, is bound to lead to misrepresentation in return, and earns for the Company an unpleasant name. Such tactics belong to the past; they may succeed in isolated cases, but salesmen are quick to detect such methods and to take appropriate defensive measures.

Fair dealing requires that advantage will not be taken of an obviously incorrect quotation which will mean a loss to the supplier. If a price which will not produce a profit is deliberately quoted, and known to be so, that is a different matter, but in general the Buyer expects the seller to make an adequate profit. How else can the supplier continue in business and to give service? A fair price which enables a manufacturer to make a reasonable profit and supply competitive goods and adequate service, including a margin for development, is essential in modern industry, and is as much a matter of interest to the Buyer as to the seller. Fair dealing also requires the Buyer to state clearly for what reason he has to turn down a quotation. This does not mean that he must disclose the competitive prices, but it is not fair to competitors to give inaccurate reasons for un-competitive prices.

There must obviously be confidence and co-operation between Buyer and seller, and in the long run a dependable supplier is a worthy partner to the Buyer. Such confidence and co-operation cannot be built up except on a basis of fair dealings.

Duties

The position of the Buyer in an organisation and the person to whom he is responsible vary more than that of any other executive in industry. He is to be found responsible to the Managing Director (and is often a Director himself), the Works Manager, the Accountant, the Chief Engineer or Chemist, or merely a Progress Engineer, and there are those who strongly support each arrangement. It is always found that persons who strongly support one arrangement do so because they have not had wide experience of other organisations and are too conscious of the peculiarities of their own organisation and not sufficiently clear on the duties of various divisions. The truth is that the relative importance of materials to the total build-up of costs of a product varies very considerably, and so, therefore, does the relative importance of the Buyer. In flour milling and sugar refining, for example, there is virtually only one material; it represents a large proportion of the total cost, and normally market fluctuations of the raw material can have a big influence on the profit of the final pro-duct. Wood case making and printing are similar, though not such extreme cases. But in most industries many diverse materials are used, prices remain relatively stable, and large contracts for supplies are not frequent. Unless it is a small company and where persons combine duties normally carried out by several, or there are unusual personnel problems, the Buyer should be responsible to either the head of the production departments (the Works or Production Manager) or to the Managing Director.

The following can be taken as representative of the duties of a Buyer:

(1) Give effect to the Company's policy relating to the purchase of material and supplies and the maintenance of stocks.

(2) Translate requisitions for supplies into orders or contracts on suppliers, and:
    (*a*) Examine requisitions to ensure that they are correctly authorised and do not exceed limits prescribed.
    (*b*) Issue enquiries to alternative suppliers.
    (*c*) Collate quotations and accept most suitable, where necessary after consultation with or reference to technical executive concerned.

(3) Interview suppliers' representatives, when advisable in collaboration with executive concerned.

(4) Maintain up-to-date records, including catalogues and trade literature, of sources of supply or material, and of supplies and equipment likely to be required by the Company.

(5) Study the commodity market and keep abreast of prices and trends. Advise executive concerned of changes in price or availability likely to affect normal routine purchasing or replacement of stocks.

(6) Progress and follow up orders and calls off contracts.

(7) Scrutinise and vouch for invoices received.

(8) Dispose of scrap, residues, surplus material and plant.

Policy

A buying policy should be laid down clearly by the Board of Directors or by the Managing Director in line with Company policy. It will be of course part of the production policy, or arise from it, and will by dictated by the kind of production programme adopted. For example, the programme may require much greater quantities at one time of the year than another, but the buying policy may be to take regular supplies over the whole year to suit the suppliers, and to take advantage of lower prices, stocking during the period of lower demand. It should not be left to the Buyer to operate as he thinks fit, with the risk of being reprimanded for what may be thought unwise use of discretion.

Three broad lines of policy are usual:

(1) *To buy on a Bargain Basis*
    This may be pursued in the case of staple commodities and for the major materials in process industries. It offers large profits on buying,

with the consequence of large risks, and it is of a speculative nature. Speculation is an activity belonging to the Stock Exchange, and should not find its place in ordinary industrial activities. If it is pursued as a policy, it is usual for the buying to be under the control of a senior executive of the Company.

(2) *To buy on Contract*

In this policy, contracts are given to suppliers for large amounts of future requirements, for a year, or for indefinite periods subject to review and cancellation with an appropriate period of notice. It has the advantage of avoiding the necessity for carrying stocks by the user and of giving a measure of stability to suppliers. It also gives the Buyer an assurance of continuity of supply and of service. Under mass-production conditions, this latter feature is most important and the policy may be well justified.

(3) *To buy against Current Market Conditions*

This is the more usual policy, giving the Buyer a wide discretion. Orders are placed for the minimum quantity required for the re-placement of stock to meet particular demands, and alternative quotations are obtained, either for each order, or occasionally as a check.

Frequently, in normal industrial conditions a combination of policies 2 and 3 are laid down, contracts being limited to certain major raw materials.

Limiting Value of Order

It is usual for a limit to be placed on the individual value of any one order. This value may vary with the type of commodity. Orders above these limits are referred to a senior executive or the Managing Director for final authority. This may be necessary to fit in with financial policy when liquid capital is strained, or when the coincidence of several large orders in a period may strain the Company's arrangements for regular settlement of accounts.

Purchase of Capital Equipment

Purchase of capital equipment, additions to plant or buildings, or replacements thereto, should be dealt with in a special manner. Expenditure on such items does not arise as a matter of routine, and must in any case fit into any capital expenditure budgets or pro-gramme. It is, therefore, essential for all items above an agreed amount to be covered by a capital sanction authorised by the execu-tive concerned. In a large concern it is advisable for certain executives only to be authorised to order capital equipment, and for the amount of capital expenditure per year and per period to be laid down for the executive concerned. In a period of expansion, it is possible, without some such control, for a Company to undertake commitments for the purchase of plant which it cannot meet.

Procedures and Order Forms

The type of order form and the procedure adopted for requisitioning and placing of orders vary widely. In all cases, however, it is strongly recommended that only the Buyer be authorised to place official orders on behalf of the firm. Works Engineers and Office Managers often contend that only they know what they require. This may be so, but the order should still go through the Buyer. Buying, and the associated records, are a specialised activity, and every use should be made of the specialised skill thus built up. In all cases, therefore, persons requiring materials should state their requirements to the Buyer on an official requisition. When the material or article must fulfil certain conditions, then the requisition must be accompanied by a specification. When the source of supply or the particular brand or maker of the article required is not stated, then it is the Buyer's responsibility to buy where he can. At other times it may be necessary for technical departments to obtain all this information first and to determine by test, or otherwise, what is most suitable.

When samples or quotations are required, then the requisition form should be used in the same way, stating that an enquiry or quotation only is required in the first place, and that these are to be submitted to the department originating the requisition, or not as stated.

Order Forms

The layout of an order form suitable for normal requirements is shown in Fig. 51. All copies are made at one typing, and different colours are used to aid sorting and distribution.

The following example of standard practice instructions for the ordering of materials, supplies and outside services through the Buyer uses the minimum possible forms for adequate control, and can be taken as a basis from which to develop a satisfactory procedure for any particular company or set of conditions. For example, it may be necessary to obtain additional authority and signature for orders over certain amounts, or for certain materials, and central buying for associated or subsidiary companies would involve a modified routine.

(1) All materials, supplies, and services from outside contractors are to be ordered through the Buyer by sending to him a requisition setting out what is required.

(2) When the originating department wants to see quotations before placing an order, a requisition form is to be used marked plainly

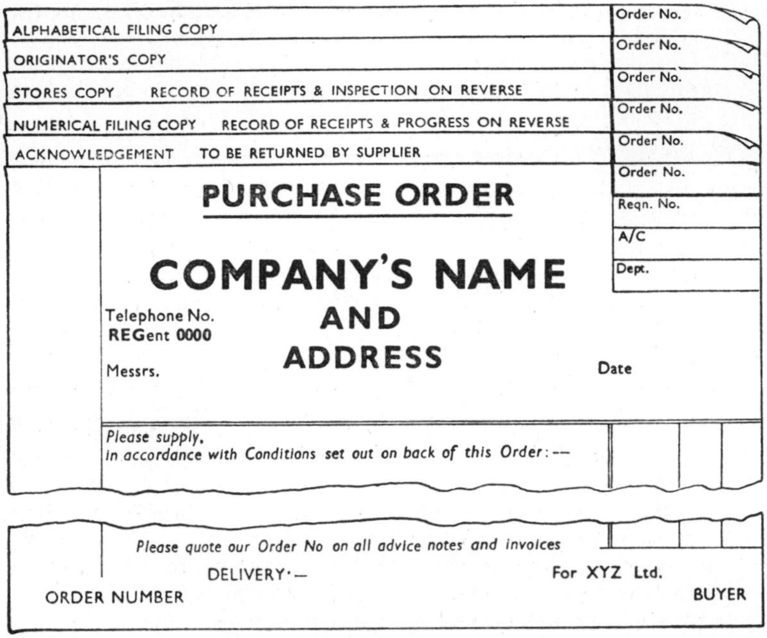

	Order No.
ALPHABETICAL FILING COPY	Order No.
ORIGINATOR'S COPY	Order No.
STORES COPY RECORD OF RECEIPTS & INSPECTION ON REVERSE	Order No.
NUMERICAL FILING COPY RECORD OF RECEIPTS & PROGRESS ON REVERSE	Order No.
ACKNOWLEDGEMENT TO BE RETURNED BY SUPPLIER	Order No.

PURCHASE ORDER

Reqn. No.

A/C

COMPANY'S NAME
Dept.

Telephone No.
REGent 0000   **AND**

Messrs.   **ADDRESS**   Date

Please supply,
in accordance with Conditions set out on back of this Order : —

Please quote our Order No on all advice notes and invoices

DELIVERY· —   For XYZ Ltd.

ORDER NUMBER   BUYER

FIG. 51.

in capitals ENQUIRY. Quotations when received are referred to the department concerned. The Buyer may at other times refer quotations obtained at his own discretion to the executive concerned for advice on selection of the most suitable.

(3) A capital sanction authorisation is to be obtained by the originating department for all purchases of a capital nature above £20.

(4) On receipt of a requisition, the Buyer translates the requisition into an order by typing out an official order set.

(5) An official order set comprises:

    (*a*) Purchase Order (white) sent to supplier.

    (*b*) Acknowledgment of Order (pink), being an exact copy sent to supplier for signature and return.

    (*c*) Buyer's copy (white) for numerical filing.

    (*d*) Stores copy (buff), with record of goods received and inspection report on reverse.

    (*e*) Originator's copy (blue), sent to department originating the requisition.

(6) The Buyer:

    (*a*) Sends first two copies to supplier.

    (*b*) Sends third copy to Stores.

    (*c*) Sends fourth copy to department originating requisition.

    (*d*) Files own numerical copy in card index

(e) Places alphabetical copy in unacknowledged file.

(f) Files requisition in box file in number sequence.

(7) Each day Buyer checks through unacknowledged file, and to firms who have not acknowledged within a week, writes an appropriate letter asking for acknowledgement and confirmation.

(8) As acknowledgement copies are received from suppliers, they are transferred to alphabetical file.

(9) When goods are received:

> (a) Stores arrange for inspection.
>
> (b) Inspection enter report on reverse side of Stores copy of order.
>
> (c) Stores copy of order is then sent to Buying Office, who transfer record to their copy, and take up any discrepancy, and report rejects to suppliers.
>
> (d) Buyer sends Stores copy of order, on same day, to stock control section of Planning Office, who transfer information to stock records.
>
> (e) For single or last consignments, Stores copy of order is returned to Buyer. For part consignments, Stores copy of order is returned to Stores.

(10) Invoices for goods received are submitted to Buyer for checking and authorisation.

(11) The following departments are authorised to use requisitions:

> Drawing Office—materials requiring long delivery periods.
> Stores Control—special materials and supplies.
> Stores—general consumable supplies and hardware.
> Production Engineers—plant, tools and equipment.
> Tool Stores—tool replacements.
> General Office—stationery.
> Pattern Shop—timber supplies and maintenance.

Records

It is essential for the Buyer to build up reliable records which will give him control of orders placed and comprehensive information regarding materials available and likely to be required, and standard and competitive prices. The extent of these records will depend upon the size of the firm, but the following records are the minimum which are required for effective control.

Copies of Orders

Two copies of the order should be filed, one filed under the Company's order number numerically, and the other under the supplier's name alphabetically. It is essential that one copy is available for very rapid reference. It is usual for the order to be known internally, and therefore the numerical copy is filed under its order number for rapid reference. Using the order set on page 341, the length of the order form is made $\frac{1}{2}$ inch shorter than a quarto-size sheet, i.e. $9\frac{1}{2} \times 8$

inches. The numerical copy is folded to within $\frac{1}{2}$ inch of the bottom, where the order number is repeated, making it 8×5 inches and suitable for inserting in a visible-edge cabinet, the quickest form of reference file. The top half of the back of the form, which is printed to receive delivery records, is uppermost after folding and filing in the cabinet. The alphabetical copy is filed in whatever way is found most convenient, and forms a cross index with the order file.

Record of Purchases

It is also necessary to keep a record of all purchases of each material or part. This is best done on a card file, with one card for each material or part. Each order placed should be entered with particulars of the supplier from whom ordered, the price and quantity. Suitable headings for such a card record are given at Fig. 52. It is not necessary

STANDARD PRICE		MATL		CODE No.		
SUPPLIER	DESCRIPTION	PRICE	DATE	ORDER No.	QUANTITY	

FIG. 52.

to keep a record of the value of purchases made for each supplier. This information can always be obtained, if required, from the Accounts Department.

Catalogues

A library of catalogues of suppliers of material and equipment likely to be used is invaluable, and should be kept in good condition, up-to-date and adequately indexed. Because of the varying size of catalogues, it often proves to be a difficult job, and it is frequently found that the simplest way is to use box files. Because many suppliers have a wide range of products, it is usually found impossible to file according to the kind of product or associated products, and one must rely on a straightforward numerical or alphabetical filing with a cross index. These indexes of catalogues can be broadened to include an index of suppliers of materials, whether catalogued or not. Although it may duplicate some of the information in trade directories, the latter can never be completely comprehensive.

Progress and Follow Up

It is as essential to progress orders on suppliers as it is to progress orders in the Company's works. Continuity of supplies can be as important as cost. Indeed, in mass production it is the essential pre-requisite. Those connected with manufacturing industry in the period following the Second World War have had frequent and bitter experience of this. Running out of stock of odd items, often quite small, has resulted in products being held up in a half-finished or almost completed state for weeks on end. At such times very inflated prices have been paid for supplies from alternative sources; output is more valuable than the increased cost incurred, and it is not only in mass-production factories that the delay is serious, the restriction on turn-over in any factory can be and has been quite large.

In difficult times, as in times of shortage, an outside progress man who visits suppliers personally and can get on personal terms with the man who matters, Works Manager or Planning Engineer, can be most effective. When much work is subcontracted it is almost essential, and advisable when there are running contracts that have to be co-ordinated with flow production programmes which are subject to acceleration or modification.

Progress can only be measured against a predetermined require-ment, and the requirement in this case is the delivery date, which forms part of the contract to supply, accepted by the supplier when he accepts the order. In order that progress can be 100 per cent. effective, it is essential to know of every order not delivered to time. The simplest way of throwing up such orders is to keep the reverse of a Delivery Promise book, i.e. a Delivery Due book. Each order made out is entered in the Delivery Due book on the page for the day (or week) when delivery is due. Each day (or week) orders appearing as due should be checked with the order record, and if a delivery has not been received, follow-up action should be initiated.

Follow-up action will depend on circumstances, but usually starts with an "urge" letter or reminder. Such letters must not appear casual or mere routine, and for this reason must be as carefully com-piled as any other letter. Although a standard form of letter can be used, it is better to have several forms (which can be selected to suit the circumstances or supplier), and individually typed letters are likely to command more attention than duplicated ones. Further promises given should be followed up with increasing pressure, and it is in difficult cases that the personal contact or outside progress man can be more effective.

Specifications

It is essential for the Buyer to make absolutely clear to the supplier exactly what is required, the tests, if any, to be passed, and the con-ditions attached to an order, which, when accepted, becomes a con-tract in law. In order to state clearly what is required, Buyers are strongly recommended to use specifications, and wherever possible to use those published by the British Standards Institution, since they are likely to avoid special production—and hence higher prices. If there is not a British Standards Specification applicable, a specification should be obtained from or drawn up in collaboration with Designers, Technical Chief, or the Production Engineers. Such specifications can be made to cover general classes or particular goods, and do help to maintain uniform quality and avoid misunderstandings.

Conditions attached to the placing of an order and to which the supplier is to be held to comply should be drawn up in collaboration with the Technical departments and the Accountant. The following can be taken as typical, although much more detailed and complex conditions are sometimes laid down:

Official Order.—No goods will be paid for unless an official order can be produced if required. Any specifications, drawings, patterns, etc., supplied by us with reference to this order remain our property.

Rejections.—Any article found to be defective, inferior in quality, or in excess of the quantity ordered, may be rejected and returned to you at your own risk and expense. A debit note will be sent informing you whether replacement is desired or not.

Suspension.—In the event of strikes, accidents, or other unforeseen contingencies, delivery may be suspended at our request.

Cancellation.—Undue delay in delivery or a continuation of defective supplies shall entitle us to cancel the order.

Advising.—An advice note quoting our order number must accompany the goods or be sent by post same day as goods are dispatched.

Invoicing.—An invoice must be sent on same day as goods are dispatched, and must quote our order number, failing which invoice may be returned.

Statements.—Monthly statements of account to be received by us not later than the 5th of the month following invoice date, otherwise payment may be deferred a month beyond the ordinary due date.

Terms.—Payment will be made during month following that in which goods are invoiced.

Liability for Injury or Damage. This order is subject to the condition that in so far as it relates to erection or other work to be carried out on our premises or elsewhere to our instructions, you accept liability for and will indemnify us against all claims, costs or expenses arising in connection with such work, whether at common law or under statute, as a result of injury to or death of any person, or to loss of or damage to any property unless such claim arises solely as a result of neglect, default, or omission by ourselves or our servants.

Delivery.—To these works unless otherwise instructed. In case of overdue orders we shall be entitled to claim delivery by passenger train or other special transport at your expense.

Carriage.—All goods to be delivered carriage paid unless otherwise arranged.

Empties.—No charge for any form of packing, including cases, barrels, etc., will be acknowledged except when expressly arranged, but every effort will be made to return such packages to you.

STOREKEEPING

The importance of storekeeping in modern industry is not always appreciated as it should be. Whilst the production departments are well equipped, the storekeepers are hidden away in cramped quarters, ill-equipped and with poor lighting conditions, and are generally underpaid in comparison with operators on production. It is not to be wondered at that loss of stock, wrong issues, unexpected running out of stock, and incorrect vouchers are a continual source of delay to production and of worry to production staff. To see the issue in its right perspective, it is only necessary to realise that the few persons in the Stores are responsible for and handle at one stage or another the whole of the material used by production. This may be worth 50 per cent. or more of the total sales value of production; the value of receipts and issues into and from Stores in a factory is greater than the total works cost, and at any time there is likely to be in stock material, components and finished products worth a quarter of the annual turnover—and yet frequently unskilled labourers are expected to be storekeepers. The truth is that storekeeping is more than a labouring job, and should be remunerated as such in order to attract and retain the quality of personnel.

It may be said in answer that card indexes, stock control "systems" and good bins deskill the job. But card indexes are no substitute for good storekeeping; they do not work of themselves, but must be used. A good storekeeper can have an amazingly comprehensive and detailed knowledge of a firm's products, which can be used by him rapidly and in a fraction of the time it takes to refer to an index or other record. Theirs is one of the few occupations in which a man's value to the Company arises more from his experience with the Company than from his technical or practical ability.

Persons should be selected for storekeeping who are tidy minded, and neat and tidy in their habits, and have a good memory. Tidiness can be taught, but whilst a person's memory can be improved, there are some who start with a big advantage by having a naturally good memory. It is essential also for a storekeeper to be good at figures or at least not to be bad at them. Whilst it may not be necessary for the ordinary storekeeper to enter up records, and it is in fact unwise for this to be necessary, he must be able to count and to count accurately without checking. It is surprising how often persons are selected for storekeeping who are constitutionally unable to concentrate sufficiently to count up to reasonable large numbers. Certainly far more care than is usually the case should be taken in selecting persons who have either the right training or the right aptitude.

Kind of Stores

Stores are places where material is kept and therefore the kind of stores will vary with all the materials in use in industry. Nevertheless, the kinds of stores and organisation required do fall into certain broad classifications as follows:
   (1) Raw material.
   (2) Component or piece-part.
   (3) General supplies or expense materials.
   (4) Finished product or warehouse.
   (5) Tool.
The last two of these classes are dealt with elsewhere in this book, No. 4, the Warehouse, in Part One, Chapter IX, and No. 5, the Tool Stores, in the next subsequent section of this chapter under Works Engineering. Nevertheless, the principles and methods of storekeeping, layout and records recommended in this section are generally applicable to all types of stores.

Raw Material Stores

These are of two kinds, those dealing with bulk storage so frequent in the extractive and processing industries, and the ordinary kind of stores in which a range of raw materials are kept in bins or rooms. Stores for bulk storage are usually specially designed for their purpose, for example, silos for the storage of grain and bunkers for coal, and are in reality a stage in the manufacturing process and should be dealt with as such. Handling in these is a mechanical problem. In the case too of certain materials which are subject to excise duty, like tobacco, cocoa, tea, etc., there is the need for a "bonded" side of the stores under the close check and inspection of a representative of the Customs and Excise Department of the Government, from which material cannot be withdrawn until the appropriate duty has been paid or vouched for.

The layout and organisation of the ordinary kind of raw material store varies widely with the industry and size of factory, though principles are still generally applicable. In engineering, pig iron for the foundry, and rough castings and rolled steel sections for the machine shops, are frequently stored outside, as they are unaffected by climatic conditions. In large factories a separate store for each material, or similar kind of material, is justified. In large food factories the main ingredients, colours and essences, and packing materials, are stored in separate stores; in textile factories the different types of fabric are kept separate; in printing, the paper, sundries and inks are kept in different stores. In large factories, each main shop may have its own raw material stores supplied from the main stores.

In all cases it is advisable, and essential for smooth production flow, for the raw material stores to be at the input end of the factory. Unless production flow is arranged in the form of a U, this means that the raw material stores must be separate from the component and finished product stores.

Component Stores

Component stores, and here we are not concerned with process factories, are of four kinds:

(1) Standard stock used in a variety of assemblies or finished products—
    (*a*) Made on the premises.
    (*b*) Bought out.
(2) Made to order, or specials required only for one order or too frequently to justify carrying stocks—
    (*a*) Made on the premises.
    (*b*) Bought out.

These stores employ the majority of storekeepers in manufacturing industry, present the most diverse problems, and require the greatest skill and ingenuity to render first-class service. Layout invariably involves racks or bins, and adequate space is always a problem.

General Stores

For a variety of reasons it is often found advisable for all or most of the consumable (indirect or expense) materials, those which do not go directly into the product, to be stored on their own. Oils, greases, paint and rags are messy, and soon make a stores dirty and untidy. Furthermore, when the Component Stores is organised on a pre-selection and accumulation basis for assembly, it diverts the storekeeper's mind from his job to have to attend to individual wants for small supplies like files, emery cloth, wipers and so on.

Duties

There are conflicting opinions and there is a good deal of loose thinking as to what a storekeeper's duties should include and to whom he should be responsible. It is maintained by some that, in addition to looking after stores, he should keep all stock records and be responsible for ordering material. It is also maintained that the Head Storekeeper should be responsible to the Buyer, or to the Secretary, or to the Accountant, or to Production Control, or for sections of stores to be responsible to departmental foremen, and all these arrangements can be met with in practice. A storekeeper's job is to keep stocks, to receive and issue them, and in between to store them tidily in a minimum of space with the minimum of labour. It is a physical job. It is not his job to keep records: that is part of stock recording, which in turn is part of production planning. To function effectively, production planning must have up-to-date information of stocks, and must be able to refer to stock records immediately in building up production programmes. This cannot be done if the records are not in the Production Planning office, and duplication should be avoided both on the score of cost and of accuracy.

As was made clear in Chapter III, the head of production planning is a specialist in the compilation and use of records; a storekeeper is not, but he must be a specialist in the physical handling and storing of materials. It is wrong therefore to ask a storekeeper to maintain records, or to expect it to be done as accurately in the works as it can in an office staffed with persons trained in the work. This does not mean that a storekeeper can forget all about stocks held; he can, by suitable technique, act as a back stop on the need for stock replacement or adjustment.

Since the storing of material is clearly a physical job, the Stores should be considered a works department, and storekeeping a works job, and the storekeeper therefore should be responsible to the Works Manager or Superintendent. As it is a specialist's job, all Stores should be under the supervision of one person, the Head Storekeeper (or alternative title).

The foreman or head storekeeper is then able to co-ordinate the activities of the various stores and economise in labour. He is able to call on other sections of the stores when any one is suddenly overloaded, as frequently happens when large consignments of materials arrive, and in times of illness.

In view of the above, the following can be taken as the duties of a head storekeeper:

A. Generally to

    (1) Supervise the work of storekeepers, and to instruct and guide them in carrying out their duties, ensuring that they are effectively performed.

    (2) Ensure cleanliness and tidiness in the Stores.

    (3) Co-operate closely with the Buyer, Chief Planning Engineer, Inspection Department, and with production foremen generally.

    (4) Adhere to the Company's personnel policy, and ensure that sub-ordinates do so.

    (5) Ensure that any records required are promptly and accurately made

    (6) Provide a prompt and efficient stores service to all departments.

B. Specifically to—

    (1) Receive goods from outside suppliers, check-count and arrange for inspection of quality. Report to Buyer deviation from specification or order.

    (2) Receive components produced in the works, and check-count.

    (3) Store all materials and components safely and tidily, and in a manner in which they are immediately available.

    (4) Check actual stock of every item, preferably once every three months, but at least once every six months, and advise Stores Control of any corrections required.

    (5) On receipt of appropriate release instructions, issue materials and components called for. Issue surplus to original requisitions only against Excess Material Requisition, and receive back materials in excess of requirements only against Material Returned to Stores Note.

    (6) Record accurately—

        (*a*) Receipt of all outside supplies on back of copy of order arranging for inspection report on each consignment.

        (*b*) Receipt of parts manufactured in works on Deliver to Stores Note.

        (*c*) Issue of material on Material Release Note.

        (*d*) Issue of finished parts on Part List.

Storekeeping Methods

More "systems" have been sold to industry for storekeeping and stock control than for any other business activity. What are really offered are tools, and these are mostly to do with stock records already dealt with in Chapter III. In this section we are concerned with the use of such tools and with methods of actually storing the goods and materials.

The first fundamental principle of good storekeeping is the old maxim for good housekeeping, "a place for everything and everything in its place". To which should be added—"and know where it is!" Nowhere else in a factory is tidiness more important. Whether or not bins or shelves are used, materials and parts should be neatly arranged, and the whole stores should present an orderly appearance. If goods have to be stored on the floor, as they may be, it is essential to arrange them in bays with gangways and to keep them as tidy as if in bins.

Equipment and Layout

The equipment now available is so varied and most of it so well known that it is unnecessary to deal with it in detail here—a study of catalogues is a fruitful way of getting new ideas to meet specific problems. However, there are certain precepts, modern developments and pitfalls which should be generally known.

In the first place, it should be remembered that it is false economy not to have adequate space and adequate bins or racks (with a margin for growth). Since floor area is expensive, this means that the maximum use has to be made of height. When the goods to be stored stack easily and the quantities are large, equipment for stacking should be used. Stacking trucks with forked tables which can be raised by power and wooden or steel platforms or pallets answer the problem. When the goods do not stack, or the quantities are small, shelves or bins should be used, and again to economise in floor space these should be as high as possible. Bins up to 12 or even 15 feet high are quite satisfactory provided that light parts only are stored in the top half and that safe, convenient and easily moved steps can be provided.

A recent development makes the maximum use of floor space by building the racks or bins in short self-contained sections, and erecting these on rollers which ride on rails let into the floor. Rows of these

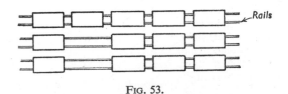

FIG. 53.

sections are placed close together, and in each row there is one section missing, so that any section can be uncovered in any row as illustrated at Fig. 53.

Long bars or tube, or lengths of timber, should be stacked on end in racks which can be built up inexpensively of angle iron. Rods or stays are fixed to a horizontal back rail, so that they stand forward from the rails to act as divisions or compartments for the different sections of material. Very heavy bar for safety must be stored horizontally.

In general, metal racks or bins are preferable to wooden ones, they take up less space for the same load, and are more easily erected and adjusted afterwards. There are several manufacturers who supply standard equipment which is so made that it can be adjusted to suit the particular requirements of the stores.

Stores should be arranged so that goods are not received through the same entrance as that from which they are issued. Gangways should be sufficient to allow trolleys to pass and slopes or different levels should be avoided if at all possible. In Component Stores supplying an Assembly or Packing Department, the goods should be so stored that it is possible to work from one end of the store to the other, gradually accumulating components for an order or requisition in the sequence stated on the requisition. When a Store serves more than one department, each requiring substantially different materials or parts, the ideal layout is for the stores to be arranged past the end of each department and the goods to be stored as near as possibly adjacent to the department issuing them, thus:

Stores		
Dept. A	Dept. B	Dept. C

Storing and Locating

There are broadly three alternative methods of storing a mixed variety of articles in a Store:

(1) When consignments are large or bulky, to carry the bulk stock in a reserve store and a small quantity of each article in the active store.

(2) To keep the whole stock of each article together, all articles of a like kind being stored together.

(3) As 2, but articles stored, irrespective of kind, in the order in which required in a normal list.

The second is usual and more satisfactory in practice. It makes for neatness and orderliness so vital in Stores, and storekeepers find it easier to memorise where everything is when articles of a like kind are stored together. Although there must be a record of where everything is, it would be obviously a very slow job if a storekeeper had to go to an index for many items. A person who knows where everything is is a treasure (and not such an uncommon one) and everything possible should be done to enable a storekeeper to become one.

A logical system of numbering items or parts is a further aid to memory, both for identity of a part and for location. If the part can be given a number according to its location in the Stores, it simplifies matters considerably for the storekeeper, but this is not recommended for general use. Almost invariably there are overriding demands from other departments for a system of code numbers which classifies parts or materials strictly according to kind and size, or to product, or model and so on. (Methods of numbering which ensure minimum inventory, maximum flexibility, and avoid duplication, are described on page 189.) A code of numbering for parts and materials which is built up according to kind and size is easier to remember than one built up according to location. However, it is essential to have in the Stores an index of location, and this should be based on a code built up logically. A simple code capable of unlimited expansion can be built up as illustrated at Fig. 54.

Number each bay or section of racks from 0 to 9 or 99.
Number each row of racks 0 to 9.
Number horizontal rows of bins or shelves in each rack 0 to 9.
Number vertical rows of bins in divisions or shelves in each rack 0 to 9.

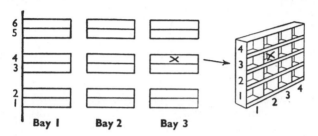

The bin marked X would be 3423.

FIG. 54.—Numbering of Stores Bins.

As stated earlier, recording of stock in the Stores is not in general recommended, and requisitioning for replacement of stocks is not normally therefore a storekeeper's duty. However, there are certain classes of material and articles which have a general-purpose use and which, in normal times, can be obtained at relatively short notice so that minimum stocks are small. Storekeepers can be made responsible for maintaining stocks of these without having to keep records. The minimum quantity for each item is first calculated and authorised. This is the quantity necessary to supply normal demand (with a margin of safety) through the period required for obtaining a further supply. This minimum quantity is then boxed, wrapped, or placed at the bottom of the bin and covered with a piece of cardboard, wood or sheet metal, and the remaining stock placed on top. When the loose stock has all been used, it indicates that the re-ordering point has been reached and a requisition is placed on the Buyer for further supplies. When new supplies are received, the minimum quantity is again boxed or covered. (This method can also be used as a danger signal on those items for which Stores Control are responsible for requisitioning.)

If it is found impracticable physically to identify the minimum stock or if for other reasons it is decided to keep a record of stock balances in the Stores, the bin stock card is the simplest method. This card is hung on the front of the bin to which it refers, and is entered up and the balance struck at the time stock is put in or taken

out. This ensures promptness of records. The simplest design of card
has rulings on one side for recording quantities received and issued,
and on the reverse details of the item, its stock number, description,
location, order quantity, and minimum stock quantity. It can be originated by the Buyer and used as an advice of order placed and to be
received. It is useful to print one side red, so that it can be turned this
side uppermost when stocks are low as a visible reminder of the fact
to the storekeepers.

To avoid the rush and additional work of stocktaking once a year
at the financial year end, it is more satisfactory to arrange for what is
termed perpetual inventory check. Providing each item in stock is
checked and compared with the stock records, and the latter corrected
if necessary at least once and preferably four times a year, the stock
as recorded at the year end is usually acceptable for audit purposes.
The simplest effective alternative methods for making this perpetual
check are either for independent staff to be appointed to do nothing
else but go round the Stores checking stock, or for the storekeepers
to check so may items every day. The former, if more regular, is
likely to be very monotonous for the staff concerned; the latter gives
each storekeeper a vested interest in the accuracy of his stock. Either
method is much more accurate than the usual annual stocktaking. In
either case, to ensure that every item is checked with the required
frequency, Stock Control should issue a daily list of items to be
checked.

Receipts and Issue

A sound principle to observe in dealing with the receipt and issue
of stores materials is that nothing is received and nothing issued without a written authority and signature for receipt. If this is not faithfully adhered to, it will be found too often in practice that verbal
arrangements and memory are very unreliable. This means that a
Goods Received Note or its equivalent must be made out by the Stores
for all consignments received from outside suppliers, and an internal
Delivery Note accompany all deliveries from works departments. All
goods received from outside suppliers should be against an order
from the Buyer, and the procedure outlined earlier in this chapter,
Buying, page 340, can be used. If a consignment is received which has
not been authorised by a written order, as occasionally happens when
senior executives give verbal orders and forget to confirm by official
order, then a Goods Received Note should be written out immediately
to notify Buyer, Stock Control and Accounts. Then if so desired and
to keep records tidy, an official order set can be made out to cover the
consignment.

It is important also to ensure that every consignment is checked and inspected, and it is preferable to do this independently of the supplier's Consignment Note—knowledge of what is stated on the Consignment Note is apt to lead to only cursory examination of the consignment, on the lazy assumption that what is stated must be correct. Inspection should be prompt, so that appropriate action can be taken without delay with the supplier, in case of discrepancy or fault.

Goods received from internal departments will have been inspected, but count must be verified before signing the Delivery Note—the signature indicates responsibility for quantity and therefore records.

In order to link up planning procedures and to give the Stores an opportunity of preparing materials to be issued in advance of requirements and so avoid waiting time, requirements should be stated as far as possible, not on requisitions written by operators, but on Release Notes, issued by the Planning Office. Such notes are likely to be more legible and accurate, particularly if pre-printed. Also, since only the correct (standard) amount of material required will have been stated, more can only be obtained on presentation of another requisition or preferably an Excess Requisition, and thus there is provided an automatic check and record of excess usage, and therefore of excess cost.

If a list of materials or parts is required, a copy of the material or part list should be used, covered, if necessary, by a Material Release Note quoting the material or part list. Requisitions for long lists of parts, written out by works departments, always lead to inaccuracies. This copy of the material or part list is a Stores "tool", and therefore should be designed with this in mind, i.e. it should be set out in such a way as to minimise work in the Stores. Materials or parts which are stored together, e.g. nuts, bolts and small hardware, should be grouped together. Also if part issue of large batches are usual, provision should be made for this, with an extension margin for marking off each issue—the alternative is a separate list for each issue. The essential thing to bear in mind is to keep paper work in the works to a minimum—it is seldom expertly done outside an office properly equipped.

WORKS ENGINEERING

Buildings and Services

For production executives or those aspiring to such positions, information on the factors affecting the choice of site for a new factory or buildings is apt to be more than a little theoretical. It is given to few of us to have the opportunity of building a new factory from virgin ground—and being able to choose the ground. And even when it is decided to put up new buildings, their design is quite rightly the function of a specialist, the architect, who is, or should be, well aware of all the factors involved. Nevertheless, the production man must know of certain factors which vitally affect the production unit and the effectiveness of work done, and see to it that they are given due consideration when a new factory is built, or an existing one is extended—some of them are insufficiently understood by the technical specialist.

Choice of Site

A dominating factor affecting the choice of a site for a new factory is the availability of labour and its type or characteristics. The material factors, such as access to various means of transport, availability of services such as electricity, gas and water, drainage and foundation problems, can all be readily assessed by the technical experts, but the human factor is not so easy to assess. There has always been a tendency for industries to develop in certain towns or localities, as much because of local skill as for any other reason, e.g. needle manufacture at Redditch, chainmaking in the Black Country, and furniture-making at High Wycombe. There is more engineering skill and tradition in Birmingham than in Hereford, but there is more competition for it. Those who have tried to develop new industries in country districts or towns where the special skills which are required are not indigenous, have sometimes paid for the experience. Workers are not so mobile as one might expect, so that if local skill is not available, production methods must be de-skilled. It can and has succeeded in many cases, but the warning is that it is always more difficult, and takes longer, than is expected.

Another point to remember is that people do not like to travel far to work, so that there is likely to be more labour in or near a residential area or housing estate than in a heavily industrialised area. It has been known for a firm to build a factory and then find it just cannot get labour at all.

Another factor often miscalculated is the room required for expansion—it will almost always be more than predicted. Adequate room for expansion is always a good investment.

Type of Building and Site Layout

The type of building and layout of site necessarily affect each other but both should be considered functionally, i.e. in relation to the work being done, and the best way to do it. In process factories, extraction and chemical industries, the buildings must be built round the processes. For example, in sugar refining and flour milling advantage is taken of gravity flow resulting in tall many-floored buildings. In the more normal type of factory, just as much attention should be given to production flow. This should be in one direction only.

The following is an outstanding modern example of how buildings can be designed round the process. The major factors which had to be taken into account in designing the new factory were:

A large number of items of packing materials, cartons, labels, etc., had to be kept in stock, thus requiring a great deal of room.

An equally large number of items had to be kept in finished shelf stock, thus taking up even more room.

A small space required for process work, preferably on the ground floor.

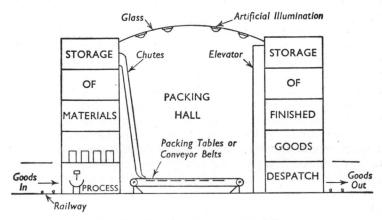

FIG. 55.—Functional Layout of Building.

Many different lines to be in production at the same time with relatively small runs.

The ultimate layout adopted is shown schematically in Fig. 55.

The actual filling, wrapping, packing, boxing, etc., is performed on conveyor belts, of which there are many, each constituting a unit, running in parallel lines across the central part of the building. Packing materials are fed mostly by chute and delivered to stock floors by continuous elevators. The administrative departments form a block across one end of the building.

This may appear a little unorthodox, but a little study will reveal its many advantages and how functionally successful it is. Equally successful results can be obtained if trouble is taken to analyse the functional requirements of production in the same way.

A factor which may have to be considered in industry more in the future than it ever has been in the past, particularly in very large concerns, is the size of the individual manufacturing units. Working groups are social groups, and play a dominating part in the building up of morale and of loyalty to either the Company's interests or to sectional interests. An employee is more likely to feel that he or she matters and to be loyal to the Company in a small unit than in a very large department or building. Research work is needed to throw light on the optimum size of units, but the point to remember with the design of buildings is that they can be too large from the human point of view.

The position of administrative and service buildings, the laboratory, drawing office, power-house, maintenance and repair department is always important, particularly in allowing for expansion. What can be the right position for the factory at one time may be quite wrong when the factory is extended.

Similarly, the position and size of canteens and parking conveniences for cycles, motor-cycles and cars must be given more consideration than used to be necessary. Canteens are an essential service in industry today, and a good deal of their undoubted value is offset if the buildings and conditions are very unsatisfactory, as they can be if of a make-shift nature. With the increasing distances which employees need to travel, and the consequent growing popularity of cycles and motor vehicles, adequate provision is required for parking. To many companies this problem is acute today; there is no need to invite the problem in the future.

The modern tendency in the design of buildings is for single-story construction. From the Production Managers' point of view this obviously has many advantages, giving greater scope for rearrangement and avoiding the transport delays inherent in multi-storied buildings. A single-storied building also is much easier to light and ventilate. When, because of the cost of floor area or restrictions of site, multi-storied buildings have to be used, windows should be as large as possible. The modern tendency is for the whole of the walls to be of glass by cantilevering the outside edge of the buildings from the main frame. Artificial lighting is expensive; the maximum possible window space avoids much of this expense. The expense is partially offset by the greater heat loss, but there is no way of compensating for the dull and depressing atmosphere of badly lighted shops, nor for continually working in artificial light.

The following is a brief summary of the advantages and disadvantages of single- and multi-story buildings:

Single-story

   Rearrangement of production and departments easier than in multi-story;

General supervision facilitated;
Good and uniform distribution of natural lighting;
Transport cheaper, quicker and easier;
Fire risks less than in multi-story;
Window maintenance less (but roof maintenance more);
Heavy machinery can be installed anywhere.

Multi-story

Departments are self-contained units and tend to better group feeling;
Factory more compact, and high-speed lifts are quicker than walking long distances;
Services (pipes and cables) shorter;
Gravity transport can be used for certain materials;
Less roof space and maintenance (gutters, covering, etc.);
Lavatory blocks more conveniently situated;
Good ventilation not so easily arranged;
Serious restriction on use of heavy machinery.

If there are strong reasons for having wide shops with a large floor area unobstructed, the lattice-girder type of construction can be used. These have been frequently used for aeroplane construction, where extremely wide shops with no roof supports at all are required; spans exceeding 100 feet have been built.

Adequate artificial illumination, heating and ventilation are an essential prerequisite of effective production and accepted without reservation by modern managements. It is impossible here to recommend standards, but the Factories Act does lay down minima which most certainly can be taken as the *absolute minimum*. Figures very much in excess of these minima are in general recommended. For lighting, a high standard of general illumination should be aimed at, providing individual lighting of a high intensity only for accurate work; for example, machining to fine limits, inspection, sewing-machine work and similar situations. As a general rule, it can be taken that general illumination should be at least 10 to 20 foot-candles. In the U.S.A. it is much more, 50 foot-candles being very common.

Heating and ventilation are problems which can only be solved in individual circumstances, but there is much to be said for the modern form of industrial fan heaters which serve a dual purpose. They not only keep warm air in circulation—and it has been proved that adequate air circulation is effective in reducing the effects of vitiated atmosphere—but they can be used for improving ventilation in the warm weather.

The painting of factory buildings and workshops, like window cleaning, is greatly neglected. There is ample evidence of the psychological effects, beneficial and otherwise, of colour schemes and general appearance of the places in which people work. The colour scheme must be chosen with as much care as the materials of which the buildings are made—and emphatically should not be a drab brown. Whilst it is true that no colour scheme can be everyone's choice, there are some that will please most, and others that can only be described as depressing—a bright and cheerful one is a good investment. The Factory Act lays down that workshops must either be painted at least once every seven years, and washed every fourteen months, or lime-washed every fourteen months. It is almost as cheap to put on a coloured distemper every year, and thus always to preserve a cheerful atmosphere, as to wash only.

The following are other problems which may arise, and which should be given full consideration in advance, when planning new buildings:

If there are many piped services in multi-story buildings, e.g. hydraulic power, gas, compressed air, in addition to the normal water and electric supply, the mains should as far as possible be taken up the building through a common shaft, like a lift shaft. This is a great convenience to the Maintenance Department.

Certain processes give off fumes or a great deal of heat. It may be advisable to site these so that they do not affect other departments. Effective extraction arrangements are necessary in any case.

High levels of vibration and noise can be minimised or insulated. It may be advisable to segregate departments in which vibration or noise cannot be avoided. The problem is accentuated if such are on upper stories.

When it is essential to divide a building into departments, standardised steel partitions, which can be ceiling height, half glass or expanded metal, are most effective, and are easily moved when rearrangement makes this necessary. Brick walls are a great deterrent to schemes of rearrangement.

Layout

The one fundamental principle to which all good factory or departmental layouts must conform, whether in workshop or office, is that production generally must flow in one direction, and must never retrace its path in the opposite direction. Flow production reaches its ultimate perfection, of course, in the mass-production layouts on the conveyor belts in the automobile industry. But the same principle of unidirectional flow should be adhered to whatever the product or process. This applies to the factory as a whole, to units of it, to departments and to sections, although it cannot apply in detail in departments doing jobbing work. In continuous-process industries especially, such as food, chemicals, metallurgical, etc., the products usually pass through a fixed sequence of machines or operations; although there are exceptions, as in bulk processing, when some of the materials, having reached one stage, are fed back to an earlier stage. But in the fabricating industries, such a fixed sequence is not usually inherent in the manufacturing methods, and as the factory develops and methods are altered, often the layout, like Topsy, just grows, and flow production is forgotten until reorganisation becomes essential.

An illustration of how a slight rearrangement of layout can greatly simplify production flow is shown at Fig. 56.

Types of Layout

There are two distinct types of layout common to all industries:
1. Group layout, common in most jobbing factories. Machines or

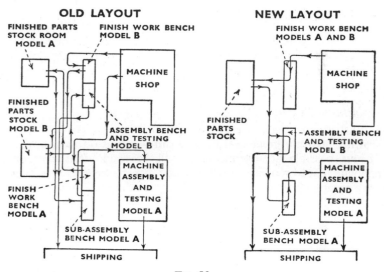

FIG. 56.

operators of a like type are grouped together, as for example in a machine shop where all centre lathes, all milling machines, all automatics, and so on, would be grouped together.

2. Line layout, where machines or operators are arranged according to the sequence of operations. This is carried to its extreme in the automobile industries.

It is usually found that a combination of both types provides the best solution in normal fabricating industries. Line layout is used when the number of a product or a component produced is sufficiently large to require certain machines or operators to be permanently engaged on that one product or component. The machines are permanently set up and arranged to produce that particular component as a line production unit, other components being dealt with on the batch system on group layout. There are certain advantages to be gained from line layout, even when used in this way for only some components, and it should be used whenever suitable. It reduces transport (and this is important for very large components), it reduces the overall production time and work in process between operations, and assures a more steady flow of products, since each machine tends to govern the flow of all the others. An example of how a department was relaid out on this basis, resulting in a considerable increase in production and reduction in cost, is shown in Fig. 57 opposite.

On the other hand, the advantages of group layout should not be lost sight of, and it should always be used in preference to a layout that merely arises out of intermittent additions to machines to increase capacity. A group layout permits the supervision of each type of operation by a person who is, or becomes, a specialist. In jobbing or mixed production shops it does tend to ensure a tidier shop and better flow.

Problems of Layout

When the arrangement of a layout is being worked out on the drawing board, a great deal of time can be spent on redrawing the various possible arrangements. It will be found that cardboard templates cut to represent each machine, bench, or other equipment, are a great help. Before cutting out they are drawn in outline, showing principal features, to the same scale as that of the outline drawing of the building or department. If there are moving portions of a machine, e.g. traversing tables, these are shown at the fully extended and closed position, and operating levers and the position taken by the operator are indicated. These templates can then be moved about the drawing until the most satisfactory layout is found, when it is drawn in and dimensioned.

It is always difficult to visualise the relative positions of plant on the floors of multi-story buildings. A very good model of the building can be made as follows. Stick on to plywood a plan of each floor, and cut out round the outline of the building. Assemble the plans in correct sequence on vertical steel bars about $\frac{1}{4}$ inch diameter, separating each floor by distance-pieces long enough to enable the middle of the floor to be seen. This vertical distance will normally be more than would be correct for true to scale, but this does not in any way spoil the general effect nor the help the model can be in studying overall layout, transport and services. Coloured tapes can be used to indicate the path of various products, components, or services.

In factories where component or material stores and service departments, such as the toolroom in engineering factories, or the maintenance department in others, serve several production departments, it is always a problem to know where best to site them. The shape of the building may allow of no alternative, but when it is a single-story rectangular building, so common in modern industry, a successful solution is to place the service departments along the outside walls, arranging the production departments at right angles to them across the shop. The sketch at Fig. 58 illustrates this for an engineering factory and shows how production is made to flow in one direction.

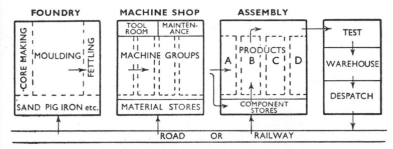

LAYOUT FOR SEPARATE SHOPS

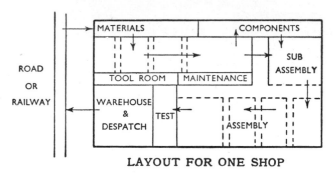

LAYOUT FOR ONE SHOP

FIG. 58

At one time problems associated with countershafting made rearrangements of layout as production developed and methods changed almost impossible, or at the least expensive. Individual motor drive provides the necessary flexibility, in addition to the important psychological benefits of an unobstructed view in the shop, and there is little excuse today for not rearranging for economical production.

Unfortunately, too little attention is paid by machine designers to the correct working height for operators at machines. The working height appears to result from constructional requirements of the machine instead of effective operating and minimum fatigue for operators. The Works Manager or Engineer of the factory using the machines, therefore, must watch this point and correct for it. Machines should be elevated, or sunk, to make the operating height correct. This is essential if machines are to be linked up with conveyors—why should it not be for operators?

In planning a layout, a frequent fault is not to allow sufficient or any room for work stations, i.e. areas where work can be kept tidily in between operations. It is useful to have one for each machine group, and certainly one for each department, preferably at the incoming end. Such stations are a great help to progress men; they are easier to control than work left around sections or machines where it so easily gets mislaid or forgotten.

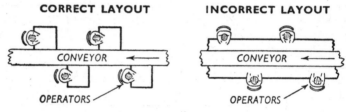

FIG. 59.

When arranging for work to be performed along conveyors, it is better to provide each operator with a small table at right angles to the conveyor and for the operator to sit facing the travel of the belt, than for the operators to sit along and facing the conveyor. The operators do not have so far to reach the belt and can more readily keep an eye on work travelling down the belt. This is illustrated in Fig. 59.

Plant and Equipment

The astonishing increases in production per man-hour obtained in many American factories (and some British ones) in the last few years are chiefly due to the use of horse-power for replacing man-power, putting machines to do the heavy work and men to do the designing, minding and maintaining. Among the conclusions that were common to almost all the reports of the Productivity Teams from Britain that visited the United States in 1950 and 1951, the greater use of tooling and power for lifting and handling was given as a primary reason for the American superiority in output per man-hour. Also, to quote Graham Hutton (*Future*, No. 2, November

1947): "Between 1924 and 1932, on the average, the annual output per worker employed in manufacturing industry in America was at least twice the volume turned out by a British worker in manufacturing industry. Today it is at least two and a half times the British figure"; and "between 1919 and 1939 American manufacturing industry as a whole used machinery of at least twice as much horsepower per employed worker as that used in British manufacturing industry; and today it is using machinery of at least two and a half times as much horse-power".

Evidently output is largely a matter of machinery and horse-power. If this is so, plant and tooling are likely to be more important than ever in the future. It is true that the larger scale of production possible in the U.S.A. with her huge home market makes elaborate tooling more economical than it can possibly be in Britain, yet much more can and will have to be done in the medium-size British factories if they are to flourish. Special assembly jigs and mechanical handling equipment (conveyors, fork-lift trucks, stillage trolleys and such like) as well as special-purpose machines can effect considerable improvements in productivity.

It is not always easy to decide on when to buy new machines or to replace old ones. Formulæ can be used, and several are given and discussed in *Engineering Economics*, Book II, by Burnham, and in the *Production Management Handbook*. In principle these set off the annual value of savings resulting from installation of the new machinery against the capital outlay and the profit the capital could earn in the business (or outside) if differently employed. Generally speaking, it is sound to err on the side of buying new plant; in the long run it pays to have modern plant. It is wise to reserve a substantial portion of annual profits for the express purpose of replacing old and buying new plant.

In general, there are two types of machines:

(1) Special-purpose—designed for a specific purpose for one article or product.

(2) General-purpose—capable of dealing with many sizes and types of work.

The special-purpose type of machine is common enough in process factories, and is much used in engineering factories on large-scale mass production. It usually enables a much higher output to be obtained than is possible on the equivalent general-purpose machine, and ensures absolute uniformity and standardisation of work turned out. It is high in capital cost, requires better toolroom service, is expensive in set-up and idle time, is soon made obsolete, and has a small secondhand value. On the other hand, the general-purpose machine is much more flexible (particularly important in times of slack trade), is cheaper to buy and maintain (spares are more likely to be available), and requires less special tooling. It may require higher skill on the part of the operators, but this is likely to be an advantage in the future.

In purchasing machines, the following points should be borne in mind:

If more than one machine of a given type and size are required, machines of the same capacity and output rate should be installed. This much simplifies machine loading, enabling Planning to load to a group instead of to individual machines.

Reliability is important—and valuable—particularly to Planning. Breakdowns not only involve maintenance costs and perhaps idle labour costs, but reduce turnover, a much more expensive matter.

Simplicity of set-up and of operating reduces idle time and human effort, expensive factors.

Automatic lubrication and totally enclosed features reduce maintenance and ensure continual operation. Too little attention is paid by designers to the need for protecting vital parts of a machine and enclosing as much of a machine as possible to protect it from dust and foreign matter. (If machines had aprons to the floor, operators could not use them for dumping rubbish beneath.)

Tools and Toolroom

It is in the engineering industry that the modern toolroom and its technique have been developed to their present high standard, partly due to the influence and enthusiasm of the youngest branch of engineering—Production Engineers. But all industries use tools, and most of them can learn quite a lot from the engineering industry of the advantages of tooling and of high-class toolroom service. In many industries the provision of small tool equipment is usually just one activity of the maintenance department, carpenter or even the Works Manager, and no attempt is made to develop the rather specialised outlook and skill required. What follows therefore deals, so far as current practice is concerned, mainly with engineering shops, but managers in other industries are strongly urged to take a leaf out of the book of experience of the engineering industry and to devote time and attention to developing a first-class "toolroom" service wherever possible.

The production of tools (and in this context tools include jigs, gauges, patterns, templates, etc., and what applies to the toolroom applies to the pattern shop) has grown from an off-shoot of the machine shop or production departments to a highly skilled expensively equipped department. Its importance is greatest in those engineering factories engaged on high-quality production, or on large-quantity repetitive production.

Experience has shown that most of the filing and fitting together of parts during assembly can be avoided by the provision of well-designed jigs, fixtures and tools, for use during the machining or fabricating stages, to ensure absolute uniformity and interchangeability. Really high-quality work to fine limits can only be executed on a production basis with the aid of specially designed tools and holding fixtures. A dictum of all craftsmen is that it is as important to hold and secure the part or article being worked as to hold the tool correctly.

Because tools and jigs must be made to finer limits than the parts with which they are used, a toolroom or pattern shop must in general be equipped with high-grade and accurate machinery and tools, and staffed with highly skilled men. In very large factories it is true that manufacture of tools can with success be put on a production basis, many of the operations being simplified and de-skilled so that they can be produced on standard machines and by semi-skilled labour, but in the small and medium-size factories, which constitute a majority of engineering factories, the need for flexibility places the emphasis on all-round skill.

When beginning to develop a toolroom, it is a common mistake to underestimate both the capital cost of equipment that is ultimately required and justified, and the room required. Because it is not a production department in the narrow sense, there is a danger of squeezing it into unsatisfactory premises or denying it the space it requires to use effectively the valuable equipment with which it is provided. With the associated tool stores, one-tenth or more of the space taken up by the shop it serves may be required by the toolroom. The layout of the toolroom in relation to the tool stores is important too. Even in large factories, where the stores can have its own tool repair section, it is advisable for the stores and toolroom to be adjacent. Tools that are returned to the stores should be examined without fail before they are put away, being reground, reset and repaired as necessary. It is usual for this to be done in the tool-room in a section set apart for the purpose, which should be under the authority of the toolroom foreman, and located immediately adjacent to the stores.

It is vitally important to integrate tool production with works manufacturing programmes. Failure to do so inevitably results in either jobs waiting while tools or jigs are rushed through, or manu-facture commencing without them, with the consequent inaccuracy and increase in costs. If it is not possible to assign a completed date to a tool when its design is first decided upon, then the toolroom must be given the tool requirements for production schedules sufficiently far ahead to enable them to make the tools in time for requirements—and tools, gauges, or patterns, and so on, are not made in a day or two. Because of this need to integrate the work of the toolroom with production, it is advisable in engineering factories for the toolroom to be under the authority of the Works Manager or Works Superintendent. In non-engineering factories tool production, or its equivalent, is normally the responsibility of the Works Engineer.

Tool Stores

The organisation of tool issue, receipt and storage depends on the number of tools stored and handled, and the number of tools required per job. The simplest method, and one quite adequate for small tool stores in engineering and other factories, is the check system. The operator asks for the tool he requires, either by description or number, and in exchange for the tool hands in a metal disc on which is stamped his own name and number. This disc is hung or placed on the hook or space occupied by the tool. Normally an operator is only allowed a small number of discs, 5 usually being adequate. When, however, this results in too much waiting time at the stores serving hatch, or the jigs, tools, or gauges required for jobs are numerous and complex, other methods are adopted for tool issue. The production department notifies the toolroom a day or two ahead of jobs which will require tools (a copy of production schedules is often sufficient). The toolroom have an indexed record of the tools used for each job, and from this the storekeeper collects the set of tools in advance. Each tool number is entered on a Tool Receipt, which the operator requiring the tools signs before being allowed to take them away. From this receipt the operator's check number is transferred to the Tool Record Card, so that at all times there is a record of where every tool is. The Tool Receipt is cancelled when the tools are returned and the entry on the Tool Record is cancelled.

Maintenance

The need in all industries, manufacture, mines, docks, or transport for the efficient upkeep of buildings, plant and equipment is, one would think, too self-evident to need emphasising, yet its importance is not always realised. Most firms know the total cost of their maintenance staff, but few could say what is the excess cost of production due to plant failure and other production delays due to poor maintenance. It can be surprisingly high, up to 5 per cent. and even 10 per cent. of the total cost of direct labour, and with only 200 operators (male and female) on direct production at an average of say £6 per week, that is an excess cost of between £3,000 and £6,000 per annum! In certain types of industries, for example, glass making, and similar process industries, with a high capital investment in plant, the maintenance department is nearly as important and has nearly as many employees as the production departments. In many companies in all industries, the controllable expenditure in overhead cost on buildings, plant and equipment, e.g. on repairs, renewals, services (heat, power), etc., may be equivalent to anything up to 25 per cent. of the cost of direct labour on production.

In large firms the maintenance department includes most of the skilled trades, each perhaps with its own department; a small firm is likely to need only one or two men in each of several trades, usually millwrights, electricians and carpenters. In medium-size firms, particularly those not engaged in skilled engineering, there is likely to be upwards of 10 or 20—and it may be found that each trade has its own foreman, each responsible to the Works Manager. This is wrong. Unless the skilled trades are also production departments, as happens in general engineering, all maintenance men should be in one department responsible to one person, who is in turn responsible to the Works Manager (or other executive). Even in general engineering there is everything to be said for keeping maintenance apart from production and responsible to a maintenance foreman. Maintenance then is much more likely to be planned, and production executives, particularly the Works Manager, released from the disproportionate amount of time which breakdown problems absorb.

Duties

What should such a maintenance foreman's duties be then? The following can be taken as typical:

(1) Maintain all property, buildings, plant and machinery in good working order and ensure continuous supply of power, water, gas and air supplies and the efficient working of the sewage system.

(2) Periodically inspect and overhaul as necessary all such property, buildings, plant and machinery.

(3) Attend to breakdowns and other repair work promptly, so as to minimise to the utmost production delays or interferences with services.

(4) Supervise and control all personal work done in the section.

(5) Maintain discipline in the department.

(6) Adhere to the Company's personnel policy and ensure that subordinates do so.

(7) Establish and encourage among personnel in the department a spirit of service to production departments.

(8) Ensure that care is taken of tools and equipment used by the department.

(9) Ensure that operators make accurately any records required of them (e.g. time spent, work done).

(10) Continually watch all forms of excess costs (particularly waste of power) and reduce to a minimum.

In larger firms these duties would need to be shared by operators or sections in the following manner:

Millwrights or Mechanics Department.—Responsible for installation, upkeep and repair of all mechanical plant. It may have its own machine tools, and would be likely to include millwrights (who are skilled in moving and installing plant and machines), machinists, fitters, pipe-fitters and sheet-metal men. If the factory produces its own power, or steam, for process it will be responsible for the boilers and engines.

Electricians Department.—Responsible for electrical plant, motors, wiring, lighting, substation and switchboard, and if the factory produces its own power, the generating equipment.

Carpenters and Building Department.—Responsible for upkeep and repair, and small extensions of all buildings and furniture. It would include, besides carpenters, plumbers, bricklayers and painters.

When it is necessary to design special plant and machinery for the Company's own use, or to rearrange plant frequently, a small Drawing Office is needed. In addition, there may be a small "outside" staff responsible for grounds, cleaning windows, lavatories and so on.

It is essential to have in the maintenance departments men who can work with little supervision and have a large amount of initiative, because by the very nature of the work they must at times work on their own, frequently outside normal working hours, and in conditions of emergency when just the right tackle or materials may not be available. It is necessary, too, to imbue the department with the idea of "service to production". Wage incentives for maintenance operators, which depend on overall effectiveness or performance of the departments they serve, are useful in this connection, though they cannot succeed if the attitude of prompt and ungrudging service is not always shown by the foremen and executives in the maintenance department.

Preventive Maintenance

The effectiveness of a maintenance department is indicated, not so much by the speed with which it does a repair, as by the way it keeps a plant running and free from any breakdowns and delays. It cannot of course be held responsible for neglect or misuse by operators; that is a major responsibility of supervision. A well-devised scheme of preventive maintenance strictly adhered to is the soundest way of ensuring the minimum trouble from plant breakdowns.

Such a scheme is based on the regular periodic inspection of every item of plant likely to give trouble, from boilers and large machines to steam traps and portable tools. It is often maintained that there is not time, or the staff is not available to carry out the necessary inspection; the truth is more often that the staff who should be doing preventive work are absorbed in "shutting the stable door". Once a system of routine inspection and of planned overhaul and repair has been running for some time, there is a net saving in time and labour.

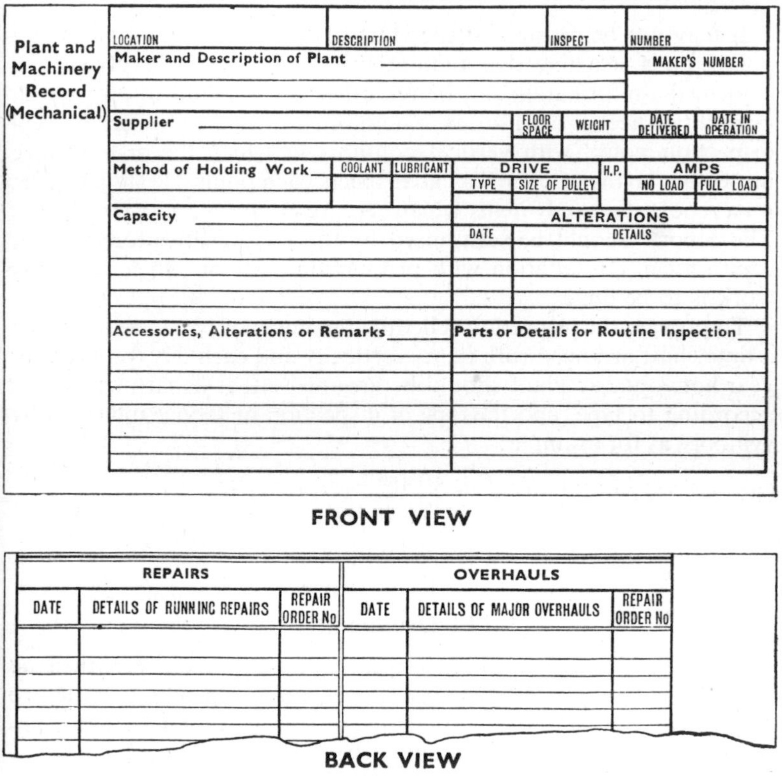

FRONT VIEW

BACK VIEW

Fig. 60.

In order to install a comprehensive scheme of preventive maintenance, the following steps are necessary:

(1) A plant inventory (if one does not exist) must be prepared, and, what is not usually included—the inventory details of parts of the equipment which are subject to wear, unexpected breakdown or neglect must be recorded. A suitable form for use in visible-edge binders as an inventory book is shown in Fig. 60.

(2) Determine the frequency of inspection and of lubrication or other service, if this is to be done at the same time, for each item of plant and machinery.

(3) Prepare inspection schedules in terms of location of plant and frequency of inspection.

(4) Assess standard times for the work. If in large works, routine maintenance work can be done on piecework.

(5) Prepare schedule of regular overhauls for equipment which needs them whatever its condition, e.g. boilers.

It may not be possible at the start to define exactly all parts and points on a machine that require inspection, but as experience is gained, the information can be recorded. It is useful to prepare an inspection sheet or card for each item of plant, listing vertically each inspection point, with vertical columns in which the maintenance inspector can insert a mark as he inspects each point. He should enter on a report sheet only items which require attention, with comments. The reports should be scrutinised by the maintenance foreman for decisions, in consultation with production staff on when necessary work is to be done.

To prepare the inspection schedule the items of plant are set out in a time chart arranged with items vertically and each day (or week) of year horizontally. Plant should be grouped either departmentally or according to type, and the type of inspection or service indicated by symbols, as for example:

I Inspect.

○ Oil and grease

△ Take up wear.

◇ Replace parts.

Η Overhaul.

All inspections, etc., falling on each day (or week) can then be brought on to a daily (or weekly) tour or tours, depending on the size of plant and number of maintenance inspectors required. The tours must be so arranged as to minimise walking time, take advantage of specialisation on certain type of plant if the quantity makes it possible, and to provide a certain amount of spare time for exceptional difficulties which may be encountered. It may be necessary, of course, to arrange for some of this work to be done outside normal production times. It is also important to attach to each tour, or to give to each inspector an exact definition of the duties to be covered.

Preventive maintenance cannot be said to be effectively under control unless, in addition to the routine inspection, there is also a record of breakdowns, which brings to the attention of management the frequency and causes of such breakdowns, and management do something about the evidence thus presented. Such records would need to classify breakdowns under the following headings, which show where the responsibility lies:

1. Faulty or insufficient maintenance.
2. Faulty design.
3. Faulty operator.
4. Unknown causes.

To collect and present the facts, the production supervision of the department or section in which the breakdown delaying production for an appreciable period, say a quarter of an hour, occurs, should record the breakdown on a Breakdown Report and send it to the Cost Office, via the Maintenance Engineer, giving the following information:

(a) Plant affected.
(b) Cause of breakdown.
(c) Period of breakdown.
(d) Loss of production.
(e) Urgency.

The Maintenance Engineer should add his comments and ensure that the Report No. is quoted on the job cards of the men doing the repair, or alternatively record the hours and names of mechanics in the report. The Cost Office can then calculate the cost of the breakdown, and render a summary report to both Works Management and Maintenance Management showing the cost under responsibility, as illustrated at Fig. 61.

WEEKLY REPORT ON COST OF PLANT BREAKDOWNS

Department	RESPONSIBILITY AND COST									
	Maint.		Operator		Design		Unknown		Total	
	Prod. Loss	Repair Cost	Prod. Loss	Repair Cost	Prod. Loss	Repair Cost	Prod. Loss	Repair Cost	Prod. Loss	Repair Cost
Total										

Fig. 61.

Such a report brings home to those responsible, not only cost of repairing, but the value of the production lost; both are excess costs, reducing potentially available profit.

In the very small firm an elaborate scheme of preventive maintenance is not required, and it is always more important to get a repair done than to record its cost. Excessive repair costs will be evident to Manager or engineer. Nevertheless, preventive inspection should be practised, and it ensures that it will get the attention it requires if the person responsible is methodical; and this involves some simple form of inspection routine or schedule, perhaps one machine a day, which is rigidly adhered to.

INSPECTION

Need for Inspection

Inspection these days is taken for granted, but it is pertinent to ask why inspection is necessary. It is as nearly non-productive as any department or function in a factory can be, and to that extent can be considered an excess cost—and one of the aims of management is to reduce excess costs to a minimum. Then why inspection? One can still come across factories where there is no inspection department. In these it is usually found that either the foremen fulfil the function or else the employees are craftsmen skilled in their particular job, the works relatively small, and all employees, operators, supervision and administration distinctly above average. It is a human problem. The truth is that inspection is necessary because human beings are fallible, and unless each person is a craftsman concerned only with producing a perfect article, bad work is likely to be passed off as good—particularly if there is anything to be gained by it. That is the reason, of course, why payment by results—quantity results—*tends* to lower the quality standard. (Payment by results can include a factor for quality and entirely successful schemes on process work have been applied which pay a maximum bonus when standard quality and output is attained, bonus decreasing when output is higher and quality consequently lower.)

All this does not mean that a lot of inspection is essential. It does mean that it is, or the extent of its need is, primarily a management problem. The higher the morale, quality and type of work, and the better the management, the less the need for inspection (and the less there are of all other excess costs as well, of course). But human nature being what it is, some inspection is always necessary. It is necessary to maintain a standard of quality and/or interchangeability of component. This latter has had the biggest influence on the growth of the inspection function. Interchangeability (that is, every repeat of a component being exactly identical within narrowly prescribed limits in size or vital dimensions), by eliminating all fitting and matching, reduces production time enormously. Without interchangeability the modern asembly-belt method would be impossible. Similarly, the repetition of process in say textiles or foodstuffs would be impossible without reliance on the quality of materials used, and this is only ensured by inspection during manufacture of the materials. And the making-up sections of the textile industry, as in the finishing sections of all industries, must depend on earlier processes for reliable standards of quality to avoid matching problems and to maintain production flow.

Aims and Objects of Inspection

But the aims and objects of an Inspection Department should be wider than merely to ensure interchangeability, important though it is. Its primary object of course is to control the Company's standard of workmanship and finish. This standard forms part of the Company's sales policy, and is interpreted in turn by the Managing Director, Works Manager and Chief Inspector. The quality of products and standard of finish should be as high as economically possible; that is, as high as costs and an adequate profit margin will allow. In practice this is a difficult matter, because there is inevitably a tug-of-war between the desire for high quality, strongly supported by the sales staff and designer, and greater output at less cost, the aim of the works departments. It is not made easier because quality is often impossible to specify precisely and is only arrived at empirically. Nevertheless, there is ample evidence that a high quality is the best form of advertising. It is especially true where reliability is more important than appearance or personal preference and for English manufacturers who do, or should, make for the quality market rather than for the cheap mass-production one.

In order to maintain these standards of quality and interchangeability, the first object of the Inspection Department in the works is to prevent faulty work from passing forward, either to next operation or to Stores; that is, to act as a kind of sieve or back stop. This is a negative kind of function. The inspection staff can and should have an equally valuable positive one not often appreciated: they should aim at preventing faulty work. From their observations of the nature and incidence of faults, inspectors should point out weaknesses, failings and faulty operation to production foremen, wherever possible suggesting where or how they may be prevented. The emphasis, of course, is on prevention. Tactful and intelligent inspectors working harmoniously with the production staff can do much to direct the latter's attention towards the prevention of faulty work and scrap.

In order that the inspection staff shall not be overridden by the production departments, the Chief Inspector should be independent of production, and responsible therefore either to the Chief Engineer or Chemist, or to the Works Manager (if he is also responsible for the technical and production administration departments). This is most important. It does not mean that in status the Chief Inspector is necessarily on the same level as the head of the Production or Technical Departments, but it does mean that he has direct access to an executive at that or a higher level who is not primarily concerned with output. Strictly speaking, he represents the customer for quality of the final product, and the assembly departments for the quality of products from component manufacturing departments. He must be quite free from undue influence. He must of course use his discretion, and to do this wisely in a company manufacturing to customer's order he must be in close contact with the Sales Department. Although an inspector has no responsibility for the quality of work *produced*, he is responsible for what is *accepted*, and in order to prevent waste production it may be customary to authorise inspectors to stop production which is continuing to fall below standard, insisting that the foreman responsible is immediately informed. Alternatively, there may be standing orders to those in charge of operating personnel, for production to be suspended if rejects have exceeded a given figure.

Duties

The following are the normal duties of a Chief Inspector:

(1) Organise and supervise the work of inspectors, testers and viewers.
(2) Instruct and train staff in carrying out their duties and ensure that they are effectively performed.
(3) Adhere to the Company's personnel policy and ensure that subordinates do so.
(4) Give effect to the Company's policy relating to quality of products and standards of finish and performance.
(5) Inspect firsts-off and finished components and products, and carry out periodic check inspection during production. Report to operator and supervisor when processes or operations are not producing to standard. Reject work not up to standard.
(6) Carry out final running tests on finished products. Record results on official test sheets and pass for delivery only those up to the Company's standard. Refer back for rectification products not up to standard.

(7) Render reports on work inspected, recommending corrections to methods and equipment where such may be necessary to maintain standards of finish and performance or to increase productivity.

(8) Advise foremen on methods of gauging and inspection carried out by operators.

(9) Ensure that care is taken of tools, gauges and other equipment used in the Inspection Department.

(10) Inspect consignments received of bought out materials and parts when requested by Stores, and render a report to the Stores and Buying Department on quality and adherence to specification or order.

(11) Record work passed, rejected and to be rectified, arranging with the foreman for rectification when necessary.

(12) Count and vouch for work passed forward and to be paid for.

(13) Keep abreast of developments in methods of inspection and collaborate with the production departments in improvements to current practice.

These duties call for persons with special characteristics, developed spontaneously or else by training, in addition to skill in the technique of inspection. An inspector must, above all, be absolutely impartial at all times, and must always be able to make a decision which is unpleasant to workers who may be his friends. There can be no compromise with the facts and his judgment of them. This is much easier of course when the inspector is not responsible to the production staff, but he still has to live and work with his workmates, and some can be very unpleasant if they disagree with a decision, or if their wages are considerably affected by it. An inspector cannot afford to be persuaded against his judgment, nor to alter a decision against the facts; it is the kind of precedent of which operators always take advantage—and quality always suffers. Then too, sound judgment is called for, that is, the ability to review quickly the various facts and factors which affect the suitability or adequacy of a job in borderline cases. When there are dimensional limits, a decision is easy, but when the standard relates to finish or appearance, the standard must be carried in the mind yet not vary from day to day. Even in the case of dimensions, there can be a combination of borderline results which has to be set against the value of an expensive component scrapped or delay in delivery if it has to be remade. This is partly skill, but a person who is capable of sound judgment on any issue makes the more skilful inspector. Lastly, the kind of person who, as a rule, does not make a good inspector is the very fast skilled worker. Inspection work proves too slow for him and does not provide the opportunity for rapid rhythmic work and higher earnings for extra effort to satisfy his ambition.

If it is desired to pay inspectors on an incentive scheme, and this is often justified and can be successful when the kind of inspection is of a routine nature and not highly skilled, there must always be a second overriding check, quite independent of the first. The person making this second check must not be paid on an incentive scheme based on output. Associated with this check must be a severe penalty for any work passed which should not have been, e.g. loss of bonus for the whole of week.

Types of Inspection

There are very nearly as many types of inspection as there are industries and jobs in them. In transport there are inspectors who check service as well as tickets, and wheel tappers who ensure safety, and in drawing offices there are frequently checkers who inspect all drawings before these are passed out. But in manufacturing industry, with which which we are primarily concerned, inspection falls into the following categories:

1. Inspection of Raw Material

This involves chemical or microscopic tests for checking the ingredients or structure of a material, tests for hardness, durability and similar properties, and for moisture content, colour, or just appearance.

2. Inspection of Work in Process

This covers the whole range of factory inspection of parts and final assemblies with all the skilled technique and accurate instruments for measuring to final limits on a production as distinct from a laboratory basis. Tests are made to determine either accuracy of form or dimension or degree of finish.

3. Process Control

Inspection of process conditions is required in chemical, food, paint and similar manufacture, heat treatment, drying and electrolysis, and other electrical treatment. When the correct conditions have been determined for production of a satisfactory material and uniform raw materials are ensured, tests which maintain these correct conditions automatically ensure correct products.

4. Running Tests

When the end product is a machine, it is usual to make running tests in conditions as similar as possible to those in which the machine will be working in service. Motor-cars have road tests; electric motors and generators, cranes and machinery designed to a customer's requirements are run on a test bed often in the presence of the customer or his representative, or tested on site before acceptance. When tests cannot exactly reproduce conditions (as for example with cars and electric motors), tests are carried out which exceed the severity of working conditions by a standard amount, so that uniformity of results is ensured. The amount by which conditions are more severe than normal is a factor of safety (or more strictly of ignorance, since it is an acknowledgment that occasionally conditions may be worse than normal by an amount not precisely known).

5. Quality Control

This is a statistical method of measuring deviation from standard quality by recording sample tests on a chart which immediately shows when work is being produced outside previously approved limits. It is applicable to all cases where limits can be worked to and is most suitable for continuous manufacture. This method has been developed and extensively used and tried out in engineering factories during the 1939–45 war, and is strongly recommended wherever it is applicable. It has the virtues of low cost and of early warning of a falling off in quality. It is simply explained in British Standards (War Emergency Publication) No. 1008 : 1942.

The following extract from page 299 of *Institution of Mechanical Engineers Proceedings*, 1947, vol. 157, "Gauging & Metrology," by John E. Sears, C.B.E., M.A., M.I.Mech.E., is a summarised description:

"*Quality Control.*—This is a new procedure which has come into vogue during the past twenty years for the control of mass-produced articles by the application of the theory of probability to the results of examination of samples. A very important feature is that the examination is made close to the machine, and as soon as possible after the articles are produced, so that the results serve to give a direct indication of tendencies in the production process, and enable corrective action to be taken before excessive errors arise, thereby avoiding unnecessary scrap. The method can be of very wide application, and is, of course, particularly useful in any case where test to destruction is required.

"From the point of view of gauging between limits, two variants are possible. Control may be based either on the percentage of defectives found in samples (for which purpose provisional 'control' limits should be set inside the ultimate work limits) or on recorded measurements of the individual parts in the samples. In either case there is a considerable saving in the number of gauges required; but for the second alternative, which is to be preferred, gauges of the indicating type are necessary.

"It is claimed that the proper application of quality control can give as sure a result as 100 per cent. gauging, when due regard is had to the possibilities of human error due to fatigue in continuous operation of the latter.

"Study of the data accumulated from the application of quality control should also afford information as to the performance of machine tools of the greatest value to designers in assessing tolerances for machined parts on a rational basis."

Limits

It will be realised, from what has already been said, that quality, accuracy and finish are relative; there is, in a practical manufacturing sense, no absolute measurement. To an engineer dead size means as accurate as he can measure with his micrometer, e.g. to a ten-thousandth part of an inch (·0001″). In setting up any standard, therefore, it is not sufficient to state a single unit (of length, degree of heat, etc.), but to express the standard as a permissible variation between upper and lower limits, unless the accuracy obtainable with instruments normally in use is good enough, e.g. foot rule, or commercial scales for weight. When other than commercial accuracy is required, limits are essential, and the standard is specified as a unit with a variation "higher or lower" or "up or down" not to exceed given amounts. In engineering this is expressed thus: 2″ plus and minus 0·005 inch, meaning a dimension of 2 inches plus or minus 5 thousandths, or between the limits of 2·005 inch and 1·995 inch.

In the British Standards and other standards of limits frequently used in industry, the following terms are used:

(a) *Limits*
Limits for a dimension or other unit of measurement are the two extreme permissible sizes (measurements) for that dimension (unit).

(b) *Tolerance*
The tolerance on a dimension (measurement) is the difference between the high and low limits of size for that dimension (measurement); it is the variation tolerated in the size of that dimension (measurement), to cover reasonable imperfection in workmanship. In connection with the fit of a part into another, e.g. a shaft into a hole or bore, the following further terms are used:

(c) *Allowances*
The allowance is the prescribed difference between the high limit for a shaft and the low limit for a hole to provide a certain class of fit.

(d) *Fit*
The fit between two mating parts is the relationship existing between them with respect to the amount of play or interference which is present when they are assembled together. In general shop terms, a fit can vary between a "heavy drive" to a "coarse clearance", and British Standards lists fourteen such fits, including various classes of push and running fits.

A full, but simple, explanation of Limits and Fits for Engineering is given in B.S.S. 164: Part I.

A much more comprehensive analysis of tolerances and fits, and of inspection problems and methods connected with engineering designs, is given in *Dimensional Analysis of Engineering Designs*, vol. I, "Components" (Part 1), prepared by the Inter-Services Committee for Dimensioning and Tolerancing of Drawings for the Ministry of Supply and published by the Stationery Office in 1948.

Organisation of Inspection

In order that the function of inspection shall not be negative only, it is essential to recognise that its task is to *control* the *quality* of production. Applying the principles of "control" set out on pages 40–41, there must be:

(*a*) Standards of quality laid down.

(*b*) Records of deviation from standards, i.e. records, not only of rejects, but also evidence of frequency and importance of rejects and where occurring.

(*c*) Action to prevent recurrence as far as possible or to minimise frequency and to rectify if possible work rejected.

Standards should be laid down in writing in specifications or on drawings, and on the latter it is important to remember that a dimension has no meaning if not associated with a tolerance. It is essential that it is clearly understood in a shop, and stated on all drawings, that dimensions to which no tolerance is specifically given, i.e. open dimensions, are to be to a standard tolerance. In practice, dimensions relating to rough castings and other non-machined parts of a component are required to be to a tolerance of $\frac{1}{16}$ inch ($\pm\frac{1}{32}$ inch), and open dimensions of machined surfaces to a tolerance of twenty thousandths ($\pm$ 0·010 inch).

The actual organisation of the work of inspecting, recording and taking of corrective action must obviously vary very widely with the type of product, process and scale of manufacture. With armament and aeroplane manufacture, 100 per cent. inspection at all stages and operations is usually called for. In the manufacture of barrows, agricultural machinery, etc., a much less rigid inspection is required, and in the chemical process industries a different type of inspection altogether is required. The first and major factor affecting the organisation of the work is whether 100 per cent. inspection or only sampling is necessary. This is mainly an economic question, although as in the case of armament and aeroplane manufacture, absolute reliability is an overriding factor. The fact that 100 per cent. inspection results in a high proportion of inspectors ("non-producers") to operators, as high even as 1 in 3, and the fact that sample or check inspection which does reveal errors is usually sufficient to maintain a reasonably satisfactory standard, suggests that sample inspection is usually adequate, and in practice this is so. When, however, work which slips through sample checks creates serious assembly delays or expensive reactions from customers, then 100 per cent. inspection may justify its cost.

When sample inspection is adopted, it is essential for firsts off a run or set-up to be inspected thoroughly. Thereafter, not only must samples be taken at a frequency to assure an adequate percentage check as indicated by experience, but there should also be random checks at irregular periods and of the batch. Although not foolproof, this usually reveals persistent faults and really bad work. The frequency of sample inspection must be laid down as part of the standard for each operator or process. A method of doing this for machining operation is illustrated on the specimen operation layout shown in Fig. 9.

It remains then to decide on either centralised or floor inspection. In the former method all work from a department is sent to the Inspection Department or made to pass through an inspection crib before passing on to the next operation. In the latter method inspectors go on to the floor and inspect work at the machine or bench. Only a study of the conditions on the spot can reveal which of these methods will give the best or cheapest results. In considering which to adopt, the following advantages of each should be borne in mind:

Advantages of Centralised Inspection

Easier and better supervision.

Division of labour possible, permitting employment of less skilled labour.

More thorough and less liable to interruption.

Tidier shops, and therefore easier to control flow of work.

More accurate checking for wage payment, and less chance of falsification.

Easier to progress.

Losses from lost or stolen work and hidden scrap at a minimum.

Advantages of Floor Inspection

Far less handling. (In the case of very large components, transport to inspection crib is prohibitive.)

Less delay due to time lag in Inspection Department.

Less work in progress.

Shorter production cycle time.

Faults can often be rectified *immediately* and by operator *responsible*.

Inspector can act as adviser to operator, with aim of *preventing* faulty work (particularly helpful with learners.)

It is not proposed to illustrate all the kind of records that should be made of the results of inspection, since these vary so widely, and obviously must be designed to suit the product and the organisation. As a help in the design of a Scrap Note, a very suitable form is illustrated in Fig. 46. Certain principles, however, must be adhered to if the amount of faulty work is to be controlled and steps taken to minimise what does occur. These are:

(1) Records must be rendered as soon after the event as possible and to the person first able to do something about it.

(2) To this end foreman should be supplied with a report item by item on the rejects in his department daily (or weekly or monthly). He should sign this and indicate action taken, and send on to the Works Manager (or other senior production executive). If he can scrutinise each scrap note, so much the better.

(3) The cost of scrap (material and labour) should be rendered to foremen on weekly cost control reports.

(4) Only inspectors should be allowed to reject or scrap any work, and scrap should not be received by Reclaiming or Stores Departments without a covering note signed by an inspector.

(5) Inspectors should be responsible for documents, arranging for the re-processing or rectification of faulty work, and ensuring that the need for so doing is brought to the attention of Production Planning.

In a small firm, where personal contact between the higher management and the operator at the bench is both intimate and frequent, and operators consequently are more aware of the significance of their work and can be made more aware of the need for quality, few, if any, inspectors are required. Except for a final inspection of the completed product, it is likely to be more successful to put the onus of passing forward only good work on the operator. It cannot be done, however, if any slackness or slipshod work is allowed to pass unnoticed or uncorrected. There must be pride in maintaining a definite standard. By and large, workmen prefer to do good work and will do so if put on their honour and if the general standard is set by example.

BIBLIOGRAPHY

1. P. H. Miller: *The Practice of Engineering Estimating*. (Oxford University Press, 1934).
2. R. O. Kapp: *The Presentation of Technical Information*. (Constable, London, 1948.)
3. R. L. Morrow: *Time and Study Motion Economy*. (Ronald Press, New York, 1946.)
4. H. B. Maynard and G. J. Stegmerton: *Operation Analysis*. (McGraw Hill, New York, 1938.)
5. Anne G. Shaw: *Introduction to Theory and Application of Motion Study*. (H.M.S.O., London, 1945.)
6. "Office Aids to the Factory" Series, Nos. 1–5: *Application of Production Control*. (British Institute of Management, London (1943–45).)
7. C. W. Lytle: *Job Evaluation Methods*. (Ronald Press, New York, 1946.)
8. C. W. Lytle: *Wage Incentive Methods*. (Ronald Press, New York, 1942.)
9. J. J. Gracie: *Job Evaluation*. (British Institute of Management, 1950.)
10. H. T. Lewis: *Procurement—Principles and Cases*. (Irwin, Chicago, 1949.)
11. H. H. Farquar: *Factory Storekeeping: The Control and Storage of Materials*. (McGraw Hill, New York, 1922.)
12. W. R. J. Griffiths: *Works Engineer*. (Pitman, London, 1943.)
13. *Quality Control:* BS. 1008/BS. 600R. (British Standards Institution, London, 1942.)

PERSONNEL

By R. M. ALDRICH

CHAPTER I

THE PERSONNEL FUNCTION—THE NERVOUS SYSTEM OF THE ORGANISATION STRUCTURE

Personnel Management. The Aims of Personnel Management. The Personnel Department's Position in the Company's Structure. Responsibilities of the Personnel Department. Financial Budget for Personnel Management

PERSONNEL MANAGEMENT

PERSONNEL management may be conveniently described as part of the management process which is primarily concerned with the human constituents of an organisation. Its object is the maintenance of human relationships on a basis which, by consideration of the well-being of the individual, enables all those engaged in the undertaking to make their maximum personal contribution to the effective working of that undertaking. The first and very obvious implication is that it cannot possibly be something apart from or extraneous to the process of management as a whole, but is an essential element in its effectiveness closely interrelated with that of management as a whole. Illustrations of this can only be too readily found from the annals of industry. Of what use is good personnel management when the organisation of production control is so weak that material or components do not consistently flow forward to the machining or assembly points, and accordingly prevent the operators in these shops from earning the incentive bonuses contained in the piece prices? Or again, what can be the meaning of good personnel management in an organisation in which there is no stable policy, or in which no definitions of executive responsibilities are set up? To argue the reverse, viz. that no other function of management can be effective without good personnel management, is certainly correct, but it serves only to emphasise the point at issue—that the personnel aspect or function is inherent in the process of management itself, and in consequence is applied by all executives and supervisors throughout the organisation rather than by the Personnel Manager or his department.

Strictly speaking, the personnel function has two aspects: there is, in the first place, this responsibility attaching to all executives and supervisors for the way in which they manage their people and weld this human material into the team that carries out effectively the activities of the operating departments or sections. While this is primarily a matter of the exercise of leadership, it is also linked up with the carrying out of the established personnel policy and the smooth application of the procedures designed to secure the fulfilment of that policy. It necessarily entails on the part of the executives and supervisors an understanding of the principles of personnel management as well as close acquaintance with the personnel procedures and methods of the organisation itself.

A "Service" Facility

The second aspect is the specialised responsibility which falls to the charge of the personnel executive. His task includes advising the Company's Managing Director or General Manager, and through him the Board of Directors, on the formulation of personnel policy, and planning and supervising the procedures by which that policy is to be carried into effect. He is, as it were, the expert retained to deal with all policy, planning and methods concerning the management of people, parallel, for instance, to the engineering expert who has to deal with production policy, process layouts, engineering methods, tooling and the like, or to the chemist who is responsible for formulæ and quality standards. The Personnel Manager's responsibility entails in the main rendering a service to other executives, as well as advising them in the discharge of their own human responsibilities. He serves the other executives by many of the activities which are carried on within his own specialist department: the procedures of selection and engaging, the records and returns, the statistics and study of absenteeism, the provision of canteen and medical services, and numerous other facilities. In the language of organisation theory, he holds a functional responsibility for all personnel matters.

The nearest analogy is in the human body. Personnel management is not the brain, the controller, nor only just a limb, a member, nor yet the bloodstream, the energising force. But it is the nervous system. It is centred in the controlling unit of the brain, for personnel policy is a Board responsibility and it is interpreted through the Managing Director. It is a two-way channel of information reaching out to every part of the body organisation. It is a live channel, not just a duct, and in some respects has automotive force. It is used in every action; if it atrophies, partial paralysis results; if it gets out of balance, there issues instability, chaotic action, disequilibrium, which can be found in all stages of advancement, in close parallel with neurosis. But, above all this, it is inherent in the whole body and intimately associated with its every movement. The nervous system can never be thought of as an adjunct of the body—no more can personnel management be an extraneous or superimposed element on the structure of organisation. The personnel function lies embedded in the structure, is inherent in the dynamism of that structure, an integral part of the process of management itself.

THE AIMS OF PERSONNEL MANAGEMENT

Getting the best out of Employees

The central purpose of the personnel function is the promotion of effectiveness of the people employed in the organisation in the performance of their allotted duties, by the substitution of co-operation in the common task in place of the suspicion and hostility which have so long been characteristic of relations between employers and employed. Put in simpler terms, this means getting the "best" out of the people by winning and maintaining their wholehearted collaboration. The personnel function does not exist for any such primary purpose as "making conditions easier" or "improving the lot of the worker": this is one of the *means*, though best regarded as one of the ordinary social responsibilities of management. Personnel management must be among the means by which effectiveness and economy of operation are attained.

The Hawthorne Investigations

Among the research carried out, particularly in America, with a view to finding out what makes people give of their best, the well-known programme was that carried out by the Western Electric Company of Chicago, popularly referred to as the Hawthorne experiment. This extended over many years, during which a systematic study was made of the behaviour and attitudes of groups of employees. The Company learned a great deal about the force of personal relations as a factor in management, and became aware of the influence that is exerted on the outlook and effectiveness of workers by the way in which authority over them is exercised or by the manner in which their services are appreciated or noticed.[1]

The major significant feature of the five and a half years of the Relay Assembly Room activities was the overall trend of output; the upward movement for something like three years and the following decline. One can forget for the moment the important variations within the general trend or the specific motivating forces at given stages and take only the broad curve. As to the final downward phase, we have the known evidence of one of the girls herself: "We lost our pride" was her own comment. For the earlier years the little team of workers had been the centre of interest for the whole factory, for its

[1] For a review of the whole programme, see *The Making of Scientific Management*, Vol. III, by L. Urwick and E. F. L. Brech (Management Publications Trust, London, 1948).

top executives, for a University Department, almost for a whole nation. "We mattered . . ." was the dominant emotion in the minds of those whose work lay in the glare of the limelight; and thus unfettered by regulative restrictions, and fostered by being consulted and expected to contribute to their own government, the subconscious power of contentment and achievement drove them to ever higher levels of physical effort and an upward streaming output curve. Even when physical working conditions were taken down to the lowest levels, output soared to unprecedented heights. "We mattered . . .", the impetus of interest and group loyalty devoted to a common purpose—not deliberate or conscious, but directed simply by unthwarted emotions harnessed in the service of the group.

Then came the turn. With the deepening of depression even an experiment in living human beings could not continue to absorb attention. Problems of output and markets began to claim more and more of the light, and as conditions worsened, the fear of unemployment—following in the wake of friends and colleagues—threw its ugly shadow ahead. Surely in these circumstances more earnings were essential to provide the standby for the threatening idleness. But the irrational emotion is stronger than the rational logic—output began to fall despite the financial incentives available. What was happening? "We were losing our pride—we were ceasing to matter."

For those who care to think about the fundamental realities of our management responsibilities there is a lot to be learned here—and the lessons it teaches are a chapter in the textbook of the Personnel Function of Management.

The Hawthorne Interview Programme may be more briefly disposed of in this connection, for in its later stages it was deliberately conceived for the purpose of providing material for the training of supervisors and superintendents. The Company had by this time learned enough about the force of relations as a factor to be fully aware of the significance of the influence that is exerted on the outlook and effectiveness of workers by the way in which authority over them is exercised. As was said in an earlier section, where a knowledge of the essentials and implications of personnel management is most heeded is in those who hold the responsibility for leadership and governances as executives and supervisors.

An earlier investigation on different lines but pointing in the same direction was Matthewson's study of restriction of output among workers in a number of American factories. Some of his findings are almost unbelievable, and most of them are incomprehensible, unless we have a belief in the influence of human emotions and feelings. All through the descriptions and analysis of the restriction of output by the spontaneous action of groups of workers, we are brought face to face with a new logic. What impels these workers to withhold their work and thus deliberately curtail their own earnings, building up elaborate precautions to attain the restriction—is not so much bitter individual experience, but a "belief" that management will cut down their rates, or a "feeling" that they will not be allowed to earn more than a given sum, or a "feeling" of improving their own security— when, in point of *fact*, they might be driving the organisation into bankruptcy. Once again the motivating force is found in emotional reactions, and lowered effectiveness is seen as a direct result of lack of good relations and consultations between management and employees.

These illustrations point right to the heart of the personnel function —the human being has powerful innate forces of an emotional kind; he has desires that are akin to the instinctive. These forces influence his behaviour both as an individual and as a member of the group. They may be thwarted—and so make him a restricted collaborator, or even an unwitting saboteur. On the other hand, they can be harnessed, and thus weld him into a group as an active contributor, and so become an important element in achieving high morale. The task of personnel management lies just here—to harness, to weld, to foster human energies and emotions for the attainment of the purposes of the organisation, to the benefit of employees themselves, of the Company, and—most important of all—of the Community of which it forms a part.

THE PERSONNEL DEPARTMENT'S POSITION IN THE COMPANY'S STRUCTURE

It has already been indicated that normally the Personnel Manager must be responsible to the chief executive of the organisation. Nothing is to be read into this as regards personal status or salary: it is meant solely in terms of executive responsibility. There is, of course, a very strong case for the view that the personnel executive ought to be of the calibre to carry a place on the "top line". This is a point which will be considered from another angle later.

In effect, the Personnel Manager's task entails discharging a part of the responsibility of the Chief Executive himself. Put into other words, his is a "General Management" function, and all his actions are really carried out on behalf of the General Manager. His position is simply an illustration of the ordinary principle of specialisation, the General Manager passing over to a suitably qualified person certain aspects of his own responsibility, in which expert knowledge and assistance are called for. As a consequence, it can be argued that a Personnel Manager's correct location in the organisation structure is that of "Personal Assistant to the Chief Executive," i.e. serving in "staff relation" to him. That he has both a functional responsibility to discharge in respect of the other sections of the organisation and a direct responsibility in relation to the activities covered by his own Department does not in any way detract from or interfere with this conception in principle, even though in practice it may be both customary and convenient to find the personnel specialist shown in an ordinary "line" executive position in the structure. This is likely to persist until such time as the principles of organisation are more fully appreciated throughout industry.

No matter how small the Company, whether employing twenty persons or two thousand, the managerial function of "personnel" must be performed. Employees have to be recruited and paid; they must have provision made for their food and drink; someone has to deal with their complaints; lavatories and cloakrooms have to be provided, and so on—the personnel work is there, even if frequently not in sufficient volume to require a full-time official. The point of growth at which it becomes necessary or desirable to appoint a full-time official cannot be laid down as a hard-and-fast rule. A number of employees of 400–500 is often quoted as a useful minimum, though during the recent war years many firms with as few as 200 employees found a specialist Personnel Officer invaluable, and numerous instances can be cited from among firms employing fewer than 150.

There is no set standard of personnel management. It varies from one works to another, or from one type of industry to another. Frequently it is practised more successfully in family concerns, where there is a long history of good individual relations than in the larger-scale organisation or nationalised concern, despite the existence in the latter of considerable formal attention to personnel activities and procedures.

The function of the Personnel Department is twofold—it is advisory and yet executive: advisory in the help that it gives to executives and supervisors in the daily discharge of their human responsibilities, and executive in the activities that it carries out and the services that it renders. As an illustration for a contribution to efficiency and for the benefit of employees, take the case of lighting in a manufacturing department. It is the Personnel Department's duty to ensure that conditions are of a certain standard, partly because the law requires it to be so, but more important because adequate lighting is an essential to effective work. Suppose in a certain Company a worker complains about the light, possibly to a member of the personnel staff while making a periodic visit to the factory. That official takes the point up with the departmental manager or foreman, tests are made to ascertain the quality of light, and perhaps the results do show a poor standard. The matter is for remedy—it may involve a complete overhaul of lighting in the department, or it may mean altering only one lamp. The action of the Personnel Department has been a service to the employee, and perhaps advisory to the electrical section in indicating the standard of illumination recommended for that particular job, leaving the electrical people to decide the means of attaining the standard and to give the instructions for the work to be carried out.

The responsibilities and status of the Personnel Manager will also vary from one firm to another, for they must depend largely on the circumstances of the organisation. But the general principle of reporting to the chief executive can always be preserved. In the following diagram the Works Manager, the Sales Manager and the Personnel Manager are all responsible to the General Manager, and all three have equal status. It is unlikely that the Personnel Manager's salary will be as high as those of the Works Manager or Sales Manager, but he has the same direct line of approach to the General Manager in the discharge of his responsibilities:

In another case, the status of the Personnel Manager is at the level of the Assistant Works Manager, but he still has direct access to the General Manager; in other words, the importance of his function is recognised, even though conditions require him to have a more junior status:

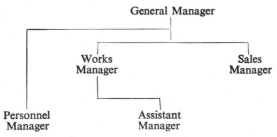

Dealing with other Managers

Questions of discipline and working conditions throw further light on the position of the Personnel Manager. The employee in a job is responsible to his chargehand, foreman or manager. Undoubtedly, were the Personnel Manager, during his walks round the factory or office departments, to observe anything wrong—such as unsafe conditions, time wasting, etc.—he would report it to the foreman or the manager of the particular section, and not try to give instructions or reprimand to the employee. A good Personnel Manager will at all times make the position so clear that there is never any doubt in the minds of his colleagues as to his intentions or any cause for doubt that he is endeavouring "to do their job" or "to undermine their authority". The Personnel Manager exercises "line" control only over the specialised activities which come within his direct jurisdiction: in a large organisation, such sections as those of the Employment Manager, the Canteen Manager, the Education Officer, the Safety Officer and Sports Secretary. The position of a full-time Medical Officer raises some difficulty, because of the medical profession's feeling that etiquette requires their direct report to the Managing Director, in regard to the medical service in the organisation, though a Personnel Manager would be responsible for the day-to-day routine and procedures connected with the medical services. This attitude is due to a failure to appreciate organisation principle—the Medical Department is part of the personnel activity, and the Medical Officer should be seen as a specialist consultant advising the Personnel Manager, and through him the Managing Director.

The arrangement of responsibility of the Personnel Manager and the status which he is given reflect a great deal on the way in which he can do his work. He must be able to deal with the other managers on a basis of a "Staff Officer," irrespective of his status in the Company being inferior to those with whom he must discuss policy and give guidance on personnel matters. To do this successfully he needs to know that he has the complete sympathy and support of the Managing Director or the head of the concern, and, by his own personality and strength of leadership, be able to attain agreement with his colleagues on everyday problems. Whenever this is not so, he should always obtain "agreement to differ", he cannot allow friction to develop between a manager or foreman and himself or any member of his team. Similarly, there must be no feeling that he is condescending to give information or that he is withholding information to prop up his own importance. He must always be frank and make a strong point of keeping foremen or managers aware of negotiations or developments which may be going on in reference to members of their department. In his general day-to-day life, he must also be careful never to do things which are prohibited to other people by the code of rules or regulations.

A good Personnel Manager is generally popular with the employees in the factory and offices and with all whom he comes into contact. Cheap popularity can be obtained by propping up the bar in the local pub, but this type of "hail fellow, well met" popularity is not the kind which a Personnel Manager should seek. He should try to be scrupulously fair in his dealings with employees, ready and willing to give assistance to any member of his supervisory staff, sufficiently near to the ground to be able to talk to the man at the bench and the girl at her desk, about their problems in a way which inspires confidence and respect. He should have an inexhaustible fund of patience, and be prepared time after time to build his castles, see them smashed to pieces, and yet be ready to start all over again in another way. Above all, he needs to be completely impartial, and make it apparent in everything he does that he is unbiased. Decisions on any matter on which his advice is requested and in which it is his duty to intervene should be given only after an investigation of the facts and without fear and favour to either party.

Finally, the status of the Personnel Manager cannot be made by flowery language or extravagant claims of his importance; neither will he be able to function effectively unless he has the support of the chief executive on a policy which is genuinely seeking sound relationships with the employees, and accepted by all members of the management.

*　　　*　　　*

The following principles have been laid down by one authoritative writer as a guide to the place of the personnel executive in organisation:

"1. Personnel management can never be completely isolated as a function. It is concerned with good industrial relations in the broadest sense. Consequently its results accrue in every contact between representatives of the management and their colleagues and subordinates. It cannot therefore be entirely 'specialised'. It should permeate every corner of the undertaking and every managerial action. On the other hand, there must be some specialisation if the undertaking is to remain up to date.

"2. The determination of the personnel policy must therefore be a central function, the responsibility of the administrative authority (the Board), which looks to the chief executive to see that it is carried out.

"3. The execution of that policy must also be a central function, since it penetrates every other function of the organisation. This is to say, if a specialised personnel manager is appointed, he should be responsible directly either to the administrative authority (the Board) or to the chief executive.

"4. This does not imply that he need be equal in status to any other executive of second rank in the undertaking. The function is one with which the chief executive must concern himself personally to an exceptional degree (*vide* 6 below). If it is clear that the Personnel

Manager speaks with his authority, the question of relative status is unimportant.

"5. The Personnel Manager should be in direct 'line' control of all units in the organisation specialising in various aspects of personnel work—employment, medical, welfare, etc.

"6. There are, however, three aspects of personnel work—general relations between the undertaking and its employees, trade union negotiations and the development and promotion of higher executives—which are of such a character that they can only be handled effectively in the last resort by the chief executive directly. Where a Personnel Manager assists a chief executive in the preliminary stages of such matters, he should act in a 'staff' capacity.

"7. In order to secure uniformity of policy and integration of action in personnel questions between large production departments, branches, etc., and the Personnel Manager and the specialised personnel units, specialised personnel assistants should be appointed in such departments or branches. Such personnel assistants should be directly responsible to the manager concerned (a line relationship), but should be responsible to the Personnel Manager for training methods, etc. (a functional relationship)."[1]

RESPONSIBILITIES OF THE PERSONNEL DEPARTMENT

One cannot closely define the activities of the Personnel Manager because of their variety and scope. One interesting summary is given in Fig. 62. How these activities are carried out in practice form the matter of following sections of this part of the volume.

Variations in scope of activity are matched by variety of title: here it is "Employment Manager", there "Labour Superintendent", elsewhere "Labour Manager", or "Welfare Officer". Yet, there may be little or no difference in the responsibilities carried out. Gradually the title of "Personnel Manager" or "Personnel Officer" is gaining ground, and some degree of conformity is beginning to emerge in regard to the main lines of activity undertaken.[2]

The smaller organisations often present interesting illustrations. Take the case of a factory employing 300 people, where the Personnel Manager is responsible for engaging both operating and clerical employees. With the assistance of a secretary or a junior clerk, he

---

[1] Extracted from "Personnel Management in Relation to Factory Organisation," by L. Urwick; published as a broadsheet of the Institute of Personnel Management.

[2] In the present text, the term "Personnel Manager" and "Personnel Officer" will be used indiscriminately, with precisely the same significance. The other terms will not be used. The habitual reference in the MASCULINE gender is nothing more than a *matter of textual convenience*. It in no way suggests lack of appreciation of the excellent responsible personnel service rendered by many hundreds of women Personnel Officers up and down the country. Similarly, save where specifically called for otherwise, reference to the employee(s) is in the masculine form.

FUNCTIONS OF A PERSONNEL DEPARTMENT [1]

Employment	Wages	Joint Consultation	Health and Safety	Welfare—Employee Services	Education and Training
Liaison with Ministry of Labour and sources of supply.	Maintenance of Company's accepted wage structure.	Act as Negotiating Officer with Trade Unions.	Application of provisions of Factories Act.	Administration of Canteen policy.	Training of new starters, apprentices, employees for transfer and promotion, instructors, supervisors.
Interview applicants, engagements, transfers, releases, dismissals.	Authorise changes in individual rates.	Knowledge of Conciliation and Arbitration procedure.	Contact with Factory Inspector.	Sick Club and Benevolent Schemes.	Encourage additional education through Day Continuation Schools, Attendance at Technical and Evening Institutes, Evening Classes, Lectures, Films, Dramatic, Musical and other societies.
Introduction of new starters to foremen.	Assessment and control of differential rates and special payments.	Maintain and improve machinery for Joint Consultations, i.e. Joint Production Committees and Works Committees, etc.	Works Medical Services.	Long-service Grants.	
Follow-up of new starters.	Workroom and individual efficiencies.		Arrange (in co-operation with Medical Service): Medical Exam. of employees, Health Records, Supervision of hazardous jobs, Sick Visiting, Convalescence.	Pension and Superannuation Funds or Leave Grants.	
Maintenance of employee records.	Consultation with time study or outside consultants in respect of incentives.	Maintain and improve procedure for ventilating and dealing with workroom grievances.		Granting of Loans.	Supervision and control of Notice Boards and Information Bulletins.
Personnel statistics.			Fatigue studies and Rest pauses.	Legal Aid.	
Employee interviews and consultations.	Authorisation of deductions from wages.	Interpret and ensure understanding of Company personnel policy.	Accident Prevention and supervision of Safety Committees, Systematic Plant Inspection, Safety Education, Investigation of Accidents, Accident Statistics, etc.	Advice on Individual problems.	Suggestion schemes.
Grading of employees.		Advise and counsel junior staff and employees in collective dealing.		Assist employees in Transport, Housing, Billeting, Shopping and other problems.	Works Tours.
Hours of work and overtime.			Administration of Workmen's Compensation.	Provision of social and recreational facilities.	Library.
Legislation relating to employment.		Act as Company representative in outside negotiations affecting personnel.		Supervision of Committees, Red Cross, National Savings, Welfare of employees, etc.	Works Magazine.
Attendance at appropriate Committees relating to employment.					

Extracted from the broadsheet of the Institute of Personnel Management, by G. R. Moxon.

FIG. 62.

keeps all the records (using only a single card index); looks after the half-dozen apprentices, arranging with the local technical college their different courses; takes visitors round the plant when they come either by invitation of the Managing Director or Sales Department; in addition, he is responsible for seeing that no unauthorised person gets into the factory during the day-time, controls the commissionaire, issues clean overalls on Monday morning, makes up the pay cards, and finally, acts as the wages clerk on Friday night by helping the clerk in the Accounts Department to prepare and issue the pay packets. The number of applicants he would interview for employment would probably be very small, and the majority of his time could be devoted to doing these other tasks, while as long as morale remained good he would not be heavily occupied in dealing with terminations of employment.

In contrast, take a large organisation with a number of factories spread throughout the country. Here we should expect to find a central Personnel Department controlled by a high-ranking executive, possibly serving as a member of the Board. His job would be the interpretation and maintenance of Company policy, advising on the attitude the Company should adopt in trade union negotiations, alterations in conditions, rates, bonus, and so on. He might have three or four Personnel Officers to deal with day-to-day activities and a large staff to look after routine matters, records and statistics, the operation of training schemes, supplemented by specialists for health, safety and first-aid. Each of the factories would have a responsible Personnel Manager on the site, with a close link with the central Personnel Department on matters of policy. In such an instance, the local Personnel Officer would probably be responsible for receiving requests for labour and supplying by promotion or engagement the people necessary to the production or service departments. It would be his job to contact the Employment Exchanges, advertise and take other necessary action to fill the vacancies, to interview applicants for employment and deal with people who wished to leave.

On the clerical side, most of the work may be covered by a Staff Manager; he or she would be responsible for engaging all clerical staff and would assist the Personnel Manager when appointments of a senior kind were being made. At set periods during the year the Staff Manager would prepare lists and, in conjunction with the departmental manager or section head, recommend to the Personnel Manager increases in pay or bonuses where they were paid. Separate records would be kept by the Staff Manager in regard to the clerical employees, and he would also be expected to examine the methods of work and to suggest improvements or economies whenever appropriate.

Interpreting the Company's Policy

Interpreting the Company's employment policy is one of the major functions of the Personnel Manager. The Company's policy is, of course, decided by the Board of Directors and sent through the Managing Director to all executives, managers and supervisors, for them to carry out. Some comply with the spirit of the policy, while others may become rigid and pedantic, interested more in the letter and in compliance with rules and regulations. This is particularly so where trade union consultation is newly accepted, and members of management have an "anti-union" attitude, which leads them to take the law into their own hands, completely ignoring the fact that the Board have entered into a local or national agreement with the trade unions. This is where the personnel specialist can exercise a valuable educational influence, and can also play a very big part in co-ordinating the executives' and supervisors' response to the Board's lead.

The Company's personnel policy should be clearly defined and opportunity should be given for those whose responsibility it is to administer the policy to have their say in what shall or shall not be done, before the Board reaches a final decision. The Personnel Manager can also serve as a two-way channel of communication, so that employees too can have an opportunity of contributing to policy. In some organisations a Joint Consultative Committee serves this purpose in a more formal way. But it remains the task of the personnel specialist to ensure that whatever is decided by the Company should always be made known throughout the works, either by public notices or through the managers and supervisors.

The value of a sound personnel policy cannot be over-estimated. It does not mean lavish expenditure, or spectacular welfare amenities. It means broad lines of guidance for managers and foremen, to encourage them to maintain standards of justice and supervision which will keep morale on a high level and so contribute to effectiveness of operation.

As an illustration of what a statement of personnel policy can include, the following schedule is reproduced[1]:

A. *Aims*

    (1) To enable the organisation to fulfil or carry out the main items which have been laid down as the desirable minima of general industrial employment policy.

    (2) To ensure that the employees of an organisation are fully informed on these main items of policy and to ensure co-operation in their attainment.

---

[1] Extracted from a *Report on the Administrative and Executive Problems in the Transition from War to Peace* (Appendix I), published by the London Centre of the Institute of Industrial Administration, 1945.

(3) To provide within the organisation such conditions of employment and procedures as will enable all employees to develop a sincere sense of unity with the enterprise and to carry out their duties in the most willing and effective manner.

(4) To provide the organisation continuously with adequate, competent and suitable personnel for all levels and types of occupations required.

B. *Principles*

(1) To establish and maintain a Personnel Management function, responsible to the chief executive, and adequately financed for the fulfilment of its responsibilities.

As a corollary, the broad lines of the Personnel Policy of the organisation should be defined by the Board of Directors on a parity of importance with other major aspects of policy.

(2) To guarantee to all employees a right of personal and confidential access to the personnel executive(s) or the executive acting in that capacity.

(3) To afford the greatest possible degree of stability in employment. This implies:

(a) Opportunity of permanent and continuous employment for competent employees.

(b) Adequate and objective methods of selection prior to engagement and of review during employment.

(c) The provision of appropriate training facilities (within or without the enterprise) to enable employees to secure the competence required—

(i) For effective performance of duties; and

(ii) For promotion when so selected.

(d) The filling of senior vacancies by up-grading and promotion so long as actually or potentially competent candidates are available.

(e) A guarantee against unfair dismissal.

(f) Adequate consideration of the influence of the employment on the organisation's policies and plans regarding production and distribution, so as to avoid employee displacement so far as is at all possible.

(4) To observe the recognised standards of Fair Wages. (This would not preclude the determination of standard Job Classifications and Base Rates or the operation of Output and other Bonus Schemes, provided they fall within the definition of Fair Wages.)

(5) To encourage fairness in the maintenance of discipline and to encourage employees to accept responsibility for discipline.

(6) To maintain a high level of working conditions, but regarding as a minimum the fulfilment—in letter and spirit—of the Factories Acts and other industrial Legislation and Regulations, with particular reference to adequate provision for the prevention of accidents, the rendering of first-aid, and the safeguarding and maintenance of health.

(7) To establish effective procedures for regular consultation between management and employees, in a genuine desire to keep employees fully informed of all matters bearing on their employment and to enable them to contribute to the effective management of the enterprise.

(8) To welcome and accord full freedom of association in membership of trade unions, but to accord equality of treatment to members and non-members alike.

(9) To assist employees in the development of social, educational and recreational amenities, and to encourage their collaboration with nationally or regionally established facilities; also to avoid the provision of amenities as an inducement to employment.

(10) To maintain these aims and principles of personnel policy without discrimination—though with the necessary differences of application—in respect of all types and grades of employees, using that term in its widest sense.

Negotiations

An important phase of the Personnel Manager's work is his participation in labour negotiations on behalf of his Company. These may be of the informal kind at shop floor level, involving discussions with a shop steward and a foreman, or of the more formal kind laid down in various trade union agreements. To some extent, of course, the greater part of the Personnel Manager's week is spent in discussions with individuals or groups of employees, but the more formal negotiations place on him a particularly important responsibility, which he carries on behalf of the chief executive.

The following case illustrates the significance of this responsibility:

In a London works, some 150 men were employed on a shift basis on production. The shop steward of the production departments and his deputy approached the foreman about an arrangement they would like to make during the Easter holiday. The suggestion was that instead of working on Monday, Tuesday, Wednesday and Thursday nights and finishing at 6 a.m. on Good Friday morning, the men should start work on the Sunday night, and thus be able to have as holiday from the end of the Wednesday night shift until the following Tuesday night, when they were due to return to work. The foreman, in discussing this with the stewards, said he could see no objection so far as he was concerned, and provided the four shifts were worked during the week it was immaterial to him on which nights the men came in. A few days later the Personnel Manager was approached by the head of the department, who repeated what had taken place between the foreman and men, and said that he was in agreement as, of course, it would mean they could clean down on the Thursday afternoon instead of having to employ an additional shift on the Friday for this purpose; he asked that the Personnel Manager should round off the matter with his shop stewards and give confirmation that the Company had agreed.

A meeting was arranged, at which two stewards and two of the men from the shift were present. At the outset it was pointed out that this alteration was at their own specific request, and favourable consideration would be given to it in order that, firstly, the men might have the longer holiday, and secondly, as it would avoid some of the workers having to hang about on the Good Friday waiting for transport before they could get home. The Personnel Manager agreed to ascertain what other factors were involved before announcing the decision. He then found that in addition to the production workers, who received a fixed amount as a shift differential, there was an electrician, a fitter and a boilerman on the shift with varying ways of payment, so that three other unions would need to be consulted before agreement could be reached. The shop stewards of the various unions were then approached, but they immediately objected. Their first objection was that the negotiations had been conducted piecemeal, that they were parties to the Agreement covering shift work in the same way as were the production people, and had been ignored. Further, if work was started on the Sunday night, their National Agreement provided for payment at double time, whereas the production people could only claim time and a half in view of the Agreement in that industry; it was doubtful whether their District Organiser would agree to the fitter participating in this arrangement, particularly as the management had already accepted the offer of the production workers to do the additional shift without consulting them. The steward of the Electrical Union repeated the comments of his engineering colleagues. Suspicion was aroused in the minds of the maintenance workers that the negotiations which had taken place between the production workers and the management had been carried out in this way so as to "force" the maintenance people into accepting the time and a half instead of double time.

The matter was sorted out in due course—the night shift was worked, and everyone paid at their proper rate of overtime according to the agreed conditions, but not before there had been a good deal of high feeling generated.

The lesson to be learned from this example is to ensure that, before negotiations are entered into on any subject, enquiries are made so that everyone who could possibly be a party to the negotiations is represented from the start. A Personnel Manager alive to his job would take such precautions almost as a matter of course. Equal care needs to be taken to make sure that answers or decisions given in negotiations do not conflict with agreements or arrangements already entered into. Many so-called "local agreements" are in fact never written down, but have been accepted as valid by dint of long observance.

Representation on Committees

Very frequently—if not customarily—the Personnel Officer is a management representative on consultative committees functioning within the organisation. He has also often to sit on official or un-official committees outside as Company's representative. In other words, active membership of deliberating groups can be a substantial element in the Personnel Manager's daily work. He needs, therefore, to be broadly familiar with committee procedure, and to train him-self to be a constructive participant in such gatherings.

FINANCIAL BUDGET FOR PERSONNEL MANAGEMENT

The principle of setting a financial budget of the personnel manage-ment function does not appear so far to have secured any wide-spread recognition; neither does there appear to have been any con-sistent action in the recording and control of the costs of a personnel department, and it is difficult to obtain any reliable evidence as to the general amount of money spent by companies on this func-tion.

Some guide may be found from investigations made a year or two ago by the Industrial Welfare Society: a trial survey produced the following results:

Number of firms submitting replies, 5.

Size of Groups (Numbers of employees), 500; 1,000; 1,500; 3,000; 20,000.

Average weekly wage paid from £4 0s. 10d. to £7 4s. 4d.

Expense Items	Per cent. Wages Bill. Range of replies		Cost per head per annum. Range of replies	
	From per cent.	To per cent.	From s. d.	To £ s. d.
I. Personnel Department sal-aries (all members directly employed in department and their personal expenses)	0·24	1·17	12 1	3 2 10
II. Personnel Department over-heads (lighting, heating, fur-niture, space, stationery, postage, telephones, adver-tisements) . . .	0·05	0·20	2 8	14 0

Expense Items	Per cent. Wages Bill. Range of replies		Cost per head per annum. Range of replies	
	From per cent.	To per cent.	From £ s. d.	To £ s. d.
III. Health, Welfare and Safety (Salaries of M.O., nurses, etc.; auxiliary medical services; safety officer; medical and first-aid supplies, allocation for overheads) .	0·32	0·88	11 10	2 4 3
IV. Education and Training (Salaries of training officers; fees to lecturers; fees for employees to colleges, etc.; allocation for overheads; library charges) . .	0·06	0·94	2 0	3 10 4
Totals Sections I–IV . .	0·97	2·59	2 9 7	9 13 11
V. General Welfare Services:				
(a) Canteen (net contribution)	0·04	0·96	0 2 0	3 12 3
(b) Journal, house magazine, handbooks . . .	Nil	0·12	Nil	0 6 4
(c) Sickness and Benevolent funds	Nil	0·24	Nil	0 12 3
(d) Social and Recreational activities (net contribution)	Nil	0·19	Nil	0 14 7
(e) Grants for hostels, living accommodation . .	Nil	0·03	Nil	0 1 6
(f) Overalls, caps, etc., in excess of essential protective clothing	Nil	0·38	Nil	1 8 9
(g) Pension schemes . .	0·60	1·23	1 10 7	5 13 4
(h) Long Service awards and gratuities . . .	0·04	0·10	2 11	0 10 0
(i) Grants to Service men and families	Nil	0·06	Nil	0 13 4
(j) Holidays in excess of national agreements . .	Nil	0·89	Nil	3 6 6
(k) Suggestion Schemes .	Nil	0·12	Nil	0 6 2
(l) Research in personnel work, contributions to societies, etc.	Nil	0·04	Nil	0 1 9
Total Section V . .	1·02	3·66	2 15 0	13 14 9
TOTAL SECTIONS I–V (inclusive) . .	2·75	6·25	7 7 8	23 8 8

Two Companies also provided information about their turnover, and the costs were expressed as a percentage of the turnover in those cases:

Sections I–IV	.	.	.	0·70 and 1·44
Section V	.	.	.	0·42 and 0·69
Total Sections I–V	.	.	.	1·12 and 2·13

To make a survey of this kind of real practical value, it needs to be more widespread, and to take into consideration the smaller firms. The method adopted of relating personnel costs to the total wages bill is quite a useful basis.

One important factor which needs to be borne in mind is that a number of the costs which are borne by the personnel management function would still be incurred and absorbed in the general costs of management or administration even if the Personnel Department did not exist. There is no sound reason why the activities of personnel management should not be costed and appropriate financial standards set, so that current expense can be controlled. Working on a budget basis, with need for specific permission to go outside the budget figure, would be one practical way.

No hard-and-fast rule can be laid down, and each individual concern would have to decide for itself a satisfactory financial level which would be justified by the contributions which personnel management makes to the effectiveness of management as a whole.

CHAPTER II

INDUSTRIAL RELATIONS

MORALE AND CONSULTATION

IT would not be untrue to say that "industrial relations" is but another term for "personnel management", the emphasis being placed on the aspect of employee relationships rather than on the executive policies and activities that are set up to foster good relations. Both are also closely allied to morale, which may be described as a readiness to co-operate warmly in the tasks and purposes of a given group or organisation. High morale makes for effective work and economical operation. High morale is a by-product of good industrial relations, which in turn are among the consequences of sound personnel management. In few British firms is there found a department specifically concerned with industrial relations as a distinct phase of personnel work. Special attention has, however, been given to this aspect by the Ministry of Labour and National Service, where an Industrial Relations Department exists. This consists of a Headquarters Staff and a Staff of Conciliation Officers in each of the regions into which the country is divided. It is the duty of this staff to keep in close touch with all industrial developments. The main functions of the Industrial Relations Department are:

(1) Assistance in the formation and maintenance of joint voluntary machinery in industry;

(2) The prevention and settlement of trade disputes;

(3) Maintaining continuous touch with the state of relations between employers and workpeople.

The Headquarters Staff are also responsible for:

(4) The examination of all questions brought to the notice of the Government in regard to the relations between the employers and workpeople;

(5) The tendering of advice to Government Departments on industrial relations questions in general, and in respect of their responsibilities for wages and working conditions either on contracts or in respect of direct labour in their employment.

The necessities of war required the introduction of certain measures to avoid stoppages of work and consequent interferences with essential production and services. These measures which are embodied in the Conditions of Employment and National Arbitration Orders,

1940–42, are dealt with in detail in a later section, but it may here be noted that they were framed on the basis of recommendations made by the national bodies representative of employers and workers, to supplement and not to supersede voluntary methods and joint machinery.

The normal methods by which the Ministry of Labour and National Service renders assistance in the prevention and settlement of industrial disputes are based on the legislative authority of the Conciliation Act, 1896, and the Industrial Courts Act, 1919, and may be summarised as:

(1) Conciliation.
(2) Arbitration.
(3) Investigation by formal enquiry.

Morale.—Management's responsibility for the promotion of morale is not a new development in industry. Even in the days of master craftsmen, the man had to be encouraged to give the highest value to his employer, by applying his knowledge and skill to the making of the article which the employer hoped to sell in order to pay wages and make his profit. At the time he was making the article he knew whom it was for, why he was making it, what sort of a job it would be used on, how much the master would charge, how much the material cost, and where it would come from. In all probability his work would be discussed at the local hostelry during the evening. Because he knew what he was doing, and why, and appreciated his significance in the chain of events, he could have a sense of pride and participation in his work—his morale was high. There is no fundamental difference to-day in dealing with morale—the atmosphere or spirit of an organisation; the happiness of its members; co-operation of one executive or one workman with another, and the indefinable "something" which impels the human being to work with a will or to do as *little* as possible in the available time—all is influenced by the outlook towards the job in hand and the general spirit of the workplace.

What are the factors which contribute towards a happy and successful organisation? The factors which the employee expects to be taken into consideration and on which he bases his value of the job in a factory or office? They are:

(*a*) Security.
(*b*) Good wages.
(*c*) Opportunity.
(*d*) Justice.
(*e*) Status.
(*f*) To know.
(*g*) Leadership.

(h) Getting the job done.
(i) Pride of product, etc.
(j) Suggestions schemes.
(k) Joint consultation.

(a) Security

One of the most important desires of an employee is to feel secure in his job, to know that at the end of each week he has a certain income, itself a foundation on which to build his future, and around which he can establish his home, the upbringing of his children and his social life. For centuries to come, industry will remember the devastation caused in the country in the 1930s: men who were unable to obtain work for years or who managed to do only a minimum of two or three days a week, the balance of time being what was known as "on the dole".

Many employees think it is better to have a steady job in an industry which is not likely to be seriously affected at times of trade depression than being able intermittently to earn very high wages for a shorter period. The prospects of full employment in this country in recent years have tended to lessen the desire for security in one particular firm, because of the opportunities which exist elsewhere, and owing to a shortage of labour, many more jobs are available than there are people to fill them.

(b) Good Wages

The employee of to-day expects to be paid a wage, firstly, which is nationally agreed between his employer and the union; secondly, which will be sufficient to provide for his family at a reasonable level of subsistence, including entertainment and a modicum of savings. He does not necessarily work for the employer who pays the highest starting rate, but is much more concerned with the long-term prospect and opportunity for earning higher wages as a result of his own individual effort. *Good employers* emphasise the opportunity of *bonus* earnings based on sound incentive schemes. Good wages are an important contribution to a happy factory.

(c) Opportunity

A large percentage of employees never wish to do other than remain in their normal jobs, skilled in their trade; operatives often refuse promotion because of reluctance to undertake the additional responsibility. But there are others again for whom the opportunity of growth in responsibility and scope is an important stimulus, men whose morale is impaired if their chance of promotion is arbitrarily blocked. There is also a widespread social satisfaction felt when a fellow employee is promoted to a supervisory or managerial position. The wise employer will provide such opportunities for those who are able and willing to accept them.

The procedure of filling vacant posts is, of course, a matter closely bound up in the Company's policy, and no strict ruling can be laid down. Differences in circumstances and conditions have to be taken into account; for instance, even in a Company which normally promotes from within, it is conceivable that at certain times due to expansion there are not available on the staff candidates adequately qualified for a given post, and in consequence an outsider, suitably skilled, would need to be engaged. The prospect of promotion only on length of service, on the basis of "waiting for dead men's shoes", is bad in any industrial undertaking. Even the most recent member of a department should be made to feel that the Company is always on the lookout for eager and ambitious employees who are willing to move about from one job to another, and in the process to expand their knowledge as a prelude to improving their position.

(d) Justice

Justice in dealing with industrial conditions and discipline is now much more common than it was even a few years ago, largely due to the influence of the trade unions as well as a more enlightened outlook on the part of managers and employers. During the recent war years, the Essential Work Orders made it impossible to discharge or suspend an employee without good and valid reason. It was no longer possible to dismiss an employee without clearly defined reasons, adequate to stand examination before an Appeal Board, consisting of an independent Chairman and a representative from a trade union and from an employers' organisation. This procedure did a great deal to get rid of arbitrary and ill-considered dismissals, and to promote a more tolerant attitude to alleged breaches of regulations or refusal to work to instructions.

The shortage of labour has always contributed to an improvement in the attitude of managers and a greater sense of justice in the control of factory and office discipline. The extent to which this more positive atmosphere contributes to the enhancement of morale and so to a better working spirit is widely recognised from practical experience gained in recent years.

(e) Status

The employee likes to feel that, in the eyes of his foreman and manager, he is regarded as having an important and responsible contribution to make to the work and progress of the organisation. He is also jealous of his skill, his craft, his status, or if in the ranks of supervision, of his responsibility. Recognition of this expectation can be a valuable factor in morale. The more important an employee can be made to feel, the better work he is likely to do.

During the war, a Company in the London area were asked by the Ministry to undertake some very important work. The factory was already widely using the slogan—"it all depends on me". Over the loud-speaker the Managing Director explained what had to be done, how, when, and why, implying expectation of a response on the basis of the slogan. Nor was he mistaken. Employees eagerly played their part, producing the most they could or doing their job in the quickest or best possible way. A feeling of pride that everyone mattered and that the Company was on its mettle, that the prospects of Britain depended on what they did at that moment, enabled the almost impossible task to be fulfilled, although some of the employees had worked almost until they had dropped asleep by the side of their machines, rather than go home before the maximum amount of work had been produced.

(f) *To know*

The communicating of information is one of the best ways of improving morale. Being "in the know" promotes co-operation, both because it gives the employee an understanding of what is going on, and because it encourages a sense of participation, of recognition. Many lessons in this direction were learned in the factories during the recent war.

(g) *Leadership*

In the Navy they use the expression "a happy ship" to denote a high level of morale in the ship's company. The "happy ship" is brought about in the first instance by the captain and his officers, who are all determined to make conditions on board pleasant and enjoyable, despite the handicaps of physical limitation and the trials and tribulations of battle. The captain of a ship is in a very similar position to that of a Managing Director or General Manager in an industrial undertaking. From him must come the example. His attitude will set the tone and his actions copied down to the lower levels of supervision. The way in which he deals with people will set the standard for relationships amongst individuals throughout the Company. His sense of respect for the employees, the interest he takes in the individual's problems, his appearance at social functions or his friendly words whilst walking through the factory, afford a pattern which will rapidly improve the worker/employer relationships throughout the organisation. Some organisations are too vast for the Managing Director to be more than a figure-head, and in these the responsibility depends on the senior executives in charge of the operating units. The importance of the influence of the men at the top cannot be over-emphasised as a factor making for high—or low—morale. A large element in the skill of management at all levels is the capacity to get subordinates to give of their best in the team. Much of the capacity depends on personal attitude—the genuine willingness to develop in everyday contacts with subordinates the spirit of "informal consultation" will bring in its train the sense of "participation".

(h) *Getting the job done*

Planning may produce the machines, the materials and all the necessary tools—they may all be on the spot in their right places at the right time—but getting the best out of people in their day-to-day lives is not by any means so easy a job. The variety of factors which make a human being decide not to start work, or to go slow, or to refuse to work, are all due to influence of mind and emotion of body. If the lead from the mind produces a negative attitude, the work will not be done or will be done poorly.

One of the special fields of personnel management is to ascertain "what makes the worker like—or not like—to work" and to be in a position to advise other executives or supervisors on this all-important subject. One factor known to be of special significance is the attitude and outlook of the supervisor himself—the way in which he speaks to the men and women, his response when asked for information, assistance or advice, the impression he gives by his own everyday behaviour in the department, and the confidence he instils in the employees with whom he is associated. His influence probably contributes more than anything else to the attitude which the worker adopts towards his job and to the Company in general.

Supervisors vary considerably, and it is impossible to lay down a formula which will produce the ideal. There are, however, two common types frequently met in industry : the easy-going, happy-go-lucky individual who takes life very much as it comes, who never has cause to complain about the work, and has the knack of getting up a sense of enthusiasm in people ; he criticises when necessary, in a friendly way, sometimes in a half-bantering, half-joking manner ; yet while he disciplines his workers, they retain an affectionate regard for him— " 'Old so-and-so' is a jolly decent fellow to work for" !! When things are difficult or production becomes more urgent, then usually he is able to ask for—and get—from each individual that extra little effort which collectively means so much. When it comes to a social function of any kind, he can throw off his day-time responsibility and enjoy the fun and games with the rest. One cannot define what the peculiar "something" is that goes to make up this type of supervisor, but his presence in a factory is readily recognised.

The other common type stands in marked contrast—often a highly skilled technician and more knowledgeable than the one we have previously discussed, but the employees in his department avoid going to him on any personal matter: they prefer to seek the advice of the shop stewards or take some other line of approach. The happy atmosphere is missing, few smiles appear, and there is a tenseness about the department because the men and women are too acutely alive to a sense of "being supervised", expected to work on without regard to their personal problems and difficulties, and governed by a man whose main interest lies in the slide rule and the stop watch, and how much he can get out in how little time. To be caught missing from the machine or bench means a "ticking off", and even minor faults mean "the carpet" and a serious reprimand. Inevitably, employee turnover in such a department will be considerably higher, absence greater, and requests for transfers to other departments frequent whenever a pretext offers an opportunity. When that extra spurt is needed, there is nothing more to come, for the real enjoyment of work is missing. At social events, this same type of person is conspicuous by his absence, or if there, makes a hasty exit as soon as possible on some flimsy excuse, but mainly because he feels his position so important that he will jeopardise his dignity by remaining in so informal an atmosphere with men and women who are formally his subordinates.

What the supervisor is may seem at first to be a topic far removed from personnel management. So long as this function is thought of in terms of the records and activities of the Personnel Department, the relations may be difficult to grasp. When it is accepted as belonging equally to the managers and foremen, their influence on morale is among the most important factors in the human element of management—especially as it bears on getting the job done, and getting it done effectively and economically.

(i) Pride of Job, Product and Company

The importance of the human relationship factor brings in its train a danger, the danger of encouraging unnecessary sentiment and emotional mollycoddling. The foreman is not expected to go about flattering his people or "treating 'em soft". What is wanted is something more substantial, an attitude that reflects the policy of the Company and suggests a readiness to make them full participants in its development. Fostering pride in his job is one of the most useful means, especially if backed up by the full information of a Company's policy, plans, progress and problems. The supervisor can encourage his employees to be proud of their work, help them to see where they fit in the general scheme of things, what their part of the finished product is and what the final article itself is like. This is done in some Companies by means of a display case, in which materials, components and finished products are set out in stages. A good deal can be done in this direction by suitable explanatory talks and demonstrations in the training courses for new employees, particularly if coupled with tours of various departments. A few firms have gone to the length of inviting employees' wives and families to see the factory.

Manufacturers of raw materials, sheet metal, and the like, may find it more difficult than in those Companies where a finished article is placed on the market. A very successful way of demonstrating to the employees the final conclusion of their work is by having a number of completed products sent down for exhibition purposes from the firms who buy the Company's goods, or alternatively to allow small groups of employees to visit other works or factories where the raw material is fabricated. Visits of this kind can, however, sometimes have unexpected repercussions.

In one Company, where copper strip was finished to a very high specification, which included completely freeing it from scratches, burrs and blemishes and very elaborate packing arrangements, a party of workers visiting a customer firm where the strip was used found it treated no better than rough bar iron—stripped of its covering, thrown down, stood on and run over by trucks. The fine-limit specification obviously had no significance—worse than that, for the customer's insistence on supply in exact 20-foot lengths had no other consequence than being chopped up into 3-inch pieces by teams of young boys and girls! What happened at the strip factory when the visit was over can safely be left to the imagination!!

An employee likes to feel that the firm for which he works is a good one. He likes, when talking to his friends and colleagues, to feel that his job is as good as or better than any elsewhere. Instilling this pride, however, must be based on reality and on a policy that gives substance and truth to it. One of its consequences will be a more positive attitude in the worker—he will avoid wasting material, make sure that the dripping tap is turned off, use up material which others might scrap, and return to the stores nails, screws and other small items at the completion of the job. Little things of this kind can mount up and make a useful contribution to the right side of the profit and loss account. The larger consequence will be reflected in productivity.

(j) Suggestion Schemes

This is another means by which a Company can promote the morale of its employees. Frequently, in the daily performance of their job, they have bright ideas about the way in which things should or could be done. These ideas are often good ones, and if there is an opportunity for putting them forward, valuable improvements may result. But even more important is the emotional influence on the employees themselves: to them the scheme means first and foremost that the Company is aware of them and interested in their contribution.

The usual way of conducting the scheme is through "Suggestion Boxes" installed in each department, with public announcements of awards for ideas which are original and are usable or adopted. Some firms leave the boxes permanently in position, repainting them in a different colour each month as a reminder and a stimulus to their use. Other firms, again, run the boxes, aided by a propaganda campaign, for a brief period every few months in the belief that familiarity or staleness will defeat the whole object of the scheme.

It is customary for a Suggestions Scheme to be supervised by a committee comprising five or six people representative of different parts of the organisation and competent to assess the ideas put forward and thus be able to recommend the award.

It is not often that we find Suggestion Schemes set up for office staffs, although in the modern office there are frequently numerous opportunities for economies in paper work and for the improvement of methods in routine clerical work. The re-drafting or re-routeing of a form might save considerable labour and time, and be worth an award comparable with those offered for factory ideas. The morale value of the scheme is, of course, also comparable.

A good deal of careful preparation must precede the establishment of one of these schemes, for the machinery has to work rapidly. Ideas will be killed if months elapse between their submission and their consideration. And the morale value will disappear if no answer at all is received by the suggester or if the scheme is conducted with an air of casualness and indifference. A badly run scheme may well damage morale.

(k) Joint Consultation

Of all the schemes by which management seeks to bring its employees into responsible and full participation in the activities, the purposes of the enterprise, the process of "joint consultation" has attracted the greatest interest in industrial circles in recent years. Considerable impetus was given to this line of development by the special agreement in the engineering industry in 1942, supported officially by the Ministry of Supply as an employer. This agreement, within the framework of the Essential Work Orders, provided for the establishment of "Joint Production (Advisory and Consultative) Committees", representative of management and employees through the trade unions, for the mutual discussion of difficulties and problems and the improvement of methods of production and of pro-ductivity. The principle of such Committees was not, of course, new; it had a precedent in the Whitley Committee scheme, and had proto-types of a kind in the several "Works Councils" which, in the more far-sighted organisations, survived the retrogressive atmosphere of the 1920s and 1930s.

The purpose of any form of "joint consultation" is precisely what the title implies—a means of exchanging views and information, and of promoting communications among the various functions or sec-tions or layers of the organisation. There is a growing weight of opinion now against the commonly accepted view of consultation as a joint action between "sides": many a spokesman has praised the "bringing together of the two sides" in a joint committee, without realising how negative is this approach. There are—or should be—no "sides" in an industrial organisation: there are differences of activity, of responsibility, of task, but all directed to the same purpose. What a joint committee bridges is this difference of function, not of interest or of aims. Without such a basis of honest principle and intention no scheme of joint consultation is of much practical use.

The representative committee form has been the most common pattern in British industry, even in those companies which had the consultative process in action for many years. The object is to provide a common understanding aimed at the betterment of relationships between worker and employer. Frequently in recent years there has developed a spate of committees, many of which have had similar functions but different names, often within one organisation. Wher-ever possible, it is advisable to have only one committee within an organisation, and its terms of reference should be sufficiently wide to deal with any matters arising. As already indicated, the importance is not in the committee itself, but in the sincerity behind the words "joint consultation". It is quite useless for a Company to have twelve or twenty people sitting round a table once a month to deal with minor complaints when neither side is being frank or genuine with the other, where the committee is a farce, where workers put forward ridiculous and extravagant demands, and the management on the other side find equally ridiculous excuses for not meeting or for ex-plaining away alleged deficiencies. Time is wasted, tempers frayed, frustration built up, and suspicion created which may take many years to eradicate. Where good intentions are only superficial, it does not take more than a few meetings for this to become apparent, and the continuance of the committee may then do far more harm than good.

Publicity alone will not make a successful committee, but it is an important element in its work; high value is to be attached to a proper channel by which information about the committee's work, progress and achievement is provided for the individual worker.

The question of how many committees should exist or what their functions are to be, is one which is rarely given sufficient consideration by top management. Frequently one finds five or six committees working in an organisation, totally unrelated to one another, sometimes having the same members sitting on each of the Committees, discussing item by item the work which could be done quite easily in one full Committee. There may, for example, be a Joint Production Committee, a Safety Committee, a Fire Committee and a Works Committee, with Subcommittees for Canteen and Social, and a Foremen's Committee. On all of these Committees, with the exception of the last, one would expect to find representatives of the employees, probably shop stewards representing the trade unions. There is hardly one item which could be put on the agenda of any of these Committees which cannot adequately be successfully dealt with by a single body with wider terms of reference centring on production.

Safety affects production; canteen arrangements affect production, in so far as they must be co-ordinated with the meal breaks for the employees. Fire precautions obviously affect production; and so on. Where circumstances require it, the single Works Council or Works Committee can be supplemented by *ad hoc* Subcommittees, set up to deal with these various matters in detail.

Subject-matters for discussion at Joint Consultation, while mainly restricted to matters which merely affect the particular concern, may, on occasions, have to pay regard to local questions of wider interest. This is particularly the case when a single industry or trade is predominant in the locality. Matters concerned with wages, piece-rates and bonuses are usually excluded from the scope of the Committees; these are usually considered more appropriate to direct negotiations.

Negotiations with the trade unions, as in many instances National Agreement, have to be considered in relation to the wage problems, and it is not always possible to find wage problems an agreeable subject for discussion by large groups of people, some of whom may have no knowledge whatever of the technicalities of the subject.

A summary of matters usually covered in joint committees may be listed as follows:

(1) Absentees and lateness.
(2) Accident prevention.
(3) Avoidance of waste of time, labour and materials.
(4) Canteens.
(5) Holiday arrangements.
(6) Issue and revision of works rules.
(7) Distribution of working hours, breaks, time recording, etc.

(8) Physical welfare questions—meals, drinking water, washing and cloakroom facilities, heating, safety, first-aid, etc.

(9) Questions of discipline and conduct as between management and workpeople.

(10) Terms of engagement for workpeople.

(11) Training of apprentices, etc.

(12) Library, lectures and social aspects of industry.

(13) Suggestions and testing of method and organisation improvements.

(14) Entertainments and sport.

(15) Improving production.

(16) Welfare fund, Sports Club funds, etc.

(17) Grievances.

(18) Canteens.

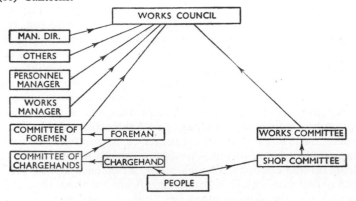

FIG. 63.—A Framework for Joint Consultation.

The whole object of joint consultation is to get rid of the division into "sides" within the factory, and to weld the workpeople and the management into a team. Exchange of information is therefore of great importance. Workpeople may give assistance on technical or mechanical matters in addition to ideas submitted through the Suggestion Scheme, and they can discuss with management likely reactions to proposals for new methods. Equally, from management's part there must be a readiness to impart information about progress, plans, proposals for development and other factors that bear on the stability and security of employment and all the well-being of the concern.

Joint consultation Committees vary in name, but are mostly similar in functions and certainly identical in purpose. It is of little avail to try to draw differences in scope or activity from differences in name. In general, however, the title "Works Council" or Works Committee" refers to the bodies with a full range of terms of reference, while the "Joint Production Committees" pay more detailed attention to matters directly concerned with production. Some of the problems frequently met are:

(a) Maximum utilisation of existing machinery;
(b) Upkeep of fixtures, jigs, tools and gauges;
(c) Improvement in methods of production;
(d) Efficient use of the maximum number of productive hours;
(e) Elimination of defective work and waste;
(f) Efficient use of material supplies;
(g) Efficient use of safety precautions and devices.

Just as the details of subject-matter brought up and the line of treatment taken in regard to them must vary according to local conditions, so, too, questions of constitution and operation of these consultative committees cannot be decided by hard-and-fast rules. Clearly, certain broad principles can be laid down, especially as such bodies are mostly elected from among employees of the various parts of the organisation. These constitutional points have been the centre of a good deal of controversy over the years—two of the most debated issues being the size of the management representation and the eligibility of employees who are not members of trade unions. Committees set up under the terms of an Agreement customarily have equal numbers of employee and manager representatives, the former being composed only of union members, though non-members participate in the elections. Though more progressive minds are inclined to feel that both these arrangements are unsound, the trend of common opinion today is along the "line of least resistance", and consequently opposed to the freedom that is offered by the more open-minded constitution. There are arguments for and against both points of view; one aspect that is frequently overlooked is this—that as matters covered by union negotiations are practically always excluded from the agenda of consultative committees, the case for restriction to union members means the arbitrary exclusion of the "independent" from independent representation.

As the basis for the constitution of joint committees, one study group with a good deal of experience of their working has laid down the following principles[1]:

1. *Structure*

The consultative mechanism should be composed of two parts, viz.:
(a) A council or Committee composed of elected representatives of Management, Supervisory Staffs and Employees; and
(b) The ordinary mechanism for negotiations between representatives of Management and the Trade Unions.

[1] Extracted from the Institute of Industrial Administration Report already cited at page 399.

2. *Terms of Reference*

   (a) The Council or Committee should have as its terms of reference all matters affecting the employee during the continuance of his employment, except questions of wages where these are covered by Agreements and are dealt with by the organised negotiations referred to in item 1 (b) above.

   Where special Committees are thought desirable for deliberation on specific issues, they should take the form of Subcommittees of the main Council or Committee, with the right to co-opt persons with special knowledge or experience of the issues under deliberation.

   (b) For the second element, the terms of reference to be wages and conditions of employment in accordance with the national, regional or individual Agreements signed between the representatives of the Employers and the Trade Unions.

3. *Constitution of Council or Committee*

   (a) Employee and Supervisory Staff representatives should be elected; those of Management should be nominated by the Chief Executive. The Personnel Executive should be an ex-officio member.

   (b) All employees should have the right to vote for representation from the outset of their employment.

   (c) Eligibility for election to membership of the Council or Committee should be restricted to employees with a minimum of twelve months' service in the enterprise, but there should be equal eligibility as between members and non-members of the Trade Unions.

   (d) Representatives of the Supervisory Staffs should be elected by and from the Supervisory Staffs themselves, on the basis of appropriate qualifying conditions, which should not include the restriction of membership of a Trade Union.

   (e) The establishment of the "constituencies" for representation purposes should provide for adequate representation of the technical and administrative (including clerical) staffs as distinct from the Supervisory and Management staffs.

   (f) The Management representatives should be few in number, leaving the employee representatives with a clear majority. The Management representatives should be responsible Executives.

   (g) All elected or nominated members of the Council or Committee should serve for a period of two years, with the proviso that there shall be an annual nomination or election of half the members in each category.

Supervisors' Committee

The idea that supervisors should have a Committee at which to discuss matters of general interest among themselves is rapidly gaining ground as a counterpart to employee consultation, because of the growing recognition of the importance of the foreman's function.

The foreman is management's representative, and in closer touch with the individual worker than anyone else; he has more opportunity of improving—or marring—relationships between the Company and the worker, through the very nature of his day-to-day contacts within the working group. This is a principle which has received considerable emphasis in earlier pages. It is therefore equally important to provide a channel of communication between supervision and management, and to provide an opportunity for consultation among the supervisors themselves, recognising the extent to which they are isolated in their own job. This means of mutual discussion at their own level and from their own peculiar standpoint is in addition to their participation, through a supervisor representative serving on the main committees, in the general process of consultation. They are also brought more closely into touch with management, so that they can discuss common problems, suggest improvements, and advise on matters likely to affect Company policy or industrial relationships, or production, technical development, etc. Information regarding costing, overheads, sales possibilities and problems can be brought to such a committee for discussion with great advantage. To have the foremen "in the know" on what the Company wants done is, of course, as important as telling the driver of the taxi where you want to go.

Shop Meetings

Some large firms have found useful the practice of holding a weekly meeting at which the Shop Stewards attend and bring forward all the difficulties or queries which have accumulated during the week. The Stewards keep their points for discussion until midday on Friday, anything arising after that (other than items of emergency) being dealt with by the following week's meeting. At noon on Friday, the list or agenda is handed to the manager by the convener or the senior shop steward in the department. Immediately after this, a typed agenda is posted on the notice board, so that the opportunity is given to all in the department to see the points which are being brought up for discussion on that day. The meeting starts at four o'clock; all the shop stewards in the department are present, including any who may be on shift work. The senior foreman and one other foreman and the manager of the department are also present. The items on the agenda vary considerably. A typical works agenda might be as follows:

(1) The reason for Smith's transfer from the large guillotine to the small one.
(2) Loss of earnings of an operator due to the late start of the Maintenance Department on the machine breakdown.
(3) The rate to be paid for a new job to be done in the department.

(4) The possibility of redundancy as the result of the mechanisation of the cold-rolling process.

(5) The number of sheets to be put through when rolling 14-gauge zinc.

(6) Investigation of the accident to a juvenile in the Press Shop.

(7) Lack of cakes on the tea trolley on Wednesday afternoon.

The Chairman of the meeting will be the Manager. Minutes will be made immediately after the meeting, and posted not later than lunch-time on Monday. Before the minutes are posted, they will be agreed with a shop steward in the department.

An occasional visitor (chiefly to emphasise the importance of the meetings) should be the Managing Director or the Director responsible for production in that department, or the Personnel Manager.

Joint Consultative Committee

Firms in which several trade unions are represented among the employees have to face a special problem in consultation, which can often be met only by the establishment of an *ad hoc* committee. The purpose of this is to bring together all the unions, so that a two-way channel of information is formed, and that matters may be discussed between the management and the union representatives in an organised way. It is usual for such a committee to be formed through the negotiation and acceptance of an Agreement, specifically determining the scope of the committee and incorporating detailed procedures to be adopted.

The items usually dealt with by such a committee are:

(1) Differentiation or variation from the basic union rates.

(2) Variation in the normal working conditions.

(3) General working conditions.

It is important to note the difference in dealing with a dispute within the works where a Joint Consultative Committee is in existence and the normal disputes procedure used in other cases. Where the Committee is in existence the matter cannot go to an outside organisation or to a Trade Union headquarters until it has been discussed within the works, and there is a "failure to agree" between the management and the employees. This type of committee has definite disadvantages for both employees and management. In the first place, many matters which might be the subject of a National Agreement or which have been laid down as a basis of discussion between the industries and the unions might be overruled by a Joint Consultative Committee, where members might act in ignorance of what was being done on the National or Industrial basis.

Another snag which arises frequently is that the shop stewards endeavour to negotiate matters with the management and register a "failure to agree", whereas if the item had to be taken direct to the union headquarters or division, advice could then be given to show that it was contrary to the desires of the trade union or had already been discussed and agreed at some other level. Thus a certain amount of time may be wasted on items which never need be discussed at all, or in any case delay carrying out the disputes procedure. Another disadvantage of the Joint Consultative Committee appears to be the antagonism which arises among non-union employees, who feel that the management are paying undue recognition to the unions as compared with the non-unionists in the organisation.

The terms of reference are set, but it is a little difficult, unless the meeting is in the hands of a strong Chairman, to avoid dealing with items which are not strictly the concern of the committee, without a certain amount of overlapping.

Joint Industrial Councils

The Joint Industrial Councils are a recognised mechanism of consultation between the Employers' Associations and the Trade Union at the level of an industry as a whole.

The subjects covered by such Councils are generally of the following order:

(1) Securing the largest possible measure of joint action between employers and workpeople for the development of the industry as part of national life, and for the improvement of the conditions of all engaged in that particular industry.

(2) Wages, hours and working conditions of the industry as a whole to be taken into regular consideration.

(3) Measures for regularising employment and production also to be taken into consideration.

(4) The consideration for settlement between different parties and sections of the industry, of any existing machinery—and, with the object of securing the speedy settlement of difficulties, the establishment of machinery where it does not already exist.

(5) Collection of information and statistics on matters relating to the industry.

(6) Encouragement of design and processes study and also of research with the view to perfecting the industry's products.

(7) Provision of facilities for consideration of any improvement in machinery or method and utilisation of inventions, also adequate safeguarding of such improvements, and to secure that such improvement shall give to each party a share of the benefits arising therefrom.

(8) Publication of reports and enquiries into special problems of the industry, including the methods and comparative study of the organisation of the industry in this and other countries.

(9) Improvement of health conditions in the industry and, where necessary, special treatment for workers.

(10) Co-operation in all branches of the industry, for arranging education with the authorities and the supervision of entry into and training for the industry.

(11) Issue of authoritative statements to the Press upon matters of general interest to the community affecting the industry.

(12) Representation of opinions and needs of the industry to the Government, Government Departments and other authorities.

(13) Consideration of other matters which may be referred to by the Government or any Government Departments.

(14) Proposals for District Councils and Works Committees put forward in the Whitley Report, having regard in each case to any organisation which may be already in existence, to be taken into consideration.

The following three functions have also been included in some of the constitutions:

(1) Consideration of measures for securing inclusion of all employees and employers in their respective associations.

(2) Arrangements for holding conferences and lectures on subjects of general interest to the industry.

(3) Co-operation in dealing with problems of common interest to the Joint Industrial Council and other industries.

DISCIPLINE

Discipline is essential in any undertaking where there is to be order instead of chaos. In industry it is essential to the attainment of the maximum productivity. The underlying philosophy of discipline is conceived in the proper thinking of the whole field of industrial relations. Its methods are profoundly influenced by the conditions of employment and by legislation, by the attitude of organised labour, and by the state of the productive processes at a given period. The modern conception of discipline is that it provides a pattern of acceptable behaviour and performance, as against the old-fashioned idea of chastisement or punishment for wrong-doing. There is now a more sincere attempt to arrive at the real cause of indiscipline, when dealing with irregularities of one kind and another. There is an evident trend that the power of the foreman to administer discipline without reference to anyone else is disappearing, and the imposing of any serious penalties now usually becomes the consideration of higher executives or even of a committee. It is, in other words, recognised that discipline obtained by fear is not a successful way of conducting affairs, and has a detrimental effect on the morale of the organisation. The imposition of a penalty must be decided upon after careful examination of all the facts in an atmosphere where everyone is "cool, calm and collected".

The position of the Personnel Manager with regard to discipline should always be made clear. His service is advisory; he can assist in investigation and explain what is the right penalty to impose, but must never attempt to usurp the position of the foreman, Departmental Manager or other "line" executive, by taking away his responsibility for discipline. His own major task is to ensure that no reprimand or penalty is inflicted unless it is just, and that the decision arrived at is in accordance with the facts.

There is only one real way in which to provide a sound foundation for discipline; that is, to draw up a code of regulations and conditions agreed between representatives of employees and to supplement this by a recognised mechanism which provides for an employee to get a fair hearing when alleged wrongful acts are committed.

The following are typical examples of the cases that happen from day to day in a factory and with which a Personnel Manager might be called upon to deal:

(a) A telephone message was received in the Personnel Department from Mr. Smith, Manager of the Foundry, complaining of the persistent habit of an employee named Blank who rides his bicycle through the foundry yard every day and leaves it underneath the crane instead of in the shed provided. Smith asked for the employee's instant dismissal. The Personnel Manager immediately went along to see the Foundry Manager and to investigate the facts. After a while, they agreed to call in the employee's foreman, who would be able to confirm how many times the employee had been warned to keep his bicycle in the proper rack provided. The foreman stated that he had warned the employee once only and that unofficially about six weeks previously; he was, however, aware that Blank had continued the practice. It was then decided to interview Blank, and he was told that he could be accompanied by his shop steward if he belonged to a trade union (this step being taken in case it was subsequently decided to discharge the employee).

Smith, the Manager, left the interview in the hands of the Personnel Manager, who drew the employee's attention to the alleged breach of the Works Rules and asked if there was any explanation. Blank admitted the offence, but said he had not realised that this was a serious breach. When he was first employed with the Company, he went on, there had been no room in the cycle rack, so he left his cycle with some others in the shed. After about a week, his lamp and pump were stolen, he reported his loss to the Works Security Officer, but the articles were not returned, so he decided that as his bicycle was worth about £10 he would leave it where he could keep an eye on it. But this was the first time in two years that a complaint had been made about it. The Personnel Manager then pointed out that he was being pulled up, not because he left his bicycle under the crane, although this was admittedly wrong, but because he cycled through the foundry yard, which was against the rules. To this he replied that he usually arrived fifteen minutes before time in order to get things ready and have the machinery and equipment going by the time the shift would be starting work again. No notice had been posted in the department forbidding the riding of a bicycle through the yard, or he would not have done so.

Although a rule had been broken, there was no case for a penalty; it was doubtful whether he had ever been specifically told not to ride in the yard, and he had certainly had no real warning from the foreman that he was committing an offence. He was a most conscientious worker, and it was doubtful whether adequate cycle accommodation had been provided for at that particular site.

It was unlikely that he would offend again, as the interview had brought home to him the existence and purpose of the ruling relative to cycling within the works and the proper storage of cycles.

It had also been established that accommodation for cycles was now insufficient, a matter clearly calling for attention by the management. The whole case had contributed to maintaining discipline in the department, and had enhanced the status of the Departmental Manager, foreman and Personnel Manager by the constructive way in which it had been handled.

(b) The Personnel Officer in a certain factory was asked by a Manager to take up a case of lateness. He had the employee's record traced back twelve months, and this investigation showed that the man had been most regular in his time-keeping up to a certain point, but had been thrown out of gear by some domestic trouble and had temporarily become a bad time-keeper. This was the first occasion he had been pulled up, so the Personnel Manager had no intention of dealing seriously with the matter, but gave a verbal warning, pointing out that home conditions had apparently now improved. If the man failed to respond, a more serious view would be taken.

(c) Another case was one of alleged slackness with which the foreman of the department was apparently able to make no headway. The Personnel Manager interviewed first the foreman and then the man, having obtained detailed evidence of what had not been done efficiently and how the employee was cited as being neglectful, careless, thoughtless and generally inattentive at his work. The man's attendance record was also obtained and a general opinion asked for from his Departmental Manager.

Armed with these facts, the Personnel Manager was able to send for the man and tell him quite pleasantly that reports had been received from his department that he was not giving satisfactory service, and perhaps he would like to talk the matter over. The foreman had complained that Blank was frequently missing from his job and spent a lot of time in the lavatory smoking. His lateness record was pretty bad, and generally speaking he gave the impression of being a man who was "fed up to the back teeth" with his job and would really like to pack up work altogether. The Personnel Manager put the last part over with a smile, and gave the employee the impression that whatever else had been said about him to his detriment, the Personnel Manager was still quite able to be sceptical, and, having engaged him when he first joined the firm, was prepared to listen to his story in a friendly way.

Blank then put up his side of the picture with a good deal of confidence; he was allowed to continue uninterrupted by questions. This enhanced the good impression that the Personnel Manager would listen to all he had to say—but he could be fairly sure that he couldn't get away with any bluff or soft soap! The Personnel Manager decided, as the other side of the story came out, that there were some genuine facts in this case that needed further consideration, and that it would not be wise to stage a straight talk from the foreman in his presence. Clearly, this man—a relatively new employee—had been the victim of circumstances, treated harshly in a previous job, and had not been properly run in his new department. A little bit of closer watch, and some help in the tricky bits of his job, would probably put him right. A friendly chat with the foreman brought to light that he had rather neglected Blank. . . . Three or four weeks later the foreman was the first to admit that he had got the makings of a good chap!

These cases throw some further light on the relationship of the personnel specialist to the "line" executives and supervisors, and illustrate the general principles outlined overleaf. The Personnel Manager is seen operating as a "safety valve", the foreman accepts his position in the organisation (which foremen will gladly do when the personnel man is of good salt, knows his job and wins respect by his skill) and appreciates the practical value of being able to refer such matters to him. But the Personnel Manager does not pose as an arbiter; he prefers to see his rôle as more of a fact-finding one. So his first reaction is to get fuller details so that he can justify his position as an intelligent and informed onlooker. His second major contribution is to remove this highly emotional personal problem of discipline into a more detached atmosphere, and then his third task can be more effectively carried out—the careful interview of both parties, which will bring to the surface real causes which may be underlying the employee's bad behaviour, will afford an opportunity of any special mitigatory circumstances to be explained, and will bring home to the individual concerned the fact of his wrongdoing seen in proper perspective. Of course, there will be many cases when the man or woman is seriously at fault, and, maybe, recalcitrant; no other solution but removal will be of any use, as both Personnel Officer and foreman can see. But if there is a genuine human policy in the organisation and an appreciation of the high value of the asset represented by good morale, every endeavour will be made to avoid the solution of dismissal, which can rightly be regarded as a confession of failure or surrender.

At no point in this process of probing the human problems with which all disciplinary situations are fraught does the Personnel Officer remove or undermine the responsibility of the "line" manager or foreman. He is their trusted "assistant", and they have referred these cases to him because they know that he will investigate the issue thoroughly to their satisfaction, and that of the employee concerned —they realise, too, how important this latter respect is, and how easily any suspicion of unfairness or arbitrariness in matters of discipline can damage morale. The Personnel Officer does not make the decision as to the final solution; he discusses his finding with the manager or foreman, and recommends which line they should take. It is usually wiser for the foreman himself to communicate the decision to the employee, though frequently the supervisors may prefer to settle the matter with the employee in the presence of the Personnel Officer, especially if there has been any occasion for outspoken words earlier in the case.

The handling of discipline is a matter deeply embedded in the human responsibilities of management and supervision. It is one of the main factors in the practical skill of the manager or foreman, something to which their personal abilities and their training can both contribute, but the soundness of discipline in any organisation also depends largely on its personnel policy; where the process of consultation is well developed as a genuine element in the practice of management, discipline is nearly always better. It has been found of particular value for factory and office rules to be planned, not by the decision of management alone, but by joint deliberations among top management, supervisors and employees. Some firms have gone to the length of giving full responsibility for the maintenance of discipline to a representative panel which sits as a "court" or Appeals Tribunal to hear the more serious cases referred to it by the foreman or the Personnel Officer. The spirit underlying this development has been the belief that the more responsibility is given to people, the more positive is their response.

Without going further into details, this question of discipline may perhaps be summarised in the following principles, which were submitted to a conference of supervisors and endorsed by them [1] :

---

[1] Extracted from a paper on "The Administration of Discipline", given at a Conference organised by the Industrial Welfare Society, 1947, by Mr. E. F. L. Brech.

A. *Setting the Code*

(1) Discipline means securing normally consistent behaviour in accordance with accepted rules. Discipline is essential to an ordered life, and especially to a democratic way of life. This means that it is essential to modern industrial administration, and we recognise this to be as true of the Socialist state as to any other political form.

(2) Because of the inevitable group structure of industry, discipline is intimately bound up with relations within the organisation, and in consequence is affected by such factors as the background, social environment and emotional outlook of the employees concerned.

(3) Because in essence discipline is the interpretation of a code, it is also closely tied up with personal feelings (sentiments, as they are called) —those non-logical emotional factors that determine so much of the behaviour of the average individual. In consequence, the effective application of discipline depends primarily on an understanding of the human being and of oneself in administering the code.

(4) Discipline is also closely connected with the policy and conditions of employment of the organisation concerned. The more broad-minded these are, the more stable and the easier is discipline likely to be.

(5) The code of discipline (including the section pertaining to it) must be decided in consultation with those who are to be under its jurisdiction or concerned in its application.

(6) The standards should be objectively the same for everyone. Where variations are obviously required for special categories owing to peculiarities of circumstances, these are to be admitted as based on objective grounds and so do not give rise to privileges.

(7) The code of discipline must be reasonable and simple, and not contain rules for the sake of rules.

(8) A good scheme of discipline entails the existence of a judicial machinery for appeals, preferably internal to the organisation concerned. In this connection it will be noted that a well-established Personnel Management function affords a useful contribution, though of a somewhat different character from that of an Appeals Tribunal.

B. *Carrying the Code into Effect*

(9) The maintenance of discipline is the core of the foreman's human responsibilities. He can achieve success only to the extent to which he regards his task as one involving constructive human principles in which the personal circumstances of the individual as well as the objective surrounding circumstances are taken into account.

(10) The maintenance of discipline is the responsibility of Managers and Supervisors by function. But in discharging this responsibility they should endeavour to share it as much as possible with the employees themselves, and thus encourage self-responsibility for discipline. Granted that a good code exists, it can surely be agreed that discipline is best where authority is least in evidence.

(11) In the last analysis, the effectiveness of discipline turns both on
the soundness of the relations within the organisation and on the
calibre and competence of the managers and supervisors, as well
as on the ability of the latter to take a positive instead of a negative
approach to their responsibilities in regard to discipline.

Misfits

It is inevitable that from time to time people will be placed in jobs
which they do not like or for which they are not particularly suited.
A variety of reasons may include this—environment, the dirty nature
of the work, smells, lighting, the heat and, more rarely, incompati-
bility with foreman or chargehand. The Personnel Manager must be
prepared to deal with these problems as they arise and to give a sympathetic hearing in every case. Where there is any suggestion that the
person is medically unfit for the job, the advice of a Medical Officer
should be sought. The case of a man who is unhappy because of in-
compatibility of temperament needs particularly careful diagnosis
by interview. Sometimes, after hearing separately the stories of the
two parties, a joint interview may enable the difficulties to be smoothed
out. But there will always be the cases where the "misfit" can be
solved only by transfer to another department, or termination of the
employment. Once again the most important aspect of the matter
from the point of view of morale lies in the mere fact that the employee has had his case sympathetically reviewed.

An illustration of some of the difficulties was given by a recent
event concerning two departments of a factory. In Department A the
average wage was in the region of £7 per week, and in Department B
between £8 and £11 per week. When certificates for light work had
been given to certain employees in Department A by a doctor, they
were transferred to tying up bundles of scrap in Department B: this
meant a transfer from a hard and strenuous job to much easier and
less-important work—and at the same time being given another £2
a week in their wage packets for doing less! Many applications for
transfer from Department A followed, appearing to be perfectly
genuine and alleging the need for "light work". This placed a good
deal of work on the Medical Department and the Manager before
the real reason for the applications was realised.

During war-time, when people were being directed to industry,
there were many classes of employees deliberately refusing to settle
down, doing their best to get the sack in the hope of transfer into
another industry where the pay was higher and the work lighter. One
young man was sent as a pipe-fitter to a large works in the "heavy
industry" category. For fifteen years previously he had been engaged
on the manufacture and assembly of bicycles. He was placed in the

plumbing department as a pipe-fitter on maintenance work, but before two or three days had passed was doing everything he could, short of violence, to get the sack. The Personnel Manager saw him on many occasions, and finally transferred him to an entirely different job and department, having made it quite clear that the Company were anxious he should settle down, and, by appealing to his better nature, got him to try again. This he did, and although he previously had a record for being late every day, refusing to work overtime, insolence and other misdemeanours, he proved before long to be one of the best employees in the Company's service in his new job.

This type of change, however, is not made without considerable interest being taken by the Manager, the foreman, the chargehand and the Personnel Manager, who must all be prepared to see such human problems as a common task which they can successfully accomplish only by co-operation.

The Worker with a Personal Problem

When an employee has a grouse or a grumble, or is troubled by a personal worry, he is not concentrating on doing his work or producing the goods, and it is therefore a direct contribution to efficiency to make provision for such problems to be dealt with or for advisory assistance to be given to the workers. The worker's first line of approach is to the foreman, or to whomever may be his immediate boss; in a small Company, this may be the owner himself.

Careful listening is the main requirement in such an interview. The reputation of management, and certainly the morale of many employees, may rest on the foreman, or the person who is dealing with the case. It is he who has to make the decision, to work out in his mind what is the right thing to do in the circumstances, what replies to give and how they will affect other things or other people. Sometimes the problem is beyond the foreman, and it is in circumstances like this, especially in the larger organisations, that the skill of the personnel specialist comes into its own. So the foreman or manager makes an appointment for the employee to see the Personnel Manager, who, with his wider view of the organisation and special training in human problems, may be able to get to the heart of the difficulty immediately and take a decision on this issue. Or he may see that there is a genuine grievance here which can be solved only at a higher level, or which requires investigation on a wider basis.

Whatever the answer, it is essential that the foreman or supervisor be put in the know at once: nothing can be more annoying than to put forward a problem to the Personnel Department and then to find that the worker has the answer before the supervisor himself has been told. Normally, proper co-operation would mean that the opinion of the supervisor would be sought before a decision is arrived at, and the answer may be given in his presence. In the case of a more personal or domestic problem, of course, the Personnel Manager may deem it necessary to treat the matter as confidential, but he should tell the foreman so at once.

Absence and Lateness

These are only special aspects of discipline, and all that was said above in that connection applies here. From the standpoint of the manager or foreman, lost time means lost output and jobs not done; it also means lower utilisation of capacity and so increased costs of operation. There are three aspects of this problem to consider:

(*a*) The responsibility of the foreman or manager for dealing with the individual, part of his ordinary responsibility for the maintenance of discipline. To a very large extent the question here is the attitude of the foreman—whether he has a human skill which enables him to deal properly with offenders and yet keep up morale, or whether his negative and unsympathetic reprimands earn for him the disfavour of his workers. The good foreman tends to be less troubled by absence and lost time.

(*b*) The difficult cases, the persistent offenders, with whom the foreman finds himself beaten. Here reference to the Personnel Manager raises the enquiry to a plane of higher and more objective analysis, which can lead to the uncovering of important matters affecting that worker's attitude to his job.

(*c*) The records and procedures for keeping track of absence and lost time. These provide the data for the study of individual cases, as well as the analysis for assessing the position in the departments and factories. Figures of lost time, coupled with figures of personnel turnover, often provide an invaluable index to the state of morale in a department or a whole factory. (Further details on procedures are given in a later chapter.)

Levels of absence vary enormously from factory to factory, and from trade to trade, so that general comparisons serve very little purpose. But when the figure is going up to the 10 and 15 per cent. level, a serious situation is clearly revealed, unless there are specific emergencies such as an epidemic. Analysis of causes is very helpful. The main break should be into the two main categories—avoidable and unavoidable. Unavoidable absence is by far the easiest to deal with, as this is usually caused through ill-health and sickness certified by a doctor, and accidents will happen at work which are covered by the First-Aid records, the information relating to the injury and possible length of absence being passed to the Personnel Manager and the Production Manager.

Avoidable absence can be subdivided into, say, domestic affairs, lassitude, lack of interest in the job, though there is also the one- or two-day sickness not certified, which may be genuine indisposition. The difficulty of knowing whether these cases are genuine or not is certainly great, and is a matter that the Personnel Manager should probe on behalf of the foreman. Careful interviewing may bring to light a sense of "fed-up-ness" in the individual, or definite low state of health (which can at once be referred to a doctor), or some domestic issue—at any rate, something which is not only impairing work when present, but also leading the employee to a remedy of spasmodic time off, so incurring a double loss of output.

The apathy of a man to his job must be very great if it is of such an intensity that it influences him to the extent that he stays away from work. Cases of this kind require a good deal of patient investigation; it must be found out whether there is something in connection with his job which he really dislikes; whether there is friction with the person in charge of him, or with whom he comes in contact. The Personnel Officer must quietly find out if his health is good and try to get information about his home. A man who is living apart from his wife, or having a domestic upheaval, may feel a lack of interest in everything he does, including his work; in tackling a subject of this kind, one needs to be very careful indeed, as a wrong impression is easily created, and instead of being able to help the man, one builds up a reputation of being a "busy-body". The quiet, frank, confidential talk with the Personnel Manager is the main line of diagnosis and remedy.

This situation is made more difficult when the Company have a Sick Benefit Scheme; the only safeguard is the insistence on the production of a Medical Certificate as the basis for the claim for payment. A point worth mentioning here is that it is not a good thing to specify a week as the minimum absence in order to qualify for sick pay; this may lead to the situation where two or three days would be the absence if no sick pay was forthcoming, but the period develops into the week in order to qualify.

Perhaps one important point of principle that emerges here is this, that these individual cases of human problems should rest in the hands of the experienced personnel specialist and should never be left to junior staff of the Personnel Department.

Domestic Affairs

This is a problem always met with, when, owing to the death of a relative or some illness, an employee is unable to come to work.

These cases need to be dealt with very carefully. Firstly, make sure that the excuse is genuine, then see whether there is an opportunity for the Company to help by any of their Welfare Schemes or by giving advice to the individual. A man who has a family of small children is put into a very difficult position when his wife is ill, and it may quite well be that it would take a day or so to obtain some domestic help or a relative who would look after the children. No one would expect a husband to leave home for work knowing that at home there is a family of young children, with a wife who is unable to get up. Even if the man did attend his work, he would be a most unusual person if he devotes his normal energy and gives his thought to the job in the way that he should.

There is only one thing that a person with domestic troubles can be expected to do, and this should be insisted upon throughout the Works Rules, namely, to see that a message is sent to the foreman or the manager of the department at starting time, so that the man's job is not left for an hour or two in the hope that he will turn up. This information will enable the foreman to see that the work goes on.

CHAPTER III

TRAINING, PROMOTION AND WITHDRAWALS

TRAINING POLICY AND PROGRAMMES

IN the form of apprenticeships often under written agreement, training has long been a recognised practice in industry. What is new in present-day arrangements is the development of systematic training for semi-skilled operations; this is, of course, of rather short-period duration, as against the years usually required for an apprenticeship to a skilled trade. Another feature that has accompanied recent training plans is the "introduction course", consisting of information about the firm, its policy and products, general layout, history and regulations. Visits to various departments are often included in the programme.

Contemporary interest in industrial training is based on the belief that the following advantages accrue:

(a) More rapid development to full proficiency.
(b) Increased production.
(c) Improved quality of workmanship.
(d) Less waste of material.
(e) Better utilisation of machines.
(f) Less damage to machines and tools.
(g) Reduced unit costs and increased profit to the Company.
(h) Decreasing the amount of supervision.
(i) Diminishing labour turnover.
(j) Revealing special talents of employees.
(k) Increasing the versatility of employees.
(l) Improvement in employee morale.

Systematic instruction of new-comers in the activities of the firm and in the conditions which appertain to the whole range of its operation, from obtaining raw material at its source to the marketing of its products, will promote co-operation, as well as enhancing the individual's status when he can say to himself and to others—"I am a trained man". The co-ordination of methods is another important result, which can be particularly valuable where a similar operation occurs in different sections of the factory.

Once it is accepted that training is an asset to an organisation, it should be obvious that it needs to be based on a defined policy, and all schemes need to be properly planned and controlled. The idea has to be put across to all ranks of managers and supervisors, and regarded as a continuous process to be brought into operation when called for. The very large concern can have a training centre which is kept in unbroken session, but it is a mistake to think that systematic training has therefore no part in the organisation of the smaller unit.

It is equally important and applicable in the workshop employing 20 people, as in the mammoth factory where 10,000 are at work. Policy and effective plans are just as necessary, even though they are brought into use only now and again every few months. In the smaller concern, it will be the foreman's job to carry out the training or to allocate a skilled man to do the instruction according to the standards and methods laid down. Whatever the size of the unit, the content of training needs to be agreed by all who are likely to be responsible for it; it must be made quite clear what is to be taught, how it should be taught, and what degrees of accuracy are to be attained. How much can be achieved by systematic plans on the lines in even very small concerns has been shown in recent years through the special method of "Job Instruction Training" in the T.W.I. programme, by means of which foremen were taught just how to attain with their own new employees all the advantages of planned analytical instruction that could be acquired in a fully established training centre.

In the large organisation which carries out a full programme, the following training procedures are likely to be found:

(a) Introductory course (sometimes referred to by the American phrase "induction training").

(b) Training for semi-skilled work.

(c) Craft apprenticeship.

(d) Training for technical appointments.

(e) Training for clerical work.

(f) Education for juveniles.

(g) Students.

(h) Training for supervision.

(i) Training for management.

(a) *Introductory Course.*—This is the method of introducing new entrants to an organisation, with the object of gaining their confidence and promoting a high sense of co-operation. If the new employee is to become an effective member of the working force, he must be able to understand where he fits in, what the Company does, how it serves the community, and how the employees get their information to or from the higher levels of the executives, what the rules and working conditions are, and a general picture of the activities of the organisation.

Procedures and methods would vary according to the age and

grade of the employees being introduced. It was found during the war that with women employees, it was most valuable to let them spend a few days in an improvised training centre where they received this general instruction, as well as preliminary instruction in the job. Sometimes, especially for machine operations, this could be extended to a week or ten days of systematic training, which gave the newcomers a much better sense of self-confidence and efficiency in using the machine. When introduced into the machine shop, they had no fears of the machines or undue apprehension of the noise; concentration on the machine itself was easier, and settling down was also made easier through making friends with someone in the training centre—all of which help to develop participation in the social atmosphere of the workshop.

The introductory course need not be a lengthy procedure: it need not be done on the day that the employee starts work, although this is desirable. What must be ensured is that the employee, before he has been with the Company many days, has been given information sufficient to hold his or her interest in the work he is about to do. In one large factory the range of information covered in the course is as follows:

1. *The Company and its Products.*—The history of the Company and its place in industry; the nature and uses of its products; the organisation of the Company and the functions of the main departments.
2. *The Management.*—The management structure of the Company; the names and functions of its principal officials, and others with whom the employee will be concerned in the course of his employment.
3. *Amenities and Employee Services.*—The location and facilities of the canteen, cloakroom, rest rooms, etc.; sickness benefit, pensions, benevolent, recreational and other employee services provided.
4. *Sources of Information.*—Where and from whom the employee can obtain information on such matters as wages, income tax, holidays, leave of absence; how he can obtain advice and assistance in connection with personal problems.
5. *Health, Hygiene and Accident Prevention.*—The health and safety practices necessary in the particular type of employment; the function and services of the medical department; the accident prevention organisation.
6. *Personnel Policy.*—"Standing Orders" and the reasons for them; wages policy; principles of discipline; the aims of, and existing machinery for joint consultation between management and employees; training, education, and promotion policy; employment opportunities; work of the Personnel Department.
7. *Working Routines and Procedures.*—Starting and stopping times; time recording system; meal breaks; the basis of payment of the wage or salary, how it is computed, where and when it is paid.
8. *The Employee's own Department.*—Introduction to the supervisor of

the employee's own department, and to employee representatives and fellow workers; location of the department; work of the department in relation to other departments; the part played by the employee's job in the work of the department.

The question of whether all this information should be given at one time is a matter of opinion. Some feel that it is best to give it in small doses and to have the employee back again at various intervals over a period of about a month. There is a danger to be considered in this method, in so far that the average employee dislikes being what he calls "mucked about". Once he starts work producing nuts and bolts, he wants to get on with the job, and it is sometimes difficult to explain to him why he must pass through a course of general information—especially if he soon comes to feel that he knows all about it.

(b) *Training for Semi-skilled Work.*—That there is valuable advantage to be drawn from a policy and a systematic programme for the training of employees engaged on semi-skilled work was a lesson taught by the experiences of war. Traditionally, the semi-skilled job has always been learned—"picked up" would be a more accurate description—by a new employee from one already experienced. That the new-comer learned all the bad habits of the established operative, and that of an unnecessarily low tempo of work as well, was a feature which seemed not to attract attention; its significance in terms of costs had apparently never been appreciated. The traditional practice is, of course, still very widespread, probably even still the common practice.

It must be borne in mind that the range of occupations covered in the category "semi-skilled" is wide, and that the numbers of persons included are considerable, far in excess of those in the "skilled" trades. In some industries the line of demarcation is not easily fixed, whereas in others the existence of defined crafts and apprenticeships make the break-point quite clear. But if we take the general field of machine-minders, machine-operators on pre-set work, sewing machinists on straightforward garments, assemblers in a variety of components and products, gauges, many occupations in textile spinning and weaving, transport operatives and so on, it will be clear that the question of training for such employees is of no mean order, and that if each individual suffers a deficiency in development and proficiency of only 10–15 per cent. due to inadequate instruction, the loss of productivity to industry and of wealth to the community is nothing short of enormous!

As with most other aspects of employment, there have always been the few firms that have been fully alive to this point and have therefore long maintained systematic schemes of training for their semi-skilled employees, to parallel those for the craftsmen—even if the training required was only a matter of a few days' deliberate instruction by an older operative specially ear-marked for the purpose. Outstanding examples could be quoted like Metropolitan Vickers Electrical Company, which maintained a training centre, using the most advanced methods based on the application of motion study.

In the war years, the first serious move in the development of training for semi-skilled operatives was taken by the Ministry of Labour and National Service in the rapid extension of the Government Training Centres. The need arose chiefly through the introduction of women into industry in large numbers and in the demand for quick training in certain widely used engineering operations. Many of the jobs hitherto done by tradesmen were broken down into simpler stages, and by the use of jigs and fixtures, reduced to routine processes of semi-skilled character. This made possible short intensive training courses, composed of general instruction in the form of lectures, usually with illustrations and models, followed by gradual "coaching" on the job stage by stage in the quieter atmosphere of the centre, removed from the hurly-burly of a workship. Later, the principle was adopted by many of the larger concerns, which established training centres of their own. In many of these, quite often recourse was had to the latest psychological knowledge on training methods, and the whole process of instructing semi-skilled workers made considerable strides forward.

The experience gained in the use of "element by element" training was sometimes applied to even skilled jobs, and it has certainly pointed the way to considerable possibilities of improvement in training methods.

The principle adopted is an extension both of motion study and of job analysis. By careful study of an operation, it is broken up into major parts, or phases or elements; quite often the breakdown of a job for time-study purposes affords a very useful analysis as the basis for training. In each element, a pattern of movement and action is then worked out. These, covering all the elements of the job, thus form an "operation specification" from the human point of view. The training consists of the two parts just referred to, i.e. the general knowledge of the operation—materials used, purpose, machine or tools, bench, special features, dangers and so on; plus specific instruction in performance. This latter part is taking one element in the early stages, so that the trainee gets ample opportunity of acquiring proficiency in each part without mental strain.

In the more complicated operations, the course of tuition in the general aspects of the job may also be given in graded stages.

The approach to training—often referred to as "part training"—

will be recognised as the care of the Job Instruction Training Programme in the T.W.I. Course for supervisors. One or two organisations specifically concerned with research and development in this field have experimented with an additional feature, the use of exercises designed to train the finger or hand muscles, and so to develop dexterities particularly required for various phases of the operation. When the operation specification is being prepared, the analysis is taken a stage farther, and the particular dexterities involved are isolated. The special exercises are performed on "gadgets" which are so designed as to develop a particular pattern of muscular movement reproducing that required for the phase of the operation. Results are not yet available of adequate reliability to confirm or reject the worthwhileness of this development. There has apparently been a long controversy in the scientific psychological circles over the "Whole Method" versus the "Part Method"; that is to say, a controversy as to whether proficiency in training is greater when a job is taught in its entirety, or whether learning is facilitated by breaking the job into suitable parts and concentrating the training effort on each part separately. To some extent the controversy has of course been academic, because every job, apart from the very simple ones, has to be broken into some stages before it can be taught. The protagonists of the "Part Method" believe that such element of the operation should be treated separately as a training project, and the skill developed to a high level before the trainee progresses to another element; this raises integration problems, which in turn become part of the training process. The experimental attitude of many firms during the war years made possible practical demonstrations of this controversy; broadly, much of the evidence pointed to the superior value of the "Part Method," provided that the breakdown of the job is not carried too far and that adequate attention is given to the integration of the stages of training.

Another important principle drawn from war-time experience lay in the high value of a systematic approach to training, a view running counter to the long tradition of British industry that a skill is best acquired by gradual practice under the eye of a master craftsman. War-time experience provided many demonstrations of even complicated skills being acquired in short intensive training courses set up on a systematic programme.

According to this programme the new recruit does not report on the job immediately on taking up employment, but spends one, two or three days in preliminary instruction, often in a specific Training Centre. There, apart from general information about the firm and its products, factory or office regulations and other such items of background information which will assist the employee in settling down, there is a brief training programme relating to the essential features of the technical operations. Where the skill is of high level, the programme is limited to the basic principles of the operation and further training is given under the supervision of the department foreman.

In most of these induction courses, training is assisted by pictorial or other aids—either photographs or diagrams illustrating the operations or the product, or charts, models, etc., that will assist in the better understanding of the nature and purpose of the operations being taught. Here and there films are used for training purposes, but only the really large organisations with extensive recruitment programmes can find this worth while. One particular device developed for war-time purposes was the "Synchrophone", a combination of gramophone and still picture automatically interlinked; the gramophone record contained a simple lecture on, for instance, the operation of a machine tool, the picture frame is a large-scale presentation of the machine; as the lecture proceeds, special features of the machine are thrown into relief by automatic light signals wired within the frame and linked up with the words of the lecturer.

At first sight many of these schemes may sound as though they are of relevance only to the larger organisations. In the sense of establishing a Training Centre with continuous arrangements for induction courses, such as this, the comment may undoubtedly be true. But the principles upon which this approach to training has been built are of equal application in the smaller firms, and in a few cases in this country effective introduction and training schemes have been developed in even quite small organisations. The difficulty usually is that the senior executives of the small firms are not alive to the importance of training, and tend to hide behind their small size as an excuse for not taking any action. Admittedly in this case of small firms, the organisation of training is more difficult, because their needs are both smaller and less continuous; their recruitment programme may need nothing more than a few additional people here and there spaced out over the year.

Experience in the few cases where systematic training has been undertaken in small British firms underlines the importance of earmarking one person, perhaps a foreman, to be responsible for the planning and supervision of such training. An illustration from a small food manufacturer may be of interest. The significance of training was first realised in this firm when on a certain occasion the manager found himself faced with an official contract which necessitated the packing of certain supplies in steel-hooped wooden cases sent in by the purchaser. Hitherto, packing had been in cartons, and there now arose the need for nailing—a skill not customary for women. It might almost sound ridiculous to talk of "training" for so simple an operation. Fortunately, however, the supervisor of the department realised that if he allowed one or two of his women to damage their thumbs in the first half-hour of nailing, his chance of getting teams regularly to work would be materially decreased. He therefore decided to deal with the problem systematically, and organised a brief training course, based on breaking the job into its essential elements. Stage one was how to hold and wield a hammer, taking into consideration the fact that women in general have had little previous experience of this implement and that their natural tendency is for a wrong grip that would lose a good deal of the weight of the blow. The second stage was the positioning of boards and the holding of the nail whilst the first blow is struck, particular attention being given to hand and eye co-ordination, so as to hit the nail rather than the thumb! Stage three was concerned with guiding the nail by the direction of the hammer blow. These three stages were very easily trained on pieces of wood suitably marked out, so that by the time the trainees were transferred to nailing a case, they had acquired adequate skill to direct the nail into the $\frac{3}{8}$-in. thickness of the side-boards without protrusions. Similar further stages of training were devoted to the positioning of the hoop (using the hammer as a lever), the use of a steel punch for piercing the hoop, linking up again with the earlier element of driving in the nail to complete the operation.

The main feature about this operational illustration is its simplicity, but it does indicate the underlying principles of breaking the job into parts so that each one can separately be learned, and of planning the training of a well-defined programme. The foreman was able to train half a dozen women at a time, and needed to devote only about twenty minutes of his time in each two or three hours to explaining and practising the elements, leaving the team for the next thirty to forty minutes carrying out practical exercises. The half-day devoted to this scheme meant a considerable difference to the efficiency and the productivity of the nailers.

Another small firm was concerned with the manufacture of lenses, involving a rather tricky setting operation. It had been said that no one was ever "trained" for this job, but that the skill was acquired by a long period of gradual experience. Anything from twelve to eighteen months was regarded as quite common. The firm employed only thirty-five persons, of whom about ten were on the particular process. It was the probability of expanding markets after the war that led to consideration of training, and the General Manager decided to have the assistance of a Training Consultant. Careful analysis of the operation by the Consultant revealed that the job was very much more simple than was commonly supposed, and that by some modification in the approach to it, it was possible to lay down specific elements each open to instruction, in place of the "judgment" which had hitherto been regarded as the key to the skill. Working along "part training" lines, with the aid of one or two simple off-the-job exercises to develop particular finger dexterities, a training programme of three weeks' duration was devised, in which the whole of the skill was acquired at a comparable level of quality of output, supplemented by a further three-week period in which the trainee's quantity of output was raised virtually to the level of the skilled operative.

In the course of the analysis of the job, the Consultant raised a considerable number of technical questions, points on which the operating instructions were not clear, variations in quality specifications, and many other technical details which indicated that the designing and tooling of the operation were still far from satisfactory. The manager was himself a technician of a high order, and confessed astonishment at the questions being asked on points of technical detail which suggested incomplete knowledge or development of the process. Before the training programme could be devised, these items had to be settled; the outcome of the whole review was, therefore, not only a considerable improvement in training, but also important modifications in the layout of the job in quality standards and in tools.

This incident is not an isolated case; frequently one of the by-products of systematic training built up on a part basis and thus necessitating a closer review of operations, machines and tools, has been technical improvements of a far-reaching character.

Publications in one or two journals have drawn a certain amount of attention to training programmes which have been worked out in one or two of the British hosiery manufacturing firms and which are likely to spread through the industry. Large numbers of female operatives are employed, and there has been the traditional policy of letting new-comers "pick up the job" from a neighbour. Some of the operations, however, involve rather special skills and learning periods, for these often stretch out over eighteen months or two years. This is too serious a drawback in face of the acute shortage of female labour, particularly juveniles, in recent years, and so the hosiery concerns have begun to pay more regard to training. Apart from getting their new recruits to a higher level of productivity quickly, one or two firms (large and small) have found that the assistance of organised training is a valuable publicity aid to recruitment. Results accruing from systematic programmes for the higher skilled operations have been little short of spectacular—for instance, training times for outer-wear lockstitch machinists were reduced from eighteen months to fourteen weeks, and even then with a higher standard of workmanship than in the case of the traditional worker. The organisation of this programme provided a very good example of the part-training approach. Analysis of the operation of machining the various parts of, say, a dress, revealed that the key to the skill lay in the control of the fabric as it ran under the needle, and that broadly five different patterns of handling were required to control the fabric at the different stages of making up the dress. Differences in fabric had also to be taken into account: knitted fabrics, for example, stretch easily, while some of the more open woven ones will easily fray. Hence one basic requirement in the programme was a series of exercises (especially devised away from the machine) for training in the handling of various fabrics—aligning edges, folding, turning in, guiding through a dummy machine for straight runs, corners and reverses. Following closely on this came the specific training in disposition of the fingers for the various types of seam (i.e. the five "patterns" of handling referred to above). This was devised in the form of some twelve to fifteen types of seam actually run up on the machine, using waste strips of fabric and assisted by a set of finished seams displayed on the wall. These seams were, of course, graded for difficulty. (Learners who had no previous contact with a sewing machine, or any who found certain stages particularly difficult, could be taught and practised on a specially devised machine which formed a chain stitch for easy removal and correction.) As each phase of the machining was mastered at an approved level of quality and speed, the trainee began to spend part of the day making up those parts of garments where such seams or machining were required. In this way, the trainee was never confronted by a whole garment or a difficult operation until the basic skill entailed had been mastered.

Later in the programme, special exercises were provided for fancy machining and for the finishing of the dress (which entailed special dexterity in knitted lines, because of the bulk and weight to be handled). Similarly, at appropriate intervals other special off-the-job exercises were included as necessary, and in the earlier phases the programme provided eye-muscle exercises to reduce the eye-strain from the concentration in learning. Throughout, pictorial aids, devices, etc., were carefully worked into the scheme.

Naturally such a programme is more easily carried out by the medium or large firms within a separate Training Centre, but the approach has been found just as valuable for smaller units, provided there is a forewoman or other person adequately trained in the method. Expense is very reasonable, and is easily off-set by the rapid climb of new recruits to proficiency.

Similar schemes have also been developed on the stocking and sock side of the industry, for the more difficult manual operations, such, for instance, as linking and seaming. They have proved more difficult to analyse, but two cases are known in which a systematic training course for linking (looping) has been developed with an improvement in training time almost as outstanding as that of the dress machinists. The difficulty in this case has arisen because of the more continuous nature of the operation, and the very fine and delicate dexterities involved in the finger work.

Brief reference is made in a later paragraph to training for clerical staffs, but it may be pertinent to observe here that the principles outlined above could be made of special value to the trainings of many of the operations in offices, particularly those involving the use of hand-operated mechanical equipment. Most work of this kind is directly concerned with the semi-skilled work in factories, and there is a big pioneer-field waiting to be explored in the application of "part-training" methods to the office.

(c) *Craft Apprenticeship.*—This is usually the title given to the apprenticeship of engineers and electricians, builders and the like, and consists of a period of training to be provided by the employer either with or without indentures. Some large firms provide practical training in model workshops, with their own school and gymnasium in the factory, and assist the youth by obtaining deferment from his call-up until such time as he has passed a recognised examination. Most training schemes are satisfied by the Higher National Certificate, but in a number of cases boys are encouraged to go farther and obtain their Degree in engineering or electrical work.

Another type of training is for the shop lad, and here the work would be done in the normal way with part-time day release, so that he can attend the local Technical College for courses. Apprentices should always be under good supervision, and it is important that someone who is genuinely interested in the boys' welfare should also be concerned. A useful method of obtaining interest is to get a skilled craftsman to take a boy under his wing or for the boy to adopt him as an "uncle", thus being able to discuss the many problems which arise from day to day in connection with his practical work.

The majority of our engineering shops are small ones, and the provision of adequate supervision when practical work is involved is one of the essentials with any scheme of craft training. Records should be kept of the amount of time the boy has spent on the different phases of work or machines, so that he can be transferred at regular intervals to the next stage of his training. At the end of his period of training he should receive a letter from the Company confirming that he has satisfactorily completed his training and giving other information which might prove useful to a prospective employer at some later date.

(d) *Training for Technical Appointments.*—Some of the youths who have passed through their practical training are considered sufficiently bright to make it worth while for the management to have them trained in some other branch of the profession or trade. An electrical apprentice might be considered for training as a technical engineer or draughtsman, whilst a mechanical engineer might be considered for time-study work, designer, production engineering, planning or progress chasing. This may mean additional study in the new job or a period of practical training in the department to which he would be attached. Some Companies insist that when an apprentice has completed his training he is attached for a period of one to three months to every department in the firm before finally deciding where he should be employed. The type of training necessary may differ according to the ideas of the particular Company, but it is always a useful guide to discuss the youth's possibilities and prospects in conjunction with his parents and the Principal of the local Technical College. By this means a wider background to the problem and the various matters for consideration can be looked into.

It is the practice of some Companies to engage for training young men who have come from the Universities or who have already reached a definite position in theoretical work together with a practical experience. It is an advantage, as a rule, to start young men in this position with a definite curriculum agreed upon, but without defining closely the final job which it is intended the Company should give him. That depends to a large extent on the suitability of the individual, the flair which he may have for a particular type of work and many other factors which can be judged only as they arise. Trainees of this kind should be attached primarily to the head executive, who should make it clear that he has an interest in their well-being.

(e) *Training in Clerical Work.*—There seems to be a widespread popular view that anyone can be a clerk, that no particular skill or experience is required to deal with paper work, but those with knowledge of what really goes on in the offices are well aware of the extent to which good training can contribute to effective work. Moreover, sound training of clerical workers has proved of great value in providing experienced people capable of promotion to higher responsibilities. The maintaining of production records for storekeeping work may not, at first sight, appear to be important, until it is realised that the whole flow of output may depend on their accuracy; production lines could be held up if the information on the bin card or records were inaccurate—the record may point to adequate quantities of material in stock, but the bin is in fact empty! Practical training of this kind is a matter for individual firms, to teach the new employee methods for dealing with papers in that particular office. The amount of skill required for this purpose by the instructor is great, for not only does he need to be able to give a lucid explanation of the "whys and wherefores", but also be able to convince his "pupils" that the job is important and that it is being done in the best possible way. Operators of machines (comptometers, typewriters and the like) can often be taught their work by the machine manufacturers, which has the big advantage that they are skilfully instructed in the special characteristics of the machines and will be trained to handle these expensive instruments with the necessary care. The training of typists is one of the jobs being given more prominence than any other today, owing to their shortage.

None of this special training, however, should be done without bearing in mind the practical aspects of what the person will be expected to do when trained : how futile, for instance, to insist on a girl reaching 140 words per minute at shorthand class only to be delegated to a person whose dictating speed never rises above 40!

(*f*) *Education of Juveniles.*—All juveniles should receive practical training on the job from the supervisor of his or her section in a similar way to new adult labour. In addition, it is considered that all juveniles need further education. Some will undertake evening classes on their own initiative, and should be released earlier in the afternoon to attend such classes. Some watch should, however, be kept on this, as attending evening school two or three times a week, after working all day, may prove detrimental to the vigour of young people and hence to their efficiency as workers. It is for this reason that many firms prefer to send their youngsters to school for one full day a week (or two half-days).

The advantages of day-time education may be summarised thus :

(i) This continued education will become compulsory in due course; in the meantime, the benefit is spread to those juveniles who do not attend evening classes voluntarily.

(ii) Those who would normally attend would be able to go less often, with consequent improvement in their health, vigour, industrial output and accuracy. Study during the day would produce much better results.

(iii) The scheme would be attractive to parents and boys and girls with ambition; therefore recruitment should be aided.

The obvious disadvantages are that the juveniles would always be away from their job on two half-days each week and would be paid for this time. However, it is considered that the fact that wages are paid during "school time" would be compensated later on by the increased usefulness of these juveniles.

(*g*) *Students.*—These would be specially selected and would have attained a minimum educational level. They would be required to attend classes on two evenings a week in addition to two half-days. In this time (day and evening) their study would be directed towards an approved examination, normally taken at age 19–21. They could apply for deferment of military service, providing the college considered that they had a good chance of passing the examination.

No hard-and-fast rule can be applied regarding time off, as this will vary according to the classes that are available locally, but it is recommended that two afternoons and not one whole day should be allocated to students who attend Technical College. Whenever possible, evening classes should be on the same day as the afternoon classes, and students could then have tea in the college canteen.

It is quite a good idea, when numbers justify it, to form a Students' Committee representing all types of students. The Personnel Officer and/or the Training Officer would be *ex-officio* members, but eventually the students should be able to manage their own meetings. The committee should have no executive power, all its recommendations and deliberations being passed on through the Personnel or Training Officer.

Students would need to be very carefully selected, and they should be interviewed by the head of the department concerned as well as the Personnel and Training Officers. School reports, too, would need to be reviewed, and each student given a test to ascertain his suitability for training. These facts and details of progress in training should be entered on the record card to save setting up a separate juvenile training card index.

There should be every incentive to cause a boy or girl to wish to attend evening classes and to study for examinations. Preferential rates of pay might be considered, and any existing schemes of increments should take care of examinations passed.

Students should not be allowed to remain at one job or in one department, but should be moved about according to a prearranged scheme, which has been agreed by all concerned. Thus an engineering apprentice or student should spend some time in Stores, Fitting, Machine Shop, Assembly, Cost Office, Time Study, Sales Department and Personnel Department during his period of training.

Four types of student are suggested:

1. *Technical Students*

   (a) Students who have been employed in the Engineering, Electrical and Works Services Departments. Alternative names are Engineering Students or even Apprentices.

   (b) Age for acceptance about 15.

   (c) A good general education would be required with a good grounding in mathematics and/or physics for intending engineers. Careful selection would be necessary, and a probationary period of from three to six months is suggested.

(d) The students would study for National Certificates in an appropriate branch of engineering, or would learn the theoretical side of their trade as craftsmen (e.g. carpenter) at the technical college.

2. *Commerce Students*

(a) Specially selected students who would be employed in the office or warehouse departments.

(b) Age for acceptance about 16+.

(c) School-leaving Examination would be a prerequisite.

(d) Different examinations for these students are held, depending on their interests, ability and ultimate department in their firm.

3. *General Students*

(a) Besides these Technical, Commercial and Laboratory students, there may remain some juveniles who would like to study at evening classes (as well as at compulsory day-time classes). They might be employed in any department.

(b) Age for acceptance 16–18.

(c) Of good general education and adjudged capable of passing an examination in general higher education by the age of 19, science usually being one of the subjects studied.

4. *Laboratory Staff*

These would be mainly Chemists and Physicists, and would study for the Inter B.Sc., preferably in Chemistry, Physics, Biology and Pure Mathematics.

(h) *Training for Supervisors.*—Of all the aspects of industrial training that have claimed attention in recent years, the development of plans for the training of foremen have probably been both the centre of greatest interest and the line of most important advance. Some firms, of course, have maintained training schemes for supervisory staffs for many years, but these were among the exceptional rather than the common. As part of the earlier phases of the "management" movement, there were always one or two activities specifically devoted to foremen; for instance, the occasional week-end conferences organised by the Industrial Welfare Society and the two-year Certificate Course in Supervision sponsored by the Institute of Industrial Administration and covered by study courses at certain Technical Colleges (evening sessions). Broadly, however, real interest on any measurable scale did not emerge until 1940–1, when the impact of war-time expansion brought home to industry the deficiencies in the supervisory levels and the inadequate existing methods— mainly in terms of technical prowess—to make any real contribution to filling the gap.

Naturally enough, the first forward move was based on existing schemes; with the collaboration of the Institute of Industrial Administration, the Ministry of Labour and National Service evolved the three-month study course covering in concentrated form most of the matter of the pre-war two-year course. Colleges up and down the country co-operated, and very soon some thousands of foremen were able to get rudimentary basic instruction in the essentials of their supervisory tasks—principles and practice of production planning and control, the significance of cost control, the human aspects, personnel relations, the maintenance of discipline and so on.

Before long the "students" themselves began to show a measure of initiative; appreciation of their course led to reorganisation of how much farther they had still to go, and the particular need that they felt was for some means by which the general and basic instruction gained at the College course could be interpreted into dealing with their individual daily responsibilities and problems. In many parts of the country, nothing at all was even done about it, but in some of the more thickly populated industrial areas, the scheme of "Supervisor Discussion Groups" was soon evolved. (The pioneer Group was formed in North-east London in the spring of 1942.) Their purpose was to provide an occasion for periodic informal meetings of foremen and similar staffs from a variety of firms in the locality, and for discussion of the practice of supervision on the basis of the principles learned in the course. These Groups are still flourishing and still making an important contribution to the strengthening of supervisors.

The next official development was the Training Within Industry (T.W.I.) Programme for Supervisors. With its origin in America, this scheme was adapted by the Ministry of Labour and National Service to British conditions and a service set up for its establishment in industrial organisations here. As the title implies, its central thesis is the principle that the greatest benefit for supervisors in training is drawn from a scheme that links up closely and immediately with their own every-day tasks.

Whether the Training Within Industry Programme has been an unmitigated success or not is open to question. Some firms have been enthusiastic in its praise, while others have felt that its pattern was somewhat stereotyped, and in consequence foremen have felt the training to be both artificial and superficial. To overcome this difficulty, one or two firms have experimented with internal group discussion methods. One of the leading Management Consultant firms has also done some pioneer work in this direction, using the small group technique and working to a scheme in which all the subject-matter which forms the basis of training is provided by the participating foremen themselves; thus the foremen can feel that they are actively sharing in a "review of management and supervision" rather than undergoing instruction. Experience is proving this approach to be of very great value, especially from the standpoint of the older foremen. The soundness of the group discussion technique as a constructive means of training has long been recognised, and in the case of its application to the development of foremen, there is the added benefit that the "matter" of the discussions is directly concerned with the daily tasks of those who are participating.

In the field of educational instruction the most important development has been the successful experiment with a three-week full-time study course for Supervisors at the Leicester College of Technology. Proof of the success of this venture is best seen from the fact that in a recent session the College had to put on 15–20 repeat courses to meet the demand from entrants from all over the country.

What should be the content of the supervisor training schemes? The answer must to some extent depend on the conditions prevailing in the firms concerned. For instance, in some industries the foreman necessarily has highly important technical functions which may deeply colour the pattern of his responsibilities. In many chemical and other process lines, problems of production planning and control do not arise at the foremen level, and little purpose is served by supervisors "devoting" more than general and superficial attention to studies of production and cost control. On the other hand, virtually every foreman will have human responsibilities, of wider or narrower scope, so that this field will need to figure in every programme. Broadly, the matter may be summarised in the generalisation that the requirements of any supervisory post are a combination of the following three factors: the arrangement, balance and emphasis being determined according to the particular circumstances of each post:

(1) Technical ability, covering both knowledge and skill.
(2) Personal qualities, centring round leadership and co-operation.
(3) Administrative ability, comprising mainly a knowledge and understanding of the significance of the organisation and control of production.

1. *Technical Ability*

From the nature of the responsibilities put upon the foreman or supervisor in a production department, it is clear that he must possess a minimum level of skill and knowledge of the processes under his jurisdiction. The more highly technical the processes, the greater the significance of this factor. But it still remains true that, whatever the process, no amount of technical ability is by itself sufficient for effective supervision.

2. Personal Qualities

The foreman or supervisor has to govern men and women in the performance of a task; he has to secure their effective co-operation in the common aim; he has to maintain law and order, settle disputes, meet complaints and grumbles. He has also to work in harmony with his counterpart in other sections, and with the management to which he is responsible. These personal qualities are usually summed up in the terms "leadership and co-operation", and are made up of varying combinations of many characteristics.

3. Administrative Ability

Supervision involves responsibility for interpreting "management" to operatives and for contributing to the control of production. The supervisor must therefore understand something about production and personnel management; and his effectiveness (if he is suitable on other grounds) can be increased only by the acquisition of a deeper knowledge of the administrative process; he is part of the executive scheme, and the more he understands what that scheme stands for, the more readily can he pull his weight in it.

It can be safely assumed that the training programme for supervisors will need, in most cases, to contain no items that are specifically devoted to the purely technical aspect of their responsibilities; that they will usually have acquired in the course of their service in the trade concerned. The training called for has to deal with the human and the administrative sides of their tasks, in general terms as well as in special relation to the methods of their own firm. Proficiency in these directions will require a twofold line of training: the acquisition of knowledge, plus some instruction or guidance in the daily application of that knowledge. This approach shows the value of the different phases of supervisor training referred to above—for instance, the Technical College course as a source of general knowledge, plus the internal group technique as a translation of that knowledge into practice. Broadly, the total content of this double training process may perhaps be summed up as follows:

(a) The acquisition of a certain body of knowledge: this will consist of:
  (1) General principles of production control and of methods which are frequently adopted in industry as a whole.
  (2) The specific methods of control used in the firm itself.
  (3) General knowledge of some of the specialised field of personnel management, as applied through the foreman.
(b) The growth in supervisory experience:
  (1) In the exercise of responsibility, leadership and co-operation.
  (2) In the use and application of control methods in so far as they form part of the foreman's or supervisor's function.

To a very large extent the first aspect will be very much the same in most firms, or at least in firms of comparable sizes. The variable element will be the study of the particular methods adopted in the firm concerned. In other words, there is a large part of the content of the training scheme under aspect (*a*) that could conform to a certain centrally established scheme; a complementary and very important part, however, will be peculiar to each firm itself, and will in particular include the second aspect of training.

In the main, the training under the second head will consist of what might be called "organised growth", consisting of systematic assistance in the acquisition and/or development of certain personal qualities—making up leadership and co-operation. Example, especially deliberate example from the supervisor's immediate chief, can play a very important part in this process, and ought certainly to have a place in the training scheme; for the rest, encouragement and guidance by group talks, discussions and conferences, or by across-the-table interviews, will form the most appropriate methods. The personal qualities to be inculcated should also include such items as the following, which are particularly important from the supervisor's point of view:

(*a*) Confidence in management and how to maintain it, especially in face of circumstances that give rise to doubts.

(*b*) Interest in the tasks of supervision.

(*c*) Ability to think objectively and constructively.

(*d*) Understanding of the value of self-analysis and constructive self-criticism.

(*e*) Ability to avoid worrying or being worried.

(*f*) Ability to apply job analysis and to realise the significance.

It is almost inevitable that much of the emphasis in training programmes for supervisors will be on the human aspects of their responsibilities. With most foremen already established, this will be the side of their task for which they have hitherto had little, if any, specific preparation. There are, undoubtedly, many foremen with the inherent skill of successful dealings with their fellow men: they need but little supplementary knowledge of the best practices of personnel management. But these gifted few stand in contrast to thousands who have no special flair, but who have adequate abilities and disposition to learn, and who thus need the special training that will enable them to copy the skill of those who are the "born leaders". Clearly, the question of selection of candidates for promotion is vitally linked up with this aspect of training. Nothing has been said here, so far, about the provision for training for potential supervisors, as distinct from those already in office: this, because the issue is one more relevant to selection than to training. The course of study and the subject-matter to be covered would be very similar in both cases, though of rather more generalised character in the case of the potential supervisors.

What are the qualities relevant to successful foremanship? Many lists have been drawn up and considerable controversy has taken place over them. Perhaps the sensible answer is that much will depend on the prevailing circumstances of the appointment, including the personalities to be contacted in the management structure in the course of discharging the supervisory responsibilities. In general terms, the following list has been drawn up as an open combination of desirable qualities for the average run of industrial foremanship appointments : [1]

(a) *Main:*
    Self-control.
    Fairmindedness.
    Honesty and sincerity.
    Tact.
    Mental alertness.
    Initiative.

(b) *Subsidiary:*
    Sense of perspective.
    Tenacity and courage.
    Patience.
    Courtesy.
    Observation.

In the industrial world of today, no firm, large or small, can afford not to develop sound levels of supervision, which in effect means having a training policy and a plan of campaign for foremen. The plan should envisage preparatory training prior to appointment or in the early stages after taking over responsibility, as well as supplementary "refresher" sessions at later intervals. These could be in the form of the group discussions referred to above as organised within the medium-sized and larger organisations, or in the case of the smaller firms, these needs could be adequately met by active participation in the local Supervisor Discussion Groups which are to be found in many districts.

The planning of a supervisor training policy should be based on a

---

[1] This list was privately prepared. For a fuller review of the problem of selection, see *The New Foremanship*, by H. G. Burns Morton (Chapman & Hall), and occasional articles in the journals of the Institute of Personnel Management, the National Institute of Industrial Psychology and the Industrial Welfare Society.

clear aim—its purpose is to improve the effectiveness of supervisors in that capacity; it is NOT intended as a surreptitious means of pushing them forward for promotion. Devising the programme to carry out the policy is likely, very quickly, to bring home to top management the need for two further fundamental principles. The one is the classification and definition of the responsibilities of the supervisors, especially in relation to "line" executives (e.g. Factory and Departmental Managers) and to service specialists. Experience with these programmes has almost invariably thrown into relief confusions over the distribution of responsibilities, and a good deal of difficulty can be avoided if the clarification takes place prior to the training, or at least as an early phase of the training programme itself. The second point calling for consideration is the status and conditions of service of the foremen. Their participation in the scheme emphasises the importance of their responsibility; it is highly important for the maintenance of their morale that the Company's policy ensures that their conditions of service are of adequate standard in relation to other members of the staff.

*   *   *   *   *

The wording of the foregoing paragraphs appears to have been planned specifically in reference to manufacturing organisations. But everything that has been said has exactly the same application to supervisors in commercial organisations, or clerical departments. In an accounts section, for instance, the supervisor's "technical" field will be his or her knowledge of accountancy and the machines used. The "administrative" group refers again to the procedures or methods according to which the section works. The "human" facet is precisely as in the factory—save that the girls work with pen or typewriter and brain, instead of with hands and dexterity: it is doubtful whether even this distinction is valid or justified.

Training of supervisory staffs in clerical and commercial operations has been even worse neglected than on the industrial side, but is no less significant.

PROMOTION

A defined promotion policy should be the natural accompaniment of systematic selection, placement and training of employees. The underlying principle would be to fill all appointments from within whenever there is a suitable candidate qualified for promotion; in practice this means a regular procedure for advertising or notifying all vacancies to employees, and for ensuring that when foremen or managers have a job to fill, they think first of upgrading and not of looking for an outsider.

The Personnel Department—where one exists—would be one of the first to know that a vacancy for a chargehand, foreman or junior executive had occurred. Applications should be invited from suitably qualified employees who are interested, and the Personnel Manager should interview each one. He will need to be particularly careful to make objective assessments of the candidates, unbiased by partial knowledge from personal contacts. The interview should serve too to give applicants further knowledge about the appointment. Other relevant information would be the absent and lateness records of the past five years, together with a short report from the departments where he had previously worked.

Once the appointment has been made and the man or woman has been selected, they should be interviewed again and congratulated on their appointment, by both the Personnel and Works Managers. A letter setting out their new terms and conditions of employment and stating when this takes place should be given to the employee, and no interview of this kind should ever be completed without asking a question—"Is there anything else you would like to know about the job?" It is often wise to ask the Managing Director to have a few words with the man, or woman, just prior to his taking over the new appointment: this would do a great deal towards convincing the ordinary man that the Board of Directors and the executives are really interested in him.

Sometimes a promotion means sitting in a different part of the canteen, and this is where the Personnel Manager again should take care to see that he lunches with the new person and introduces him where necessary, so that he suffers no embarrassment.

WITHDRAWALS

1. Retirements

The Personnel Manager's part in dealing with the older employee reaching retiring age is the complement of his tasks in recruitment, training and promotion. Time was when the main problem in retirement lay in the financial position of the old people, but recent developments in National Insurance, supplemented by the much wider existence of contributory and savings clubs, have removed the greater part of this problem. Moreover, there is now greater readiness to stay at work to a later age, and far more opportunities of continuing in employment, in the interests of the country's economic progress.

From the Company's standpoint, the more important aspect is morale value of the retirement; this turns on the Personnel Manager's attitude. Some reference will necessarily have been made to the impending termination during the preceding few months, but at the point of parting the Personnel Manager should arrange a special interview, with adequate time to make the employee feel that it is an important occasion. In the smaller firms, this pleasant task will naturally be taken over by the owner or chief director himself. The firm's policy may make this the occasion for a souvenir presentation. In any case it will be made clear to the retiring employee that the Company is still interested in him, anxious to be kept in touch with him and always ready to help. All legal obligation to this employee may indeed have ceased, but there is no doubt that where a man has given a major portion of his working life to a firm, they have a moral duty to extend a considerate and helping hand to him—and they undoubtedly draw benefit from this contribution that such an attitude makes to the morale of all employees in the firm.

2. Terminations

For one reason or another, there will always be some employee whose service with the Company comes to an end. For the Personnel Department a termination of employment involves a task with two distinct phases. There is the purely mechanical task of carrying out certain things to ensure that the departing employee is paid all money due, returns tools or equipment belonging to the Company, gets back his Insurance card, and so on. But there is also the human side, the face-to-face contact with the employee concerned, and this should be an important personal responsibility of the Personnel Officer or his immediate functional deputy.

It is characteristic of the previous era that employees (then called "hands") were dismissed at an hour's or a day's notice without regard to the personal damage done to the individual by the shattering of security, to the morale of the factory or office, or to the fabric of society.The rising generation that does not know the industrial world of the pre-Essential Work Order days cannot readily appreciate the significance of the contemporary cry for "security" or the almost unreasonable tenacity against even glaringly obvious redundancy.

The existence of a personnel policy usually means the inclusion of a guarantee against unfair dismissal, and the Personnel Manager is primarily responsible for seeing that the guarantee is upheld. Hence the importance of his personal task—in a case of dismissal to be sure of the facts, to know the employee's side, to make an objective appraisal to uphold the agreed decision, but to see to it also that the employee leaves with a sense of justice done rather than injustice suffered, and that his former mates do not bear a self-justified resentment.

The other side of the picture has a similar importance. The employee wishing to leave may be a genuine case—with reasons patently obvious. He may, however, bring forward a seemingly factual reason as the means of an underlying disgruntlement—perhaps unfair treatment, perhaps dissatisfaction with conditions or the progress, or perhaps the reflection of a sorry state of morale in the department. It must be among the Personnel Officer's most important tasks to interview all employees wishing to terminate their service, not as a formality, but as an occasion for letting the individual make a contribution to his knowledge of the social relations of the organisation. From the employee whose termination is simply on factual grounds— getting married, removal from district, etc.—the Personnel Officer may get little but pleasant reminiscence. From those whose leaving reflects a sense of discontentment, this may become a valuable guide to weaknesses in organisation or supervision, or unsuspected grievances, and may perhaps disclose a chance of retaining the employee after all.

In a period of man-power shortage, wastage of employees can be a source of serious loss, and the Personnel Officer is making his most valuable contribution towards his real purpose in the organisation every time he avoids the termination of service of a good employee, especially if at the same time he is able to set in train correctives for adverse conditions hitherto unsuspected.

3. *Redundancy*

It happens in many Companies that conclusions or cancellations of contract or other outside economic factors bring about a redundancy of operatives which looks like being longstanding. Where this takes place, it is usual for the last employees to come to be the first to leave, and this kind of clause will be found in many Trade Union Agreements. If the discharges are to be on a considerable scale, the detailed work needs to be carefully planned beforehand. In every case, the employees should be given either adequate notice or, alternatively, a week or two's pay in lieu of notice, so that they have the opportunity of seeking employment without being thrust on to public funds straightway. The Personnel Manager should plan to carry the Shop Stewards with him from the outset. The reasons for the redundancy should be carefully and fully explained. If there are to be several stages, this should be disclosed at the first meeting. Reference to the records or to specially prepared lists will enable, in each section or category, the principle of "last come, first go" to be observed. Where the lists are considerable, it is best to allow the Stewards a day or two to investigate the matter themselves; it will then be easy to find out how many cases are agreed and how many are queried. For those that are agreed, discharging machinery and a posting of notices can be arranged in the shop, and then individual notice given to each man. Whatever happens, the Personnel Manager should make sure that these notices are handed out in the department by himself, or by one of his representatives. They should not, in any case, be put into the pay packet, for wherever possible a full explanation should be given to each individual employee. The queries can be carefully scrutinised and finally agreed by the Personnel Officer and the Shop Stewards.

Apprentices and students under training are usually excluded by an Agreement which has been made either individually or by the Unions, and where the number of employees is reduced owing to redundancy they are kept on.

There will undoubtedly be the odd case which cannot be agreed, and this needs to be treated with a great deal of care, particularly if there is any suggestion that an employee is being unfairly treated. In such a case, it should be made clear that the person will be kept in the Company's employ until such time as the matter is disposed of by negotiation, and this may, in fact, mean taking it either to a Joint Industrial Council in the industry or, alternatively, to notify the Ministry of Labour of the failure to agree and ask for an independent arbitrator to be appointed.

There is nothing that can injure a Company so quickly as the apathetic attitude to a job which becomes apparent as soon as the word "redundancy" is whispered around. Men get restless and start looking around for other jobs, thinking the firm is going bankrupt; rumour follows rumour, and unless the Personnel Manager is alive to the situation, much damage can be done externally, as well as within the works.

4. *Disorderly Conduct*

Under this heading the decision to discharge an employee is usually based on some definite evidence. It may be a breach of the works rules, a brawl or fight between two employees, the merits of which will need to be gone into very carefully by the Personnel Manager or sometimes by the Managing Director himself. In highly emotional cases, including drunkenness, it is wise never to make a decision on the day that the incident happens, but to wait until the next day. People who are giving an account of what has happened will give an entirely different story when they are cool, calm and collected, than they will when tempers are frayed.

5. *The Unsatisfactory Worker*

Some reference was made to this type of problem in an earlier section on morale. It may be that complaints drift into the Personnel

Manager about an employee in such-and-such a department, until, finally, a definite request is received by the Personnel Manager to discharge the employee. The Personnel Manager usually handles this type of case by seeing the man to explain that he has been unsatisfactory from a work point of view over a long period, that he has had several warnings and, despite these, no improvement has been shown, and finally it is felt that he must go. Where a man belongs to a union, he has the right to have his Shop Steward present if he wishes. Always try to discharge employees in a friendly way; there is no need to be hostile, abrupt or unkind. The Personnel Manager must, however, be very frank, and if the man being discharged protests that this, that or the other fact is incorrect, the person who made the allegations should be sent for immediately, and be required to repeat them in the presence of the employee. Hearing the facts on both sides, the Personnel Manager will have the final word, but it is much better to get agreement from the man that he has been unsatisfactory and that it is a logical thing for him to be discharged, as he has not improved.

The question of whether a discharged person should work out the notice is debatable. Most Personnel Managers think that an employee who is discharged—whether from factory or office—is best out of the gates as soon as it has been decided, and that he should be paid wages in lieu of notice rather than have him about the place, a misery to himself and everyone else, whilst he is serving his notice.

Finally, when it comes to the end, the man should be given a friendly hand-shake and wished good luck in whatever job he takes up. The fact that he has not been successful in one Company is no criterion that he will not be an outstanding success in the next. He may well be helped to obtain a suitable job elsewhere, a matter in which the good Personnel Manager can really demonstrate his own skill.

THE ACTIVITIES OF A PERSONNEL DEPARTMEN1

The Personnel Department Office. Sources of Recruitment. Reception on Recruitment. Selection Tests. Employee Records. Wages. Job Analysis and Specification. Medical Department

THE PERSONNEL DEPARTMENT OFFICE

AMONG the functions of a Personnel Manager is that of supplying the factory and offices with recruits as required by the production or load of work, and of keeping up-to-date information about the personnel employed. This and many other activities necessitate the provision of suitable accommodation. Where to place the department is determined by such factors as:

(1) Policy in regard to separate or central records.
(2) The location of the production departments.
(3) Location of main administrative offices.
(4) Access from the road.
(5) Availability to all employees.

The size of the staff required in the department must also be considered. Most factories have their Personnel Department near the works entrance, so that applicants for jobs and other visitors can be directed to the appropriate reception without getting lost in a maze of factory departments or without having to go through a number of offices, stores, etc. On the other hand, it is necessary to bear in mind that the Personnel Department must also be easily accessible to the employees, so that they are not discouraged from coming there with problems because it is situated in an out-of-the-way part of the factory, and involves a journey of several minutes. To arrive at a balance of these conflicting issues needs a careful review of all the relevant factors in each particular case.

Where the factory is a large one, with many big departments, it is advisable to have a separate small Personnel Office in each main department. This might also be an advantage where there are a number of storeys to the building, and time might be wasted by the employees leaving their jobs for a long time in order to visit the Personnel Department with their particular problem.

The layout of an ordinary Personnel Department needs to be given careful consideration, and a number of plans have been prepared for both simple and extensive departments. Wherever possible, the whole of the Personnel Department should be located together. This is particularly important where a Medical Section is concerned, as the amount of work which goes on between the two sections is considerable, and co-operation is made easier on many matters if they are situated in the same building, and can possibly use the same records, apart from the confidential professional information which the Medical Officer must keep himself in private custody.

SOURCES OF RECRUITMENT

It would depend on the size of the Company whether the Personnel Department was split up into different sections. In a factory employing, say, about 500 people, it would be usual for the Personnel Manager himself to take on all new employees. The sources of supply are :

(*a*) Casual callers.
(*b*) Employees sent by the Ministry of Labour.
(*c*) Introductions from friends or relatives.
(*d*) Persons attracted by advertisements.

(*a*) In the first place, the *casual caller*. This is the person who, for some reason best known to himself, does not wish to go to the Employment Exchange in his search for work. Many men object to having to register with the Employment Exchange in order to get a job. Some, remembering the 1930s—Means Tests and transitional payments and unpleasant things of that kind—have sworn that they will never go near an Employment Exchange again. Others feel that they can find employment for themselves, and in touring around for a job, do so, not with the particular object of taking the first job that they find vacant, but finding somewhere that suits their idea of a reasonable place in which to be employed. (The Personnel Officer, in dealing with these applicants, has to bear in mind any limitations on engagement which may be currently in force under Statutory Orders.)

(*b*) *Employees directed by the Ministry of Labour.*—"Directed" does not necessarily mean under war-time measures of direction. These apply only to a limited number of cases, governed in the main by special engagement orders. The normal method when a person ceases to be employed at one place and is searching for work elsewhere is to go to a central spot in the locality where this information is available—that is, the Ministry of Labour Employment Exchange. Here details of every known vacancy in the locality are kept. The vacancies are filed in occupational order, and when a worker calls at the Employment Exchange for a job,

SUGGESTED PROVISION FOR WELFARE

Size of Firm	Staff	Accommodation Required

1.—Under 200 [1]: Director, manager or executive responsible, among other duties, for welfare and employment policy
Secretary-assistant (qualified in first-aid) carrying out most of the routine work
Clerk or clerical assistance (part-time)
N.B.—*Much of the work may be deputed to the secretary-assistant, in which case she will need clerical help; otherwise, in the smaller firm, she may combine the duties of secretary and records clerk, or a part-time clerk may be employed on records.*

Executive's office
Secretarial and records office
Waiting and/or interview room
First-aid room
Small extra room for interviews or committees may be an advantage

2.—200–300: Executive responsible as in (1) *or*
Personnel Officer
Secretary-assistant
Clerk
N.B.—*The firm will not be large enough to justify the employment of a nurse, unless she has also certain welfare duties. Either the Personnel Officer or secretary-assistant should be qualified in first-aid.*
Whether a separate clerk will be required will depend on the scope of the work. As in (1), it should be possible to combine the secretarial and records work.

Private office
Secretarial and records office
Waiting-room
Committee room (which can also be used for interviews)
First-aid room (with screened rest couch or separate rest room)
Store cupboard for protective clothing and first-aid supplies

3.—300–500: Personnel Officer
Secretary-assistant
Clerical assistance according to need
N.B.—*In the firm of 300+, the appointment of a Personnel Officer should be made unless an executive can devote most of his time to the work. Secretary-assistant and clerical assistant now become essential. It may be worth considering the appointment of a nurse. Normally she would not have enough to keep her busy unless there were special hazards, a part-time medical service, sick visiting, etc., and unless she assisted the Personnel Officer in certain duties. Otherwise the arrangement should be as in (2).*

Accommodation as in (2), but separate rest room is necessary.

[1] It is deliberately assumed that progress has been made in the organisation of employment, welfare and health services in this size of firm. The small firm about to consider the whole subject should seek the assistance of the Industrial Welfare Society.

FIG. 64.—Extracted from a pamphlet

Size of Firm	Staff	Accommodation Required

4.—500–1,000: Personnel Officer
Assistant
Secretary
Records clerk and other clerical assistance according to the scope of the department
Nurse

N.B.—*One of the staff should be qualified in first-aid to assist the nurse when required or to take her place when she has to go out.*

Private office
Office for assistant, secretary and records
Waiting-room
Interview room
Committee room (*this can be used as additional waiting-room or interview room*)

Surgery
Nurse's room
Waiting-room   (preferably divided for men and women)
Washrooms and w.c. for men and women
Rest room
Store for surgery supplies and protective clothing

4a.—500–1,000 (with part-time medical service):
As above, with addition of part-time medical officer, and assistant to nurse (full or part-time according to scope of work in surgery)

As above, with addition of doctor's   consulting-room and separate waiting-rooms for men and women

---

5.—1,000–3,000: Personnel Manager
Two or three assistants, with duties divided between them (e.g. employment, reinstatement, training, employee services)
Secretarial and clerical staff according to the scope of the work
Part-time Medical Officer
Nurse
Assistant nurse

N.B. (*a*)—*When clerical assistance is required in the surgery, the staff of the personnel office can usually assist. Additional nurses will be required if the firm works on shifts.*
(*b*)—*Firms in this category should consider the advisability of decentralising the work, i.e. placing certain services in the works proper instead of segregating them in the Personnel Department.*
(*c*)—*In this category, there might often be a good case for a full-time Medical Officer.*

Private office
One or more offices for assistants
Secretarial and records office
Waiting-room
Interview room
Conference room

Surgery (preferably divided into two for men and women)
Doctor's consulting-room
Nurse's office
Waiting-rooms for men and women

Washrooms and w.c. for men and women

Rest room divided for men and women
Store for surgery supplies

Store for protective clothing
Staff cloakroom

published by the Industrial Welfare Society.

he is interviewed, in the first instance, by the counter clerk and given a classification, and passed on to the Placement Officer, who, after a confidential chat, looks through the list of vacancies, firstly, in the home locality, and later in other jobs outside the radius of his own Exchange. Usually the applicant is given two or three jobs to go to before he is registered as unemployed, and an Introduction Card is issued by the Ministry, which is an introduction to the Personnel Department of the firm where the vacancy exists. The Ministry make a point of trying to place workers in the job which they want, or in the locality where they prefer to work and they will circulate particulars to exchanges within a given area, or throughout the country.

Clerical workers or office staffs are usually dealt with through the same channels, but persons in technical or managerial grades are referred to the Appointments Departments. These are situated in different regions throughout the country, and specialise in finding employment for people with managerial or specialist qualifications. They are linked up by teleprinter, and a person registering at one can be assured that his particulars will be circulated should a vacancy exist in another area. Similarly, this service to employers is a very useful one, for it means that where an important position has to be filled, details can be given to the Appointments Manager, who will pre-select applicants who appear to be suitable for the job, and send them along by appointment for interview. A large number of persons are usually registered on these Appointments Departments, although they are in work elsewhere, but waiting for a suitable opportunity at which they can be transferred to a more senior appointment or a better job, and it is not necessary for a person to be completely out of work before his particulars can be registered with the Appointments Department.

(c) *Introductions from Friends or Relatives already employed.*—Some Companies pay a great deal of attention to these introductions, and from a morale point of view it is a channel that should be considered of great importance. The goodwill of the Company has already been partly won before the employee starts work, by reason of his knowledge of conditions as gathered from his friends or relatives. He is therefore anxious to start. In some areas, particularly in many of the older industries, Companies have for generations employed father and son, mother and daughter, in the same works, and applications for employment in the Company are made when the children reach the age of twelve or thirteen. This often helps to weld employees together with the Company, and one gets the impression of it being a "family concern". Priority, generally, should be given to introduction of relatives, but a danger here to be considered is the position when an old servant or employee asks for a vacancy to be found in respect of one of his relatives, and it is not possible to do this without increasing the agreed number of employees.

(d) *Persons attracted by Advertisements.*—The method of advertising varies according to the Company's policy. Some firms prefer to place their own advertisements and give their name for interested applicants to know who they are. Others make a practice of never advertising their identity, but prefer to have a Box number; others an Advertising Agency—the advantages are that they are not bothered by people who have applied for a position and been considered unsuitable, whereas by the other method more people feel disposed to apply. The small service which should be given to all applicants for a job advertised in the Press is for the employer to take the trouble to acknowledge the application. To a person who has taken the trouble to sit down and write a letter applying for a job, it is most disheartening if, after watching the postman day after day, there is no reply to the letter he has written, whereas, for the sake of a stamp and a plain piece of paper and a plain envelope, the person may be told that his application was considered, but that his experience did not fill the qualifications desired, or that he was otherwise unsuitable. No name may even be mentioned, for the note may be typed on a plain piece of paper without any reference to the name of the employer.

Some Companies make a practice, when inserting advertisements, of saying that the job has already been offered to members of their staff, and from this one presumes that a notice has been placed in the works advertising the job without success. This is important, and is a practice which the majority of people recommend to be followed, as it does prevent people employed by the Company from replying to an advertisement inserted by their own employers—a situation which sometimes has unfortunate after-effects for the applicant.

RECEPTION ON RECRUITMENT

Having attracted the prospective employee by advertisement or introduction, we next need to see him and find out if he complies with our requirements. He also needs to see us, to find out if we can offer him the kind of employment he wants. The first impressions a new employee receives when he enters the Personnel Department—the way in which he is treated, the environment, cleanliness, lighting and heating—are all most important. The personality of the receptionist and the friendliness of the greeting do much to impress the man or woman with the attitude they are likely to meet as an employee.

To make him comfortable in a physical manner is perhaps the easiest, for one can provide a clean room with a comfortable chair, and some reading matter in case—by accident—he has to wait to be

P.P.M.—16

seen. In the interview room itself another important thing is to avoid placing the candidate so that he faces the window or other source of strong light. Interviewer and candidate should each be able to see the other comfortably and clearly.

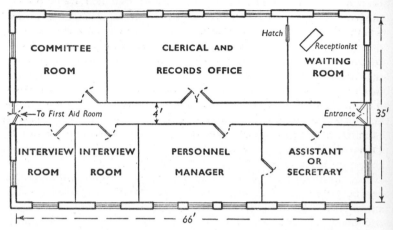

FIG. 65.—The Layout of a Personnel Department in a Small Factory.

In a small Company, the person acting as the receptionist is probably a clerk or typist, and on her would fall the job of receiving the applicant, getting from him what was required, or keeping him interested for the brief waiting period which is often unavoidable. In the large Company, the receptionist would probably be a full-time job. A good receptionist is of great value. The manner in which she receives the new-comers to the Company helps them to feel at home whilst sitting in the waiting-room. She should be able to sense the mood of the individual and be able to converse intelligently, whether the applicant is looking for a junior clerical job or for a more senior appointment. The receptionist may often serve to receive all callers as well as those for the Personnel Department, an arrangement which often makes possible the employment in the capacity of a better-grade adequately trained girl.

Contrast this with the all-too-frequent procedure that one meets—a hard chair in a draughty corridor, to which one may be directed by a gruff, uniformed commissionaire, and there left to wait until some-one decides at his convenience to see you.

Application Forms provide a useful basis for the employment interview, though opinion is divided as to whether they should be completed by the applicant in advance or by the interviewer from responses to questions put. To some extent the form needs to be related to the job, but information is a valuable guide to assessment. One would hardly think of asking for the schooling and academic qualifications, special training or professional organisations, in the case of applicants for routine labouring jobs. The information that is necessary in such cases consists of the name and address of the employee, his age, for whom he has worked in recent years, rates earned, whether he is suffering from dermatitis or any other similar industrial disease which may be influenced by the type of work being offered, reasons for leaving, military service and similar general points. On the other hand, some Companies like to have very detailed information about all their employees—they want information about families (children and ages), past national service, medals and awards. References are also required by some employers, so that details are needed of names and addresses of past employers and information about the Department or Section in which the man or woman worked, so that they can easily be traced.

For junior or technically trained people, particulars of education are important, and it is also useful to know the type of college or the subjects studied and whether they are members of any professional organisations, have special interests or the like. Information should be as complete as possible, so that it is not necessary to bother the employee to answer questions once he has been engaged and has started work. Everything that is likely to be wanted should be obtained at the original interview.

The more common method of obtaining this information is by a question and answer at the interview; getting answers to questions is not always easy, and some Personnel Managers take the view that the subject is best dealt with by having a general talk with the individual about his past experiences and the type of job he would like. The first thing to do is to put the man or woman completely at ease, perhaps by a few minutes' conversation about general topics of the day, or whether they have had a good journey (if relevant). The serious business then begins more smoothly. One method is to ask the applicant to give a brief story of what he has done since leaving school. Quite probably much information is irrelevant, particularly if he has been at work several years. The details of previous employment, reasons for leaving, comments on health, obvious physical defects, and other such points of interest are noted. During the telling of the story, the applicant gains confidence and the interview becomes quite fruitful.

Completing the Application Form before the interview is held by many to be the better practice, though it has disadvantages, particularly when dealing with clerical or senior posts; some persons are rather sensitive and object to a person of a junior status, such as a receptionist, asking them for information which they regard as confidential. It can have a bad effect on the whole of the interview if the prospective employee has been "ruffled" before he gets to the Personnel Manager. In such cases, of course, the difficulty is often overcome by having written applications in advance (through the post) and interviews held by appointment.

Another disadvantage from the prior completion of the Form may be in this, that quite early in the interview either party may learn that there is no suitable job available or no basis for considering the candidate further.

Interviews differ according to the type of job which is vacant. Generally, these fall into three categories : unskilled or skilled labour ; clerical ; sales or supervisory staff. The interviewing of unskilled labour is usually undertaken by the Personnel Manager for and on behalf of the Production Departments. The Personnel Manager does the engaging, because it is more convenient or because there is an agreement between the Production and Personnel Managers that this is the best arrangement. In all cases, however, the foreman should be asked whether he would like to see the person, and frequently it is desirable that he should be present at the interview, or should have an interview with the applicant alone. It is important to note that the underlying principle here, namely, that the foreman or manager of the department is responsible for the engagement and acceptance of the new employee, the Personnel Department acting in the capacity of agent.

By the time the foreman is called in to the interview, the Application Form should be completed and be available for his inspection, so that it is not necessary for the same questions to be gone all over again. The foreman can carry on the interview half-way through by explaining what has to be done in the department and the type of work which the prospective employee would do if employed.

There may be some differences in the routine for engaging clerical or office workers, but quite frequently in a large Company the Section Leader or Departmental Manager would interview them, whereas in a small concern they are usually taken on by the Chief Accountant or someone acting for him. The terms of their engagement are set out by letter, which offers employment or confirms the arrangements reached verbally by the interview. The testing of shorthand-typists is usual, allowances being made for errors believed to be due to nervousness.

In the case of the Sales Staff, engagement is usually dealt with by the Sales Manager, the Personnel Manager serving as an assistant and a consultant. It is becoming more common for similar service to be given in the case of responsible technical staffs engaged for the Chief Engineer or Chemist. There are Personnel Managers whose acceptance has won such confidence that they play an *active* part in all appointments, even up to senior levels. In principle this is perfectly sound, and it is so far chiefly the limited experience and outlook of many Personnel Officers that has withheld their participation in these wider responsibilities.

Contract of Employment

When an employee accepts a job, he does so in the belief that certain conditions will be kept by the employer; namely, that he will be paid his appropriate rate of pay agreed at the interview and that certain other conditions will be maintained. The exchange of service or work in return for money constitutes the contract. The employee contracts to work for an employer for a given number of hours in return for consideration by way of wages. Contracts of employment are becoming more common in this country, and it is no longer unusual for an employee to be asked to sign a form agreeing to the terms and conditions on which he is engaged.

Contracts of employment are particularly used for senior officials. Such documents usually show the date on which work is to start, the rate of pay, the amount of notice to be given, the holidays granted and similar matters about the general affairs. The acceptance of the contract is proved by the person starting work. A contract used in a small works is reproduced below:

TERMS OF EMPLOYMENT

Employment with the Company is subject to the following conditions:

1. Each employee is required to pass a standard medical examination by the Company's doctor upon engagement, and upon return to work after sickness.
2. Engagement is subject to satisfactory references being obtained.
3. Employees are required to adhere to the regulations for employees of the Company as set out in the Works Handbook provided.
4. Employees must join the Life Assurance and Pension Scheme when eligible.
5. Employment may be terminated by 44 hours' notice on either side unless otherwise agreed in writing. Notice to be given by noon Friday.

RATE OF PAY AND WEEKLY DEDUCTIONS

Wages are based on a rate of   per 44 hours worked according to the Company's time clocks.

1. *Lateness.*—Time lost during the week will be deducted at the appropriate hourly rate.
2. *Absence.*—Absence for any cause other than sickness will not be paid for.

3. *Sick Pay.*—An ex-gratia payment in respect of sick pay may be made at the discretion of the Company.

Deductions from pay are made each week for the following:

INSURANCE   SPORTS CLUB   PENSIONS[1]

I have received a copy of the Works Handbook, and agree to the above terms of employment of the Company. I authorise, also, the deductions shown above to be made from my pay each week.

SIGNATURE..

WITNESS..   DATE........................

[1] Premiums will be deducted without further notice when employees become eligible.

A corresponding illustration for office staff is in the form of a letter which embodies the following points:

The terms and conditions of the appointment are as follows:

1. *Salary.*—The initial salary will be £   per week.
2. *Hours of Work.*—Mondays to Fridays, 9 a.m.–6 p.m.
3. *Date of Starting.*—Monday, 24th October. Please bring with you Insurance Cards and Income Tax Form, and report to the Employment Department at 10 a.m.
4. *Termination of the Appointment.*—Will be subject to one clear week's notice by either side; such notice to be given by noon on Friday.
5. *Holidays.*—You will be entitled to two weeks' holiday annually, in addition to the usual Bank Holidays.
6. *References.*—The appointment is subject to our obtaining a satisfactory reference from your previous employer and to your passing a standard medical examination by the Company's doctor.
7. *Pension Scheme.*—It is a condition of employment that employees, as soon as they become eligible, shall join the Pension and Life Assurance Scheme.

We shall be glad to receive your letter confirming acceptance of the appointment, and this correspondence can then form the contract between us.

SELECTION TESTS

There has been a good deal of loose talk regarding intelligence, aptitude and other formal tests applied in the selection of employees during the past years, and a tendency to overrate their significance. The novice in Personnel Management should regard such tests with some caution, and with an eye to the many other factors involved in the assessment of the individual. Authoritative bodies, such as the National Institute of Industrial Psychology, have made it clear that they do not regard intelligence or aptitude tests as the sole, or even most important, part of good selection; any such test should be taken as one of a number of points for consideration when deciding if an applicant is suitable for a particular job.

Selection comprises the whole process of assessing a candidate for a (more or less) specific job. It should start with the basic facts set out on an application form, and may include formal intelligence and aptitude tests. It must include an interview ; this alone makes possible the interpretation of all the information and pointers about the individual, gathered from tests, application form and verbal questions. These, put together and rounded off, give a coherent and complete account of the individual, which, when related to the job in question, puts the decision as to suitability on reasonably firm ground.

It is not possible to measure mental ability directly, but that with a well-validated intelligence test some indication is attained of the effect mental ability has had in enabling a person to acquire a certain knowledge or mental skill. Thus, if a large number of people of varying ages complete an approved test, from their scores it is possible to establish a fair average for age, and, on this basis, judgment of an individual's intelligence or special aptitude can be made with a reasonable chance of accuracy by a comparison of that person's performance with the performance of others. The average performance in fact becomes the yardstick by which the individual is measured. Tests vary considerably, especially in their suitability for different ages, or even for different educational backgrounds. Most include questions centring on vocabulary, arithmetic and reasoning processes, such as shape and space tests. Many Personnel Managers have been impressed by the experiments carried out during the war years, in which a good measure of accuracy was obtained in suiting certain people for jobs in the Armed Forces. The value of tests in these circumstances became widely recognised.

Obviously, the desirability of using formal tests for selection purposes must depend on the work to be undertaken ; they are of little relevance to unskilled manual occupations, but may be of considerable significance for technical, skilled, operative or office occupations.

The design of tests is, of course, a task for the qualified psychologist. There is also a good case for their use in selection procedures to be avoided by the Personnel Manager unless he is able to call on the advice of an experienced psychologist in the choice and establishment of the tests to be used.[1]

EMPLOYEE RECORDS

The maintenance of information about the employees and the preparation of periodic reports and returns, summaries, changes and

---

[1] No reference is made here to "temperament tests," because their application to industrial selection is still in an experimental stage.

movements are among the best-known activities of any Personnel Department. It is, in fact, often said that too much attention is given to this aspect of the Department's responsibilities. In many instances, the allegation may indeed be true, but this should not be allowed to overshadow the real importance of the recording activities. Information—correct and reliable information—is a necessary basis for dealing with management problems, whether relating to individual cases or departmental matters. It is one of the essential functions of the Personnel Department to build up and maintain such information in up-to-date form. Similarly, the Department provides a service to other parts of the organisation in compiling periodic returns of employees engaged or leaving, lost time, apprentices in training and other matters of interest.

What information is recorded and what returns compiled must be determined by the needs of the organisation concerned—by the responsibilities of the Personnel Officer, reflecting the policy and aims of management. Some of the items of information that are likely to be required may be stated as follows:

(1) Personal data about individual employees prior to engagement. Source: Application Form.

(2) Any assessments made at engagement, including medical report.

(3) Employment history—transfers, promotions, wage and salary changes, etc.

(4) Absence and lost-time records.

(5) Weekly and monthly statements of engagements, losses and lost time. Analysis of terminations.

(6) Periodic returns of accidents and consequent lost time.

(7) Statements of strength, against planned requirements.

In addition, the work of the Personnel Department will necessitate the use of forms to carry out various procedures in a systematic way, for instance: requisitions of personnel wanted; advice of engagement; routine for termination.

Many methods and systems have been devised for carrying out these procedures, and no useful purpose would be served in the present context by outlining any one approach, to the exclusion of others. There is indeed a danger in suggesting anything like a "standard" form of records and procedures for a Personnel Department. Valuable guidance in designing or selecting systems may be had from publications of the Industrial Welfare Society, the Institute of Personnel Management and the British Institute of Management.

Certain fundamental points are of importance in devising a scheme:

(1) The first essential is to know clearly what activities within the Personnel Department are to be covered by the scheme, and what other departments or executives (if any) are to be brought into the procedures.

(2) Consultation with other interested parties in regard to planning the scheme will serve as a useful preliminary to its inauguration when ready. This will also ensure that the procedures are in line with the responsibilities and interrelations of the various parties concerned.

(3) Aim at simplicity in the design of all procedures and forms and records. Include only items for which there is a genuine need.

(4) Aim also at keeping the number and circulation of records and forms to the essential minimum. One copy of a notification form, for instance, can be made to circulate to two or three persons instead of each having a copy; its return to the Personnel Department will provide evidence that the necessary notifications have been made. (Many a Personnel Department has experienced the misfortune of earning the nickname of "paper-production department".)

(5) There should be a unity in the conception of a scheme of routines and records, even though various ones are introduced from time to time. There is, in fact, great value in introducing new procedures gradually, but this ought not to mean that there are discrepancies or lack of interrelation between one procedure or record and another.

(6) Wherever possible the routines of a Personnel Office should be tied in with related activities carried on elsewhere, e.g. in a Wages Office, or in a Time Recording Section. This does not mean that the Personnel Department should have control of these activities: that must depend on circumstances. It is, however, a wasteful approach to duplicate work that is already being done elsewhere, or to draw up a procedure that does not tie in with a related routine carried on in another section.

(7) Avoid "bits and pieces" of records and forms. A single visible-index record, with appropriate markings and signals, is usually much more effective if well designed than a series of records and files for each employee. Another common error in this connection is the filing, or "hoarding", of papers for which there is really no permanent use.

WAGES

The subject of "wages" provides a very good illustration of the "functional" character of the Personnel Manager's position. He cannot decide rates or earnings alone; nor can the Factory and Office Managers. Regard has to be paid to National and Local Agreements, to local conditions, to the responsibilities of the job, and to the ability of the individual. These latter aspects are the province of the Personnel

Manager, the field in which he is expected to bring to bear his specialised knowledge. It could be argued that "wages" is a subject belonging to the personnel function; but it is also a significant element in costs, and so is of major concern to the "line" executives—the more so when wages schemes include payments by way of bonus on output.

From the point of view of its position in the working of management, the question of wages needs to be considered from several aspects, which may be summarised as follows:

1. *Determining Basic Rates or Grades.*—This is a field for joint action by the Personnel Manager and the Factory Manager or Office Manager, or other appropriate "line" executive.

2. *Conformity with Agreements.*—This is an item on which the Personnel Manager is rightly to be regarded as the specialist, and the Managing Director would hold him responsible for ensuring that the Company does not go wrong under this heading. (Here the Personnel Manager's functional responsibility comes into play: if he cannot get a "line" executive to conform, he has the duty of reporting back, to secure remedial action at a higher level.)

3. *Conformity with Local Levels.*—Again an item for the Personnel Manager's special responsibility.

4. *Comparative Grading of Rates.*—This is really an aspect of the first item, and must be covered by the joint consideration of the Personnel Manager and "line" executives. The technique known as Job Evaluation or Base Rate Analysis is used in order to secure the correct comparative grading of jobs with the factory or the offices.

5. *Bonus Schemes.*—These depend upon output or some other criterion of performance and proficiency. They are closely linked up with the planning of production, and may be based on the same standards (see, for instance, Chapter IV in Part II). Hence they are primarily the province of the "line" executives concerned, with the Personnel Manager holding a watching brief.

6. *Merit Rating Awards.*—These may be regarded as an individual counterpart of the foregoing items, and responsibility for them is distributed in the same way. The Personnel Manager may, however, play a bigger part in two ways: (i) as the person who carries out the mechanics of rating, and (ii) as the safeguard against any unintentional unfairness between one individual and another.

7. *Wage and Other Payments.*—This is solely a matter of the mechanics of the Wages Office. The Personnel Manager serves as the contact between employee and Wages Office in the event of queries, discrepancies, etc.

8. *Information to Employees.*—This is an aspect in which again the Personnel Manager exercises an advisory rôle. He must ensure that

employees are properly informed of wage rates, bonus schemes, deductions, etc., at commencement with the firm or whenever changes are made. He must also assist Wages Office in securing an adequate presentation of weekly earnings and deductions on the pay-packet. Quite often, one of the Personnel Manager's most important tasks in this field is helping to make bonus schemes simple to present and easy for the employee to understand.

9. *Queries and Discrepancies.*—It is the Personnel Manager's primary responsibility to clear up doubts and difficulties raised by employees. Queries on wages, deductions, etc., are better directed to this department than to the Wages Office, and his staff should be trained in the sympathetic handling of such matters, especially in dealing with the less well-educated persons who may find genuine difficulty in understanding the compilation of a weekly wage or the correctness of income-tax deductions. The Personnel Department should see this as one of their opportunities for promoting good employee relations. (This does not mean that the Personnel Manager and his staff have to acquire detailed knowledge of wage computations, income tax, etc.; they may themselves go to the Wages Office for the explanation of a query and then "relay" it to the employee concerned.)

10. *Holidays, Sickness Schemes, etc.*—Wage payments for periods of non-working depend on the policy of the firm, and the only practical problem arising is that of the mechanics of payment.

11. *Guaranteed Week.*—This may be seen as the modern form of minimum wage legislation, supplementing a guaranteed minimum base rate for the job with a guaranteed payment for so many hours' attendance. It is, of course, the Personnel Manager's functional responsibility to see that the guarantees are honoured.

Whatever may be the importance of other non-financial factors in development of morale and contentment at work, there can be no gainsaying the basic significance of wages or remuneration for work. While most Personnel Managers will *not* subscribe to the view that "the pay packet at the end of the week" is the only, or even the chief, motive for work, they will equally recognise the primary economic motive in work. Earnings are the means of livelihood; they must, therefore, rank very high in importance to every employee. It is for this reason that difficulties and disputes so often centre on wage matters, even though the real causes of the high antagonistic feelings revealed in a dispute may be in other aspects of manager-employee relations. Wages questions are largely factual, so that there is no excuse for their being a source of difficulty or confusion within a single organisation. The Personnel Manager has here a field in which to prove the importance and value of his own functional position.

JOB ANALYSIS AND SPECIFICATION

Job analysis and specification have been described as the scientific study and statement of all the facts about a job which reveal its content and the modifying factors around it. This is a study that is of considerable value to the beginner in personnel management. As a basis there is needed a background knowledge of the structure of organisation of the Company, the functions and relationships between the different departments, the processes of the firm's products and what they are used for. The purpose of Job Analysis and Specification in relation to personnel management is for guidance in the selection, engagement or transfer of employees, but they can also serve for the benefit of training schemes and the establishment of comparative wage sales.

Maine, in his *Job Analysis for Employment Purposes*, published in 1923, gave the following four reasons for introducing Job Analysis:

(1) For improving working methods and processes.
(2) For protecting health and safety.
(3) As a basis for training employees.
(4) For employment purposes: (*a*) selection, transfer and promotion, and (*b*) the establishment of wage schedules and the adjustments and revisions.

The information given may be reproduced as a tabulated list or may be designed in a form. The details wanted are:

(1) The title of the job.
(2) The department in which the work is to be done.
(3) A description of the duties or work.
(4) The physical conditions of the job.
(5) The rate of pay, bonus or piecework.
(6) Any particular hazards, disadvantages or benefits.
(7) The length of training necessary.
(8) Opportunities for promotion.
(9) Personal qualifications required, including any special skills.

The application of job analysis and grading for the purposes of comparative rate-setting has been dealt with above in Chapter IV of Part II.

MEDICAL DEPARTMENT

This specialist section of the personnel field is still relatively unusual, though increasing numbers of firms are coming to recognise the value of its contribution, and the loss of time from illness in the normal factory is considerable, rarely less than 10 per cent. One estimate has put it as at least 270 times as great as that due to strikes or industrial upsets. Numerous studies on fatigue, ill-health, and their effect on output, have been made by research bodies, with regard to both the physiological and the psychological aspects. Bodies, such as the Industrial Health Research Board and the Tavistock Institute of Human Relations, have singled out such problems for investigation, and the latter organisation is prepared to advise firms as to ways of dealing with such problems. On the purely physical side there has already been a considerable extension of industrial medical services, which are becoming valuable assets in the pattern of industrial relations.

A Medical Officer attached to a factory, full-time or part-time, becomes the confidant of all employed, worker and management alike. The ethical doctor-patient relation must, at all times, be maintained, and everyone feel quite sure that information given to the Medical Officer at the factory will be as sacred as though given in the consulting-room of the private practitioner. Frequently, when a Medical Officer starts at a factory in a full-time capacity, he has to be prepared for a number of setbacks—to be misunderstood, and to have prejudice against him. When employees are first told they must report to the Works Doctor, they often express resentment, refuse to be examined or to have anything whatever to do with the Medical Service. This is but a passing phase, for in a short time the surgery will be full of people who wish to see the doctor or nurse on all kinds of illnesses, domestic problems, and also those seeking advice on behalf of other members of their family. The patients, finding that they can obtain information and treatment within the works, rapidly become accustomed to the idea of seeing the Works Doctor on matters which they would hesitate to take to their own practitioner. Frequently those who have objected in the strongest way are among the first to be converted.

The work of the Medical Department varies according to the size of the firm. Where only 100 or 200 employees are concerned, a Rest Room or Ambulance Room with facilities for treating minor injuries is all that is necessary, often with only part-time service from a specially trained employee. For the medium-sized firm, State Registered Nurses with industrial training may be able to give adequate service under the professional guidance of a local doctor on a part-time basis. A doctor should be employed wherever possible, if only in an advisory capacity.

The work of a Medical Department will consist of:

(a) Assisting in fitting the individual into the most suitable job.
(b) Medical examination prior to engagement.
(c) Attending minor accidents and re-dressings.

(*d*) **Giving** advice on physical working conditions with special reference to the suitability of persons.

(*e*) General advice on the health of the employees.

(*f*) Accident prevention methods, by co-operation with the Safety Officer.

(*g*) Periodical examination of all juveniles.

In large factories where considerable numbers are employed, the Medical Department (or Clinic, as it is becoming more popularly

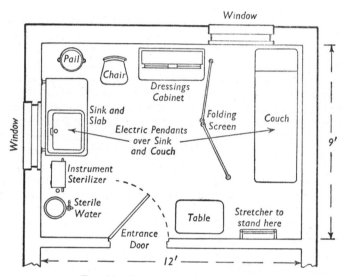

FIG. 66.—Layout of a First-aid Room.

known) covers services other than the first-aid, and many now include dentistry, ophthalmology, chiropody and electrotherapy.

Medical Examination before Engagement

Medical examination before employment should be the aim of all employers in industry. It induces turnover by making sure that the people taken into the Company's employ are physically suitable for the job, and creates contentment amongst the workers, because each employee himself is able to do work which he is asked and the heavy jobs do not fall on a few, the burden being equally shared. Some people occasionally object to being medically examined; when this happens, the Personnel Manager should make a point of explaining to the applicant that it is in his own interests, because the Medical Officer has the knowledge to see how the individual can undertake the work. Applicants for employment should always have an appointment made for them with the Medical Officer, so that waiting is avoided.

Medical Examination during Employment

Some Companies insist on employees reporting back to the Medical Department if they have been away ill; this is a wise precaution, for there are a number of people who will return to work long before they are physically capable of renewing their normal job. Some try to return because of the money factor: having families to support, they are anxious to resume their normal earnings without delay. Others do it from the point of view of loyalty to the Company, feeling that they are letting the firm down by being absent, if only for a few days. When an employee returns to work after being ill, he should not normally be allowed to start until he has seen a member of the medical staff. This is for two reasons: firstly, to ensure that the individual is physically able to do his normal job, and secondly, to protect other employees from possible lingering infection. A third subsidiary reason is to make possible the completion of the Medical History Record. Close liaison is always required here between the Personnel Department and the Medical Staff, and particularly if the illness has been severe and necessitates transfer to other work, maybe in a category where a lower level of pay is normally applicable. Where an employee is unfit for the job, he should be told so by the Works Medical Officer. It may be that the reason for unsuitability is one which the man would not wish to be made public, and the Personnel Department need only know that he is medically unfit for the work for which he was employed. A special problem for the Personnel Officer is created if there should happen to be no other suitable job immediately available.

Disabled Persons

Disabled persons should always be under the care of the Medical Officer and notice taken of the job on which they are engaged. A visit in the works to the man on his job is greatly appreciated, and on these occasions the Medical Officer should make sure that the work being done by a disabled person is within his limits.

CHAPTER V

PHYSICAL WORKING CONDITIONS

*Information. Recreation. Canteens. Amenities. Heating and Ventilation.
Lighting. Factory Legislation. Other Legislation regarding Employment.
Safety and the Safety Officer*

INFORMATION

Booklets

THE practice of issuing a booklet to employees giving them information about the factory, working conditions, rules and other information is becoming increasingly popular.[1] The handbook is given to the employee on starting work; no charge is made and it remains his property. Sometimes supplementary booklets are issued to cover such subjects as Safety, Joint Consultation arrangements, Fire Precautions, Contributory Schemes and Pensions, etc. As a matter of principle any handbook of information for employees should always be prepared in conjunction with employee representatives and it is particularly important to have joint agreement on the conditions of employment and regulations, etc., which are published. Personnel Managers will know that, so far as Union members are concerned, it is not possible to alter works rules or impose new conditions of employment without prior consultation.

Notice Boards

A notice board is a useful method of distributing current information, for most employees find time to look at it either in the break period or at the end of the day. The practice of having separate notice boards for various items is not advisable. It is better to have in each Department one notice board which covers all information: it can be divided into sections—one for official notices or announcements from the Company of interest to the employees in general, e.g. appointments of the Board, the financial results of the Company, and similar general announcements; another for departmental notices, to include minutes of Committee and other meetings, shift lists, special instructions for dealing with the product, changes in hours or working conditions, or other items agreed at joint discussions. A Trade Union section would be placed at the disposal of

---

[1] The Institute of Personnel Management have published a broadsheet entitled "Preparing an Employees' Handbook", which deals in detail with the type of matter to be covered in such booklets.

the shop stewards in the department, who would be entitled to place any notice on that section which referred to the activities of the branch of which employees of the Company were members. There would need to be some policy agreed with the shop stewards as to the type of notice which might or might not be placed on the board; for example, it would be undesirable for a notice to be posted in one Company asking for pickets to be provided for another Company, the employees of which were on strike. Similarly, political notices would be banned. A Sports Club section would be at the disposal of the Sports and Social Clubs, to cover announcements of dances, amateur dramatic and theatrical shows, and any other items of sporting or social interest to the Company's employees.[1]

Magazines

The practice of issuing a magazine or news letter is also one that has been more widely developed in recent years. Quite simple leaflets are used in some firms, while large organisations with a big pay-roll that justifies the higher expenditure go in for an expensive booklet with many photographs, and printed on good paper with a stiff cover. The contents will be current information about the firm and its people, including topical items, family news, etc.; also sports results and club announcements. The more elaborate magazines, issued monthly or quarterly, have articles written by employees as well as special contributions, either dealing with problems particular to the industry and the work of departments in the Company, or with wider contemporary events. Much thought and a great deal of detailed work are involved in producing a magazine of this kind, and it should never be started until the basic material for three or four editions is in hand or in sight.

The problem of whether to give these publications away or to sell them to employees is one which needs to be dealt with in each individual concern. There is no doubt that the majority of employees find them interesting and instructive, and where a factory consists of many departments, they can be of considerable educational value by descriptions of the work done in the various parts of the organisation, and by the news given about them.

A few firms adopt the practice of contracting with a publishing house, who specialise in works magazines, to supply them with a given quantity of a general magazine in which the majority of the material is written by well-known writers, and two or three pages are

---

[1] A suitable notice board can be made from hardboard about 8 feet long by 3 feet wide and divided into strips, allowing approximately 2 feet for each of the sections. A suitable heading piece with the name of the Company might quite well be added. Paint in a distinctive colour: cream and red have been found both attractive and serviceable.

specially inserted covering domestic matters pertaining to the Company. The main advantage of this method is relative cheapness.

RECREATION

Sports Clubs

Sports Clubs attached to factories and commercial organisations seem to be more popular in the Midlands and the North of England than they are in the South. This is possibly due to the fact that in the Midlands and North, employees, generally speaking, live nearer to their work than in other areas. Many of the big London commercial houses, however, have had flourishing sports grounds for a good many years.

It is usual for the Company to provide ground, or, where the numbers do not warrant this, to give financial assistance to facilitate a link-up with other sports organisations in the area. But the Company should not seek to exercise control over the activities. Running expenses are met by voluntary subscriptions from employees who participate, supplemented by the proceeds of dances, musical and dramatic shows, socials and concerts—especially when the club premises carry a licence!!

The usual constitution of a social club is in the form of a committee elected by members, i.e. interested employees, with the addition of one or two representatives of the Company, often an Accountant and a Personnel Manager, to maintain liaison with the Company, to provide secretarial service and to assist the club generally. The management and finances of the club should be in the hands of a strong Committee. Each section should prepare a budget, and expenditure above this amount must be subject to approval by the whole Committee. The accounts should be audited half-yearly and a statement made by the auditors. Any item covered by Company payments should be included, so that members do not take them for granted.

The sectional interests—social, educational, different games and sports—can best be served by sub-committees which have a responsibility for planning, but which report back to the main Committee. An Annual General Meeting of members should be held and a report made of the activities and progress during the year.

In a small Company it is usual for one of the employees to act as secretary and to do all the necessary work in connection with the club, receiving telephone calls and visitors with the permission of the management. But where a large number of employees are concerned, it has been known for the club to be looked after by a full-time secretary, whose wages and other administrative costs would be paid by the Company, though perhaps with some arrangement for offsetting the Club profits.

CANTEENS

Under the Statutory Rules and Orders No. 373, it is essential for canteens to be provided where the number of employees exceeds 250. The nature and extent of the accommodation will necessarily vary a great deal. This is a rather specialised field, and a Personnel Manager would be well advised not to rely entirely on his own knowledge and judgment. A body like the Industrial Welfare Society provides specialist information and assistance in this direction to its member-firms, and there are also professional firms of Catering Consultants or Contractors.

A canteen need not be elaborate; neither need great expense be incurred, and with very small firms a mess-room with tea facilities is often better than nothing.[1]

A few general points may be recorded as a matter of interest:

1. *The Main Meal.*—This may be the midday dinner or might quite well be breakfast or supper in the case of shift workers. The main meal is usually meat or fish and vegetables with a sweet. The amount of food and the way in which it is cooked are usually of greater importance to the working man than the way it is served. On the other hand, office workers seem to prefer a smaller meal served in pleasant surroundings.

2. *Snacks.*—Snacks, consisting of tea and cakes, sandwiches or rolls and butter, are sold by the canteen in the morning and afternoon breaks. In some factories tea trolleys are employed in order to take the food to the workers, who are able to eat it by their machines, whereas other managements find it more convenient for employees to go to the tea stations set up in the departments or to the main canteen.

3. *Tea.*—Tea is usually made in urns. Some of these, known as thermal urns, will keep tea hot for as long as eight hours. This is very helpful, particularly where it is necessary to make the tea in the canteen and to distribute it around the works if the area to be covered is great.

Cleanliness in scalding out the urns after use is most important, and a frequent cause of complaint about the quality of the tea may be traced to the improper cleaning of the urn. Tea is one of the most profitable products of the canteen, but at the present time the regulations of the Ministry of Food make it impossible to improve the standard beyond certain limits.

[1] The Official Factory Department Welfare Pamphlet No. 2, entitled "Mess Rooms and Canteens in Small Factories", will be found most helpful in giving details of the equipment and accommodation.

4. *Cleanliness.*—A Personnel Manager should always insist on cleanliness being a most important factor in the canteen. There should always be provision for the washing of hands by employees who are engaged in the plating or handling of food in any way. A wash basin with hot and cold water should be in the centre of the kitchen and a good supply of soap and towels should be available. Epidemics can be passed on to a large number of people through contamination of food, and the recent drive by the Ministry of Health for cleanliness in catering establishments should be observed.

5. *Outside Catering.*—As catering is a specialised field, some Companies have found it advantageous to place their catering in the hands of outside specialists. It is usual for the Company itself to provide the premises and equipment, and for the caterer to provide the meals and service to the Company's requirements, taking all profits. An advantage of this system is that the Company is able to have a fixed amount set aside for catering, whereas in most instances when they do their own catering there is an indefinite loss, sometimes of considerable amount.

6. *Canteen Committees.*—Canteen Committees representative of employees are usually a source of great help, particularly in dealing with the day-to-day problems and grumbles which arise. Committees of this kind need to be positive in their action, as well as being the safety-valve for complaints and the source of investigations.

AMENITIES

Lavatories

Legal requirements with regard to lavatories both for men and women are defined in Section 46 of the Factories Act, which sets out the minimum standard. There are also local authority prescriptions to be taken into account. The field of factory hygiene is one now becoming recognised as a good mirror to reflect the attitude of management; the factory with a good policy and good executives wisely provides pleasant amenities, realising the value of their contribution to morals.

The amount of space devoted to this purpose and the cost entailed need not be great. Location and convenience of access are important, particularly bearing in mind means of avoiding congestion, the proximity of cloakrooms, etc. To some extent, so far as washing facilities are concerned, the nature of the work and the needs of the very dirty departments may affect planning.

In some organisations the provision of sanitary accommodation has been laid before a Works Committee for consideration.

Cloakrooms

Since a cloakroom is where the employee keeps outdoor clothing for the time he is at work, the most satisfactory method is to have a steel cabinet handy to where he is working. This, however, is not always practicable, although a bank of steel cabinets can often usefully be employed as a screen within the factory. Where general accommodation is being provided, the cloakroom should be a self-contained unit which can be locked up at a given time each morning and only opened at leaving-off time. This is probably the only way in which petty thieving or pilfering can be satisfactorily stopped. Some employers have numbered containers in cloakrooms, and have so arranged these that clock number and cabinet number tally. The manner in which the employees' clothes are to be kept depends to a certain extent on the amount of space available. The Factory Department Welfare Pamphlet on cloakrooms gives examples of clothing suspended from the ceiling or placed in containers. The more crude method of hanging hats and coats on pegs, which should be at least 18 inches apart, is still to be found in some works. The Factories Act requires that clothing is to be dried whilst the employee is at work, a point which is often overlooked; so the cloakroom needs to be heated—a point which raises but little trouble to add an additional radiator or two where steam is employed in the factory.

There should always be seats on which the employees can change their shoes; this does not mean anything more elaborate than a form or seat attached to a wall.

Whether a cloakroom attendant is employed full-time will depend on the number of people using the facilities. It is of great advantage, particularly where large numbers of women are employed, to have someone in charge of the lavatories and cloakrooms and available throughout the day. One aspect which needs to be carefully watched is to make sure that the cloakroom attendant does not usurp the duties of the medical staff by attempting to "doctor" female employees who may feel ill, instead of referring them to the nurse, from whom they could receive proper attention. This is a small point, but it is one which should be made abundantly clear to the cloakroom attendant at the time of her engagement.

The responsibility for lavatories and cloakrooms falls to the Personnel Manager, and it is a good plan to have the lavatory cleaners and attendants made directly responsible to him, to enable him to maintain high standards of cleanliness.

Complaints are sometimes heard from management that the employees do not appreciate decent lavatories and that they wilfully despoil them. This is not usually proved by facts, for where a high standard is provided and the shop stewards or other representatives of the men and women are asked to co-operate, they take a pride in keeping the lavatories and cloakrooms in the same condition as they would if they were at home.

HEATING AND VENTILATION

The importance of adequate ventilation has latterly been realised more than ever before, partly as an outcome of the blackout conditions which were enforced so rigidly during war-time, and partly because it has been widely realised that heating and ventilation are closely interrelated. One of the major problems in older factories has been "draughts," often giving rise to industrial unrest, poor morale and a sense of grievance in employees when nothing is done by management to relieve the unsatisfactory conditions. Lift shafts can be a particularly troublesome item in winter, as also are open doors where loading or unloading of vans or lorries has to be undertaken.

To ensure a comfortable and healthy working atmosphere, it is necessary to provide a definite circulation of air, warmed to a given temperature and evenly distributed throughout the factory. Fans drawing in cold air only may be worse than useless in severe weather conditions, and may easily exaggerate an already difficult situation. One method of introducing an adequate amount of air into a factory without causing draughts is by means of a fresh-air inlet fan, air-heating batteries controlled by modulating thermostats, and ranges of air distribution trunking fitted with draughtless air diffusers at regular intervals. With this system, the vitiated air from the factory can be extracted at high level, through ring-mounted exhaust fans, fitted in the walls or roofs. A plant of this type ensures an even temperature throughout. There is air movement over the entire factory, without cause of discomfort to the workers. Location of the plant above truss level ensures the saving of valuable floor space. The maintenance entailed on this equipment is small compared with a system made up of separate units.

Experience has proved it necessary to provide four changes of air per hour through the summer months and to make provision for recirculating during the winter a percentage of warmed air, as conditions allow. This may not prove suitable in all cases, particularly with work which involves hot processes; here it is better to have cold air under pressure a short distance above the employees' heads; or alternatively, on trunking with a swivelled funnel, so that it can be directed by the operator at his discretion.

The solution adopted in one case is an example of what can be done by a large Company to provide adequate ventilation:

The floor space of the main factory covers an area of approximately 200,000 square feet, and comprises eleven main bays, four of which are of the lofty travelling-crane type. Roofing materials are all of light construction, and insulation of the outer shell of the factory is poor.

To provide a temperature of 60 deg. F. throughout, in conditions of 30 deg. F. outside, the losses through the fabric of the building amounted to approximately 10,000,000 British Thermal Units per hour.

It was decided to provide equipment capable of diffusing four air changes per hour, with 50 per cent. of the air being returned to the plant and mixed with fresh air for re-heating to the required temperature. On this basis, under the coldest conditions, the highest temperature of the air being diffused into the factory was calculated at 95 deg. F. The total heat requirements were then found to be within the spare capacity of the existing boiler equipment, which comprised five Lancashire steam boilers, with a working pressure of 100 lb. per square inch.

Twelve plants were installed, having a total capacity of 10,800,000 cubic feet of air per hour. High-efficiency axial-flow fans, directly connected to totally enclosed motors, enabled the equipment to be accommodated above truss level. Fresh air was drawn from suitable positions, well above the floor level or through the end walls of the factory. Adjustable air-mixing dampers were fitted in the fresh-air intakes, to enable the percentage of the warmed air to be re-circulated. For warming the air to the required temperature, copper gilled-type air-heating batteries, served with steam at 100 lb. pressure per square inch, were installed on the discharge side of the fans, with thermostatic control. This control was provided by modulating motorised valves operating in conjunction with room-type thermostats, the latter being set to a predetermined temperature. Each centralised plant was carried on a steel grillage supported above the roof trusses.

From the air-heating batteries, ranges of steel sheet trunking were fixed on wrought-iron cradles, having circular double-cone air diffusers and adjustable air-deflecting louvres. The air distributors were zoned to cover the entire floor area of the factory. They were designed to eliminate uncomfortable draughts. To avoid all shadow they were arranged at a suitable height above the factory lighting.

To deal effectively with the high travelling-crane bays previously mentioned, the main air distribution trunking was fixed above truss level. Rectangular branch ducts were carried down from it to within 13 feet of the floor, and were terminated with adjustable air-deflecting louvres. The branch ducts were so arranged as to conform with the width of the vertical stanchions supporting the crane rails, thus eliminating any obstruction.

The exhaust system comprised approximately forty ring-mounted propeller fans, direct-coupled to totally enclosed motors of the fractional horse-power type. Each fan is mounted in the highest point of the roof, and each is wired independently to a hand-operated push-button starting switch.

From the existing boilers, steam and condensate mains were carried at

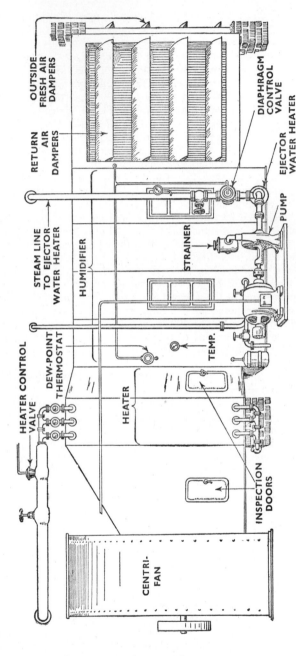

FIG. 67.—Illustration of Main Heating Unit.

(*Adapted from Ministry of Labour and National Service Pamphlet No. 5 by permission of the Controller of H.M. Stationery Office.*)

high level, with connections taken off to the air-heating batteries. The opportunity was taken, at the same time, to reorganise all steam-using appliances in the factory, and to bring all condensate back to the boilers through the new mains.

A great variety of old equipment was disconnected and salvaged when the new plants were brought into commission. Heaters of many different types, accumulated over many years, and operated by gas, electricity, hot water and steam, were all removed. An important incidental effect was that a considerable fire-risk was removed with some of the heaters. Cosy corners and cold patches gave way to evenly warmed floor space, constant change of atmosphere and no draughts.

The heating and ventilation of a modern woodworking shop, attached to the same factory, are assisted by the use of wood chips, shavings and sawdust, which are extracted from the various machines and conveyed to a separate boiler-house, there to be utilised for fuel, etc. The heating and ventilating equipment is similar to the installation previously described, the fan being designed to provide an output of approximately 10 per cent. in excess of the air being exhausted through the conveying plant. The air is warmed by an air-heating battery served with steam from the boiler plant, and is thermostatically controlled by a modulating motorised valve and room-type thermostat. From the air-heating battery, sheet steel trunking—rectangular in section—is fixed at ceiling level to give maximum head room, and is fitted with adjustable air-deflecting louvres. The air is diffused evenly throughout, and is extracted at various points at floor level through the exhaust system, thus ensuring a balanced distribution of air.

All these installations maintain comfortable conditions during both summer and winter throughout the factory, and the running costs are low. In workshops, where fumes, smells and metallic dust were always in suspension in the atmosphere, clean warm air is now the rule; and it is no longer necessary to have a permanent "fog" in cold weather, nor to dodge from one cold spot to the next. As a result the incidence of colds and infections should be substantially reduced.

It is perhaps of importance to emphasise that heating and ventilating is a specialist technological field about which the Personnel Officer should have general knowledge, but in which he should not lay claim to expert views unless he is qualified to do so by adequate training.

LIGHTING

Piccadilly Circus Station on London's Underground is most noticeable to travellers because of its intensity and colour of lighting, equivalent to daylight. The effect of good lighting in a factory is twofold: the benefit to output from clearer vision and the benefit to morale through the effect on the individual. Few conditions are more irritating than those associated with bad lighting, whether due to insufficient illumination or incorrect placing of the fittings.

The Factories Act provides certain minima, but these are low—too low for good and efficient working. As a guide to managers, the Illuminating Engineering Society has laid down certain standards as follows:

RECOMMENDED VALUES OF ILLUMINATION FOR SELECTED INDUSTRIAL OCCUPATIONS

(Extracted from the Code Published by the Illuminating Engineering Society)

	Lumens per sq. ft.
Assembly:	
Very small	100
Small	50
Ordinary	10
Large	7
Carpets:	
Weaving, designing, Jacquard card cutting, tapestry setting and beaming, mending, sewing and fringing . . .	20
Clothing Manufacture:	
Cutting, sewing, inspecting medium colours . . .	20
Pressing	10
Cotton Industry:	
Weaving, dark colours, fine counts	30
Light colours, fine counts	20
Grey cloth	10
Spinning, bale breaking, blowing, carding, combing, conditioning, twining, roving, slubbing, doubling (plain) .	7
Food Manufacturing and Preserving:	
Inspecting and grading	50
Refining, mixing, blending, cleaning, sweet making and confectionery	10
Bottling, canning, packing, flour-milling, bakehouses and cutting benches	10
Glass Works:	
Fine inspection and glass cutting (cut glass) . . .	50
Bevelling, decorations, etching, fine grinding and inspection	20
Cutting glass to size, glass-blowing machines, grinding, pressing and silvering	10
Furnace rooms and mixing	5
Hosiery:	
Lockstitch and overlocking machines:	
Dark	30
Light	15
Mending, examining and hand-finishing:	
Dark	50
Light	20

Lumens per

Hosiery—continued.   *sq. ft.*
    Circular and flat knitting machines, universal winders, cutting
        out, folding and pressing   15
    Linking of running on   .   .   .   .   .   Special Lighting

Inspection (General):
    Minute   200
    Very small   100
    Small   50
    Fairly small   20
    Ordinary   10

Machine and Fitting Shops:
    Very small bench and machine work, tool and die making,
        gauge inspection and precision grinding   100
    Small bench and machine work, medium grinding, setting
        automatic machines   50
    Fairly small bench and machine work, rough grinding .   .   20
    Ordinary bench and machine work   10

Shoe and Boot Manufacturing:
    Stitching, inspecting and sorting   20
    Cutting, hand turning, lasting and welting, miscellaneous
        bench and machine work   15
    Closing and clicking .   .   .   .   .   .   Special Lighting

Woodworking:
    Fairly small bench and machine work, fine sanding and
        finishing   20
    Cooperage, gluing, medium machine and bench work,
        planning rough sanding, sizing, veneering and pattern-
        making   15
    Sawmills   7

Woollen and Worsted Industry:
    Perching   70
    Burling and mending   50
    Weaving fine worsteds   50
    Weaving medium worsteds and fine woollen   .   .   .   30
    Weaving heavy woollen   10
    Warping, including balloon warping and warp dressing   .   20
    Spinning (mule and frame), winding, cropping, sorting
        (including rag sorting and grinding), combing (coloured),
        twisting (doubling)   15

Fluorescent lighting is now used extensively, and the wide area
of light which this gives has made it most popular in factories.
Great advances have been made in obtaining a pure white light or
imitation daylight. The provision of light and the type of fittings and
standards are usually the responsibility of the electrical department.

but the Personnel Manager will be expected to express an opinion from the human standpoint and to deal with complaints which arise from poor lighting. Glare is often the cause of complaint, and is due to the effect of looking directly at a bright source of light, or at a direct reflection from a shiny surface. Vision is temporarily impaired, maybe not seriously, but with sufficient inconvenience to deflect attention from the job, and it is also a source of fatigue. Glare can usually be avoided quite easily by a change of working position.

For some types of close machine work it is usual to have what is known as local lighting, which is a low-voltage bulb fixed in such a position that it throws a light directly on to the machine. This has an important advantage, as it precludes any shadow being thrown on the work.

It need hardly be said that wherever daylight can be obtained, it should be provided in preference to artificial, however good. The cleaning of windows on a regular service basis will often provide additional daylight. Stacking boxes and goods against windows should be vigorously watched as a channel of serious loss of natural light.

The foregoing are points of general interest to the Personnel Officer or other manager. Lighting, again, is a special technical field in which the Personnel Officer cannot and should not pretend to be an expert—unless adequately qualified by appropriate technical training.

FACTORY LEGISLATION

The history of the legislation by Statute and by Orders, governing the conditions of work in factories, has long been a major item in the training of the Personnel Officer. One hundred and fifty years have provided the stage for that story, since the Health and Morals Act of 1802, and for more than a century there has been a Factories Inspectorate to watch over the administration of the legislation. But the average Manager or Personnel Manager to-day is in a position where he is concerned with a level of conditions far above that prescribed: in other words, the Factories Acts are still of interest in detail primarily to those few employers—often in the smaller firms— who are unable to grasp the wisdom of high standards as an incentive to good work, and need the pressure and the threat of a penalty to conform even to the bare outline of officially prescribed minima.

The Personnel Officer needs to know his way about the Factories Act and the related legislation, including the Statutory Rules and Orders. To know these in detail is not an essential item in his competence, but he needs to know where to turn for this and that: it is no part of the function of the present volume to attempt to cover ground that is already well provided for in other publications, including the official *Guide to the Factories Acts* (H.M.S.O.).

A word on the position of the Factories Inspector may be in place. For most employers and managers, he or she has long ceased to be but the shadow of the law, something like an un-uniformed policeman. To their great credit, the Staff of the Factories Department have kept well abreast of new developments in the field of employment and personnel relations, and have been able to render invaluable help both to Personnel Officers and to the many concerns which have not been able to develop their own personnel executive. Moreover, the department has gone to the length of establishing a specialist "Personnel Management Advisory Service" (since transferred to a parallel department) in order to be able to extend the scope of the assistance that they can render in the improvement of conditions and the betterment of employee morale.

The Annual Report of H.M. Chief Inspector of Factories has in recent years been not so much a vindication of the strong arm of the law as an annotated commentary on the progress of Britain's proficiency in the practice of personnel management.

OTHER LEGISLATION REGARDING EMPLOYMENT

Of the legislation regarding employment to which the Personnel Officer is most likely to refer, the Truck Act is probably one of the foremost.

The *Truck Act* was first passed in 1831, and was subsequently amended in 1887, 1896 and again in 1940. The object of the Act is to prevent an employer paying the wages of his workers in kind. That is to say, he must pay the employee the total amount of his wages, and cannot make deductions from them for food and tools or things of this kind. Another stipulation which is made by the Act is that the employee must be free to spend his money with whom he likes, and the employer cannot give directions to him as to where the wages are to be spent.

It should be understood, however, that certain deductions may be made providing there is a contract in writing signed by the workman. The deductions to which he can lawfully agree are:

(*a*) Medicine or medical attention.
(*b*) Fuel.
(*c*) Materials, tools or implements if employed in mining.
(*d*) Provender to be consumed by a horse or other beast of burden used by the workman.
(*e*) Rent of a house let by the employer to the workman.

(*f*) Victuals dressed or prepared under the roof of the employer and there consumed by the workman.

Provision is made in the Act that the amount deducted for any of the above items must not exceed the real and true value of the goods, etc., supplied. Where it is a condition of employment that deductions may be made for the loss of tools or scrapped work and similar matters, the employer must keep posted in the workshop a copy of the notice.

The employer must give particulars of the amount of fines or deductions and must be fair and reasonable. The employee is entitled to have details of the specific amounts deducted. There have been a number of cases in connection with this matter, but Bird and the British Celanese in 1945 and Pratt *v*. Cook & Son in 1940 were two which were given a good deal of publicity in the Press. In the case of Pratt, it was decided that the workman could recover the amount of such deductions for a period longer than the statutory period of limitation which is six years, and in the case in point, deductions for a period of the preceding twenty years were repaid.

In the ordinary course of events, a deduction from wages in respect of damaged work, tools or the like can only be recovered by the employee provided he commences his proceedings within six months from the date of deduction.

Disabled Persons Employment Act, 1944

The Disabled Persons Employment Act was passed in 1944, and provides that the Minister of Labour may instruct employers to take on a standard percentage of disabled persons. The standard percentage is now fixed at 3 per cent. under S.R.O. 1258. All employers are obliged to keep a register of disabled people in their employ, and a factory employing 1,000 people would have to find jobs for at least thirty who had registered as disabled persons.

Disablement does not necessarily mean the loss of a limb. All registered disabled persons carry with them a card showing that they have registered at the Ministry of Labour and are regarded as coming within the scope of the Act. It is important to note that an employer may not discharge a disabled person if by doing so he would bring the number of disabled persons employed below the standard percentage.

Reinstatement in Civil Employment Act, 1944

This Act provided that a person who had undergone a period of war service and who, on release from that service, desired to return to his pre-war civil employment, was entitled to reinstatement by his former employers subject to conditions and qualifications laid down in the Act. This Act will also apply to youths called to compulsory military service, and employers must give the same facilities of reinstatement whether an employee volunteered or was conscripted.

The Act provides for the employee to do certain things. He must apply for reinstatement on Form RE1 which he obtains from his demobilisation centre, or Employment Exchange. The application must be made within a period of four weeks of the end of his demobilisation leave, and he must be prepared to accept an alternative job if, due to circumstances beyond the control of the employer, there is no longer work available for him in his old job or occupation. Should the employer refuse to reinstate him or offer reinstatement in a position which is worse than previously held, the employee may refer his case to an Appeal Board, who have power to award either reinstatement or payment of compensation in lieu of reinstatement. The Reinstatement Committee have wide powers to exercise their discretion on the question of awarding compensation.

Should either party be aggrieved at the decision given by the Reinstatement Committee, the case can then be referred to an umpire. His decision is final, and certain selected decisions are published at various intervals by the Stationery Office.

The effect of the Act applies to any class of employee called to National Service, and where necessary a person engaged may have to be discharged in order to provide a job for the returning ex-forces employee.

SAFETY AND SAFETY OFFICER

One of the most important functions of modern industrial management is that of maintaining safe working conditions within the undertaking, with a continuous effort to prevent accidents when and wherever possible. During the past ten years, and especially during the 1939–1945 war, it became appreciated, owing to labour shortages, that accidents to employees were a serious drain on production, and consequently, like medical practice and treatment, the science of "accident prevention" made great progress. Enquiries into high accident rates revealed all-too-frequent physical or mechanical causes.

Accident prevention is the responsibility of management, and in a large number of industrial undertakings this responsibility rests with the Personnel Department or Manager. In some, however, depending on the size of the undertaking and type of plant installed, the carrying out of this function is delegated to a specialist known as the Works Safety Officer or Accident Prevention Officer or Plant Safety Engineer.

Under the Building (Safety, Health & Welfare) Regulation, 1948, an employer employing more than fifty persons on building work is required to nominate a Safety Officer or "competent person". Thus, for the first time in industrial history, such person is given an official status, but in other industries it still remains the prerogative of the owner of the undertaking to decide how his accident prevention policy shall be put into effect and by whom. Opinion may differ as to the "line" of responsibility of such an officer, whether full-time or part-time. There is a good case to be made out for his being responsible to either the Personnel Manager or the Works Executive. The stronger argument is on the side of the latter—pinning on to the executive managers clear responsibility for safe working, with the specialist assistance provided. In the larger process plants, such as chemical works, steel works and so on, there is an equal case for "line" responsibility to the Chief Engineer, with functional liaison with the Personnel Manager.

The Safety Officer should be a man of qualities rather than qualifications; his efficiency and sincerity of purpose should be above question, and he should possess moral courage to a high degree, and so command respect of those with whom he comes into contact. He should be a good mixer. Technically, he must have had good experience of the industry in which he is employed, with an aptitude for approaching all his problems with a detached, impersonal and common-sense attitude.

The size of the undertaking and the nature of the process will determine whether he shall be a full-time Safety Officer or one who carries out safety work in conjunction with other responsibilities. Where there exists a well-developed Personnel Department, the need for a full-time safety specialist is often reduced.

Broadly, the functions of the Safety Officer may be described as the prevention of accidents by:

(a) Routine inspection of plant, buildings, gangways, materials, etc.

(b) Creating an active interest in safe working by means of propaganda.

(c) Training employees and advising members of the Supervisory Staff in methods of safe working.

(d) The supervision of works employees in respect of protective equipment and clothing, and compliance with works safety regulations.

(e) Advice, from the safety standpoint, on plant, layouts of shops, working methods, conditions, etc.

(f) Analysis of accidents and keeping historical (statistical) records.

Naturally, many of his activities have a direct relation to the requirements of the Factories Act (1937) and the Factory Orders, together with any special regulations for safety issued from time to time by the Minister; it is therefore highly important that he should have a comprehensive and up-to-date knowledge of them to a standard where he is in a position to advise management. Responsibility for compliance with legal requirements rests clearly on management, as the representative of the Board or the owner, and it cannot be passed on to, or usurped by, the Safety Officer.

The important obligation of maintaining good relations between a Company and H.M. Factory Inspectorate should be a particular feature of the Safety Officer's duties by reason of his knowledge of the Acts, his specific industrial experience, as well as his intimate knowledge of the reasons for any accident that may occasion an investigation by H.M. District Inspector.

His association with the Personnel Department facilitates the routines attaching to his work, such as attending to Insurance Claims and making reports to H.M. District Inspector of Factories and the Ministry of National Insurance. This functional contact will also be of value in cases where legal proceedings ensue or where an accident gives rise to any strong feelings among employees. There is, too, a further advantage: the Safety Officer is, strictly speaking, a *technical* man whose particular qualifications lie in his knowledge of the plant and equipment and of the regulations. There is, however, a large *human* element, both in the cause of accidents and in the promotion of accident prevention: this is a fact on which the Personnel Officer is much better able to be the source of knowledge and advice. A safety scheme should never overlook the possibility of "accident-proneness" or other factors in the personal make-up of some individual employees who may sustain injury in circumstances which may have left other individuals unharmed. The investigation of any accident should always include—on the initiative of the Personnel Officer —reference to the purely human aspect.

In regard to the official requirement and procedures under factory and insurance legislation, the most desirable arrangement would appear to be:

(*a*) Primary responsibility vested in the Personnel Manager.

(*b*) Detailed work managed by the Safety Officer, where appointed.

(*c*) Liaison with factory and technical executives, as safety is part of their normal "human responsibilities".

In all aspects of his work, liaison with the Medical Clinic by the Safety Officer is all-important, for it is through the medium of "case" reports and records that he will get indication of accident trends, and the statistics so necessary in indicating the accident potential. He should make a daily visit to the clinic to study the Minor Accident Log Sheets, abstracting from them such information as may be necessary for him to carry out investigations. Of course, he plays no part in the treatment of "cases".

The keeping of statistical records is important, especially in the form of graphs and charts, so that the appropriate steps are taken to investigate and correct any adverse trends at the earliest opportunity.

Liaison with the Surgery or Medical Department is an important factor in the human aspect of safety, to which reference was made above. The doctor or nurse may often be well placed to collaborate with the Safety Officer (and perhaps with the Personnel Officer himself) in the approach to the individual cases of recurrent accidents, having features which suggest that the cause lies in the human element instead of in the mechanical. In one engineering factory, recently, negligence in this direction allowed a young lad of sixteen and a half to persist on the same machine job without anyone bothering to make special enquiries, although he had attended at the clinic seventeen times in eight months for minor cuts and injuries!

The efficiency of a safety or accident prevention scheme depends on the co-operation of employees as well as on the skill of the Safety Officer. This is often a matter of training. Some Companies incorporate training in safe working with their "Training within Industry" schemes; others use the discussion group method; but none of these methods can be more effective than informal talks to employees on the job, and instructive discussions with supervisors. A short informal talk to new entrants is useful to point out the specific hazards associated with the work upon which the employees are to be engaged, but not in a manner liable to give rise to fear, as this would defeat the object of the talk.

The investigation of accidents is an extremely important part of the Safety Officer's work. The investigation should be made as soon as possible after the occurrence, and should be approached with an open mind, free from any preconceived conceptions of a hypothetical nature. The plant should be examined for material evidence, and statements taken from witnesses and from the injured person, if possible. A conclusion should be arrived at only after careful consideration of the evidence in all its aspects, and great care should be taken to see that one does not become confused between the cause of the accident and the cause of the injury.

Unfortunately, many accidents and unsafe conditions arise in the general layout of the plant during the design stage in the Drawing Office—largely due to the "safety aspect" not being part of the draughtsman's outlook and to concentration on the engineering aspects in machine or plant design.

For these reasons, and providing the Safety Officer has the necessary experience and/or training, he should be given facilities for examining layouts in the initial stages, for the purpose of advising on any special measures he might consider should be taken to make the plant safe and, perhaps, to bring it into line with the requirements of the Factories Act. The "initial stage" means first of all in the Drawing Office, otherwise it may be too late to remedy an unsafe condition once drawings have been passed.

Routine inspection of gangways and sites will take up much of the Safety Officer's time. This should be carried out methodically and thoroughly, and, in the case of specific plant units or departments, it should always be carried out in the company of the person responsible for their running: this will avoid the impression that the Safety Officer is acting the part of a "snooper"—an outlook well calculated to destroy co-operation. The inspection should cover proper use of protective gear, operatives' attention to instructions, notices, faults in guarding, moving projections outside guards, lighting and general floor conditions in the immediate area. Operations that appear to be unsafe should be queried and constructive advice offered whenever possible. These routine inspections should always be made an opportunity of studying the working methods of employees in respect of machine operations, and particularly the handling of heavy goods.

The development of protective gear has been an encouraging feature in the present decade. Each industry has its own hazards, and these require the use of specific protective equipment, such as goggles, eye-shields, protective footwear, gloves, aprons, protective suits, respirators and breathing apparatus. In some industries, e.g. the Chemical Industry, the occupier or owner of the factory is by law required to supply protective equipment, and the employee himself has a legal obligation to wear it if there is risk of injury. Human beings are, however, often perverse about such matters, and many do their best to avoid wearing the equipment. These are the persons for whom the Safety Officer will always have to be on the alert.

Unless danger is immediate, the correction of employees found acting in this manner must, of course, always be left to the person responsible for their control.

From this brief review of the field of safety and accident prevention, it will be readily apparent that there is a call for special knowledge, a blending of human and technical. It is a channel through which the co-operation of supervisors and managers with personnel officers can be sought, either by direct contact in the promotion of supervision of safety measures, or by the intermediary of a Safety Officer if one is appointed. The range of knowledge required is too wide to be within the scope of one individual, though length of service in one plant does enable the quick-minded man to acquire a good measure of valuable detail about its equipment and operation. The knowledge required, either in the Safety Officer himself, or in the combination of personnel and technical persons, say, sitting as an expert Safety Panel, may be summarised as follows:

(*a*) Full acquaintance with the site and plant of their own factory.

(*b*) General knowledge of electrical circuits and good "earthing".

(*c*) Elementary hydraulics and an understanding of the term "pressure".

(*d*) Elementary principles of engineering in so far as it relates to the particular industry.

(*e*) Outline of the production processes used.

(*f*) Factories Acts and special regulations.

(*g*) National Insurance requirements and official procedures.

(*h*) The human factors in accident causation.

(*i*) How to keep records and compile simple statistics.

When a Safety Officer is employed, either full-time or part-time, it is advisable for him to belong to an appropriate local organisation.

In many factories, it has been found valuable to make accident prevention one of the subjects of joint consultation, in order to encourage a high level of employee participation and responsibility. The large organisations may find it useful to have a series of Departmental Safety Committees, each undertaking the review of conditions in its own area, and following out many of the activities of the Safety Officer. On the other hand, even when a full-time man is employed in this capacity, the existence of an employee-management committee can do a great deal to promote safe working and to foster a sound conception of "prevention is better than cure".

These deliberations on the detailed working and requirements of the safety factor in production might easily give the impression that special provision is called for only in the larger organisations. This, however, is far from true. In most enterprises some danger arises; and it is the nature of the process, the layout of buildings, the character of the plant, and other such technical factors, rather than any matter of size, that brings the question of danger and safety into prominence. There may be, and often is, just as much call for "accident prevention" in the tiny concern as in the mammoth works. In the smaller unit, of course, no question of full-time service arises. Many a small firm has met this need and built upon it—built up an efficient "safety organisation" round the enthusiasm and interest of a foreman or other member of the staff. With the policy laid down and the necessary support and assistance given by the management, a foreman can learn a good deal about regulations, hazards, safety practices and so on, and be able to render invaluable service as an "honorary or part-time Safety Officer". All that has been said in the foregoing paragraphs then applies to him and his activities with equal validity.

CHAPTER VI

EMPLOYEE SERVICES

MOST employees at some time or other have a problem which they want solved even though it is outside the scope of their employment. It may be advice on a legal matter, some question on a building society loan, how to get to a hospital, housing or accommodation difficulties, inadequate transport facilities, or some other general problem which affects them as individuals. A good personnel policy in a Company provides an opportunity for dealing with these queries, sometimes in the employee's own time—for instance, during a break or dinner-hour. Assistance of this kind is known as "Employee Services", and is undoubtedly a great asset to a Company in promoting goodwill and creating good morale. This is also one of the ways in which management discharges part of the "social responsibility" inherent in its role. Some of the common items arising are dealt with below.

1. *Lodgings*

During the war years, employees were directed under Defence Regulations from one part of the country to another, in order to fill vacancies at shadow factories and disposal units. As a result of this transfer, the difficulties connected with housing and lodgings became more and more acute. Unfortunately, due to the war years, the situation has not yet righted itself, and almost everywhere in the country it is difficult to obtain accommodation for employees who live outside the district.

A Personnel Manager will often be expected to find lodgings and accommodation for new employees, and frequently his assistance will be called upon when employees marry and wish to set up home. Without turning himself into a "local billeting official", he can often be of considerable help, either in an advisory capacity, or by keeping track of opportunities for accommodation that happen to come to his notice through local contacts. He is often also well placed to be in close touch with the official local Housing Authorities. It is easy to maintain in the department a register or record of the names of people in the locality who are willing to take a man or woman and to classify whether they are prepared to take a permanent lodger or merely willing to do it for a few nights. Usually after a matter of a few weeks, the new employee finds a home with one of his workmates or their relatives, and it is the exception to find that the worker remains at the same premises as those which are chosen for him. A plan which has been followed with some success is to insert a printed slip in all pay packets stating that the Company is constantly being asked for lodgings, and if employees know of any addresses, would they let the Personnel Manager know. He should then make a practice of following up these addresses to ascertain details, especially the standard of comfort and cleanliness.

While the Personnel Officer will give every help to employees in this matter, he must avoid becoming implicated in responsibility for the rental or for the behaviour of the "lodger".

2. Housing

To some extent, the location of the works or factory will determine whether housing is an acute problem or not. To the average man with a family the importance of obtaining a suitable home cannot be over-emphasised. To many men with families the prospects of obtaining a house are more important than those offered by the job, and many a man has had to turn down a promising opening because of inability to secure suitable accommodation.

There are a number of schemes by which assistance can be given.

(a) *Houses for Key Workers.*—Generally in the Development Areas, priority has been afforded in providing houses for key people, and licences are granted in order for firms which otherwise would not have been able to start their factories without key workers to build houses for them at the same time as the factory is taken over, or, in the case of new factories, to include them in the scheme. The cost of these houses is sometimes borne partly by the Government Department and partly by the occupier of the new factory.

New factories under consideration would of course be planned by the Development Authority, having in mind the number of employees who would require to be housed at or near the factory site.

(b) *Small Dwellings Acquisition Act.*—This Act provided for houses to be purchased over a number of years (fifteen to twenty) at low rates of interest, where the house is required for the personal occupation of the owner. This is a very useful service, for it means that an employee is able to purchase a house for almost the same amount as he would be able to rent it. The amount of the loan in many approved cases is up to 95 per cent. of the total value of the property. Application for a loan in such cases should be made to the treasurer of the Loan Authority.

(c) *The Company Tied Houses.*—Some industrial undertakings, particularly in coal-mining areas, erected houses for their employees when the mines were first opened and developed. The houses were let at normal rents, some as low as 6*d*. a week. The accommodation was not good by present-day standards. Generally speaking, the houses were in rows and terraced, opening on to the street, with a back-yard of a few square yards of concrete or rubble. Many of these houses can be seen on the north-east coast and in Wales; some of course have fallen down, whilst others have been maintained in a good condition and are quite habitable. Employees living in these houses are able to work only for the particular firm which owns the houses. Should they decide to leave the employ of that Company, they are legally bound to give up possession of the house, and this is incorporated in their contract of employment, either in writing or as a result of practice.

The Company tied house has many advantages, and in recent years has been applied much more to executives and managers. It functions well, and has many points to its credit, although there are still a few people who would prefer to pay higher rent and not be under an obligation to their employers.

Where the Company owns houses, it is usually the Personnel Department's job to collect the rents and to arrange details of tenancies, to keep a waiting list of people who are anxious to become tenants, and to regard the housing situation as one of the jobs to be looked after. A strong point in its favour is the good relationship which can be built up by the Personnel Department in their weekly rent collection visits with the wives and children and the personal interest which can be shown in the welfare of the employee.

(*d*) *Housing Schemes*.—Yet another way for a Company to assist their employees in connection with housing is by the formation of a building society, financed by the Company and receiving Government support or subsidy. In this case the employee becomes the lessor of the property, the owner for the time being is the Company, and after a period of years the title in the property passes to the local council or some other body appointed by the Ministry concerned.

This is a particularly good scheme, and helpful when a new factory is being formed in an area where no houses exist to "let". It provides a great deal of flexibility in the design of the houses, and enables an estate to be laid out on rather better lines than would be possible were the cost to be fully borne by the Company. The usual system in letting the houses of this kind is to allocate the first few to specially selected key people and the balance to be let on a necessity basis, those men with the most children or dependents getting first choice.

3. *Legal Aid*

From time to time, employees have troubles which mean attendance at a police-court or county court, and when these problems arise the employee often comes to the Personnel Manager for assistance. Some large Companies have legal members among the staff, and so expert advice can be had forthwith. Legal problems should be treated with great reserve, and a Personnel Manager should be cautious about attempting to give advice unaided.

Where an employee is involved in police-court proceedings, it is not unusual for the Company or the man's trade union to provide a solicitor and for the costs to be repaid by the man at a later date, or alternatively treated as a works charge and given to the emplo yee. Each case would, of course, need to be dealt with on its merits. A frequent problem which arises in this way is the possession of premises by a landlord, and often the threat of a county summons for possession of the rooms or premises in which a man lives can completely upset his normal work and cause absence, and it is well worth the few pounds which it will cost for the matter to be dealt with by the Company's solicitor or someone specifically instructed to act on his behalf.

4. Contributory Schemes

With the coming of the National Health Act in 1948, a number of contributory schemes which were then in existence were dissolved. There are, however, still a number of funds to which employees contribute; the most common of these are the Sick Club, the Loan Club, the Christmas Club and the Clothing Club.

(a) Sick Club.—This is operated by a weekly payment, usually of 6d. per week from each member of the firm, occasionally collected through the Wages Department as a deduction. Payments of varying amounts are made to employees when they are absent owing to sickness: the amount may be £1 per week for the first six weeks, and 10s. per week for a further six weeks. Payment is usually made by the secretary of the Sick Club on production of a medical certificate. To obtain benefit, an employee must have been a contributor to the scheme for a given period, usually three months, and a medical certificate has to be produced each week that the employee claims payment. The first three or four days are not recognised, and the amount of sick pay in any one year is limited.

Accident pay, which is usually covered by the same Club, is sometimes on the same basis, and, in addition, a death benefit is payable.

It is not unusual for a Company to be asked to make a grant on the formation of a Sick Club, and in some cases the members of the Accounts Department are asked by the workpeople to act as treasurer and auditor. Generally speaking, it is not desirable for the money to be paid into the Company's accounts, for the reason that the employees often resent the Company holding their money, and, of course, in the event of financial difficulties on the part of the Company, the Sick Club money might be inadvertently commandeered.

(b) *Loan Club.*—Loan Clubs are usually operated departmentally. The man pays in to the collector whatever sum he wishes to save that week. There is no fixed limit, and he has the opportunity of withdrawing a given sum in a fixed time which he arranges with the secretary. If he fails to take a loan he has to pay a fine, and at the end of the year the accounts break even, or the contributions are returned with interest which has accumulated as a result of the fines paid by the non-borrowing members.

It is not often that the management are asked to handle the money in connection with such a Club. The money, collected by subscription each week, passes on to various members, who return it on given dates.

(c) *Christmas Club.*—A number of Companies, in order to encourage thrift amongst their employees, offer, as an inducement, to pay interest on the money collected by the Christmas Club in any year. The usual procedure is to have sixpenny shares, with a maximum number which any one employee can hold. Payments start the first week in January, and continue until the middle of December, including payments during the holiday weeks. It is not usual for anyone to be allowed to withdraw the Christmas Club contributions until the end of the year, and interest is paid at about 5 per cent. on the money saved, that is to say, 2s. 6d. on 50s.

The share-out of the Christmas Club money is made by special payment through the Wages Department, who are also responsible for the deductions from earnings throughout the year. Every endeavour should be made for the money to be paid out before the last Saturday before Christmas.

(d) *Clothing Club.*—Some firms provide overalls, others do not. There are a number of schemes for the provision of clothing to the worker on the job. One scheme, known as the Industrial Overall Scheme, provides for two sets of overalls each year on payment of a fixed sum each week. The same scheme also provides for the overalls to be cleaned, and this is a great help to the housewife.

Where overalls are provided and laundered free, employees rapidly get used to the idea of not purchasing their own overalls, and some become careless in the way in which they are looked after.

5. *Loans*

The problem of lending money to employees is a difficult one, and at the same time one which requires to be dealt with with a good deal of flexibility. The budgeting of the working-man's household expenditure is generally so near the line that there is little left to put away for a rainy day. When an emergency arises, the problem of finding a large sum of money is also one of great difficulty. Going to a pawnbroker and borrowing at a rate of interest sometimes solves the problem, but more often than not an approach is made to the employer with a view to obtaining a loan.

Loans generally fall into two categories. First, a "sub" or "a little on account". There is no reason why an employee should not be paid by way of a loan an amount which he has already earned, and which, by custom of trade, is held in hand until the next pay day. Many employers are diffident about making arrangements for this facility, but there seems to be no reason for this obstacle being placed in the way of the working man. The usual procedure is for the man to apply to his foreman for two or three pounds as a "sub", and for the foreman to refer to the Personnel Department, who should readily accede to the man's request. There will, of course, always be the inveterate liar who will produce heartrending stories each week in order to obtain his money, but it is for the Personnel Manager to put an end to this type of borrowing as soon as he is satisfied that there is any suggestion of the man not being genuinely in need.

Secondly, there is the man who requires to borrow a sum of twenty to fifty pounds, perhaps as a deposit on a house or to purchase furniture when getting married, or for some other genuine reason. A loan in this case might be given after investigation of the facts by a responsible person employed in the Company, and a proper statement setting out the amount of the loan and the basis on which it is to be repaid should be drawn up. The agreement should be stamped, and a copy of it handed to the employee at the same time as the authorisation is given for the amount which is to be deducted week by week until such time as it is repaid. Any question of a loan of a large sum of money should always be regarded confidentially, but the manager of the department in which the man works would undoubtedly be asked for his views before a decision was made or a request granted.

6. Transport Problems

The problem of getting employees to and from work affects only those factories which have to draw from a scattered area, or are isolated in rural surroundings. In the London area the travelling problem is probably more acute than anywhere else in the country, for it is not unusual for workers to travel from one side of the metropolis to the other, a journey which may take anything up to $1\frac{1}{2}$ hours morning and evening.

A Personnel Manager is expected to have a good knowledge of local transport conditions, to know the schedules of trams, buses and trains around the starting and finishing times of the factory and to be able to deal with the problems which arise. A frequent complaint is the lateness and irregularity of the running of a bus. Sometimes the bus runs early, other times it is late, and thus causes an appreciable number of employees to be late for work. Of course, it is quite use-less for a Personnel Manager to refer a complaint to a transport

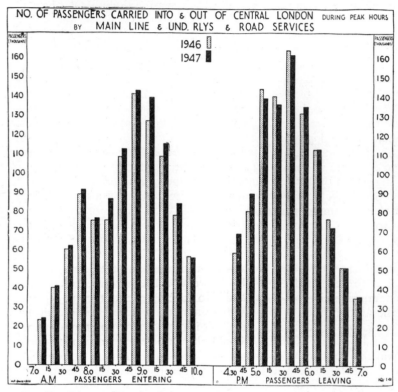

FIG. 68.—Diagram Showing Passengers Conveyed into and out of London.

(Reproduced from J. E. Cowderoy, Public Co-operation in Transport, 2, by permission of London Transport Executive.)

undertaking without being able to give factual information. The type of detail which the transport authority will want is the time at which the incident took place, the number of the bus, the number of people affected and the amount of time lost, also the cost of wages to the individuals where they are paid on a time-worked basis.

Usually, transport officials are most helpful when properly ap-proached, and will go to considerable lengths in order to ensure that the services for workpeople run smoothly, efficiently and on time.

Where more people travel than the vehicle can cater for, additional services, particularly on short runs, can be provided by the local garage manager without reference to anyone else. On the other hand, if the number of people travelling to a given area becomes great, it is probable that the headquarters of the transport executive would arrange for a re-routeing or re-timing of transport to meet the demand.

Some factories operate their own transport, and in the Midlands

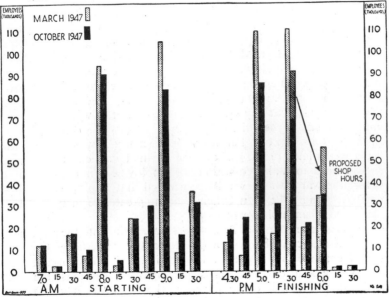

STARTING AND FINISHING TIMES OF STAFF EMPLOYED BY
1,321 INDUSTRIAL AND COMMERCIAL FIRMS IN CENTRAL LONDON

FIG. 69.—Diagram Showing Redistribution.

(*Reproduced from J. E. Cowderoy, Public Co-operation in Transport, 2, by permission of London Transport Executive.*)

districts buses leave for outlying places at given times, the driver remains on some light work in the factory until the end of the work period, and then takes the bus back to the city centre. Another system is for the employers to hire coaches, and for the employees to pay a normal fare, sometimes deducted from their earnings by special authorisation.

The most difficult section of transport with which to arrange alterations is probably the railways, and here the network of junctions and intricate timing of trains frequently make it impossible for immediate alterations to be made. One train made to run five minutes earlier or later may throw out the whole time-table for a system.

When transport problems of this kind are being dealt with, the joint consultation machinery should always be used in order that the information of what is being done to rectify the complaints may be passed on to the workers.

7. Pension Schemes

With the new National Health Act and the provision for higher rates of pension at retirement age of sixty-five, Pension Schemes received something of a setback. This was rapidly put right, however, when the relative value of money before and after the war began to be properly assessed. The object of a Pension Scheme is to try to provide a standard of living which will be in keeping with the person's position at retirement. Many people retire and have nothing to live on except a few pounds which may have been scraped together during the latter part of their lifetime. Others are more prudent, and have saved against the "rainy day", whilst still further people decide that they cannot retire at any age and must continue to work in harness until such time as they die.

The introduction of a Pension Scheme, many of which came into being in the later 1930s, was another means by which management endeavoured to make conditions of employment more attractive. Before the war it was generally considered that employment with a firm operating a Pension Scheme meant greater security and less likelihood of unemployment.

There are many types of Pension Scheme, falling into the categories of (a) the non-contributory, or (b) the contributory. Large Government Departments, the police and some industrial concerns set aside each year a contribution towards the employees' pensions; the right to pension continues only so long as the person remains in that employment. Should he leave before pension age, special circumstances come into operation, but generally speaking he does not obtain any material benefit. Under the contributory schemes, the employee makes a contribution from salary or wages by deduction at an agreed scale. To this is usually added the contribution from the employer, who pays a block sum in accordance with an agreement with an Insurance Company. Conditions for membership of the Pension Scheme may be by length of service, and, where a large group scheme is concerned, it is not usual for a medical examination to be asked for. The Insurance Company take the view that the risk is sufficiently widespread amongst the whole of the employees for them not to insist on making sure that they are taking only good lives on their risk. Frequently, the Pension Scheme also covers Life Insurance, and the following tables give typical examples of the rates of contributions, amount of life insurance, and the amount of pension which one may expect in a given time:

TABLE OF BENEFITS AND CONTRIBUTIONS

The benefits and contributions under the Scheme are shown in the following table:

Salary or Wage Class	Annual Salary or Wages	Annual Pension payable from normal pension date [1] for each complete year as a contributor in Salary Class			Employee's weekly contribution payable while in Salary Class		Life Assurance payable on death while in Salary Class
		£	s.	d.	s.	d.	£
A	Not exceeding £104	0	8	0	0	6	50
B	Over £104 to £130	0	16	0	1	0	100
C	Over £130 to £156	1	4	0	1	6	150
D	Over £156 to £182	1	12	0	2	0	200
E	Over £182 to £208	2	0	0	2	6	250
F	Over £208 to £250	2	8	0	3	0	300
G	Over £250 to £300	2	16	0	3	6	350
H	Over £300 to £350	3	8	0	4	3	425
J	Over £350 to £400	4	0	0	5	0	500
K	Over £400 to £450	4	16	0	6	0	600
L	Over £450 to £500	5	12	0	7	0	700
M	Over £500 to £550	6	8	0	8	0	800
N	Over £550 to £600	7	4	0	9	0	900
O	Over £600 to £650	8	0	0	10	0	1,000
P	Over £650 to £700	9	0	0	11	3	1,125
Q	Over £700 to £750	10	0	0	12	6	1,250
R	Over £750 to £800	11	0	0	13	9	1,375
S	Over £800 to £850	12	0	0	15	0	1,500
T	Over £850 to £900	13	0	0	16	3	1,625
U	Over £900 to £950	14	0	0	17	6	1,750
V	Over £950 to £1,000	15	0	0	18	9	1,875

and so on in increasing multiples, with a maximum to be agreed between the Company and the Assurance Society.

[1] The Normal Pension Date is the anniversary of a member's entry into the Scheme which is nearest to attainment of age 65 in the case of males and age 60 in the case of females.

For example: A male employee aged 21 at his nearest birthday joins the Scheme in Salary Class B. Assuming that his salary is increased from time to time, eventually reaching £234 per annum (i.e. £4 10s. per week), so that he contributes to the Scheme for 44 years in all in the Salary Classes set out below, he will retire with a pension of £90 16*s*. per annum, made up as follows:

						£	*s.*	*d.*
For, say,	2 years of service in Salary Class B at 16*s*. p.a.				.	. 1	12	0
,,	3	,,	,,	,,	,, C at £1 4*s*. p.a.	. . 3	12	0
,,	5	,,	,,	,,	,, D at £1 12*s*. p.a.	. . 8	0	0
,,	10	,,	,,	,,	,, E at £2 p.a.	. . 20	0	0
,,	24	,,	,,	,,	,, F at £2 8*s*. p.a.	. . 57	12	0
	44	Total annual pension at normal pension date payable for a minimum period of five years			.	. £90	16	0

In addition, the member has been covered for Life Assurance while in service, rising to a maximum for Salary Class F, of £300.

Note I.—Changes of Salary or Wage Class shall, for the purposes of the Scheme, take effect only from the anniversary of the date of a member's entry into the Scheme next following the date of change in salary or wages. If at the time when an increase in Life Assurance benefit is due to take effect a member is away owing to injury or illness, such increase will not take effect until the 28th day of the month which follows completion of two months' continuous active service after return to work.

Note II.—The term "Annual Salary or Wages" shall mean basic salary or wages only, and shall not include bonuses, commission, overtime or any other emoluments.

Note III.—All contributions shall be deducted from salary or wages by the Company. Contributions of members whose salaries are paid monthly will be deducted at the rate of four and one-third times the weekly rate.

Note IV.—For the purposes of calculating pensions under the above table, ages are reckoned as at the birthday nearest to the date of joining the Scheme or any anniversary of that date.

Note V.—The masculine shall, where the context so admits, include the feminine.

The table on p. 511 should be read as illustrative of general arrangements of benefits and contributions; actual values change in the course of years in line with changes in the value of money. Acknowledgment for permission to quote the table is offered to the Legal and General Insurance Company and the Metropolitan Pensions Association.—EDITOR.

CHAPTER VII

TAKING A CASE TO ARBITRATION

Case History of a Reference to Arbitration

IN the majority of industries, rates of pay and certain basic conditions of employment are agreed between the headquarters of interested Trade Unions and the Association of Employers. Details are laid down in what are known as National Agreements, and their observance is one of the responsibilities of the Personnel Manager. These rates are known as "basic rates," and it is not unusual to find firms paying higher than these minimum figures. As a general rule, wage claims arise from disagreements between operatives and foremen on how much should be earned for a particular job; from such a humble beginning troubles can arise, which, if not settled within the works, become serious differences requiring settlement ultimately by "arbitration".

Within the framework of the Agreements, Companies vary in the way in which they conduct negotiations with "organised labour". In the small firm the manager or foreman, or the owner, would probably deal directly with the individual employee, taking a stand on what he can afford to pay in the way of "piecework" prices or bonus earnings, in relation to the profit he is making out of the sale of his products. By contrast, the large firm, employing some thousands of people spread in various factories all over the country, would have a central Personnel Department, the head of which would be responsible for negotiations arising out of the Agreements, as well as for participating in discussions in regard to modifications or the drawing up of new Agreements.

In the small firm, it is unlikely that there would be a Shop Steward: employees who are members of a Trade Union would accept employment only providing they were to receive the nationally agreed basic rate and other defined conditions as a minimum. In the event of any difficulty arising the District Organiser of the Union concerned would come in to help in solving the problem.

In many Agreements, the procedure in dealing with problems or disputes arising is laid down. Some Employers' Associations also insist on their members dealing along certain lines: in some cases, the matter must be referred to the Association, and negotiations from there on are taken out of the hands of the individual employer. He is called upon to give such evidence and data as the Association will require in conducting negotiations with the Unions according to the appropriate procedure.

In major matters of policy, it is not always the Personnel Manager who participates in the meetings as the Company's sole representative. With the medium-sized concerns, that is, the majority of the factories in this country, negotiations are usually conducted by the Works Manager, the General Manager or the Managing Director, perhaps with the Personnel Manager in attendance. This is not necessarily a reflection on the latter's competence, but an admission of the part that the "line" executives play in employee relations. It also helps to arrive at earlier conclusions, because these executives are able to take binding decisions. There is nothing more aggravating to a group of employees or to an organiser of a Trade Union than to spend time and energy in putting forward a case and in full discussion of the pros and cons, only to find later in the meeting that the person present on behalf of the management has no authority to give a firm reply or take a conclusive decision—which means that the whole discussion must be repeated at another level. On the other hand, where a Personnel Manager has been established in an organisation, it is highly important that he should attend at all negotiations.

Until such time as the functional position of the Personnel Officer becomes really established, there is much to be said for negotiations being conducted by a top-line executive, who may be better acquainted with all the financial implications and better able to give a quick decision, provided he has the advice of the Personnel Manager on procedure and on what is being done elsewhere on similar problems. One advantage from this arrangement is that it keeps the Personnel Manager in a neutral position, serving as the source of expert knowledge and advice, but at the same time *au fait* with the details discussed: he avoids becoming suspect among the employees as having worked against them in connection with their application.

Broadly described, the procedure laid down for dealing with problems or disputes arising in the interpretation of Agreements is something like this:

The employee concerned raises a matter with his foreman, and if no satisfaction is obtained he calls in the Shop Steward. These two then go as a deputation to the Department Superintendent, the Personnel Manager, or the Works Manager, according to the arrangements laid down by the Company itself. Failure to agree at this stage means that the matter is taken to the outside Organisers, either the Employers' Association or the Trade Union District Office. A defined "disputes procedure" applicable to the industry is then followed.

The sequence may be illustrated by the procedure applied in the Heavy Chemical Industry, which is laid down as follows:

(a) Any question in dispute arising out of this Agreement between an employer and his employees should be dealt with in the first place by an employee or the Trade Union Shop Steward on his behalf, and by the appropriate representative of the Management.

(b) Failing a settlement within the works, the question should be discussed by a Trade Union officer and by the appropriate representative of the management, who may avail themselves of the services of the Association of Chemical and Allied Employers.

(c) In the event of local agreement not being reached, the question should be referred for settlement to the appropriate Trade Union headquarters and to the Association of Chemical and Allied Employers.

(d) In the cases where the Trade Union headquarters and the Association of the Chemical and Allied Employers fail to arrive at a settlement, the difference is to be reported forthwith to the Joint Secretaries of the Joint Conference.

(e) If the Joint Industrial Council fails to settle a dispute, the aggrieved party should have recourse—

(1) To the Industrial Relations Department of the Ministry of Labour; and

(2) To arbitration, before giving the legal notice of cessation of work.

"Arbitration" will mean the formality of submitting the case for objective external investigation through the machinery of the National Arbitration Tribunal set up by the Industrial Court Act of 1919 (see page 536). This prescribes that any matter referred to the Court may be heard and determined (a) by a single member of the Court, or (b) by the President and such other Assessors as might be thought fit. In addition, there are the facilities afforded by the 1951 Industrial Disputes Order No. 1376 (see page 537), which provides that the Ministry of Labour may set up an Industrial Disputes Tribunal. Any aggrieved party is able to take a case to the Ministry, who are then under obligation to refer the matter to the Industrial Disputes Tribunal for settlement. Alternatively, at the discretion of the Ministry, the matter could be dealt with under the conciliation procedure provided for in the Conciliation Act of 1896: this prescribes for the parties to meet under the chairmanship of an individual nominated by the Minister, or agreed among the parties, to act as a conciliator. The decisions arrived at, however, are not legally binding, although in practice it has been customary for them to be accepted and acted upon.

Under the Industrial Courts Act (1919) procedure, the consent of both sides has to be obtained by the Ministry, and no case may go to an Arbitration Court if there exists within the industry any other form of conciliation procedure by which the dispute can be settled. This is not so under the 1951 Order 1376, according to which either party may advise the Ministry of Labour of the existence of a dispute and upon such notification the Ministry must act.

The Industrial Court is a permanent institution, but is not in any way subject to Government control. The assessors are appointed from panels comprising persons representing the industry and the Trade Unions. Whilst it is possible for the parties to be represented by counsel or solicitors, this practice is unusual. It is more often that the Trade Union side is represented by their National or District Official and the Company by the Personnel Manager and/or one of the Directors.

The rules of the Court are flexible, and allow the President a good deal of scope in the way in which the evidence and information are to be given. They are not given on oath, and the rules of procedure provide for both sides to be given a proper and full hearing, irrespective of the length of time taken. It is very rare for the Court to be unable to agree, but in such instances provision has been made in the Act for the matter to be referred to an umpire.

In practice it rarely happens that a case is taken to arbitration without agreement by both sides as to the procedure to be adopted or the terms of reference of the matter in dispute.

The decision made by the Court is known as the "Award". It sometimes happens that an "Award" is not clear or is difficult to understand, in consequence of which the matter may be referred back to the Arbitrators for further interpretation.

The Industrial Disputes Tribunal consists of a chairman (usually a barrister or judge), with two or four assessors representing employers and workpeople in equal number. Their decision, once given, is irrevocable and binding on both parties.

A case taken to arbitration usually has to follow certain recognised rules of procedure. There are instances where arbitration is reached only after protracted negotiation through the earlier disputes procedure: several meetings may be prescribed, at which the subject-matter is discussed in the hope of reaching a decision. Arbitration is, of necessity, a final stage, resorted to only after all direct channels have failed. The amount of detail required in connection with a case going to arbitration is considerable. Factual information of every kind has to be sought, for a case presented to the Tribunal is as serious as a High Court action. Personnel Managers realise that the point in dispute may be an extremely costly one: it may mean a permanent addition to the Company's wages bill as a result of the award.

As a matter of interest, and because many Managers and Personnel Managers have little opportunity of personal experience of arbitration before they are plunged into their first case, a hypothetical reference to the Tribunal is set out in detail in the following story:

CASE HISTORY OF A REFERENCE TO ARBITRATION

(Entirely fictitious characters)

The Personnel Manager, J. J. Green, of a metal company, Smith & Smith, Ltd., not belonging to a Trade Association or Federation, heard from a workman that at a Branch meeting held recently, it was unanimously decided to ask for another 2d. per hour for all unskilled workers and 4d. per hour for skilled and semi-skilled workers.

The same day the Branch Secretary, T. Jones, who was also the Convener of the Shop Stewards in the factory, asked for an interview with the Personnel Manager, who, having granted the interview, had this claim put before him. He rejected the claim, saying that the Company were not prepared to accept any further increases above the existing rates—pointing out that the Company's rates were amongst the highest in the industry. After a lengthy meeting and hearing the arguments, they registered a "failure to agree". The Personnel Manager suggested that if the stewards wanted to take the matter any further, the best thing to do was to get the claim in correspondence. He suggested that a letter be written by the Union putting their claim formally before the Company.

A few days later a letter was received by the Personnel Manager:

Document No. 1

From the Union of Metal Workers.
T. Jones (Cardiff No. 1 Branch).

THE PERSONNEL MANAGER,
SMITH & SMITH LTD.,   1st April 1951[1]
CARDIFF.

DEAR SIR,

At a meeting held on the 27th March, it was unanimously agreed to inform you and the Company that we wished to make a claim in regard to our members as follows:

[1] Subsequent dates are omitted in this correspondence.

2*d*. per hour increase for unskilled workers,
4*d*. per hour increase for semi-skilled and skilled workers,

with appropriate increases in respect of youths and women. As this matter has been outstanding already for some time, we shall be glad to have your advice as to an early date for the meeting.

Yours fraternally,
T. JONES,
Branch Secretary.

This letter was received by the Personnel Manager and the following reply was sent:

Document No. 2

From Smith & Smith Ltd.,
The Personnel Manager.

T. JONES,
BRANCH SECRETARY,
METAL WORKERS UNION.

DEAR MR. JONES,

We thank you for your letter of the 1st April, in which you make a claim on behalf of your members, and we suggest Tuesday or Friday next as the most convenient time to hold a meeting to discuss this matter.

Will you please let us know by return which of these days will suit you, and at the same time let us know the names of the employees whom you will wish to be present at the meeting, so that arrangements can be made for them to be released and substitutes found for their work.

Yours faithfully,
J. J. GREEN,
Personnel Manager.

Document No. 3

MINUTES OF MEETING held in the office of the Managing Director, on Friday 10th April.

Present: L. J. Head   .   Managing Director (*Chairman*).
E. G. Worker   .   Production Manager.
J. J. Green   .   Personnel Manager.
H. Brown .   .   Foreman.
T. Jones   .   .   Branch Secretary.
G. Gray   .   .   District Organiser.
L. Brother   .   Branch Chairman.
G. Black   .   .   Shop Steward.
D. Fence .   .   Shop Steward.
G. Wall   .   .   Shop Steward.

The Chairman opened the case by saying that the meeting had been held at the Union's request, to consider a claim for increases in wages, and he felt that in the circumstances it would be best if Mr. Gray would state the case on behalf of the workpeople.

Mr. Gray said that he had known of this claim for a long time, but had persuaded his members to delay asking for any increase in wages, although they were fully justified some months back in asking for it; the time had come when the employees unanimously decided that the case must be pressed with all speed for this claim to be brought forward.

The wages of the firm did not compare favourably with others in the same industry, and many good people had left the firm in recent months, simply and solely because of the appalling level of the wages paid. It was quite impossible to ask a man today to live on any wage which is under £5 per week, as the cost of living had gone up so rapidly that, on that ground alone, the Union felt there could be no doubt as to the validity of their case. But this was not their only ground: they felt their members were unfairly treated because the conditions of employment within the Company were poor, the factory was very dirty, the work arduous in the extreme, and it was quite clear that the wages were not attractive to new employees, otherwise the Company would not still be wanting the fifty men they had been trying to get for the Melting Department for the last six months. Finally, the work itself was not congenial, it was not a simple straightforward job, it required a man to be above the average intelligence, and the dangers which the men had to undergo were out of proportion to the wages which were received. He asked that the management would consider this very carefully, because there was strong feeling about it in his Union, and he would not want the men to take any kind of action which might be considered precipitous.

The Chairman then called upon the Personnel Manager who in reply said the letter from the Union was not correct, there had been no delay in dealing with the application, that the Company's average wages showed them to be in the region of £7 per week, instead of £5, as stated by Mr. Gray. They were paying considerably above the basic rate for the industry, and the Company felt it would not be prepared to make increases of this kind. The amount of money which was now being asked for in respect of skilled and semi-skilled workers would mean that their rates of pay would be 3s. an hour instead of 2s. 8d. which was the rate, and the cost of this additional increase in the wages would be in the region of £10,000 per year on the Company's wage bill.

Mr. Black, Shop Steward, said that the wages paid in their department weren't anything like that which the Personnel Manager had stated. Very few of them got a chance to do overtime, and they were on the basic of 44 hours. The bonus was set wrong, so that the men got about 8s. instead of the 23s. the ratefixer said they should earn as the result of their piecework prices, and that the men would all leave if something wasn't done.

Mr. Jones, the Branch Secretary, pointed out that what the Shop Steward said was true, that in this particular department no one ever stayed more than a week, the Employment Department could not get people to take the job, the type of employee they did get was not good, and the job they were expected to do required the strength of a horse, and was in a department where it was terribly hot all day long, where clothes got burnt, and it was a lie to say they had never heard of this before, because the Company knew months ago that the claim was coming up and the foreman had been asked very often to put this rise forward and had done nothing. He felt the men were not getting a square deal by the Company, and they should be warned that no matter what advice they were given by the Headquarters of the Union, the men might ignore it.

Mr. Fence, Shop Steward, said this was quite true. Men were always trying to get in his department, because the rate there was better, the bonus came out at 18s. a week, and in his opinion the job in the other department was twice as bad as the one they had to do and yet they got their 18s. a week without any trouble.

Mr. Brother, the Branch Chairman of the Union, suggested it was quite true what the Branch Secretary had said, that they had had the claim before them for a long time and tried to hold it back, but their members were now getting out of temper, and unless the Company agreed to make the payment, anything might happen. The advice of the Union would be to stay at work and follow through the negotiations, but he could not speak for the men, who would quite likely take no notice of what the Union advised and the Company should grant this increase without any more trouble. The profits of the Company showed that they had paid a dividend of 7 per cent. as against 6 per cent. the year before, and the members thought that they should share in the Company's prosperity.

Mr. Brown, Foreman, said he would like to make one thing quite clear, that he had heard nothing previously of any claim for an additional increase: the first he ever knew of this claim was when he was asked to come to this meeting to discuss it, and although the Shop Steward said it had been mentioned on a number of occasions, he could not agree that this was so.

Mr. Worker, Production Manager, said that he could not agree with the accusation that the conditions in the Melting Department were any worse than elsewhere. One did not expect to come into a metal works and find the works the same as assembling wireless sets. The men knew the type of job they were coming into, and it was quite wrong to say the Company could not get labour in a particular section; the trouble was that the plant which had been due for delivery in that department had not arrived, and production was not ready as had been expected, due to unforeseen delays, and that was the real reason why he had not attempted to recruit the fifty which had been mentioned.

The Chairman then asked if there could be a short adjournment.

Upon resuming, the Chairman said that the Company had given careful consideration to the claim made by the Union, and regretted that it was not possible at the moment to accede the claim for the reasons which had been outlined in detail at the earlier part of the meeting.

The District Organiser said that he was not satisfied with this answer, and that he proposed to take the matter up elsewhere.

About a month later, the Company received a further letter reading as follows:

Document No. 4

From the Union of Metal Workers.

T. Jones (Cardiff No. 1 Branch).

PERSONNEL MANAGER,
SMITH & SMITH, LTD.

DEAR SIR,

Re our claim for increased wages, 2*d.* per hour for unskilled workers and 4*d.* per hour for semi-skilled and skilled workers.

At a Branch meeting held on Sunday last, it was unanimously agreed that further steps should be taken in connection with our claim, and in view of our failure to agree at the last meeting, we should be glad to know whether you are willing for this matter to be placed before an individual assessor or arbitrator?

Yours fraternally,

T. JONES,

Branch Secretary.

On receipt of the letter, the Personnel Manager discussed it with the Managing Director and the Works Manager, with particular reference to which form of approach should be adopted by the Company in dealing with these disputes; two channels had to be considered:

(*a*) THE INDUSTRIAL COURTS ACT, 1919.

INDUSTRIAL COURT PROCEDURE RULES, 1920.

(*b*) THE INDUSTRIAL DISPUTES ORDER No. 1376.

Having considered the various aspects, it was decided that the Company would insist on the claim going before the Industrial Disputes Tribunal, and in consequence the following letter was sent:

Document No. 5

THE METAL WORKERS UNION,
CARDIFF NO. 1 BRANCH.

DEAR SIR,

Further to our acknowledgement, we have considered your suggestion that this claim should go before a single arbitrator, and hereby give notice that it is our intention that the case should go before the Industrial Tribunal.

A copy of this letter is being sent to the Industrial Relations Officer of the Ministry of Labour for information purposes.

Yours faithfully,

J. J. GREEN,

Personnel Manager.

In addition, the following letters were sent:

Document No. 6

To the Chief Wages Clerk,

From the Personnel Manager.

Will you please let me have the wages sheets in respect of the X, Y, Z, A and B Departments for the past twelve months?

Will you also let me have these split down for each man showing his:

    (*a*) Basic rate.

    (*b*) Number of hours worked.

    (*c*) Basic rate earnings per week.

    (*d*) Overtime.

    (*e*) Bonus per hour.

    (*f*) Bonus earnings per week?

    (*g*) Total gross earnings.

This information is required in connection with a case which is being prepared for arbitration, and I shall be glad if you will make sure that it is checked carefully, and that no amounts of money refunded or credited for such things as dirty money, expenses, income tax and travelling time, etc., are included. Will you please prepare this information, giving the same detail in respect of departments C and D for the past three years. Please let me have your reply with six copies.

J. J. GREEN,
Personnel Manager.

Document No. 7

STATISTICS DEPARTMENT,
MINISTRY OF LABOUR & NATIONAL SERVICE,
BLACKPOOL.

DEAR SIR,

We shall be glad if you will let us have the rates paid by firms in the Metal Industry, together with details of any increases which have been made either in basic rate or bonuses for the last twelve months.

    Can you also give:

    (*a*) The average earnings for the industry as a whole.

    (*b*) Average earnings for the Cardiff area?

Yours faithfully,
J. J. GREEN,
Personnel Manager.

Document No. 8

To the Federation of Metal Working Manufacturers.

DEAR SIRS,

Although we are not members of your Federation, we should be grateful to have information concerning rates of pay and bonus which may be paid by your members. We are faced with a claim from the Union of Metal Workers for a further 4*d*. per hour for skilled and semi-skilled workers and 2*d*. per hour for unskilled.

Any information which you agree to give us will be treated as confidential, and we shall not disclose it to the other side without first obtaining your permission. If the details can be given covering the period of the past twelve months we should be very grateful.

Yours faithfully,
J. J. GREEN,
Personnel Manager.

Copy of a letter sent to ten firms in the Metal Industry in various parts of the country:

Document No. 9

THE MANAGING DIRECTOR.

DEAR SIR,

We should be glad to have your assistance in connection with a claim made by the Union of Metal Workers for increased rates of pay amounting to 4*d.* per hour for skilled and semi-skilled workers and 2*d.* per hour for unskilled. Could you please let us know the earnings of employees in your departments? It would be of great assistance if you could give the information in the following form:

(a) Basic rate.
(b) Number of hours worked.
(c) Rate for overtime.
(d) Rate of bonus.
(e) Average weekly bonus earned by male adults.
(f) Additional remuneration by way of dirty money and the like.

We should be grateful for this information as quickly as possible, and would confirm our willingness to reciprocate in a similar way should an opportunity arise.

Thanking you in advance.

Yours faithfully,
J. J. GREEN,
Personnel Manager.

Document No. 10

To CHIEF INDUSTRIAL RELATIONS OFFICER,
MINISTRY OF LABOUR & NATIONAL SERVICE,
ST. JAMES'S SQUARE,
LONDON.

DEAR SIR,

Industrial Disputes Order, No. 1376.

We have to give notice of a dispute arising between the Union of Metal Workers, Cardiff No. 1 Branch, and ourselves.

The claim made by the Union is as follows: 2*d.* per hour for unskilled workers, 4*d.* per hour for skilled and semi-skilled workers, with proportionate increases for women and juveniles. We understand that the Union are writing you direct, registering the claim, and we enclose a copy of our letter in which we express our desire that this matter shall be referred to Industrial Disputes Tribunal. Conferences have been held with the Union and all existing machinery exhausted without producing a settlement.

We shall be glad to hear from you of the approximate date on which this matter may come before the Court and its constitution.

Thanking you,

Yours faithfully,

J. J. GREEN,

Personnel Manager.

Document No. 11

THE SECRETARY,
INDUSTRIAL DISPUTES TRIBUNAL,
25–28, BUCKINGHAM GATE,
LONDON.

DEAR SIR,

We thank you for your letter, enclosing the minute in respect of the dispute that exists between this Company and the members of the Metal Workers Union. We note that the case has been fixed for Wednesday, the 10th September, at 10 a.m. at your address, and that you require seven copies of our Statement of Claim. These, together with other relevant documents, will reach you not later than the 27th August, in accordance with your request. The following members will attend on the Company's behalf:

Mr. Head—Managing Director.

Mr. Robinson—Works Manager.

Mr. Green—Personnel Manager.

Mr. Worker—Production Manager.

Yours faithfully,

J. J. GREEN,

Personnel Manager.

Document No. 12

THE SECRETARY,
INDUSTRIAL DISPUTES TRIBUNAL,
25–28, BUCKINGHAM GATE,
LONDON.

DEAR SIR,

Dispute between this Company and the Metal Workers Union.

As requested, we enclose seven copies of the Company's case, Nos. 1–7. Copy No. 8 has been sent at the same time to the Secretary of the Metal Workers Union, Cardiff.

Yours faithfully,

J. J. GREEN,

Personnel Manager.

Your Ref. NAT/XYZ.

Document No. 13

Statement of the Company's Case in respect of the Dispute between the Company and the Metal Workers Union.

1. This Company is concerned with the manufacture of products from all kinds of metal, and consists of five different departments, situated at High Street, Cardiff.

The Departments of the Company are as follows:

Refinery	60 workers, all on bonus work.
Foundry	100 workers, all on bonus work.
Sheet and Strip Mills . .	1,600 workers, all on bonus work, except 4 Mess-room Attendants.
Engineering Department .	120 workers, all on basic tradesmen's rates.
Factory Service Department (Builders, Electricians, etc.)	80 workers, all on basic tradesmen's rates

2. The type of work in the respective departments and the base rates per hour for the different jobs throughout the factory, all of which have been agreed with the Unions, compare favourably with those paid by other similar Companies.

They have been calculated according to the type of work and the skill and effort needed. In addition to the base rates and national bonus, a production bonus is paid to all employees.

The production bonus is paid on two schedules:

(a) *Individual or Team Bonus.*—This is directly related to the output obtained by an individual or a team of men working on a machine or a series of machines interdependent on each other, the amount of bonus depending on the effort of the individual or the team.

(b) *Group Bonus.*—In this case the bonus is paid on the output produced by a group of workers engaged on machines that are not interdependent on each other, and is calculated on the total output, being equally divided between all, according to the number of shifts worked.

The Company has offered to meet the Union claim by payment of an additional 1*d.* per hour in respect of skilled and semi-skilled and ½*d.* in respect of unskilled workers. This was rejected by the Trade Union at a meeting held at the works on the 30th June. The Company have rejected the claim for an overall increase of 4*d.* because the earnings of the people employed compare very favourably with those in similar firms in this industry. The Union having declined to accept the proposal put forward by the

Company as stated earlier, namely, for an increase of 1*d*. and ½*d*., it was suggested that the dispute should be settled by the Industrial Disputes Tribunal.

Appendix I shows the present rates paid by the Company and compares them with the average rates paid elsewhere.

Details of the bonus earnings are also shown for the whole of the Company's employees, and from which it will be seen the majority of employees are able to earn bonuses of 40*s*. upwards per week of 44 hours. Additional bonus is payable to those who work overtime.

The facts given are taken from a representative week. Other matters which the Union have mentioned in support of their claim are:

(1) Company's profits for the last three years.
(2) Increased production by comparison between five years ago and now.
(3) Increase of 5*s*. per week for workers in the cable industry.
(4) Holiday pay comparing unfavourably with other industries.

If the Unions wish to put forward these claims at the hearing and they

are considered to be relevant, the Company is prepared to answer any of them. They have not been incorporated in the main statement of the Company's case, ' ɔcause the Company consider them to be irrelevant.

APPENDIX I

Rates per Hour

		Time Work	*Payment by Result*
BIRMINGHAM	Engineers .	2/6·25	2/4·21
	Metal . .	2/6·38	2/4·24
LONDON	Engineers .	2/7·08	2/5·05
CARDIFF	Existing .	2/6	2/5·19
	Proposed .	2/7	2/6·19

APPENDIX II

Range of Bonus Earnings per Man, based on a 44-hour Week

Up to 20*s*. . .	9
20*s*. to 40*s*. . .	219
40*s*. to 60*s*. . .	1,302
60*s*. to 80*s*. . .	49
Over 80*s*. . .	37
	1,616

It will be noted that 1,388 of our employees are in receipt of weekly bonus earnings of over 40*s*.

APPENDIX III

Comparison of Earnings in Metal Industry
Firms in all Areas of Country
Week of 44 Hours

Job	Earnings per 44 hours—Basic rate plus National Award				
	Blue Metal Co.	Smith & Jones	Black & White	Bee Sons	Smith & Smith
Rollers 1 . . .	98/6	98/6	91/–	109/9	189/6 to 156/11
Rollers 2	96/–	96/–	—	—	157/3 to 120/10
Rollers 3	88/–	88/–	89/–	—	119/11 to 116/–
Rollers Assistants . .	—	75/–	78/–	85/7	152/11 to 108/2
Annealers . . .	78/4 to 81/3	81/6 to 89/–	117/–	93/7	132/4 to 110/2
Picklers . . .	76/6 to 87/6	76/6 to 87/6	131/–	85/6 to 96/–	132/4 to 112/1
Warehousemen . .	105/–	105/–	117/8	106/4	130/7 to 113/3
Warehousemen Assistants .	—	110/–	110/–	85/7	100/3
Straighteners . . .	—	80/6 to 87/–	—	85/–	134/5 to 112/1
General Labourers . .	—	72/–	78/–	78/–	113/3 to 89/1
Drawbenches . . .	80/4 to 99/10	—	—	—	180/– to 121/3
Sawyers . . .	80/4 to 95/–	—	—	—	134/5 to 119/–
Electric Furnaces:					
Furnacemen . . .	113/7	113/6	113/6	110/–	118/6
Mouldmen . . .	111/8	111/6	113/6	112/–	114/10

The Company's rate is believed to be the second highest in the industry, and, as will be seen, compares very favourably with other earnings in similar manufacturers.

UNION'S CASE

Document No. 14

Case to be submitted to the Industrial Disputes Tribunal concerning Wage Dispute between Smith & Smith and the Metal Workers Union

The claim for an increase of 4*d.* per hour for adult skilled and semi-skilled workers and 2*d.* per hour for unskilled, with proportionate increases for women and juveniles, was first placed by worker delegates to the management on the 10th March. As no settlement was reached, the matter was referred to our Trade Union, and I wrote to the Company on the 1st April, Document A submitted.

A conference was held with the management on the 10th June, when the management said they had investigated the claim very carefully and that they could not make any further offer. In June, in view of the fact that the men were becoming restive and talking about strike action unless a favourable decision was given by the management, I convened another meeting, which was held at the works on the 30th June and at which time an offer was made of 1*d*. and ½*d*. per hour respectively. This was unanimously rejected by the representatives of the men, who instructed my Union to take this matter to arbitration. The men in the Smelting Department have been particularly restive because of the appalling conditions under which they work, and our members generally in the Works, when informed that the management had turned down our application for an increase, threatened to stop work. Having been advised by the Branch Secretary during the Whitsun holiday of what was likely to take place, I was at the works at starting time on the Tuesday after Whitsun, and was successful in persuading them to carry on with their work on the understanding—

(*a*) That there would be an early conference with the management under the auspices of the Ministry of Labour;

(*b*) That if no settlement was reached at the conference, the case should be referred to this Tribunal; and

(*c*) That particular stress would be made at this hearing so that any adjustment in wages should date from the 10th March, when the case was first brought to the management's attention.

Although the claim is for 4*d*. an hour on the basic rates, it means, in fact, that the men would have a substantial increase in their gross wages to an extent equal to 4*d*. per hour, and as the majority of them work on shift basis, this increase would proportionately be more favourable, as it would rank for additional payment by way of overtime.

The claim for the 4*d*. and 2*d*. is submitted on three bases:

(*a*) That the wages in the works are not commensurate with the skilled and arduous nature of the work performed.

(*b*) That the gross earnings have not increased over the period equivalent to the increase in other firms in the industry.

(*c*) That the cost of living has gone up by 98 per cent., to such an extent that some adjustment in the base rate must now be applied.

The type of work on which these men are employed is of different kinds but it will be appreciated that in a metal works there is much skilled and arduous work which has to be carried out under trying conditions of heat, dirt, dust and fumes. It is difficult to explain the type of conditions to this Tribunal, and they have to be seen to be really appreciated. If you can imagine the heat which will come from a number of furnaces and visualise a man employed for eight or ten hours each day in the vicinity of a smelting furnace with the fumes and the smoke, some idea of the unpleasant nature of the work may be appreciated.

I attach Document B showing the wages paid in five other firms which are doing work of a similar nature to Smith & Smith. You will notice that in the case of Document C the wages per week are £13 0s. 0d., in Document D £13 10s. 5d., Document E £7 14s. 6d., Document F £6 5s. 0d., and Document G £9 7s. 0d. These earnings are worked on a basis of a 44-hour week against the average paid by Smith & Smith of £6 10s. 6d., and you will notice that the wages are unfavourable by comparison. I have calculated that the average increase over the last five years in this Company is only 20 per cent.

As against this, I would refer the Tribunal to the July issue of the *Ministry of Labour Gazette*, page 71, where it states that the average increase in weekly earnings between October 1943 and 1950 for the sixteen groups of important industries amounts to 64 per cent., and the Tribunal will appreciate that the workers at Smith & Smith have not had any increases so favourable. In fact, the only increases which have been given are on the production bonus, and nothing additional has been paid on the base rate.

I also enclose in my statement of case, Document L, showing that railway men have had their basic earnings increased in the corresponding period by £1 0s. 6d. per week. Miners had several increases during the comparable period totalling on average 37s. per week.

The tribunal are also asked to take into consideration factors other than those covered by the *Ministry of Labour Gazette* figures for the cost of living. As an example, the price of cigarettes, beer, bus fares, clothing, boot and shoe repairs have all increased out of all proportion during this period. Similarly, the cost of living figures of the Ministry of Labour do not take into consideration the extremely high rents which are paid by our members owing to the shortage of houses, and whilst it may be true that in some parts of the country the average rental of a working man is 12s. 6d., I find that many of the members of my Union pay anything from 25s. to 35s. per week for two or three rooms, and I could quote instances of rents even higher than these being paid by the working man.

Our members also feel that the profits of the Company have been such as would enable them to grant this increase without undue hardship or embarrassment, as the profits have increased from £20,000 in 1941 to £100,000 last year, and our members believe that this is due to their increased efforts to gain more production and that they should share in some measure in the Company's prosperity.

Document No. 15

To The Personnel Manager,
Messrs. Smith & Smith,
High Street,
Cardiff.

Dear Mr. Green,
    Our members have reported to us that there are a number of outstanding matters which are not being dealt with in the way they feel right.

I should therefore be glad if you would let me know when I could have a meeting with you to discuss their claims.

Yours faithfully,
G. GRAY,
District Organiser.

Document No. 16

TO THE MANAGING DIRECTOR,
EXETER ROLLING MILLS.

DEAR SIR,

This Trade Union has an Arbitration case pending concerning the rates paid by a firm in Cardiff engaged on similar work to yourselves. It would be helpful to the Disputes Tribunal if they could have, therefore, details of wages paid by your Company.

Our members who work in your Metal Department inform us that their rate of pay per shift is as follows: £3 3s. 8d. per shift of 12 hours, inclusive of production bonus, dirty money and danger money. We should be glad to know if this information is correct.

Yours faithfully,
G. GRAY,
District Organiser.

Document No. 17

TO THE MANAGING DIRECTOR,
MESSRS. DAVIES & PETERS,
BRISTOL.

DEAR SIR,

This Trade Union has an Arbitration case pending concerning the rates paid by a firm in Cardiff engaged on similar work to yourselves. It would be helpful to the Disputes Tribunal if they could have before them details of wages paid by your Company.

Our members who work in your Metal Department inform us that their rate of pay is £2 7s. 6d. per shift of 12 hours. We should be glad to know if this information is correct.

Yours faithfully,
G. GRAY,
District Organiser.

Document No. 18

TO THE MANAGING DIRECTOR,
MESSRS. J. PHILLIPS & SONS,
TAUNTON.

DEAR SIR,

This Trade Union has an Arbitration case pending concerning the rates of pay at a firm in Cardiff engaged on similar work to yourselves. It would be helpful to the Disputes Tribunal if they could have before them details of wages paid by your Company.

We are informed that your Company pay 2*s*. 6*d*. per hour, plus a production bonus, with a guaranteed minimum of 20*s*. per week. We should be glad to know if this information is correct.

Yours faithfully,
G. GRAY,
District Organiser.

Document No. 19

TO THE MANAGING DIRECTOR,
A. H. PARKER & CO., LTD.,
GLOUCESTER.

DEAR SIR,
This Trade Union has an Arbitration case pending concerning rates paid by a firm in Cardiff engaged on similar work to yourselves. It would be helpful to the Disputes Tribunal if they could have before them details of wages paid by your Company.

We are informed by our members who work with your Company that they are paid for all classes of semi-skilled work an inclusive rate of 3*s*. per hour for 44 hours and double time for all hours which are worked outside the normal shift.

Yours faithfully,
G. GRAY,
District Organiser.

Document No. 20

TO THE MANAGING DIRECTOR,
MESSRS. ANDREWS & JAMES,
WINCHESTER.

DEAR SIR,
This Trade Union has an Arbitration case pending concerning the rates paid by a firm in Cardiff engaged on similar work to yourselves. It would be helpful to the Disputes Tribunal if they could have before them details of wages paid by your Company.

We understand from our members who are employed within your firm, that furnacemen earn £8 0*s*. 0*d*. to £8 10*s*. 0*d*. per week of 44 hours, and in addition have two weeks' holiday with full pay at their average earnings for the preceding twelve months.

Yours faithfully,
G. GRAY,
District Organiser.

Document No. 21

Extract of Meeting with Railway Executives

Negotiations on the wages of railway workers were resumed at the meeting of the National Council on Monday, the 19th July, and the following settlement was made :

Adult Males, total increase   20s. 6d.
Adult Females, total increase 15s. 4d.
Proportionate increases to youths and women.

This settlement applies to time workers and piece workers, to take effect retrospectively from April 1948.

Document No. 22

TO THE SECRETARY,
TIN WORKERS FEDERATION,
GREAT BRITAIN.

DEAR SIR,
This Trade Union has an Arbitration case pending concerning the rates paid by a firm in Cardiff engaged on similar work to yourselves. It would be helpful to the Disputes Tribunal if they could have before them details of wages paid by you. We understand that during the past five years there has been an increase in payment of 6s. 2d. per shift, which, on a normal week of six shifts, gives 37s. per week.

Yours faithfully,
G. GRAY,
District Organiser.

Document No. 23

To the Works Manager.
From the Personnel Manager.

At an arbitration case which is to be held next Monday, the following employees will be required to represent the Union side:

Mr. A. J. Griffiths.
Mr. R. N. Mason.
Mr. L. Smith.

Will you please make all arrangements for them to be released during the day, and if any of the workers are on night shift, will you make sure that they have adequate leave and do not work the night preceding the case. Wages will be paid by the Company for all time lost during attendance at the hearing.

J. J. GREEN,
Personnel Manager.

Document No. 24

List of Documents to be taken by the Personnel Manager to Tribunal.
Wednesday, 10th September, 1950.

Company strength.
Wage sheets.
Bonus files.
Correspondence with the Union.
Correspondence *re* this case.

Minutes of Trade Union meetings.
Copy of Published Accounts for last year.
Ministry of Labour Gazette from March to date.

Document No. 25

To all Departmental Managers and Foremen.
From the Managing Director.

10*th September,* 1950.

For your information, the Arbitration case in which we were concerned was heard today in front of Mr. Justice Evans and other members of the Tribunal. The Company's case was read out by me, and after the District Organiser had read his case also, we were allowed to exchange questions and to deal with the many matters which were not mentioned in the written statement.

The District Organiser made a number of points regarding the working conditions in the Company, delays in dealing with the men's claims, unhelpful attitude of supervisory staff, and I shall be discussing these with you at our next meeting.

We shall not know the result of the case for a few days, but I have formed the impression that the Tribunal will find in our favour. A copy of the award will be sent to you as soon as the result becomes known.

L. J. HEAD,
Managing Director.

Document No. 26

Copy to Cost Department.
To Wages Department.
From the Personnel Manager.

Will you please note that as from the 15th September, all rates of pay will be increased as follows:

Skilled and semi-skilled—1*d.* per hour.
Unskilled   —½*d.* per hour.

This is to comply with the interpretation of award No. 595 dated the 10th September, 1950.

J. J. GREEN,
Personnel Manager.

Document No. 27

TO THE MANAGING DIRECTOR,
MESSRS. SMITH & SMITH.

FROM THE SECRETARY,
INDUSTRIAL DISPUTES TRIBUNAL.

DEAR SIR,

I have to transmit herewith, for your information, an advance copy of the award made by the Industrial Disputes Tribunal in the case in which Smith & Smith and the Metal Workers Union were concerned, and which was heard by the Tribunal on the 10th September last. Copies of the award will shortly be on sale by H.M. Stationery Office.

Yours faithfully,

F. JOHNSON,

Secretary.

Document No. 28

INDUSTRIAL DISPUTES TRIBUNAL
Award No. 595

RATES OF REMUNERATION OF EMPLOYEES OF A CARDIFF FIRM ENGAGED IN THE METAL TRADE

Constitution of the Tribunal in this case:

Appointed Members:

The Hon. Mr. Justice Evans (*Chairman*).
Sir John Robinson.
Sir William Davies.

Panel Members:

Mr. E. W. James.
Mr. F. L. Jones.

Parties:

Messers. Smith & Smith

and

Certain workers employed by them.

Claim: For an increase in base rates of 4*d.* an hour for adult male skilled and semi-skilled workers and 2*d.* an hour for unskilled workers with proportionate increases for women and juveniles.

1. The Ministry of Labour and National Service, on 10th September, 1951, referred to the Industrial Disputes Tribunal for settlement, in accordance with the provisions of the Order No. 1376, a trade dispute existing between the parties specified in the First Schedule hereto, which had been reported to the Minister by Messrs. Smith & Smith, the employers mentioned in the said First Schedule (being one of the parties to the said dispute), particulars of the dispute being those set out in the Second Schedule hereto.

FIRST SCHEDULE

PARTIES TO THE TRADE DISPUTE

(*a*) Employers: Messrs. Smith & Smith, High Street, Cardiff.

(*b*) Workmen: Members of the Metal Workers Union, in employment of the above-mentioned employers, being of the following classes: Skilled Tradesman, Semi-skilled Operative and Labourers.

SECOND SCHEDULE

PARTICULARS OF THE TRADE DISPUTES

The dispute arises out of an application made on behalf of the workmen mentioned in the First Schedule by the Metal Workers Union for an increase in base rates throughout the works of 4*d*. an hour for adult male skilled and semi-skilled workers and 2*d*. an hour for unskilled workers, with proportionate increases for women and juveniles.

2. Representatives of the parties were heard at a sitting of the Tribunal held in London on the 10th September, 1951. Statements were made and documents submitted as to : the work in which the firm was engaged; the departments in which the work is organised, and the number of workers employed in each department; the basis of remuneration, which consists, as respects one department with another, of a base rate varying according to the type of job, a bonus on production (individual, team or group), the present base rates and the method of computation between the earnings of the firm in Cardiff on the one hand and other firms in the metal trades in other parts of the country, particularly Birmingham and Wolverhampton, Glasgow and London. The wages and earnings of workers on whose behalf the claim is made compared with the wage rates and earnings of employees in other establishments and employed in metal trades. The offer made by the Company of 1*d*. for skilled and semi-skilled and ½*d*. for unskilled workers which was rejected by the Trade Union, and the fluctuation in the cost of living and matters appertaining thereto and the profits made by the Company over the period 1941 to 1948, and that the workmen should participate in these increased profits.

3. The Tribunal have given careful consideration to the above-mentioned statements and submission made on behalf of the parties. On the footing that the firm give effect as from the beginning of the first full pay period following the date hereof to the offer made to them as referred to in paragraph 2 above and specified in the written statement submitted to the Tribunal at the hearing, the Tribunal find against the claim of the workmen specified in the Second Schedule in paragraph 1 above and they award accordingly.

G. T. EVANS,
Chairman.

F. JOHNSON,
   Secretary.

NOTE.—It is provided in the Schedule to the Industrial Disputes Order that if any question arises as to the interpretation of any award of the Tribunal, the Minister or any party to the award may apply for a decision on such question, and the Tribunal shall decide the matter after hearing the parties, or without such hearing provided the consent of the parties has first been obtained.

Document No. 29

Letter to firms and others who supplied information :

THE MANAGING DIRECTOR.

DEAR SIR,

You will remember our correspondence earlier this year, when you were kind enough to give us certain statistical information regarding rates of pay and bonus paid to your employees.

The matter in question was dealt with by Arbitration on the 10th September last, and we have pleasure in enclosing a copy of the award, from which you will see that the Tribunal found in our favour and awarded the Union the penny and halfpenny which we had previously offered.

May we take this opportunity of thanking you for the great assistance which you rendered us on this occasion, and to reaffirm our willingness to assist you in a similar way should the opportunity arise?

Yours faithfully,
L. J. HEAD,
Managing Director.

Below are the two Acts as mentioned in the previous pages:

(a) *The Industrial Courts Act,* 1919.
The Industrial Court (Procedure) Rules, 1920.

Dated fifteenth day of March, 1920.

Made by the Minister of Labour by virtue of powers vested in him by the Industrial Courts Act, 1919, and of all other powers enabling him in that behalf.

1. In these Rules:

the expression "Act" means the Industrial Courts Act, 1919, and the expression "Minister" means the Minister of Labour; and the expression "Court" means the Industrial Court established by the Act and includes (unless the contrary intention appears) any division thereof and any single member of the Court to whom a matter may be referred to for determination; and the expression "President" means the President of the Industrial Court; and the expression "Division" means any group of members of the Court constituted as the President may direct to hear and determine any matter referred to the Court.

2. The Court may sit in two or more Divisions.

3. Any matter referred to the Court for settlement may, at the discretion of the President, be heard and determined by a single member of the Court.

4. The Court may, at the discretion of the President, in any matter in which it appears expedient to do so, call in the aid of one or more assessors and may settle the matter wholly or partially with the assistance of such assessor or assessors.

5. The Court may, with the consent of the parties act, notwithstanding any vacancy in their number, and no act, proceeding or determination of the Court shall be called in question or invalidated by reason of any such vacancy, provided such consent has first been obtained.

6. The Court may correct in any award, any clerical mistake or error arising from an accidental slip or omission.

7. If any question arises as to the interpretation of any award of the Court, the Minister or any party to the award may apply for a decision on such question, and the Court shall decide the matter after hearing the parties, or without such hearing, provided the consent of the parties has first been obtained. The decision of the Court shall be notified to the parties, and shall be final in the same manner as the decision in an original award.

8. Persons may appear by counsel or solicitor on proceedings before the Court with the permission of the Court.

9. Subject to these rules, the Court may regulate their own procedure as they think fit.

10. These rules may be cited as the Industrial Court (Procedure) Rules, 1920.

GIVEN UNDER THE OFFICIAL SEAL OF THE MINISTER OF LABOUR THIS FIFTEENTH DAY OF MARCH, ONE THOUSAND NINE HUNDRED AND TWENTY.

Seal.

Signed—D. J. SHACKLETON,
Secretary.

(*b*) *The Industrial Disputes Order No.* 1376 : *promulgated* 1951 *to replace the Conditions of Employment and National Arbitration Orders* 1940–42.

Essential features may be summarised as follows:

1. There are to be no penal sanctions against strikes and lock-outs, although the Minister may delay action on disputes if stoppages are in progress.

2. Disputes can be reported only by employers, employers' organisations and trade unions (not by individual employees).

3. There is no general obligation on employers to observe recognised terms and conditions, though awards can be obtained from the new Industrial Disputes Tribunal to force them to do so.

4. The term "dispute" is to apply only to differences about terms and conditions of employment, not about employment itself, or about membership.

THINGS A PERSONNEL MANAGER SHOULD KNOW

IN SOME DETAIL

THESE are matters which are his particular responsibility, and in which he would be regarded as the expert.

1. *Termination of Employment*
Time necessary to terminate the employment of a person paid by the hour, the week or the month.

Wages Structure
Within the industry, and rates paid by other firms doing similar work.

Rates Paid
Rates paid in other industries, particularly engineering, electrical, building trades, for his own Company's maintenance workers. Rates for canteen workers and the Rail and Road Haulage rates covering drivers and van-guards.

4. *Agreements*
Details of procedure Agreements within his own Company and any arrangements in the industry.

5. *Bonus Rates*
Make-up of bonus or piecework, how calculated and when paid.

6. *Wages*
The method of calculating wages, deducting lost time, rates for overtime payment and the extension of wages on a clock card or wages slip.

7. *Labour*
How to obtain through employment exchanges. How to obtain circulation at Regional level, or ensure demands circulated in likely areas.

8. *Labour Exchange Procedure*
What happens to a person when he visits the Labour Exchange and the procedure used there for coding by occupation. The resettling of ex-servicemen and the placing of disabled persons.

9. *Time Lost*
The monthly average of time lost for lateness and sickness for men and women employed in similar factories to his own.

10. *Notices*
Organise distribution of notices; responsibility for posting and removing (except those of the trade unions).

11. *Statutory Notices*
To know that Statutory Notices have to be posted within the works and to cover the following official registers to comply with the Factories Act:

Factories Act.—(*a*) Give details to Factory Inspector one month after occupation of any premises as a factory, giving details of nature of work and if mechanical power is used, etc.

(*b*) Post at factory entrance abstracts of Factory Act, containing the address of the Factory Inspector and the Examining Surgeon.

12. *Registers*

The keeping up-to-date of the following registers:

General Register.

Register for Young Persons.

Register showing dates of whitewashing, cleaning, etc.

Register for reporting accidents and industrial disease.

IN GENERAL PRINCIPLE

There are many matters in the day-to-day life of a Personnel Manager, about which he will be asked and on which he should be able to give advice. His personal opinion on matters of this kind will, of course, carry great weight, and he will become the "Advice Bureau" for the employees in the factory.

1. *Pension and Life Assurance Schemes*

These vary according to whether the Pension Scheme is contributed to by the employee or if it is a scheme financed by the Company. In the former, when the employee leaves, he receives back the contributions which he has paid, and generally speaking he has been covered for a Life Policy. Generally, the cover for a Life Policy is regarded as more than compensation for the loss of interest on the money invested in the Pension Scheme. Advice will frequently be sought by employees today, taking out additional Life cover, and the Personnel Manager may be expected to know the difference between an Endowment Policy and one which covers the whole life. It is usual to have in the office one or two copies of a prospectus, so that some idea can be given of a weekly cost of such a scheme.

2. *Right of Search*

An employer is not entitled to search an employee, except in two circumstances. The first is where he has reason to believe that the employee has in his possession stolen property, and in the second, where the employee has agreed to be searched as one of the conditions of employment. The searching of individuals is a matter to be dealt with in a most careful way, and special arrangements should be made where women are employed, so that the searching is carried out by a matron or some other reliable woman employee.

3. *Job Analysis*

The Personnel Manager would be expected to know the methods by which a job is broken down and to have a general knowledge of the whole of the jobs which have to be done in each department.

4. *Legislation Affecting Industry* (*S.R. & O.*), *etc.*

Information on these matters can nearly always be obtained from the Government Stationery Office, who will arrange to send on to employers copies of Orders which affect their industry.

5. Moving Machinery Regulations

Regulations regarding moving machinery, fire and lifting tackle, are dealt with in detail in the Factory Act. Constant reference to the Factory Act will need to be made as the points arise, but a copy of Redgrave and Owners Factory, Shop and Truck Act will be found invaluable.

6. Training and Education Schemes

Schemes which are available in other works, or at local Technical Schools, should be known in broad outline. Specific information on the training for a particular subject can be obtained by referring to the Principal of the local Technical College.

7. Joint Consultation Committee

The procedure and minutes should be carefully studied, and the methods of conducting a meeting on proper lines, the numbers needed to make a quorum and similar matters affecting committees should be studied. A good book on this subject is available from the Industrial Welfare Society and entitled "Works Committees".

8. Works Outings

The Personnel Manager will be expected to know how outdoor functions, such as Works Outings, Beanfeasts, Sports Days, etc., should be arranged, and he should make himself familiar with the organisation which is needed for this type of amenity, the towns which are able to cater for large numbers, the transport services required and available, and so on.

9. Sports Club and Welfare Schemes

These should be known in broad outline. Organising a Sick Club where none exists and the co-ordination of social events in which people at the Company are interested. The Sports Secretary must be a man prepared to accept a lot of hard knocks, without ever receiving the bouquets.

10. Works Magazines

These need to be carefully planned, and a committee is usually appointed, as this tends to spread the number of contributors and the amount of copy available. Some Companies believe this to be a matter for their Advertising Department. Suggestions from other firms can usually be obtained by asking for details from the Personnel Department. A useful guide on prices and the like is given by the Industrial Welfare Society.

11. Labour Turnover

Reduction of labour turnover is the aim of each Personnel Manager. Constant review of the Exit Book tends to lessen the number of people leaving. Labour turnover is unsatisfactory from every point of view.

12. Court of Referees

Procedure at Court of Referees should be understood, and the Personnel Manager should have a general knowledge as to how to prepare a case for presentation to such a body. Statements of the evidence to be given should always be obtained before the hearing, and witnesses need to be warned of the time at which they are to attend.

13. *National Insurance Act,* 1946

This Act should be considered and carefully read, so that it is possible to discuss matters which arise and on which information may be asked.

14. *National Insurance and Industrial Injuries Scheme*

This scheme has replaced the old Compensation Act, and an employee is no longer precluded from accepting money from his employers as sick pay, pending the settlement of his case by the National Insurance Office.

15. *Civilian Employment Act of* 1944

Reinstatement in Civilian Employment Act of 1944 makes it compulsory for an employer to take back into his service anyone conscripted into the services. Where an employee has been engaged to fill the vacancy caused by the call-up of the conscript, that person must be discharged in order to reinstate the original employee. Details of the Act should be studied.

16. *The Truck Acts* 1891 *and* 1940

These make it clear that an employer may not deduct money without written authority.

17. *The Personnel Policy of the Company*

This has to be interpreted through the medium of the Personnel Manager, who should make it clear to all concerned of the capacity in which he is acting. The Company's policy should be clearly stated and re-examined from time to time at meetings, at which the Managing Director is present.

18. *Accident Prevention*

This is a specialised subject, and should be treated as such. The numerous references to the Factory Acts will need to be made; in connection with this matter, previous reference is made in pages 492–5.

19. *Medical Department*

The function of the Medical Department is to maintain and improve the health of the employees. Medical records should always be treated as confidential.

WHERE TO FIND

The Personnel Manager should know where to find information in books of reference, from technical bodies and other organisations from whom up-to-date and detailed knowledge of the particular problem can be obtained, and it is the duty of the Personnel Manager to see that he is quite familiar with its various aspects.

1. *Clocking*

Time Recording Systems vary a great deal. The usual type punches the card with a time stamp, and by this means a record is made on the clock card showing the attendance day by day. The ideal system is to have a master clock which controls all other clocking stations in the works. For the smaller unit the single clock is sufficient, and information about the various types offered can always be obtained from the clock manufacturers or by reference to such journals as the *Factory Manager, Industrial Welfare Society's Bulletin, Industry Illustrated,* etc.

2. *Income-tax Allowances*

Special allowances are granted to workmen in respect of tools and clothing. Details of these are not usually given in the Notes of Reference, but most books on income tax set out the details of allowances due in this respect. Alternatively, direct application could be made to the local Inspector of Taxes.

3. *Fair Wage Resolution*

It is usual for the Government, when placing a contract, to overstamp or overprint the documents with a special clause to ensure good working conditions and fair rates of pay. This is to ensure that labour employed for the contract enjoy conditions of a minimum guaranteed standard.

4. *Ventilation and Seating Accommodation*

In work-rooms, these two problems are dealt with by the Factories Act. Guidance can be obtained by reference to Part I, Section 4 (Ventilation) and Section 44 (Seating). The amendments of the Act in 1948 (Section 6) make it compulsory to provide seating accommodation for all classes of employees whenever practicable. This is a matter of fact which has to be established in each works. A knowledge of the law relating to employment and the various Orders which are issued from time to time are explained in the *Ministry of Labour Gazette* and commented upon in other journals. Reference to the Ministry of Labour should be made to clear up any doubtful points.

5. *Women's Problems*

Problems relating to women's work are discussed at meetings of the Industrial Welfare Society held in various parts of the country from time to time, and information relating to the particular problems on the employment of women is frequently given from this source. The Ministry of Labour Factory Inspectorate Department have a special section dealing with women's employment problems, and information can be obtained from the local office.

6. *Fatigue Problems*

Problems relating to fatigue are best handled in conjunction with the Medical Officer. Reference can be made to the Industrial Health Research Board, the National Institute of Industrial Psychology and the Institute of Personnel Management, who have available information from practical studies on this point.

7. *Mental Disorders*

These call for specialised treatment by a psychiatrist, who should be called in through the medium of the works doctor. Rehabilitation Centres, such as Rothey Park, Horsham, specialise in dealing with such disorders.

8. *Juveniles*

Juvenile employees present problems which are peculiar to adolescence. Co-operation with the Manager of the Juvenile Employment Bureau and the Headmasters or Headmistresses Department and the Ministry of Education can be very helpful.

9. *Cost of Living*

Problems on the cost of living are undertaken by the Government, who have research workers continually investigating. Comparisons are shown in the *Ministry of Labour Gazette* issued monthly, and a new basis for the cost of living came into operation in 1948. Details of the items which have a bearing on the cost of living are included.

10. *Telephone Numbers*

Telephone numbers of Trade Unions, Ministry of Labour, Factories Inspector, Police-station, Railway Station, Works Doctor and Fire Brigades should be posted in the Watchman's Office, and copies should be available at the Works Manager's Office, Medical Department and Personnel Department.

BIBLIOGRAPHY

THE following is a brief selected list of references on various aspects of personnel practice covered in this section. The literature on this subject is now very considerable, books by American authors and publishers being particularly numerous.

1. C. H. Northcott: *Personnel Management: its Scope and Practice.* (Pitman, London, 1950; 2nd edit.)

2. May Smith: *An Introduction to Industrial Psychology.* (Cassell, London, 1945.)

3. R. F. Tredgold: *Human Relations in Modern Industry.* (Duckworth, London, 1949.)

4. W. B. D. Brown & W. Raphael: *Managers, Men and Morale.* (Macdonald & Evans, London, 1948.)

5. G. S. Walpole: *Management and Men.* (Jonathan Cape, London, 1944.)

6. C. Conway Plumbe: *Factory Well-being.* (Sevenoaks Press, 1949.)

7. J. Munro Fraser: *A Handbook of Employment Interviewing.* (Macdonald & Evans, London, 1950.)

8. For details and illustrations of various techniques and procedures in the practice of "Personnel Management", including joint consultation and employee records, see the various broadsheets and pamphlets published by:
    The Institute of Personnel Management.
    The Industrial Welfare Society.
    The British Institute of Management.

9. O. Tead and H. C. Metcalf: *Personnel Administration.* (McGraw Hill, New York, 1947; 4th edit.)

10. Burleigh B. Gardner: *Human Relations in Industry.* (Irwin, Chicago, 1945.)

11. T. W. Harrell: *Industrial Psychology.* (Rinehart, U.S.A., 1949.)

12. V. Clarke: *New Times, New Methods and New Men.* (Allen & Unwin, 1950.)

13. Redgrave: *Factories, Truck and Shop Acts.* Thompson and Rogers. (Butterworth, 1949; 17th edit.)

14. *A Short Guide to the Factories Act.* (H.M. Stationery Office, 1949.)

CONTROL

By J. MADDOCK

CHAPTER I

THE NATURE AND PURPOSE OF CONTROL IN MANAGEMENT

Definition. The Development of Control. The Objects of Control. Control a Process in Management. The Control Activity in Organisation Structure. Organisation for the Control Activity. The Detail of Control. Introducing Control Information

DEFINITION

CONTROL is the continuing process of measuring the actual results of the operations of an organisation in relation to the results which were planned for that organisation, either as a whole, or in its various parts, and of direction and action accordingly.

THE DEVELOPMENT OF CONTROL

Industrial activities have always been subject to some form of control process. At the time when the industrial unit was small, simple and controlled directly in all its features by an individual, organisational control was altogether a matter of individual application arising from the concentration of functions in the individual. Thus the proprietor of a business personally would carry out most of his buying and selling, supervise manufacture, and keep his own record of his assets and liabilities.

In the early stages of the development of industry, solvency, ability to meet liabilities, was probably the only overall test of management. The application of what have since been identified as processes of management, e.g. forecasting, planning, was ill-developed. Often it was unconscious; or, if conscious, was merely in relation to a single transaction or a group of transactions.

Manifestations of control could be found in action to avoid obvious waste of materials or time, or in adjustment to meet changed requirements, e.g. engaging or dismissing labour in accordance with the state of the order book. Such manifestations cannot be regarded as control as a function of management owing to their intermittent nature, lack of relationship to an overall plan, and because they dealt only with what was obvious. With the growth of larger and more complex enterprises it became necessary to delegate duties and authority, and the need for means to assess the results of delegation followed.

The development of book-keeping and accountancy made it possible to measure the results of business operations much more accurately, but control from annual accounts, in orthodox form, with insufficient or inappropriate detail, was too remote from performance to be a factor in effective management. Also, during the period between the annual accounts there was often a complete lack of current information regarding the progress of operations, or, where there was some information, it was incomplete. In many instances action taken could not be governed by anything except a translation of current problems into terms of past results, irrespective of the fact that the conditions of the past results would rarely apply to current problems.

Few attempts were made to use accounting information in the management of industrial affairs. Cost finding had to be carried out for selling price purposes, but it was empirical, and its effectiveness could be judged only in relation to the balance sheet. Except in general terms, the relative cost advantages of different manufacturing methods could not be measured; adverse trends, except those of the most obvious kind, were not revealed until long after they had started, and identification of the causes of high costs or poor trading results was often difficult, if not impossible, owing to lack of information.

With the increased rate of technical development and the more acute competition in world markets towards the end of the nineteenth century, there was a growing need for reliable and current information about business affairs, and cost-finding systems began to be applied extensively, particularly during the period 1914–18. Many of these systems, however, were subject to severe drawbacks such as:

Insufficient attention to the accuracy of first entries;
Over-elaboration; unnecessary figures, and delay in presenting results;
Classification of costs in terms of expense headings, without regard to organisation structure, so that action could not be taken through individuals.

Nevertheless, the development of cost finding was a marked advance in the control of industrial organisations. It introduced the techniques of analysis, measurement and comparison into the relationship between work done or service rendered and value in exchange.

Coincident with the introduction of costing systems, development took place in the science of management, and whereas in the first place the introduction of cost-finding systems was not recognised altogether as an aid in effective management, it became clear that cost finding was in fact part of a process in management. Recognition of this led to corresponding developments in accounting, and improvements were made in the technique of assembling, presenting and using information. The emphasis now is on control, on providing information whereby individuals in charge of industrial activities may be able to control those activities economically as well as technically.

THE OBJECTS OF CONTROL

The objects of control are:

By means of budgets and accounts, to relate income and expenditure to performance requirements, and to provide the means whereby expenditure can be controlled in relation to the net result of operating.

By means of standards and costs to disclose technical efficiencies and the advantages or disadvantages of alternative processes, or of alternative courses of action, e.g. the relative results of capital or revenue expenditure.

This statement of the objects of control is but an elaboration of the definition given. It permits of expression in great detail, and of grouping of the detail under three main headings: general financial control; performance control; and cost control, all of which are interrelated. It is much more important, however, to understand control in organisation as a factor which operates at and through all levels in the organisation, a factor operated by people, and not as a schedule of advantages described in the terminology of accounting.

Control implies a plan, a basis for comparison. One main object of control information, and one which is often overlooked, is that of establishing data for future plans.

CONTROL, A PROCESS IN MANAGEMENT

The purpose of management is co-ordination in the achievement of an object. Control—itself a process—is most concerned with the management processes of: forecasting, determining the object; planning, establishing what is necessary to achieve the object; operating, carrying out the plan; and accounting, recording variations in assets and liabilities as a result of operating.

There are other processes in management concerned with the achievement of an object. Examples are leadership and co-ordination. These and similar processes, dealing with the more intangible aspects of organised human relationships, do not permit of objective and definitive comparison, but the application of the control process to the results of operating will be significant of their effectiveness or otherwise.

It is important to distinguish between the preparation of control information and its use. Accounting, costing and recording, as such, are not control, and in management do not confer any right to exercise authority or direction over other activities. Control, the process in management, can be exercised effectively only through the organisation structure, i.e. by individuals, each in relation to his responsibilities, and the purpose of accounting, costing and recording in relation to control is to provide information as a guide to decisions or action.

Failure to appreciate this distinction is a common reason for regarding control information with suspicion. An accountant responsible for preparing certain control information may tend to assume an authority of information; or an executive may tend to resent the presentation to him of information which does not represent the position as he sees it, or the preparation of which he does not understand.

Therefore, if control is to be effective, it is essential from the outset that there should be complete understanding that control is a process in management, to be applied through the organisation structure, and that accounting, costing and recording are not control so much as means for control.

It is equally important to understand that the real value of control information is the use made of it. The best of systems and the greatest degree of detail do not guaranteee sound and effective management. Management information is not a substitute for management action. The need for judgment, for intelligent interpretation of figures and assessment of probabilities is paramount.

THE CONTROL ACTIVITY IN ORGANISATION STRUCTURE

The expression "control activity" refers to the preparation of control information. The application of that information to management problems is the "control function".

Even the largest organisation must be headed-up by an individual, and similarly there is need for the control activity to present an overall review of what was planned and what is happening. This necessarily involves centralisation of the final assembly of control information, but the detail may be widely decentralised. Also, there must be a centralised, i.e. overall, review of the application of accounting and costing practice to control function requirements in order to avoid unnecessary variations in recording methods, in expense classification, and in the presentation of detailed control information. Otherwise comparison is vitiated.

The degree of centralisation or decentralisation in the preparation of control information is a particular matter. It has to be worked out

for each enterprise or part thereof, and there are no general rules
Typical factors to be considered are:

The size of the business.
The size of the units, if any, within the business. (Size may refer to
number of employees, number and complexity of different manufactures,
capital employed, turnover, etc., either separately or in combination.
One or several establishments, and their geographical location.
Vertical or horizontal organisation of manufacture.
Whether or not the establishments make completed articles or pro-
ducts for sale, or whether they are "feeder" to other establishments.
Organisation structure, and the extent to which responsibility and
authority are delegated.
Whether or not the establishments are separate financial and legal
entities.

The dangers of over-centralisation are those of remoteness, duplication, loss of time, suspicion and lack of understanding of local
problems. The danger of too much decentralisation lies in the possibility of variations in method, in losing sight of the total position,
in inability to synchronise the presentation of results, and in variations
in comparative methods. Usually, the dangers of decentralisation are
less in effect and more easy to deal with than are those of centralisation.

A business enterprise need not necessarily be large, with a number
of establishments, to over-centralise or over-decentralise the preparation of its control information. A small concern may find
difficulty because the preparation of its control information is not
appropriate to its real needs.

Whilst there are no general rules, the position of the control
activity may be summarised with reference to:

(1) The assembly of control information for the enterprise as a whole.
    This necessarily involves a centralisation of authority in the control
    activity.
(2) Detail should be decentralised as far as possible, to produce local
    information which can be used promptly, maintaining at the same
    time an appropriate relationship with the centralised authority.
(3) Control of methods, expense classifications, etc., should be cen-
    tralised.
(4) Economy in the preparation of control information is secondary to
    effectiveness in use. It may be possible to aggregate certain clerical
    work of the control activity, to obtain economy in clerical effort,
    and yet, because of aggregation, suffer a net loss owing to ineffective
    use of information obtained.

ORGANISATION FOR THE CONTROL ACTIVITY

By its nature, involving the use of specialist techniques and knowledge, and because it involves some degree of centralisation to secure

the necessary overall review, the control activity must be set up as a separate activity. The preparation of control information is a major task in organisation; it cannot be dealt with satisfactorily as an adjunct to another main task.

The detailed organisation of the control activity depends altogether on factors such as those affecting centralisation or decentralisation. Where the entire control activity can be centralised, it is necessary only to break it down into its main divisions, the degree and level of breakdown being dependent upon the size and nature of the particular undertaking. In a small business, for example, the Accountant personally might supervise budgeting, accounting and costing. In a large business he might have two or three principal assistants, each responsible for a main division of work, his own work being that of co-ordination, interpretation and method. In a still larger and more complex business, with perhaps many establishments, the division of work would be carried farther, co-ordination, method and group account assembly being dealt with by the principal executive of the control activity—the Chief Accountant—with decentralisation of detail to the various establishments, under local executives, each responsible to the Chief Accountant for that part of the control activity associated with the establishment to which he is attached.

There may be many variants between the extremes. There is *no one* organisation for the control activity which, in the pattern of its organisation, should follow the general organisational arrangements. Decentralisation of detail should be designed to provide for the control information requirements of the decentralised operating activities, and should be organised accordingly, with reference to what is required locally as well as to what is required centrally. Control information is for use by executives responsible for operations, and not merely for the interest of the executive responsible for its preparation. Decentralisation of control therefore must be more than a projection of "head office" into the "field"; whilst retaining its correct relationships with the centralised authority, it must also be a working part of the operating activity or activities it serves. Decentralisation of any aspect of the preparation of control information should not mean that a departmental, i.e. centralised, structure is superimposed on a general arrangement of decentralised operating. Adaptations, e.g. of method and system, should be permitted where they can be justified, the burden of justification resting with the executive who requires the modification. Inflexibility based upon "head office" practice is dangerous.

The usual main divisions of the control activity are accounting and costing. Each of these divisions has its appropriate parts: accounting for purchases, for sales, for wages, for assets and so on; or, in costing, for utilisation of time and materials, and allocation or recovery of overhead expenditure. Accounting and costing are different aspects of the control activity. Costing is part of accounting, though it is sometimes regarded as being quite separate and distinct. In fact, it is analysis and sub-analysis of expenditure recorded in accounts and related to performance, i.e. to units of production or service. Consequently, in organisation for the control activity it is incorrect to set up separate Accounting and Costing Departments without a common head. The two are parts of the same whole.

It is sometimes found that one part of the control activity, accounting, is a direct responsibility of the Accountant, whereas another part, costing, may be a direct responsibility of the Works Manager. An arrangement of this type is illogical, and shows a lack of understanding of the control function. Not only are accounting and costing parts of the same subject, the recording of business transactions, but they require a common technique in many of their applications, and the one, costing, cannot be completed except from the other, accounting.

The most important control document in any Company or business enterprise is the balance sheet. The preparation of the balance sheet is an accomplishment of accounting. Costs, representing the application of accounting practice and information to operations, should have their relationship to accounts recognised in the organisation for their preparation, so that they may be integrated into the sum of records which find final expression in the balance sheet.

Unless, therefore, costs and accounts are recognised for what they are, parts of the same whole, their application and usefulness will suffer. Costs prepared in a Works Office, without liaison or link with accounts, are useless. They are not a tool of management. They are often misleading, and an avoidable duplication.

In practice, this is often a difficult question to resolve. Executives responsible for operations may take the view that they must have their own costing if costing is to be useful, or, where costing is not established as part of their duties, that the costs are therefore incorrect and inappropriate. This attitude finds its counterpart in the accountants who will give other executives figures which they, the accountants, think should be given, with no regard for what is really required. The problem can be dealt with:

By recognising that the control activity is a main activity, to be set up as such.

By establishing that the control activity has to produce control information required by operational executives, as this may be determined from time to time by the operational executives and the Accountant or bv the Board or the principal executive.

By explanation of methods and by relating accounts AND costs to the balance sheet.

By checking frequently that this general arrangement is strictly followed.

To the executive in charge of the control activity, this activity itself represents operations. Just as the costs of the operations of production and distribution require control by the executives responsible for them, so also is it necessary for the cost and effectiveness of the control activity itself to be measured.

There are no absolute standards whereby this can be achieved. The costs of the activity should be budgeted and performance measurement may be applied where appropriate, e.g. for a typing pool in a large undertaking. On the whole, however, the work of the control activity does not permit of precise measurement or the ready attachment of cash values. Assessment of the effectiveness of the activity is chiefly a matter of judgment. Things to look for are unnecessary elaboration of figures and undue refinement in detail. The object of control of the control activity is to ensure as far as possible that its cost is not more than the value of the results obtained. If the control activity is costed as such, the expenditure involved may be compared with that for other main activities, and over a period a relationship may be established. This is probably the best way in which to control the cost of the control activity, namely, to compare the level of expenditure with that of other main activities, and to control that expenditure against a forecast.

A part of the control activity often overlooked is that concerned with clerical management. This is the process of ensuring that throughout an organisation clerical methods and procedures are carried out with minimum cost and maximum effectiveness. Clerical management is the method study and planning of the control activity.

THE DETAIL OF CONTROL

Control information must:

(1) Be classified in accordance with expense responsibility.
(2) Present results in a comparative manner and on a consistent, though not rigid, basis.
(3) Be presented for a time period appropriate to the objects of the organisation, and be available at a time when the factors represented by the control information can be influenced by decisions based on the control information.
(4) Be the minimum to meet the real needs of those whose duty it is to use control information.
(5) Show clearly the exceptions to the plan or to the general arrangement in order to conserve management effort.

In general, the detail of control is the detail of accounting, using this term in the wider sense of recorded information relative to all aspects of business affairs. For control, therefore, what has to be done is to take all recording work and relate it to organisation so that it may be used by individuals in the organisation. This requires:

A. The establishment of a plan, first in terms of performance, e.g. in terms of quantities planned for sale or production, and then in terms of money.

The plan is in fact the sum of a number of separate forecasts, made by individuals each in relation to his responsibility and authority. It is therefore a model to which accounting and recording can be adapted to present the results of working for comparative purposes.

B. The modification of the accounting system to reclassify expenditure so that each classification is significant of the organisation structure, and to present short-term and up-to-date statements of the results of working as shown in accounts.

C. The analysis of expenditure to units of production or service, in order to enable cost prices to be determined, and to provide data for the measurement of work and utilisation of plant, materials, etc.

Within these requirements it is necessary to restrict detail to limits dictated by its usefulness. A surfeit of information may be opposed to the principle of control. It may well result in attention being directed wrongly, or in inability to assess the results of working and the interrelationship of the various parts of an enterprise.

INTRODUCING CONTROL INFORMATION

There are two main approaches to the problem of introducing control information: either broad control may be introduced generally, or detailed control may be introduced for a particular feature of the economy of the business. Subsequently, broad control may be broken down to detail as the need for detail becomes apparent, or detailed control may be built up to give broad control.

Of these approaches, the introduction of broad control first is unquestionably the more satisfactory. Not only does it give general information more quickly: it permits also of introduction without major upheavals in clerical systems; it is more easily understood and appreciated, and its extension to detail can usually be carried out with a minimum of staff.

Attempts to introduce full detailed costing, budgetary control, and other control information in a short space of time invariably fail. Usually they lead to the adoption of some form of broad control which later is broken down to detail as may be required. Often the chaos resulting from attempts to do too much in too short a period of time leads to control information being viewed with suspicion. Rarely too are the results accurate or up-to-date.

It is desirable, therefore, to introduce control information first of all in general terms, say, in blocks of expenditure or departmental costs, which in the course of time may be modified and adapted to produce necessary details.

CHAPTER II

OUTLINE OF CONTROL IN OPERATION

Control and Organisation Structure. Establishing Control Data. Comparison and Variations. Account Classification. Control through Activities. The Time Element in Comparison. Avoiding Unnecessary Information. Information must be Related to a Period. Simple Presentation of Comparisons. Definition in Control and its Effect on Organisation Structure. Summary

CONTROL AND ORGANISATION STRUCTURE

CONTROL in operation may well be illustrated by an example. Assume a Company with an organisation structure as in Fig. 70.

FIG. 70.

The example is a representative simple arrangement, and contains the essential features of most industrial organisation structures. It is worth while examining two ways in which it might be adapted and extended to more complicated requirements, because in this way it will be understood more clearly that control as a function is an integral part in organisation, and that, whilst the features of control in any given case are governed by the organisational arrangement, the underlying principles and their application are the same in all cases.

In the example shown in Fig. 71 below, the main activities of production and sales are brought together under general managers for each related product group, or for each factory, e.g. where one works serves a prescribed area, whilst activities which are common to the producing and selling units are established as service, with centralisation of control and decentralisation of detail. The basic pattern of the

557

first example (Fig. 70) is still maintained. Where, however, activities of a common nature are brought together, the pattern of organisation immediately follows that given in Fig. 71, with the basic pattern of the first example still maintained.

The second illustration is based on a holding company, as in Fig. 72 (opposite). In this case the relationship between the various parts is altogether financial.

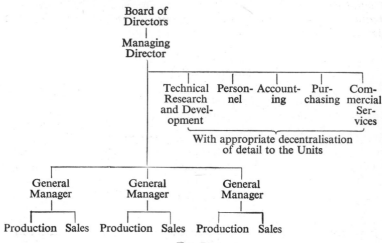

Board of
Directors

Managing
Director

Technical	Person-	Account-	Pur-	Com-
Research	nel	ing	chasing	mercial
and Devel-				Ser-
opment				vices

With appropriate decentralisation
of detail to the Units

| General | General | General |
| Manager | Manager | Manager |

Production   Sales   Production   Sales   Production   Sales

FIG. 71.

The outline in Fig. 71 does not show the relative importance of activities which together make up an enterprise. It is typical[1] and significant, not absolute. In a large retail business, for example, production activities would be replaced altogether by purchasing, and technical research and development would be displaced by consumer research. That is to say, in the particular case one activity, namely, purchasing, would assume a position of exceptional importance, in the place of production, which, with related activities, would be carried on by other concerns, and technical research and development would cease to be so directly significant. Market research, which would displace technical research and development, would do so because of its greater significance in relation to the problems of the particular enterprise. The essential features of the organisation structure would be therefore purchasing, distribution—warehousing, market research, selling, transport—and accounting.

[1] The Introduction of this book warns against facile use of the word "typical" in relation to organisation structure. In the context above, "typical" refers to the divisions of work, the grouping of activities, and *not* to the organisation structure.

Similarly, in a concern providing a service such as transport, the actual operation of the service would take the place of production, and distribution could well be confined to publicity and consumer research. A large service, e.g. transport, organisation might well have an actual production activity, say, for vehicles. In this case the organisation pattern would follow the outline in Fig. 71, the actual control of service operations, the main activity, being organised under a manager or managers responsible for areas or sections, the "production" activity being set up on a common basis, i.e. on a line with the common activities shown in Fig. 71 (opposite).

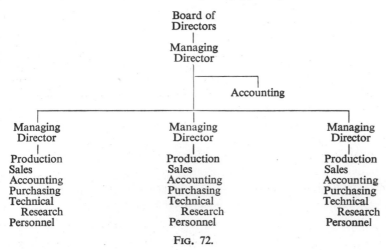

FIG. 72.

Taking an opposite extreme, a small business might combine one or more of the activities shown under one executive. Control in management is not something which can be applied only to the large business: it is necessary for the sound management of all economic enterprises, large or small. The combination of activities in a small business does not mean that these activities lose their identity; it means merely that a convenient aggregation has been adopted because it is practicable or expedient, or perhaps because the organisational requirements of the business are not understood. Whatever the reason or reasons, the small business can identify the elements of organisation and the divisions of work in its own structure, and provide for control accordingly, whether or not control is exercised through one, two, or several executives. All well-founded structures of organisation, even those which appear most complicated, can be reduced to an outline form which can be related to a simple division and/or grouping of activities. Therefore, in its essentials, control can be considered in relation to the simple form of organisation, which by division or division and aggregation may assume what appear to be and often are complex forms, with many interconnections between the various parts.

The outline in Fig. 70 is therefore taken for purposes of illustration as being representative of what is found, however it may be modified, in all industrial enterprises.[1] There is:

I. A Board of Directors whose principal duty is the determination o policy.

II. A Managing Director whose duty is to interpret policy and plan and co-ordinate its execution through his subordinate executives.

III. A Works Manager who is responsible for producing planned output at planned cost, with a Purchasing Officer responsible for obtaining raw and service materials in sufficient quantity at the time required to enable planned output to be made at planned raw material cost.

IV. A Sales Manager responsible for disposing of planned output at planned selling prices.

V. A Technical Research and Development Manager responsible for giving technical service to the Works and Sales Managers, and for providing a technical basis for continuity in operations.

VI. A Personnel Manager responsible for applying or ensuring the application of the personnel policy of the enterprise.

VII. An Accountant responsible for recording the business and internal operating transactions of the enterprise.

This summary emphasises the planning element in the duties of the executives named, or, in another enterprise, their equivalents. Planning is not mentioned specifically in the duties of the Technical Research and Development Manager, the Personnel Manager and the Accountant. Yet even in these cases there is a substantial element of planning. Research must for ever be looking ahead, and estimating the cost of projects which will mature in the future. Personnel management must forecast labour requirements and what should be done to meet them. Accounting has to be planned for staffing and for producing control information. The important thing to recognise is that there is this element of planning, no matter what it is called, in all business activities. How, then, does it take effect: in what form and by what means?

---

[1] The Introduction sets out the nine aspects of the whole Management field found in the Ministry of Education Report on *Education for Management*. It points out, too, that in arrangement these aspects do not conform to a type. Hence, and again, illustration is made with reference to a grouping of activities.

ESTABLISHING CONTROL DATA

The Board of Directors is concerned to show a profit from which the business of the enterprise may be financed in the future and a return may be made on capital invested. Both these items are matters of policy; amounts placed to reserve, or used for financing projects, i.e. capitalised directly, may be greater or smaller; dividends may bear a reasonable relationship to the cost of acquiring other capital, to risk and so on, or they may be disproportionate. It is necessary to determine the minimum net sum which, obtained from trading, and after making full allowance for the obligations of the business, e.g. to pay wages at agreed rates, is satisfactory for dividend purposes and appropriate to the continuity of the undertaking by enabling sums to be set aside for contingencies, replacement of fixed assets, financing trade, or development.

Once this sum has been determined, the Board requires its principal officer and his executives to submit their plans for achieving the desired net result.

A. *Distribution*

The first step is that of forecasting,[1] budgeting, for revenue, involving estimates of sales at estimated average realised selling prices. The sales budget is the responsibility of the executive in charge of distribution, and should be in two parts: the budget for what can be achieved with the manufacturing facilities available, and the extended budget giving effect to trends and market potential as a basis for expansion, contraction, or modification of the product range.

In addition to forecasting revenue, the distribution executive must forecast—budget—the expenditure in respect of detailed activities under his control, necessary to achieve that revenue. Thus he would budget for publicity, salaries, commissions, rent of sales offices and so on.

At this stage there are two items, one, a credit, revenue, and one, a debit, for expenditure associated with the work of distribution in relation to that revenue. There are, of course, many factors in budgeting for revenue; e.g. market conditions, stock policy, sales trends, price trends, Government policy. These are matters for separate con-

---

[1] The forecast of demand may lead to production problems which have to be resolved before a firm estimate of the demand for a product can be made. The level of production required to meet first estimates of demand may not be sufficient to permit of economic manufacture. This is especially important in new or expanding industries, wherein it is necessary to calculate the investment necessary before production is practicable. Where demand is elastic, the economics of production at different levels is a principal determinant in estimating the volume of demand.

sideration; here the object is to illustrate in general terms how control operates.

The quantitative sales budgets, possible and potential, should be submitted to the production executive and, after evaluation, to the accountant.

B. *Production*

From the sales budgets the production executive should review available plant capacity in relation to both budgets and, if need be, prepare an estimate of capital expenditure necessary to meet the requirements of the potential budget. He should take the finished product stock position and stock policy into account, and determine what has to be made in order to meet sales requirements, forecasting raw and service material requirements accordingly.

The official responsible for purchasing should examine raw and service material estimated requirements in relation to stocks, price trends, availability or otherwise of supply, and estimate the cost of providing the raw and service materials required by the production budget. This cost, applied to the production budget, forms part of the budget cost of manufacture.

The cost of operating purchasing during the budget period should also be forecast.

If it is assumed that cost control is established, standards can be applied to the production requirements to give theoretical costs for materials and labour, and the production executive's next task is to forecast expenditure on services, such as power generation and transmission, internal transport, canteen, etc. To some extent these charges may be matters of policy, but from their total and the prime costs established from standards, estimated costs of manufacture are determined.

C. *Technical Research and Development*

This item is almost altogether a matter of policy. Budgets should be established in relation to projects, i.e. the introduction of budgetary control implies that there must be planning of what is to be done. Any plan, of course, should provide some marginal allowance for contingencies. The budget for the Technical Research and Development activity should be prepared, in the first place, on the widest possible basis. The aim is to establish what is desirable; there follows the question of what can be afforded.

For immediate budget preparation purposes the Technical Research and Development budget will be in two parts: a "normal" amount based on experience and related to projects, and a desired amount, also related to projects. The presentation of the budgets should show the detail of their make-up, e.g. salaries and wages, materials, power, etc.

D. *Personnel*

The budget for this function is the estimated cost of carrying out the personnel policy of the enterprise in the budget period. Examples of expense headings are given later (Chapter V, Factory Expense Budgets).

E. *Accounting*

The accountant should estimate the costs of his department. Copies of all budget statements should be sent to the accountant who, including the budget for his department, should assemble them into the form of a budget profit and loss account.

This is his main task in the preparation of budgets. He can, how-ever, assist his co-executives greatly in the compilation of their budgets, both operating and expense. For example, the accountant should apply cost information to the preliminary quantitative sales budget, possible and potential, as a first guide to profitability. From this, it may be desirable to amend the sales budget, assuming that amendment is possible.

Similarly, the accountant can assist other executives in the preparation of their expenditure budgets, dealing with and advising upon budget distribution or recovery of overheads, trends of expenditure and provisions for, e.g., stock losses.

The assembled budgets form the budget for the enterprise as a whole. Consideration of this budget is a matter for the principal executive. Normally, he would discuss each stage with the executive concerned, and depending upon the results shown, would require alterations, such as reduction in expenditure under certain heads, until a final satisfactory budget was established, for Board approval, as a "target" for operations in the budget period.

Reference has been made to cost control and cost standards in manufacture. Standards are established by measurement, by observation and by study, and represent the one best—or acceptable—way of performing any job or operating any process at a given time. They find expression in material, labour, and plant utilisation, and can be extended to include services such as power or internal transport. Their effect is to provide, by comparison between actual and standard utilisation of materials, labour, and equipment a means whereby detail control of operations can be made effective within the broader framework of budgets, which are more concerned with "blocks" or groups of expenditure. The principle in both cases is the same, namely, comparison.

COMPARISON AND VARIATIONS

The next stage in control is, through the medium of the accounting and recording systems, to compare actual results with those which were planned. This stage introduces another element, namely, variations owing to changes in the load factor. There are possibly a few instances wherein operations can be forecast with an accuracy which almost renders the plan unnecessary, but, owing to the limitations which, for practical purposes, are found in the planning of all industrial activities, it is found almost always that variations from the plan become apparent as soon as the plan is put into operation. This is not to state that, for this reason only, a plan is unnecessary and useless because of the variations from it which inevitably arise during its currency. Indeed, the contrary is true, that it is the possibility of variations and unusual circumstances, which, over a period, make a plan an essential feature in the sound conduct of industrial affairs. The load factor element in budgets may be illustrated simply by considering that if the actual load on a plant is less than planned load, then a direct comparison between budget and actual expenditure will show an advantage in favour of actual. Budgeted expenditure, therefore, must be established on a basis which permits of modification for changes in load. There are two principal means whereby this can be achieved. The first is to have budgets for various levels of activity; the second is to reduce budget expenditure to a unit basis, i.e. to so much expenditure for each unit of production or service. The first method is complicated; a net fall in activity may be made up of a number of increases and a larger number of decreases, either numerically or quantitatively. The unit budget cost method is simple in application, the budget cost of any volume of, e.g., production being the product of the number of units at a unit budget cost in which an allowance for the effect of volume has been made. The problem of load introduces many complications into control; here its incidence is noted generally as an item for which special measures are necessary.

ACCOUNT CLASSIFICATION

Some of the means whereby comparison is effected are altogether matters of accounting; others are matters of factory recording. Generally, however, where a comparison is made in terms of money, the accounting system is, or should be, involved. Budgets and accounts therefore should be set up on a comparable basis. This may seem elementary; it is sometimes overlooked, budgets being prepared on one basis of account classification, accounts being prepared on another, with the need for reconciliations and the delay occasioned thereby. Account classification should be built up from the organisation structure. Items of expenditure, no matter what their nature, should be grouped in relation to the expense responsibility involved. This is a simple matter in the case of major items of expenditure, such as raw materials or direct wages; it is more difficult in the case of certain items of overhead expenses. Who, for example, is responsible for repairs expenditure? The Engineers' Department or the department for which the work is done? This point, with others similar, is discussed in detail later. It is introduced here in order to bring out what is basically the only method of dealing with the problem, namely, it does not matter so much whether or not the responsibility is placed on one executive or another, provided that responsibility corresponds with authority and that what is established is clearly understood.

That is to say, the niceties of accounting theory are much less important than a practical grouping of expense items under the positions in the organisation responsible for incurring expenditure. In this connection, too, it has to be remembered that as the subject of organisation is people, with all their imperfections, there will always be some difference of opinion between those who are responsible for expenditure and those who think they should be responsible. Hence the importance of a simple, readily understood, generally acceptable arrangement of expense headings, not necessarily rigid and determined for all time, but sufficiently representative and acceptable to be applied for long periods of time without major change, unless, of course, major changes are in fact required owing to fundamental changes in the nature, organisation, or practices of the enterprise.

CONTROL THROUGH ACTIVITIES

Net profit is a residue made up of a number of profits and losses which may be identified either against products or activities, e.g. purchasing, manufacturing, distribution. Normally, the amount of detail involved makes it impracticable to effect an identification of profit or loss in relation to single transactions. "Control" in this way is unwieldy, and indeed is not control because of itself it does not provide the means for actually affecting the course of what is happening in any part of the business. Consequently, the method to be adopted for control is that of identifying profits or losses with activities. The actual isolation of the profit or loss element in any activity would be a painstaking and very contentious affair. If, however, the revenue and expense aspects of industrial activities are planned in relation to a desired result, by means of budgets and standards, then control can be achieved quite readily by recording and acting upon variations between what was planned to happen and what has in fact happened. For control, therefore, accounting and recording are concerned chiefly to reveal, in sufficient detail for action to be taken, the nature of variations from any aspect of the budgets or standards.

THE TIME ELEMENT IN COMPARISON

The prompt presentation of the actual results of working, for comparison with budgets or standards, is of the utmost importance. One object of control is to enable corrective action to be taken, and this cannot be done if the subject of the action has long been completed. Unless control information is up-to-date, it is useless; the very pressure of day-to-day affairs makes enquiries into results long past a matter of small significance; current affairs may demand something entirely different. More important, the individuals concerned may have forgotten the details of the item under review owing to lapse of time, and "escape routes" may have presented themselves or be invented without possibility of denial. Effective control cannot be remote, and whilst sound conclusions may be drawn long after any event, it is too often the case that effective remedial action, especially in matters of detail, cannot be taken owing to lapse of time, and to the details available being blurred in the minds of those concerned. Yet the presentation of up-to-date control information is a major problem in accounting and recording. There are several reasons for this: suppliers may not send in their invoices, errors in recording may be found, and yet be difficult to trace and correct; clerical work, anyway, tends towards "peaks" which disturb normal routine; the incidence of holidays, with perhaps the need to make up and pay wages a day or two in advance of the normal day; these and similar factors have to be dealt with.

They may be dealt with in many ways which depend altogether on particular circumstances. Whatever detailed steps are adopted, however, must be preceded by an appreciation of the place of accounting and recording in control; by a full understanding that the purpose of accounting is to aid the achievement of the objects of the enterprise and that businesses do not exist so that accounts may be kept. Accounting and recording must be adapted to the needs of the business in which they are to be used.

AVOIDING UNNECESSARY INFORMATION

An additional complication is sometimes introduced at the stage wherein comparative information is being prepared. It is inevitably the case that execution of one part of the comparative work will open up new possibilities for further information. Some of this further information may be of value; often it is merely of interest. There is a natural tendency to elaborate figure information, perhaps to meet requests for particular detail from time to time, or because of excessive enthusiasm. This tendency has to be controlled carefully, and this control falls chiefly to the accountant. Unless it is controlled, there is more delay in presenting results which are important, and executives become overburdened with figures. Information should always be the minimum necessary, not the maximum which may be obtained, and in all cases the test should be: Can action be taken?

INFORMATION MUST BE RELATED TO A PERIOD

The information produced by the accounts and records relates to:

Short-term requirements.
Accounting period requirements.
Forecasting requirements.

Short-term requirements are concerned mainly with control of the practical operations of manufacture and distribution. The period may be taken generally as one week; but in some instances it may be daily, or it may be the production cycle, which may be more or less than one week. Typical short-term control information is for:

(1) Turnover.
(2) Production.
(3) Plant utilisation.
(4) Material supplies.
(5) Labour utilisation.
(6) Material utilisation.
(7) Services (power, transport, etc.) utilisation.

Except in very few instances, it is unnecessary to have short-term product or service costs.[1] If the elements of costs are controlled, the actual costs may be said to look after themselves.

The actual preparation of the short-term information is governed by organisational arrangements. It involves the Accountant's Department, the Sales Office, the Production Offices, and the Purchasing Office, and it presents the results of operating against the principal factors affecting them, internal and external. Internal factors are the standards and, where they apply, budgets. Budgets normally do not afford a satisfactory basis for comparison in the short term, but each

---

[1] Control may be achieved by working from product or service costs, i.e. the cost of part A is £1, whereas it should be 18s., or the cost of product B is 5s. per lb., whereas it should be 4s. This involves breaking down the part or product cost into its elements, often a lengthy and involved business, in order to ascertain where the "loss" has occurred. It is more practical to deal with the elements of cost in total in relation to actual production, estimated production and estimated cost.

business has to be considered on its merits. A departmental store working on a cash basis, or a biscuit manufacturer, might well be able to budget weekly; a manufacturer of heavy engineering products might not find it practicable so to do.

Short-term control information should be distributed appropriately amongst those responsible for operations, i.e. to each in relation to his responsibilities. Some of the figures would be quantities, e.g. man- or machine-hours lost, pounds of material used in excess of standard. Others would be in cash. At some stage all the figures would be expressed in terms of cash, departmental executives and higher management would certainly require to know the cash results of operating. On the other hand, it might be undesirable, or it might be less significant, to show production gains or losses in terms of cash. Spoiled articles, or pounds of material, or hours lost might be more readily appreciated.

Accounting period control information requirements consist of summaries of the short-term information, under all headings, with the addition of statements of overhead expenditure and recovery, a trading account, cost statements and a statement of assets and liabilities. All the items of revenue and expenditure are compared with the budgets and standards, variations being noted for reconciliation between budget and actual results. It is desirable, too, to prepare a summary of capital expenditure, which should have been budgeted, for monthly comparison with the budget. Distribution of this information should be appropriate to expense and performance responsibility in the organisation structure.

Forecasting requirements are simply a further aggregation and subsequent condensing of short-term and accounting period control information, carried out at three- or six-monthly intervals to bring out the significance of longer term trends. The longer term information may be supplemented by various ratios and comparisons of a financial nature.

SIMPLE PRESENTATION OF COMPARISONS

The effect of introducing control information is to enable those responsible for the various activities, or the parts of activities, in an enterprise, to know, not only what are the results of their work, but also how those results compare with what they were planned to be, or what they should have been. It is not sufficient, however, merely to know the factors in any situation; the knowledge has to be put to use.

Now the mass of intricate detail involved in any but the smallest and simplest business means that if the control information is to be of real value, it must be presented in a form which enables those concerned to see at once what items require their attention. Executives are not concerned so much with what is right as with what is wrong. This "what is wrong" must be made to stand out; it must not require extracting from the total amount of information available. Unless this is achieved, so that executives can concentrate on their jobs and *not* on interpreting and studying figures, control information loses its value, leading, not to control but to lack of control, for those who should be leading and acting have perforce to deal with extracting and interpreting information, often a tedious and lengthy task, or else have to decide to act without the aid of control information. Usually, in these circumstances, as practice counts for more than theory, the second course is taken.

Hence it follows that whilst appropriate information should be given to executives, it is more important that they should consider and deal with departures from the budgets and standards. These items should be shown separately as variations, gains or losses, or gains and excess costs. Once variations are noted, the task of management is to ascertain causes, thus achieving the real purpose of control information, namely, presenting the financial and operating results of any activity so that action directed to the end of controlling that activity in relation to a plan may be taken promptly and effectively.

It is not necessary to strive rigidly to adhere to the plan. Performances which are better than those planned should be encouraged. The purpose of the plan, in the form of budgets and standards, is to assist managers to achieve results at least equal to a minimum acceptable level, not to establish a basis from which variation is not permitted.

Often a more important thing than a variation itself is the reason for it. The business of investigating variations, of ascertaining reasons, cannot but lead to an improved understanding of the "Why" of proved results, and to a better application of the specialist technique of any executive, be he concerned with buying, design, manufacturing, or selling.

DEFINITION IN CONTROL AND ITS EFFECT ON ORGANISATION STRUCTURE

An important feature of the application of control information is its effect on organisation structure. An organisation structure may have grown over a period of years, may appear satisfactory, and yet be unwieldy, uneconomic and faulty. Control, with its emphasis on definition in organisation, reveals the need for improvement or adaptation in organisation structure and relationships because its application inevitably concentrates attention on the arrangements there are for responsibility and authority.

SUMMARY

(1) Control in management must be based upon organisation structure and defined executive responsibilities within the organisation structure.

(2) The establishment of control data requires that executives responsible for main divisions of activity must forecast the performances and costs of those activities.

(3) Control operates through positions in the organisation structure.

(4) Control information consists essentially of comparisons between planned and actual performances and costs, with accent on variations. It requires that account classification should be in terms of organisation structure.

(5) Control information must be prepared and presented promptly, simply and appropriately, and be related to a time period.

(6) Unnecessary information—information which cannot be used for action—should be avoided

CHAPTER III

BUDGETS—GENERAL CONSIDERATIONS

Introductory. The Period of Budgets. Change of Budgets during their Currency. The Nature of Budgets. Making "Targets" too Easy. Revenue and Expense Budgets are part only of Total Budgets. The Limitations of Planning. Organisation for Budgets. The Starting-point for Budgets. Budgets and the Smaller Business. The Degree of Variations. The Introduction of Budgets

INTRODUCTORY

CERTAIN general conclusions relative to budgets may be drawn from the detail given in the preceding chapter:

(1) Budgets are an expression of the objectives of a business, and provide a means whereby business operations can be directed in relation to the objective.

(2) The budget for a business as a whole is the sum of the budgets for each of the main divisions of the business. Similarly, the budgets for the main divisions of the business may be supported by subsidiary budgets.

(3) The introduction of budgets enables:

(*a*) Policies to be expressed with reference to defined plans and objectives.

(*b*) Co-ordination in the execution of policies to be improved by imposing an objective which has been accepted, i.e. a common objective.

(*c*) Measurement to be applied to the operations of a business by means of comparison between budget and actual results.

(*d*) Minimum net revenue and expense limits to be established with confidence.

(*e*) Financial requirements to be planned by showing what funds will be required, when they will be required, and towards what ends they are to be applied.

(*f*) Policies and practices to be changed in order that the objective may be achieved altogether or as nearly as may be possible.

(*g*) A greater degree of delegation to be exercised, and more freedom in the use of initiative and judgment within the framework and scope of the budgets. Men can direct their efforts to known ends, and, because the ends are known, can be given greater freedom in their actions accordingly.

(*h*) An improved factual basis to be adopted for planning future operations. Experience is not only recorded; it is recorded in relation to a plan.

(4) Control of the detail of manufacture or service requires that budgets should be related to performance and cost standards. These standards are not budgets, neither do they take the place of budgets, but they are essential if the budgets are to be more than financial estimates which are unrelated to production, distribution and service performances.

(5) Budgets require:

(*a*) Clearly established and definitive policies.

(*b*) A defined, logical and well-founded organisation structure.

(*c*) Active application of the policies which were in mind when the budgets were drafted.

(*d*) Account classification, not only in terms of expense headings, but also in terms of organisation structure.

(*e*) Comprehensive accounting and costing systems capable of producing promptly information for comparison with budgets and standards.

THE PERIOD OF BUDGETS

The most important single item in determining the budget period is that it must be appropriate, in the sense that it reflects and allows for the various influences and forces to which the business is subject. A year is a common budget period. It may be the calendar year, or it may be a year ahead from the end of each quarter. In the first instance the budgets are prepared for a year and reviewed yearly; in the second instance they are prepared for a year and reviewed quarterly. In some cases budgets are prepared monthly, and reviewed at the end of each month for a period, a quarter, six months, or a year ahead. In all cases it is necessary that the budget is continuous in its nature. It may be convenient and proper for one day's transactions to fall into one accounting or budget period, and the next in another accounting or budget period, but in fact one day's transactions are very much like those of the next day. Business is a continuing process, and budgets which are significant of its continuity are to be preferred.

The nature and characteristics of various industries and trades also are important when the budget period is being determined. The budgets should bring out the normal economic period relative to the particular business. The gas and electricity supply industries expect to make and sell more of their products in the winter months. A preserved foodstuffs industry may find that its main manufacture must be carried out in a period of two or three months, whilst distribution of the product is spread evenly over the months of the year. A garments factory may be making winter articles of clothing in the preceding spring or summer, and clothes for summer wear in the winter, the main product groups having different cost and sales values. Retail stores may be consistently busy, yet the sales value of articles sold may show substantial differences from time to time owing to seasonal requirements. In all these instances, yearly averages of sales, expenses, costs, or performances are unsatisfactory for short-term budget purposes, although, if they are continuing, i.e. based on a longer period which makes allowance for all the normal periodical fluctuations, they are not without their uses. That is to say there may be, and should be where conditions permit, a short-term and a long-term budget, and the budget period must be such that it represents fairly what is expected to take place.

Many industries, however, do not require that seasonal fluctuations should be brought into the budgets. In all probability the fluctuations are present, but they are of minor degree, and control against budgets can be effected readily by ignoring their existence. In these instances averages based on a long period may be used successfully, but the budgets should be reviewed at least twice a year, at six-monthly intervals, and preferably at quarterly intervals for a determined time ahead. It is essential to keep the distinction between short-term and long-term planning and control well in mind, and all results should be established for significant periods, i.e. periods significant of trends. One month's results may be unfavourable, another month's may be especially good, when compared with the budget. This is the short term; but unless the budget period is devised to take account of short-term fluctuations, the monthly results alone may be misleading, i.e. they are significant only in relation to averages over previous months which do take the longer term, the particular economic cycle, into account. The important feature, therefore, of a budget period is not the time it represents, but the appropriateness of that time to the particular business.

One factor which has to be borne in mind is ability to prepare accounting and cost information promptly in relation to the budget period. There is no purpose in having a supposedly short-term control if the actual results cannot be obtained until long after the period is ended. In certain industries, invoices are not rendered until the month after goods have been dispatched, so that a two- or, where there is delay, three-months' interval may rest between receipt of goods and invoice. Estimates may be used; in effect, they double recording work. In these circumstances, therefore, two or three months is the minimum time for the budget period in order not to confuse comparison by short-term fluctuations. It is not by any means the case that one month's excesses are roughly equal to another month's shortages. This rule may be applied to invoices outstanding in a manufacturing or other business where the total may be small compared with total purchases invoices. It does not permit of universal application.

Lastly, a too-short budget period may mean that the detail involved in providing comparative information promptly is such that it cannot be handled except by excessive staffing. Whether or not this applies can be judged only by experience in particular cases. The "excess" staffing may be justified. Equally, it may represent unnecessary refinement. Budget periods must be regarded critically in the light of what is needed to meet their requirements, and whether or not these requirements are essential.

CHANGE OF BUDGETS DURING THEIR CURRENCY

If the budget period is short term, or if the budgets are reviewed at say quarterly intervals, it should not be necessary to change the budgets within the budget period. Longer term, e.g. yearly budgets, may require to be changed. There are two principal reasons for changing budgets before the normal time for change:

A. When the basis on which the budgets were first drawn up, and the conditions affecting it, have changed materially, or no longer apply, so that the budgets become impossible of achievement. An example is a change from peace-time to war-time economy in an industry whose productions are affected by the change.

B. When the budgets are proved to be ill-founded and faulty.

It is not possible to prescribe general rules which can be used to determine when budgets should be changed during their currency, i.e. to define what is meant by "changed materially". An example is given (A above); other examples are:

(1) The closing of large export markets for political or financial reasons.
(2) The incidence of new invention, which, if readily available, makes the use of an older technique or product obsolete, and, if they cannot be improved, limits or eliminates their sale potential accordingly.

Budgets should not be changed just because variations arise between any aspects of budget and actual results. It is only where examination of the variations reveals that the budgets are no longer significant that interim changes should be made. With short-term continuing budgets this is an unlikely happening.

THE NATURE OF BUDGETS

All budgets, whether departmental, divisional, or total, should represent the minimum it is proposed to do or to accept. Performances should not be restricted because budgets have been set; budgets do not say, "Thus far and no farther". They point the way, but they may not be able to indicate how far along that way progress might be made. As net results they are the minimum acceptable and not the maximum possible.

The successful preparation and use of budgets for control is largely a matter of personal qualities. It is emphatically not a matter of statistics, averages, calculus, or actuarial science. The budget is more of the nature of a plan of campaign. It represents what many individuals are going to try to do in order to achieve a certain objective. Statistics, averages and so on are tools to be used in budgeting, and they are useful chiefly in so far as they show trends. In budgeting, nothing can take the place of individual and corporate judgment, and budgets should give ample scope for the exercise of initiative in achieving results. Arithmetic might show that a certain volume of production from a plant is normal, and budgets might be calculated accordingly. But a man with ideas might revise the work of that plant to produce a surprising increase. Sales of a commodity may have tended to a normal, everyone concerned accepting the mathematics of averaging as being all that can be done. But a new competitor with an improved and cheaper product or manufacturing method might just be ready to enter the market, or a market survey may open up completely new applications. Trends, therefore, must be looked at in the light of current knowledge and experience. Merely to accept certain figures because, over a period, they represent the trend, is not budgeting. It is stagnating. It is in the nature of budgets to establish targets which, with normal effort, should be and in fact are possible of attainment.

MAKING "TARGETS" TOO EASY

An obvious criticism of budgeting is that those concerned might set the budgets at levels easily achieved. Sales executives may set their turnover figures on the low side in order to be sure of reaching them. Production executives may set their output figures low, their budget costs being correspondingly high, in order to be sure of satisfactory output performances. Nor are accountants able to exercise any correcting influence in these technical matters as they may find expression in the budgets. It will be observed that the two tendencies have a similar effect on profitability, namely, they tend to reduce it. It might be, of course, that the limitations deliberately set upon sales targets include the least profitable lines, so that budget net profitability shows a fortuitous increase. This is beside the point; the effect of setting targets at such a level that their achievement is more easy in the longer term is reflected directly in net profitability. The tendency to "play safe" is very human, and it must be guarded against. Consciously or otherwise, it is a factor affecting the judgment of all who attempt business forecasting in any of its features. Budgeting demands an objective outlook, honesty and a realistic approach.

A certain measure of protection is afforded by discussion in the stages of budget preparation, and in particular the principal executive should allow for natural precautions. Equally he should allow for excessive enthusiasm and zeal. In a business with a marketing department and an effective production standards department there are existent more checks on budget estimates, e.g. the market estimates and statements of consumer trends, and the production and cost standards.

It may be argued that if the final budget net profit is satisfactory, then also the budgets are satisfactory, i.e. it may not appear to matter that sales targets are set too low and expense items too high. Such a proposition can be accepted, but it is not good budgeting. It is more typical of an approach which places emphasis on safety, even if it involves a measure of self-deception. Budgets aim, amongst other things, at showing a better or, in given conditions, the best way, whether or not that way is of policy or of detail within a policy. They demand that the supporting detail can be substantiated and supported, that reasons can be given for all figures submitted. Most of all they require the moral qualities of uprightness and honesty.

REVENUE AND EXPENSE BUDGETS ARE PART ONLY OF TOTAL BUDGETS

Budgets are usually thought of in terms of revenue and expenditure. This may be by an association of budgets with national and local government income and expenditure, but in business more is required than mere forecasts of revenue and expenditure. The final criterion of the conduct of a business is its overall soundness or otherwise, for immediate purposes, as it is expressed in the balance sheet. Consequently, the revenue and expenditure budgets should be regarded as means of approach to a position shown in a balance sheet, their effect being related to a current balance sheet, which, in this way, can be projected into the future. That is to say, there is more in the conduct of a business than control of income and expenditure, important though this control is. There are the relationships which exist between groups of assets, fixed and current, between debtors and stocks, creditors and invested capital and so on. These relationships are usually described as ratios, and they may be applied to actual and budget balance sheets. Budget balance sheets may be prepared by applying revenue and expenditure budgets for a period to the balance sheet as at the commencement of that period, to give a balance sheet as it should be if the budget forecasts are realised (see Chapter VI). One difficulty in achieving this is that the balance sheet as at the commencement of a budget period is not often available at the commencement of that period. It is prepared during the currency of the budget to which it is an essential prelude. There are two ways in which this problem may be met. If the budget period is long, say a year, then, if the application of the budgets for any year to the balance sheet as at the commencement of the year shows an unsatisfactory budget balance sheet position, there is at once a case for review of the budgets. This may apply even if the budget period is shorter in term, say, three or six months, but in these instances, and this is the second method, the position as it may appear from the application of budgets to the balance sheet provides a basis for corrective measures in the budget period immediately following. That is to say, budgets for the next following period must be designed to take account of balance sheet trends which appeared in the preceding budget period.

Also it is necessary to take account of the budget rates of income and expenditure, in order to ensure that adequate finances are available for commitments, or, if they are not as it may appear from the forecasts of trading, to determine what steps are necessary for financing operations. This too is an important subsidiary use of budgets, namely, information is made available whereby financial operations can be planned to the best advantage, adjustments in the financial plan being made as actual results become available for comparison with budget.

THE LIMITATIONS OF PLANNING

Budgets are the financial and operational control aspects of planning. They are based upon plans, and they are subject to the ordinary limitations of planning. It is therefore pointless to insist that budget results *must* be achieved. It is not in the natural order of things that future detail can be predicted with accuracy. What can be done, and this is what budgets purport to do, is to assess available data about a business undertaking, to note trends, and to interpret them intelligently in relation to a desired objective. There is nothing rigid in this, nor can there be. Budgets must be applied with the knowledge that should the need arise, they must be flexible to meet changed or changing conditions. On the other hand, it is just as necessary to guard against the mind which accepts all deviations from the budget as being inevitable, simply because planning has its limitations. It has been observed earlier that budgets should represent the minimum it is intended to do.

From this and what has been stated about other general aspects of budgets, it will be obvious that, of themselves, budgets do not guarantee success. There have been instances wherein budgetary control has been introduced and has failed in its purpose because the error has been made of regarding a system as an end in itself. Budgets, like cost and performance standards, costs, accounts, and so on, are just as good as the use made of them. An imperfect or incomplete system applied and interpreted intelligently is far better than the most complete aggregation of systems, methods and gadgets which, pretending to ensure control, mislead men into thinking that the system is the control.

ORGANISATION FOR BUDGETS

The preparation of budgets must be organised. Each person concerned must know for what part of the total budget he is responsible, to whom he is responsible, and when he is required to do the work involved. As in the organisation of all work, co-ordination is necessary, and it may be exercised by the principal executive, or, when he has issued the necessary instructions, by one of his immediate subordinates. The accountant is in a useful position to co-ordinate the preparation of budgets and to facilitate the adjustments which follow discussions on the departmental or divisional budgets, wherein opposing points of view have to be reconciled. The accountant's work in this connection must be understood clearly as that of co-ordination and assembly. He is often in a position to advise or guide, but by status, experience, or knowledge, he is rarely in a position to *direct* budgets for other activities. His advice and guidance, however, can be invaluable.

Budgets should be prepared before the period to which they relate, and a programme of the various parts and sub-budgets is essential to secure co-ordination. Such a programme should be drawn up with reference to the organisation structure, each grouping of activities having set against it the budgets for which it is responsible, the normal time by which the budgets are required and the order of preparation. The programme can well be set out in the form of a timetable, each executive concerned receiving a copy of the part for which he is responsible.

THE STARTING-POINT FOR BUDGETS

In the example given in the preceding chapter, budgets begin with profitability. Profitability is taken as the starting-point, because at present it is the measure by which the acceptability or otherwise of operations is determined. A business exists to meet a demand; the extent of its success in meeting the demand is measured by its profitability. Whilst the profit figure is therefore the final arbiter, in practice budgets may start with volume of turnover or with expense levels. In some businesses it is not easy or practical to forecast sales, an example is a specialist engineering business making "one off" articles or dealing with specialist repairs. In such a case the level of expenditure is as good a practical basis as can be found for budgeting purposes. Over a period it is invariably found that constant relationships are set up between groups of expenditure and/or sales levels. A sales budget can therefore be based upon the expense ratios. Again, it is emphasised that whatever ideas may exist regarding the basis for budgets, it is only in so far as expense levels indicate a level of turnover yielding an acceptable profit level that they become really significant for budget purposes.

If volume of turnover is used, values must be applied to it and costs must be calculated in order to determine profit. Turnover may be the beginning, but profitability is the determinant.

BUDGETS AND THE SMALLER BUSINESS

It may be thought that budgets are necessary only in the case of a large, complex enterprise, wherein the mere fact of there being several departments or sections makes it imperative that each departmental or sectional executive should have some performance target; that the smaller business, owing to the greater ease with which its various parts can be visualised in relation to the whole, has no need for such mechanisms.

In the preceding chapter it is observed that control—the function in management—is necessary in all economic enterprises, large or small. It is perhaps true that owing to its greater size and complexity the large business must rely more upon and use more records, in the place of the memory of an individual, so often found in the smaller business. Apart from the succession problem; when the individual goes his memory goes with him, it is found invariably that recorded practice and results vary, often considerably, from the impressions which were in the minds of individuals. The degree of variance may not be important, but this cannot be assumed.

Control is a function in management. It is carried out in some degree or form in all enterprises, but can be most effective only where it is recognised and accepted, provision being made accordingly. In the smaller business this provision can be more simple and easily visualised in relation to the business. Budgets do not mean elaborate "systems" and paper work, or the substitution of routines for judgment. They are part of the application of a technique of recording and comparing without which judgment can be based only on impressions, not on facts.

THE DEGREE OF VARIATIONS

A question sometimes asked is, "How accurate should budgeting be?" Alternatively, "Is budgeting satisfactory when the variations are within 5 per cent. or 2 per cent?"

At the outset there is *no* general answer to a question of this nature. Not only has each case to be considered on its merits; in one industry it might be possible to forecast repeatedly within a 5 per cent. limit, in another the margin might be 20 per cent.; but also the incidence of general economic affairs over a period necessarily affects performances in relation to forecasts.

In any event, the purpose of budgets is not to set a series of targets which must just be reached. It is more the forward expression of a policy, applied to resources available and expected to be available, in order to express a minimum result in relation to what is required to achieve it. From this, it follows that, as has been observed already, control against budgets is concerned much more with the reasons for than the extent of variations. The extent of variations is a reconciliation between actual and budget performance, and is the financial effect of the factors which have caused the variations. It is this which is important: to know the financial effect or trend of variation factors so that action can be taken regarding them or allowance can be made for them in the future. Whilst it is true that action following variations is directed towards allowance or correction for the future in order to minimise variations, this is not to say that "satisfactory" budgeting is measured altogether by the absence of variations.

THE INTRODUCTION OF BUDGETS

The introduction of budgetary control is usually a long-term job. Apart from the many problems connected with devising budgets and organising accordingly, most instances require adaptations or modifications in accounting in order that the budgets may be supported by reliable data regarding what is taking place. The main steps are few and, in their essential features, simple:

(1) Relate budgets to established chart of organisation and established policies.
(2) Draw up expense responsibility account classification accordingly.
(3) Prepare schedule of performance responsibility.
(4) Prepare budget programme.
(5) Determine the form of account presentation necessary for budget comparisons.

In this, as in many other matters, the gradual approach is invariably the best. Amongst other things, the successful operation of budgetary control usually requires a period of re-education. The first reactions towards control of expenditure and of performance are hardly likely to be encouraging. The individuals concerned have to see for themselves just how budgetary control can be of advantage to them in carrying out their work before they can support the idea fully, without reserve. Also, some time is necessary in order that the possibility of making targets too easy, dealt with earlier, can be avoided. Almost invariably at the outset sales cannot be budgeted because "this is a very special business which can be dealt with only on a day-to-day basis". Similarly, production can be planned in broad terms only "because of the inconsistency of sales demands". Also, it may be argued that customers are odd people, who would resent strongly any attempt at a planning of production which might not quite meet their individual requirements. These objections cannot be dismissed as being of no consequence; they contain certain elements of truth which are concerned, not so much with establishing budgets, as they are with the operations of the business. In many instances, too, there may not be standard cost information to be used in establishing or checking the detail of budgets. The examples given are but typical of what is found; they are not an exhaustive list of the reasons why budgeting is thought to be impossible in certain cases.

The gradual introduction of budgetary control starts with "blocks" of expenditure or of revenue. It is necessary only to estimate on a broad basis, and past records, adjusted for current policy and trends, provide the information required. In effect, control on this basis is a form of comparison with previous periods' results. Comparison, however, should be made more significant by relating the average, if an average is chosen as the basis, or the preceding period's figures, if they are chosen, to policy. If advertising expenditure has been about £10,000 per annum, it is pointless to use £10,000 for comparative purposes if it is known that the advertising programme will require £15,000. If wages have been increased by say 1*d.* per hour, the effect of this increase must be added to whatever figure, derived from preceding years, is to be used as a budget for wages. Usually too accounts have to be recast in order to arrange items of expense responsibility properly in the structure of responsibility. This in itself is a useful step towards the introduction of control. Attempts at forecasting from orthodox accounts quickly reveal the limitations of these accounts in the control of business operations, mainly because the classification of expenditure is not representative of the organisation responsible for the expenditure.

Before any attempt is made to break down the broad control figures or to introduce refinements, it is highly desirable that the broad control should be working effectively and be well understood. Time taken in ensuring smooth working and successful application in the early stages is amply repaid by the more rapid development of control technique which it encourages. The next step is to break down the broad expenditure or performance figures to detail as it may be required. The important words are "as it (detail) may be required". Figures lead to more figures; there is always a tendency for control information to expand into a mass of detail never envisaged when the control was introduced and impossible of application to business problems. Every breakdown of control information should be examined critically, the advantages should be real and well understood, and the cost of achieving the breakdown should be assessed.

Again, it is always wiser to proceed slowly, not to endeavour to introduce too much control information at one time. The amount of detail required under the main divisions of expense and performance grouping should be regarded in the light of the use that can be made of it. Control in management—like control of anything, machine, vehicle, or piece of equipment—has to be learned, and whilst the amount of detail which can be assimilated by individuals in a given time varies, the habit of using information for control purposes takes time to acquire. A little control information used really well is much better than a mass of detail which leads but to superficial attention to fundamentals. With the natural development of the technique of using control information which comes from practice, more detail can be dealt with readily, placed rightly in the control scheme of which it is part, or, should it prove unnecessary, confidence will normally have been developed whereby what is not required can be expunged.

CHAPTER IV

SALES BUDGETS

Introductory. The Form and Presentation of Sales Budgets and Sales. The Treatment of Selling Prices and Carriage Costs in Sales Budgets. Responsibility for the Sales Budgets. Comparison: Deliveries Invoiced or Orders Received. The Period of Comparative Statements. Prompt Presentation of Sales Information. Using Sales Control Information. Sales Budgets in the Smaller Business. Expense Control for Distribution

INTRODUCTORY

PRACTICAL factors underlying the preparation of sales budgets are dealt with in Part I, Distribution. Here it is assumed that a sales forecast has been made, at least quantitatively, and that its practical requirements have been established. The Distribution Executive may attach values to his sales forecast, based on what the market will bear, or on his experience and knowledge, or he may request the Accountant to place values on the budget forecasts. There are instances wherein a quantitative sales budget is unnecessary; examples are certain wholesale or retail trades in which the products sold carry fixed profit margins, so that the turnover in each line is automatically significant of contribution to net profitability. The budgets for departments or branches might be shown in some detail, and obviously the greater the number of lines and the more the variations in the profit margins between the lines, the greater the complexity of forecasting. Often considerable judgment and skill is required in forecasting such things as fashion trends or what is and what is not likely to be required. Once these forecasts have been made, control is relatively simple, and, unless direct manufacture, i.e. manufacture by the firm concerned, is involved, the sales budgets are the key budgets for control purposes.

It may be convenient to digress upon the operation of control in a typical case. Sales budgets are determined for a range of products carrying fixed "profit" margins. These margins have to provide for the expenses of selling, most if not all of which may be regarded as fixed, and profit. Also, they have to provide for stock losses, "sales", and redundant stocks. Estimates of reduced margins for these contingencies and conditions are a matter of experience and policy. The important thing in businesses of this type is to maintain volume of turnover and to control expenses within the limits of the margins. Control must be short-term; frequent in its application. The period may be one week; it should not be greater than a month. As sales are made, they build up, in effect, a fund from which the cost of the goods sold and the expenses of selling them have to be paid. The first item, the cost of the goods sold, is a simple matter of receiving invoices and paying them, involving the control technique, e.g. to the extent that more than was forecast should not be paid for goods unless profit margins are increased accordingly, or unless more can be sold at a reduced margin to achieve the forecast of profit in total.

Administrative control is therefore concerned with turnover, ensuring that the turnover is adequate to meet the expenses of achieving it, and controlling those expenses within the margins allowed to leave a margin for contingencies and a satisfactory profit. Where business is conducted on a cash basis, both for purchases and sales, the problem of control is made yet more simple. Indeed, in these instances the chief difficulty is that caused by the sheer volume of transactions and the possibly very large number of different products sold. The importance of this digression rests in its emphasis upon dealing with the problems of control by means of contribution, i.e. by means of turnover which, after charging the cost of goods sold, should leave a margin for expenses and profits. It is unnecessary to complicate control by elaborate arbitrary allocations of expenditure; expenditure can well be controlled within the predetermined limits for which a given turnover is required. This is important, and is dealt with in more detail under expenditure control.

THE FORM AND PRESENTATION OF SALES BUDGETS AND SALES

The precise form of the sales budget, or of the presentation of the sales results of trading, is different in each business. Similarly, the comparative period may and does vary. What is necessary for control purposes is a comparison between what has been achieved and what has been forecast. Wherever possible in a manufacturing business it is desirable to show comparisons quantitatively as well as in value. The comparative statement should be designed to show variations and cumulative totals within the budget period. The actual comparative period is usually taken as the month, either the calendar month or a four-weekly period. Weekly statements of turnover are valuable, but it is rare that any real purpose is served by showing budget comparisons against them. The period is too short; budget comparisons should be made at the end of periods which are significant of trends.

No purpose would be served by illustrating typical presentation of sales against budgets. Whatever the precise form comparison may take, it consists fundamentally of information as follows:

Budget Quantity Sales compared with Actual Quantity Sales.
Variations between Budget Quantity Sales and Actual Quantity Sales.
Budget Realised Selling Prices compared with Actual Realised Selling Prices.
Budget Value of Sales compared with Actual Value of Sales.
Variations between Budget Value of Sales and Actual Value of Sales.

To be most useful, the figures should be presented for the normal comparative period and the budget period to date. Another useful comparison is for similar information shown as the average of a number of preceding comparative periods.

It is necessary to know the total position, and it is necessary to know the detail position. Total sales may compare favourably with the budget, yet there may be wide variations in the detail; the sales of any product may compare favourably with the budget, because losses in one territory or industry are made up by gains in other territories or industries.

Accordingly, the total budget for sales may be subdivided into detail budgets for various aspects of sales activity. The more usual division is to sales territories or areas, but it might be to industries or uses, with or without further territorial subdivision. There may be a separate budget statement for each product, with the required "breakdown" of detail shown on it; or there may be statements including *all* products, with supporting detail statements. There are no overriding merits about one form of presentation when compared with another. It all depends on what the man concerned wants to know and the way in which he wants the detail put to him in order to acquire knowledge. On the other hand, except in the most simple cases, one statement which attempts to portray all the aspects of control is unwieldy and so obscured by detail that it is almost useless for action. Control has to operate through men in relation to things, and the presentation of control information should indicate clearly the direct relationship between individuals and performances.

Graphs and charts may be useful. Some people prefer them; others find they can grasp the significance of columns of figures more readily. In all instances, too, it will be the case that various methods will be tried over a period. Hence, in dealing with presentation, it is essential to be flexible, ready to try new arrangements of figures, or new forms of graphical presentation, and to be co-operative in the trial.

An accountant responsible for the preparation of certain detailed comparative statements for sales control purposes may know that modifications are nothing more than a whim. If his arguments are inconclusive or unacceptable, if the executive concerned wants the figures that way, then "that way" is the way to present them. The reason is that this other executive, whatever activity he is concerned with, is the executive responsible for performance in that activity.

The information to be shown by comparative statements naturally varies with each business. Generally, and elaborating what is described above, information as follows is required for budgetary control purposes:

(1) Actual deliveries invoiced compared with the forecast of deliveries invoiced for the same period, in quantity and value.

(2) Prices realised, either gross (including packages, carriage, etc.) or net, compared with the forecast.

(3) Cumulative figures from the commencement of the budget period for deliveries invoiced and prices realised.

(4) Appropriate subdivision of the total comparative figures to sales territories, industries, products, etc.

(5) Orders received and executed in the budget period, with the balance of orders outstanding and corresponding stocks at the beginning and the end of the budget period.

(6) Analysis of sales credits.

The preparation of detail under items (1) to (4) and item (6) is usually carried out by the Accountant's Department; the detail under item (5) is obtained from sales records and stock records, the stock records also being a responsibility of the Accountant. A typical comparative statement is shown at Fig. 73.

Product	This Period						Totals to Date					
	Budget			Actual			Budget			Actual		
	Qty.	Price	Value	Qty.	Price	Value	Qty.	Price	Value	Qty.	Price	Value

Note.—The comparative columns would be repeated for variations and, if they are used, for the moving average or average to date figures.

Fig. 73.

This general form contains the essential features of any comparative sales control statement. The detail on the statement might be arranged under territories, departments, e.g.:

<table>
<tr><td>Territory 1.
Products</td><td rowspan="2">Comparative
Columns</td><td>Department A.
Products</td><td rowspan="2">Comparative
Columns</td></tr>
<tr><td>Territory 2.
Products</td><td>Department B.
Products</td></tr>
</table>

The typical statement shown in Fig. 73 is concerned with deliveries invoiced. The order and stock position may be shown in Fig. 74.

| Product | Stock | | | | | Orders | | | | |
	Open-ing	Produc-tion	Total	Dis-patches	Clos-ing	Blnce. Out-standing	Recd.	Total	Dis-patches	Blnce. Out-standing

FIG. 74.

This form too is an outline of the main features of information required for control of sales. It can be adapted to conform with the detail requirements of any business; it is not to be regarded as a form for universal application. The "Orders" part of the form should also be presented in detail similar to that in the deliveries—accounting sales—statement. This is necessary if the true nature of variations is to be understood. Suppose, for example, that sales of a product by Salesman A show a marked gain over budget, whilst the sales of Salesman B are below budget. Examination of the order statement may show that Salesman B has much more to his credit as unexecuted orders. The reason may be that for special reasons deliveries to customers in Salesman A's territory had to be given priority, or perhaps that adverse weather or a carriage embargo affected deliveries in Salesman B's territory. This leads to an important conclusion, namely, that the purpose of comparative statements is twofold: to show variations, and to be significant of the reasons for variations. Comparative statements can well show variations, the comparative figures are on them. Often, however, it is useful to extract the variations on to a Variations Summary which, after investigation, can be extended to show an analysis of variations under the main headings applicable in the particular case. This understanding of the reasons for variations cannot be emphasised too strongly. It would be futile to blame a salesman for a reduction in sales value if his quantity sales had been maintained and the reduction had occurred because of a general reduction in selling prices over which he had no control. This is obvious, but it might be overlooked by a harassed executive unless he had an analysis of variations. Control of sales from budgets is not merely a matter of dealing with single items or isolated cases so much as of ascertainment of all the factors affecting a situation and assessing their interaction. Single items and isolated cases have to be dealt with, but action is, or should be, based on thinking from the general to the particular.

THE TREATMENT OF SELLING PRICES AND CARRIAGE COSTS IN SALES BUDGETS

The price figures may present difficulty. In some instances carriage charges are included in selling prices, in others they are shown and charged separately on invoices for goods sold. Where carriage charges are included in selling prices no problem arises, the budget, actual and variation columns would deal with established figures, which, in their various parts—materials, labour, carriage, etc.—should be the subject of expense control. On the other hand, where goods are quoted at ex-works prices, the significant figure is the ex-works price. Carriage charges added to invoice values are what the carrier has charged, or, in accordance with established rates, will charge for delivery. They contain no profit element. The problem for control purposes may be expressed thus:

A. If carriage charges (or similar charges, e.g. insurance) are included in the comparative figures, then the total ex-works value of sales cannot readily be established.

B. The extraction of carriage charges from invoice values to obtain ex-works values may be a long job, expensive in clerical labour.

C. Geographical variations in distribution will cause fluctuations in average realised selling prices, and the average of the carriage, etc., charges may be of no significance when translated into places, i.e. the average will be significant only of an average haul, an interesting but hardly useful figure which anyway is complicated by different rates for the various means of transport to the same destination. Also, in instances customers may, probably will, collect their own goods, so that the average figure of realised price becomes even less significant.

D. Carriage charges have to be paid; they are part of total cost which is recovered from the customer. Why therefore select them for special treatment any more than another element in cost? That is to say, why should they be omitted from the average of prices realised; in fact, they are part of that price.

In practice, the disadvantages of taking total average prices are much less than might be concluded from a study of the factors in the problem. Even with all variations in distance, with corresponding variations in carriage, etc., charges between one year or period and another, it will be found that average realised selling prices tend to a normal and show trends. They are significant and may be used. The key to whether or not they should be used rests chiefly in the amount of clerical effort necessary for their extraction of carriage, etc., charges from invoice values. If the extraction can be carried out quickly, without incurring additional cost for clerical labour or with but a small increase in clerical costs, then on balance it is desirable to have ex-works prices and separate carriage, etc., charges. If the extraction cannot be carried out readily, the average realised selling prices, including carriage, etc., are still useful.

In the case of goods which include the costs of distribution in the selling price there is an important distinction in that a contribution to profit or loss may be made by carriage charges in costs. This is quite opposed to the practice wherein carriage charges shown on invoices are the actual costs of delivery paid by the seller. The alternative involves adding an item for cost of carriage in cost computations. This can be an average based on experience, or a fixed rate, or an area rate. As goods are sold they contribute in effect towards the cost of carriage to the extent that each sale includes a carriage element in the price. If the total recovered in this way is regarded as the credit to the carriage charges account, actual expenditure being the debit, the effectiveness or otherwise of the carriage allowances in costs is shown clearly by the balance, a credit balance showing that more is being recovered in selling prices than is being spent, a debit balance showing that more is being spent than is being recovered. This comes properly within the sphere of expense control, but it is a matter with which the Distribution Executive of a business is very much concerned, and it has to be borne well in mind when dealing with sales comparisons.

RESPONSIBILITY FOR THE SALES BUDGETS

The preparation of the sales budget is a responsibility of the Distribution executive; the preparation of the comparative statements for control purposes may be, and is usually, a responsibility of the accountant. This is because the documents and routines concerned are part of accounting practice; in fact, the comparative statement, whatever form it may take, is an analysis or series of analyses of the nominal ledger account for sales. There are instances wherein sales ledgers are kept and invoicing is carried out in the Sales Department. In these instances the analysis and summary work necessary for the comparative statement also would be carried out in the Sales Department.

Where the comparative statements are prepared by the accountant for the Distribution executive, the form and presentation should be agreed between these executives. The analysis required, or thought to be required, for sales control might be impossible without special staff and equipment. Equally, the accountant might be able to suggest methods of achieving what was required by the Distribution activity, and might have useful ideas regarding the presentation of data to bring out clearly the significant trends.

COMPARISON: DELIVERIES INVOICED OR ORDERS RECEIVED

When comparisons are being considered the question arises: "What is being compared?" The answer, of course, is sales, but to the accountant, sales are usually taken to mean deliveries invoiced, whereas a Sales executive is probably more interested in orders received. To him, an order is a sale. Comparative sales figures are useful to the extent that they take both factors into account. The sales budget itself is usually based upon deliveries invoiced, i.e. upon sales according to the accounts. The Sales executive also wants to know what is the up-to-date order position, because it is this which precedes and eventually takes the form of deliveries invoiced. The deliveries invoiced figure should be net, after allowing for credits for returned goods, discounts, etc. It may be that the Distribution activity is not responsible for some of the credits, e.g. for faulty materials. Sales comparisons may be affected adversely by bad work in the production departments. It is possible to "work" these items through accounts and budget comparisons to figure as excess costs against production, but this is unwieldy. What is more practical is to analyse credits under their main groupings, so that the expense against each heading can be shown as so much for discounts, so much for returns and so on. Information is then available for action to be taken as it may be appropriate.

THE PERIOD OF COMPARATIVE STATEMENTS

The control statements should be prepared for the normal comparative period within the budget. For day-to-day sales control this period may be too long, and almost invariably sales figures are required at weekly, in some instances at daily, intervals. It is not necessary that these figures should be in the same detail as the budget period comparisons. What is sought is a day-to-day guide to sales activity, but the information obtained for this purpose should be arranged to correspond with that in the budget period statements.

The budget period statements are but totals of the, say, weekly state-ments, with additional classifications and the addition of comparisons, variations and analyses of variations. Where, therefore, shorter period information is required, it should be compiled and presented in a manner similar to its presentation for the longer period, i.e. as shown in the budget period statement. That is to say, that certain details for the budget period statements are compiled at, say, weekly instead of four-weekly intervals, the budget period statements being completed from the weekly statements. In some instances, weekly or shorter term information is not related to the budget period state-ments, with the result that when the budget period statements are available, there is considerable activity reconciling and agreeing the different presentation of what are the same figures.

PROMPT PRESENTATION OF SALES INFORMATION

With control information for sales, as with other control informa-tion, prompt presentation of results is of first importance. The control information is compiled from records of orders received; orders executed and deliveries invoiced; and, for stock purposes, from accounting records. The first point of note in ensuring prompt pre-sentation of results is not to make the comparative statements so elaborate that the time taken to complete them defeats a major con-dition of their use: promptness. The second point is similar to the first, but distinct from it. It is to study the information required in relation to resources of staff and equipment available, with the definite aim of achieving the maximum degree of simplification. It has been remarked previously that figures lead to more figures, and there is always a tendency to carry analysis work to an extreme degree. All analysis work adds to cost, and successive analyses can increase the costs of control substantially. There are, of course, many aids to analysis work, but they involve expenditure. It may be attractive to have a series of analyses from punched cards, but the items have to be coded, cards have to be sorted, tabulated and inter-pretative notes have to be added to the tabulations. Every copying operation increases the possibility of error.

It is not possible to generalise on the degree of analysis work required. Some industries permit of invoicing one article on one in-voice; others usually require that many items are on one invoice. In the first instance adequate sales information can be obtained by sorting and listing invoices; in the second instance this may not be possible, although certain major control information, such as terri-torial sales, can be obtained in this way. If product sales are required, recourse is often made to "sorting" from the invoices. There is, of course, another way in which adequate product sales figures can be obtained, namely, from stock records. These figures, however, are in total, and cannot be allocated to territories, industries, etc. Where detail is necessary, a useful method is to analyse by sections. In one budget period sales are analysed in detail under any one or two headings, say industries in a representative's sales territory.

In the following period another territory is taken and so on, so that over a year analyses are taken one or more times as it may be decided, to give a representative selection of detail. Such figures suffer the drawback that what happened in the particular analysis period for a given territory or product application may not happen in another period for which no analyses are made. Over a period, however, it is possible in this way to build up information which shows broad trends.

Where a concern operates on a cash basis, the compilation of weekly sales is a matter of accounting for cash, but this does not solve the problem of analysis to show for what products in what departments the cash was received. This again is the example of control by profitability, the products sold carrying fixed gross profits. For practical general control purposes it is sufficient to know that actual sales, in total, have resulted in a total profit which approximates closely to or is greater than budget profits. If, however, sales development is required, then detail analysis of sales must be undertaken, but it should be discontinued when the immediate purpose has been carried out. Sales development work would be carried out in order to increase profitability; normally associated with increase in turnover, but which may be associated with decrease in turnover, e.g. by discontinuing the sale of lines with a low gross profit. Once a "target" profitability has been set for a given cash volume of sales at established gross profit rates, the detailed analyses of sales in a budget period would not be required.

Public utilities metering their products cannot hope to read their consumers' meters and send out bills at weekly intervals. They provide a clear example wherein quantities sold are, in effect, the quantities made, subject to stocks, and short-term control can be devised accordingly. The figure of output which goes through the main distribution meters will not necessarily represent the full quantity registered by consumers' meters, but it provides a reliable guide. Its conversion to cash values is but an estimate based on an average price, because, without consumer meter reading, the make distributed cannot be related to price differentials.

These examples, however, are good illustrations of the practical approach to a complicated problem. For short-term control a unit of measurement directly significant of activity is chosen. The detail required beyond that unit of measurement is another matter; one which may be required from time to time, or for a period, but which has no place in normal short-period control. This is the only way in which detailed analyses of sales for control purposes may be viewed; are their production practical in relation to requirements? It is in fact a matter of judgment. Normally analysis work should be the minimum; additional analysis tends to delay the preparation of information and is expensive, but the expense has to be considered in relation to the value which may be derived from the information obtained. The main advantages of detailed analysis may, in appropriate cases, be obtained by selection and analysis of groups within the total of sales.

Apart from this question, which is contentious and which can be resolved only by individuals for their own requirements, there are other factors which may delay the preparation of control information for distribution. Pressure of work causes invoicing to fall into arrears; dispatch documents may not be cleared as promptly as they should be; holidays disturb the ordinary flow of work. These items cannot always be foreseen. Their correction is a matter for management action, but full allowance for them should be made when the preparation and presentation of sales control information is being planned.

Comparative sales statements show how sales are progressing in relation to a target which in turn is related to other targets, e.g. production budgets, and to profitability. Whilst comparison with a target figure is much more important than a comparison only with what happened in the past, e.g. in the same month last year, comparisons with previous years' results are not without value. These comparative figures can well be inserted in the control statement in columns, e.g. (1) sales for the same period last year, and (2) average sales in the accounting periods for the preceding financial year, or for the year to date. They show longer-term trends, and are useful accordingly.

USING SALES CONTROL INFORMATION

Control information should be used for action, and action on sales control information is a matter for the executive in charge of distribution. His most important duty before deciding on action, or, as it may be, a recommendation for a change in policy, is to ascertain and understand the reasons for variations. As far as possible these reasons should be shown on the variations summary, so that valuable executive time is not spent in seeking what should be given.

The precise action to be taken in any case must depend upon the circumstances of that case. Already it has been stated that sales budgets are not merely maximum figures to be achieved; rather are they minimum below which performance should not fall. On the other hand, in the case of two or more products made on one piece of plant, an excess sale of one product, in itself a satisfactory feature, may react with an even greater opposite effect on profitability by restricting the make and therefore the sale of the other products also made on that one piece of plant. Examples of this kind emphasise the need to look at comparative results as a whole before endeavouring to draw particular conclusions.

An important subsidiary use of sales comparative information is that of providing a basis for a bonus payment to representatives, sales managers, etc. Before any such scheme is adopted, great care should be taken to ensure that it is thoroughly understood by those concerned, and that the targets set are possible and within the control of those who will be held responsible should they not be met. This subject is described in Part I, Distribution; it is mentioned here because the mechanisms whereby a bonus scheme is in fact operated are those of the preparation and use of sales control information, and of the control statements prepared the most important for bonus purposes is the analysis of variations, wherein what is and what is not under the control of the individual is shown.

SALES BUDGETS IN THE SMALLER BUSINESS

Special reference has been made previously to the application of control in the smaller business. The reason principally is that it is so often assumed that because descriptions of control in operation are necessarily more or less comprehensive or relate to a case which may be hypothetical or otherwise, then because the smaller business is usually more simple, in the sense that its activities and their implications can be more readily grasped, there is not the same need for organisation and paper work which may in other businesses seem to be an unavoidable feature of control in operation.

In fact, descriptions of control in operation in any of its aspects may appear complicated because they usually deal with the more complex arrangements associated with a larger business unit. Of themselves the arrangements for control should be complex only when they have to deal with complex conditions.

This may be understood with reference to budgeting for sales as it is described in this chapter. The principles employed are those of forecasting and comparison; even the smallest business may forecast what its revenue from sales will be, and from this it is a simple matter to establish comparison with results actually achieved. Because in this chapter some attention is given, e.g., to the problems encountered in determining and applying budget selling prices and comparing them with actual selling prices, it must not be assumed that if a business is not troubled with the complications described, then *ipso facto* it has no need to provide for the control activity in its affairs. It is emphasised that the principles underlying the operations of the control activity essentially are few; they can be applied to all business activities, and this work is more concerned to deal with principles and their application than to describe systems. Consequently, this chapter and others should be read with the idea well in mind that what is described in detail is illustrative of the principles defined in the opening chapter, and not a description of the peculiar factors found in any one undertaking.

EXPENSE CONTROL FOR DISTRIBUTION

Expense control in relation to distribution is dealt with in a following chapter under that heading.

CHAPTER V

EXPENDITURE BUDGETS

Manufacturing Expenditure Budgets. Research and Development Expenditure Budgets. Distribution Expenditure Budgets. Other Expenditure Budgets. Limited Budgets

MANUFACTURING EXPENDITURE BUDGETS

Purpose and Nature

MANUFACTURING expenditure budgets are used to control generally the actual expenditure incurred in manufacture against the expenditure which was planned for a predetermined volume of production. The volume of production required may or may not correspond with the requirements of the sales budget. It may be that stocks are such that the actual make of an article may be more or less than the sales budget requirements, or, in some instances wherein manufacture has to be carried out long before goods are offered for sale, current manufacture may not be related at all to the current sales budget. In these instances it should be related to a forward sales plan, but such a plan is not a budget so much as a basis for a future budget.

The first stage in preparing manufacturing budgets is to determine what is to be made, and in what quantity. In the great majority of cases this is done from a consideration of the requirements of the sales budget in relation to stocks. A further point to which attention should be given is the "when" of manufacture. Sales of a commodity may be spread evenly over a period; manufacture accordingly may not be economic nor possible. It may have to be carried out in a shorter period to meet sales requirements over a longer period. On the other hand, sales may be seasonal, but manufacture may be regular, over a longer period than the sales demand, and designed to meet that demand at the proper time. The importance of considerations of this nature again lies in the fact that the budgets must not be averages of expenditure where averages are not appropriate. The forecasts of expenditure to meet the manufacturing programme should represent that programme as nearly as possible. Even over a long period averages will not become representative where there are wide fluctuations in the level of monthly expenditure, and if averages are used for budget purposes management may be seeking variations which in fact do not exist. An example will make this clear.

Item	Budget Charge per Month based on Average of Past Expenditure	Actual Charge when Product A is being made	Variation	Actual Charge when Product B is being made	Variation
Materials	£ 10,000	£ 12,000	£ + 2,000	£ 8,000	£ − 2,000

Whilst averages of past expenditure may be used for comparison with actual expenditure, it is always much better to calculate a theoretical cost for the budget production actually required in the comparative period.

It is necessary to establish what is or should be included in the manufacturing budgets. It has been said that the first item is what is going to be manufactured, a quantitative figure established from the sales budgets, stocks, stock policy, and from the requirements of manufacturing technique. If stocks of a product are high at the commencement of an accounting period, and stock policy is to reduce them, then the manufacturing expenditure budget will be so much less than the manufacturing cost of sales budget requirements. Conversely, if stocks are low, and policy is to increase them, the manufacturing expenditure budget will be greater than the manufacturing cost of sales budget requirements. The position is complicated where the manufacturing cycle is long-term, continuous and large-scale. The sales budget quantity requirements may represent $3\frac{1}{2}$ production cycles in a given period, but $3\frac{1}{2}$ cycles may be an impossibility: the number may be 3 or 4. In these cases the production of the "unwanted" half-cycle is an addition to stock, for sale in a subsequent period.

Production Budgets

Production budgets are required not only to establish what should be made to meet sales requirements. Possibly their most important use is that of providing information for production planning. From them factory loading and departmental loading can be worked out to obtain regularity and evenness in production, and to enable the movement of raw and partly finished materials and finished production to be planned. It may be that the first production budget does not permit of the best utilisation of plant, equipment, etc., and of labour owing to the irregularities of its loading or the relationship of quantities required to the most economical quantities which may be made. In this event the sales budget should be reviewed to ascertain whether or not adjustments can be made to enable the maximum economies and advantages in manufacture to be obtained.

Wherever possible, actual production should be compared with budget production over the shortest convenient and appropriate period, usually the week. In making these comparisons, it may or may not be necessary to take work in progress into account. Where plant is fully loaded and is running continuously, the quantity of work in progress may be omitted from the comparison unless there has been a major change in the nature of the output. If, on the other hand, the production cycle exceeds the comparative period, and if the production cycle time cannot be used as a comparative period, work in progress must be taken into account if a true comparison is to be made. It is rare, however, to find a need to take work in progress at weekly intervals. If figures are required, they can be estimated quite accurately from suitable records.

The figures required for control of output against budget are obtained from production records, and, provided adequate records of output are available, this comparison does not present any difficulty. It aims merely to show that in the budget period so many articles or pounds or gallons were to have been made, and that in the budget period the actual make was more or less than the forecast. Obviously this applies only in those industries wherein there is a natural measure of output which can be applied conveniently; it would be useless in a major constructional engineering job, although even in such an instance a great deal can be accomplished by means of a time plan for work and actual progress against that plan. That is merely to say that each example must be considered on its merits, the progress control being set up appropriately. The presentation of output figures against budgets is essentially a simple comparison, for example:

Period ended...................

Product	This Period				Cumulative			
	Budget	*Actual*	*Variation* +	*Variation* −	*Budget*	*Actual*	*Variation* +	*Variation* −

Action on variations is a matter for Production Management. As in the case of sales budgets, what matters far more than the variations is an understanding of them. However important detail may be, it is essential that the total position should be kept well in mind. When sales budgets were discussed, it was described how a certain traveller's sales might be affected by influences and factors outside his control, e.g. adverse weather affecting deliveries. The results of these adverse influences and factors might find their way through to production budgets, to show a minus variation, i.e. actual production being less than budget production. A similar variation might be caused by an epidemic, or by a major plant breakdown. Minus variations are not necessarily significant of poor Production Management.

Evaluating Production Budgets

Manufacturing expense budgets are established from production budgets, to which values are attached to give a theoretical cost of manufacture. If the cost so calculated is too high to give the required profitability, then adjustment is called for, either in manufacturing expenses (and/or other expenses) and/or the sales programme. It is not usually possible to calculate the cost of a manufacturing programme without breaking the total cost into its elements. A business may have production costs, which can be applied to the manufacturing programme. This, however, is merely carrying forward to the future established or, as they often are, hypothetical costs to the factory cost stage. Apart from the fact that this is not budgeting, it does not give the broad details necessary for control, although the detail for control purposes can be obtained. Consider an example:

Budget Requirements Article	Manufacturing Cost per Article (from Cost Records)	Budget Cost
	£	£
1,000 (A)	2	2,000
500 (B)	3	1,500
1,500 (C)	4	6,000
2,000 (D)	5	10,000
		£19,500

The totals for each item and the grand total can be shown in detail, e.g. assume the costing is as follows:

Article	A			B			C			D		
	£	s.	d.	£	s.	d.	£	s.	d.	£	s.	d.
Materials	0	15	0	1	0	0	2	0	0	1	10	0
Direct Labour	0	10	0	0	15	0	0	10	0	1	10	0
Repairs	0	2	0	0	5	0	0	10	0	0	10	0
Factory Services	0	5	0	0	10	0	0	10	0	0	15	0
Variable Manufacturing Overheads .	0	4	0	0	2	0	0	5	0	0	10	0
Fixed Manufacturing Overheads .	0	4	0	0	8	0	0	5	0	0	5	0
	£2	0	0	£3	0	0	£4	0	0	£5	0	0

On these figures a "budget" cost could be calculated:

	A 1,000	B 500	C 1,500	D 2,000	Total
	£	£	£	£	£
Materials	750	500	3,000	3,000	7,250
Direct Labour	500	375	750	3,000	4,625
Repairs	100	125	750	1,000	1,975
Factory Services	250	250	750	1,500	2,750
Variable Manufacturing Overheads	200	50	375	1,000	1,625
Fixed Manufacturing Overheads .	200	200	375	500	1,275
	£2,000	£1,500	£6,000	£10,000	£19,500

Where the cost detail is available, this method appears to provide an easy way in which to calculate budget costs, but in fact the method is incorrect and the detail will not serve. The method assumes that costs in the future will be the same as they were in the past. This, however, may not be the case. In some ways budgeting is a projection of the past into the future, but the projection has to be consistent with conditions as they may be expected in the future. This method of estimating for budgets takes no account of factors such as:

A. Raw material price trends. The costs for the previous period may be based on purchases when prices were higher or lower, or, e.g. new methods of buying or delivery may effect economies whereby the cost of this element can be reduced in the future.

B. The trend of wage rates, e.g. rates might be subject to an increase during the budget period, but this does not show in previous costs.

C. Improved utilisation of materials, machinery, equipment and labour, whereby reductions in unit costs will be secured.

D. The possibility of a previous period's costs bearing heavy or light charges, quite fortuitously, for, e.g., repairs.

E. The effect of volume on the incidence of fixed overheads.

Neither does this approach to forecasting costs show the way towards improvement. It implies contentment with the established position.

The presentation of this example, however, does show certain things. It shows that a forecast must take current information which, to become a budget, must be judged in relation to current trends and policy; and it shows too that a budget for manufacturing expenses must be in certain detail if it is to be at all useful for action. The second aspect requires attention first. It is useless to budget the cost of an activity in such a way that the forecast is a "blanket" covering the work of many executives. The budget must be broken down to departments or sections corresponding with the organisation structure, and each man in that organisation structure must know precisely for what expenditure headings he is responsible. This is no more than expense classification in terms of organisation structure, and is simple in so far as direct charges are concerned; the expenditure headings can be assembled quite easily under the various divisions of activity: production, in its various parts, e.g. processes, shops, departments; repairs and maintenance; power generation and transmission; internal transport, etc. The cost of the service activities also has to be recovered by production; how, therefore, is it to be "spread" over, charged to, productive departments? The point is that no matter how much is done towards measuring material usage, time or, e.g., consumption of power, there remains a burden of common expenditure which cannot be allocated directly to productive departments, but which has yet to be controlled in relation to those departments if expenditure budgets are to serve their purpose.

There are several ways in which this problem may be met, and they are dealt with in a later section. For immediate purposes it is necessary only to note that budgets for manufacturing expenditure must be built-up with reference to:

Subdivisions of the Production Activity and Production Departments
———————————→

Items of Expenditure
|
|
↓

Each of the items of expenditure has to be considered separately, in relation to the subdivisions or departments with which it is concerned.

Before the budgets for expenditure can be prepared, final production requirements should be analysed to their antecedent processes and output targets set accordingly. For example:

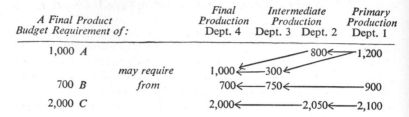

From these output targets departmental budgets must be worked out for the expense headings—materials are sometimes excluded—under the control of the executives in charge of production. With the budgets for the service departments and those for common manufacturing variable and fixed expenses, the total of the departmental budgets is the budget for the manufacturing activity.

The Main Divisions of Manufacturing Expenditure Budgets

At this stage it is more convenient to deal with budgets for manufacture under the main divisions. These main divisions will vary with every factory, and the general classification given in the example on pages 599–600 is taken as being representative. It is:

  i. Materials.
  ii. Direct Labour.
  iii. Repairs and Maintenance.
  iv. Services.
  v. Variable Manufacturing Overheads.
  vi. Fixed Manufacturing Overheads.

(i) *Material Budgets.*—The responsibility for the material budget rests with the chief executive in charge of manufacture. From the production budgets it is necessary to calculate how much raw material will be required for production, and, taking stocks of raw materials into account, how much will have to be bought. This last item is the purchasing budget for raw materials. The two aspects of the raw materials budget—consumption and purchases—are quite separate, though closely related. They must not be confused. The actual calculation for raw materials is a matter for each industry, and it is made more easy when the productive processes have been studied to provide standards for material utilisation.

Parts lists, specifications, formulæ, the stoichiometry of processes and wastage allowances are applied to finished production in order to calculate what types and quantities of raw materials will be required for that finished production. The theoretical calculations of what materials will be required for budget production should be checked with cost accounting records, which, if well designed, contain much information regarding materials consumed for each type or style of production and the production losses which are regarded as being normal.

It is not always necessary to set materials budgets for the various stages through which a product passes before completion (see Chapter VI). What raw materials budgeting sets out to determine is that for x lb. of finished production y lb. of raw materials are required. The y lb. of raw material may, of course, consist of many different raw materials passing through many processes or operations, the "finished product" of one being the "raw material" of the next until the product is in saleable form. It is important to know at what stages in manufacture losses occur, but this is the concern of cost control, and not that of budgetary control, which deals with the broad expense headings. A desirable quantitative record covering the budget period consists of the columnar presentation of:

Commencing stocks (Inventory),
Estimated deliveries (Purchasing Budget),
Estimated usage (Raw Materials Budget),
Closing stocks (Estimate of Inventory),

for each item of raw materials. The important comparison is that of actual usage with budget usage in relation to actual production and budget production.

Whatever method is used for determining quantitative material requirements for budget purposes, it is the case that unless it includes a standard, a measurement of what materials should be used, the budget is more in the nature of a guess than an estimate. Standards for material usage have the added advantage that they associate budgets directly with cost standards and cost control, i.e. variations from a budget during its currency are but the total of the variations from the standard cost; and a common basis is provided for budgets, costs and accounts. It may be that in the first place budgets are calculated from standards, but that as a matter of policy the standards are relaxed temporarily for actual budget purposes. The standard raw material usage for 100 lb. of finished production may be 110 lb. of raw material A. It is known, however, that the standard is unlikely to be reached, and in this case it may be desirable to allow say 112 lb. or 115 lb. for budget purposes. Action of this type has drawbacks; it tends to obscure the standard, to encourage satisfaction with what is really not the best. In suitable circumstances it has merits, these merits depending altogether on the soundness or otherwise of the judgment used in making the decision to depart from standard for budget purposes. The merit of the method in those cases where it can apply is that in the budgets it presents a realistic view of what it is hoped to achieve.

Values must be applied to the raw material consumption forecasts. Where the budget period is short-term, this can be done from stock valuations; but it should be noted that stock valuations are not necessarily values to be applied to budget usage of raw materials. Stocks may have been written down as a matter of policy. Except on special occasions wherein it is desired to use stocks at written-down values—a matter of policy—the values to be applied where budget requirements can be met from stocks should be the current cost of replacement as nearly as it can be estimated.[1] It is unusual to find that budget raw material requirements can be met from stock. Usually purchases have to be made, and the purchasing budget is an essential preliminary to evaluating budget raw material requirements.

The purchasing budget shows the cost of buying the materials which will be used in production, adjusted for such items as working out old materials not to be replaced, e.g. because an improved alternative has been found, and policy on stock levels, e.g. it may be desired to purchase more or less than budget requirements in order to increase or decrease stocks. The full purchasing budget includes all the materials and supplies required by an enterprise; here it is dealt with solely in relation to raw materials, i.e. materials for conversion or processing. The purposes of the purchasing budget are the same for all materials:

  (i) To enable purchasing to be planned to the best advantage, to take advantage of market conditions, etc.
 (ii) To ensure that materials are available in adequate quantity and at the right price for production requirements.
(iii) To enable financial cover for purchases to be planned.
(iv) To relate inventory investment to requirements and market conditions.

Purchasing may be an activity directly responsible to the executive in charge of production, or it may be established as a separate department responsible to the principal executive. The first step in budgeting

---

[1] The statement that current cost of replacement for materials used for production should be that used for budget purposes is a general guide which must be interpreted in relation to price trends. For example, on a falling market it might be that stocks have to be written down in accordance with the usual formula—cost or lower market value. Losses of this nature, however, are outside the scope of budgets and should be shown separately. Thus, in this example, budget figures will be based upon current cost of replacement, whilst the additional cost item for loss of stock values will be shown as such in total as a deduction from budget profitability when this is being reconciled with the actual profit earned. Where, however, a stock loss of this nature can be foreseen, it should be shown in the budgets, i.e. as a loss of a special nature.

for purchases of raw materials is to ascertain stocks and to apply budget raw material requirements to them for monthly periods, to show stocks at the end of each monthly period. From this information the quantities to be bought can be ascertained readily, and these quantities have next to be related to stock policy and the purchasing executive's assessment of forward market conditions. On a rising market it may be desirable to purchase at more than the normal or budget rate; on a falling market it may be desirable to withhold ordering. Whatever the position is, the most important aspect of the purchasing executive's work is that of ensuring as far as possible that production is not delayed by shortages of raw materials. On his assessment of price trends, too, there depends substantially the values to be applied to the raw materials budget. There are many problems connected with budgeting for purchases: production requirements in the short term may not represent economical purchasing quantities; some materials deteriorate in stock, the time between purchase and use having to be correspondingly short; deliveries may be affected by factors outside the control of the purchasing concern, and opportunities may occur to purchase special consignments at low prices. The purchasing budget must be flexible in that it would be folly to restrict purchasing severely solely because a budget had been set. Flexibility in operating a purchasing budget is chiefly a matter of co-operation between the purchasing executive and his co-executives. Problems or possibilities arising during the course of a budget should be discussed immediately with others who may be concerned, and a course of action based on conjoint thinking should be determined. There are very few occasions when decisions have to be given on the spot, and a purchasing executive cannot shelter for long behind the "plan as it was laid down", i.e. behind the budget, for failure to take advantage of offers to purchase at lower rates or to secure the supply position for an extended period ahead. The purchasing budget is made to ensure that the raw materials budget can be applied—it might even be necessary to modify the raw materials budget when its requirements and stock policy are translated into purchases—and to provide information for evaluating the raw materials budget.

In many businesses it is usual to find that at the end of an accounting period adjustments have to be made for stock losses, e.g. actual shortage, or by deterioration, or in stock values. No purpose is served by endeavouring to include charges of this type in the raw materials budget, which is concerned with the effective or ineffective use of material for a predetermined volume of production. The adjustments in stock values are substantially a matter of policy, but they may have been made necessary by careless purchasing or poor storekeeping. Stocks of raw materials are held for use, for conversion into finished production, and not in order that they may deteriorate. Deterioration, involving a reduction in value, may be due to faulty stocking: it may also be due to provision for an expected sales demand which was never realised. Examples of this kind are outside budgets; they should be shown in the accounting period in which they are charged as special losses, i.e. as deductions from budget profitability, and, depending upon the nature of the business, budget profitability should be set to allow a margin for contingencies of this kind. Another way of presenting such losses is to add them to the costs of the department or activity, which, after enquiry, is found to be responsible for them, although this course has the disadvantage that there are many instances wherein responsibility cannot be placed precisely. For instance, a writing-off necessary because certain raw materials become redundant owing to reduced sales demand might be charged to sales, or to production, or to both in some proportion, but unless the instance were very clear, such action would probably lead only to argument and a sense of aggrievement. Similarly, a charge to purchasing for a stock loss might leave but a feeling of injustice, unless there was no possible doubt that the purchasing executive had in fact erred. Finding scapegoats is no part of the conduct of a business, and leads usually to timidity, to fear of risk-taking, however slight the risk might be, because of the possibility of unpleasant consequences. Executives "play for safety". It is better as a rule to regard losses such as those described as Company losses, and where admonishment is necessary, to deal with it by explanation and discussion, not by figures on paper.

(ii) *Direct Labour Budgets.*—Budgets for direct labour charges are forecasts of the direct labour charges necessary to achieve the level of production required by the production budget at the time when it is required, with the raw materials available in accordance with the raw materials budget. Whilst the primary purpose of a direct labour budget is that of expense control for a given volume of production, the budget serves also to indicate what will be required of labour policies. It should show labour requirements over the budget period, to enable recruitment or displacement policies to be arranged accordingly. By showing the labour requirements of the production budget it enables fluctuations in these requirements to be controlled, either by adjustment in the production programme or by planning internal arrangements to ensure an adequate volume of work for the maximum utilisation of labour.

There is no one way of preparing a budget for direct labour. The first step is to define what is meant by "direct labour"; to ensure that the classification of employees for budget purposes is the same as that for accounting purposes. The direct labour budget should be confined to those workers whose wages can be associated directly with a unit of production or service where the rendering of a service, e.g. transport, is the object of the enterprise. The second step is to apply standards and cost accounting information to the requirements of the production budget in order to convert it into units which are significant of labour requirements. These units may be man-hours; or they may be machine-hours, which can be translated into man-hours by applying the normal employee requirements of a machine-hour. The method of analysis under processes may also be used, whereby estimated labour requirements of operating process equipment are applied, after checking against standards or information contained in previous records. If incentives are used, allowance must be made for them.

The evaluation of the unit requirements is effected by converting the units into the normal basis on which wages are calculated, under the various classes of labour engaged, so that hourly, daily, or weekly rates can be applied. Thereafter the calculation of the budget is a matter of arithmetic, which, in total, should be compared with the totals for previous budget periods. Allowance should be made, too, for trends in wage-rates. If it is known that an increased rate will apply during the budget period, an addition should be made accordingly for the period to which it refers.

The direct labour budgets should be presented in detail corresponding with the main departments, sections, or processes, to represent the responsibility in the organisation for the utilisation of direct labour, and to provide a means whereby responsibility for performances can be identified with individuals, i.e. with supervision.

(iii) *Factory Expense Budgets* (Repairs and Maintenance, Manufacturing Services and Miscellaneous Manufacturing Variable and Fixed Expenses).—Budgeting for factory expenses is usually more difficult than is budgeting for raw material and direct labour expenditure. Both raw materials and direct labour are tangible and can be identified closely with executive supervision. Many expenses, however, are general, common to all the productive departments, and others, though still general, are peculiar to services, which, whilst they must exist, often seem remote from the point of view of the production executive. Also, expenses contain several points where opposing interests clash and provide grounds for conflict of interest. A production executive will accept a budget for output, raw materials and direct labour. What is his position regarding repairs and maintenance charged to the products made in the departments under his control? The budget for repairs and maintenance is the responsibility of the plant engineer or his equivalent. The production executive may contend that the burden of engineering cost which his department has to carry is too heavy, that the central services of the engineering department, e.g. the drawing office, involve a staff and expenditure not warranted by the requirements of his department. Alternatively, he might argue that his production performances are not what they could be owing to inadequate engineering, quite contrary to the view expressed by the engineer. Conflict of this nature must be resolved, not only in order to budget, but also in order to obtain co-ordination in work. Organisation structure provides the means. A production executive is held responsible for defined expenditure only, and if the definition excludes repairs and maintenance, say these are the province and responsibility of the plant engineer, then he is not concerned with their volume, provided the engineering service is sufficient to keep his plant in operation. If the expenditure on repairs and maintenance is insufficient, one of two things, or both of them, will happen; either there will be excessive delay owing to breakdowns, a question of fact, or the plant will deteriorate more rapidly than it should, and the production executive might be held responsible. There is no way of dealing positively and generally with this last aspect. In every case there comes a point when the truth of any matter is a question of judgment on the facts available. If the production executive has repeatedly called attention to deficient maintenance work, and has pointed to its results, then the responsibility is that of the plant engineer and of general works management. If, on the other hand, he has accepted an unsatisfactory position, he has a responsibility accordingly. Items of this nature are outside the scope of budgeting, but they are met frequently when budgets are being established. For budget purposes the rule is that given already, to classify expenditure in relation to responsibility.

Another problem connected with budgeting for factory expenses is that connected with the level of activity. Although it is not strictly true, it is convenient to assume that certain expenses vary in direct relationship to the volume of production, and that other expenses are constant, no matter what the activity level is at any time. This element need not enter into the determination of expense budgets unless alternative budgets are set for various levels of production, i.e. if one budget fails, there is another on which to fall back, the budget expenses of the first budget being $£x$ and of the second budget $£y$. It has been indicated already that unless special circumstances apply, this is the negation of budgeting. The budgets should represent targets which are capable of achievement, and which it is intended shall in fact be achieved unless the whole basis on which they are drawn up is changed. Consequently, any alternative expense budgets are unnecessary complications. Their object is clear and understandable. It is to show that a level of expenditure below that of the budget first established, say at 100 per cent. activity, is not necessarily a gain over budget. It may be, and in most instances is, due merely to a reduced level of activity. A secondary object is to establish the ratio between the variable and fixed expenses at different levels of activity. As activity falls, fixed expenses are naturally a greater proportion of the total.

Now the first object can be achieved from a comparison between the production budget and actual production. Activity is most clear in the form in which it is best understood, and most significant. This form is output, not idle machine time or any cost figure; records of idle machine time are of course significant, but not wholly significant, of activity. The second object can be achieved from short-term accounts, without the complications of many expense budgets for various theoretical activity levels. The danger in all complications is that of introducing a mechanism which cannot be operated because of its complications. It is often impracticable to budget for expenses at 80 per cent. of activity, 60 per cent. of activity and so on. What do these terms mean, especially in a business making a variety of products? A definition can be applied, say machine time, operator time theoretical against actual output and so on, but these definitions serve merely to obscure the real use of budgets as aids in running a business. To be practical, budgeting for factory expenses is approached best by estimating for the budget volume of production, leaving any departures or results of departures from that volume of production and the expenditure forecast to show themselves as under- or over-production and, in relation to actual expenses incurred, as expense variations. A general classification of factory expenses is:

	Dept.	Dept.	Dept.	Dept.	Total
Repairs and Maintenance Details	.				
Power Generation Details	.	.			
Internal Transport Details	.	.			
Variable Expenses Details	.	.			
Fixed Expenses Details	.	.			

Some of these expenses are charged, not only to departments, or, as they may be, to processes, etc., but also to other headings of expenditure. Internal transport is probably used by the power-house, and both require the services of the Engineers' Department. For budget purposes items such as these can be provided for by memorandum figures showing the total cost of the particular activity and the amounts transferred to other headings, leaving the remainder to be charged to production departments or processes.

Another important activity for which it is necessary to budget is that of the Personnel Department. In some large companies the Personnel Department is a main activity responsible to the principal

executive. More often it is confined to employees engaged in manufacture and the services ancillary thereto. This item is dealt with
under "Factory Expenses" because the detail is usually set up as
part of the organisation for manufacture; the methods of forecasting
would apply equally well if the Personnel Department were a main
activity.

The most important aspect of budgeting for the Personnel Department is that the budgets should represent policy relating to personnel
rather than the detail of expenditure allocated to the department on
some arbitrary basis. It should show the expenditure over which the
personnel executive has direct control, and which he can influence
readily in the discharge of his duties. Consequently, it is unnecessary
to estimate the cost of the department with reference to square feet
occupied (for rates, heating, etc.) or lighting points. The need is to
estimate expenditure under the main activities concerned, e.g. :

(a) *Administration.*
   Salaries, stationery, travelling.
(b) *Publicity and Entertainment.*
   Works magazine, lunch-time concerts.
(c) *Medical.*
   Salaries, or salaries and fees, of doctor and nurses, medical
   supplies and equipment.
(d) *Education and Training.*
   Salaries, University and Technical College fees, library subscriptions.
(e) *Canteen.*
   Wages and salaries, cost of foodstuffs.
(f) *General.*
   Estimate of cost of sports clubs, e.g. groundsman's wages,
   accommodation allowances; clothing allowances; visiting.

Attention to budgeting in this way means that the total cost of
running the department is not known; the method omits incidental
expenses, which should be regarded as general factory expenses. It
does include all the major items of expenditure, the items omitted
being relatively small in amount, and it presents the cost of policy in
relation to the activity. All the expense headings are positive; they
mean that something tangible is to be done, and this effect is not
obscured by the arithmetic of allocations.

The stages in budgeting for manufacturing expenses are:

A. Classify expenses into main groups, i.e. those which are controlled
directly by executives responsible for them, such as repairs and maintenance, internal transport, and those of a common or policy (e.g. in-

surance, depreciation) nature, arranged as miscellaneous variable, or fixed, expenses.

B. From past accounts ascertain what has been spent against each item.

C. Consider policy as it applies to each item. Repairs may have been haphazard, whereas it may be decided that in future a certain sum shall be spent; welfare facilities may have been extended, and so on. In these instances the amount determined as a matter of policy is the budget.

D. Examine each item and forecast its cost. Depreciation, insurances and other fixed expenses are usually easy to forecast. Salaries may be regarded as fixed expenses, or part of them may be regarded as a departmental or activity charge. It does not matter so much what is done provided it presents the basis for action on the comparative figures obtained. Normal salary increases should be allowed when calculating the budget charge.

When items such as repairs expenditure budgets are being considered, allowance should be made for the value of materials recovered during repair jobs. For budget purposes the value placed on materials recovered may be an estimate of their current market value, or an estimated or actual purchase price, generally reduced for normal depreciation. In those instances wherein recovered materials can be sold for more than their first or written-down cost, the profit on sale can be taken into the budgets in the estimate of realisable value: it should not be taken into account, for comparative purposes, until the materials have been sold and the profit has in fact been earned. A business cannot make a profit out of itself merely by transferring materials from one place to another.

E. As far as possible, items of expenditure should be converted into numbers of men, materials required, etc. Yard cleaning requires so many men. The budget should be considered as one for a number of men as well as for the expenditure in wages which they involve. The first-aid and ambulance room may be staffed by a trained nurse with an assistant, or in a small factory first-aid may be the part-time work of an ambulance trained man. Items of expenditure should not be regarded merely as figures, but as people using equipment to perform tasks.

F. Examine the total and ascertain whether or not it is within or in excess of the provision which can be allowed for these items. Some re-budgeting may be required; policy on repairs may be adjusted to reduce or increase the amount to be spent, or economies may have to be sought in incidental expenses.

G. Present the budgets to those concerned with operating under them and obtain agreement.

The executive most concerned with preparing the detail for expense budgets is the accountant, but in its preparation he should work in close co-operation with the factory executives concerned. The budgets are for the use of the factory executives in discharging their duty; they are the cash expressions of what will be the overhead elements required for budget production. The budgets therefore are the budgets of the factory executives.

(iv) *Summary.*—The preparation of budgets for manufacturing expenditure may be summarised as follows:

A. Determine from sales budgets, stocks and stock policy what has to be manufactured, in what quantity, and its distribution over the budget period. This is the production budget.

B. From standards, cost information, or investigation, establish the raw material requirements of the production budget, taking raw material stock policy and market trends into account. Calculate the estimated cost of raw materials.

C. From standards, cost information and accounting records, calculate the budget direct labour cost of producing the budget quantities of finished production from the budget raw materials.

D. Calculate the estimated cost of factory services, and general expenses, in the budget period.

E. Present the budgets under departments, processes, etc., as far as direct expenditure is concerned, to the total of which must be added the costs of services and other expenses set out under executive expense responsibility. This is the manufacturing expenditure budget with which actual expenditure is to be compared at stated periods.

F. Where the information is available, from standards or cost records, calculate to the direct cost stage the unit budget cost of the budget production. It is unnecessary at this stage to allocate general factory expenses, services, etc., to give unit manufacturing costs. The unit budget costs multiplied by budget production should equal the total budget direct cost shown under departments and in total. The acceptability or otherwise of the budget expenditure levels can be established by working backwards from the revenue budget:

	£
Revenue (Sales) Budget . . .	a
Deduct Profit Required . . .	b
Available for Total Expenditure . .	$a - b$
Deduct Direct Costs of Manufacture .	c
Available for Manufacturing and Other Expenses	$(a - b) - c$

The amount available $(a - b) - c$ should be compared with the total of the budget manufacturing and other expenses of the business. If it is insufficient, then profit must be reduced, or the expenses must be reduced, or revenue must be increased.

RESEARCH AND DEVELOPMENT EXPENDITURE BUDGETS

Budgets for technical research and development may be set in a number of ways:

A. By establishing as a matter of policy that a sum certain shall be spent in any budget period. This sum may be varied from time to time.

B. By scheduling the projects on which research and development expenditure is required and budgeting for an amount against each project.

C. By budgeting for a sum to be expended for each employee, or for classes of employee, e.g. section leaders, engaged in research and development.

D. By allocating a fixed proportion of gross turnover, say 3 per cent., for research and development.

Research and development expenditure is in the nature of an insurance. The longer-term view must prevail when it is being considered. The work involved in the activity should be the basis for future turnover. Whilst all this is true, it is true equally that too much can be spent on the activity; too much in the sense of more than can be afforded at current levels of revenue and expenditure. If too much is spent, then, because revenue from sales is not so flexible, too little will be spent on other necessary work, or profits will be insufficient to give a reasonable return on invested capital and provide finance for the future. Balance between the expenditure on the various activities of an enterprise must be maintained; otherwise those parts which are out of balance, disproportionately low in relation to requirements, will suffer and react to the detriment of the whole enterprise, making it impossible to achieve the full benefits of those activities for which more than ample provision is made.

The most important aspect of expenditure on research and development is not the amount but the use made of the amount. All concerns find a tendency to attempt to deal with too many problems at one time, and this tendency has to be controlled carefully. Consequently, however the sum for the total expenditure of the activity is determined, it is essential that it should be assigned to projects in order that the activity can in fact be controlled. It is desirable to assign the whole amount to projects; but part may be left unassigned except in so far as it is regarded as being available for fundamental work of a general kind which may lead to new discoveries, or for special problems which may arise during the budget period.

As well as being set out under projects, the budget also should have its expense items arranged under the ordinary account headings. The effect is that the Research and Development Executive is shown to be responsible for expenditure under normal account headings: salaries, materials and so on, and this expenditure is shown in relation to the projects on which it is to be spent:

BUDGET

Expense Item	Total	Project 1	Project 2	Project 3	Project 4
Salaries . .					
Materials . .					
Depreciation .					
Insurances, etc. .					

Except in those instances wherein the Research and Development activity is on a large scale, with perhaps its own establishment, it is not necessary to include in the budget expense items other than what may be regarded as direct charges. A staff of a research department on a works site would probably use the works canteen; therefore it may be argued that the Research Department budget should include an item for canteen. This, however, is carrying analysis too far; it is impracticable and quite unnecessary.

In some industries a complication sometimes arises when a Research and Development Department is required to do certain work for actual sale. During the course of a budget period a customer may require a small quantity of a special material or a special article or part. Production is hardly a factory job, so it is handled by the laboratory or experimental shop. Now this cannot be budgeted. Normally, such items are special in the sense that they are carried out because of longer-term possibilities or because the customer requiring the material is sufficiently important to merit extra attention. Yet if they are excluded from the budget, the comparisons with actual expenditure may show an excess of actual over budget, or budget may appear more than actual, because staff and materials have been directed to projects other than budget projects, for which no provision is made in the budgets and which, under "Actual Expenditure", are therefore omitted from the comparative statement. The simplest way in which to deal with this complication is to provide a margin for incidental work and to feature it as a project in the budget. If more is spent than was provided in the budget, or less as the case may be, the full position is at once apparent when comparisons with actual expenditure are made. It does not matter in the least that budgeting for such expenditure is altogether guessing; what does matter is that the possibility of expenditure under a given "project" is brought into the budgets. Another way in which the item can be dealt with is to omit it from the budget, and to show actual expenditure in detail only in so far as the corresponding detail appears in the budget. Then, to the actual expenditure shown against the budget items, there must be added the additional expenditure on special work in order to obtain the total cost of operating the activity. Against this item there may be shown the sales value of the work done, with a memorandum "profit or loss" accordingly.

When expenditure is being apportioned to projects, provision must be made for those items which will be completed or perhaps dropped during the budget period, and for the introduction of new items. This can be done by providing several columns in which additional figures can be entered for the new projects. Where a project is completed or is dropped before it is completed, and the team

engaged on it is transferred to other work, there is for budget purposes a simple transfer of budget expenditure accordingly, from the
old project to the new one. It may happen that a completely new venture, not foreseen when the budgets were prepared, has to be undertaken. This is a change in the budget, and has to be looked at in
relation to resources in men and equipment available. If existing projects are so important that they must be continued, the new venture
requires additional staff, equipment, etc., with expenditure accordingly. An addition of this nature to an established budget must be
sanctioned by the authority which sanctioned the first budget, normally the Board of a Company. If, however, the new venture can be
or has to be met from existing resources in staff and equipment, it
can be treated in the budgets as a transfer of budget expenditure from
one project heading to another, the projects from which the transfer
is made being the subject of reduced activity accordingly.

DISTRIBUTION EXPENDITURE BUDGETS

Distribution expenditure budgets are set for the estimated expenses
of the distribution activity in achieving planned sales under the sales
budget. The expenses include:

Wages and salaries (in sales offices, or travellers, sales managers, etc.).
Travelling expenses incurred by the sales staff.
Office rents, insurances, rates, lighting, etc.
Depreciation on travellers' cars.
Publicity and advertising.
Cost of samples.
Commissions.

These items are fairly common. In some instances the responsibility of the production function ceases with the completion of the
finished article; warehousing, storing, dispatching and transport
being included within the responsibility of the distribution executive.
In other instances main warehousing, dispatch and transport may be
organised under production, but there may be depots carrying out
similar work on a local basis, being "fed" from the main warehouse,
and under the direct control of the distribution executive. Whatever
the facts in any case expenditure must be classified accordingly for
budget purposes. Carriage on finished production sold may be
charged to the customer as a separate item, which, depending on
whether or not carriage charges can readily and economically be
extracted from invoices, may or may not require budgeting, or the
goods may be sold at a delivered price, in which case the carriage
costs must be budgeted in the same way as other items of expense. If
the organisation for warehousing and transport is part of production,

then budgeting for its cost will be a responsibility of the production executive; if it is a part of distribution, then budgeting will be a responsibility of the distribution executive. In those cases where budgeting for this expense is a production responsibility, the production executive should consult with the distribution executive when establishing his budget.

The actual technique of estimating the cost of carriage where this item is included in costs depends altogether upon the type of article and the physical method of distribution: by road, by rail, by post and so on. Unless there is a marked change in the distribution of customers or the nature of the goods being sold, and allowing for increases or decreases in carriage rates in the budget period, past experience is usually a reliable guide to the level of carriage outwards charges. It is quite useless to aim to be too exact, analysing budget sales in great detail, calculating carriage rates accordingly, applying them to sales, and so on. The work involved in this task in many instances would be enormous, so that budgets would be out-of-date before they were ready. More important, such a detailed analysis presupposes a greater degree of control over the detail of distribution than can in fact exist; sales cannot be planned in advance in fine detail, so that the method is based on a wrong premise. An intelligent interpretation of past experience, as revealed by accounting records, with an assessment of current trends, will usually be sufficiently accurate for practical purposes. Where a concern operates its own delivery arrangements, say by its own lorries or vans, the budget for carriage on goods sold can be fixed with reference to estimated cost of operating the service; depreciation on the vehicles, wages, petrol, oil, etc.

The other items in the sales expense budget can be estimated readily from the accounting records, adjustments being made for any policy changes or normal variations in expenditure, such as increases in salaries, or a decision to open a new branch sales office. Advertising is often made the subject of a separate budget, and the approach to budgeting is similar to that used for technical research and development. Expenditure on advertising is almost altogether a matter of policy, say a fixed sum, or a percentage of budget turnover, or of the turnover of each product. Within the sum determined as a budget it is necessary to show the allocation to products, schemes, exhibits, etc., for control purposes. The budget expenditure may be further analysed to lay and technical press, brochures and leaflets.

OTHER EXPENDITURE BUDGETS

Other activities for which expenditure budgets are required are those of purchasing (where this is organised as a separate activity), personnel, accounting and general administration. These expenses consist substantially of wage and salary costs, stationery, rents, postages, telephones, etc., and budgeting for them is chiefly a question of examining what the expense levels have been in previous periods and adjusting accordingly for the budget period. The adjustments may be increases, say additions to staff or for normal wage and salary increases, or decreases, where economy is required, or where clerical work is reorganised to effect economy or to substitute mechanical methods for manual methods. It is necessary to note only:

A. That each division of activity must have its own budget.

B. That expenditure headings must be shown in that budget.

C. That as far as possible the expenditure headings must be associated with physical and measurable factors, e.g. number of clerks.

D. That certain expenses of a particular nature may be included in the budgets. For example, in the accounting budget for a mechanised department it would be necessary to include a depreciation charge for the accounting machines.

E. That generally it is unnecessary to make fine allocations for budget purposes. The budgets should be confined to main groups of expenditure over which the executive concerned has direct control. There is no point in the Accountant estimating an insurance charge for his department, or the proportion of rates it might carry. These expenses should be dealt with by budgets under "General Administration".

LIMITED BUDGETS

What is described in the preceding pages applies to the majority of manufacturing businesses, wherein what is to be made and sold can be and is decided before actual make and sale. There are other businesses wherein budgets cannot be set for the main items of expenditure. A jobbing or repairing business is a good example. In these cases budgets, as they have been described, should be set only for those items of expenditure which can be forecast reasonably. Accounting and administrative expenses, and sales expenses, are typical items of this nature.

It may be possible, too, to budget for direct labour costs, e.g. where the concern has a labour force which is regarded as the establishment for the volume of work which is anticipated. Materials are more difficult; they depend almost entirely on the type of job which has to be done. It has been observed previously that over a period expenses tend towards a normal, although averages may be upset by changes in the type of work done, or by exceptional demands of a specialised nature. "Budgets" set on such averages are a guide: they are not a means for control. Control in these instances operates through sound estimating and cost control, and, for those expense items which are sufficiently stable for forecasts to be made, through budgets. Control of expenditure by means of budgets cannot apply where budgets cannot be set, and no purpose is served by devising expenditure budgets which are not related to what may happen. The approach to control has to take other courses; those of limited budgets for general expenses and where there is an "establishment" for direct labour, for wages, and what in effect are budgets for materials (and for wages where there is no "establishment") set by estimating for each job. The principles of control involved are precisely the same as those in a business wherein all manufacture is predetermined. Their application is modified to suit the requirements of the particular business.

CHAPTER VI

THE APPLICATION OF BUDGETARY CONTROL

Accounting Against Budgets. Using Budget Information. Control and the Balance Sheet. Summary. Example

THE preparation of budgets for the parts of an enterprise and for the enterprise itself leads to comparative revenue and expenditure statements and a theoretical trading account showing the estimated profit effect of trading at the level of activity of the sales budget and the manufacturing budget. The next stages in control are:

1. Accounting against budgets; the preparation of short-term comparative statements and trading accounts.
2. Using the information provided by the comparative statements.

ACCOUNTING AGAINST BUDGETS

Accounting against budgets is a part of the work of the accountant, and it can be considered conveniently under the headings used in the descriptions of budget preparation.

(1) *Revenue*

The preparation and presentation of comparative statements for revenue from sales is dealt with under "Sales Budgets". It is short-term, and shows how actual sales compare with those which were planned.

In addition, there are other items of revenue which should be estimated for financial control purposes. In a manufacturing business these are incidental to budgetary control; and the forecast for them is concerned chiefly with cash budgets, a responsibility of the accountant. These other items are those such as rents receivable and investment income.

(2) *Production*

The comparative production statement is written up from production records. It may be prepared in the factory offices, or in the Cost Accounting Department from production returns for costing purposes. It shows simply how actual production of each article or type of product compares with what was planned. If the planned production is related to theoretical capacity, in simple cases it provides a means for assessing the activity level. Where products made are numerous and complex, this comparison cannot be made without resolving the production into work content, except in so far as money value can be taken as a measure of volume, as it is frequently.

(3) *Expenditure*

(*a*) *General.*—Budgetary control presupposes that there are systems and methods for recording the actual expenditure incurred in running the business. It is the duty of the accountant to ensure that the classification of expenditure used for budget compilation is used also in account preparation, and that the accounting records are adequate to furnish the comparative statements required.

(*b*) *Materials.*—The actual cost of materials consumed is obtained from summaries of material requisitions evaluated in accordance with normal practice, which may be an average, or actual, or current replacement cost, or, where measurement of issues is not practicable, from material accounts whereby an estimated consumption is calculated from commencing stocks plus purchases less closing stocks.

The comparative figure should be the budget cost of actual output. If the budget material cost of planned output is used, and for any reason actual output is more or less than the planned output, then an incomplete comparison is being made and variations will be shown with no existence except on paper, e.g.:

> Planned output is 1,000 at a budget raw material cost of 10*s*. — £500.
> Owing to a power supply failure, actual output is 800, at an actual cost of 10*s*. 3*d*. = £410.
> A comparison of the budget and actual material costs is £500 compared with £410, or a gain over budget.

The real comparison is in two parts:

> (*i*) Actual production with budget production, i.e. 800 instead of 1,000.
> (*ii*) The actual cost of production with the budget cost *of that production*, i.e. 800 at 10*s*. 3*d*. = £410, with 800 at 10*s*. = £400.

Nevertheless, it is quite impossible in practice to adjust the budget Profit and Loss Account continuously for items of this nature. The budget Profit and Loss Account charge for raw materials could remain at 1,000 at 10*s*. = £500, but it should be supported by a memorandum entry showing the budget cost of actual production, to be significant of activity and a true comparison of values. This point arises whenever comparisons are being made between expenditure forecasts and actual expenditure, which varies directly with the volume of output.

(c) *Direct Labour.*—Comparative statements for direct labour costs can be written up readily from a suitably analysed pay-roll, i.e. to departments or processes. In presenting the comparisons, provision must be made for the possibility of variation owing to activity, as described under 3 (b) above, Materials.

(d) *Factory Expense Accounts.*—The treatment of these must vary with each case. The greatest difficulties usually are those of ensuring that all purchase accounts are brought in to charge, and that, as regards the internal systems, correct allocations are made on the originating documents.

The accounting system must show:

(i) The total expenditure in the comparative period against each expense heading.
(ii) How the various items are dealt with in costs.

Budgetary control is concerned only with (i), the expenditure actually incurred on any account against the forecast made by the executive responsible. Certain items are made up of charges for wages as well as for materials and expenses. Examples are steam-raising, repairs and maintenance and yard cleaning. The pay-roll should be arranged to enable expense assembly to be carried out in accordance with budget expense classification requirements.

Certain expenses relate to a period, e.g. rates, insurances. These items are dealt with simply by making a proportionate charge in each accounting period. For example, if rates are paid in advance for six months, and the calendar month is the comparative period, each accounting period (calendar month) would be charged with one-sixth of the payment for rates, a memorandum account being used to record the amount of rates "absorbed" until the charges equalled the payment. Payments "in arrears" can be dealt with similarly, a proportion of the total amount due some time in the future being charged in each month's accounts and credited to a memorandum account to which the actual payment would be debited when made. Any balance over- or under-charged could be dealt with by carry forward, adjusting the charge in the periods following accordingly, or by transfer to general overheads. Items such as depreciation, which are matters of policy, should be the subject of schedules showing the charge over the full budget period, so that short-term charges can be brought into the accounts, e.g. if the total depreciation charge is £26,000 for a full budget period of thirteen four-weekly periods, then each four-weekly period must be charged with £2,000 for depreciation.

(e) *Departmental Budgets.*—In Chapter V it is stated that budgets for manufacturing expenditure must be built-up with reference to:

Subdivisions of the Production Activity and
Production Departments
———————————————→

Items of Expenditure

An arrangement of budget detail along these lines leads to sub-divisional and/or departmental budgets. Items included under production departments should be those for which the various production executives are responsible; under subdivisions, e.g. Repairs and Maintenance, those for which the plant engineer is responsible, and there will be a residue of general expenses which should be shown as general expenses. In the example given later in this chapter the departmental budgets for manufacture would be:

Expense Item	Production Manager					*Works Engineer*	*Power Plant Supt.*	*Purchasing Manager*	*Variable Expenses*	*Fixed Expenses*
	R.M. Stockkeeping	*Dept. 1*	*Dept. 2*	*Dept. 3*	*F.P. Stockkeeping*					
Materials Wages, etc.										

Manufacturing Variable and Fixed Expenses are shown under "Works Manager". In another organisation some items included might be under a Services Superintendent, or be a responsibility of the Production Manager, or they might be shown in detail under each main classification, e.g.:

In the column "Expense Item", there would appear the headings "Variable Expenses" and "Fixed Expenses", with details under each heading, the budget charges being extended under the executive responsibility headings, so that each department of subdivision of activity would carry its own fixed and variable charges.

Also, in the example given later in this chapter it is observed that there is no one perfect method of grouping and classifying expenditure, so that the guiding principle in each case is appropriateness. Transfers, e.g. for power charges, might be shown in order to complete the departmental budget summary. In the first place, transfer items would be shown in full, to give the total budget cost of the service activity concerned, and from the total deductions would be made to represent the proportion of the service charge to be debited to other departments on a budget basis. The other departments would have corresponding additions made to their budget costs.

A question which arises when departmental budgets are being considered is whether or not there should be a budget charge for materials in each column. Obviously the departments or subdivisions using prime raw materials should have a budget charge accordingly. The engineer's department would have a budget charge for engineers' stores, tools, etc.; the power plant would have a budget charge for fuel and water. There is, however, a difficulty when production departments budgets are being prepared.

Raw materials may enter into production at the first process or operation, or series thereof covered by a department, and not in subsequent processes or operations covered by other departments, the "raw materials" of which would be the finished production of the department(s) concerned with preceding processes or operations. Alternatively, production departments may make one product or product range only, with no relationship or movement of materials between them, each department having its own raw materials; or prime raw materials as well as the production of earlier process or operation stages may be introduced at any stage in manufacture. In other instances production departments are feeder or service to other production departments; they may be said to have no raw materials of their own, they carry out a service.

Say a raw material passes through four stages: A, B, C and D. It may appear desirable or even necessary to know that the budget cost of the raw materials used in stage A is £x, compared with an actual cost of £y; that the "raw materials" used in stage B—the finished production stage A—have a budget cost of £m and an actual cost of £n, and so on. Arrangements for achieving this can be worked out, but, except in the simplest cases, the intricacies involved and the detail recording required are such that accounting may become excessively complicated.

Quantitative material requirements for each stage may be established from the analysis of the production budget (see p. 602). The difficulty is that of attaching values to the partly processed materials, but the problem can be dealt with in two main ways:

(*i*) By confining departmental budgets strictly to actual raw material costs, leaving the actual control of material usage to cost control. There would be departmental budgets for raw materials only for those departments wherein actual raw materials were used in manufacture, and inter-process transfers would be omitted.

(*ii*) By showing raw material budget costs under departments, and the estimated departmental cost of partly finished materials transferred on a standard cost basis. Budget costs for materials would be inflated to the extent that the same raw material would be brought into the budgets a number of times, and allowance accordingly would have to be made for reconciliation with the total budget which aims to establish that for a production of x units y units of raw material at a cost of £z should have been used. This allowance could be arranged by providing a budget "credit" for budget quantities of intermediate production transferred.

In both instances the analysis of variations, actual from budget, should show:

The extent to which cost variations are dependent upon a production variation, actual against budget.

The losses or gains which have occurred in operations or processes and their cost, actual against standard; a matter for cost control.

The extent to which variations are dependent upon price variations.

The position may be summarised by stating that the inclusion of material charges in *all* departmental budgets depends upon the practicability of using standard cost information for this purpose. If the amount of detail is too great for practical application, satisfactory control can be achieved by omitting other than actual raw material charges from budgets; by using the budgets for broad control, and by using standards for detail control.

(*f*) *Other Expenditure Accounts.*—Other expenditure statements for the remaining activities of an enterprise are a matter of extraction from a suitably analysed nominal ledger. The detail in these statements too should be similar to that of the budgets.

In the case of research, etc., work, where the budget may be presented in terms of forecasts of expenditure on projects as well as in terms of salaries, materials, etc., comparative statements for actual expenditure should be drawn up accordingly. This involves provision for booking expenditure to projects.

The expenditure statements with budget comparisons should be designed to form part of the ordinary accounting routines. It cannot be emphasised too strongly that accounting against budgets is substantially a question of suitable classification and analysis of nominal ledger accounts, with the object also of enabling a short-term profit statement to be prepared as well as enabling actual expenditure to be presented against the forecast. The final stage in accounting against budgets is that of preparing this short-term profit statement.

A budget which is altogether within the province of the accountant is the cash budget. This budget takes the cash position at the commencement of the budget period, and applies the budget revenue from sales and the budget expenditure in order to provide information for improved financial control. Receipts from miscellaneous income, and from investments, should be included in the cash budget. The cash budget is useful when attention is being given to finance; it assists when answers are being sought to typical questions such as that implied in a position wherein the bulk of receipts fall in a shorter period, and payments have to be made more regularly over a longer period.

Forecasts of capital expenditure are necessary for the cash budget, in turn leading to capital expenditure budgets with which actual capital expenditure can be compared. Capital expenditure budgets should be approved by the Board of a Company—or its equivalent in another form of business enterprise—and finance accordingly should be planned at the same time, either from ordinary revenue, per the cash budget, or by borrowing.

In order to prepare accounts and comparative statements promptly, it may be necessary to make certain assumptions. Typical examples are that book stocks are represented by physical stocks; that work in progress at the beginning and end of the accounting period has the same value; that invoices not received in one period are balanced by invoices brought in from another period. The point about assumptions of this kind—provided they are appropriate—is that it is much better to make them and prepare accounts quickly than it is to wait until their substance can be dealt with properly. The extent to which such assumptions vitiate the accuracy of accounts is usually small, each period's errors being corrected in the next and so on. At least twice a year, however, the assumptions should be tested by preparing accounts, including them, and carrying out the detail work, or waiting for invoices, which they avoid, in order to check their application.

USING BUDGET INFORMATION

At the outset when budgets were being discussed generally, it was stated that their purpose is not that of establishing a master plan to which actual work must in fact conform. Detail planning in this sense is impossible; it is not in the nature of affairs to permit of detail forecasting. Too many things may arise to upset the plan. The use of budgets therefore is based more on an analysis and interpretation of variations, actual from budget, in order to determine precisely where actual operating has deviated from what was planned, to take corrective action if this is possible, or to acquire knowledge from experience in order to plan better in the future.

The establishment of the reasons for variations is the most important aspect of preparation for control—a function of Management—from budgets. Consider these typical examples:

(1) Raw materials consumed may exceed budget because:

(*a*) Output exceeds budget, and more raw materials have been used accordingly.

(*b*) Prices have increased more than was foreseen in the budgets.

(*c*) Wastage is higher than budget, or effective use is less than what was planned.

(*d*) Unavoidable losses have taken place.

(*e*) Budgets were based on incorrect data.

(*f*) Any combination of (*a*) to (*e*).

(2) A common cause of budget/actual raw materials variation is the holding of stocks at written-down value:

(*a*) *Stock Increase*

				£
Opening Stock	100 at 10*s*.	. . .		50
Purchases	500 at £3	. . .		1,500
				1,550
Closing Stock	100 at 10*s*.	.	50	
	100 at £3	.	300	
			—	350
Materials Consumed	400 at £3	. . .		£1,200

or, assume *all* stocks are held at written-down value:

			£
Opening Stock	100 at 10*s*.	. . .	50
Purchases	500 at £3	. . .	1,500
			1,550
Closing Stocks	200 at 10*s*.	. . .	100
Materials Consumed	400 at £3 12*s*. 6*d*. .	.	£1,450

If the budget cost of the raw materials is based upon purchasing, say £3, then a "loss" variation arises because of the practice of valuing *all* stocks at the written-down value, i.e. the real cost of the materials used is £3 per unit, but this is increased by 12*s*. 6*d*. per unit because of the writing down.

(*b*) *Stock Decrease*

			£
Opening Stock	100 at 10*s*.	. . .	50
Purchases	500 at £3	. . .	1,500
			1,550
Closing Stock	50 at £3	. . .	150
Materials Consumed	550 at £2 10*s*. 11*d*.	.	£1,400

or, assume *all* stocks are held at written-down value:

			£
Opening Stock	100 at 10*s*. . . .		50
Purchases	500 at £3 . . .		1,500
			1,550
Closing Stock	50 at 10*s*. . . .		25
Materials Consumed	550 at £2 15*s*. 5*d*. .	.	£1,525

In this case there is a gain variation, because for budget purposes production is charged at £3, whilst actual production is charged partly at £3 and partly at 10*s*.

(3) Direct Wages may be less than budget because:

(*a*) Output is low. Output might still be low and direct wages approximate closely to or even exceed budget.

(*b*) Employees are working more effectively.

(*c*) The budgets were based on incorrect data.

(*d*) Any combination of (*a*) to (*c*).

(4) Actual and budget sales may vary because quantities sold are above or below budget levels, or because average realised selling prices have been exceeded or have not been realised.

(5) Variations may consist of over- or under-spending, either as such or caused by variations in the volume of production and sales.

Not only do these considerations apply to the enterprise as a whole; they apply equally to the departments or divisions of the enterprise, so that the net variation, in fact, is made up of many variations, some working in one direction, some in another. Hence the analysis of variations is the most important document for use in budgetary control.

It has been described already that action is a matter for executives, each in his own sphere, and the comparative statements prepared by accounting should be distributed appropriately to those concerned with them, either in part or as a whole.

CONTROL AND THE BALANCE SHEET

In Chapter III it is explained that revenue and expense budgets are part only of the total budgets; that to be complete they have to be related to the financial position of the business enterprise as expressed in the balance sheet. In the example given later in this chapter, budgets for revenue and expenses are shown between two balance sheets; one assumed to be actual, though as budgets must be prepared before the period to which they relate, in practice it would be an estimate which would be compared with the actual balance sheet, the effect of changes on the budgets being noted; the other hypothetical, a budget balance sheet.

(1) The Purpose of the Budget Balance Sheet

The budget balance sheet serves to show what variations in assets and liabilities are expected as a result of budget trading. Some of these variations are part of trading, e.g. the relationship between debtors, stocks and cash, which are affected by sales, stock and credit policies, and the effectiveness or otherwise with which these policies are applied. Other variations are altogether matters of policy, i.e. questions of effectiveness or ineffectiveness do not arise, e.g. appropriations to reserve.

The importance of comparison between a budget balance sheet and an actual balance sheet also lies in the attention it draws to the "reason for variations". Comparison reveals and provides the means for measuring the factors which affect the conduct of a business and the results of its working, so that over a period data is established for use where decisions affecting current or future operations are being made.

The expressions of forward policy shown in a budget balance sheet are affected by:

A. Variations between budget and actual trading

This item is not concerned solely with the available balance on the Profit and Loss Account, e.g. budget profit and actual profit may approximate closely, yet the details of trading—sales and expense levels, cash collected, etc.—may show wide variations between budget and actual, affecting stocks, debtors, creditors and cash in the balance sheet.

B. Changed conditions leading to changed policies

At the start of a budget period the Directors of a business might have had in mind that free reserves should be increased by £10,000, and that fixed assets should be written down by £5,000. At the end of the budget period the trading profit might be satisfactory and compare favourably with the budget, but because of changes in taxation it might be necessary to reserve more on that account than had been anticipated, thus reducing the appropriation to the reserve account, and because of a continuing rise in the cost of plant and buildings, it might be more appropriate to take advantage of the opportunity to write off intangible assets such as goodwill and preliminary expenses.

(2) The Form of Control

It may be thought that if a budget balance sheet is prepared as at the end of a budget period, no purpose is served by balance sheet comparisons, actual with budget, during the budget period. On the contrary, if budgets are accepted as guides to action, there is every reason for short-term comparison between actual and budget balance sheets in order that the trend of affairs towards a desired result can be noted for action.

Where budgets are prepared, say, at quarterly intervals for a period ahead, actual and budget balance sheet comparisons should be made as soon as possible after the end of any quarter. Where budgets are for say a year, two courses are open:

A. A budget balance sheet may be prepared for each short-term (four/five weeks or calendar month) comparative period, for comparison with an actual balance sheet prepared as soon as possible after the end of the short-term comparative period.

B. A budget balance sheet may be prepared for the full budget period, showing the budget position as at the end of that period. During the currency of the budgets, actual balance sheets would be prepared and compared at short intervals (four/five weeks or the calendar month) with the budget balance sheet, in order that the trend towards the budget balance sheet can be noted.

(3) *The Use of Ratios*

Budget "balance sheets" are sometimes set out in the form of asset, liability and revenue ratio statements. There is no special merit about this method; it is merely one more way of setting targets and relating results of working to them. Balance sheet ratios are described in a number of standard works, the more usual ratios described being:

Current Assets/Current Liabilities: to give relative liquidity and the availability of assets to meet current claims upon them.

Capital Invested, Reserves, Profit and Loss Account Balance/ Creditors: to give the relationship between capital owned by a business and capital loaned by creditors.

Capital Invested, Reserves, Profit and Loss Account Balance/Fixed Assets: is significant of the availability of liquid capital from capital owned by showing the relationship between capital owned and capital invested in fixed assets.

Finished Product Stocks/Debtors: used to check movements in the current ratio, i.e. to determine whether or not any change in that ratio is fundamental or merely owing to changes in the distribution of assets in the current ratio, stock and debtors normally being the main current assets.

Sales/Debtors: over a period is significant of the time taken for debts to be paid; it reflects trade activity in the relationship between sales and paying for them.

Sales/Finished Product Stocks: is significant of the rate of turnover of finished product stocks, and may reveal trends towards excessive or inadequate inventories.

Sales/Fixed Assets: shows the sales productivity of capital invested in fixed assets.

Sales/Capital Invested, Reserves, Profit and Loss Account Balance: shows the sales productivity of owned capital.

Net Profit/Sales: shows the relative net earning power of sales.

Net Profit/Capital Invested, Reserves, Profit and Loss Account Balance: shows the relationship between capital owned and earnings.

Two drawbacks to the use of ratios for budget purposes are that many people do not appreciate their significance or understand them, and that from ratios alone it is difficult to visualise the complete balance sheet from which the ratios must be calculated. Sometimes too there may be difficulty in setting ratios for target purposes. Individuals may have different opinions regarding what is a satisfactory ratio in given circumstances, and ratios naturally reflect any policy decisions affecting the value of assets, e.g. an unusual degree of writing-down fixed assets, or stocks, for which allowance should be made when computing ratios. On the whole, ratios can be most useful for establishing trends in the relationships between groups of assets and liabilities, for revealing conditions such as over-trading on owned capital, ability or inability to meet current obligations, rate of debt collection, over-investment in stocks, etc. It is advisable to read them in conjunction with the balance sheet(s) to which they relate.

SUMMARY

1. The characteristics of control against budgets are:
   (a) Short-term comparison between estimated and actual performances as expressed in revenue and expenditure.
   (b) Individual responsibility for performances as expressed in revenue and expenditure must be shown on separate comparative statements.

2. Variations are of two types:
   (a) Over- or under-spending;
   (b) Over- or under-recovery;
and they may be caused by several factors working in any combination. Therefore, an analysis of variations is required so that necessary action can be taken.

EXAMPLE

The detail described in this and previous chapters may be illustrated by an example. At the outset it is necessary to emphasise the limitations of examples, which too often are accepted as easy ways of understanding mechanisms of control in the place of understanding of principles and objectives. A fully detailed example would be too lengthy for a textbook. Also, examples must be general and hypo thetical. Forms, comparative statements, and rules may be drawn from practice, but practice must vary in every instance. There have been too many instances of taking what Company A does and applying it *in toto* to Company B. The purpose of the example is to illustrate, not to provide a general solution, in potted form, to all problems.

The method illustrated is not a system. It is one way only of applying the principles and practices described in this and the preceding chapters. The detail shown is not exhaustive; raw materials and direct labour costs and production could be shown under departmental responsibility (in the example, under the three departmental superintendents) as well as in total. Separate statements are given for main groups of expenditure to bring out the idea of showing expenditure against the executives responsible for it.

Example

(1) A.B., Ltd., is a Company which makes and sells five products. Also it factors two other products. Its organisation structure is:

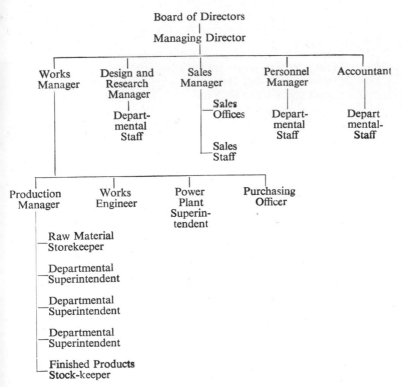

(2) At the 31st of December, 19—, its Balance Sheet is:

BALANCE SHEET

Liabilities		£	*Assets*		£
Issued Capital .	.	150,000	Fixed Assets .	.	90,000
Reserves .	. .	30,000	Investments .	.	40,000
Profit and Loss Ac-			Stock .	. .	66,000
count Balance	.	10,000	Debtors .	. .	50,000
Trade Creditors	.	55,000	Cash .	. .	1,000
Bank Overdraft	.	10,000	Preliminary Expenses		
			and Goodwill	.	8,000
		£255,000			£255,000

(3) Expense responsibility is established by the Managing Director as follows:

A. *Works Manager*

Raw Materials: consumption and stock losses.
Service Materials: consumption and stock losses.
Finished Products: losses of finished stock owing to faulty stock-keeping.
Direct Wages: wages expended directly upon manufacture.
Indirect Wages: wages paid to labourers; wages and salaries for maintenance and factory services; factory office clerical and typing wages and salaries.
Fuel and Wages: for power generation.
General Factory Expenses: lighting, maintenance of roadways, etc.
Salaries: of factory executives.

The Works Manager takes this general classification, and with the aid of the Accountant rearranges it so that it shows expense responsibility within the manufacturing organisation:

Production Manager

Raw Material Storekeeper:
Stock losses.
Wages.
Departmental Superintendent:
Departmental stocks.
Materials consumed.
Direct wages.
Wages of labourers, etc.
Wages and salaries of supervision.
Power consumed.
Departmental clerical wages and salaries.

Departmental Superintendent:
Departmental stocks.
Materials consumed.
Direct wages.
Wages of labourers, etc.
Wages and salaries of supervision.
Power consumed.
Departmental clerical wages and salaries.
Departmental Superintendent:
Departmental stocks.
Materials consumed.
Direct wages.
Wages of labourers, etc.
Wages and salaries of supervision.
Power consumed.
Departmental clerical wages and salaries.
Finished Product Stock-keeper:
Stock losses.
Wages.

Works Engineer

Wages in service machine shop and for repairs and maintenance
men, plumbers, joiners, buildings maintenance employees.
Consumption of engineers' stores, and stock losses.
Salaries: drawing office and supervision.

Power Plant Superintendent

Wages and salaries of employees in boiler house and electricity
generating station.
Consumption of fuel and stock losses.
Sundry supplies.

Purchasing Officer

Expenditure on materials purchased (see page 604).
Wages and salaries; it is decided that these relatively small
items shall be included in fixed overheads for purposes of
comparison.

There remain certain items of general expenditure which it is
decided shall be grouped as Variable and Fixed Expenses, although executive responsibility for the activities they represent
may rest with any one of the Works Manager's subordinate
executives. These items of general expenditure are for the Works
Manager's personal attention, and they complete the classification under "Works Manager":

Variable Expenses

Stationery.
Telephone.

Variable Expenses (continued)

Laundry.
Protective clothing.
General lighting and power.
Yard cleaning.
Test and inspection.
Security.
Postages.
Carriage.
Works Manager's Office wages.
General expenses.

Fixed Expenses

First-aid and Ambulance.
Salaries, Works Manager's principal subordinates and Works
    Manager's Office, and Purchasing Office.
Rates and Schedule A.
Insurances.
Depreciation.

The object of expense grouping in this way is to classify
expenditure to individuals in accordance with their power to
influence that expenditure in relation to an object, and in
accordance with their power to control that expenditure.

B. *Design and Research Manager*

Salaries and wages of staff and employees in his department.
Materials used for experimental work.
Power and light.
Depreciation of equipment in experimental department.
Stationery and general expenses, telephone, etc.

C. *Sales Manager*

Salaries and wages: sales and sales office staff.
Advertising.
Commissions.
Travelling expenses.
Rent and rates of sales office.
Depreciation of motor-cars used by sales force.
Stationery and general expenses, telephone, etc.

D. *Personnel Manager*

Departmental wages, salaries, stationery, travelling.
Printing works magazine.
Canteen wages and cost of foodstuffs purchased, power, heating
    and lighting.
Medical officer's fee.

E. *Accountant*

    Wages and salaries.

    Stationery.

    Depreciation of office equipment.

F. *General Administration*

    Salaries of Managing Director, Works Manager, Design and Research Manager, Sales Manager, Personnel Manager, Accountant.

    Salary of Managing Director's Secretary.

    Managing Director's travelling expenses.

Notes

  (i) This classification, like all others, contains items, the placing of which may be contested.

  (ii) The Works Manager is responsible for finished product stock losses owing to faulty stock-keeping. What is faulty stock-keeping? It might be argued that certain stock losses occurred because of sales inability to sell the items concerned before they deteriorated.

  (iii) The salaries of the principal executive and his principal subordinates are included in "General Administration". This is because they are regarded as being expenses controlled directly by the Managing Director. They could be included in the divisions of activity with which they are concerned, e.g. Works Manager's salary under "Works Manager", and so on.

  (iv) There is no perfect method of grouping and classifying expenses. Items in any classification may be contested by individuals according to their interests or points of view. Nevertheless, some classification has to be accepted. What matters more than argument is that whatever arrangement is adopted is understood by those concerned, that definition is clear and as free from ambiguity as possible.

  (v) It is assumed that with the exception of a sales office, all activities are on the one site. This could lead to an apportionment of common charges such as rates, so much to manufacture, so much for sales and so on. It is decided, however, that the sum involved does not justify the apportionment, and Rates and Schedule A are included in "Manufacturing Fixed Expenses".

(4) The position shown in the balance sheet under (2) above was known generally by the Board before the balance sheet was prepared, from the Company's internal, i.e. control, accounts. The balance sheet confirms and establishes the position as at a date.

    Board policy for trading during the year following that for which a balance sheet is given was formulated with reference to:

A. Reducing Stocks.
B. Reducing Creditors.
C. Earning a profit which would:

(i) Enable a gross dividend of 10 per cent. to be paid.
(ii) Enable the Reserve Account to be increased by £5,000.
(iii) Enable £4,000 to be written off Preliminary Expenses and Goodwill.

It is calculated, i.e. after taking taxation into account at say 10s. in the £, that the trading profit required is:

(a) For Dividend . . .		15,000
(b) For Reserve		10,000
(c) For Writing off Preliminary Expenses and Goodwill . .		8,000
		£33,000

D. In addition, the Board wish to incur capital expendi ture o £8,000 on fixed assets. If necessary, this expenditure can be financed to the extent of £4,000 by increasing the bank overdraft, although the Board do not want the overdraft increased to finance current trading. If necessary, investments can be sold, but the Board would like the cash position improved to enable as much as possible of the capital expenditure to be financed out of trading.

(5) Sales budgets are prepared:

A. After investigation the Sales Manager considers the total market to be:

	Quantity p.a.	Estd. Realised Selling Price	Value p.a.
		£	£
Product 1	2,000	25	50,000
Product 2	4,000	30	120,000
Product 3	10,000	20	200,000
Product 4	15,000	15	225,000
Product 5	10,000	10	100,000
			£695,000

With the production facilities available (i.e. excluding the anticipated increased output from the budget capital expenditure) output as follows can be obtained:

	Quantity p.a.	Estd. Realised Selling Price	Value p.a.
		£	£
Product 1	1,000	25	25,000
Product 2	2,000	30	60,000
Product 3	4,000	20	80,000
Product 4	10,000	15	150,000
Product 5	15,000	10	150,000
			£465,000

OR

	Quantity p.a.	Estd. Realised Selling Price	Value p.a.
		£	£
Product 1	1,500	25	37,500
Product 2	2,000	30	60,000
Product 3	4,500	20	90,000
Product 4	12,000	15	180,000
Product 5	10,000	10	100,000
			£467,500

The quantities required by these preliminary budgets are submitted to the Works Manager.

B. Products 6 and 7, which are factored, are service accessories to products 1 to 5, and the Sales Manager makes an estimate as follows:

	Estd. Number Reqd. for Sale	Selling Price	Value of Sales	Cost per unit	Total Cost	Gross Profit
			£		£	£
Product 6	6,000	£1	6,000	14s.	4,200	1,800
Product 7	12,000	15s.	9,000	10s.	6,000	3,000
			£15,000		£10,200	£4,800

He finds that there will be approximately 1,000 of Product 6 and 3,000 of Product 7 in stock, at cost price, at the commencement of the budget period. These levels have proved to be too high, 500 of Product 6 and 1,000 of Product 7 being adequate. Purchases therefore can be reduced to:

$$
\begin{array}{ll}
 & £ \\
5{,}500 \text{ of Product 6 at } 14s. = & 3{,}850 \\
10{,}000 \text{ of Product 7 at } 10s. = & 5{,}000 \\
\hline
 & £8{,}850 \\
\end{array}
$$

Stocks will be reduced by: £

> 500 of Product 6 at 14*s.* =   350
> 2,000 of Product 7 at 10*s.* = 1,000
>
>   £1,350

C. The Sales Manager estimates the costs of his activity as follows:

	£
Salaries and Wages	23,000
Advertising	8,000
Commissions	1,500
Travelling Expenses	4,000
Rent and Rates of Sales Office . . .	800
Depreciation of Cars	2,000
Stationery, Telephone and General Expenses .	700
	£40,000

(6) Manufacturing budgets are prepared:

A. Finished product stock levels, previously agreed with the Sales Manager and approved by the Managing Director, are:

Product 1	75
Product 2	200
Product 3	300
Product 4	1,000
Product 5	1,000

In view of the Board's policy to reduce stocks, these levels are reviewed and agreed as follows:

Product 1	75
Product 2	150
Product 3	250
Product 4	750
Product 5	600

Stocks at the date of the balance sheet are estimated to be:

Product 1	100
Product 2	180
Product 3	240
Product 4	1,200
Product 5	1,300

The production budget is therefore calculated as follows:

(i) *First Budget*

	Quantity Required	Deduct Est. Stock Commencement	Total	Add Stock Reqmnts. (Closing)	Production Required
Product 1	1,000	100	900	75	975
Product 2	2,000	180	1,820	150	1,970
Product 3	4,000	240	3,760	250	4,010
Product 4	10,000	1,200	8,800	750	9,550
Product 5	15,000	1,300	13,700	600	14,300

OR

(ii) *Second Budget*

	Quantity Required	Deduct Est. Stock (Commencement)	Total	Add Stock Reqmnts. (Closing)	Production Required
Product 1	1,500	100	1,400	75	1,475
Product 2	2,000	180	1,820	150	1,970
Product 3	4,500	240	4,260	250	4,510
Product 4	12,000	1,200	10,800	750	11,550
Product 5	10,000	1,300	8,700	600	9,300

B. The alternative production budgets are broken down into their component process requirements and considered in relation to:

(i) The load each provides on the factory in order to permit of maximum plant utilisation, full employment of labour force, possible labour requirements, and provision of the widest basis for the recovery of overheads.

It may be, for example, that Product 5 is more expensive in relation to its selling price than is Product 1, that whereas production of 1,475 of Product 1 provides a theoretical margin for works overheads of, say, £5,900, production of 14,300 of Product 5 provides but, say, £4,766.

The alternative budgets therefore could be viewed along the lines of discontinuing the manufacture and sale of Product 5 in order to make more of the other products, say, more of Product 1, which would lead to increased profitability if the additional output could be sold. On the other hand, Product 5 might meet a wider market not yet fully developed, but which has greater potential. This is a question of judgment on the facts available: assume it is decided to retain Product 5 in the range.

(ii) Raw material stock and supply position, and stock policy.

After investigation it is reported by the Production Manager to the Works Manager that the second budget provides a more effective load, a greater contribution to factory overheads, and permits of more ready execution of the policy to reduce stocks. Nevertheless, the Works Manager decides to calculate a theoretical materials and labour cost for both budgets.

C. Standard costs, raw materials and labour for the products made are:

	Materials	*Direct Wages*	*Total*
	£	£	£
Product 1	7	3	10
Product 2	9	4	13
Product 3	6	4	10
Product 4	4	3	7
Product 5	3	2	5

Whilst these standards are set in order to be attained, the Works Manager decides it would be prudent to make an allowance of 5 per cent. on total cost to provide for contingencies. These costs are then applied to the production budgets:

(i) *First Budget*

	Production Required	*Material Cost per Unit*	*Total for Materials*	*Direct Wages Cost per Unit*	*Total for Direct Wages*
		£	£	£	£
Product 1	975	7	6,825	3	2,925
Product 2	1,970	9	17,730	4	7,880
Product 3	4,010	6	24,060	4	16,040
Product 4	9,550	4	38,200	3	28,650
Product 5	14,300	3	42,900	2	28,600
			129,715		84,005
		Add 5 per cent.	6,486	Add 5 per cent.	4,205
			£136,201		£88,300

(ii) *Second Budget*

	Production Required	Material Cost per Unit	Total for Materials	Direct Wages Cost per Unit	Total for Direct Wages
		£	£	£	£
Product 1	1,475	7	10,325	3	4,425
Product 2	1,970	9	17,730	4	7,880
Product 3	4,510	6	27,060	4	18,040
Product 4	11,550	4	46,200	3	34,650
Product 5	9,300	3	27,900	2	18,600
			129,215		83,595
		Add 5 per cent.	6,461	Add 5 per cent.	4,180
			£135,676		£87,775

In practice a number of considerations would have to be dealt with, e.g. in the example the same standard cost has been used for both budget calculations. It might be that redistribution of the load on the factory (Budget (ii) compared with Budget (i)) would affect the theoretical costs owing to factors such as economical batch sizes, accord of load with process sequence, longer "runs", etc.

D. Manufacturing expenditure budgets are prepared:

(i) For the general expenses of the production departments:

Item	Dept. 1	Dept. 2	Dept. 3	Total
	£	£	£	£
Indirect Wages (1)	2,000	3,000	4,000	9,000
Salaries (2) .	2,000	3,000	3,000	8,000
Miscellaneous Expenses	500	700	800	2,000
Clerical Salaries (3) and Sundry Expenses.	1,000	1,250	750	3,000
Power and Lighting (4)	8,000	10,000	4,000	22,000
	£13,500	£17,950	£12,550	£44,000

Notes.—Items (1), (2) and (3) are calculated with reference to numbers of employees, employee turnover, wage and salary rates, and normal increases in remuneration which may be expected in the budget period.

Item (4) is calculated with reference to estimated consumption of electric current for power and lighting, based on past records, h.p. of motors, lighting points and wattage. It is a credit to the Power Plant Account.

(ii) For repairs and maintenance; for wages, salaries, etc., with reference to the number of employees, their wage rates and the trend in wage rates, etc., and for materials with reference to experience and established programmes, e.g. a piece of large equipment which once every five years has to be stripped and reconditioned would require an allowance accordingly. The Engineer's estimates are:

	£
Wages and Salaries	11,000
Materials	10,000
Materials for Special Repairs	2,000
Drawing Office, Clerical and Supervision . .	3,500
	£26,500

(iii) For power generation: for wages and salaries with reference to number of employees, wage and salary rates and trends; cost of fuel and water with reference to stocks and price trends, normal usage, estimated load expected, etc. The Power House Superintendent's estimates are:

	£
Wages and Salaries	6,000
Fuel	17,000
Sundry Supplies	2,000
	£25,000

(iv) For purchasing, a straightforward calculation based on salaries; say £1,800 (include in fixed expenses for comparative purposes).

(v) For variable expenses, in detail, say £20,000.

(vi) For fixed expenses, in detail, say £38,000.

E. At this stage the manufacturing expenditure budget may be summarised as follows:

	First Budget		Second Budget	
		£		£
Raw Materials . .		136,201		135,676
Direct Wages . . .		88,300		87,775
General Factory Expenses		44,000		44,000
Repairs and Maintenance .		26,500		26,500
Power Generation . .	25,000		25,000	
Less Transferred to General Factory Expenses .	22,000	3,000	22,000	3,000
Purchasing . . .		1,800		1,800
Variable Expenses . .		20,000		20,000
Fixed Expenses . .		38,000		38,000
		£357,801		£356,751

Budget costs per unit of production can be calculated; standard costs are available for materials and labour, and it would be necessary to allocate other expense items in accordance with previous results and/or some arbitrary bases, either "allocation" or "recovery" (see Chapter VII).

For purposes of illustration, the budget calculations use the same figures for both budgets. It might be that a change in load would influence cost items other than those mentioned at the conclusion of 6 (C) above. One product, say 5, might require more power than another, say 4. Therefore, a reduction in the quantitative requirements of 5, and a less than proportionate increase in the quantitative requirements of 4, would reduce the demands for power, with the possibility of economy accordingly.

It would be necessary:

(i) For the Works Manager and the Sales Manager to discuss the alternative budgets in relation to their respective requirements. The Sales Manager would probably conclude that the second budget was more appropriate to the market, and that it offered a greater revenue for a slightly reduced cost. The Works Manager, on the other hand, is more concerned with maintaining the load on his factory in order to produce the greatest volume of finished articles of the right quality at the lowest cost. Let it be assumed that he too concludes that the second budget has the greater advantages.

(ii) For the Works Manager and the Sales Manager to discuss with the Accountant the general levels of expenditure forecast and to compare them with the results of current and previous operating. Standard costs are taken for direct materials and labour; whilst the standards are set to be achieved, it might be that actual working showed a consistent excess of actual over standard. If this is likely to continue, the budget calculations should be adjusted accordingly.

(iii) For the Works Manager to review again the trend of his expense items and factors affecting them. In the example, 5 per cent. is added to the cost of raw materials and direct wages for contingencies. Let it be assumed that this 5 per cent. is to provide for (a) a probable increase in basic wage rates, (b) a possible increase in raw material costs, and (c) excess of actual costs over standard. In practice, each factor would have to be assessed separately.

At this stage too the budgets should be considered by the principal executive. In all cases wherein budgets are being prepared, much is gained by informal discussion regarding problems involved before the budgets have to be considered formally, i.e. the need is for continuous integration.

(7) Budgets are prepared for Design and Research:

A. General policy within the Company is that 2½ per cent. of budget turnover should be spent on design and research, and for budget purposes turnover is estimated to be of the order of £475,000. If general policy were to be followed strictly, the turnover level taken would be one of the alternatives given under (5) above, sales budgets, namely, the one finally adopted. Practically, the small difference between the assumed figure of turnover (£475,000) and the budget turnover (£465,000 or £467,500) is so small as to be of no moment.

B. The budget sum available for design and research is therefore £11,875, say £12,000.

C. The Design and Research Manager first of all considers this sum in relation to the expense headings for which he is responsible. These are:

Wages and Salaries.
Materials.
Power and Light.
Depreciation.
Stationery and General Expenses.

During the first ten months of the year preceding that for which budgets are being prepared, these expenses have been as follows, and the Design and Research Manager converts them to an estimate for the year by adding one-fifth:

	Ten Months	One-fifth	Estimate for one Year
	£	£	£
Wages and Salaries . .	5,000	1,000	6,000
Materials	2,900	580	3,480
Power and Light . .	500	100	600
Depreciation . . .	400	80	480
Stationery and General Expenses . . .	200	40	240
	£9,000	£1,800	£10,800

The estimate for the year is compared with previous years' expenses:

	Est. this year	Last Year	Year ...	Year ...
	£	£	£	£
Wages and Salaries . .	6,000	5,400	4,200	4,500
Materials . . .	3,480	3,600	2,600	2,800
Power and Light . .	600	720	400	400
Depreciation . . .	480	500	300	350
Stationery and General				
Expenses . . .	240	200	150	180
	£10,800	£10,420	£7,650	£8,230

D. During the budget period, the Design and Research Manager knows he has eight projects on which work has to be done, one being a major development; that he must provide technical service to the manufacturing and sales activities, and that a margin of effort should be available for contingencies.

The approximate time plan for the projects is:

```
Project   J. F. M. A. M. J. Jy. A. S. O. N. D.
   1          ———————
   2             ——————————————————
   3                         ————————————————————————
   4              ——————————————
   5          ——————————————————————————————————————
   6          ——————————————————————
   7          ——————————————————————————————
   8             ——————————————————————————————————
```

The requirements of these projects have to be considered in terms of men and materials, bearing in mind that as one project is finished the staff concerned can be transferred to another, either planned already or which may arise during the budget period. From these considerations it is estimated that:

(i) Additional expenditure on materials will have to be incurred in the budget period, £800, but as some projects will be concluded, there will be a corresponding reduction in material requirements, say £600.

(ii) Additional staff will be required, £1,500.

(iii) Power charges will probably increase by £100.

The Design and Research Manager's preliminary budget is therefore:

	£
Wages and Salaries	7,500
Materials	3,680
Power and Light	700
Depreciation	400*
Stationery and General Expenses . .	250*
	£12,530

* Estimates based on preceding year and policy.

This budget is submitted to the Managing Director, who examines it with the Design and Research Manager, the Works Manager and the Sales Manager. It is concluded that whilst the amount required is somewhat above the budget "allowance", all the work represented is necessary and that the budget should stand.

(8) Budgets are prepared for (A) Personnel, (B) Accounting, (C) General Administration. These expenditure budgets would probably be prepared in the first place by the Accountant, in the form of expense statements based on previous results and current working:

A. The Personnel Manager would make his budget with reference to policy on personnel, normal changes in expense levels, e.g. salary increases, each item of expenditure being considered separately. Assume the budget is £3,000.

B. The Accountant would forecast the wage, salary and normal operating costs of his department, make allowance for normal changes in expense levels. Assume the budget is £5,000.

C. The Managing Director would review the expense information submitted to him by the Accountant for those items of expenditure included under "General Administration", and forecast expenditure for the budget period in accordance with his judgment and interpretation of policy. Assume the budget is £14,000.

(9) The Accountant is now in a position to prepare a budget profit and loss statement.

Budget Profit and Loss Statement for the Year Ending 31*st December*, 19. . .

	£	£
Product Sales		467,500
Accessories Sales	15,000	
Deduct Cost of Accessories . . .	10,200	
		4,800
	Carried forward :	£472,300

	Brought forward :	£472,300
Manufacturing Expenses (in detail) . . .	356,751	
Design and Research Expenses (in detail) . .	12,530	
Sales Expenses (in detail)	40,000	
Personnel Expenses (in detail)	3,000	
Accounting Expenses (in detail) . . .	5,000	
General Administration Expenses (in detail) .	14,000	
		431,281
		£41,019

Difference between opening and closing finished product stocks (assume finished product stocks are valued at the cost of direct materials and direct wages only):

	Stock Decrease	Stock Increase	at £	£	£
Product 1 .	. 25	—	10	250	
Product 2 .	. 30	—	13	390	
Product 3 .	. —	10	10	—	100
Product 4 .	. 450	—	7	3,150	
Product 5 .	. 700	—	5	3,500	
				7,290	100
				100	
				7,190	7,190

Budget Profit	£33,829

(10) This statement can be set out in account form:

Budget Manufacturing Account for the Year Ending 31*st December,* 19. . .

	£		£
Commencing Stock of Raw		Manufacturing Cost of	
Materials . . .	33,160	Finished Production 356,751	
Purchases . . .	131,516		
	164,676		
Closing Stocks of Raw			
Materials . . .	29,000		
Raw Materials Consumed .	135,676		
Direct Wages . . .	87,775		
General Factory Expenses .	22,000		
Purchasing . . .	1,800		
Variable Expenses . .	20,000		
Fixed Expenses . . .	38,000		

Repairs and Maintenance:

	£
Stores, commencing	4,000
Purchases . .	11,000
	15,000
Stores, closing . .	3,000
Materials Consumed .	12,000
Wages and Expenses .	14,500
	26,500

Carried forward : £331,751		*Carried forward :* £356,751	

Brought forward: £331,751   *Brought forward:* £356,751

Power Generation:
Stocks of Fuel, com-

mencing . .	6,000	
Purchases . .	15,000	
	21,000	
Stocks, closing . .	4,000	
Fuel consumed . .	17,000	
Wages and Expenses .	8,000	
		25,000
		£356,751

        £356,751

Budget Trading Account for the Year Ending 31st December, 19. . .

	£		£
Commencing Stocks, Finished Products . . .	20,640	Product Sales .	467,500
Manufacturing Cost of Production	356,751	Accessory Sales .	15,000
	377,391		
Closing Stock of Finished Products . . .	13,450		
	363,941		
Commencing Stocks, Accessories . 2,200			
Purchases . . 8,850			
11,050			
Closing Stocks, Accessories . 850			
	10,200		
Design and Research Expenses (details) . .	12,530		
Sales Expenses (details) .	40,000		
Personnel Expenses (details)	3,000		
Accounting Expenses (details)	5,000		
General Administration (details)	14,000		
Budget profit . . .	33,829		
	£482,500		£482,500

11) The budget must be examined in relation to Board policy:

(*a*) *Stocks*

	Commencing Stock	Closing Stock	Decrease
	£	£	£
Raw Materials . .	33,160	29,000	4,160
Stores . . .	4,000	3,000	1,000
Fuel . . .	6,000	4,000	2,000
Finished Products .	20,640	13,450	7,190
Accessories . .	2,200	850	1,350
	£66,000	£50,300	£15,700

There is therefore a "budget" reduction in stock levels.

(b) *Creditors*

A reduction in stocks of purchased materials may imply a reduction in supplies; or it may be caused by increased manufacture. In the first instance, and other things being equal, i.e. payments being made, a reduction in creditors on purchases account could be expected.

(c) *Profitability*

The budget profit compares favourably with the profit required.

(12) A budget balance sheet can now be prepared:

A. *Liabilities*

£

(i) *Issued Capital. This item will remain at* . . . 150,000

(ii) The Reserve Account should be:

	£	
Reserve at 1st January	30,000	
Add Transfer from Profit and Loss Account .	5,000	
		35,000

(iii) Creditors:

		£	
Balance at 1st January		55,000	
Purchases:			
Raw Materials . . .	131,516		
Stores	11,000		
Fuel	15,000		
Accessories	8,850		
		166,366	
General Factory Expenses		2,000	
Sundry Supplies, Power Generation . .		2,000	
Variable Expenses on Creditors' Account (say) .		5,000	
Fixed Expenses on Creditors' Account (say) .		4,000	
Distribution Expenses on Creditors' Account (say)		10,000	
Design and Research Expenses on Creditors' Account (say)		4,500	
		248,866	
Capital Expenditure		8,000	
		256,866	
Deduct			
Payments required to reduce Creditors to £45,000		211,866	
			45,000

(iv) Bank:

	£	
Overdraft	10,000	
Payments to Creditors	211,866	
Cash Payments	223,305	
	445,171	
Receipts from Debtors (say) . . .	445,171	

Carried forward: £230,000

Brought forward : £230,000

		£		
(v) Profit and Loss Account:				
Balance at 1st January	. . . .	10,000		
Budget Profit for year to 31st December	.	33,829		
		43,829		

Deduct

	£		
Provision for Dividend and Tax thereon	15,000		
Provision for Tax . . .	9,000		
Transfer to Reserve Account . .	5,000		
Written off Preliminary Expenses and Goodwill	4,000		
		33,000	
			10,829

(vi) Provisions:		
Dividend and Tax thereon	15,000	
Income Tax	9,000	
		£264,829

B. *Assets*

(i) Fixed Assets	90,000		
Additions	8,000		
	98,000		
Depreciation	15,000		
		83,000	
(ii) Investments		40,000	
(iii) Stock		50,300	
(iv) Debtors:			
Balance at 1st January	50,000		
Sales	482,500		
	532,500		
Receipts required from Debtors (say) . .	445,171		
		87,329	

	£	
(v) Cash:		
Balance at 1st January	1,000	
Transfer from Bank Account . . .	223,305	
	£224,305	

Cash Payments:	£
Direct Wages	87,775
General Factory Expenses . .	20,000
Purchasing Expenses . . .	1,800
Variable Expenses . . .	15,000
Fixed Expenses	19,000
Repairs and Maintenance Wages .	11,000
Repairs and Maintenance Expenses	3,500
Power Generation, Wages . .	6,000
Distribution, Wages and Expenses	30,000
Design and Research, Wages and Expenses	8,030
Personnel	3,000
Accounting	5,000
General Administration . .	14,000

	224,105
	200

Carried forward : £260,829

Brought forward: £260,829

(vi) Preliminary Expenses and Goodwill: £
    Balance at 1st January   .   .   .   8,000
    Amount written off at 31st December .   .   4,000
                                      4,000

                                   £264,829

This preliminary statement of the balance sheet position is satisfactory, but the Sales Manager does not expect that payments by debtors will be as much as the statement shows. Accordingly, it is decided that the bank overdraft will have to be maintained, debtors being increased accordingly. The budget balance sheet now becomes:

Balance Sheet

Liabilities		Assets	
	£		£
Issued Capital . .	150,000	Fixed Assets . .	83,000
Reserve Account .	35,000	Investments . .	40,000
Creditors . .	45,000	Stock . . .	50,300
Bank Overdraft .	10,000	Debtors . . .	97,329
Profit and Loss Account	10,829	Cash	200
Provisions . .	24,000	Preliminary Expenses and Goodwill . .	4,000
	£274,829		£274,829

Alternatively, because of the improved position, creditors could remain at £55,000, thus eliminating the bank overdraft.

Summary

Budgets start with a statement of fact, the balance sheet.

Premises are made and a policy is formulated.

Policy is applied to the balance sheet, leading to the budget balance sheet.

    The position shown in the budget balance sheet leads to further policy considerations, leading to a final policy for application.

(13) There is now a series of "targets", for performance and expenditure in relation to an objective:

    A. The Works Manager has to produce a defined quantity of each of several products in a range, at a predetermined cost; and the responsibility for expenditure on manufacture has been allocated to the Works Manager's subordinates, each in accordance with his duties.

    B. The Sales Manager has to sell a defined quantity of each of several products at a price which he has forecast, and to control the costs of his activity within the limits of the budget for distribution expenditure.

C. The Design and Research Manager has to work upon and complete certain projects, and to give technical service, whilst controlling the costs of his activity within agreed limits.

D. The Personnel Manager and the Accountant are responsible for providing defined services at an agreed cost.

E. The cost of General Administration is estimated at a sum certain for a given level of profitability arising from operating at established levels of activity.

Whilst the objectives are described by stating that executives have to do something at a predetermined cost, it is understood that the budget figures are not fixed and unalterable. In their total and in their parts they represent what the enterprise has set itself to achieve, and the contributions of the various parts of the enterprise towards that achievement.

The next stage is that of comparing the results of actual working with the budget results. It is decided that certain comparative information is required at weekly intervals and that other comparative information is required at monthly intervals. The problem now is to decide what is a monthly interval; a period of four weeks or the calendar month?

The four-weekly "month" has many advantages, the chief being that it can be related quickly and easily to the week. On the other hand, owing to statutory holidays, it does not always give a strict comparison period by period; some "months" may contain more working days than others. Also it involves difficulties, inasmuch as suppliers invoice by the calendar month, and sales invoiced are related to the calendar month. This involves estimating at the end of each four-weekly period.

The calendar month also does not provide strictly comparable periods owing to the varying number of days in months and the incidence of statutory holidays, and it involves fractions of a week. Its chief merit rests in its being the period recognised for accounting with debtors and creditors.

After consideration, it is decided that the estimation of debtor and creditor items, with their corresponding revenue and charge accounts, is more practicable than the apportionment of terminal weeks over calendar months. It is decided too that each quarter shall consist of two periods each of four weeks and one period of five weeks.

The budgets for the year are now arranged over this basis by the Accountant, i.e. instead of being shown only for the yearly period, the budgets are reduced to a weekly basis and shown also for four weeks and five weeks. In the particular case, manufacture can proceed steadily throughout the year, but sales are always greater in the months from September to January. Short-term, weekly and "monthly", budgets for expenditure are therefore shown as equivalent proportions of the year's budget: for one week, one fifty-second; for four weeks, four fifty-seconds; and for five weeks, five fifty-seconds; but sales budgets are presented in relation to the Sales Manager's estimate of actual sales performance, i.e. the spread of sales over the year.

Weekly control information required is for:

(1) Works Manager:
   Materials consumed.
   Expenditure on direct wages.
   Production.
   Repairs and maintenance materials consumed.
   Repairs and maintenance wages.
   Fuel consumed.

(2) Sales Manager:
   Orders received.
   Deliveries invoiced.

Monthly control information required is in general a series of statements presented in the form in which the budgets were drawn up, showing actual and budget activity, revenue and expenditure, with variations. The preparation of the monthly control information is the work of the Accountant; with the exception of the Orders Received summary, the preparation of the weekly control information also falls within the scope of the Accountant's duties.

Notes.—The control information required is selected for purposes of illustration. It is not necessarily that which should be prepared in other examples, i.e. it is related to the assumed requirements of this example.

If sales invoicing were carried out in the Sales Office, under the Sales Manager, then summaries of deliveries invoiced also would be prepared in that office. This point is made merely to emphasise that different businesses adopt different arrangements, and the preparation of control information has to be adapted accordingly. To say, for purposes of illustration, that the preparation of certain control information falls within the scope of the Accountant's duties is not to establish a general rule or principle.

(14) Budgets for the year are now complete. It remains to illustrate the weekly and monthly control information.

A. *Weekly*

(1) The weekly Manufacturing Control Statement is shown in Fig. 75 on page 656.

(*a*) The statement provides a general guide only. Details under any variation would have to be sought in the supporting manufacturing, accounting and costing records. Daily figures of performance might be required for day-to-day control; for output, materials, wages, etc. Wages would not be wages paid, but an evaluation of time booked. Wherever possible, daily control detail should be prepared, especially for the main items of expenditure under the direct control of production supervision.

(*b*) It deals with finished production only, omitting work in progress.

(*c*) Action would be taken only in case of excessive variations. The week is too short a period for long-term trends to become apparent and noted for action.

(*d*) Cumulative statements also would be used, showing the position at the end of any week in a four/five-weekly period.

(2) The weekly Sales Control Statement is shown in Fig. 76 on page 657.

B. *Monthly*

(1) *Manufacture*

(a) *Direct Material Control*   *Month ended....   ....*

Product	This Month					Year to Date				
	Budget[1]	Actual	Variation			Budget	Actual	Variation		
			+	−				+	−	
	£	£	£	£						
1	661	701	40	—						
2	1,210	1,200	—	10						
3	2,520	2,670	150	—						
4	3,780	3,840	60	—						
5	2,016	2,000	—	16						
£	10,187	10,411	250	26						

[1] This column contains the budget cost of actual production figure.

(b) *Direct Wages Control*   *Month ended............*

Product	This Month				Year to Date			
	Budget[1]	Actual	Variation +	Variation −	Budget	Actual	Variation +	Variation −
	£	£	£	£				
1	283	303	20	—				
2	538	578	40	—				
3	1,680	1,760	80	—				
4	2,835	2,780	—	55				
5	1,344	1,320	—	24				
£	6,680	6,741	140	79				

[1] This column contains the budget cost of actual production figure.

(c) *Production*   *Month ended............*

Product	This Month				Year to Date			
	Budget	Actual	Variation +	Variation −	Budget	Actual	Variation +	Variation −
1	112	90	—	22				
2	152	128	—	24				
3	348	400	52	—				
4	888	900	12	—				
5	716	640	—	76				

These columns also would be
completed.

(d) *Actual Production at Budget Rates and Budget Production at Budget Rates*

Month ended............

Product	Production				Materials — £				Direct Wages — £			
	Budget	Actual	Variation +	Variation −	Budget	Act. at Budget	Variation +	Variation −	Budget	Act. at Budget	Variation +	Variation −
					£	£	£	£	£	£	£	£
1	112	90	—	22	834	661	—	173	357	283	—	74
2	152	128	—	24	1,432	1,210	—	222	636	538	—	98
3	348	400	52	—	2,186	2,520	334	—	1,457	1,680	223	—
4	888	900	12	—	3,732	3,780	48	—	2,798	2,835	37	—
5	716	640	—	76	2,253	2,016	—	237	1,504	1,344	—	160
£					10,437	10,187	382	632	6,752	6,680	260	332

WEEKLY CONTROL STATEMENT—MANUFACTURE

Week ended............

Product	Production Budget	Production Actual	Prod. Var. +	Prod. Var. −	Raw Materials Budget	Raw Materials Actual Prodctn. at Budget Rate	Raw Materials Actual	R.M. Var. +	R.M. Var. −	Direct Wages Budget	Direct Wages Actual Prodctn. at Budget Rate	Direct Wages Actual	D.W. Var. +	D.W. Var. −	Total Budget	Total Actual
1	28	20		8	206	147	155	8		88	63	70	7		210	225
2	38	32		6	359	302	320	18		159	134	120		14	436	440
3	87	98	11		548	618	600		18	366	412	440	28		1,030	1,040
4	222	244	22		932	1,025	1,048	23		699	768	785	17		1,793	1,833
5	179	160		19	564	504	524	20		376	336	319		17	840	843
£					2,609	2,596	2,647	69	18	1,688	1,713	1,734	52	31	4,309	4,381

Repair and Maintenance Materials

Budget	Actual	Variation +	Variation −
231	258		27
231	258		27

Repair and Maintenance Wages

Budget	Actual	Variation +	Variation −	Total Budget	Total Actual
212	242	30		443	500
212	242	30			

Fuel Consumed

Budget	Actual	Variation +	Variation −	Total Budget	Total Actual
327	343	16		327	343
327	343	16			

£5,079 £5,224

WEEKLY CONTROL STATEMENT—SALES

Week ended. . . . .

Product	Previous Week Stock	Production this Week	Total	Deliveries this Week	Stock	Value of Deliveries £	Average Selling Price £	Orders Outstanding Previous Week	Orders Received	Total	Deliveries this week	Orders Outstanding car. fwd.	Delivery Required Jan.	Feb.	Etc.
1	100	20	120	5	115	130	26	120	30	150	5	145	30	45	
2	180	32	212	8	204	248	31	120	40	160	8	152	44	80	
3	240	98	338	74	264	1,406	19	250	90	340	74	266	100	80	
4	1,200	244	1,444	200	1,244	3,200	16	1,200	500	1,700	200	1,500	600	700	
5	1,300	160	1,460	120	1,340	1,200	10	800	400	1,200	120	1,080	250	275	
6	1,000	—	1,000	40	960	40	1	200	300	500	40	460	240	160	
7	3,000	—	3,000	100	2,900	75	15s.	300	400	700	100	600	300	200	
						6,299									

Fig. 76

(e) *Manufacturing Expenses* Month ended..........

Item	This Month				Year to Date			
	Budget	Actual	Variation +	Variation −	Budget	Actual	Variation +	Variation −
	£	£	£	£				
Indirect Wages . .	692	708	16	—				
Salaries . . .	615	600	—	15				
Miscellaneous Expenses	154	188	34	—				
Sundry Expenses . .	231	262	31	—				
Power and Lighting .	1,694	1,786	92	—				
£	3,386	3,544	173	15				

(f) *Repairs and Maintenance* Month ended..........

Item	This Month				Year to Date			
	Budget	Actual	Variation +	Variation −	Budget	Actual	Variation +	Variation −
	£	£	£	£				
Wages and Salaries .	846	906	60	—				
Materials . . .	769	705	—	64				
Special Materials . .	154	104	—	50				
D.O. and Clerical . .	269	275	6	—				
£	2,038	1,990	66	114				

(g) *Power Generation* Month ended...........

Item	This Month				Year to Date			
	Budget	Actual	Variation +	Variation −	Budget	Actual	Variation +	Variation −
	£	£	£	£				
Wages and Salaries .	462	482	20	—				
Fuel	1,307	1,400	93	—				
Sundry Supplies . .	154	134	—	20				
£	1,923	2,016	113	20				
Less Transfer to Manu-facturing Expenses .	1,694	1,786	—	—				
£	229	230	1	—				

(h) *Variable Expenses*   *Month ended*............

Item	This Month				Year to Date			
	Budget	Actual	Variation		Budget	Actual	Variation	
			+	−			+	−
Variable Expenses (in detail) . . .	£ 1,538	£ 1,620	£ 82	£ —				
£	1,538	1,620	82					

(i) *Fixed Expenses*   *Month ended*............

Item	This Month				Year to Date			
	Budget	Actual	Variation		Budget	Actual	Variation	
			+	−			+	−
Fixed Expenses (in detail)	£ 3,062	£ 2,950	£ —	£ 112				
£	3,062	2,950	—	112				

(2) *Design and Research*   *Month ended*............

Item	This Month				Year to Date			
	Budget	Actual	Variation		Budget	Actual	Variation	
			+	−			+	−
Design and Research Expenses (in detail) .	£ 964	£ 1,064	£ 100	£ —				
£	964	1,064	100	—				

3) *Distribution*   *Month ended*............

Item	This Month				Year to Date			
	Budget	Actual	Variation		Budget	Actual	Variation	
			+	−			+	−
Distribution Expenses (in detail) . . .	£ 3,077	£ 3,000	£ —	£ 77				
£	3,077	3,000	—	77				

(4) *Personnel*   *Month ended*............

Item	This Month				Year to Date			
	Budget	Actual	Variation +	Variation −	Budget	Actual	Variation +	Variation −
Personnel Expenses (in detail) . . .	£ 231	£ 204	£	£ 27 −				
£	231	204		27 −				

(5) *Accounting*   *Month ended*............

Item	This Month				Year to Date			
	Budget	Actual	Variation +	Variation −	Budget	Actual	Variation +	Variation −
Accounting Expenses (in detail) . . .	£ 385	£ 351	£	£ 34 −				
£	385	351		34 −				

(6) *General Administration*   *Month ended*............

Item	This Month				Year to Date			
	Budget	Actual	Variation +	Variation −	Budget	Actual	Variation +	Variation −
Administration Expenses (in detail) . . .	£ 1,077	£ 1,000	£	£ 77 −				
£	1,077	1,000		77 −				

Note.—For expenditure, a plus variation equals a "loss", an excess of actual over budget, and a minus variation equals a "gain", an excess of budget over actual.

(7) *Sales*

Pro-duct	Quantity				Price				Value				
	Bud-get	Act-ual	Variation +	Variation −	Bud-get	Act-ual	Variation +	Variation −	Bud-get	Act-ual	Variation +	Variation −	
					£	£	£	£	£	£	£	£	*(Repeat for "Year to Date")*
1	80	60	—	20	25	26	1	—	2,000	1,560	—	440	
2	140	120	—	20	30	28	—	2	4,200	3,360	—	840	
3	360	400	40	—	20	20	—	—	7,200	8,000	800	—	
4	800	680	—	120	15	15	—	—	12,000	10,200	—	1,800	
5	800	760	—	40	10	11	1	—	8,000	8,360	360	—	
6	480	520	40	—	1	1	—	—	480	520	40	—	
7	960	880	—	80	15s.	15s.	—	—	720	660	—	60	
								£	34,600	32,660	1,200	3,140	

(8) *Summary*

	Trading Account							
	This Month				Year to Date			
	Budget	Actual	Variation +	Variation −	Budget	Actual	Variation +	Variation −
Manufacture:	£	£	£	£				
Materials Consumed	10,187	10,411	224	—				
Direct Wages .	6,680	6,741	61	—				
Manufacturing Expenses . .	3,386	3,544	158	—				
Repairs and Maintenance . .	2,038	1,990	—	48				
Power Generation (Net) . . .	229	230	1	—				
Variable Expenses .	1,538	1,620	82	—				
Fixed Expenses .	3,062	2,950	—	112				
	£27,120	27,486	526	160				
Design—Research .	964	1,064	100	—				
Distribution . .	3,077	3,000	—	77				
Personnel . .	231	204	—	27				
Accounting . .	385	351	—	34				
General Administration	1,077	1,000	—	77				
	32,854	33,105	626	375				
Add Cost of Accessories . . .	816	804	—	12				
TOTAL EXPENDITURE .	33,670	33,909	626	387				
Deduct Value of Increase in Finished Product Stocks .	553	1,344	—	—				
	33,117	32,565	—	—				
SALES . . .	34,600	32,660	—	1,940				
PROFIT . . .	£1,483	95	—	—				

(9) *Variation Summary*   *Month ended*..............

	This Month		Brought Forward		Year to Date	
	Gain	Loss	Gain	Loss	Gain	Loss
Manufacture:	£	£				
Materials . . .	—	224				
Direct Wages . .	—	61				
Manufacturing Expenses.	—	158				
Repairs and Maintenance	48	—				
Power Generation (Net) .	—	1				
Variable Expenses . .	—	82				
Fixed Expenses . .	112	—				
	160	526				
Design and Research .	—	100				
Distribution . . .	77	—				
Accessories . . .	12	—				
Personnel . . .	27	—				
Accounting . . .	34	—				
General Administration .	77	—				
TOTAL VARIATION: UNDER/ OVER-SPENDING . .	387	626				
Sales	—	1,940				
TOTAL VARIATIONS: UNDER/ OVER-RECOVERY . .	—	1,940				

The variation summary is primarily a statement for the principal executive, the Managing Director, who would require from his subordinate executives explanations of variations and suggestions for action to be taken, or a report on action taken, or, where appropriate, suggestions for changed policy. The variation summary would be supported by the separate control statements from which it is prepared, and copies of the control statements would be given to executives in accordance with their responsibility, e.g. the Works Manager would have copies of each statement under "Manufacture"; the Sales Manager would have copies of the statements against "Distribution", "Accessories", and "Sales", and so on.

The first step would be to examine the make-up of each variation, because a net loss variation of £10 may be made up of a gain variation of £990 and a loss variation of £1,000, and the Managing Director's questions would be framed with reference to ascertaining the reasons for variations. Where variations were relatively small, i.e. normal owing to the limitations of all forms of planning, it would not be necessary to seek reasons for variations unless over a period there was a marked trend either as "loss" or "gain".

Immediately upon receipt of control information, the Works Manager, the Sales Manager and the other chief executives should issue copies of the various parts appropriately to their subordinate executives in order (1) to ascertain reasons for variations to enable them to deal with questions which they could expect from the Managing Director, and (2) to take corrective action where necessary. Their enquiries and the results of them should be reported to the Managing Director; in fact, the Managing Director's questions would probably not be asked until he had received explanatory reports from his subordinates, and they would deal with those items with which he was dissatisfied.

(10) *Over/Under Recovery of Expenditure*

In addition to the variation because of under/over-spending, actual against budget, variation also arises because of under/over recovery of expenditure. Because, as stated, budget sales activity is not uniform in each four-weekly period, the Trading Account budget comparison figures are adjusted accordingly to give a better comparison of budget and actual results; to relate what has happened to what was planned to happen *in the particular period*:

Expense Item	Theoretical Four-weekly (Monthly) Budget (1)	Budgets for the Four Weeks (Month) Ended............	
	£	£	
Materials Consumed . .	10,437	10,187 ⎱	(2)
Direct Wages . .	6,752	6,680 ⎰	
Manufacturing Expenses . .	3,386	3,386 ⎫	
Repairs and Maintenance .	2,038	2,038 ⎪	
Power Generation (Net) .	229	229 ⎬	(3)
Variable Expenses . .	1,538	1,538 ⎪	
Fixed Expenses . . .	3,062	3,062 ⎭	
	27,442	27,120	
Design and Research . .	964	964 ⎫	
Distribution	3,077	3,077 ⎪	
Personnel	231	231 ⎬	(3)
Accounting	385	385 ⎪	
General Administration . .	1,077	1,077 ⎭	
	33,176	32,854	
Accessories	785	816	(4)
Finished Product Stock Reduction	553 (Decrease)	553 (Increase)	(5)
TOTAL	£34,514	£33,117	
Revenue Item			
Sales	£37,115	£34,600	(6)

(1) These figures are an average over the budget period; as the particular period is of four weeks, they are one-thirteenth of the annual budget.
(2) These figures are the budget cost of actual production, i.e. actual production multiplied by budget rates for materials and direct wages.

(3) These figures are averages; one-thirteenth of the annual budget.
(4) This figure is the budget cost of the budget sales of accessories in the particular period.
(5) This figure is the budget cost of the estimated increase in Finished Product stocks in the particular period. Whilst the Company's policy is to reduce its investment in stocks, owing to the "spread" of sales and the build-up of production to meet them, there is an increase in stocks of finished products whilst sales are at the lower level.
(6) This figure is the sales budget for the particular period.

There is, therefore:

A. A variation between a four-weekly average of the annual budget and the budget for any four-weekly period.
B. A variation between the budget for any four-weekly period and actual revenue and expenditure in that period.

The total of the expenditure variation under (B) is shown on the Variation Summary against *Total Variation: Under/Over-spending*, and in the *Trading Account* against the total of expenditure excluding the finished product stock variation.

A small profit only is earned, chiefly because of manufacture for future sale being taken into stock at the cost of raw materials and direct wages only. (*Note.*—This basis of valuation is taken only for purposes of illustration.)

The actual total cost of producing:

90 of Product 1,
128 of Product 2,
400 of Product 3,
900 of Product 4,
640 of Product 5,

and of Selling

60 of Product 1,
120 of Product 2,
400 of Product 3,
680 of Product 4,
760 of Product 5,

is £33,105.

The difference between quantities made and sold goes into or comes from stock, i.e.:

	Production	Sales	Stock Increase	Stock Decrease
Product 1 . .	90	60	30	—
Product 2 . .	128	120	8	—
Product 3 . .	400	400	—	—
Product 4 . .	900	680	220	—
Product 5 . .	640	760	—	120

The value at which this variation is taken into account is:

	Increase	Decrease	At	Increase in £	Decrease in £
Product 1 .	30	—	10	300	—
Product 2 .	8	—	13	104	—
Product 4 .	220	—	7	1,540	—
Product 5 .	—	120	5	—	600
				£1,944	£600
				600	
		Net Increase		£1,344	

The increase, however, has cost more than £1,344. Expenditure on manufacturing and general overheads has been incurred, and part of this expenditure is attributable to the increase in the quantities held in stock. Assume that the total cost of manufacturing the production during the four weeks is:

		Balance	Expenditure per Trading Account
	£	£	£
Total Cost of Manufacture .	27,486	—	27,486
Allocation for Design and Research	374	690	1,064
Allocation for Personnel .	180	24	204
Allocation for Accounting .	150	201	351
Allocation for General Administration	400	600	1,000
	£28,590	£1,515	30,105
Distribution			3,000
			£33,105

Assume too that costing records show the analysis of this total cost to be:

Product	Production	Cost per Unit	Total Cost
		£	£
1	90	20	1,800
2	128	25	3,200
3	400	17 5s.	6,900
4	900	12 10s.	11,250
5	640	8 10s.	5,440
			£28,590

The cost of the stock increase is therefore:

Product	Stock Increase	Stock Decrease	At £ per unit	Increase in £	Decrease in £
1	30	—	20	600	—
2	8	—	25	200	—
3	—	—	17 5s.	—	—
4	220	—	12 10s.	2,750	—
5	—	120	8 10s.	—	1,020
				3,550	£1,020
				1,020	
				£2,530	

Therefore a stock increase valued at cost at £2,530 has been taken into account at £1,344; an under-recovery or reduction in profit of £1,186. The total position may be summarised as follows:

		£
Revenue from Sales		32,660

Expenses Recovered in Sales:

	Sales	At Cost in £	£	£	£
Product 1	60	20	1,200		
Product 2	120	25	3,000		
Product 3	400	17 5s.	6,900		
Product 4	680	12 10s.	8,500		
Product 5	760	8 10s.	6,460		
				26,060	
Product 6	520	14s.	364		
Product 7	880	10s.	440		
				804	
					26,864

Surplus £5,796

Expenses Not Recovered in Sales:

		£	
General Expenses . . .	1,515		
Distribution Expenses . .	3,000		
Stock "Loss" . . .	1,186		
		5,701	

Profit per Trading Account . . . . £ 95

(11) *Profit Reconciliation*

(*Note.*—This statement is included for purposes of completion; it is not a control document for executive use.)

(a) *Adjusted Budget*

		£	£
Budget Profit			1,483
Add Variation for Under-spending . .		387	
Variation for Stock Difference . .		794	
			1,178
			2,661
Deduct Variation for Over-spending . .		626	
Variation for Under-recovery . .		1,940	
			2,566
Profit per Trading Account . . . . . £			95

(b) *Original Budget*

		£
Budget Profit for a four-week period		2,601
Adjustment for Variations in Activity :	£	
Add Raw Materials Budget	10,437	
Actual Production at Budget Rate .	10,187	
	250	
Direct Wages Budget	6,752	
Actual Production and Budget Rate .	6,680	
	72	
		322
		£2,923

Deduct : Sales Budget for period is less than average of sales, per yearly budget, because of the "spread" of sales:

	£	
Sales per budget average .	37,115	
Budget this period . .	34,600	
		2,515
Adjusted Profit		408
Add Gains per Variation Summary		387
		795
Deduct Losses per Variation Summary		626
		£169

Average budget requires a charge in each four weeks for finished product stock reduction, but owing to the "spread" of sales a finished product stock increase takes place in this period, therefore *Add* £553 (normal stock decrease) to £1,344 (stock increase this period)   1,897

	£	2,066
Deduct Excess cost of accessories monthly budget/		
Average budget	31	
Actual sales below adjusted budget sales	1,940	
		1,971
Profit per Trading Account . . . . . . £		95

CHAPTER VII

COST CONTROL

General Considerations. Cost Control, Cost Finding and Budgets.
Standard Costs. Cost Accounting. Raw Materials. Work in Progress.
Direct Wages. Overhead Expenses. Cost Assembly for Control

GENERAL CONSIDERATIONS

WHEREAS control against budgets deals mainly with groups of expenditure, cost control applies the techniques of measurement and comparison to the detailed operations of running a business. It finds its widest application in the manufacturing industries, although certain aspects of cost control, particularly those concerned with overhead expenses, can be applied to other types of business, e.g. to retailing. Merely to know the cost of an activity, or of a unit of production or service, is not cost control. Cost control requires that there should be standards of performance and related expenditure with which actual costs can be compared, and in this way it shows, not only what is cost, but also what it ought to be in given conditions. The detail of cost control relates chiefly to manufacture and its ancillaries, because in most businesses the expenditure on production and production services is by far the largest part of total expenditure, and because the very complications and details involved in manufacture mean that effective control of expenditure can be exercised only if there is available such detail as will enable expenditure to be identified with tangible factors in respect of which action can be taken. Budgets may be calculated to show that the raw material costs of making 1,000 gross each of finished products (*a*), (*b*) and (*c*) are £25,000, but unless there is cost detail to show precisely where losses or gains have taken place or have been made, effective action cannot be taken to deal with a total excess cost of £1,000, i.e. the reasons for variations cannot be established. Without this detail control is general, and serves not so much to enable corrections to be made as to show where what actually happened differed in total from what was planned to happen.

The same considerations do not apply to other groups of expenditure; to sales expenses, administration and so on. This is because budgets are built-up in relation to the tangible physical factors underlying these expenses; e.g., so many men at such and such salaries, with allowances for expenses. In these instances control can be exercised from budget comparisons because the items involved can be recognised from the comparisons. The very detail of manufacture makes a different approach imperative.

The means for cost control described in this chapter are based upon a practical identification of expenditure with tangible factors, so that control of costs is obtained as follows:

A. *Direct Expenses*
   By identification of costs with the utilisation of materials, labour and equipment, to the extent that it is possible to establish measurement of these items.

B. *Indirect Expenses*
   By comparison between actual expenditure and budget expenditure.

The control of expenditure against budgets is discussed in Chapters V and VI, and this chapter deals with cost control for direct expenses. For the sake of completeness, however, further reference is made to the control of indirect expenses against budgets.

COST CONTROL, COST FINDING AND BUDGETS

Circumstances can be visualised wherein a manufacturer makes one product only, say x, the raw materials being prepared and processed through stages 1, 2, 3 and 4. From drawings he knows what materials are required for one x; from experience he thinks he knows what material losses occur in manufacture, and he considers he knows what labour force is required to operate the equipment necessary to make 5,000 x in a four-weekly period. He can therefore budget for the production of 5,000 x:

Raw Materials Budget
   5,000 times the estimated raw material cost of one
     x plus normal spoilage . . . . = £A

Direct Labour Budget
   Number of employees at, e.g., rate per hour multi-
     plied by hours per week multiplied by four . = £B

He is now in a position to compare his actual expenditure with his budget. Of itself this is better than no comparison at all. Presumably the manufacturer thinks, when compiling his budget, about the "how" and "why" of the costs included, and endeavours to set targets accordingly. When the actual expenditure comparisons are made, however, assume that raw materials are over-spent by £500 and direct labour is under budget by £100. This information is useful. It shows the manufacturer generally where actual working has deviated from the plan, and it provides a reconciliation between the profit he planned to earn and that in fact earned, e.g.:

		£
Budget profit for the four weeks		
Deduct Raw Materials in excess of budget . .		500
Add Direct Labour costs below budget . . .		100
Actual profit		—

To this extent it provides data for the broad control of expenditure, but, of itself, this information is of little value for controlling costs, in the sense of taking action to ascertain the causes of excess costs, or the reasons for gains over budget, so that improvement can be made in future. Consider the two items:

A. The excess cost of £500 on materials may be because of:
  (1) Faulty estimating.
  (2) Increase in purchase price over that estimated for budget purposes.
  (3) Excessive consumption, or spoiled production.
  (4) Incorrect allowances for process waste.

B. The "gain" of £100 on direct labour may be because of:
  (1) Faulty estimating.
  (2) Improved utilisation of labour.

In this instance, merely to know the general position as it is shown by a budget comparison does not give any information about the cause of the variations. Neither does it show where losses or gains arise; in the example, in stage 1, 2, 3, or 4, the £500 excess on materials might have occurred in stage 2, or stages 1 and 4, or in all the process stages. The "gain" on direct labour also might have arisen at any one or at any combination of stages. Also the "gain", being net, might conceal losses, say an excess of £50 at stage 1, of £30 at stage 3, a "gain" of £110 at stage 2, and a "gain" of £70 at stage 4. It is therefore necessary to go to more detail if the principal detailed items of expenditure are in fact to be controlled.

The example takes the manufacture of one product only. It will be readily understood that where more than one product or product type is made, the position will be complicated more.

Cost finding is of great help in cost control, but of itself it is insufficient. It is part only of cost control. Cost finding tells what is the cost of a process or product, but it does not tell what that cost should or could be, although, where they apply, it can be compared with estimates worked out primarily for selling-price purposes. For cost control, however, estimates are required for the theoretical possible cost of the work, job or product under predetermined conditions, so that actual costs ascertained from a costing system can be compared with theoretical costs.

In order to make effective comparisons, it must be remembered that costing systems using arbitrary allocations of, e.g., overhead expenses, produce costs which are arbitrary and approximate to that extent. To avoid this and to relate costs of overhead expenditure items to their recovery in selling prices, it is desirable to deal with the elements of cost involved more by control against budgets, and by a recovery method, rather than by allocation.

When budgets were being discussed, it was explained that budget calculations for the principal items of expenditure in a manufacturing business, raw materials and direct labour, should be made from cost standards, thereby associating them directly with cost control data. If this is done, the budget cost of raw materials and direct labour is theoretical production at the standard cost of these items, and variations from budget will be caused and affected by the difference between theoretical and actual production and the variations of actual costs from the standards. Cost control against standards usually stops at this stage. It can be extended to other items, such as warehousing, and where this is practicable standards and budgets can be related in precisely the same way as for raw materials and direct labour. The other main expense groups involved in running a business, the overhead expenses, require a different approach. Budgeting for them is more a matter of policy and forecasting from facts, trends and financial and cost records, not from standards, and control is a matter of ensuring as far as possible that what is spent is recovered in selling prices. To achieve this the overhead expenses may be allocated to products on a combination of arbitrary bases, e.g. canteen expenses according to number of employees in departments and time spent on various products, or sales expenses on a value of sales basis, or they may be dealt with by charging products in accordance with what it is thought the market will bear. For example, of two products, one might have a much higher margin over its cost of direct materials and direct labour than another, and be able to "carry" more overheads. From the point of view of control, every sale represents a credit to an account for the unit cost element of the items of overhead expenses included, against the total of which actual expenses have to be set to show over- or under-recovery. Control of costs cannot operate in the abstract; it requires comparison both of actual costs with cost standards, where they can apply, and with amounts recovered in selling prices. It operates through budgets and cost standards and by means of the costing and accounting systems.

Before dealing with standards and the costing system, it may be useful to recapitulate from the discussion on budgets to show the interrelationship between budgetary control and cost control:

Item	Budgetary Control	Cost Control	Variation
Raw Materials.	Estimates or cost standards, supported by accounts for total check, with reference to stocks and trend of purchase prices, or at standard price.	Utilisation standards for quantity, evaluated with reference to stocks, and purchase price trends, or at a standard price.	Price change. Standard set incorrectly. Excess material usage. Material usage less than Standard. Actual production above or below budget.
Direct Labour.	Estimates or cost standards, supported by accounts for total check, with reference to trend of labour requirements and wage rates.	Utilisation standards, either in cash or as time to be evaluated at rates in force.	Wage-rate change. Standard set incorrectly. Excess labour utilisation. Labour utilisation better than standard. Actual production above or below budget.
Manufacturing General Overheads and Manufacturing Services.	Policy, estimates related to requirements, or estimate from accounts and cost accounts.	Cost standards may be set for certain items, in which case budgets should be calculated accordingly. Otherwise, as budgets.	Variations in level of production. Actual expenditure above or below estimate. Overheads recovered in selling prices more or less than charges.
Other Overhead Expenses.	Policy, estimates related to requirements or estimate from accounts.	Not applicable. Control operates from and by means of budget comparisons.	Variations in level of sales. Actual expenditure above or below estimate. Overheads recovered in selling prices more or less than charges.

STANDARD COSTS

Standard costs are the predetermined costs of operating any process or performing any job in a defined way at a given level of output, and the standard—defined—method of operating a process or performing an operation is regarded as the best method available. Standards for control and cost purposes are not rigid; one of their merits is that of pointing the way towards improvement, and they should be kept under constant review.

A standard can be worked out for all the expenses of any operation or process, but normally it is sufficient to set standards for the use of materials and the utilisation of labour. Overhead expenses representing services such as power, steam, internal transport and normal repairs and maintenance can also be subject to standards, but general manufacturing overhead expenses are in their nature not appropriate for measurement and are dealt with best by control against budgets. Similarly, general overheads, sales expenses and so on, are controlled best against budgets because their nature does not permit generally of the setting of standards. There are instances wherein standards can be set for certain items of general expenditure. An example is transport, or, in a retail business, expenses can be compared with a standard for "turnover per man-hour", as opposed to production per man-hour in a manufacturing business.

Standards for manufacturing or service operations can be determined only by study, analysis and measurement of the cost value of each element involved. The setting of standards involves time and method study, i.e. observation and measurement, and the application of theory to ascertain what is required to produce a unit of finished production. This is described in detail in Part II: see Chapters III and IV. For immediate purposes the principal factors involved in setting standards are:

(1) Theoretical machine or equipment outputs, subject to an allowance for contingencies and an allowance to enable a wage incentive scheme to be coupled with the standards.

(2) Theoretical requirements of materials for the adjusted theoretical machine capacity.

(3) Theoretical requirements of labour, based upon the true work required.

Control of expenditure against cost standards is, like the control of expenditure against budgets, a matter of comparison, in this case between actual and standard. At some stage the comparisons must be expressed in money values, but it may not be desirable to give indications of money values to foremen, chargehands and operatives; or it may be more significant to express a loss or gain, against standard, as so many pounds or units of material or so many man-hours. To·be effective, the comparison between standard and actual results must be made frequently. A week is a usual period, and where the week is used the actual results should be available for comparison with standards not later than the end of the week following that to which they relate. Otherwise, it is too late to take effective action. In certain work the comparison may be made with reference to the number of jobs, or the output, in a given period, which may be more or less than a week. That is to say, the production cycle provides a useful basis for comparison.

The operation of cost standards may be illustrated by a simple example:

Standard Cost of 1 lb. of Finished Product P

48 lb. of product P requires:

		s.	d.
(1) *Materials:*			
Raw Material A, 12 lb. at 2s.	=	24	0
Raw Material B, 30 lb. at 6d.	=	15	0
Raw Material C, 12 lb. at 3s. 6d. . . .	=	42	0
		81	0
(2) *Labour:*			
2 Operatives at 2s. 3d. per hour . . .	=	4	6
1 Operative at 2s. 6d. per hour	=	2	6
Proportion of labourer's rate at 1s. 10d. per hour	=	0	11
Hourly cost of supervision, chargeable to product P	=	2	1
		10	0
(3) *Services:*			
Steam, 400 lb. at 5s. per 1,000 lb. . . .	=	2	0
Power	=	3	0
		5	0
Total (for 48 lb.)	=	96	0
Standard cost for direct expenses, per lb. . .		2	0

Notes

(1) The product P, requiring raw materials A, B and C, is made in three stages; (i) at which raw materials A and B are mixed and processed; (ii) at which raw material C is added, and (iii) the final process. An example could apply equally well with a product—or part—which passes through a series of operations, as in engineering practice. Alternatively, the standard could be set with reference to a machine or equipment, i.e. a certain machine should produce a given number of a defined article or product in a predetermined time. No purpose would be served by endeavouring to illustrate all the many ways there are to set standards for cost purposes. Instead, attention is drawn particularly to principles, not so much "what" is done, but "why".

The first stage in setting the standard is therefore to determine exactly what is the process or operation sequence, and what happens at each stage.

(2) The second stage is to establish what production should be obtained from the processes or operation sequences in a given time. The ascertainment of the theoretical output possible may be altogether a question of observation—time and method study—or it may be one of calculation from specifications, machine speeds, or the stoichiometry of processes. Whatever theoretical output is accepted must be modified for losses owing to contingencies, necessary stoppages such as loading the machine or removing the finished production, and often the theoretical output is subject to an allowance to make possible the application of an output bonus. In the example the position may be shown as follows:

	Theoretical Output lb./hr.	Theoretical Output adjusted for Contingencies and Necessary Stoppages lb./hr.	Allowance to make it possible for Operatives to earn 33⅓ per cent. bonus lb./hr.	Standard Output lb./hr.
Process 1	100	88	22	66
Process 2	80	64	16	48
Process 3	120	112	28	84

It will be noted that there is an obvious lack of balance between the processes, final output being governed by the output of process 2, with a standard output of 48 lb. per hour. This might be corrected by adding other units of plant at processes 1 and 2, to bring the output at each stage up to 84 lb. per hour, the output of process 3, or the processes 1 and 2 might be worked proportionately longer than the process 3. Both courses would increase the depreciation and other fixed expense elements and operating costs, and a new standard would have to be calculated, e.g.

Assume the introduction of equipment sufficient to bring the total output up to 84 lb. per hour:

Additional fixed expenses consequent upon purchase of new equipment .   .   .   .

Additional operating costs of new equipment, power supplies, maintenance, etc. .   .

Additional process labour (assuming that additional labour is required)   .   .   .

Carried forward: £.

Brought forward : £

Deduct

Normal under-recovery of fixed overhead expenses before installing additional plant owing to idle time in processes 1 and 2   .

Net Increase in Expenditure, say   .   .   .   £720 p.a.

The cost standard is calculated only for raw materials, labour and steam and power. The additional cost of these elements should be extracted from the total additional costs and applied to the standard. At 2,400 hours p.a., £720 is equal to 6*s.* per hour, and the additional cost of labour and services can be assumed at 4*s.* per hour, the balance, 2*s.*, being the net addition for fixed expenses not included in the standard cost. The new standard is therefore:

$$\begin{array}{lll} & s. & d. \\ \text{Materials } \frac{81s.}{48} \times 84 \quad . \quad . \quad . \quad . \quad = & 141 & 9 \\ \text{Labour and Services, } 15s. + 4s. \quad . \quad . \quad = & 19 & 0 \\ & \overline{} & \\ \text{Total} & 160 & 9 \end{array}$$

Standard Cost for Direct Expenses .   .   1*s.* 11*d.*

Thus, for an annual expenditure of £720 there is a demonstrated prime cost reduction of 1*d.* per lb. or 7*s.* per hour, or £840 p.a. Other economies, of course, would be secured in the distribution of general overhead expenses over an increased volume of production.

(3) The third stage is to determine what are the theoretical material and labour requirements of the standard output.

Material requirements can be calculated from drawings, from the stoichiometry of chemical processes, or from the quantity of the "end" product required. Calculations should be checked by observations, by measurement on the job, especially to determine normal process losses and operating efficiencies. Also, it is necessary to establish those points in the operation or process sequence at which material content is to be measured. In certain industries, e.g. textile spinning, the product weight may vary considerably from stage to stage owing to changes in the moisture content. Where the yarn is conditioned, it is essential to define whether or not weighing takes place before or after conditioning. This illustrates the importance of approaching all questions of standards with due regard to the technical variables and peculiarities involved. In one industry material control can be exercised well by knowing that for every 100 of finished product x, 106 of component y, 208 of component z, etc., are required, and by controlling issues of raw materials in relation to planned output accordingly. This is the principle underlying material control, namely, to issue no more raw materials than are required for a given volume of finished production: the business of establishing what is this "no more than is required" is that of the setting of standards for materials. In other industries the relationship between a given volume of finished production and its raw material requirements is by no means so clear, and may be complicated by any one or combination of a number of factors. For example, in certain textile processes, on one day more may . be made than was issued owing to moisture absorption, whilst on another the opposite may be true.

It would be an impossible task to account in detail for all such variations, and the practical approach towards dealing with them is, through the study necessary in setting standards, to establish what can be regarded as the normal over a period.

Standards for labour can be established only by observation and measurement, by method and time study.

(4) Material and labour requirements must be evaluated. Materials may be valued, e.g. at a price based upon stock valuations, or current market prices, with allowance for price trends (see page 604). Values calculated in this way should apply for the budget period or for a period of up to six months, unless there is a substantial change in price trends. Labour requirements have to be evaluated with reference to Trade Union Agreements, special risks, unusual conditions, or special responsibilities.

(5) In the example the standard is limited to materials, labour and steam and power charges. In other instances steam and power charges might be omitted, or other expenses of manufacture could be included if desired, either on some arbitrary basis related to the budgets for those items of expenditure, or, where the technical conditions permit, against a measurement factor.

There is no one stage to which a standard cost may be taken, the principal determinant being practical working. It is necessary to note too the distinction between standard costs for cost control purposes and for price purposes. This distinction is but one of application, the same information being used for different though related purposes. It will be apparent that just as standards are desirable if not essential when budgets are being established for those items capable of measurement, e.g. materials and labour, so also are budgets desirable for those expenditure items of a service or general nature in order that predetermined costs for price purposes can be assembled. The application of the overhead, etc., expense items to the standard costs used involves allocation, either by means of distributing the expenses on various bases, or by working from an assumed or known selling price to make each product carry what it will bear in overhead expenses. The two methods may be shown as follows:

A. *Allocation*

The various items of overhead expenditure are budgeted, allocated to departments, shops, processes on a combination of arbitrary bases, and so are charged to production.

	s.	d.
Standard cost per example (page 674) . . .	2	0
Add proportion of budget cost of overheads (in detail)	1	0
	3	0

B. *By Recovery*

The selling price of the product P, which has a standard direct cost of 2s. per lb., is 5s. per lb. If 20 per cent. on selling price is accepted as the profit margin, then each pound of product P sold contributes 2s. to the cost of overhead expenditure. This 2s. may be allocated to the expenes accounts included in overhead expenses on an arbitrary basis.

Taking the example further:

Standard output is 48 lb. per hour, for 2,400 hours p.a. = 115,200 lb. per annum.

If standard output is sold at budget selling price (5s.), and direct costs are controlled at or within standard (2s.), then product P contributes £11,520 towards manufacturing and general overhead expenditure. This sum is its budget contribution.

If output exceeds standard, and/or actual costs show a gain over standard, the output being sold, then product P makes a proportionately greater contribution towards overhead expenses, and conversely if budget sales are not achieved, or standard costs are exceeded.

The final stage in cost control is to set up a cost accounting system which enables prompt comparison of actual and standard costs to be made, and shows the allocation or the recovery of overhead expenses in costs. Cost accounting is therefore the next consideration.

COST ACCOUNTING

It is not the purpose of this book to describe costing systems or the particular treatment of expenditure in cost assembly. Costing generally, and in its application to a number of industries, is already the subject of many excellent textbooks. This chapter is concerned more with the general subject of costing for control purposes; with the general requirements necessary if the costing system is to fulfil its purpose; with practical difficulties, and with the use of information obtained.

Cost accounting is the systematic analysis of expenditure in relation to significant units of production or service, and a costing system must:

(a) Record raw and service materials consumed; interprocess or interdepartmental transfers; finished production; stocks of raw and service materials and finished products; and identify raw material usages against finished production.

(b) Analyse wage charges to jobs, operations, processes or departments, or to services and activities classified as overhead expenses.

(c) Accumulate items of overhead expenditure under appropriate headings, and provide for their identification with finished production and sales.

In outline the necessary records are:

(1) *Stock Records* for raw materials, service materials, e.g. engineers' stores, fuel and finished products, in quantity only, with a separate account for each item.

    The opening and closing entries on these accounts are balances representing stocks on hand; receipts of raw and service materials and fuel are obtained from goods received records; issues, either to production or to an overhead expense account, are obtained nominally from requisitions, though there are many instances where requisitions cannot be used for measuring issues. "Issues" of finished products are obtained from dispatch records or their equivalent.

    Intermediate stores or stocks are maintained in some industries, in effect, stocks of work-in-progress. These too should be the subject of stock accounts.

(2) *Wages Analysis*, an abstract of gross wages taken from the pay-roll, and written-up by direct analysis, or from time analysis forms, such as clock cards or time sheets.

(3) *Overhead Expenditure Accounts*, written-up partly from invoices, for direct charges partly from summaries of material

requisitions, for issues of, e.g., repair materials chargeable to an overhead expenditure account, partly from the wage analysis, for those wages chargeable to an overhead expenditure account, and from salaries records.

(4) *Production Records*, appropriate to the type of production being measured. They must be kept for finished production, and they may be required also at intermediate stages in the production processes, for partly finished production or components.

(5) *Cost Accounts*, which assemble the various cost elements to give product, or component, or process, or operating, etc., costs.

This outline is illustrated in account form below:

Raw Materials Stock Account

	£			£
Commencing Stock .	1,000	Issues, Process A .	.	200
Purchases	400	Issues, Process B .	.	300
		Balance carried down .	.	900
	£1,400			£1,400
Balance brought down	£900			

Service Materials Account

	£			£
Commencing Stock .	200	Issues, Process A .	.	40
Purchases	90	Issues, Overhead Account	.	30
		Balance carried down .	.	220
	£290			£290
Balance brought down	£220			

(*Note.*—For purposes of illustration, these accounts are shown in terms of value. In most instances it is unnecessary to keep stock and stores records in quantity AND value.)

Wages Account

	£			£
Wages per Pay-roll .	600	Process A . . .	.	200
		Process B . .	.	300
		Overhead Account	.	100
	£600			£600

Overhead Expenses Account

	£			£
Expenses, per invoices	180	Process A . . .	.	180
Service Materials .	30	Process B . .	.	100
Wages . . .	100	Balance under-recovered carried forward . .	.	30
	£310			£310
Balance brought down	£30			

Process A

	£		£
Work in Process brought forward	30	Value of Finished Production, 100 tons	600
Raw Materials . . .	200		
Service Materials . .	40		
Wages	200		
Overheads	180	Work in Process carried forward	50
	£650		£650

Work in Process brought forward £50

Process B

	£		£
Work in Process brought forward	50	Value of Finished Production 27 tons	675
Raw Materials . . .	300	Work in Process carried forward	75
Wages	300		
Overheads	100		
	£750		£750

Work in process brought forward £75

Finished Production Account

	£
Production from Process A .	600
Production from Process B .	675

Total Account

	£	£		£	£
Value of Finished Production:			Opening Balances brought forward:		
Process A . .	600		Raw Materials .	1,000	
Process B . .	675		Service Materials .	200	
	—	1,275	Work in Process:		
			Carried forward Process A .	30	
			Carried forward Process B .	50	
				—	1,280
			Purchases:		
			Raw Materials .	400	
			Service Materials .	90	
			Expenses . .	180	
				—	670
	£		Wages, per Pay-roll . .		600
Closing Balances carried forward:					
Raw Materials .	900				
Service Materials .	220				
Overheads under-recovered	30				
Work in Process:					
Process A . .	50				
Process B . .	75				
	—	1,275			
		£2,550			£2,550

Cost accounts are analyses and sub-analyses of nominal ledger accounts, and the example given shows in principle the main features of all cost accounting, no matter how involved it may appear. The first requirement of costing for control purposes is that the cost system and the presentation of costs should be appropriate. There is no one "system" which can be applied to all industries or factories. In some businesses the variety of products dealt with, and perhaps the small proportion that any one line bears to the total volume of business, means that detailed costing is impossible, and in these circumstances cost control naturally finds expression in expense control—against budgets—and estimates to which gross profit additions are made. The principles involved are precisely the same as those used in a manufacturing business, wherein detailed costing can be applied; the application of these principles is modified to meet the practical conditions of the particular industry.

RAW MATERIALS

Turning again to the illustration, raw material accounts—stock accounts—are familiar in all accounting systems. The principal problem connected with their application is that of ensuring that all issues from stock are measured, authorised, correctly described and entered on the requisition or other document of authorisation, and correctly booked. This problem cannot be met by "system", although a well-designed system will reduce the possibility of error. In order to ensure as far as possible that the system is thoroughly understood, it should be written-up in a manual which should be issued as a whole, or in appropriate part, to those concerned with its operation. Afterwards, good supervision and checks on detail are necessary if full accuracy is to be obtained and maintained. Also, if the materials records are to be used, as they should be, for control of quantities in stock, it is essential that the physical arrangements for stock-keeping are adequate, and that responsibility for stocks is defined, particularly the point at which the stock-keeper assumes responsibility for materials, and the point at which he relinquishes responsibility, i.e. upon issue.

In some industries it is not practicable to measure materials issued for processing, and consumption is obtained by deducting stocks at the end of an accounting period from the total of stocks at the commencement of the period and receipts (purchases and returns to stock) during the period. This method of calculating issues is satisfactory where stocks can be taken accurately, and stock records must be kept. Book and physical stocks should be agreed or reconciled at frequent intervals. Where these conditions apply, it is usual to find that there are unaccounted-for quantities of materials, which

can be dealt with as additional charges to the manufacturing operations, or as overhead charges, the total amount being shown as a
separate item in the expenditure summaries.

In some instances quantities of materials issued can be measured,
but stocks cannot readily be taken accurately. Where these conditions apply, materials should be issued in predetermined quantities,
or units of predetermined quantities, related to the calculated usage
of raw materials for a volume of finished production required. Book
stocks have to serve for short-term accounting purposes, but at least
twice in each year an attempt should be made to ascertain accurately
the quantities of stocks held.

Where issues from stock cannot be measured at the time of issue,
there is always the possibility of "raiding" raw material stocks in
order to cover spoiled production. Spoiled production, however,
represents so much lost material and time, which, subject to work in
progress, is revealed when actual production is compared with
standard production over the time cycle. Also, if materials are issued
in predetermined quantities or units or multiples of such quantities,
there is the check that more has been issued than can be accounted
for in finished production.

Materials used in production may be evaluated in many ways, of
which the principal are:

(a) Actual cost, which, if purchase prices vary frequently and
appreciably, is much less simple in use than would appear at
first sight.

Actual cost may be applied either as "first in, first out" or
as "last in, first out". Depending on the frequency of stock
turnover, "first in, first out" gives high costs and low profits
on a falling market, and low costs and high profits on a rising
market. Also it gives high inventory values on a falling market
and low inventory values on a rising market.

It is therefore not representative of current market conditions,
for which a manufacturer designs his product, or the price
factor which governs his profitability and ability to continue
in business.

(b) Average costs, which require that a new issue price should be
calculated after each purchase. This is often cumbersome in
operation.

(c) Market price, the price taken being that current at the date of
issue. Market price is closely related to "last in, first out", and
has the merit of relating business results more closely to current market conditions, avoiding or minimising profits or
losses on inventories.

(*d*) Predetermined—or standard—issue prices current for a de-fined future period, say six months. These prices are calculated with reference to stock values and probable purchase-price trends, i.e. they are a breakdown of budget purchases.

Stock valuations affect profitability directly, and the method of evaluating stocks of raw materials AND finished products is an item of major policy. A safe rule for evaluating issues from stock is to use a method which gives as nearly as possible the current replacement cost of the items of stores and stock, i.e. a predetermined, or a "last in, first out", method.

Stock values are often written-down as a matter of prudent financial policy. Such writing-off is in effect an additional charge against profits in the period when it is made. Normally, written-down values would not be used for pricing issues; the effect would be fictitious costs, but there might be occasions when written-down values could be used with justification. Assume a Company has adopted a prudent financial policy in profitable years, and has written-off against profits con-siderable sums for stock depreciation. In less profitable years an average stock price, or a standard price, based upon averages, might be used with advantage, to recover profits previously reduced by writing-down stocks. This operation has to be carried out with extreme care; it might readily lead to writing-up stock values on a falling market.

Example   *Profit and Loss Account*

	£			£
Commencing Stock:		Sales		22,000
1,000 units at £1 (cost price)	1,000			
		Closing Stock:	£	
Purchases, 10,000 units at		900 units at £1 2s.	. 990	
£1 2s.	11,000	*Less* written-off	. 90	
Expenses	8,000		——	900
Profit	2,900			
	£22,900			£22,900

Notes

(1) If stocks had not been written-down by £90, the profit would have been £2,990.

(2) The example reduces the closing stock valuation to the open-ing stock valuation, i.e. it assumes that the items in stock at the end of the accounting period were the same as those in stock at the commencement of the accounting period. Physically, the opening stock has probably changed; it is as-sumed that it remained as it was.

(3) The writing-down might have been more than 2s. on £1 2s., in which case correspondingly more profit would have been

"lost". If it had been 4s. the closing stock valuation would have been £810, and the profit £2,810.

(4) If, in the following accounting period, issues are priced at the written-down value of £1, costs receive the advantage of 2s. for every unit issued, because that 2s. has been written-off out of previous profits. The costs are not thereby improved except on paper, so that a more normal method of pricing issues, i.e. average, actual, or standard, etc., is desirable.

(5) The effect of recovering in issue prices amounts previously written-off leads to a profit on the stock account, i.e. the stock accounts are credited with more than they are debited, so that the closing balance has to be reduced, or a profit—part or whole of that previously written-off—shown.

(6) When average values are used for issue prices, the stock account values tend to move towards actual purchase prices. It is necessary to ensure that written-down values are not applied to stock issues when there is no balance of stock brought forward at written-down values from which issues at the same price can be made. Additional writing-down of stock values is necessary when this position arises and actual stock values are below book values.

WORK IN PROGRESS

Work in progress represents expenditure of materials, labour, services and overhead charges not yet recoverable in finished production, and which has to be borne by production yet to be finished. In some instances it may be ignored in costs, the finished production carrying all the expenses of its production and the expense properly chargeable to work in progress. Provided there is no great short-term variation in the quantity of work in progress, this method may work out well, one period's excess costs being cancelled by the output at a theoretical no-cost in the next period and so on.

The principal reason for omitting work in progress from costs is that as work in progress it is of no realisable value. Where, however, it is desirable that work in progress should be brought into costs, the quantity of partly finished production may be dealt with:

(1) By estimation, based on theoretical capacity of plant.
(2) By measurement, by counting, weighing and so on.
(3) By accounting, e.g.:

	£	£
Work in progress at commencement .		100
Raw materials issued	1,000	
Direct wages	500	
		1,500
Carried forward :		£1,600

Brought forward : £1,600
Finished production (say at standard cost
  adjusted for variations on account of
  raw material and direct wages)   .   1,400

Work in progress at end   .   .   .   £200

Work in progress may be defined to include intermediate stocks of partly finished production. Records kept for these intermediate stocks should be used to estimate that part of the work in progress which is in the intermediate stores. The accounting method (3 above) is a form of estimating, and where the nature of the finished production is such that quantity variations can operate through factors such as moisture absorption, allowances should be made. It is much more safe to understate than to overstate work in progress, and as a rule much more easy to overstate than to understate the quantities.

Work in progress values are usually confined to the direct labour and direct material content, excluding all overhead charges. Where, however, the nature of the work is such that the production time is long, overheads should be brought into charge. Similarly, in determining the treatment of work in progress in costing, the time period of the production cycle should be taken into account. The output and cost results of manufacture should be presented in relation to the short term, say the week. If, however, the production cycle exceeds one week, weekly costs will fluctuate widely unless work in progress is taken fully into account.

A convenient way of valuing work in progress is to apply half the previous period's cost of the direct items involved, on the assumption that work in progress is half-way through the production stages. The effect of this is that the proportion of direct charges not credited as work in progress is charged to finished production, and of course there is a correction in the next period following, the work in progress at the beginning becoming finished production, credited at the full value of finished production, there being a carry forward of closing work in progress at a hypothetical value, and so on.

Whatever method is adopted, work in progress should be checked at least twice in each year. It is assumed too often that expenditure "is in work in progress" and when the actual work in progress is measured, substantial osses may be found. This is the important aspect of accounting for work in progress for control purposes, namely, to ensure as far as possible that what is done is adequate. If six-monthly measurement is adequate for a check upon records, and experience only will tell, then the six-monthly period can be adopted as normal. If three-monthly checks are necessary, there are no short cuts or gadget methods which will avoid the three-monthly checks·

The very detail and complexity of measuring work in progress is usually a deterrent against too frequent measurement. Nevertheless, measurement is the only real check, and accounts and records are working substitutes which are useful over limited periods only. Evaluating work in progress is a question of policy, and much depends on the nature of the product. Some work in progress has a value in exchange, it could be sold. Other work in progress, as work in progress, is so much waste material. Quantitative measurement is more easy in some industries than in others, and where it is relatively easy the checks on records should be made more frequently than the minimum required. In more complex and larger concerns, the records for dealing with work in progress must be so much more detailed because of the difficulties in measurement. Yet it is not necessary for them to be so involved that they set up an accounting system within a system. The detail refers to "breaking bulk" in the records to make each work-in-progress account represent a defined part of the production process to which responsibility can be attached positively, and so that parts of the work of the enterprise can have the work in progress in them measured for comparison with the records, the whole being covered two or three times in a year.

DIRECT WAGES

Accounting for wages also presents a number of problems. It is important to ensure that the analysis of wages to products and processes agrees or is reconciled with the pay-roll. Transfers may present a problem, which can be dealt with only by centralised authorisation of the transfers. Unauthorised transfers should not be accepted. In addition to serving as a means whereby transfer forms may be initiated, a centralised check by a competent department also provides for changes between jobs at different rates of pay. Copies of transfer authorisations should be sent to the costing department for wage-analysis adjustment purposes.

Booking of time to work done is the main problem in accounting for wages, and it requires a comprehensive system of agreeing or reconciling total time with time spent on production. The work-booking system must reveal lost time, such as waiting for work, or plant breakdowns, and also it must show what overtime is worked and on what jobs or processes. Also, of course, it must identify wages paid with work done.

For cost-control purposes the charging out of wages to production must be identical with the set-up used for standards. Alternatively, the standard for the wages element in costs must be designed for comparison with a practical method of analysing wages paid for production.

The many methods of dealing with wages in costing records are described in textbooks on costing. The method used in any instance must be adapted to the conditions and circumstances found, and for control purposes the wages accounting system must give a comparison with whatever operation, group of operations, job, or process, is selected for standard purposes. From this, it provides the means for operating the detail of an incentive method based on standard performances. Incentive payments can be made only on completed work. It happens often that an operation is commenced towards the end of a wage week, and completed in the wage week following. In these cases there may not be a straight comparison between work done in the week and standard for the week's work on a given task, although, as in most instances where there is a carry forward, after the first week the "shortage" in one week is balanced by the "excess" brought forward from the week preceding. Where this does not apply, standard and actual wage costs should be compared for finished production only, the balance of wages for uncompleted work usually being made up on day rates.

OVERHEAD EXPENSES

For cost-control purposes overhead expenses should be arranged in three main categories:

A. Services, those activities which may be regarded as being almost in the nature of trading activities, and which are ancillary to the main activity. Examples are repairs and maintenance, power or steam generation and transmission or distribution, internal transport organised centrally.

B. Indirect Expenses associated with manufacture, in two main groups: (i) Fixed, e.g. depreciation, insurances, rates; and (ii) Variable, e.g. canteen, protective clothing, general labourers.

C. Indirect Expenses of a general nature, in two main groups: (i) Fixed, e.g. purchasing department expenses, selling expenses such as salaries, and (ii) Variable, e.g. sales commissions, telephone, stationery.

The term "Indirect" is used to contrast the expenditure included in the classification with that, such as materials and labour, which can be associated directly with the unit of production or service. The manufacturing and general overhead expenses are sometimes subdivided into three main groups—variable, semi-variable and fixed. The terms variable, semi-variable and fixed are used in relation to volume of business, whether expressed as turnover or production, and the introduction of the third group, semi-variable, is a refinement of no great significance. It is used for expense items which are considered to vary not directly with, say, turnover, but in some proportion, which is altogether a matter of conjecture. The terms variable and fixed too are more statements of tendencies and convenience than of fact: but they are undoubtedly convenient for expense control.

It will be appreciated that overhead expenses, as a group, are dissimilar from direct charges—materials and wages—because they consist of expenditure on materials, wages and salaries, and services such as those implied in, e.g., local rates, which cannot be identified with the unit of production or service. Materials for production are usually bought, and accounting for them is a matter of accounting for purchase invoices and subsidiary documents, requisitions or their equivalent. Direct wages are represented by the pay-roll (*Note.*—The pay-roll also includes indirect wages, but it should be so arranged that the direct items are arranged as such) and accounting for them is a matter of identifying money paid in wages with work done or time spent. Overhead expenses too may involve a considerable amount of transfer work between one group of expenses and another. For example, salaries are taken as fixed expenses. Factory management wants to know the total of fixed expenses, including salaries, and the total cost of, say, repairs and maintenance. The total cost of this heading of expenditure must include a sum for the salary of the engineer in charge, his staff and the drawing office. Hence expenses must be assembled first under their significant heading, in this case salaries, and then, by transfer from salaries, under the activity headings. Also, a machine shop used for plant maintenance work uses power generated by the power-house, which in turn uses the services of the machine shop.

Another distinction rests in the nature of control. Materials and labour are controlled against standards established from observation and measurement. Certain items of overhead expenditure also may be the subject of standards, e.g. steam and power generation, or, as in some industries, repairs and maintenance can be planned to a quite substantial extent, with standards accordingly. When those items of overhead expenditure which can be controlled against standards are dealt with, there remains a substantial amount of overhead expenses for which no standard can be set. For these items the control operates against budgets, and has two aspects: control in total compared with budget total for any period, and control in detail, i.e. the proportions carried by the various products in relation to what they were planned (budgeted) to carry. These two aspects of control, of course, apply equally to direct expenses and those overhead expenses which can be controlled against standards.

The technique of dealing with the various types of overhead expense is as follows:

(1) *Services*

In an undertaking of any size where the service activities are substantial, they should be costed as separate activities, and charged to production either as the cost of work actually done, e.g. for engineering repairs and maintenance, or by charge rates, say per 1,000 lb. of steam consumed, or per hour for crane or locomotive "hire". The charge to the production departments should be credited to the cost account of the particular service activity, to which actual expenses are debited. This is the equivalent of the Production Department's purchasing services, the service activities being established as units which, by the periodical adjustment of charge rates, should neither make a profit nor incur a loss.

Control operates through (i) budgets, for the total expenditure of each service activity, and (ii) standards set for those service activities or parts of service activities which permit of measurement.

Whilst over a period service activities should neither make a profit nor incur a loss, at the end of each accounting period—not budget period—there is usually a small balance over- or under-recovered. This should be credited or charged to general manufacturing overheads and dealt with as part of them.

(2) *Indirect Manufacturing Expenses and General Indirect Expenses*

These expenses are controlled against budgets, and may be charged to production by allocation, or dealt with by recovery.

Where overhead expenses are charged to production by allocation, the basis of charging each item is made appropriate to its nature, e.g. canteen charges may be distributed in accordance with the number of employees engaged in each production department, or part may be charged first, e.g. to a service account and thence to production: analytical testing charges by the number of batches made; power charges on h.p. installed; lighting by a points-wattage method and so on. The charge to production departments is added to the direct charges and expressed in the total of the cost per unit of production.

The principle of dealing with overhead expenses by recovery is contribution. The price range in which a product will sell is in general reasonably easy to establish. Consequently, if direct expenses, materials, labour and perhaps certain services are measured, it is possible to determine a margin from which overhead expenses must be paid and a profit must be earned. This may be illustrated as follows:

		s.	d.
(*a*)	The standard raw material cost of a product is	50	0
(*b*)	The standard cost for direct labour is .	30	0
(*c*)	The standard cost of manufacturing services is .	15	0
		95	0

		s.	d.

(*d*) Selling price is 140   0

(*e*) Leaving a sum out of which manufacturing and
general overhead expenses have to be paid, and
a profit earned 45   0

Say budget sales in a period are 10,000. Therefore, there is a sum of
£22,500 as a contribution to overhead expenses and profitability.

If the process is repeated for other products, it is calculated that
there is a total of £150,000 for overhead expenses and profit. Assume
£50,000 is the minimum profit required, then there is a sum of
£100,000 available for overhead expenses. This should be compared
with the budgets for overhead expenses; the sum might be more than
adequate, to give a theoretical increase in profitability, or it might be
insufficient, thus reducing theoretical profitability, or requiring a
reduction in the amounts budgeted.

Variations will arise because of variations from the budget level of
activity; if more is sold than is budgeted, there will be a corresponding
increase in the sum available for overhead expenses, or, if less is sold
than is budgeted, there will be a decrease in the sum available for
overhead expenses; because of over- or under-spending on overhead
expense accounts, or because of excesses or gains over standard in
those items subject to standards.

The amount which is established for the unit contribution of any
product line is estimated at the total for that line divided by budget
production. In the example, if, after aggregating the contributions
of all products and deducting the amount required for profit, there
remains for the one product the sum of £12,500, i.e. on a budget basis
the profit contribution required is £10,000, then—also on this basis—
the charge for overhead expenses to each unit of production is $\dfrac{£12,500}{10,000}$,
or £1 5*s*., and the actual charge is this figure plus or minus variations.

The actual distribution of overhead expenditure to products may
be altered as a matter of policy, often based on what the market will
stand. It may be decided, for example, that a product which shows a
margin less than that really required should still be made because of
its contribution to fixed overheads, which otherwise would have to be
borne by other products. Alternatively, another product might carry
more than the minimum necessary, either because the market will
stand the additional charge, or to subsidise yet another product the
manufacture and sales of which it is desired to maintain say for prestige reasons. The method shows which sale lines are contributing to
profitability and overhead expenses, with the amounts involved, and
facilitates the making of quick decisions regarding extending,
reducing, or discontinuing the sale of any line.

Similar figures can be compiled from records showing the distribution of overhead expenses by allocation, but they involve more clerical work. It may be argued that the recovery method does not give the actual cost of a product, and that allocation does. Since, however, the exact cost of a unit of production can never be determined in practice, because different methods of allocating overhead expenses —all equitable—give different results, and because every variation in the volume of production and sales leads to variations in the incidence of overheads in total cost, the argument is academic.

The accounting detail of the recovery method may be illustrated as follows:

Manufacturing Expense Account

	£		£
Actual Expenses:		Recovery (i.e. charge to)	
Wages	8,000	Product A . . .	1,000
Invoices . . .	6,000	Recovery (i.e. charge to)	
Etc.	7,000	Product B . . .	6,500
		Etc.	12,500
		(Actual production × budget recovery rate.)	
			20,000
		Under-recovery carried forward . . .	1,000
	£21,000		**£21,000**

If the actual expenses were less than the recovery, there would be an over-recovery carried forward. Budget comparisons can well be shown against each item, debit and credit, and final recovery should be only on sales, because expenses are not recovered until the products are sold.

I n the allocation method, actual expenses are assembled from wage-books, invoices, etc., and distributed to production depart ments:

Expense Account	Total	Dept. 1	Dept. 2	Dept. 3	Dept. 4	etc.
Wages . .						
Salaries . .						
Canteen . .						
Lighting .						
Heating . .						
Power . .						
Etc. . .						

The totals are divided by the output of the departments, and may be part of the finished cost, or of intermediate cost, e.g. where the production of one department undergoes further processing in another. To the prime cost there has to be added general overheads, allocated say on a value of sales basis, to obtain the separate product overhead expense costs and total expenditure. Either method can work well, although the recovery method is more simple, and usually more useful for cost and expenditure control.

Another way in which overheads may be brought into costs is by means of machine- or man-hour rates. Machine- or man-hour rates may be set for overhead expenses only, or they may include the standard for direct labour. Where the equipment for which they are established is one purpose, using particular materials for conversion in one way only, they can also include materials, the charge being varied in accordance with activity. It is necessary, of course, to account for actual expenditure under all the expense headings included in the machine- or man-hour rates, i.e. to compare actual with theoretical expenditure and recovery.

COST ASSEMBLY FOR CONTROL

The arrangement and presentation of cost information for control purposes has a wider significance than that for cost finding only. Cost finding is often extremely detailed, yet useless for controlling the operations it represents. An engineering product may consist of many parts, each of which is subject to cost finding. This must involve the detail of accounting for materials, labour and overheads in relation to each part, and in the end gives a figure which can be assumed to be the cost. It does not and cannot give any indication of what the cost could be. Once the theory of working against standards is applied and understood, the detail of costing can be reduced to facilitate promptness in preparing comparative data. Control does not operate through an operation costing 0·32 of a penny per unit produced; it operates through the elements of cost: materials, labour and suitably classified expenses. Hence the comparative data should be presented as expenditure of materials, labour and expenses in relation to a given output AND expenditure, and not as expenditure in relation to a unit or part unit of production.

The expenditure in relation to units, or part units, of production, i.e. cost, can be ascertained from the application of variations to standard costs, e.g.:

	s.	d.
Standard Material Cost of part A . . .	8	0
Variation this week for 1,000 A is an excess of £25,		
i.e. for one A		6
Material Cost	8	6

The presentation of cost information for control should show:

A. Comparison between standard and actual for measured activities (material usage, direct wages, and, where appropriate, other measured activities).

B. Comparison between expenditure on overhead expense accounts and its recovery in production and sales.

C. Totals of expenditure under all headings for comparison and/or reconciliation with budgets.

There are therefore three elements in cost control: standards, budgets and the costing system. Budgets are concerned mainly with broad expense control, standards with operational cost control, and the costing system with assembling actual costs and expenditure in such a way that frequent comparison can be made with budgets and standards. Variations between budget and actual expenditure and standard and actual costs are the items which require attention from management, and variation columns should be provided on all cost summaries.

Cost summaries may be prepared either for operations, processes, or products, the determinants being the type of product, and whether or not one product only is made by a particular operation or process. The presentation of cost results for control purposes, with comparisons accordingly, is more useful if it is made by reference to the elements of cost in relation to operations or processes than if it is made in terms of cost of parts or units of production.

CHAPTER VIII

CLERICAL MANAGEMENT

Introductory. Organisation of Clerical Work. Clerical Management and Relationships in Organisation. Clerical Methods and Procedures. The Physical Basis of Clerical Work. Staff Management. The Arrangement of Work. Control of Clerical Work. General Office Services. Office Practices

INTRODUCTORY

THE clerical activities of a modern industrial or commercial organisation are but a natural extension of the simpler office work of bygone times, and they have become closely associated with the control activity even though their scope is much wider than the practice and procedures required by that activity alone. They are often found within the jurisdiction of the Chief Accountant, or sometimes of the Secretary, though on occasions the organisation may provide for a "Clerical Manager" on the top line, responsible directly to the Chief Executive. This close association of clerical activities with the "control" function is sound in principle: in the definition of management (see page 12) specific mention is made of the procedures or routines by which the planning and regulating of activities is attained. These procedures, which may be briefly summarised as the process of communicating and recording, are the field of "clerical management". They cover all those activities by means of which information or instructions, data or decisions, policies or practices, are put on record for future reference or conveyed from one person to another. These activities are largely carried out by means of forms—requisition notes, invoices, dispatch notes, analysis sheets of one kind or another; but a good deal are still carried on in the more generalised form of memoranda and correspondence. The telephone service is of course also a part of the communication system. So far as records are concerned, the filing system will come to mind as the most obvious activity. It is, of course, arguable that the accounts and costing records, and all the procedures connected with expense and budget controls, are part of the total scheme of "records"; though it is customary to dissociate these functional items from the more general ones, and to speak of "accounts and clerical activities". This distinction is a fiction rather than a fact, and may have its roots in the professional exclusiveness which has long been characteristic of the accountant. Some would argue that the importance of the financial procedures and documents supports the distinction; they have, however, equally to agree that many non-financial records and documents are of similar importance. In practice the distinction makes little difference, especially in view of the common tendency for the Chief Accountant to have both fields within his own scope.

With the years the existence of a "clerical aspect" of management has become widely appreciated. There has, for instance, been in existence for a long time an "Office Management Association", a professional body catering for the interests and needs of those who specialise in this field. That its recognition has been greater in the United States may be attributed to the greater prevalence of large organisations in that country.

Clearly, the larger the size of the organisation the greater and more complex will become the recording and communicating activities, and correspondingly the greater the need for specialist guidance.

In the average manufacturing or trading enterprise, clerical activities may, of course, play a somewhat limited part in the organisation as a whole: their function is essentially that of a service to the other (major) operations of making and selling. Yet there are several fields in the economic system in which the clerical activities bulk very large: banks, insurance companies, building societies, are obvious illustrations. Outside of the commercial system, the same is also true of Government Departments, the offices of Local Authorities, and, in more recent years, the Administrative Headquarters of the Nationalised Industries. In all these instances, the employees of the organisation may be numbered in the hundreds or the thousands. Virtually, all the operations are performed on paper, i.e. are basically matters of communication and record.

It is important to recognise that, whether in the offices of a small factory or in the almost "mass-production" clerical sections of the big Building Society, the process of management is at work in the same way as in the factory or the retail store. The nature of the operations is different, the details of application may also be different, but, with these appropriate adjustments made, all that has been said in the other parts of this volume apply with equal validity. In one sense, this is almost too obvious a point to make in the present context; yet strangely enough, it is widely overlooked. If the analogy is taken far enough, there is a close parallel between many of the questions which the Factory Manager must ask and answer in the course of his executive activities and those which will form the daily round of the Clerical Manager in the large organisations. For instance, the manager of a factory may analyse or study the work, the conditions, the movement of materials, the methods, etc., in order to determine whether or not machines should be grouped or placed at various points in the factory. The same issues may easily arise in connection with office machinery. Should typing be pooled? To what extent? Is all office machinery fully engaged? Is the flow of work such as to permit of minimum movement of people and paper, and the maximum utilisation of effort, time and investment in equipment? Are there alternative ways of performing a job to give advantages in time, effort and results? Are forms or documents designed in the way that best facilitates effective and economical working?

From another point of view, too, the similarity is close. Office work, just like the factory, requires man-power—human skills and capacities, human efforts and application and time. Often the clerical staff units in some commercial enterprises (not to mention Government Departments) are comparable in size with large factories. Thus the same problems of utilisation of man-power arise: the proper allocation of jobs, the selection of the right people with correct abilities for the work, training, the efficient use of special skills, the performance levels of all employees, the question of full attendance, and effective use of the man-hours available when people are on the job. The planning of work, therefore, has much the same significance as in manufacturing, and, if the staffs engaged are really large, it may well be worth while to develop appropriate control techniques to ensure adequate use of the capacity provided.

In fine, the matter is just another aspect of the general question of costs. Clerical costs may or may not be a large part of total cost: whatever their relationship to total cost, they should be regarded in the same way as expenditure on manufacture or on purchases in a merchanting business, i.e. in relation to value received. Clerical work can be carried out effectively or ineffectively. Single instances may be small, but the total of what are usually concealed losses may be substantial.

A special factor has come into play in clerical work in more recent years because of the greater quantity of information and records that are called for by official or semi-official requirements, as well as internally through the development of new techniques in management. Information may sometimes be produced in two offices or sections of an organisation for different purposes, but is really concerned with the same matter, and could easily be produced by one piece of work. But perhaps unwittingly Heads of Departments have produced two different and unrelated procedures because they have worked independently. This has frequently happened, for instance, as between a Personnel Department and a Wages Office. A more systematic and unified approach to clerical work would have obviated this source of excess cost. Or, again, a new executive coming into an organisation might bring his own "systems", and if there is no form of control

P.P.M.—23*

attention to this question of clerical methods, expensive differences and duplication can easily ensue. Clerical work is *never* an end in itself—it is essentially a service to other parts of the organisation; it is essentially a part of the process of management as a whole, that part, namely, which is concerned with communications and records.

The implication of this statement is the case for the integration of clerical work, at least to the extent of the planning of methods and determination of procedures. Whether or not there is a case for the appointment of a specialist or functional "Clerical (Office) Manager" is a point that can be decided only by circumstances. The case is clearly very strong in a large organisation with wide ramifications and a variety of different clerical activities. Yet even in a very small organisation, it would be easily possible—and might be demonstrably profitable—to allocate to one executive responsibility for the planning and integration of clerical routines and documents. (An illustration of the scope of a Clerical Manager's responsibilities is given in Document LG/7 in the schedules appended to the Introduction.)

It is argued by many people that the scope of clerical management regarded as a specialist field should be such as to include all matters concerned with the staff and working conditions. This is an issue to which there are definitely debatable sides. On the one hand, in so far as actual conditions of working are concerned, there is a good case for this approach, for the effective layout of work, determination of working methods, choice of equipment, etc., are all bound up with office conditions. Similarly, the specification of jobs and of aptitudes or skills required, the nature and extent of training, the relative grading of jobs and the salaries to be paid for them are all matters for which special knowledge of the clerical work concerned is essential. On the other hand, many of these points are such as could rightly be held to fall within the domain of the Personnel Officer, as the kind of things that he would quite naturally undertake in respect of factory staffs. Just as he would collaborate closely with the factory executives, who are directly responsible for these matters in their own departments, so too he would work with the Clerical Manager or Chief Accountant or other executive concerned with clerical work, but would take the necessary initial steps and exercise the full functional responsibility appropriate to his specialist capacity.

There is no need to resolve this issue in the present context—probably there is no single or general answer anyway. The simple fact remains that, in respect of clerical staffs as of others, there is a "personnel" aspect of employment which needs to be specifically met, and it has to do with recruitment, training, placement, physical conditions, lighting, amenities, morale. These are human factors which exert their influence on contentment and on effectiveness of work.

ORGANISATION OF CLERICAL WORK

How the clerical activities of any enterprise are to be organised must be determined by individual needs. Certain guiding principles can perhaps be laid down, such as those concerned with the grouping of activities, or the concentration of responsibility in a given person or group, e.g. for filing. The "systems" or procedures used will also play a part in determining the flow of work and documents, and so the general pattern of activities. The basic principle of all clerical work is the one already stated, namely, that clerical activities are a service intended to play a certain rôle in the working of effective management. Accordingly, the first questions to be asked in laying out the framework and content of procedures and records must be: What are they wanted for? What are they intended to do or to show? What purpose are they to serve? And to whom (i.e. to which members of the organisation)? Only when these answers are clear can the secondary questions be adequately met, namely: What is the best way of showing this information? How can these data be effectively circulated without excessive use of paper? What system should be used?

From these answers, the next questions emerge—relating to the types and numbers of staffs required, the equipment, the methods of providing documents, and so on. This approach is worth stressing because of the common tendency today to reverse the order: to decide on a certain machine, or piece of equipment, or method, and then build round that a series of procedures and a staff. All too often the outcome is a lot of information and documents of little real use to anyone in the organisation, and certainly not contributing to the effectiveness of management as a whole.

This thought leads to another important fundamental, viz. the need for *recognition* of clerical activities as specialist activities of a service nature. Their rôle properly defined is an important one, because it is an element in the effectiveness of management. Among the smaller firms, in particular, there is a readiness to belittle clerical work, and to see it only as a source of expense. But it may have much to contribute to the stability of the business. If it ensures that products are dispatched at due dates, it adds to customer satisfaction. If it ensures that invoices go out properly and reminders follow when necessary, it contributes to financial liquidity. If it enables potential customers to get prompt replies and correct information, it may promote sales. If it provides adequate manufacturing data for the control of production, it may assist in avoiding excess cost. One could work through many facets of management in practice, and find the clerical element called for time and time again.

With acceptance of the field, the next step is the functional organisation of the activities, working from the principle of ensuring a planned systematic approach to such activities and their effective integration, so as to avoid duplication and overlapping. There is no general form that can be laid down, though it would seem clear that responsibility for clerical work should normally be found within the "control" field. The following alternative bases of organisation seem to be available:

(1) Where clerical management is not a full-time specialist responsibility, it may be organised as part of the work of the Accountant or the Secretary. In a small business, either of these officials would himself undertake the responsibilities, but in a larger business it would be delegated wholly or partly to an assistant.

(2) Where clerical management is a full-time job, it may be carried out by a Clerical (or Office) Manager—

either (a) Responsible to the Accountant;

or (b) Responsible to the Chief Executive, and of status equal to that of the Accountant. This would be likely to arise only in cases where clerical methods had a particularly important rôle to play in determining the effectiveness of the enterprise.

The title used is not so important as clear definition of the responsibility which the post carries, but where it is a full-time job, there is an advantage in having a title which describes as nearly as possible what the position does in fact involve: the usual choice is Clerical or Office Manager. A difficulty in this arises from the use of the word "manager": in fact, the "Clerical Manager" does not manage (unless he also has charge of the central typing, messenger and filing services). His task is more a "designing and planning" one: the "managing" of clerical activities and staffs is done by the executives and heads of departments under whose jurisdiction these various sections of the work are carried out. It will be recalled that the same difficulty arises in the case of the "Personnel Manager" (see page 30). It can be dealt with—

By adequate and clear definition of responsibilities; and
By emphasising the service aspect of clerical management.

The Clerical Manager's job is to provide and maintain the conditions for effective work on the part of other employees. It is for this reason that the title "Clerical Methods Advisor" is used in some organisations.

Clerical management is not something which anyone can do in his spare time, or because there is no one else available, or because a job has to be found for some person. Its requirements are exacting. They call for a high degree of technical skill and personal qualities such as ability to co-operate well, sound judgment, good critical faculties and human understanding. Whether or not clerical management is carried out as a full-time job or as part of the duties of another position, it is of first importance that the individual concerned should know his subject and be able to apply his knowledge.

CLERICAL MANAGEMENT AND RELATIONSHIPS IN ORGANISATION

Most of the organisational relationships in clerical management are indirect. The clerical manager would have a direct executive responsibility for such work as telephone and postal services, office messengers, perhaps a typing pool and a central filing system. He would be responsible for ensuring that working conditions were maintained satisfactorily, and that equipment is of correct standard, etc.

Those aspects of clerical management which deal with performance factors, methods, procedures, design of forms and documents, and so on, involve indirect relationships which, unless they are well understood, may lead to difficulty. Minor variations in clerical practice in a factory may perhaps be introduced, though the person introducing them forgets to advise the Clerical Manager or to obtain his views. This may also happen within the office itself: the head of a Sales Ledger Section may introduce changes without reference. In either case the Department Manager may have made the change independently simply as an accident, genuinely forgetting to refer the matter in advance to his colleague responsible for clerical methods. Or it may have occurred deliberately, from a sense of resenting "interference" from somebody supposedly not knowing the special activities of the factory or the sales ledger. Such an attitude means virtually the breakdown of specialist clerical management, for it indicates that the purpose of this functional specialisation has not been properly understood. This may be the fault of top management; proper explanations may not have been given, or responsibilities may not have been clearly defined; or it may be the fault of the die-hards to whom any change not founded on their own unique experience and knowledge is at once condemned as impracticable, and to whom all advice is presumption. Here again the remedy must lie in the Chief Executive taking the appropriate action. It is not sufficient to make changes in organisation structure, to introduce a new concept which may or may not involve a new position, without ensuring as far as possible that the reasons for the change are really understood; and it may be necessary to repeat these reasons fairly frequently, until the idea becomes accepted as part of the normal order of the enterprise. Once the policy of specialist clerical management has been adopted, the

Chief Executive must ensure that it is accepted and supported. To some extent he must be able to rely on the skill of the executive to whom this responsibility has been entrusted to secure co-operation from his colleagues, but his own support of that executive must be clearly evident.

CLERICAL METHODS AND PROCEDURES

Even the smallest business concern can profit from a review of its clerical methods. The results may not always be in terms of economy or more effective performance of the job; often they are indirect, in the sense that they permit of increased effectiveness in those production and service jobs which are dependent upon or influenced by the clerical methods used. Where the clerical staff is large, the possibility of economy is substantial: few things grow more readily or insidiously than paper work. Often the paper work of a business is far in excess of its real needs, and constant supervision with frequent checks is necessary to minimise the possibilities of waste.

A. *Examination of Clerical Methods and Procedures*

The first step is to establish what is being done and to reduce it to writing. Where possible, this is most effectively achieved by means of "flow charts", as illustrated in Figs. 77 and 78. The examination of clerical methods and procedures should distinguish three quite different, though related, objectives:

(1) The avoidance of duplication, excessive movement of documents, unnecessary documents, excessive copying and other causes of lost effort.
(2) The performance of individuals in relation to what is required: a clerk may work hard and *effectively in relation to a given task*, and yet his work may be ineffective in relation to the objects of the enterprise.
(3) The possibility of improvement by adopting different methods.

B. *Establishing the Purpose of Documents and Records*

Different and improved ways of carrying out clerical work may range from minor changes to complete revision of method and systems. The question "What is its purpose?" should be asked in relation to every document and record, and the real use as opposed to the supposed use of records should be sought. Records are sometimes made for reference on incidental matters perhaps once or twice a year. This is not necessarily a sign of bad management; the press of current affairs often makes it impossible for executives to review and revise the detail of their departments as frequently as they would like.

C. *Forms and Documents*

Clerical work is largely paper work. Hence the design of the "papers" can be a very important element in the effectiveness of the activities. A wide range of matters comes in here for consideration: questions of quality of paper, of carbon papers, of style of typewriter, and other matters of stationery supply; the publicity aspects of letter-heading and other documents; the extent to which standardisation is to be carried in different facets of the work. The most important series of considerations are, however, those that bear on the design of the forms and documents used, for these are essentially linked up with the procedures themselves. The layout of the documents is the means by which the purpose of the communication or record is achieved, and is also the means by which economy and effectiveness in achieving that purpose are promoted.

D. *Mechanisation*

Mechanical aids and office machinery, properly applied, can be of the greatest value in improving clerical methods, and in some instances they have the incidental advantage that by mechanisation of routine work they facilitate progress control, i.e. they introduce the machine technique and its accompanying concept of measurement.

Mechanical aids, office machines, etc., should not be introduced until the work to which they are to be applied has been thoroughly studied, and the advantages and the disadvantages of proposed changes have been assessed. Gadgets are a nuisance and are costly. Many office appliances have a field of usefulness, but this field is not by any means as wide as the vendors of the equipment are apt to claim. Efficiency cannot be bought merely by installing this machine or that, this or that stationery , or visible record. Two examples may suffice:

(i) There are a number of so-called systems which claim to show at a glance, for instance, the state of stocks, or debtors, or purchases, or sales, or creditors. Usually they involve a convenient method of recording the item to which they refer, with "signals" or other devices which "automatically draw attention" to, e.g., excess stocks, short stocks, overdue accounts. The enthusiast may overlook that such records have to be written-up from documents of prime entry; they do not avoid errors on those documents, neither do they avoid errors in writing-up. Also, the movement of "signals" is not automatic; someone has to do it, and mistakes may be made. In any event, it is an additional task. In many instances the same results can be achieved more cheaply and effectively by sorting and classifying the original documents, or by using information already available.

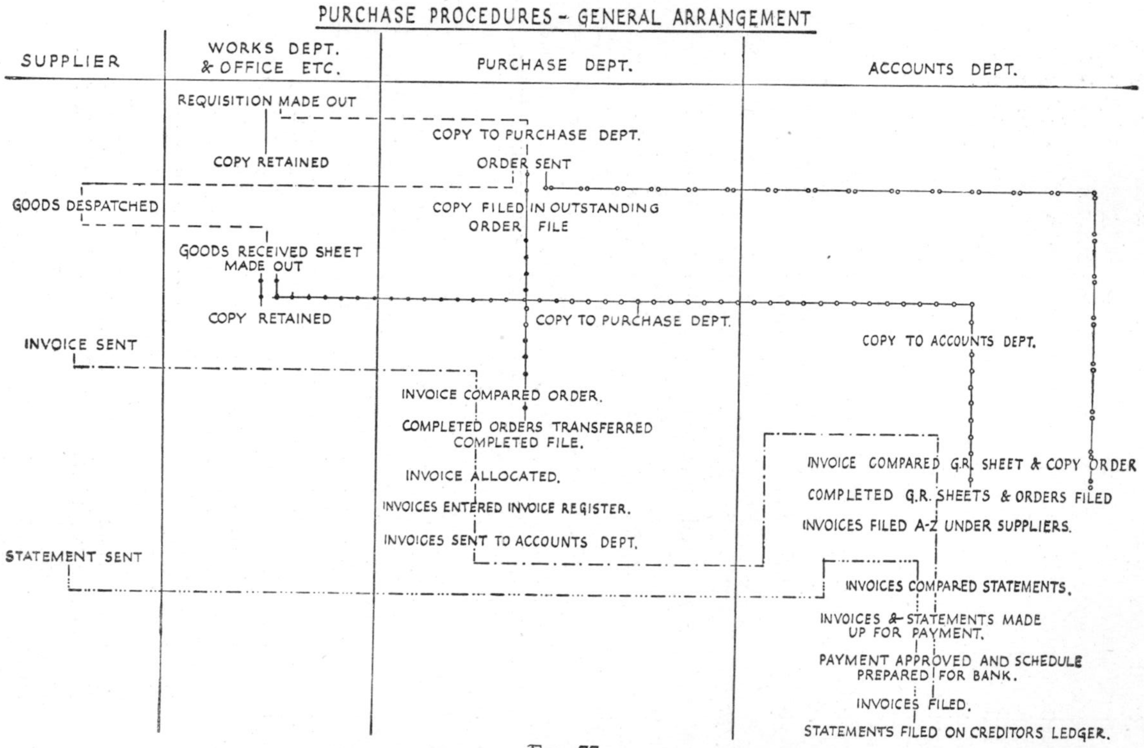

PURCHASE PROCEDURES - GENERAL ARRANGEMENT

SUPPLIER

WORKS DEPT.
& OFFICE ETC.

PURCHASE DEPT.

ACCOUNTS DEPT.

REQUISITION MADE OUT

COPY RETAINED

GOODS RECEIVED SHEET
MADE OUT

COPY RETAINED

COPY TO PURCHASE DEPT.

ORDER SENT

COPY FILED IN OUTSTANDING
ORDER FILE

COPY TO PURCHASE DEPT.

INVOICE COMPARED ORDER.

COMPLETED ORDERS TRANSFERRED
COMPLETED FILE.

INVOICE ALLOCATED.

INVOICES ENTERED INVOICE REGISTER.

INVOICES SENT TO ACCOUNTS DEPT.

COPY TO ACCOUNTS DEPT.

INVOICE COMPARED G.R. SHEET & COPY ORDER

COMPLETED Q.R. SHEETS & ORDERS FILED

INVOICES FILED A-Z UNDER SUPPLIERS.

INVOICES COMPARED STATEMENTS,

INVOICES & STATEMENTS MADE
UP FOR PAYMENT.

PAYMENT APPROVED AND SCHEDULE
PREPARED FOR BANK.

INVOICES FILED.

STATEMENTS FILED ON CREDITORS LEDGER.

GOODS DESPATCHED

INVOICE SENT

STATEMENT SENT

FIG. 77.

704

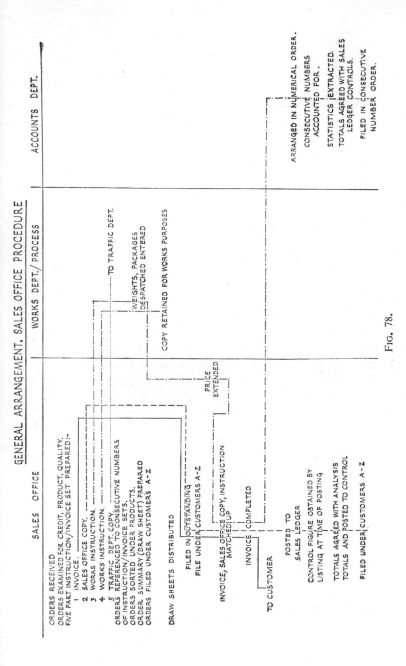

GENERAL ARRANGEMENT, SALES OFFICE PROCEDURE

SALES OFFICE | WORKS DEPT./PROCESS | ACCOUNTS DEPT.

ORDERS RECEIVED
ORDERS EXAMINED FOR CREDIT, PRODUCT, QUALITY.
FIVE PART INSTRUCTION/INVOICE SET PREPARED:-

1 INVOICE.
2 SALES OFFICE COPY.
3 WORKS INSTRUCTION.
4 WORKS INSTRUCTION.
5 TRAFFIC DEPT. COPY.
ORDERS REFERENCED TO CONSECUTIVE NUMBERS
OF INSTRUCTION/INVOICE SETS.
ORDERS SORTED UNDER PRODUCTS.
ORDER SUMMARY (DRAW SHEET) PREPARED
ORDERS FILED UNDER CUSTOMERS A-Z

DRAW SHEETS DISTRIBUTED

FILED IN OUTSTANDING
FILE UNDER CUSTOMERS A-Z

INVOICE, SALES OFFICE COPY, INSTRUCTION
MATCHED UP

INVOICE COMPLETED

TO CUSTOMER

POSTED TO
SALES LEDGER

CONTROL FIGURE OBTAINED BY
LISTING AT TIME OF POSTING

TOTALS AGREED WITH ANALYSIS
TOTALS AND POSTED TO CONTROL

FILED UNDER CUSTOMERS A-Z

.... TO TRAFFIC DEPT.

WEIGHTS, PACKAGES
DESPATCHED ENTERED

COPY RETAINED FOR WORKS PURPOSES

PRICE
EXTENDED

ARRANGED IN NUMERICAL ORDER.

CONSECUTIVE NUMBERS
ACCOUNTED FOR.

STATISTICS EXTRACTED.

TOTALS AGREED WITH SALES
LEDGER CONTROLS.

FILED IN CONSECUTIVE
NUMBER ORDER.

FIG. 78.

705

(ii) There are on the market a number of "filing systems". Strictly speaking, they are *aids to filing*. There are many such aids to filing, but *there is no filing system which guarantees that documents will fall readily to hand when required.* Filing is a personal job; it depends on good arrangements, and on individuals observing and using those arrangements. Ultimately, filing comes down to a certain person putting a piece of paper in a particular place. He or she may, however, put in it the wrong place—something no "system" will ever overcome.

Papers may be filed under subject, department, name, or other convenient classification, and the first step is to provide adequate filing accommodation with visible references. Thereafter:

(*a*) Establish a classification.

(*b*) Define responsibility for filing.

(*c*) Record issues from files by means of requisitions.

(*d*) Do not leave files open of access to anyone. The person responsible for them should put papers in the files and take them out.

E. *Manual of Procedures*

An effective means of ensuring that the full benefits of specialist clerical management are attained is the compilation of a "Manual of Clerical Procedures". This should contain specimens of all forms and documents, a description of the procedures and their purpose, and detailed instructions for carrying each into effect. If built up by sections for a large organisation, each group of procedures can be associated, so that each unit or section of the staffs can be given just that part of the Manual that concerns their work, a copy of the whole Manual being available for reference at a convenient central point. Such an arrangement facilitates the introduction and training of new members of staff; it ensures uniformity of interpretation and practice; it prevents misunderstandings; it promotes integration; it obviates independent action in modifying procedures, because only the formally issued instruction from the Manual is valid for use by members of the staff.

It is, however, important to ensure, when such a Manual is established, that there is an executive or other person made responsible for keeping it up-to-date, with modifications entered, and superseded procedures withdrawn—not only in central reference copies, but in all those outstanding. This would be a normal item among the responsibilities of the Clerical Manager, whether a full-time specialist or someone acting in that capacity.

THE PHYSICAL BASIS OF CLERICAL WORK

Many questions of premises, layout, equipment, physical conditions and so on, come into consideration in the discussion of the effectiveness of clerical activities. A good deal of what has been said earlier in this volume in relation to factory operations also applies to the office. There are, of course, a number of specialist points in addition, and a few of the main items may be usefully summarised.

A. *Buildings*

A general principle cannot be laid down that the premises used for clerical work should have been designed and built for office purposes, and not be just other buildings adapted for this purpose. There are often too many difficulties in the way of building and rebuilding to make any such prescription possible of application. Office buildings should be light, airy, quiet, with adequate toilet and washing facilities, and if possible there should be a rest-room for female staff.

B. *Layout and Arrangement*

It is usually felt to be a good practice to have as few small and private offices as possible. Executives at and above a certain level need to have a personal office, because of the nature of their responsibilities, the interviews entailed, telephone conversations and so on. Certain work, such as cash and wages, requires to be independently housed for security reasons. But for the general run of office work, the specialists seem to prefer the large open rooms, which permit of planned layout to make for simple flow of work and documents, which entail a minimum of movement, and which make direct supervision of staffs much easier.

There is, however, a human side to this, and the matter is one on which perhaps some experimental research could be conducted in order to provide reliable answers. Many girls find that working in large open offices is difficult and less effective than in smaller self-contained groups. They point to the bustle and the distraction, the never-ending general "hum" or background noise; they sometimes feel a certain soullessness in the serried ranks or planned groups of desks.

Related work being housed together is an obvious point of planning, to reduce movement. But how far to carry this in some respects is again open to question. For instance, whereas all accounting machines may be concentrated in one room, unless that room is spacious and lofty the noise may be a source of considerable fatigue and irritation to the operators as well as to others not actually engaged in machine operation. This is more true in the case of a typing pool.

Filing, on the other hand, is a case where all the points are in favour of concentration; it is also good practice to segregate filing into a separate room or into a space marked off by turning the cabinets themselves inwards, so that their backs form a barrier wall to the rest of the room.

C. Spacing

Good spacing improves control of staff and work, and promotes discipline. In some instances calculations have been made to show that each clerk should have, say, 100 square feet or some other defined area. The exact amount of space is much less important than that there should be a clear passage permitting of unobstructed movement between desks, defined "roadways", and regular arrangement.

D. Equipment

Except where special requirements dictate, equipment should be standardised. Modern designs have produced a variety of good desks and fatigue-reducing chairs. The nature of the work and the ease of the clerk for comfortable working should determine choice. Other factors may come in in certain points: for instance, in the choice of desks, the number of drawers. While providing for the convenience and comfort of the clerk as an aid to effective work, it needs also to be remembered that a surfeit of drawers sooner or later leads to an accumulation of personal effects, and it affords a convenient place wherein working papers can be lost. Books and working papers are better stored overnight in cupboards, safes, strong-rooms, etc., each section or department having its place.

E. Lighting, Heating and Ventilation

These are technical questions which have been more fully covered in Part III (see pages 486/9). There is nothing that need be further added here, except to underline the following points:

(1) The high importance to clerical work of adequate light, with absence of glare and absence of shadows at the point of work.
(2) The avoidance of too great a contrast between general and local lighting.
(3) The importance of fresh air, though not to the detriment of warmth in winter—nor warmth to the detriment of fresh air.
(4) Adequate movement of air. Movement of air is not necessarily the same thing as changing the air. Movement can be achieved by the ventilation system or by fans.
(5) The aim of heating should be to maintain an even temperature appropriate for the time and conditions of the year.

In these items there is an "efficiency" aspect as well as that of the health and comfort of the staff: poor conditions of light, ventilation and temperature mean fatigue and reduced effectiveness of work.

F. Amenities

Again, all that has been said in Part III about the beneficial effects of staff amenities—cloakrooms, canteens, rest breaks and so on—applies with equal validity to the clerical employees.

STAFF MANAGEMENT [1]

The provisions for the human aspects of the clerical field are but a repetition, with appropriate modifications, of the application of Personnel Management, covered in the preceding Part. There are, however, a few specific comments that can usefully be made.

(a) All offices, even the smallest, should have an established training scheme for clerical workers, to ensure that newcomers are trained in their tasks and are encouraged to become as skilled in them as they possibly can be. In the case of younger personnel, the training scheme should be supplemented by recognised courses of instruction, e.g. at evening classes in the local college.

(b) Many types of routine clerical work cause fatigue through boredom. Consequently, rest pauses are of value in breaking up the day and in maintaining high outputs: the loss of 15 minutes each session in breaks in the morning and afternoon is usually more than made good by improved freshness.

(c) Clerical work should be graded to provide a Staff Grading Scheme, into which all employees may be placed for salary and promotion purposes. This involves an analytical review of all activities and the allocation of points rating for various factors determining the comparative worth of the jobs.

(d) Clerical salaries are sometimes supplemented by bonuses which may be bi-annual, annual, or related to performance. The difficulty with bi-annual and annual bonuses is that they tend to be regarded as part of normal earnings to which the employee is entitled. They are not related in any way to performance and results, and consequently they are not understood by the employees. Bonuses of the type which cannot be related to known factors within the control of the individual should *not* be applied; salaries should be adequate for the task without long-term bonuses. On the other hand, there are certain jobs, particularly where work is arranged on a pool basis, which

[1] For a fuller treatment on this subject, see the broadsheet, *Staff Management*, published by the Institute of Personnel Management.

can be measured, and bonuses can be calculated on the results of the measurement. These bonuses can be paid at weekly intervals.

(e) Another device which is sometimes used with advantage is that of merit-rating, by which employee performances are reviewed as impartially as possible, rated accordingly, and remunerated in accordance with rating results applied to a salary scale. Clerical salaries should be reviewed at least four times in each year in order to note trends and the salary cost of clerical work.

The effectiveness of clerical work is principally a matter for individual judgment. Even in those cases wherein measurement can be applied, judgment is necessary before effectiveness can be gauged: a typist may have a remarkably high output of work, but also have a high "output" of errors.

On the whole, effectiveness of work is best dealt with by rating with reference to such output records as may be available, and to the ability of the individual to complete work correctly in the planned times laid down.

THE ARRANGEMENT OF WORK

How the clerical activities of an organisation are to be arranged must, of course, be determined in the first instance by the factors that were mentioned above, viz. the policy and the purposes to be attained. This is a matter which also is to some extent influenced by the pattern of management responsibilities as a whole. Thus, for instance, when an integrated scheme of budgetary control is in operation, and executive responsibilities are laid out accordingly, the details of clerical and accounting work have to be framed to fit in with the requirements of these basic factors in the working of management. So, too, in a smaller way, the arrangement of clerical work is affected if schemes for production and cost control have been established for the factory; the needs of these schemes will have repercussions on the activities of the accounting and clerical sections of the offices, if their own efforts and expenditures are not covered by the schemes.

Another factor which has a very significant influence on the organisation of clerical work is the particular type and design of procedures or "systems" in use. More correctly, it could be said that these procedures are in fact the anatomy of clerical work: they determine what detailed work has to be done by the clerks and other members of staff, how the documents will flow from one point to the next, what grouping of staff is needed, and so on. The effective performance of the various activities will be ensured by their clear definition in "standard practice instructions" as laid down in the "Clerical Procedures Manual" (see page 706). But this definition should in practice be carried a stage farther in the actual allotment of work. When an individual member of the staff is appointed to do this or that task, clear responsibility should be given; in other words, each person should have his or her tasks clearly defined and related to the manual of Clerical Procedures.

The most usual problem in offices is that concerned with grouping of activities. Certain work is specific and readily defines itself, e.g. sales ledgers, purchase ledgers. Other work is general, e.g. typing. The question is whether or not advantages can be gained by grouping general work; in the case of typing, by pooling. Pooling of work undoubtedly has advantages, especially in a large organisation, because a pool is flexible and is able to serve a number of departments quite effectively. On the other hand, where highly specialised work has to be carried out, there are advantages in having departmental typists who by specialisation increase their relative effectiveness in carrying out departmental work. This aspect of the problem of organisation is concerned chiefly to provide adequate loads and to provide maximum utilisation of equipment. If a department can provide an adequate load for its equipment and its staff, there is no virtue in pooling as such. Where, however, there are a number of departments with inadequate loads for such services as typing, pooling does offer advantages.

Similar considerations apply to accounting machines which may be grouped or sectionalised, e.g. all machine accounting can be dealt with in one department under separate control or each main department may have its own accounting machines. Again, the answer to the problem rests chiefly in the load on the accounting machines. If a department can provide an adequate load for an accounting machine, nothing is to be gained by transferring that operator to another department or section.

The policy of giving clear responsibility for specific work and encouraging the members of staff to take that responsibility fully has been strongly advocated. In regard to correspondence on customer queries, or dealing with orders or accounts, some Clerical Managers have advocated the practice of so organising the flow of work that any one clerk looks after a certain group of customers and deals with everything that affects them. The clerk gets to know the detailed position very fully and has a greater sense of a responsible self-contained job. In other cases, a similar arrangement might apply to a certain section of activities rather than to a group of customers, or to a geographical unit. The smaller office units often afford greater scope for this practice than the larger ones.

From what has been said earlier in this chapter about the significance of an analytical approach to clerical work, asking "what, why or **how**", it will be appreciated that the arrangement of such work is not a subject that readily lends itself to generalisation. The experienced Clerical Manager will have met many different ways of attaining the same purpose, and will be well aware of the extent to which the local circumstances have coloured the selection of this or that approach in each instance. The test question usually works out as: which method gives the required information most effectively and with the least cost?

CONTROL OF CLERICAL WORK

The cost aspects of clerical management were covered in earlier chapters as part of the general question of control of overhead expense. To some extent, too, the line of approach discussed in the foregoing paragraphs is an automatic contribution to control of cost. If procedures are developed only as strictly necessary to meet defined purposes and are laid down for the maximum effectiveness and economy, the expense arising from them is under control as long as they are actually working in accordance with the defined standards and methods. The uncontrolled source of loss is that of materials, i.e. waste of stationery, forms and consumable supplies, and the bad use of equipment. Appropriate controls can be developed as part of the functional clerical organisation, and a watch for proper economy will be among the responsibilities of supervisors and section heads.

The effective use of the "man-hours" available is similarly a responsibility of managers and supervisors in the commercial sections. For many of the routine tasks standards can easily be defined from observation and study of the flow of work, and from tests by competent clerks. Such standards could rarely be applied automatically but they would afford a useful guide to the head of a section in fixing the volume of work allocated to any clerk or group of clerks or in determining the rate at which work should flow in a consecutive operation. Quite apart from the cost aspect, this control of clerical work may have another purpose, namely, to ensure that tasks are completed in time: for instance, the preparation of Advice Notes or Despatch Notes may in one organisation determine the rate at which the factory or warehouse can send out its goods to customers, or alternatively establish the staffing necessary to meet despatch requirements. The timely completion of invoice preparation or monthly statements may affect the inward flow of cash. This time factor can indeed be regarded as highly important in clerical work and as one of the main bases for controlling effectiveness. The preparation of a time schedule is a valuable management tool. The object of the time schedule is to prescribe the task and the time when it should be completed in accordance with the general pattern of control, accounting, and other "administrative" activities. Properly used, a time schedule means avoidance of "arrears": arrears of clerical work usually assume importance because they are not noticed until they have attained substantial proportions. Arrears of work are not so important if they are controlled, if their extent is known. Those in charge of sections or departments can then have information available which enables them to note precisely the position of work at any time. In short, there is scope in clerical work for the application of the ordinary executive elements of "planning" and "control".

GENERAL OFFICE SERVICES

Generally speaking, the clerical activities of an industrial or commercial organisation tend to fall into certain definite categories associated with the main divisions of management—for instance: Production (Works Office or Planning) routines; Sales Office procedures; Accounts Department activities; Personnel records. But there are in addition certain further services which refer to many sections. Some of these, e.g. typing or filing, could easily be split down among the other divisions, though they can just as easily be operated as a "central service" to the organisation as a whole. Others are more difficult to make specific, e.g. the telephone switchboard, duplicating facilities (because of cost of machine), stationery stores.

In cases where specialist clerical management has been developed, it has become customary to group these services together as a "General Office" or "Central Office Service". They would include:

Telephone and Messengers;
Filing (except for confidential papers of senior executives);
Typing pool—either: copy typists only (perhaps including dictaphone typists); or copy and shorthand typists (other than senior executives' private secretaries);
Duplicating (and similar reproduction);
Stationery supplies, forms, etc.;
Office furniture and equipment.

These activities and the staffs carrying them out are under the "line" responsibility of the Clerical Manager, or of the person serving in that capacity, and the unit is regarded as providing a "service" by the loan of the member of staff or the carrying out of the job.

OFFICE PRACTICES

This chapter has not set out to provide a detailed review of the methods and facilities used or recommended for the efficient performance of clerical work. Its purpose has been a presentation of and commentary on some of the more important aspects of the general management of office activities. Questions of equipment, methods, forms and the like are of considerable importance to the Clerical or Office Manager, but they are more appropriately dealt with in the specialist textbooks or reference books. There is, in fact, a sizable literature on the detail of clerical work and methods. The following brief list of sources of information is offered as a select guide to some of the recognised authoritative British works:

A. *General Topics, Office Layout, etc.*

(1) *Office Organisation and Method,* Mills and Standingford. (Pitman.)

(2) *Office Organisation and Practice* (B.S. 1100, Part 10); published by the British Standards Institution and distributed by the British Institute of Management.

B. *Specialist Topics*

(1) Design of Forms: *Fundamentals of Office Method and Forms Design,* by Laurence H. Bunker. (Pitman.)

The Design of Forms, Organisation and Methods Division, H.M. Treasury.

(2) Stock Control: *Stock Control and Storekeeping* (B.S. 1100, Part); published by the British Standards Institution and distributed by the British Institute of Management.

(3) Equipment and Machines: *Machines and Appliances in Government Offices,* H.M. Stationery Office, 1947.

Machine Accounting and Accounts Office Practice, by P. N. Wallis. (Pitman.)

Office Mechanisation (B.S. 1100, Part 8); published by the British Standards Institution and distributed by the British Institute of Management.

(4) Wages Systems: *Pay-roll Methods, including Pay-as-you-earn Income Tax Procedure;* published by the British Standards Institution and distributed by the British Institute of Management.

(5) Grading and Rates: *Clerical Salaries Analysis,* 1948, published by the Office Managers' Association.

Clerical Job Grading Schedule, published by the Office Management Association.

BIBLIOGRAPHY

1. A. W. Willsmore: *Business Budgets and Budgetary Control.* (Pitman, London, 1949; 3rd edition.)
2. A. Bliss: *Management Through Accounts.* (Ronald Press, New York, 1924.)
3. J. A. Scott: *The Measurement of Industrial Efficiency.* (Pitman, London, 1950.)
4. Institute of Chartered Accountants: *Developments in Cost Accounting.* (Gee, London, 1947.)
5. Institute of Cost and Works Accountants: *An Introduction to Budgetary Control, Standard Costing, Material Control and Production Control.* (London, 1950.)
6. J. J. Glover and C. L. Maze: *Managerial Control.* (Ronald Press, New York, 1937.)
7. T. G. Rose: *Higher Control in Management.* (Pitman, London, 1950; 5th Edition.)
8. Editor, S. H. Gillett: *Management and the Accountant.* (Gee & Co., London, 1950.)
9. G. T. Trundle and others: *Managerial Control of Business.* (John Wiley, New York, 1949.)

CONCLUSION

MANAGEMENT IN PRACTICE

By E. F. L. BRECH

MANAGEMENT IN PRACTICE

1. CO-ORDINATION

THE layout of the management activities which form the matter of the foregoing Parts of this study might easily give an impression of four separate fields without apparent unity. This is an inevitable, if unfortunate, consequence of the form of presentation that has to be adopted in order to do justice to the expert knowledge underlying the various practices in each field. More unfortunate, however, is the fact that this apparent separation reflects the tendency, commonly met in everyday industrial life, to see and think of the practice of management itself in the same separate compartments. This tendency is found in its extreme form, of course, in the very large organisations which are actually set up on the basis of specialist divisions, in many instances often having representation at Board level through a so-called "functional director". An almost natural corollary follows in the inclination of the specialist managers or officials to think of their own particular activity as the most important item in the life of the organisation, and, on occasions, even to display an unawareness of the fact that the organisation as a whole exists for purposes other than the practice of their own specialist or functional work.

To obviate or prevent this separatism within an organisation is among the main tasks of a General Manager. To him falls the responsibility for ensuring that the basis and the framework of management (i.e. the policy and organisation of the enterprise), especially in the larger units, are determined with a clear recognition of the fundamental unity of the process of management itself. His own attitude must be characterised by a determination to preserve the unity. In this task the owner or manager of a small organisation has a big advantage; not only because in such organisations each man in the management structure customarily embraces tasks in more than one field, but also because the owner or chief executive is in a position to exercise a closer unification through the smaller personal span that has to be covered. To some extent the smaller the size of the unit, the less the danger of separatism. There is, of course, a corresponding danger in these smaller units that the bias or the deficiency of an individual may lead to the over-emphasis of some aspects of management or the neglect of others, thus leaving an out-of-balance which is not corrected by a compensating specialist in the particular fields neglected.

So far as the study of management is concerned, distinct for the moment from its practice, a line of argument developed in the Introduction (see page 13) helps to promote unity of conception. The distinction was drawn there between the "functions of management" and the "divisions" in which they are found in operation. It was pointed out that, taking the four major sections into which the practice of management is to-day customarily divided, the fields of Production and Distribution represent activities within which the two special processes of "Personnel" and "Control" are carried out. The latter two thus have a rather different character from the former, a fact which should help to underline at least the unity of Personnel and Control with Production on the one side, and their unity with Distribution on the other. How the argument is projected into practice has been shown in the matter and the illustrations set out in Parts I and II: making allowances for individual differences of treatment, it will be found that the content of Part III, in regard to the personnel aspects of management, and of Part IV, in regard to control activities, apply equally to the field of operations covered in Part I—Distribution, and that covered in Part II—Production. Moreover, throughout both the first two Parts considerable emphasis has been laid on the close interrelation of Distribution and Production activities. This is also brought out again in Part IV, in connection with the formulation and application of budgets, making clear that the forecast of manufacturing activities and expenditure is based essentially on known quantities or estimates of sales arising from Distribution activities.

2. SOME ILLUSTRATIONS

How this unity of management is borne out in practice can be shown by two illustrations:

(a) Take the case of a small firm, for instance, one manufacturing spectacle lenses, employing some 70 people all told. At its head there is a Managing Director, who is virtually the owner and is the technical brain behind product and processes. Because of the special requirements of the trade, his technical skill is of particular relevance to customers, and it is only natural therefore to find that he makes himself personally responsible for sales. In charge of the small factory he has established a Works Manager, a man who has been trained in this field and has grown up through the firm; latterly he has been devoting time to learning something about factory organisation and management. The scope of his responsibilities is, of course, small, and some of his friends from larger enterprises might well mentally classify him as "a glorified foreman". He is entrusted with full executive responsibility for production activities and carries out his tasks with the aid of three foremen: one looks after the tools and equipment, polishing heads, moulds and rough-lens stores, with a small staff working under him; a second looks after the processing operations, which for convenience are divided into four sections, each headed by a skilled working chargehand; the third foreman has responsibility for quality standards, for the inspection of lenses at intermediate and at finished stages, for opinions on flaws and faults; he also maintains the stocks of finished lenses and attends to despatch to customers, assisted by two girls for the packing and paper work. In the office, the Managing Director has a good-grade Secretary with a small staff, to whom are entrusted the keeping of books and accounts, the payment of wages, the maintenance of personnel and wage records, the issue of customer invoices, and the other processes that go to make up the routines of a General Office. Included in the responsibility of this "Secretary-cum-Office Manager" is the functional control of the girls who, under the jurisdiction of the inspector, carry out the office routines in connection with stock records and despatch.

To the Works Manager himself fall, apart from the general oversight of the factory, the special tasks of planning and progress of production, the control of quality through the definition of standards and material specifications, and a general responsibility for the human aspects of management (the personnel function), even though he expects that the detailed contacts and activities will in the main be carried out by the foremen.

Clearly the Managing Director is himself serving in three capacities —he is a General Manager, a Sales Manager, and a Technical Director or Manager.

This small organisation is representative of many thousands in British industry; perhaps its structure is more clearly defined than is customarily the case. The important point at issue is that there is no activity set out in the Introductory Chapter or in Parts I to IV that this little unit cannot carry into effect. Some of them, of course, may not be necessary in a formal way, the same purpose being attained by simpler means. Market research provides a useful instance: the Managing Director's personal contacts with the Prescription Houses, who are his wholesalers, enables him to keep track of new trends in customer demand, such as fashion in the shape of lenses. His participation in Trade Association discussions enables him to have advance information of possible lines of National development that may have a bearing on his sales programme. Or again, in the case of budgetary control, the simplicity of the range of products makes the analysis of expenses less important; but not for one moment could it be suggested that the control of operating costs and expenses is not just as necessary in this tiny unit as in one 10 or 100 times its size. The same is true in regard to the planning of production or the control of progress through the sequence of operations. Naturally, the basis on which these activities are set up and the procedures by which they are carried into effect would be very much more simple than has been suggested in the relative chapters of this study, but the principles there set out to underlie such activities will apply in just the same way, and to a very large extent it may be possible to apply, with minor modifications, even the detailed routines suggested if they are found to be justified.

In the personnel field a similar line of argument again applies: in matters of selection and training, in discipline, in consultation (especially of the informal kind), the principles described apply without variation; the techniques adopted will be much simpler and much less formal.

The unity of management is clearly emphasised by the personal control of a single Managing Director, and by the continuous personal contact between himself and the Works Manager on production matters, himself and the Secretary-cum-Office Manager on control details. It is interesting, perhaps, to conclude the illustration by pointing to a thought that has been frequently emphasised in the Introduction, namely, that it is the attitude of the chief executive that can make or mar both the unity and the efficiency of an organisation: this is no less true in this small unit than in the larger ones where it may be more obvious.

(b) A second illustration can be drawn from a firm of considerably larger size, though again representative of the units which characterise certain industries. This is a garment manufacturing firm employing about 2,300 people. Its organisation structure is something like the pattern represented in Fig. 1 in the Introduction (page 32), with obvious modifications of the division shown under the Design Engineer. This firm is of sufficient size to warrant having the full range of activities described in the foregoing Parts. (One or two exceptions might readily be envisaged; for instance, there may be no Medical Department and no separate Design Section.)

To portray the unity of management in action within such an organisation would mean little more than rewriting in specific form all that is set out in the foregoing 700 pages. The point can be made equally well in more concise form by selecting certain aspects for the purpose of illustration.

(1) The General Manager maintains co-ordination, and therefore provides the first basis of unity in management, by four particular features:

(i) He has defined in writing the responsibilities of all his major and second-line executives, and a copy of the definitions has been issued to each of them. From the outset, therefore, they are clear as to who does what, and where their fields of responsibility begin and end. His own drafting of the schedules has ensured that there are no gaps and no duplication.

(ii) It is his practice to maintain daily individual contact with each of the top-line executives, and he has encouraged these in turn to follow the same practice with their own subordinates. In this way he and they keep a finger continuously on the pulses of the organisation, and are readily in a position to spot at the very earliest moment divergencies or deficiencies before they can become serious.

(iii) In addition, he adopts the practice of a fortnightly Progress Meeting of the senior executives and two or three of the more pertinent second-line men. This meeting, while informal in character, does follow a definite Agenda, and is intended primarily for the purpose of co-ordination. There are occasions when the hour devoted to it represents more a social gathering than a serious management meeting, because there is nothing calling for serious attention. But none of those attending feel that such occasions are in the nature of a waste of time, because of the considerable contribution that these regular contacts make to the unification of knowledge and thought on the affairs of the Company.

(iv) Latterly the Board have decided to introduce a budgetary control scheme and the details are now being worked out. When complete, all costs and expenditure will be controlled by predetermined standards, and a further highly important contribution to the co-ordination of management in action will have been established.

(2) At a lower level, unity is illustrated by the attitude, for example of the Production Manager in regard to the making-up sections of the factory and the maintenance of plant. Long before the budgetary control scheme had been mooted, the Production Manager had developed well-defined plans in respect of current and future output, and had gone to the trouble of establishing a Planning Office. Thus, one of the common weaknesses of the larger manufacturing organisations has been overcome by the integration of, for instance, the purchase of materials with the known forward making-up plans; by the co-ordination of engineering activities and maintenance requirements with pre-planned production operations; by the control of work in progress in relation to available man-hour and machine capacity.

That this emphasis on co-ordination has made a serious contribution to the well-being of the manufacturing side of the organisation is evident from even a few minutes' conversation with the department heads and foremen.

(3) Further illustrations can be drawn from the Company's activities along functional lines:

(i) Plans have already been laid for determining the budgets on annual, quarterly and four-weekly bases. The basis of operation will be a regular meeting of the Sales Manager, the Production Manager and the Chief Accountant with the General Manager—of course, with adequate consultation of subordinates at a lower level who have particular knowledge and information that may be required in framing the budget.

(ii) In regard to the records maintained within the jurisdiction of the Production Manager, for instance, those of the Planning Office, there is close co-ordination with the requirements of the Accountant's Department, and now, of course, to meet the particular needs of the procedures for cost and budgetary controls. The introduction of a Clerical Methods Manager (see the chart on page 32) is a useful means of co-ordinating the planning of procedures, to ensure that full advantage is obtained from such control schemes in relation to all the recording and communicating activities carried on throughout the organisation.

(iii) The work of the Personnel Department is in turn tied in with all other activities. For instance, the absence records maintained in the Department are tied in with the time-recording and job-costing procedures carried out under the jurisdiction of the Accountant; in effect, the basic material for the Personnel Department's absence records is supplied from the Accountant's offices, leaving the Personnel Department to deal with their peculiar part of this activity, i.e. the contact with the individuals concerned, as distinct from the gathering of the information. Similarly, in regard to recruitment of new personnel, there is close co-ordination with the Production Manager; in the first place, the Personnel Officer's participation in the General Manager's Progress Meetings (see item 1 (iii) above) keeps him informed of forward plans, and accordingly all recruitment programmes are based on known or estimated future trends of output. The actual technique of recruitment is based on close co-ordination between the Personnel Department and the managers and foremen in the making-up sections, in order to ensure not only that all accepted candidates conform to the general standards required by the Company's policy, but also that they fit in with the individual supervisor's own assessment of his needs and are not likely to give rise later to incompatibilities on a personal basis. The same co-ordination is found in action in regard to the up-grading of juniors and lower-paid operatives whenever better jobs become available, as well as in regard to transfers between Departments.

In the early stages of the development of management within this organisation, it was the outlook and attitude of the Managing Director himself that set the pace and determined the tone. But gradually as the organisation structure became clearly defined, and as various procedures were formulated, the growing sense of responsibility among the senior and lower executives prompted a ready response to the lead given and gave rise to a wholehearted readiness to seek co-ordination as the natural corollary of their everyday activities.

3. THE FUNCTIONAL PRINCIPLE

Reverting to what was said in the Introduction (page 30) about the theory of the functional principle, it will be seen that the foregoing illustrations afford a number of examples of that principle at work. The responsibility of the Chief Accountant, for instance, in respect of budgetary control and cost-control techniques involves him in responsibility also for many of the planning and control routines that are carried out within the manufacturing departments and particularly within the Planning Office under the jurisdiction of the Production Manager. As was said, the schemes and the methods for operating these top management-control techniques were determined in consultations which included the Production Manager himself, but once the methods were brought into operation, responsibility for their maintenance reverted to the Chief Accountant. It is he who must "instruct" the Department Managers and the Planning Office Superintendent as to the production records that are to be maintained and the way in which they are to be completed; for instance, the filling of daily work sheets or job tickets for material requisition. Similarly, it is from the Chief Accountant's Department that the clerical methods used for stores records are determined.

The Personnel Department affords an illustration in regard to more general clerical routines: the various records and procedures used are tied in with the general principles of clerical methods laid down by the Clerical Methods Manager under the jurisdiction of the Chief Accountant. The Personnel Officer is, of course, entitled to say what particular forms of information and data he requires, but the shaping of such needs into detailed methods is a matter for which he has not sole jurisdiction. Conversely, the Personnel Officer has the main functional responsibility in his own domain—so far as the selection and engagement of staff for the Accounts Department or for the Clerical Methods Manager's office are concerned, neither of the executives immediately responsible is free to act on independent lines, but must defer to the Personnel Officer's "instructions" to ensure that the correct recruitment policy and practices are carried into effect. At lower levels in much the same way both the Chief Accountant and the Personnel Officer will have their functional contacts with the supervisors in the making-up departments.

Quite clearly, this conception of the functional principle in action cuts right across the customary authoritative isolation that is so characteristic of present-day organisations. It will work effectively and smoothly only where there is a sound "tone" of management and only where there is a chief executive who sees it as his primary responsibility to ensure co-ordination among all his subordinates. The working of the functional principle involves an interlacing of executive and specialist responsibilities that will avoid becoming chaos only in organisations which have a well-defined structure and a clear executive attitude at their head.

One special point of functional practice may perhaps be usefully referred to here: it is the question of the issue of instructions to subordinate executives and supervisors. When such instructions concern functional or specialist matters, should they be issued direct by the functional executive concerned, or should they be issued to each group of supervisors by their own direct chief? In so far as a functional principle can be said to be customary of present-day industry, the former method tends to be the more usual. There is, however, something to be said for the direct executives, each in his own domain, issuing all instructions to their own subordinates. This need not prevent common wording, with suitable modifications where required; it need not even prevent using a single printed document throughout the whole of the organisation, if each copy is signed by the appropriate head for display in his own areas of jurisdiction. The gain from this line of procedure is the emphasis placed on that executive's responsibility for all the activities that occur within his domain, and for ensuring that all the requirements of the organisation as a whole are carried into effect by his subordinates. It underlines also his own acceptance of the functional authority residing in the specialist executives, and prevents the possible emergence of so-called "conflicts" between the manager and the functional chief.

4. MORALE—A SOCIAL FACTOR

These last considerations of the working of management throw into relief another facet of the unity of the executive process, namely, its essentially human tone.

The tone of an organisation comes from its head, and is in the first place a matter of attitude. It springs from the impact of the Managing Director or General Manager on the first-line executives, an impact which gives birth to the morale of the executive team. There are, regrettably, far too many managers who, from personal experience, can confirm the extent to which low morale springs from poor-grade top management. Frustration is so readily bred, even at the executive level, by the absence of clear definitions of responsibility, the crossing of instructions between seniors, the confusions of reporting back, especially when there are two or three "Directors" acting in an executive capacity. Morale is, too, easily undermined by absence of policy or by uncertainty as to its interpretation, by unstable decisions on the part of the senior executive, or by the ragged working of relationships between the Managing Director and his immediate subordinates. There may be heroic efforts made by managers at the second and third lines to maintain a good working tone, but in the longer run the strain proves too strong, and their own sense of frustration finds itself reflected in their attitude to subordinates and in a gradual deterioration of the morale of the teams that follow them. This is an experience which has perhaps been found more frequently by supervisors than by any other grade in the industrial hierarchy: within their own relatively small jurisdiction the good supervisors can exert a good influence, can have a sound impact on their subordinates, can maintain a high level of morale in their teams, but they find themselves subject to frustrations coming from weak seniors, from poor-grade Works Managers, from an unstable structure, from confusions about instructions and policy, and sooner or later their own mental energy begins to flag; they are no longer able to carry the department, and general morale drops.

In the experience of many people, there are executives who have been able to bear incredible burdens and undertake long hours of work, endure rapid and repeated changes in product, in operations or equipment, go through very severe crises—because they enjoy a high sense of morale engendered by and maintained by a respected chief, who sets a high tone and binds the executive team into a solid, co-operative unit.

It is perhaps a point worth recording, though more in a spirit of illustration than of criticism, that most of the instances of confusion in management, and consequently of the frustration and low morale that have just been described, occur in the organisations where there are Directors (other than the Managing Director) also maintaining executive positions. Where such persons clearly *recognise their executive subordination to the Managing Director or General Manager*, the weaknesses do not emerge, but where they make the mistake of feeling that their Director status attaches itself also to their executive position, and gives them in the latter capacity something more than is inherently characteristic of it, the confusion is bound to arise. There cannot successfully be three "chief executives" responsible to the Board, each looking after a certain part of an integrated organisation; such a structure completely contradicts the unity of management and must inevitably lead to confusion.

The question of human relations is, however, not only important at the upper or executive levels, for it reappears throughout the organisation. It has been shown earlier that management is a social process in the sense that its main task lies in the planning, co-ordination and regulation of the activities of people. These people are, by the very fact of their membership of the industrial organisation in which they are employed, associated in a common task concerned with the production and distribution of goods. This task represents an economic purpose, and to that extent management may be said to have a primary economic aim. Yet, because it is concerned with the activities of these people, management also has a secondary social aim. It forms part of the pattern of social life in the wider community in which it is set, and must so carry out its tasks as to contribute to that social pattern, to maintain its standards and advance its progress. As is sometimes said, management carries "social responsibilities", which are fulfilled in part by its regard for the physical amenities of the locality in which its premises are established, and in part by its constructive attitude to the people whom it employs. The management which allows unstable policy or inefficiency or any other factors within its own control to cause serious unemployment is betraying its social responsibility. So, too, is the one which allows sprawling buildings, waste dumps or effluent to despoil the surroundings. On the more intimately personal plane, management is neglecting its social purposes if it causes among its people frustrations, discontent, conflicts, an abiding sense of grievance, suspicion and the other negative mental states that bar the way to happiness and satisfaction in the enjoyment of association in a common task well performed.

There is, as has been shown earlier, another aspect to this line of thought. By the promotion of satisfaction among employees, and the achievement of its social purposes, management is contributing, too, to its own self-interest on the economic plane, for from high morale flows efficiency of operation and lower costs. Herein lies the now commonly held justification for the elaboration of the personnel function, an active phase in the daily working of management.

There is, however, another standpoint from which these human facets of an organisation can be regarded. The phrase, "the social aspects of management", has already become part of the contemporary industrial jargon. To many writers, it represents nothing more than an elaborate term for the personnel function; few appreciate its full significance or the deeper aspects of the process of management to which it more correctly refers. For the better conduct of its activities an organisation is divided into sections, according to specialist allocations of responsibility, to lines of flow of work, to stages of production, or other such objective bases. Such divisions or sections represent the formal grouping of the persons—managers plus rank and file—who make up the enterprise. But in any human organisations of more than a few people, there are other groupings that cannot be portrayed on a chart: these are flexible groupings, at various levels or between levels. They arise among people who have some factor in common in their association at work, and they arise usually among small numbers. The basic cause may be proximity of work, or participation in related tasks; it may arise from the origin of association—for instance, new recruits who start work on the same day in the same or adjoining departments; or, again, it may spring from the fact that certain persons have come from the same home locality, and are now "strangers" in their place of work. Similar informal associations are found, for example, among inspectors working in a certain department while not belonging to that department, belonging instead to the common pool of inspection. They may even arise from a sense of negative unity of purpose, as is seen from systematic resistance to new methods of work or the extensive existence of restriction of output, which, while having no formal basis, is organised by an underlying mutual agreement. It has been found also that these informal groupings will be different for different purposes, among the same body of people.

This pattern of relationships is part of the life-blood and of the nervous system of an organisation, but it cannot be reduced to principles, to routines or to formalities. It springs from the natural human tendency to association, from the need of the individual to feel the support of his fellows, and recognition of its existence must be an essential principle in the effective working of good management. The aim of the manager, in so far as he can exert influence, must be to "direct" the force of informal association to the well-being of the enterprise as a whole, and so to the good of the people employed themselves. Success in this will be achieved, however, only if morale is good, and morale will be good only where the human outlook of management is sound—securing the genuine participation of the members of the organisation in its purposes and activities. The methods available to the manager are few and simple, and are summed up in the social skills of co-operation—informing, listening, consulting, promoting security, participation.

These skills are in the main the expression of an attitude of mind that recognises the essential contribution of people to the progress of the organisation and is reflected in a genuinely human tone in the daily working of management.[1]

There are some authorities who maintain that the promotion of contentment among employees in their social relationships within the organisation is a primary aim of management. This is not a correct line of thought, for the *primary purpose* of management in the industrial world is necessarily economic, as has been shown in the Introduction. The social responsibilities can form only a *secondary* aim. This does not reduce their importance in the sense that the heads of an organisation or the lower managers are entitled to disregard them. On the contrary, the extent to which sound social relations and high morale determine the levels of productivity and economy in operation consistently underline their significance in the process of management. What this relative placing of primary and secondary aims means in practical terms has been well illustrated in the recent history of contemporary Britain. There are many desirable improvements in living conditions that just cannot be carried into effect without incurring a cost or an interruption of productive processes that the country, for economic reasons, cannot afford. They have to become secondary aims, in spite of their intrinsic importance. Some of the older industrie provide another line of illustration: the all-too-natural human resistance to change has in a few industries widely held up the adoption of new methods of production which would substantially improve efficiency. Management has no option here but to seek every means in its power to press ahead with the improvements. Obviously, it will use the social channels of information and consultation, but even if the modifications entail a certain interim measure of discontent and insecurity—even involving short-term pockets of unemployment and transfers to new jobs—the overriding economic need of the country for the assurance of its survival must receive prior consideration.

The relative sequence of aims can be summarised in this way: the task of management is to secure the availability of goods and services at a high level of quality and a low level of cost; it can do this

---

[1] Some of the studies that have contributed to this line of thought are to be found in *The Making of Scientific Management*, vol. III, *The Hawthorne Investigations*, by L. Urwick and E. F. L. Brech (Management Publications Trust, 1948). See also *Free Expression in Industry*, by J. J. Gillespie (Pilot Press, 1948).

only by promoting the morale of the people it employs, and it can get high morale only by adequate attention to the social relations of its people.

From this line of thought there arises one interesting question on which a good deal of first-hand research is required before it can be satisfactorily answered. Does this consideration of the social factor in the practice of management mean that the smaller organisation has an advantage over the larger? The answer would seem to be a ready affirmative. Yet not all enterprises can be small; there are many technical or commercial factors that make large-scale organisation inevitable in some industries. Is there, then, to be a conflict between technical and human considerations? Is it a conflict in which a compromise can be the means of solution? It would be futile to attempt a superficial answer in the present context, but a pointer to the answer is probably this, that what really matters is the size of the *unit* on which the impact of individual management or supervision is made; in other words, a solution has to be found which makes possible a large economic organisation composed of a number of smaller human units.

5. COMMITTEES IN ORGANISATION

Reference to co-ordination necessarily brings to mind the question of committees, a subject around which considerable controversy has long existed. The controversy exists because—as in so many other aspects of management—there has been no first-hand research leading to systematic knowledge.

A committee may broadly be described as a gathering of people representing different functions or spheres of knowledge coming together to promote a common purpose or fulfil a common task by the interchange of views. It is perhaps important to note that the different persons composing the committee, strictly speaking, represent differences of function, of experience, or of knowledge, and *not* differences of self-interest. Failure to appreciate this fundamental distinction has led to the popular concept of "bringing the sides together" as the characteristic of joint consultation committees, hence giving rise to the unfortunate tendency for "conflict" rather than "common action" to result.

Of its very nature a committee can be a ready means of co-ordination: it meets Mary Follett's requirements that co-ordination should start at the early stages of a project, should be maintained by direct contact among the parties concerned, should be continuous while the matter is under consideration or development, and should entail a reciprocal relating of all the factors in the situation concerned. It can, of course, equally well be argued—and amply supported from experience—that a committee can be an occasion for friction and a source of a good deal of waste of time. The difference, perhaps, is that between good and bad committee action, which turns in the main on the attitude and outlook of the persons serving on the committee, and particularly of the chairman.

Any committee which is designed to serve the purposes of management must start with firm emphasis on the common purpose or task which is under consideration, and must be represented to those participating as simply a mechanism for pooling their respective contributions, i.e. an opportunity for each to put into the pool of available knowledge and experience his or her specific contribution, but not as an occasion for seeking or demanding the satisfaction of individual interests. The co-ordinative character of a committee, as part of the mechanism of management, is underlined by not putting the committee in a position of having to decide action by a majority vote, or even by unanimity. This is what is meant by saying that "a committee in management should not have executive functions". Giving them such functions is a common error in contemporary management. It may be done literally by requiring the committee to deliberate on certain matters and to take the relevant decisions; it is then to be held responsible for initiating and/or carrying out the necessary action and appraising the progress. In this sense, admittedly, a committee with executive functions is not often found in industry today. The other way is less conspicuous and correspondingly more common. It lies in the arrangement of putting a Managing Director or other senior executive in the chair, and looking to him to give instantaneous *executive* decisions on matters raised, in his capacity as Managing Director. This arrangement is frequently praised as an efficient method of conducting business in committee; in fact, it destroys the most valuable element in committee procedure, viz. the opportunity for detached appraisal of a subject from many points of view with the aim of submitting advice or recommendations to the executive authority, leaving that authority in the position to decide clearly on the merits or otherwise of the recommendation in relation to all other relevant factors, which may or may not have been known to the committee. All too often a Managing Director, serving as Chairman of a committee, has to turn down a "decision" reached by the members, because of aspects of policy which he knows but is not free to disclose. That members should then feel somewhat rebuffed is but a natural consequence, and confidence in the committee's usefulness inevitably suffers. But if the very same point were reached by the committee as a "recommendation", to be transmitted to the chief executive outside of the meeting, the same emotional repercussions do not ensue. With adequate time to prepare a reasoned reply, the chief executive is able to make a *constructive rejection* of the recommendation at the next meeting, and so to frame his explanation that the committee retain confidence in their own purpose.

This is not necessarily to argue that a Managing Director or other senior executive should not serve as Chairman of a committee. If he does so serve, he must invariably perform the "Jekyll and Hyde" act, distinguishing his rôle as Chairman from that of his executive position, and in all seriousness acting out the farce of transmitting to his other self away from the meeting a recommendation which he knows he will have to turn down. Any executive serving on the committee is in much the same position: he can put forward reasons why this or that could or could not be done, but he cannot accept from the committee *as such* instructions for executive action. These can come only from his own superior. In practice, it may often be possible for an executive serving on a committee to agree to carry out a certain course suggested by the meeting, because he knows that it fits with policy, that it falls within his jurisdiction, that it is in line with general plans, and that it would have the chief executive's support. In principle, this is *not* accepting an executive instruction from the committee.

Within an organisation a committee can play its most useful part in one or other of the following capacities:

(*a*) As an advisory body, to assist an executive by bringing together the knowledge and experience of various other members of the organisation, and getting them to deliberate on the particular problems allotted to them.

(*b*) As a means of consultation, to ensure that the viewpoints of persons or functions related to the matters in hand are brought forward for consideration.

(*c*) As a co-ordinated channel of information, to ensure that all the interested persons receive the information, receive the same information, and receive it in the same form, and at the same time.

(*d*) As a means for keeping harmony in development or similar activities, ensuring co-ordination of progress as well as of policy and action.

The value of a committee in these directions may perhaps be illustrated from the case of a certain manufacturing organisation during the earlier phases of the recent war—representative of many similar instances. This was a small concern, employing only about 400 people. It was faced with the gigantic project of rapidly doubling its output at a time when employees were being withdrawn for National Service purposes and when the possibility of additions (particularly of skilled personnel) was remote. In the executive structure responsible to the

Managing Director, there were some six or seven senior and junior executives covering the various activities, partly on functional lines. In the main, the Managing Director was the technical brain, but among his subordinates there were minds that had particular, if limited, qualifications in certain relevant directions. For the expansion programme to be achieved with the maximum effectiveness and economy of man-power, it was essential to maintain a continuously harmonious development, particularly ensuring balance in progress among the various contributory sections, such as purchase and installation of plant, raw material supplies, training and up-grading of personnel, availability of tools, development of inspection standards and inspection techniques, etc. As the mechanism for achieving this co-ordination, the Managing Director instituted a "Production Progress Committee", meeting at fortnightly intervals, with himself as Chairman and the six or seven subordinate executives as members. On a defined agenda, the Committee's deliberations fortnight by fortnight covered the whole programme to meet the expansion; it ensured that all the executives shared the available information and were able to see how their own contribution fitted into the general pattern. The Committee did not, in fact, take decisions, but the Chairman, as Managing Director, was able to say, after a point had been deliberated, that he proposed to accept the Committee's advice and to issue immediately after the meeting the necessary instructions for action. This enabled those executives who would be required to take the action to get moving immediately, and it also enabled them to be called on at the subsequent meeting to report progress or to submit reasons for failing to achieve progress. That there were difficulties in meeting the planned expansion, of course, goes without saying, but it is equally true that the difficulties were minimised and that the rate of progress was substantially enhanced by this effective mechanism of co-ordination.

The part that the committees can, in general, play in the structure and working of management is not a subject on which it is yet possible to lay down rules, and there is scope for a good deal of experiment by practising executives.[1]

Whatever the particular purpose that a committee has to serve, there are two or three fundamentals for its success. The first is a clear definition of its purpose or terms of reference; this affords clarity as to its membership and the reasons why each is participating, i.e. the lines along which each member is to make his contribution. The second is good chairmanship; not the imposition of the chairman's

---

[1] The only systematic study of the subject is in a booklet called *Committees in Organisation*, by L. Urwick, published by Management Journals, Ltd. (1936), and reprinted (1952) by the British Institute of Management.

will on the participating members, but the really effective chairman-ship that promotes ready contribution, that eliminates the unnecessary verbosity, and that ensures at each stage of discussion a drawing to-gether of threads and the presentation of conclusions. The third requirement is adequate documentation—the careful preparation of the agenda, the timely issue of supplementary papers when called for, and the subsequent preparation of a brief yet adequate record of main findings, of argument where particularly relevant or important, and of conclusions. The fourth factor is but the outcome of the third, namely, a competent secretary.

The corresponding dangers have already been referred to, namely, the possible emergence of friction and the waste of time through rambling and inconclusive proceedings: if the foregoing fundamentals are adequately respected, the dangers are likely to be at a minimum.

6. THE CRITERION OF MANAGEMENT

Any discussion of "criteria" in management at once focuses attention on the absence of agreed principles. If such principles had already been laid down, they would be the obvious basis for the assessment of the operations and results of management in factual terms. In their absence, however, some attempt can be made at least to lay down guiding lines according to which the practising manager may seek to assess the proficiency of his organisation.

Criteria of proficiency will necessarily be formulated in terms of the purpose that management is to serve—the fulfilment of a given task effectively and economically. This means that there are three channels along which to seek criteria:

(1) The achievement of the purpose of the organisation. In the world of industrial and commercial affairs, this purpose is ex-pressed in terms of making and selling certain goods or pro-viding certain services. Accordingly, the satisfaction of the consumer is the only really pertinent criterion that can be used. At once a difficulty emerges because there is no known means of assessing consumer satisfaction. The economist would argue, with some justification, that the continuing success of the enterprise is itself a guide, because if the consumer were not consistently or recurrently satisfied, he would not con-tinue to purchase the goods offered by an organisation, and therefore through diminution in trading it would eventually disappear in bankruptcy. Protagonists of market assessment techniques have argued that by questionnaire, opinion sampling, and other similar methods, it is possible to obtain a picture of consumer reactions and throw up a guide to the

achievement of satisfaction. There is no need in the present context to argue the merits of either course, or indeed to pursue the possibility of reaching a detailed answer: the main point to be made is the fact itself that the first basis for the assessing management lies in the achievement or otherwise of the task that the organisation has set out to accomplish. This criterion may be put another way, namely, assessing the extent to which policy is being implemented.

(2) The effectiveness and economy of the operations that are carried out within the organisation in order to put the product or service at the consumer's disposal. This is the domain of all the manufacturing and selling operations, the administrative procedures, the accounting and clerical routines, and so on, that have been subjected to systematic study in the foregoing four Parts. For this aspect, there is a ready tool available in the modern techniques of cost and performance control that have been described, for example, in Parts II and IV. The complete picture made up out of the detailed lines of control is seen in the periodic summary returns presented to the Board of Directors in the form of higher control statements, progress charts or management ratios.

(3) The third channel of assessment is one that will come readily to mind because it was dealt with a few pages back: it lies in the social aspect of management, and may be summarised as "the contentment of the people employed". It could, of course, be argued that, because of the extent to which the effectiveness and economy of operations are influenced by the morale of the people composing the organisation, there is no case for this third criterion. The level of morale, i.e. the contentment of the people employed, will be reflected in the operating standards, in the cost levels, and in the financial results as a whole. Yet, because management is a social process, there is ample justification for specifying a human or social factor in the criterion of its proficiency—an argument supported by hitherto customary omission of this element. Let the manager be required to prove his human skill by the level of social contentment that he can attain and maintain.

Certain indexes can be laid down in this direction, and can be made the subject of standards and control techniques parallel to the financial ones already known. The factors constituting such indexes—which can be made equally applicable to the organisation as a whole or to individual sections, for the whole of a year or for any shorter periods—may be summed up as follows:

(a) Personnel turnover: the number or ratio of persons leaving the organisation, especially when due to avoidable reasons. Regard has, of course, to be paid to the general trend of business, as heavy losses may be inevitable in a time of falling employment, and would not reflect any human disability on the part of management.

(b) Lost time: the levels of lost time due to short-period sickness, avoidable causes, or without cause known: punctuality may or may not be a factor of importance in this connection.

(c) Effectiveness of work: the general operating performance, in respect of quality as well as quantity; this will be revealed through the production control and quality control data.

(d) Contentment: the number of grievances or grumbles coming forward to management, particularly the proportion that turn out to be trivial or without foundation.

(e) Initiative: the readiness with which employees bring forward suggestions or ideas for improvements.

(f) The general attitude or behaviour of employees: this cannot, of course, be measured, but it can be assessed by an objective manager from his personal contacts or can be "determined" from outside by such techniques as the Attitude Survey.[1] The chief difficulty lies in this, that the poor and the non-objective manager is the one who is not likely to be able to assess the attitudes of his people, but who is most in need of the information because the attitudes are sure to be bad.

In the contemporary industrial world it is the customary practice to assess management efficiency by the final results shown in the Profit and Loss Account. The contents of this volume will have made amply clear how inadequate such a criterion is. The range of management activities is far too complex to permit of so simple or single a measure of achievement. What is really being assessed is an intricate skill, composed at once in part of a mass of technical and administrative knowledge, and in part of the human process of impact of one man on others. In the technical language of the Introduction, it represents the union of the two functions of management (personnel and control) with the greater or less technical competence that the operations (production or distribution) require. Again, the attitude of the manager himself comes into the picture. His knowledge of the management fields (the functions of personnel and control) equip him to carry out the tasks of the executive process in the discharge of his responsibilities. His success in so doing depends not only on the extent of his knowledge, but also on his personal ability—his skill in

[1] For a description of this technique see the article by Mrs. W. Raphael on "An Analysis of Strains and Stresses in the Working Group" in *Occupational Psychology*, vol. XXI, No. 2, April 1947. Also Chapter VII on "Attitudes in Industry" in Brown and Raphael's *Men, Managers and Morale* (Macdonald & Evans).

the application of planning and in the promotion of a human tone. Management has, in brief, a certain collection of "tools" fashioned out of the advancement of knowledge. In the hands of the skilled manager they will produce excellent results: a high level of operating performance and low costs, associated with contentment and high morale. In the hands of the unskilled, they will produce not only a poor factual result, but possibly also human damage in frustrations and unhappiness. British industry is, regrettably, only too well marked by illustrations of this unfortunate truth.

Recognition of it is of the utmost importance. The study of management methods (techniques or "tools") is certainly desirable, and the advances now being made in this direction are to be warmly welcomed. They must not, however, induce undue complacency, because they represent only half the factors that make up the manager's skill.

7. THE SKILL OF MANAGEMENT

If it is in a combination of knowledge and human ability that the skill of management lies, the significance of adequate standards of selection and training for those whose profession lies in the practice of management is at once apparent. This is again an aspect of the subject on which it is as yet impossible to lay down even general prescriptions, and which calls for a good deal of systematic research. What are the essential human qualities that make for success in management? Are they relative to particular circumstances? Or are there certain minimum qualities or combinations of qualities which could be specified as a necessary basis? Much of the research could be conducted along the lines of analysing known cases of managers who are proven failures, in contrast with those hailed as successful. While real knowledge is missing in this field, there have been many opinions, and the lists of qualities suggested as the specification of the good executive often read like classifications of the virtues. Tentative analysis of experience with a large number of managers has indicated the following as the optimum basic qualities required in the successful manager:

(1) Organising ability—a combination of planning sense, foresight, and orderliness of mind, which will result in willingness to think straight, thoroughness and promptness of decision.

(2) Ability to see the other person's point of view and to be as critical of self as of others. This is the basis of ability to work with other people.

(3) Integrity, in the sense of mental honesty.

(4) A restrained self-confidence, coupled with initiative and resourcefulness.

(5) A balanced temperament—particularly the absence of such negative traits as emotional instability, marked inferior sense, aggressiveness, self-centred outlook.

(6) A sense of humour or of cheerfulness.

(7) Persistence, but not to the point of obstinacy.

A fuller study will almost certainly reveal that to some extent different executive appointments (especially at different levels of responsibility) will require differences in the optimum combination of qualities.

It is encouraging to know that experimental work is going forward in this matter. Among the methods of study now proceeding, though not actually for widespread industrial application, is an examination of the selection techniques adopted for war-time purposes in the search for officer candidates (War Office Selection Board).[1] The essential purpose of such techniques is the creation of human or social situations in which the candidates have the opportunity, by assuming the rôle of "manager", to reveal to skilled observers latent talent or clear deficiency.

In regard to the field of knowledge which the skilled manager needs to acquire, there is also a good deal of development in progress. The syllabus sponsored on national lines by the Ministry of Education in 1948 has provided a framework for the study of management in selected professional fields and for the process as a whole. The very completeness of this scheme, however, enhances a danger that has long been feared in some quarters, i.e. the weakness of pumping into younger candidates quantities of factual knowledge on a variety of subjects, many of which they have no opportunity of carrying into effect or, often, of even seeing in operation. Such study is not itself "training" for management: it needs to be supplemented by an "on the job training", something on the lines of a coaching of the on-coming man by the successful practising executive. Only in this way can the essential skill entailed in the practice of such a human process of management be effectively trained. Unfortunately, the numbers of really successful managers, knowledgeable and skilled enough to undertake such coaching, are quite inadequate to meet the country's present needs. Again, however, encouragement can be taken from another new development which goes some way (even if on a restricted scale) to meeting the need: this is the training afforded for potential senior executives under the ægis of the Administrative Staff College. There, instruction is combined with a form of "coaching", which uses the experience of the highly selected men who attend, supplemented by the skill of visiting executives. By the interchange of views and the

---

[1] See, for instance, the article by Lord Piercy and J. Munro Fraser entitled "The Stoke d'Abernon Method", *Industry*, September 1948.

thrashing out of problems in small groups, the "feel" of management at higher levels is imparted to men who, in their early-to-middle-thirties, have already had many years of responsible executive experience and have given proof of professional competence at lower levels.[1]

8. MANAGEMENT IN NATIONAL AFFAIRS

The contents of this volume have been written quite deliberately from a manufacturing and trading standpoint, though at intervals suggestions have been made as to the applicability of its teaching in other economic and social fields. No slight to the increasingly important activities of national and local government is intended by referring to them only in a brief comment among these closing paragraphs. In the Government Departments and the Local Authority Offices there are carried out a wide range of activities that immediately suggest a parallel with the work of industrial and commercial organisations, even if their purpose and setting are very different. Little of what has been set out in detail in the main parts of this study would have any direct applicability, but the underlying principles and approach are certainly relevant. It is seldom overtly realised that within Government and Municipal "administration" the same process of management is at work. Differences in terminology veil the existence of the same executive process—the same four elements of planning, control, co-ordination and motivation; the same broad task of the official with its twin functional facets of "planning-control" and "co-ordination-personnel"; the same emphasis on the attitude of the official as an important factor in the proficiency of his unit and the performance and cost of his staff; in brief, the same fundamental principles of management. That so much of the work of the central and local government officials is concerned with paper, with clerical staffs, with office routines, merely means that the emphasis in management lies in the clerical and control fields—but the human tasks and the human essentials are unchanged, directly parallel with the spinners in the mills or the fitters in the engineering works.

When one turns to the nationalised industries, the relevance of this volume is, of course, more readily apparent. Even the detailed pro-

---

[1] Further comment on the subject of the training of managers, and a fuller development of the argument in favour of this latter form of training, are to be found in an article by the author entitled "The Training of Managers", in the *Journal of the Institute of Industrial Administration*, vol. VI, No. 14.

Two Reports prepared by teams visiting the United States under the auspices of the Anglo-American Productivity Council, dealing separately with the American approach to the training of supervisors and of higher executives, have been published under the titles: *Training of Supervisors* and *Education for Management*.

cedures set out in the four parts would have been directly pertinent to a privately operated coal-mine or railway workshop, or the accounting department of the electricity undertaking or road haulage concern. Nationalisation of ownership cannot change the process of management—the nationalised industries remain part of the country's manufacturing and trading system, and are included among the fields to which the content of the book is intended to apply.

It is, however, only fair to conclude these comments with the hope that the present study will have at least pointed to the need for the specialist treatment—in a companion volume—of the process of management within the field of the public services and the nationalised industries.

* * * * *

One of the most encouraging features of the contemporary industrial scene is the recognition that has been given everywhere to the importance of management as a factor in national progress. The widespread emphasis on its "professional" character, in the sense of a call for high standards of ethics and of competence, and of specifying an accepted body of knowledge as the basis of that competence, is matched by an ever-widening eagerness in the ranks of younger industrial personnel to acquire the necessary skill and to qualify for their advancement to higher responsibilities.

Britain is living through an era in which—at last—there is a genuine belief that her technical prowess must be paralleled by proficiency in management. Wealth, it is now widely admitted, does not accrue of its own momentum nor flow from haphazard endeavour. The odd individual here and there may reap a fortune overnight in a football pool or unexpectedly acquire a legacy from a more fortunate forbear; a few will also always be able to make a more than comfortable livelihood by their wits in the pursuit of nefarious practices. But the average man and woman must depend on mutual effort in organised form. The technology of twentieth-century industry does not permit of casual and chaotic working without taking its toll in loss of productive result. There can be a full and rising social standard of life only if sound management is the foundation of all economic endeavour.

That simple truth is the justification for this volume.

BIBLIOGRAPHY

THE following have become known over recent years as authoritative books of reference on various aspects of management:

1. *The Handbook of Business Administration.* Editor: W. J. Donald. (Publishers: McGraw Hill, New York, 1931.)
2. *Production Handbook.* Editors: L. P. Alford and J. R. Bangs. (Publishers: Ronald Press, New York, 1945.)
3. *Cost Accountants' Handbook.* Editor: T. Lang. (Publishers: Ronald Press, New York, 1947.)
4. *Accountants' Handbook.* Editor: W. A. Paton. (Publishers: Ronald Press, New York, 1947.)
5. *Manual of Factory Management and Maintenance.* Editor: R. C. A. Vernon. (Publishers: Production Publications, London, 1945.)
6. *Scientific Management.* F. W. Taylor. (Harper Bros., 1947: a collection of Taylor's more important works.)
7. *Fundamentals of Industrial Administration.* Author: E. T. Elbourne. 4th Edition, edited by H. MacFarland Davis. (Publishers: Macdonald & Evans, 1947.)

The following is a study of special interest relative to some aspects of the social factors in management:

The Changing Culture of a Factory. Eliot Jacques. (Tavistock Publications and Routledge-Kegan Paul, 1951.)

INDEX